TOM RIDDELL
STEVE STAMOS
JEAN SHACKELFORD

BUCKNELL UNIVERSITY

ECONOMICS
A TOOL FOR UNDERSTANDING SOCIETY

WITH CONTRIBUTIONS BY
JOAN ANDERSON
BILL COOPER
PETER KRESL

 ADDISON-WESLEY PUBLISHING COMPANY

Reading, Massachusetts • Menlo Park, California
London • Amsterdam • Don Mills, Ontario • Sydney

This book is in the
ADDISON-WESLEY SERIES IN ECONOMICS

Copyright © 1979 by Addison-Wesley Publishing Company, Inc. Philippines copyright 1979 by Addison-Wesley Publishing Company, Inc.

All rights reserved. No part of this publication may be reproduced, stored in a retrieval system, or transmitted, in any form or by any means, electronic, mechanical, photocopying, recording, or otherwise, without the prior written permission of the publisher. Printed in the United States of America. Published simultaneously in Canada. Library of Congress Catalog Card No. 78-62552.

ISBN 0-201-06352-2
CDEFGHIJK-HA-89876543210

FOREWORD AND ACKNOWLEDGMENTS

This book is one of the results of an ongoing project at Bucknell University to improve the teaching of introductory economics. This project began in earnest in 1974, when several members of the Economics Department decided to devote a substantial amount of their time to the planning and teaching of the one-semester introductory economics course at Bucknell. Simultaneously, contemporary events contributed to dramatically increasing enrollments in the course. The economy went into a severe recession in 1973-1975 and the economic future of the U.S. and the world faced increased uncertainty with resource shortages, energy crises, continuing inflation and unemployment, and persisting food shortages and poverty in the Third World. The increased enrollments and these events were part of the reason for embarking on this project. In addition, though, we wanted to do a better job of teaching what we feel will be an important tool for helping students understand their world and its problems. We feel that our commitment has paid off; our course continues to draw large numbers of students and to provide students with an appreciation of economic problems and some of the ways to think about them. We hope that this book helps you to do that; and we hope that you enjoy it.

The principal authors of this book were Tom Riddell, Jean Shackelford, and Steve Stamos. Other members of the department have contributed invaluably to the project and to the book. The primary contributors were John Anderson, Bill Cooper, and Peter Kresl. Bill Cooper, our department chairperson, was instrumental in encouraging us to pursue the project in the first place. All three of our colleagues have assisted us in writing and revising this text. In addition, Harry Blair, Mike Burnett, and David Lah have helped us to teach the course and have provided many useful and important comments and suggestions on the book itself.

We have also received assistance and suggestions from our Teaching Assistants in recent years. We are indebted to them for their assistance and ideas.

We would like to extend our appreciation to the McKenna Fund, the R. K. Mellon Foundation and Wendell Smith, the Provost of Bucknell University, for providing the financial support which made this project and this book possible. We would also like to offer our heartfelt, but often inadequately expressed, gratitude to our departmental secretary, Ann Witkowski, for her care and diligence in typing and preparing this material. Without her help, it would have been truly impossible. We are grateful to Judy Gilbert and Nancy Johnson for typing the final draft of the text. Their help has been invaluable. Extreme thanks are also in order for Bucknell's Administrative Services Office for their patient and complete help in duplicating previous versions of this book.

Foreword and Acknowledgments

Our students at Bucknell have been very patient with us as we experimented with new material and new approaches to economics. Their reactions, both positive and negative, have helped us to form the present text. We have learned from them and trust that they have learned from us.

Our editor at Addison-Wesley, Marshall Aronson, deserves credit for inspiring us to continue working on this book and for providing us with numerous and valuable suggestions for revision. His enthusiasm for the project has given us additional motivation. We have enjoyed working with him as our editor throughout the early life of this book. Thanks also to Linda J. Bedell, William J. Yskamp, and George Abbott of Addison-Wesley for their assistance. During the academic year 1978–1979, Tom Riddell was visiting at the University of Massachusetts, Amherst, in the Department of Economics. We would also like to acknowledge support for this project from that institution.

Finally, extreme thanks to our families, sources of stability, tolerance, and growth.

Lewisburg, Pennsylvania
January 1979

Tom Riddell
Steve Stamos
Jean Shackelford

PREFACE TO THE INSTRUCTOR

In recent years, there has been a good bit of dissatisfaction among teachers of introductory economics with the available textbooks. Not surprisingly, this has led to a surge of new textbooks—for both the one-semester and two-semester courses. Most of these new books have attempted to cut down on the encyclopedic nature of the Samuelson and McConnell type of text, and many have introduced readings and problems that are up to date and relevant to the current population of introductory economics students. This book is also in that tradition. Its singular contributions are that it is intended to be a one-semester book, that it focuses on a particular set of basic economic concepts, that it emphasizes active learning on the part of the student, that it includes different perspectives and, finally, that it places a good bit of responsibility on the instructor for teaching the course.

This last aspect addresses another concern that has recently surfaced among teachers of introductory economics. Many of the textbooks that were popular in the 1950s and 1960s were relatively easy to teach from; it was all there, it was all relatively straightforward, and the material was all familiar to anyone with a graduate degree in economics. Certainly, there was room for classroom innovation and experimentation to make the learning of economics exciting and lively. But the form and content of the two-semester textbook made it only too easy to lecture on the development of the theory in the text.

However, in the context of the continuing turmoil and confusion of the 1960s and 1970s, many economics teachers became dissatisfied with this approach to introductory economics. They wanted more relevance and applicability of economic concepts. Many were concerned with the lack of balance in the texts—one particular "brand" of economics would be emphasized to the exclusion of others; these teachers wanted more controversy and exposure to different points of view in their courses. They wanted less scope and less depth in the development of theory. They wanted to take a more active role in teaching their courses. It is with these kinds of concerns that we began the effort of writing this textbook.

Many of these concerns are reflected in the growing body of literature in the *Journal of Economic Education* published by the Joint Council of Economic Education, 1212 Avenue of the Americas, New York, N. Y. 10036. The Joint Council has recently published "A Framework for Teaching Economics: Basic Concepts" which attempts to distill the essence of introductory economics. See also the Joint Council's "Training People to Teach College Economics" by Philip Saunders. *Change*, the Magazine of Higher Learning, in its January 1977 issue had a selection of reports on innovations in teaching economics. The Winter 1975 issue of *The Review of Radical Political Economics* is a "Special Issue on Teaching: Approaches to Introductory Economics and Social Relations of the Classroom" which contains some thoughtful articles on the form and content of intro courses. Professional conferences of economists have had and continue to have sessions devoted to teaching economics.

This text obviously does not cover every possible topic or economic concept that one might want to teach in the ideal introductory course. Nor are the articles and examples we have chosen the ones that would be selected by everyone. The questions for the students as they read through the text might not be the ones that you would choose to emphasize the essence of a particular concept. However, we do feel that the book will help students to learn and practice economics and the economic way of thinking as they progress through your course. And it is essentially *your* course. We feel that this book leaves room for and, indeed, requires a substantial amount of imagination, work, and dedication on the part of the instructor. You will have to teach economics; and, hopefully, this text will help you in your task.

We have found the material in this book to be useful to us in teaching economics. Our students seem to have enjoyed working with and learning from it. However, we have chosen to supplement it in a variety of ways. In each of our own sections of the course, we have emphasized different parts of the book more than others, based on our own interests and conclusions about what is important. We have used different examples in explaining a certain concept. Some of us rely heavily on lecturing. Some attempt to actively involve the students in discussions and in solving problems in class. In addition, each week we meet with the entire group of students taking the course for a "common hour," or laboratory. During this session, we have shown movies and slide shows; we have had guest speakers; and we have presented mock debates. During 1976, our teaching assistants presented a debate between Jimmy Carter and Gerald Ford on the economic issues. We have shown Charlie Chaplin's classic, "Modern Times," in connection with studying the Great Depression. Guest speakers have included Barry Commoner, Leonard Silk, and Federal Reserve staff members. The purpose of these sessions is to encourage the students to grapple with economic problems and to utilize their growing knowl-

Do you know what time it is, kids? It's time for Uncle Bob's Economics 324 lecture.

edge of economics to understand them. And, oftentimes, other media and another face help to do this.

One of the most important innovations that we have made in the teaching of our course is to require the students to read a daily paper. Due to our location and the College Service which they offer we have used The *New York Times* in this way. Having students read the paper helps them to use and reinforce their economics—to formulate questions in class, to discuss controversial events or proposals, and to provide real, current examples of economic problems and the light that can be thrown on them using economics.

Hopefully, this text will encourage you and help you to continue to be creative and imaginative in the way that you teach introductory economics. It has been a lot of work for us—including many headaches and failed experiments. But then it has also been fun, exciting, and rewarding. Teaching's like that, isn't it?

PREFACE TO THE STUDENT

KELLY & DUKE   **by Jack Moore**

Copyright © 1975, Universal Press Syndicate

ECONOMICS—WHAT'S IN IT FOR YOU?

Two hundred years after the beginnings of the United States as an independent nation, we Americans live in one of the most technologically and economically advanced countries in the world. Our complex economic system produces and distributes goods and services to us daily and provides us with a high standard of living. And yet we are not satisfied because we, personally and collectively, have many economic problems. Can we find, and keep, a job that provides us with the income to support ourselves and our families? Can we find a job that we like? Inflation, unemployment, energy problems, poverty, pollution, resource shortages, underdevelopment in the Third World, and corruption in business and politics are problems that have dominated the headlines in the newspapers in the 1960s and 1970s. We have had our successes and our failures, and we continue to experience this mixed performance.

Economics, as one of the social sciences, is intended to help us in understanding, thinking, and forming opinions about, and developing responses to these economic aspects of our social experience. Economics can be a tool that aids us in defining what our successes and our failures are and in preserving success and correcting failure. In an increasingly complex and confusing world, this tool can be of service to us personally and collectively as we strive to be responsible citizens of our communities, our nation and our world. This book is dedicated to attempting to help you acquire that tool.

We want to make economics as important as baseball and football scores. The minds are out there. It's a question of getting the attention.

>Robert P. Keim, President of the Advertising Council, commenting on a new public service campaign to "improve public understanding and awareness of the system," 1975.*

Acting is a business—no more than that—a craft, like plumbing, or being an economist; it's been a good living.

>Marlon Brando, actor, in a television interview with Dick Cavett, 1973.

"An inhabitant of cloud-cuckoo land; one knowledgeable in an obsolete art; a harmless academic drudge whose theories and laws are but mere puffs of air in face of the anarchy of banditry, greed, and corruption which holds sway in the pecuniary affairs of the real world."

>A definition of "economist" that won an award from the New Statesman in England, 1976.

---

1. Would you like to be an economist? Why or why not?
   None of the questions in this book is rhetorical. Each is intended to make you pause and think. Try to answer each question as you go along.

COLLEGE ECONOMICS COURSES AT THE INTRODUCTORY LEVEL

Introductory economics courses in colleges across the U.S. have undergone significant changes in recent years. During the 1950s and 1960s most schools offered a two-semester introduction to economics course. "Everyone" wanted to, or was required to learn economics in the postwar era of American prosperity. Many textbooks appeared on the market to meet the demands from expanding enrollments. Paul Samuelson of M.I.T., a Nobel Prize winner in economics, became a millionaire through the sales of his widely used and heralded *Economics*. (He now writes a regular column on the Economy in *Newsweek*). His book became almost a bible and influenced thousands of fledgling economists.

As the enrollments increased and new postwar economic problems emerged, though, the textbooks, in an effort to remain relevant, became encyclopedic. They were also pretty dry. The books all tried to convey almost everything there was to know on an introductory level about all of economics. Some texts seemed purposefully to make economics as hard as possible to learn—to complicate and mystify.

---

*The Advertising Council's campaign produced radio and television commercials on the American economic system and a 20-page pamphlet, complete with illustrations by Charles Schulz, on "The American Economic System . . . and your part in it." The pamphlet is available without charge by writing: "Economics," Pueblo, Colorado 81009.

Ph.D. students have been known to use Samuelson's book to study for their doctoral exams! But the hitch in this approach was that not everybody was going to be a Ph.D. in economics—or even an economics major as an undergraduate. Not all students wanted to have 1000 pages of textbook economics crammed into their heads. Much of it was "irrelevant" to the students who went on to become "noneconomists." It was abstract and not related very well to real world problems. Most of it was forgotten. Very few of the economic concepts presented—beyond supply and demand—were retained for day-to-day use by most graduates of introductory economics.

In addition, real world events forced change. As the problems of race and poverty in the U.S. and the problem of development in the Third World became highlighted by riots in U.S. cities and wars in Indochina, students of economics demanded less abstraction and more relevance in their courses. Consequently, in the late 1960s and early 1970s many college economics departments began to change their approach to introducing students to economics and economic problems. They attempted to make their courses more interesting and more relevant. Many used an historical approach. Many attempted to teach only the core of elementary economic theory (to avoid getting overly abstract and technical). Many colleges and universities retreated to a one-semester introductory course that would be more attractive and useful to the student who might never take another economics course—as well as provide a foundation for those who would take more courses as nonmajors or as majors. And many new economics textbooks came along to meet these new demands.

This textbook, which we developed in connection with our introductory course at Bucknell University, is one of this new breed. This book emerged from a series of changes we made in our course to make it more effective in teaching introductory economics to college students. Our basic goal was to create an "experimental" one-semester course that enhanced the teaching and learning process in introductory economics. In this text, we have tried to compile a quality, nonencyclopedic approach that deals with the basics and doesn't overwhelm students with volume. We have tried to consistently relate these basics to real world problems, and we have tried to use uncomplicated language to simplify and demystify your study of economics. And we have included many conflicting ideas and controversial subjects to stimulate thought and to encourage critical thinking. In our course, we have also experimented with different approaches to teaching economics, including the use of movies and slide shows, outside speakers, newspapers, and other classroom innovations. The combination of these innovations seems to have worked at Bucknell in making it fun to teach and learn introductory economics.

The following *New York Times* article by Leonard Silk provides some perspective on many of the changes in teaching and learning introductory economics that have occurred in recent years. This book contains many such readings. Read the article and then try to answer the questions posed at the end. If you are diligent about doing this, it will help you to learn economics as you progress through the book and your course.

ECONOMIC STUDIES, A GROWTH INDUSTRY
LEONARD SILK

Higher prices and jobs harder-to-come-by have made economics a major political issue—and principles of economics one of the fastest growing areas of student and professorial concern.

Actually, their rising rate of interest in economics is the culmination of a long-term trend. Twenty years ago, annual sales of textbooks for "Ec. 1" totaled half a million. Ten years ago, college bookstores sold two-thirds of a million. This year—with college enrollments themselves in a zero-growth phase—sales of introductory economics textbooks will rise above one million, with an additional 350,000 students taking an Ec. 1 course in which the professor is not using a standard text, but newspapers, magazines, paperbacks, government reports, and other "real-world" materials.

That large slice of no-text courses is one reflection of the effort of many instructors to get back into the act of teaching—or helping students to learn—in a time of crisis in both economics and education.

Until a few years ago, the introductory course in economics had become a snap (for professors if not for students), thanks to what Prof. W. Lee Hansen of the University of Wisconsin calls "those superbly produced, massive forty-five chapter principles texts which, replete with color diagrams and accompanying readings and workbook, covered most everything economics had to offer."

The book, Professor Hansen adds, did the instructing. Those lush and tranquil days ended in the late sixties with the period's challenge to "the establishment," on campus and off, including to the establishment that dominated the economics profession itself.

There was, then, an upsurge of radical economics (a complex derivative of Marxian economics, loosely jelled, whose basic proposition is that orthodox economics is really a rationalization of the interests of the dominant bourgeois class). But there was, too, a more general dissatisfaction with the eminently forgettable standard principles course. There the lessons of the encyclopedic textbooks were extended by professorial monologues, sometimes brilliant, sometimes boring, but rarely involving the students.

Conceivably some subjects can be learned adequately that way, but not economics, which involves difficult passages from the concrete to the abstract—and back again. A series of tests in the early 1960s by Profs. G. L. Bach and Phillip Saunders, then of the Carnegie Institute of Technology, found that social studies teachers in high schools, eight years after they had studied college economics, knew no more than those teachers who had never taken a course in economics. The general public was in the same pickle.

For a way out, Professor Bach turned hopefully to what the psychologists called learning theory. He found no satisfactory general consensus, but at least a convincing body of expert evidence about the conditions under which learning occurs best. The most important factor, for people or for rats, is motivation—hardly a surprising discovery, except, apparently, for economics professors. There were

Copyright © 1975 by The New York Times Company. Reprinted with permission.

discoveries about the cognitive process that were relevant to the way economics ought specifically to be taught:

Effective learning is not passive. The student has to do something, talk, analyze, get involved. Economics is not a set of "truths" but a way of trying to crack problems. And it is heavily laden with social, political and moral values.

Indeed, the learning process goes much faster if the material is relevant to the learner's own life and his personal values and goals. And the student should get prompt and accurate "feedback" on how he is doing in the course.

The major economic issues of the last decade have provided far stronger motivation—not only for students but also for economics professors. Indeed, among the rash of new experimental approaches, one of the most successful is called the "issues approch," developed by Profs. Richard H. Leftwich and Ansel M. Sharp of Oklahoma State University.

The course does not stress formal economic analysis (its principles are nothing more difficult than simple supply-and-demand analysis). But it tackles very real and urgent problems: Agricultural issues—should we subsidize the rich? Economics of crime and prevention—how much is too much? Is poverty necessary? The high cost of discrimination. Why are labor resources wasted? Inflation—how to gain and lose at the same time. The economics of higher education—who benefits and who pays? Pollution problems—development or conservation?

Other new approaches include the program at Vanderbilt University, developed by Prof. Rendigs Fels with the cooperation of the Joint Council on Economic Education. It uses a case approach already familiar in the teaching of law and business. Why did the Cincinnati Bell Telephone Company start charging 20 cents for directory assistance? Why did Coca Cola get rid of returnable bottles?

The case approach goes beyond company or individual consumer matters to involve the functioning of economic systems as a whole—the overriding concern of the professional economist at the highest level of government as well as of the citizen as voter, taxpayer, bills-payer, job-hunter.

The greening of economics—all theory need not be "gray" as Goethe contended—is by no means limited only to those courses that have abandoned the standard textbook. In the fiercely competitive textbook market, the authors have been slugging it out with one another to make economics more relevant and exciting.

Economics has always been a countercyclical discipline; it flourishes when the economy founders, and vice versa. The personal impact of tougher times—the need for a job after college—is pulling students into economics as much as the quest for understanding one's period. And the course is required for majors in business and accounting. But the students pushed into Ec. 1 these days are likely to have more fun than they once would have—perhaps to compensate for less fun when they get out.

---

2. Why are you taking economics? Do you think you should "have more fun" while you do?

3. "Economics has always been a countercyclical discipline; it flourishes when the economy founders, and vice versa." Why do you suppose that's so? And is it a correct observation?

OBJECTIVES, OR WHAT WE'VE TRIED TO DESIGN THIS BOOK TO ACCOMPLISH

Before we begin our formal study, we'd like to share the following list of what we feel are the most important objectives of an introduction to modern economics:

1. To produce some "cognitive dissonance." What we mean by this is that we hope to present you with some ideas, facts, and ways of thinking that are new or different to you. It is hoped these will challenge you to think, to work a little, and to learn. *Is capitalism better than socialism?* It might be, but, then again, it might not be! We hope to open your minds to thinking about alternatives. What is "investment"? It is *not* simply buying a share of stock in a corporation! Introductory economics may shake up some of your preconceived ideas and beliefs! And it may reorganize them into a *system* of thought.

2. To give you some perspective on the historical *changes* in the material conditions, economic institutions, and social relations of human society. We haven't always been affluent, and capitalism hasn't always existed.

3. To *introduce* you to a system of economic theories and ideas about the economic institutions of societies—and how those ideas and theories have changed over time. Even the conservative Republican, Richard Nixon, became a Keynesian!

4. To convey to you *some* of the economic theories that economists, or groups of economists, regard as being accurate descriptions and predictors of economic activity. We do *not*, however, intend to attempt to give you a survey of all of economics. We want *rather* to expose you to some of the most basic, and useful, *economic concepts*. There is too much of economics to try to do all of it in one semester (or even a year); time is *scarce* (that's an economic concept).

5. To focus on some contemporary economic problems—inflation, unemployment, growth, resource shortages, the energy crisis, the ecological crisis, poverty, multinational corporations, economic growth and development, and others.

6. To expose you to the various, and contending, "schools" of economic thought. Not all economists agree on theories or even on which problems are the most important. We hope that you will at least appreciate the variety of economic opinion—no matter which, if any, particular set of economic ideas appeals to you.

7. To give you *practice* using economic concepts. We don't want you to just "tape" the concepts in your head and play them back on tests. We hope that this text gives you opportunities to use economic concepts in solving real world problems. Our intention is to provide you with numerous case studies that allow you to apply economic concepts, ideas, and theories so that you may come to better understand the world you live in (and perhaps to change it!). We encourage you to read a daily newspaper. Reading the paper on a regular basis ought to provide numerous real world examples of economic problems (to integrate theory and reality). And applying economic concepts to them ought to help us understand them and figure out their implications. We may even be able to suggest solutions to some of these problems. How would you eliminate inflation?

8. To provide you with a minimum amount of economic "literacy." You should be able to interpret some of the *jargon* of professional economists. You should also be able to identify the variables, ramifications, and possible explanations of and solutions to a variety of economic problems. We hope you develop a facility to critically evaluate economic ideas.

9. To *demystify* economics so that you do not feel that the economy and its problems are too complex to understand and solve. Economics ought not to be left only to the economists.

cpf*

10. To provide a foundation for future and continued learning. It is a complex world. But economics ought to be able to assist you in thinking critically and independently about that world you live in. It should be one more tool which allows (and encourages) you to assume a creative stance in your community, your society, and your world. Our hope is that we can turn you on to economics enough so that it becomes a useful and creative tool that you will continue to use in achieving a rich and meaningful life.

---

4. Are there any objectives we've missed? Do these make sense to you? Is this what you expected introductory economics to do for you?

---

*cpf is a graphics exchange network for original artwork and that used in community, organizational and other publications. Community Press Features is part of Urban Planning Aid, 120 Boylston St., Boston, Mass. 02116.

CONTENTS

PART I INTRODUCTION TO ECONOMICS AS A SOCIAL SCIENCE: THE EVOLUTION OF ECONOMIES AND ECONOMICS   1

1 The Evolution of Economic Systems

Introduction	3
From Feudalism to Capitalism	5
Feudalism E. K. HUNT	7
Mercantilism	15
The Rise of Classical Liberalism and the Industrial Revolution	16
The Development of Capitalism in the United States	18

2 Economics as a Social Science

Introduction	24
What Is Economics?	24
Paradigms and Ideologies	28
Radical, Liberal, and Conservative Economics DAVID GORDON	32

PART II THE DEVELOPMENT OF MODERN ECONOMIC THOUGHT   39

3 The Setting—What Is Property?

Introduction	41
The Development of Property in England	43
Those without Property—The Peasants	45
Conclusion	47

4 The Coming of Adam Smith—The Division of Labor

Introduction	49
Adam Smith and the Division of Labor	51
Adam Smith Led 1776 Revolution in Economics SOMA GOLDEN	51
Side Effects of the Division of Labor	57
Conclusion	60

5 Creating Value—Producing Goods and Services

Introduction	62
Smith and Ricardo on Value	62

xvii

	John Stuart Mill on Smith and Ricardo	67
	The Contribution of Jevons	69
	Conclusion	71

6 Dividing Value—Income Distribution

	Introduction	72
	Distributing the Goods	72
	Smith on Income Distribution	73
	Veblen on Entrepreneurs	77
	Conclusion	78

7 The Rise and Fall of Laissez-Faire

	Introduction	80
	The Flow of Economic Activity	80
	J. B. Say and Gluts	81
	Laissez-Faire	82
	Laissez-Faire and the Poor: The Socialist Critique	85
	The Flowering of Laissez-Faire	87
	The Situation in the United States	90
	The Parable of the Water Tank EDWARD BELLAMY	90
	The Keynesian Critique of Laissez-Faire	95
	The End of Laissez-Faire JOHN MAYNARD KEYNES	95

8 The Marxian Critique of Capitalism

	Introduction	98
	Karl Marx: Political Economist and Revolutionary	98
	Marx's General System of Thought	99
	The Marxian Analysis of Capitalism	102
	Social Revolution	106
	Conclusion	109

PART III MICROECONOMICS — 111

9 Scarcity: "You Can't Always Get What You Want"

	Study Forecasts Major Shortages HAROLD L. SCHMECK	113
	Scarcity: The Fundamental Economic Fact of Life	114
	The Production Possibilities Curve	116
	Graphs, Equations, and Words	117
	Defense vs. Civilian Priorities	118
	This Side of Doomsday DONALD NEFF	119
	Mobilizing for Survival THE EDITORS OF *THE PROGRESSIVE*	122
	Applying the Concept of Choice to Personal Decisions	124
	Value of a College Diploma: Center of Growing Debate	
	U.S. NEWS AND WORLD REPORT	126
	A College Degree Still Maintains Its Aura EDWARD B. FISKE	129
	Conclusion	131

10 The Theory of Markets

Introduction	133
Markets and Price Determination: Supply-and-Demand Analysis	133
Demand	135
Ceteris Paribus and the Demand Curve	138
Supply	140
Ceteris Paribus and the Supply Curve	141
The Market and Equilibrium Price	143
A Tinge of Reality: It's Not a *Ceteris Paribus* World	146
You Are What You Eat and You Pay for It	148
Hard Economics the Key to World Livestock Supply SETH S. KING	149

11 Wherein Profit Maximization and Competition Produce Consumer Sovereignty, Efficiency, and the "Invisible Hand"

Introduction	156
Profit Maximization and the Competitive Firm	157
A Digression on Total Cost and the Law of Diminishing Returns	159
Profit Maximization	160
Average Costs and Profits	162
The "Invisible Hand" and Consumer Sovereignty	164
Competition and Efficiency	167
Conclusion	168
Appendix 11A The Marxian Theory of Profit	**170**

12 Wherein Noncompetitive Market Structures Disturb Adam Smith's Perfect World

Introduction	175
Noncompetitive Market Structures	175
Monopoly	175
Oligopoly and Monopolistic Competition	178
The Importance of Noncompetitive Markets in the American Economy	180
Sources of Concentration in the Economy	182
Some Cases of Noncompetitive Market Structures	183

13 The Corporation

Introduction	196
The Corporation	196
The Role of Profits in the Corporate System	198
Profits Are for People JOHN T. CONNOR	199
The Profit System and America's Growth RICHARD C. GERSTENBERG	200
Free Enterprise vs. the Government	202
The Modern Little Red Hen WILLIAM P. DRAKE	203
The Fable, Amended BRUCE R. MOODY	204
American Corporations Go Global	205
Coping with the Nation-State: Multinationals at Bay	
GURNEY BRECKENFELD	206
Conclusion	215

PART IV MACROECONOMICS — 217

14 Macroeconomics: Issues and Problems

Goals of the United States Economy	219
Problems and Issues—From the 1930s to the 1970s	219
Poverty, Deprivation, Haunt Millions of Kids BARBARA MINER	220
Economic Theory versus Economic Reality: The Future?	224
High Price of Prodding the Economy WILLIAM C. FREUND	225

Appendix 14A Measuring GNP — 230

GNP, NNP, PI, DI. . . .	230
Problems with National Income Accounting	230

15 The Classical and Keynesian Models and the Great Depression

Introduction	237
The Classical System	237
The Flaws in the Classical System	239
The Great Depression	241
Enter John Maynard Keynes—Stage Right . . . Moving Left	243
Keynes to the Rescue	243

16 Keynes in Words and Pictures

Introduction	248
Consumption	248
Savings	252
Investment and the Two-sector Model	253
Changes in Investment and the Keynesian Multiplier	256
The Three-sector Model	258
The Four-sector Model	260
Conclusion	260

17 Fiscal Policy: Government Spending and Taxation

Introduction	263
Fiscal Policy	265
Lags, Lags, and More Lags	269
Counter-countercyclical Policy	270
The Debt	270
An Issue in Fiscal Policy–Urban Policy	274
Excerpts from the President's Message to Congress Outlining His Urban Policy	275
Conclusion	277

18 The Role of Money and Financial Intermediaries

Introduction	279
The Uses of Money	279
Demands for Money	280

	Supply of Money	282
	The Myth and Mystique of Money	286
	Money and the Keynesian System	290
	Monetary Policy—Tools of the Trade	292
	Monetarism	295
	The Effectiveness of Monetary Policy	296
	An Issue in Monetary Policy—Independence of the Fed	297
	The Independence of the Federal Reserve System ARTHUR BURNS	298
	Monetary and Fiscal Policy—A Summary	299
19	**Unemployment, Inflation, and Stability**	
	Introduction	302
	The Trade-offs: Inflation and Unemployment	302
	Inflation	304
	Inflation: A Tale of Two Decades DOLLARS & SENSE	307
	Unemployment	313
	The Hidden Costs of Unemployment JAMES P. COMER	317
	The Fear, the Numbing Fear EDWARD B. FUREY	319
	On Post-Post-Keynesianism	320
	Post-Post-Keynes: The Shattered Synthesis DANIEL R. FUSFELD	320
	Live a Little LIANE ELLISON NORMAN	324
	Conclusion	326
PART V	**INTERNATIONAL ECONOMICS**	**329**
20	**International Economic Interdependence**	
	Introduction	331
	The Balance of Payments	332
	The Decline of the Dollar DOLLARS & SENSE	337
	Trade and the Internationalization of Production: Elements of Economic Interdependence	341
21	**International Trade and Protectionism**	
	Introduction	345
	The Modern Theory of International Trade	345
	Classical Liberalism and Free Trade	349
	Restrictions to Free Trade—Protectionism	349
	Neomercantilism	351
	A Modern Trade Policy for the Seventies GEORGE MEANY	352
	Global Commerce Expands More Slowly as Barriers to It Spread ALFRED L. MALABRE, JR.	357
22	**The International Financial System**	
	Introduction	361
	The Gold Standard	361
	The International Monetary Fund and the Bretton Woods System	364

		What Went Wrong? International Monetary Crisis	366
		The Downfall of the Bretton Woods System	366
		Floating Exchange Rates	371
		Stabilizing the Ailing Dollar—Active and Passive Aspects CLYDE H. FARNSWORTH	372
	23	**Economic Problems of Developing Nations**	
		Development and Underdevelopment: What's the Difference? What Does It Matter?	377
		How Life Subsists in a Chilean Slum JONATHAN KANDELL	378
		The Quest for Economic Development	380
		The Modern Context for Developing	381
		Basic Economic Problems	382
		Competing Views of Underdevelopment: The Diffusion, Structuralist, and Dependency Models	384
		The Future of the Developing Nations	388
		Declaration on the Establishment of a New International Economic Order	389
		Helping Others—and Ourselves PETER G. PETERSON	393
		Diverse Models of Development	395
		Tanzania Hopes Model Village Will Inspire Growth of Others MICHAEL T. KAUFMAN	395
		Brazil Regime Widening State Economic Control JONATHAN KANDELL	398
		Maoist Economic Development: The New Man in the New China JOHN GURLEY	402
		Conclusion	406
PART VI	**THE FUTURE**		**409**
	24	**What Has Become of the Keynesian Revolution?**	
		Why the Question?	411
		A Brief Historical Overview: World War II to the Present	413
		The Nixon-Ford Years and the Coming of Carter	416
		Sorry, No Change MELVILLE J. ULMER	418
		The Outlook WALTER HELLER	422
		Radical Critique: Keynes and the Business Cycle	425
		Who Will Plan the Planned Economy? RAFORD BODDY AND JAMES R. CROTTY	429
		What the Marxists See in the Recession BUSINESSWEEK	433
		The Keynesian Revolution and the Future	437
		Concluding Notes on the Social Philosophy Towards Which the General Theory Might Lead JOHN MAYNARD KEYNES	438
	25	**Economic Growth, Resources, and the Environment**	
		Introduction	443
		The Problem in Historical Perspective	444

	The Economic Growth Controversy	451
	Don't Knock the $2-Trillion Economy PETER PASSELL AND LEONARD ROSS	452
	Critique of Economic Growth E. J. MISHAN	456
	The Road Ahead: Other Reflections	460
	Summary of the Future of the World Economy WASSILY LEONTIEF AND OTHERS	461
26	**The Future: A Perspective**	
	Introduction	464
	The Future of American Capitalism	464
	The Planning Controversy	466
	National Economic Planning: Pro HUBERT H. HUMPHREY	467
	National Economic Planning: Con THOMAS A. MURPHY	469
	Let's Start Talking about Socialism JOHN BUELL AND TOM DE LUCA	472
	The Visionary Future	479
	The Optimistic Vision	479
	The Pessimistic Vision	482
	Second Thoughts on the Human Prospect ROBERT L. HEILBRONER	483
	The Future and Human Nature	486
	Human Nature and the Future MIHAILO MARKOVIC	486
	Conclusion	489
	Name index	491
	Subject Index	493

INTRODUCTION TO ECONOMICS AS A SOCIAL SCIENCE: THE EVOLUTION OF ECONOMIES AND ECONOMICS

PART I

Will capitalism survive? How did the U.S. come to have a free enterprise economic system? In the near future, will the economic system of the U.S. be fundamentally altered? Will there be some form of national economic planning? Who will do the planning? for whom?

Why is inflation so high in the U.S. and in Western Europe? Can it be decreased? Why is unemployment so high now? Can *it* be decreased? Can we produce a job for every American who wants one? Why is the U.S. so affluent? Will it continue to be, especially if there are more shortages of materials like oil? Can the U.S. develop energy self-sufficiency? Have we licked pollution, or will it get worse? Why do we still have poverty? Is there a reason why a black person is more likely than a white person to be poor and unemployed? Why do we spend so much on arms? How come the U.S. produces so much food? What should we do with it? sell it to the Soviets? give it to the world's starving and poor? Will *you* be employed? rich? poor?

These are all predominantly economic problems that affect each and every one of us in our day-to-day lives—either directly or indirectly. We read about these problems in the newspapers, we hear about them on the radio and the television, politicians talk about them, and we discuss them with our friends and neighbors. They are important and interesting. We have opinions about them—and answers to some, or all, of them.

Economics is essentially an organized body of knowledge about all of these problems—some of which are current and some of which are perpetual. It seeks to understand and explain these problems and to assist us in solving them. It helps us to think about these problems by indicating important variables and relationships. It develops for us a way of approaching such problems. It is hoped that, in this course, you will learn to use economics to consider those problems that interest and/or affect you.

In the following, we will focus first of all on the subject matter of economics—the operation of economic systems. All societies must organize themselves to produce the goods and services needed for their survival. We will examine, in a general way, the different types of economic systems that human societies have developed

2 Introduction to Economics as a Social Science

Economics in the news. (Photograph by Tom Riddell.)

and how these have changed. These will be the subjects of Chapter 1. In Chapter 2, we will concentrate on economics, or political economy, *as a social science.* Human beings have developed a body of knowledge to help them understand and shape their economic systems. Over time, these economic theories and ideas have also changed. In addition, since economics deals with the social affairs of *homo sapiens,* we will discover that there is and has been controversy and disagreement among economists.

THE EVOLUTION OF ECONOMIC SYSTEMS

CHAPTER 1

INTRODUCTION

> The first premise of all human history is, of course, the existence of living human individuals. Thus the first fact to be established is the physical organization of these individuals and their consequent relation to the rest of nature. . . .
>
> . . . The writing of history must always set out from these natural bases and their modification in the course of history through the action of men.
>
> Men can be distinguished from animals by consciousness, by religion or anything else you like. They themselves begin to distinguish themselves from animals as soon as they begin to *produce* their means of subsistence, a step which is conditioned by their physical organization. By producing their means of subsistence men are indirectly producing their actual material life.
>
> The way in which men produce their means of subsistence depends first of all on the nature of the actual means of subsistence they find in existence and have to reproduce. This mode of production must not be considered simply as being the reproduction of the physical existence of the individuals. Rather it is a definite form of activity of these individuals, a definite form of expressing their life, a definite *mode of life* on their part. As individuals express their life, so they are. What they are, *therefore,* coincides with their production, both with *what* they produce and with *how* they produce. The nature of individuals thus depends on the material conditions determining their production.
>
> Karl Marx *The German Ideology*

Every society is faced with the problem of providing for the day-to-day sustenance of its people. Production of goods and services on a systematic basis is necessary for

Karl Marx, 1818–1883.

the continuance and development of any society or nation. Institutions, traditions, rules, methods, and laws are developed to determine what goods and services will be produced, how they will be produced, and how they will be distributed among the people. According to Marx, the ways in which a people organize themselves for the production and distribution, the *economic system,* constitutes "the mode of life" of any society. Understanding the economic system, then, is fundamental to understanding the history and the nature of any society and the people in it.

To "know" the United States, it is necessary to acknowledge the importance of private production and consumption in providing for our day-to-day survival. Consequently, we would want to examine the roles of specialization, division of labor and markets in the operation of our economic system. It is also important to realize that American institutions, productive methods, and material conditions have changed over time. Corporations and labor unions have emerged and developed. The standard of living has advanced remarkably. Mass production has led to the assembly line and automation. The government has accepted more direct responsibility for the health of the economy. In other words, the economic system has evolved.

Over time, all economic systems change. The present American economic system, its institutions and conditions, developed out of previous methods of production and distribution. The historical background includes both American and European experience. For example, our market system has its roots in the emergence of trade in the Middle Ages in Europe; and the modern corporation has its roots in the development of earlier European and American business enterprises. If we understand this background, perhaps we will gain some useful perspective on our current economic system.

---

1. Do you agree with Marx that the "mode of production" of a society constitutes "a definite mode of life on [its] part"?
2. "The nature of individuals thus depends on the material conditions determining their production." What does this mean? Do you think it's true?

FROM FEUDALISM TO CAPITALISM

From time to time, economic change is so wrenching that major transformations occur and completely new economic systems emerge. Such was the transition from *feudalism* to *capitalism* in Western Europe during the 12th to 18th centuries. The change occurred over several centuries but accelerated in the later periods. In the following, we will concentrate on the highlights of this transition to illustrate economic change and to show the historical roots of modern capitalism.

As we have said, all societies must organize themselves for production, distribution, and consumption. Perhaps if we are clear on what these economic activities are, we will be able to focus on the major differences among economic systems. *Production* refers to that activity which takes the *factors of production* (resources) and transforms them into goods and services. The factors of production include land, labor, and capital. *Land* includes raw materials and the land where productive activity takes place (i.e., farmland or the land on which a factory is located). *Labor* is the physical and mental effort of men and women that is necessary for all production. *Capital* refers to the technology, buildings, machinery, and equipment that are used in production, as well as the financial resources necessary to organizing production. *Consumption* is the purchasing and using up of produced goods and services. *Distribution* refers to the manner in which goods and services are apportioned among the people of a society. As we will see, feudalism accomplished all of these with institutions and methods much different from those of capitalism.

---

3. All societies must be able to organize themselves for production, distribution, and consumption. What other economic goals should a society have? List at least five.

The ancient empires of Egypt, Greece, and Rome were the precursors of modern Western societies. They were largely agricultural societies that struggled to produce enough food for continued subsistence. Tradition and custom were primarily responsible for organizing production and distribution. Things were done the way they always had been. Sons followed their fathers in occupations. Slaves remained slaves. Peasants were agricultural producers tied to the land. The priests and kings and lords continued in the role of the elite upper class removed from production. As economist Robert Heilbroner has described it in *The Making of Economic Society,* these societies had "a mode of social organization in which both production and distribution were based on procedures devised in the distant past, rigidified by a long process of historic trial and error, and maintained by heavy sanctions of law, custom, and belief."

As a result of the inability of these societies to produce much more than was needed for subsistence, they were unable to support a large nonfarming population. Throughout history, the ability to produce an agricultural and economic *surplus* (i.e., to produce more than is needed for subsistence consumption) has been a source of growth and power. The existence of an agricultural surplus allows for a geographically separate urban population. In Egypt, Greece, and Rome, cities obviously did exist, but they were not extensive enough to allow for a significant amount of nonagricultural production. Instead, the cities of ancient times were relatively parasitic and lived off the surplus of the rural area. What surplus the cities were able to produce themselves resulted from trade with other cities and from the institution of slavery, with its ability to exploit slave labor. With a largely rural population tied to tradition and an urban economy based on the unstable slave system, the ancient empires were economically stagnant—they were unable to amass economic surplus and to grow. Because of this base of internal weakness, each of these ancient empires eventually crumbled. They were replaced by feudalism during the Middle Ages.

Before we examine feudalism, it is worthwhile to pause and consider an additional aspect of *economic surplus*. As we have seen, if a society can produce more than it needs for consumption, it can use this excess to support an urban population that can pursue nonagricultural production and it can devote resources to increasing future production. The surplus can be used to further a division of tasks within an economic system and thus to spur economic growth.

By forgoing current consumption, a society can use resources to increase its ability to produce goods and services in the future. A simple example would be using excess grain to feed oxen (instead of eating it) so that more grain could be produced in the future. Another example would be transporting food to an urban area where artisans would fashion simple tools for agricultural production.

Though the surplus can thus be a source of growth, how a society uses its surplus and who controls its use tells us a lot about that society. Egypt, Greece, and Rome did succeed in producing surplus, but most of it was not used in attempting directly to further economic production. The surpluses of these societies were controlled by religious and military elites to build temples, pyramids, sphinxes, magnificent roads, and buildings that are still with us today. But little of the surplus went to the slaves, peasants, or artisans who were the producers of consumable goods and services. Nor was the surplus directed toward improving the productive potential of these sectors of the economic systems. As a result, these societies stagnated because they were not able to generate economic growth.

---

4. What does the U.S. do with its "economic surplus"? Who determines how it is used?

Feudalism

Feudalism was an economic system that dominated Western Europe throughout the Middle Ages. What exactly was feudalism? What were its major institutions, methods, and customs? The following selection by economic historian E. K. Hunt, from his book *Property and Prophets,* provides us with a concise description of feudalism.

Environmental Action,
June 5, 1976.

FEUDALISM

E. K. HUNT

The decline of the western part of the old Roman Empire left Europe without the laws and protection the empire had provided. The vacuum was filled by the creation of a feudal hierarchy. In this hierarchy, the serf, or peasant, was protected by the lord of the manor, who, in turn, owed allegiance to and was protected by a higher overlord. And so the system went, ending eventually with the king. The strong protected the weak, but they did so at a high price. In return for payments of money, food, labor, or military allegiance, overlords granted the fief, or feudum—a hereditary right to use land—to their vassals. At the bottom was the serf, a peasant who tilled the land. The vast majority of the population raised crops for food or clothing or tended sheep for wool and clothing.

Custom and tradition are the key to understanding medieval relationships. In place of laws as we know them today, the *custom of the manor* governed. There was no strong central authority in the Middle Ages that could have enforced a system of laws. The entire medieval organization was based on a system of mutual obligations and services up and down the hierarchy. Possession or use of the land obligated one to certain customary services or payments in return for protection. The lord was as obligated to protect the serf as the serf was to turn over a portion of his crop to or perform extensive labor for the lord.

Abridged from pp. 5–8 in *Property and Prophets: The Evolution of Economic Institutions and Ideologies* (2nd ed.) by E. K. Hunt. Copyright © 1972, 1975 by E. K. Hunt. Reprinted by permission of Harper & Row, Publishers, Inc.

Customs were broken, of course; no system always operates in fact as it is designed to operate in theory. One should not, however, underestimate the strength of custom and tradition in determining the lives and ideas of medieval people. Disputes between serfs were decided in the lord's court according to both the special circumstances of each case and the general customs of the manor for such cases. Of course, a dispute between a serf and a lord would usually be decided in his own favor by the lord. . . .

The extent to which the lords could enforce their "rights" varied greatly from time to time and from place to place. It was the strengthening of these obligations and the nobleman's ability to enforce them through a long hierarchy of vassals and over a wide area that eventually led to the emergence of the modern nationstates. This process occurred during the period of transition from feudalism to capitalism. Throughout most of the Middle Ages, however, many of these claims were very weak because political control was fragmented.

The basic economic institution of medieval rural life was the *manor,* which contained within it two separate and distinct classes: noblemen, or lords of the manors, and serfs (from the Latin word *servus,* "slave"). Serfs were not really slaves. Unlike a slave, who was simply property to be bought and sold at will, the serf could not be parted from either his family or his land. If his lord transferred possession of the manor to another nobleman, the serf simply had another lord. In varying degrees, however, obligations were placed upon the serfs that were sometimes very onerous and from which there was often no escape. Usually, they were far from being "free."

The lord lived off the labor of the serfs who farmed his fields and paid taxes in kind and money according to the custom of the manor. Similarly, the lord gave protection, supervision, and administration of justice according to the custom of the manor. It must be added that although the system did rest on reciprocal obligations, the concentration of economic and political power in the hands of the lord led to a system in which, by any standard, the serf was exploited in the extreme.

The Catholic church was by far the largest owner of land during the Middle Ages. . . . This was also an age during which the religious teaching of the church has a very strong and pervasive influence throughout western Europe. These factors combined to make the church the closest thing to a strong central government throughout this period.

Thus the manor might be secular or religious (many times secular lords had religious overlords and vice versa), but the essential relationships between lord and serfs were not significantly affected by this distinction. There is little evidence that serfs were treated any less harshly by religious lords than by secular ones. The religious lords and the secular nobility were the joint ruling classes; they controlled the land and the power that went with it. In return for very onerous appropriations of the serf's labor, produce, and money, the nobility provided military protection and the church provided spiritual aid.

In addition to manors, medieval Europe had many towns, which were important centers of maufacturing. Manufactured goods were sold to manors and, sometimes, traded in long-distance commerce. The dominant economic institutions in the towns were the *guilds*—craft, professional, and trade associations that had existed as far back as the Roman Empire. If anyone wanted to produce or sell any good or service, he had to join a guild.

The Wizard of Id by permission of Johnny Hart and Field Enterprises, Inc.

The guilds were as involved with social and religious questions as with economic ones. They regulated their members' conduct in all their activities: personal, social, religious, and economic. Although the guilds did regulate very carefully the production and sale of commodities, they were less concerned with making profits than with saving their members' souls. Salvation demanded that the individual lead an orderly life based on church teachings and custom. Thus the guilds exerted a powerful influence as conservators of the status quo in the medieval towns.

---

5. What were the dominant institutions of feudalism?
6. How does the feudal "custom of the manor" differ from our modern system of contracts?
7. What did the "religious lords and secular nobility" do with the economic surplus that they controlled?

The Breakdown of Feudalism

As feudalism developed, several new economic activities and trends emerged which eventually created the preconditions for a new economic order, capitalism. For brevity's sake, we will simply list and describe them. Taken together over several centuries, these factors engendered the transition from feudalism to capitalism.

Changes in Technology. In agriculture the widespread introduction of the three-field system of crop rotation about the 11th century, replacing the two-field system, allowed for a more productive use of agricultural land. In this system, all parcels of land would lie fallow every third year. This prevented the land from becoming depleted by constant planting. This simple change increased the agricultural surplus and encouraged the use of more grain in supporting field animals. With greater use of oxen and horses, agricultural production increased even further. Later consolidation of agricultural lands further increased food production. In addition, transportation of agricultural goods was facilitated by more horses and improvements in wagon technology.

Urbanization. The increasing agricultural surplus supported an expanding and more urbanized population. Larger urban centers fostered specialization in economic production; the early medieval towns and cities began to concentrate on trade and manufacturing. This specialization led to further increases in production and stimulated trading among the cities and between the cities and the countryside.

The Medieval Merchants. Given different specializations of agricultural and manufacturing production of different areas throughout Western Europe, individual merchants during the 10th to 14th centuries began traveling from place to place buying and selling and trading goods. These transient merchants exposed self-sufficient manors to the variety of products of the rest of Europe and Asia and created interdependencies that whittled away at the traditional patterns of feudal life. This very trade further encouraged the development of regional and urban–rural specialization—a source of increasing economic surplus. It also laid the roots for the later sophistication of European commerce. Traveling merchants were replaced by permanent markets in commercial cities by the 15th century.

The Crusades and Exploration. Between the 11th and 13th centuries, the Crusades brought Europeans in contact with a civilization much more concerned with trading and money-making. It also exposed them to the wealth of the Orient and its goods. This exposure encouraged an effort to expand the trading periphery of Europe. The nations of Europe began to explore Africa and Asia. These explorations ultimately led to the discovery of the New World. The example of money-making was not lost either. Merchants financed and profited from the Crusades, while European nations used their newfound exploring capability to establish colonies and reap from them raw materials and precious metals. These new forms of economic surplus would finance further development and create fledgling capitalist institutions. In fact, the inflow of gold and silver produced such rapid growth that a great price inflation occurred during the 16th century in Europe.

The Nation-State. An additional factor which broke down feudalism and, in fact, supported exploration was the creation of the nation-state. The self-sufficient and decentralized nature of feudalism began to hamper trade as manors attempted to levy tariffs and tolls on merchants. However, as centralization of political power became the goal of certain nobles and lords, these forces were joined by the commercial merchants in the cities. This coalition of economic and political power assured the emergence of nation-states. By the 16th century these newly unified *nations* within Europe were encouraging trade within and among their countries and exploring across the Atlantic and the Mediterranean. These new nation-states possessed the economic, political, and military power that formed the basis for a new economic order and increased economic growth.

The Decline of the Manor. One of the most significant trends in the transition from feudalism to capitalism occurred on the manor. Increasingly, the feudal obligations between lords and serfs became monetized. As trade expanded, the need

From Feudalism to Capitalism   11

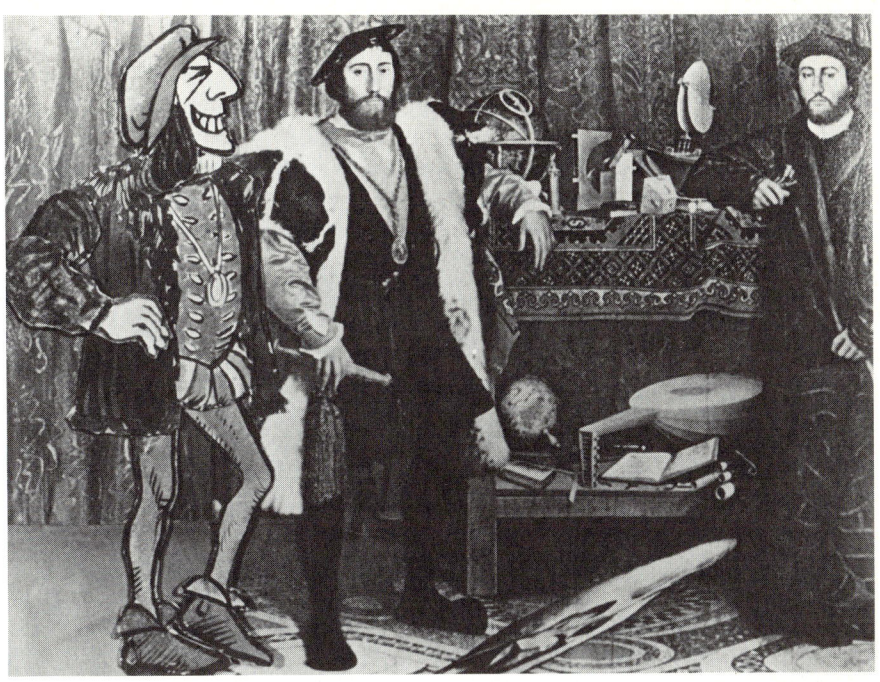

From "The History Book," a movie available from Tricontinental Films, 333 Sixth Avenue, New York City.

for money caused feudal lords to sell their crops for cash and to put their serfs on money payments for work. In turn, the serfs paid rents to the lords for the use of land. This conversion to a monetary system eventually destroyed the feudal manor as the lords were squeezed by inflation and the inability of the serfs to regularly pay their rents. Eventually the serfs lost their feudal rights to the land. *The enclosure movement* from the 13th through the 18th century sealed the fate of the manorial system. Robert Heilbroner describes this process as follows in *The Making of Economic Society:*

Starting as early as the thirteenth century, the landed aristocracy, increasingly squeezed for cash, began to view their estates not merely as the ancestral fiefs, but as potential sources of cash revenue. In order to raise larger cash crops, they therefore began to "enclose" the pasture which had previously been deemed "common land." Communal grazing fields, which had in fact always belonged to the lord despite their communal use, were now claimed for the exclusive benefit of the lord and turned into sheepwalks. Why sheepwalks? Because a rising demand for woolen cloth was making sheep-raising a highly profitable occupation.

The enclosure process in England proceeded at an irregular pace over the long centuries; not until the late eighteenth and early nineteenth centuries did it reach its engulfing climax. By its end, some ten million acres, nearly *half* the arable land of England, had been "enclosed"—in its early Tudor days by the more or less high-handed conversion of the "commons" to sheep-raising; in the final period, by the forced consolidation of tenants' strips and plots into tracts suitable for large-scale commercial farming, presumably for fair compensation.

From a strictly economic point of view, the enclosure movement was unquestionably salutary in that it brought into productive employment land which had hitherto yielded only a pittance. But there was another, crueler side to enclosure. As the common fields were enclosed, it became ever more difficult for the tenant to support himself. At first slowly, then with increasing rapidity, he was pressed off the land, until in the fifteenth and sixteenth centuries, when the initial enclosure of the commons reached its peak, as many as three-fourths to nine-tenths of the tenants of some estates were simply turned off the farm. Whole hamlets were thus wiped out. Sir Thomas More described it savagely in Book I of his *Utopia*.

> Your sheep that were want to be so meek and tame, and so small eaters, now, as I hear say, be become so great devourers and so wild, that they eat up and swallow down the very men themselves. They consume, destroy and devour whole fields, houses and cities. For look in what parts of the realm doth grow the finest, and therefore dearest wool, there noblemen and gentlemen, yea and certain abbots, holy men Got wot, not contenting themselves with the yearly revenues and profits that were wont to grow to their forefathers and predecessors of their land ... leave no ground for tillage, they enclose all into pastures, they throw down houses, they pluck down towns and leave nothing standing, but only the church to make of it a sheep house....

The enclosure process provided a powerful force for the dissolution of feudal ties and the formation of the new relationships of a market society. By dispossessing the peasant, it "created" a new kind of labor force—landless, without traditional sources of income, however meagre, impelled to find work for wages, wherever it might be available.

Robert L. Heilbroner, *The Making of Economic Society* (2nd ed.), © 1968, pp. 54–60. Reprinted by permission of Prentice-Hall, Inc., Englewood Cliffs, N.J.

---

8. What similarities and/or differences do you see between the enclosure movement in Europe and the modern replacement of family farms in the U.S. by agribusiness corporations?

The Breakdown of the Guilds. The process of the creation of a laboring class of people and the extension of the market for labor services was also accelerated by the replacement of the guilds by the putting-out system. Here, as in the enclosure movement, a new kind of labor force was created: a "free" labor force in which work was not a guarantee, and the individual was free to seek work for wages determined by emerging market forces.

Under the guild system of production, independent craftspeople utilized their own tools and shops to produce their products. The products were then sold to merchants. Production and sales were overseen by the guilds. As trade expanded and the production of manufactured goods increased, the putting-out system began in the

16th century to replace the guilds. In this arrangement, a merchant-capitalist gained control of the tools, raw materials, and work place and would hire, for wages, skilled individuals to produce the final product. Eventually this system led to the establishment of centralized industrial factories.

There were two major elements of this new system that differentiated it from the feudal guild system. First of all, production was controlled by the capitalist, the owner of the tools, buildings, and other resources involved in production (i.e., the capital). This person would also arrange for the sale of product items. The goal was monetary profit. The guild no longer influenced the production and sale of the goods. Second, this new system created a labor force that was dependent on the capitalist for work. The craftspeople no longer owned capital; they had only their skills and labor power to sell to the capitalist.

As this system further developed, markets for goods and wages and resources determined profits for capitalists. Based on these calculations and market relationships, rather than the custom and tradition of feudal relations, decisions were made about who would work, for what wages, and how the work would be performed. In this way, industrial production was organized on a capitalist, rather than feudalist, basis.

The combination of the enclosure movements and the putting-out system created a new class of individuals who controlled the productive land and resources of Western Europe and whose goal was profit. In both the countryside and the city, this centralization of control and ownership resulted in increases in economic production. In addition, a new class of landless, propertyless individuals was created—people no longer tied to their hereditary lands or their crafts. This "free" labor force responded to the forces of change by attempting to sell their only resource, their labor power, at the best possible wage. Most of these people gravitated to the cities and formed the emerging urban working class.

The Rise of Protestantism and Individualism. The final contributing factor to the decline of feudalism concerned a change in the philosophy of much of the European population as well as a decline in the power of one of feudalism's most powerful institutions, the Catholic Church. The Catholic Church emphasized in its teachings a concern with afterlife and de-emphasized material life. In fact, the Church argued against lending money for interest (usury) and profit making; if people were poor, that was their station in this life (it was God's will!). This philosophy supported the role of the Church in the society and the economic system, and downplayed the importance of the individual. The rise of the Protestant challenge to Catholicism weakened the controlling role of the Catholic Church's feudal society. In addition, it offered a philosophy more directed toward individual salvation. Calvinism, in fact, provided a justification of profit making as demonstrating service to God in one's "calling." If one worked hard, earned profits, and plowed those profits back into the business, it constituted circumstantial evidence that one was among God's chosen. This new religious idea, and the Protestant Churches as institutions, along with an increased emphasis on political freedom and liberty, supported the creation

14 The Evolution of Economic Systems

of a new *individualism*. This spirit, in turn, prompted much of the behavior necessary to the establishment of capitalist institutions.

These factors, and others, as sources of change over centuries of time in Western Europe eventually led to the destruction of feudal institutions and relationships. These were replaced by a new set of institutions and relationships that we have come to label *capitalism*.

Property rights were established following the Norman Conquest of Britain by building a castle such as this one in York. It overlooked two rivers and was perched high on a hill. Its vantage point assured the property holders that no invaders were sneaking up on them. (Photograph by Bill Cooper.)

---

9. From the material above, list the feudal relations and institutions that were destroyed by the centuries of change in Western Europe between 1000 and 1800.

10. List the new relationships and institutions that were emerging to form capitalism.

Emergent Capitalism

E. K. Hunt has provided us with a succinct description of what these centuries of change had wrought in terms of creating a new form of economic system. In *Property and Prophets*, he discusses the key elements and historical roots of capitalism:

> ... [P]rofits were accumulated as capital. *Capital* refers to the materials that are necessary for production, trade, and commerce. It consists of all tools, equipment, factories, raw materials and goods in process, means of transporting goods, and money. The essence of the capitalist system is the existence of a class of capitalists who own the capital stock. It is by virtue of their ownership of this capital that they derive their profits. These profits are then plowed back, or used to augment the capital stock. The further accumulation of capital leads to more profits, which leads to more accumulation, and the system continues in an upward spiral.
>
> The term *capitalism* describes this system of profit-seeking and accumulation very well. Capital is the source of profits and hence the source of further accumulation of capital. But this chicken–egg process had to have a beginning. The substantial initial accumulation, or *primitive accumulation*, of capital took place [during feudalism]. The four most important sources of the initial accumulation of capital were (1) the rapidly growing volume of trade and commerce, (2) the putting-out system of industry, (3) the enclosure movement, and (4) the great price inflation. There were several other sources of initial accumulations, some of which were somewhat less respectable and often forgotten—for example, colonial plunder, piracy, and the slave trade.
>
> During the sixteenth and seventeenth centuries the putting-out system was extended until it was common in most types of manufacturing. Although this was not yet the modern type of factory production, the system's increased degree of specialization led to significant increases in productivity. Technical improvements in shipbuilding and navigation also lowered transportation costs. Thus during this period capitalist production and trade and commerce thrived and grew very rapidly. The new capitalist class (or middle class or bourgeoisie) slowly but inexorably replaced the nobility as the class that dominated the economic and social system.

Abridged from p. 24 in *Property and Prophets: The Evolution of Economic Institutions and Ideologies* (2nd ed.) by E. K. Hunt. Copyright © 1972, 1975 by E. K. Hunt. Reprinted by permission of Harper & Row, Publishers, Inc.

By the late 15th and early 16th centuries in England, France, Spain, Belgium, and Holland, capitalism was emerging, and modern nation-states, involving monarchs and merchant capitalists, had effectively eliminated the decentralized power of the feudal system. This new system would also change and develop, although even today it retains its basic elements of private ownership, profit making, and markets. In the following, we will very briefly trace some of the most important periods in the development of Western capitalism.

MERCANTILISM

Mercantilism was a policy of the new nation-states to build and consolidate their political, economic, and military power. Trading was seen to be the foundation of the nation's power and prestige. The object of trading was the accumulation and retention of gold and silver bullion. These stores of precious metals could in turn be used to finance further trade or to enhance the political and military power of the nation. Obviously, this concern led to exploration in attempts to discover and hoard more precious metals. It also led to policies designed to maximize the flow of money into the nation and minimize the flow of money out. Consequently, mercantilism developed trade monopolies to minimize the prices of imports and maximize the prices of exports, controlled importing and exporting, levied tariffs on imports, subsidized exports, and controlled shipping extensively. The state, thus, took a large degree of responsibility in controlling economic activity. At first, this obviously aided some nascent capitalists, but the overriding control by the state over the economy eventually began to burden increasing numbers of individualistic and profit-motivated businesspeople.

THE RISE OF CLASSICAL LIBERALISM AND THE INDUSTRIAL REVOLUTION

Mercantilist restrictions eventually gave rise in the 18th and 19th centuries to an opposition that ultimately prevailed and drastically reduced the amount of direct interference in economic affairs by the state. The movement to end mercantilism was spearheaded by a new philosophical and economic body of thought—Classical Liberalism. In 1776, a Scottish philosopher, Adam Smith, published *The Wealth of Nations* in which he argued very strongly that mercantilist policies interfered with the ability of private individuals and markets to produce maximum social welfare. Smith felt that, although everyone was basically out to maximize his or her own welfare, private *competition* in production and consumption would ensure the best possible outcome for all. Therefore, Smith argued forcefully that the state should not be involved in economic activity; that beyond providing for law and order, national defense, and some public goods like highways, the state should take a laissez-faire attitude toward the economic system. Individuals would guide production and consumption.

This philosophy was seized by the emerging capitalist class in Western Europe and used to eventually legislate an end to most mercantilist restrictions on trade and other economic activity. Left to their own devices and the profit motive, English capitalists took early advantage of the technological advances of the Industrial Revolution. The introduction of more sophisticated machinery in textiles, transportation, iron production, and other industries led to a fantastic increase in the productive capacity of the English economic system. The Industrial Revolution, and the entrepreneurs who financed it and led it, spread throughout Western Europe and to North America. However, the increase in production was not all the Industrial Revolution and emergent capitalism brought with them, as Heilbroner explains:

... [W]e must pay heed to another immediate and visible result of the industrial revolution in England. We can characterize it as the transformation of an essentially commercial and agricultural society into one in which industrial manufacture became the dominant mode of organizing economic life. To put it more concretely, the industrial revolution was characterized by *the rise of the factory to the center of social as well as economic life.* After 1850, the factory was not only the key economic institution of England, but it was the economic institution that shaped its politics, its social problems, the character of its daily life, just as decisively as the manor or the guild had done a few centuries earlier.

The factory provided not merely a new landscape but a new and uncongenial social habitat. In our day we have become so used to urban-industrial life that we forget what a wrench is the transition from farm to city. For the peasant, this transfer requires a drastic adjustment. No longer does he work at his own pace, but at the pace of a machine. No longer are slack seasons determined by the weather, but by the state of the market. No longer is the land, however miserable its crop, an eternal source of sustenance close at hand, but only the packed and sterile earth of the industrial site.

Distasteful as was the advent of the factory itself, even more distasteful were the conditions within it. Child labor, for instance, was commonplace and sometimes began at age four; hours of work were generally dawn to dusk; abuses of every kind were all too frequent.

It was a grim age. The long hours of work, the general dirt and clangor of the factories, the lack of even the most elementary safety precautions, all combined to give early industrial capitalism a reputation from which, in the minds of many people of the world, it has never recovered. Worse yet were the slums to which the majority of workers returned after their travail. A government commissioner reports on one such workers' quarter in Glasgow called "the wynds."

> *The wynds . . . house a fluctuating population of between 15,000 and 30,000 persons. This district is composed of many narrow streets and square courts and in the middle of each court there is a dunghill. Although the outward appearance of these places was revolting, I was nevertheless quite unprepared for the filth and misery that were to be found inside. In some bedrooms we visited at night we found a whole mass of humanity stretched on the floor. There were often 15 to 20 men and women huddled together, some being clothed and others naked. There was hardly any furniture there and the only thing which gave these holes the appearance of a dwelling was fire burning on the hearth. Thieving and prostitution are the main sources of income of these people* *

Robert L. Heilbroner, *The Making of Economic Society,* (2nd ed.) Copyright © 1968. Reprinted by permission of Prentice-Hall, Inc., Englewood Cliffs, N.J.

---

11. Why were capitalists and classical liberals opposed to mercantilism?

12. Why was early capitalism so unmindful of the social effects of industrialization brought on by the Industrial Revolution?

The emergence of capitalism and a free market for labor encouraged, as well as fed on, the Industrial Revolution. These forces produced rapid economic growth

---

*Quoted in F. Engels, *The Condition of the Working Class in England in 1874* (New York: Macmillan, 1958), p. 46.

and the factory system, as well as urban slums and adverse working conditions. Central to these changes was the spread of markets for goods and services throughout Western Europe. With the diminution of the roles of tradition, custom, and the State in the economic affairs of Western Europeans, capitalism relied increasingly on *markets* to organize production and distribution.

Land, labor, and capital, as factors of production, all became commodities that were bought and sold on markets for prices. This required the emergence of a market system in which producers made calculations, based on prices of resources and products, directed towards the accumulation of profits. Economic activity was thus directed through the operation of these markets and the determination of prices in them. Again, land, labor, and capital became commodities. This was in contrast to the feudal system wherein land and labor were part of the social organization of communities (feudal manors and guilds) and were regulated by social custom, tradition, and institutions. With the emergence of capitalism, land and labor became subject to the market for their occupation and use. In this way, as the late historian Karl Polanyi has argued in *The Great Transformation,* capitalism required the subordination of social considerations to the economic dictates of the private market system. Production and distribution were organized, for the society, through markets.

13. What is the significance of markets to capitalism?

THE DEVELOPMENT OF CAPITALISM IN THE UNITED STATES

As capitalism was forming in Europe, many of its institutions and relationships were transplanted to the American colonies. When the colonists eventually removed the yoke of English political and economic control during the American Revolution, the way was cleared for the formation and development of the United States own form of capitalism. However, the Americans retained their debt to Western civilization, thought, and institutions. This lineage was important to the establishment of emerging capitalist attitudes and institutions in the colonies and their continuance after the Revolution. Most of the colonists were Protestants who emphasized individualism and hard work. Private ownership of rural and urban production was the dominant form of economic organization. International and domestic trade flourished with the goal of private gain and profit. Markets developed and guided production. In the early years of the new nation, the government utilized mercantilist policies of controlling international trade to foster economic development and to protect the emergence of the U.S. as a Western nation-state.

Before we proceed with a brief overview of the economic history of the U.S., it is important to define the term *economic development*. As was suggested at the beginning of this chapter, all societies must organize themselves for the production and distribution of goods and services. The methods and institutions for accomplishing these tasks constitute a society's economic system. Over time, as we have seen in the transition from feudalism to capitalism, economic systems change. Economic development represents progressive changes in the ability of a society to meet its economic tasks of production and distribution. Economic development contains two key elements. One concerns the total amount of goods and services that are produced and available for consumption, and the other concerns institutions. Economic development occurs when a society is able to increase its total output; it experiences economic growth through the generation and usage of its economic surplus. Very often a society's ability to produce such growth is a function of the second element of economic development. This concerns the changes in the economic institutions, relationships, and methods of the society. If the society experiences changes in its economic institutions, relationships, and methods that make it better prepared to produce a growing volume of goods and services for its people, then development will occur. The discovery of new resources will encourage economic development, as will technological improvements in the methods of production. The spread of education and attitudes toward work may facilitate the ability of a society to produce goods and services. Economic development is obviously of crucial importance to any society and its continued survival. We will now turn to a brief consideration of the development of capitalism in the U.S.

Throughout its first 100 years as a nation, the U.S. was primarily an agricultural economy. Through the mid-1870s, agricultural output accounted for more than half of total production in the U.S. It was not until the mid-1880s that the value of manufactured goods surpassed the value of agricultural goods in total U.S. production. It was also at this point in time that the nonagricultural portion of the labor force first outnumbered those who worked on farms. In fact, it wasn't until about 1920 that the urban population in the U.S. surpassed the rural population. Despite the fact that the country was primarily rural and agricultural, the development of industry began early in the 19th century. Industrial production accelerated during the middle years of the 19th century, stimulated in part by the demands of the Civil War. By the turn of the century, the United States was the leading producer in the world of both manufactured and agricultural goods.

What accounts for this tremendous economic achievement? One important source of American economic development, which is often neglected, was the role of the government. In the formative years of the nation, the government played a crucial role in the construction of a federal system in which economic trade flowed freely from one state to another. Indeed, this concern with encouraging trade within the U.S. was one of the primary reasons behind the construction and ratification of the Constitution. In addition, the government passed tariffs to protect infant industries, it established a national currency, and it created a legal framework that governed economic transactions. Later, in the 19th century, it financed and encouraged the development of different forms of transportation, along with state and local governments, that facilitated the internal trade in the expanding nation.

Another source of growth was the vast supply of land and resources available to the U.S. The country expanded westward throughout the 18th century. This expansion was made possible by the conquering of one after another of the Native American tribes, by the purchase of land from France and Russia, and by military conquest over Mexico and several European countries that still controlled land in North America. Through what Americans called Manifest Destiny, the U.S. eventually controlled from coast-to-coast the middle part of the North American continent. This expanding geographical territory supplied space for expansion and raw materials for increasing agricultural and industrial production. It also supplied an expanding volume of cotton and wheat exports for sale to Europe. This international market encouraged further agricultural production and made possible imports which facilitated industrial production.

Later, at the end of the 19th century and the beginning of the 20th century, the U.S. joined Western European countries in the process of expansion beyond their borders. American imperialism, as the U.S. pursued Manifest Destiny beyond the North American continent into the Pacific, Asia, and Latin America, provided raw materials, markets, and investments that fueled further economic expansion.

The American people themselves, both the original colonists and the later immigrants, proved to be an important source of growth and development. Strongly individualistic and dedicated to hard work, they took risks, organized productive activities, educated themselves, invented, and conquered. The U.S. became a thriving and growing economy through a primarily private economic system based on the efforts of individuals and groups of individuals tied together through an expanding system of national markets for goods and services.

Coincident with all of these sources of growth, many institutions emerged in the U.S. to stimulate development. The banking system, retail and wholesale organizations, and the transportation system facilitated the expansion of economic activity with improved organization and lower costs. Related to the development of these sectors of the economy was the emergence of one of the foremost institutions of American capitalism and economic production, the corporation. A legal combination of individuals, *the corporation* was a successful device for amassing resources for organizing and engaging in production. And in several leading industries, large corporations led the advance of American growth—oil, the railroads, banking, steel, automobiles, and so on. In a sense, the history of the American corporation and its development is the history of modern American capitalism.

By the middle of the 20th century, the U.S. was the dominant economic, political, and military country in the world. It was the most advanced nation in terms of manufacturing and agricultural techniques and production. It had the highest standard of living, on the average, for its almost 200 million citizens. And it was still a nation that valued individual economic and political freedom. For the most part its development had been a success story.

However, throughout its history, there have also been some negative aspects in American economic development. The conquest and exploitation of the American Indians must be counted as, and remains, a black mark in our history. Slavery throughout the colonial period and until the Civil War relied on the inhuman subjugation and exploitation of human beings as a source of increased production. Scandals of political and economic corruption, as both economic and political power became more concentrated, have been rife throughout our history. These range from the Crédit Mobilier affair of the 1870s to the Teapot Dome Scandal of the 1920s to more recent instances of illegal corporate campaign contributions in the U.S. and bribery abroad.

During the development of the American economy and up to the present, our country has been plagued by a host of problems that are of an economic origin or at least have an economic dimension. These include: poverty, commercialism, pollution, militarism, racism, and sexism. These problems continue to challenge our economic institutions, relationships, and methods.

An additional negative aspect of American capitalist development has been its instability. Throughout the late 19th and early 20th centuries, the U.S. suffered through repeated depressions in economic activity. Periods of prosperity and boom were regularly followed by periods of depression and bust. Figure 1.1 graphically depicts this pattern.

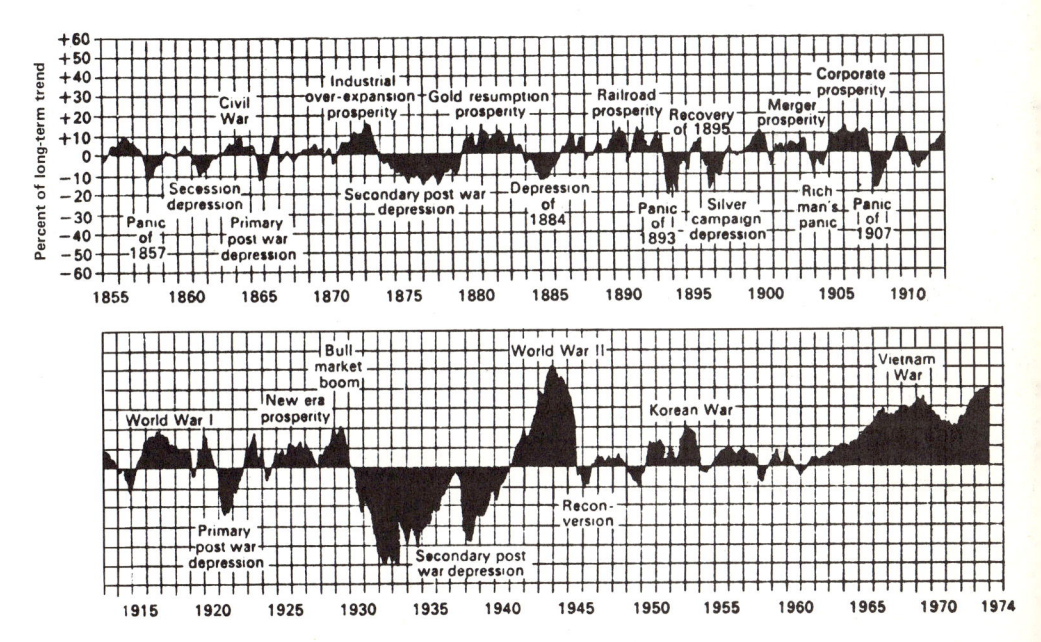

FIG. 1.1 Economic instability in the United States. (From *American Business Activity from 1790 to Today,* by the Cleveland Trust Company.)

During these depressions, unemployment and economic hardship for many people increased dramatically and tragically. The worst of these depressions occurred in the 1930s, when the decrease in economic activity spread around the world. In 1933, almost one-third of the work force in the U.S. was without employment. The Great Depression was deep and lasted throughout the 1930s.

This Depression and our "escape" from it with the increased production and employment brought about by World War II, in fact, engendered one of the more recent alterations in the American form of capitalism. Given the historical instability of capitalism's growth process, the U.S. government since the 1930s has taken a more direct responsibility for the overall health of the economy. It has attempted to prevent extremes in the cycles of boom-and-bust. Some would call this mixed capitalism; others might call it state capitalism. Still others, noting the role of the State and the role of large corporations in the economy, call it monopoly capitalism. At any rate, this expanded economic role of the state constitutes one more major change in the continuing development of American capitalism as an economic system.

14. Based on your conception of the American economic system, list its five most important attributes. Are these positive or negative attributes? Are they results of the system? or are they fundamental characteristics of it?

15. What's your name, or label, for our economic system? Why do you call it that?

The American economy has come a long way in the 200-year history of our independent nation. Sometimes, however, we are too sanguine about our success; and we retain many false impressions of our economy. But recent experiences with the deep recession of 1973–1975 and with the coexistence of high levels of inflation and unemployment have shaken confidence in the strength of our economy.

With this brief introduction to the roots and evolution of our economic system, we will now turn our attention to "economics." What is economics? Now that we know something about economic systems, what they do and how they change, what can economists tell us about them?

KEY CONCEPTS

tradition
feudalism
capitalism
production
consumption
factors of production—land, labor, capital
distribution

surplus
the manor
the guilds
the transition from feudalism to capitalism
mercantilism
classical liberalism
economic development

REVIEW QUESTIONS

1. Discuss the distinguishing characteristics of ancient economic systems.
2. What must an economic system accomplish? Why?
3. Why is surplus a source of economic growth?
4. Explain the transition from feudalism and capitalism and identify the main differences between the two systems.

5. What is the importance of markets to a capitalist economic system?
6. What accounts for the success of the American economy?
7. Given Hunt's description of capitalism in this chapter, do you think the U.S. today has a capitalist economy?

SUGGESTED READINGS

Robert Heilbroner, 1968. *The Making of Economic Society,* Prentice-Hall. This is a relatively brief introductory historical treatment of the emergence and development of Western capitalism—from its roots in feudalism to its modern manifestations. Very well written and readable.

E. K. Hunt, 1975. *Property and Prophets,* Harper & Row. Also an introductory history of the roots of modern economic institutions. In addition, this work concentrates on the relationship of social and economic change to the development of ideas.

Douglass C. North, 1966. *Growth and Welfare in the American Past,* Prentice-Hall. A brief economic history of the U.S., chock-full of interesting data detailing the economic progress of the U.S.

Karl Polanyi, 1957. *The Great Transformation,* Beacon Press. A more advanced treatment of the withering away of feudalism and the introduction of the market as one of the central foundations of the capitalist economic system.

William Appleman Williams, 1973. *The Contours of American History,* New Viewpoints. An extended social, political, and economic history of the U.S. written from a critical perspective.

ECONOMICS AS A SOCIAL SCIENCE

CHAPTER 2

INTRODUCTION

Now that we have briefly examined some economic history, what is economics? And what can it do for us?

Economics is the study of how the productive and distributive aspects of human life are organized. It studies the history of production, distribution, and consumption of goods and services in different societies and countries *and* how these aspects have changed over time. Economics, as a social science, is thus an accumulation of human knowledge about one particular segment of social life. It seeks to help us to understand the complexities and confusions of our economic system in the *modern world*.

In this chapter, we will examine the elements of economics as one of the social sciences. We will be concerned with its goals and its methods, as well as its relevance to our lives. In addition, we will introduce briefly the different branches of economics and the kinds of things that economists do. Finally, we will see that *economists* have some disagreements about what economics is and ought to be.

WHAT IS ECONOMICS?

In recent years, teachers of economics have become concerned about how best to teach economics. Their concern stems from the importance of economic knowledge in the modern world and from their inability oftentimes to teach that knowledge to students in a way that will prove useful to them. Out of this concern, many economists have attempted to define precisely what the key elements of economic understanding are and to concentrate on teaching these. Several of these economists, working with the Joint Council on Economic Education, have recently published a booklet called *A Framework for Teaching Economics: Basic Concepts.*[*] In this piece, they point out the following key elements of economic understanding: practicing a reasoned approach, mastering the basic concepts, possessing an overview of the economy, identifying the issues, applying these elements to particular issues, and reaching decisions on economic issues.

---
*W. Lee Hansen, Chairman; G. L. Bach, James D. Calderwood, and Phillip Saunders, *A Framework for Teaching Economics: Basic Concepts,* Joint Council on Economic Education, 1977.

These elements provide some insights into what economics is. Economics is the study of how the productive and distributive aspects of human life are organized. In addition, economics is a body of knowledge and a way of thinking about the economic aspects of social life. It is concerned with "practicing a reasoned approach"; that is, economics presents an organized and logical way of thinking about economic reality. It utilizes many basic concepts that focus our attention on key variables in economic activity. It provides us with an overall appreciation of the structure and complexity of the economic system in our country (as well as in others). It should help us to identify the issues that will be important to us in our individual and social lives. In addition, economics helps us to reason and to draw conclusions about specific economic problems, their ramifications, and possible solutions.

One of the central concerns of economics in attempting to accomplish all of these tasks is the development of *economic theory*. This relates to the *method* of economics. While it is concerned with social life and the vagaries of human beings, it also attempts as nearly as possible to be scientific.

Economists attempt to measure and collect facts about economic activity. In doing so, they try to discover certain similarities in the relationships between different components of economic life. These similarities can, when they are accepted as expressing a constant relationship (in normal circumstances), become *economic theories*. An example of such a theory would be the theory of supply and demand. We can use this *economic theory* to gain insight into the nature of certain goods and services—how they are valued by society's members, how costly they are to produce, and what *price* they will sell for in the society given different circumstances.

The function of an economic theory, therefore, is to allow us to examine certain limited aspects of economic life, to discover more or less constant relationships between different economic variables, and to predict possible economic events in the

I'd like you to meet Marty Thorndecker. He's an economist but he's really very nice.

Drawing by Ed Arno. Copyright © 1974, The New Yorker Magazine, Inc.

future. For example, the theory of supply and demand tells us that, most of the time, a desired article in short supply will command a relatively high price. From this, we can conclude (theorize) that *if* the supply of that article is reduced, its price is likely to go up even further. Note that such statements are based on an assumption—an *if* statement—followed by a conditional conclusion. Economists love to make assumptions. Much of their theory is based on similar assumptions. In the final analysis, however, their theories must be judged by whether their conclusions and predictions conform with what actually happens in economic reality.

In the case of supply-and-demand theory, there are constant examples where we can check out the validity of the conclusions and predictions of economic theory. For example, in 1973 when the Arab oil-producing countries embargoed shipments of oil to the U.S., Western Europe, and Japan, the supply of oil decreased and the price *did* increase. Likewise, when there are good crops of wheat in the U.S., the price of wheat is likely to go down; or when crops are bad because of the weather, the price of wheat does go up. In each of these cases, economic reality conforms with economic theory.

This aspect of economics highlights its *relevance*. Economics and economic theories are concerned with problems and activities that are crucial and/or important to all of us as individuals and to our societies. The scope of economics can be national, international, regional, local, or personal. The problems and activities that are the subject matter of economics include the following: inflation, productivity, supplies of natural resources, efficiency, debt, unemployment, technological development, product distribution, advertising, poverty, alienation, the allocation of scarce resources, income redistribution, taxation, war, and a host of others. Economics identifies such economic problems, describes their ramifications, hypothesizes about their causes, predicts their future development, and prescribes solutions to them. Economics seeks to build up our understanding of and knowledge about the fundamental economic aspects of our social lives.

To this end, there are many branches of economics, some of which will be introduced in this book. Economic history focuses on how and why economic activity has changed over time. Urban economics focuses on analyzing the economic operation and problems of cities. Microeconomics is concerned primarily with the activities of smaller economic units, such as the household or the firm. Macroeconomics has the much broader subject of the operation and health of an entire national economy. International economics deals with economic relationships and activities on a global scale. Economic thought treats the development of ideas by economists through the years. Economic development concentrates on the theories and problems associated with the economic growth and maturation of national economies. Public policy economics is concerned with the analysis of proposals for dealing with public problems. Political economy highlights the relationships between economic and political institutions and how they affect each other. This by no means exhausts the list of the different branches of economics.

Given this wide variety of branches of economics, there are lots of different things that economists do. Many people trained in economics as a discipline become teachers of economics in high schools, colleges, or universities. Many work in businesses attempting to inform decision makers on current and future economic realities. Since World War II, an increasing number of economists have found employment in government at the state, local, and federal levels. Economists also work for consulting firms, for labor unions, for public interest or lobbying groups, or for international organizations.

With this diversity of employment experiences (and hence allegiances and perspectives), it should not be very surprising that there is a healthy amount of "confusion" within the social science of economics. Economists, despite their efforts to build economic theory, often disagree among themselves and fall into different camps. They may differ about which problems are most important (or even, sometimes, that they are problems!), about what the causes of a problem are, and about which solutions to a problem are the best. Controversy in economics reflects controversy in life.

Nevertheless, there is also a large core of economic ideas that is accepted by most economists. We will study many of these ideas in this book. In addition, economists are unified by the goal of economics: building knowledge about the economic aspects of life.

Much of the debate among economists about what economics is and should be concerns its scope. The famous English economist, Alfred Marshall, thought that economics could be one of the most precise and scientific of the social sciences because it dealt with observable and measurable data in the form of prices, quantities produced and sold, and incomes. In his *Principles of Economics,* he wrote:

The advantage which economics has over other branches of social science appears then to arise from the fact that its special field of work gives rather larger opportunities for exact methods than any other branch. It concerns itself chiefly with those desires, aspirations and other affections of human nature, the outward manifestations of which appear as incentives to action in such a form that the force or quantity of the incentives can be estimated and measured with some approach to accuracy; and which therefore are in some degree amenable to treatment by scientific machinery. An opening is made for the methods and the tests of science as soon as the force of a person's motives—*not* the motives themselves—can be approximately measured by the sum of money, which he will just give up in order to secure a desired satisfaction; or again by the sum which is just required to induce him to undergo a certain fatigue.

Alfred Marshall, *Principles of Economics,* Macmillan Publishing Co., Inc., 1948.

Other economists, however, have been less convinced by this argument. They point out that economics, as one of the social sciences, cannot divorce itself from the society in which it exists. Efforts of human beings to understand reality must necessarily be influenced by morality, ideology, and value judgments. In other words, economics cannot be totally scientific because the economist's understanding of the subject matter is affected by his or her evaluation of, opinions about, and conclusions concerning social reality. Economics, as a body of thought, functions to preserve, to protect and/or to challenge existing social reality—as well as to help us to understand it. For some economists, then, economics should be a part of the effort to understand *and to improve* social existence. Joan Robinson, another English economist, has written in *Freedom and Necessity* that:

> ... The methods to which the natural sciences owe their success—controlled experiment and exact observation of continually recurring phenomena—cannot be applied to the study of human beings by human beings. So far, no equally successful method of establishing reliable natural laws has been suggested.
>
> Certainly, the social sciences should not be unscientific. Their practitioners should not jump to conclusions on inadequate evidence or propound circular statements that are true by definition as though they had some factual content; when they disagree they should not resort to abuse like theologians or literary critics, but should calmly set about to investigate the nature of the difference and to propose a plan of research to resolve it. ...
>
> The function of social science is quite different from that of the natural sciences—it is to provide society with an organ of self-consciousness.
>
> Every interconnected group of human beings has to have an ideology—that is, a conception of what is the proper way to behave and the permissible pattern of relationships in family, economic and political life.

Joan Robinson, *Freedom and Necessity,* Pantheon Books, 1970.

For Robinson, then, economics must attempt to be scientific and rigorous; but, since it is also concerned with the effort to create a better society, it must also devote itself to exploring areas that are more philosophical in nature. It must recognize its ideological elements.

Along these lines, economists often divide themselves between "economics" and what is called "political economy." Economics is more concerned with explaining what can be measured and with developing theories about "purely" economic relationships. Political economy, on the other hand, is more concerned with the relationships of the economic system and its institutions to the rest of society and social development. It is sensitive to the influence of noneconomic factors such as political institutions, morality, ideology, and so on in determining economic events.

1. "The function of social science ... is to provide society with an organ of self-consciousness." What does this mean? How does economics do this?

2. What, according to Robinson, is an ideology? What role do ideologies play in social development?

3. What does Robinson think is the task of economics as a social science? Do you agree with her or not? would Alfred Marshall?

PARADIGMS AND IDEOLOGIES

As we have seen, economists disagree about what economics is and should be. Furthermore, they often disagree about what economic problems are important, what theories are correct, and what economic policies are best. This is especially true over time as the economic problems a society is likely to face *change* as conditions change. Along with changes in economic problems and economic institutions over time, economic theories have also changed. This aspect of changing economic theory and of differences among economists has two results that will be useful to keep in mind while studying economics. The first is that there are different, and sometimes contesting, kinds of economic theory; and the second is that there are different kinds of economists with different goals, values, and beliefs.

The Realm of Theory

First of all, different periods of economic history (and different economic systems) have given rise to different types of economic theories. That is, new types of economic conditions and economic institutions have required different systems of thought and explanation.

For example, as capitalism emerged as an economic system, so did classical liberalism as an economic theory. Stated slightly differently, as crises developed in economic matters as the old gave way to the new, economic institutions changed; and, finally, economic thought also changed. The previous theories and notions were inadequate to explain the new conditions and problems. Thomas Kuhn, in *The Structure of Scientific Revolutions*, has referred to such changes in scientific theory as changes in *paradigms*. This concept can be applied to the natural sciences as well as to the social sciences. A *paradigm* serves to structure thought about a certain aspect of nature, life, or society; and, furthermore, it is *widely accepted* as doing so. However, as time passes, natural and social conditions change, new interpretations and new facts become known, and the existing paradigm may be challenged or may be inadequate to explain reality. If this happens, eventually a new and more widely accepted paradigm will be developed. An example of this in the scientific world would be the replacement of the Ptolemaic by the Copernican conception of astronomy and the universe. It is now widely accepted, because it conforms with what we know and observe, that the planets revolve around the sun. Still another example is our debt to Christopher Columbus because he was sure that the earth wasn't flat!

In addition to changing paradigms over time, there is the possibility that two contending paradigms will seek to explain the same aspect of reality. Examining the same events and facts, but differing on the use of key concepts and relationships, these contending paradigms will offer sometimes conflicting (or, at least, differing) interpretations of reality. At one time or another, or in different places, one or the other might be dominant. Marxian economists and orthodox economists have different interpretations of American business cycles. But in the U.S., orthodox economics is dominant.

This process of changing and conflicting paradigms will also be emphasized in our study of economics. As economic crises occur and economic conditions change, one economic *paradigm* will replace another. *Keynesian economics* emerged as the *dominant* economic theory out of the Great Depression of the 1930s—replacing *clas-*

A pretty girl or a witch?

sical economics. Classical economics argued that a laissez-faire, self-regulating market economic system would eliminate instability through the flexibility of markets. If there was overproduction of goods and, consequently, a decrease in production and an increase in unemployment (that is, a depression in economic activity), then the markets would respond to correct the situation. Wherever there was an oversupply of goods, prices would fall and stimulate consumption of those goods, thus eliminating the surplus. Likewise, wages would fall and stimulate the hiring of unemployed workers by business. In fact, classical economics relied on *Say's Law*, developed by the French economist, J. B. Say (1767—1832), that held that supply created its own demand, to explain why overproduction or underconsumption would be unlikely in a laissez-faire market economic system. Say theorized that incomes paid out in the process of production would always be sufficient to buy what was produced. Furthermore, the flexibility of prices and wages in self-regulating markets would ensure the result.

However, as we have seen, capitalist economies were and have been very unstable—with alternating periods of prosperity and depression. The weakness of Say's Law was especially pronounced in the severity and persistence of the Great Depression. Consequently, a new theory, a new paradigm, Keynesian economics (about which we will learn more in Part IV) emerged to explain why depressions do occur and what can be done about them.

An example of *conflicting* paradigms is the contrast between Marxian economics and orthodox economics. *Orthodox* economics accepts the institutional setting of the economy and builds a theory around how it works. *Marxian economics* assumes a critical stance toward the existing economic system and attempts to discover how it will and can be changed. Orthodox economics accepts capitalism, and Marxian economics criticizes capitalism and argues for socialism. Another example of conflicting paradigms occurs within orthodox economics: it is the difference between the Keynesian and Monetarist approaches. The Keynesian view contends that it is most important to focus on aggregate demand to understand economic events. The Monetarist view rejects this approach and argues that only through monetary changes can we understand the economy. Throughout this book, we will encounter these conflicting paradigms as they attempt to explain economic reality. But this brings us to our second point: that there are different kinds of economists.

The Realm of the Economist

There are different kinds of economists. Economists are human beings with differing ideas, theories, assumptions, and ideologies. As economic conditions and institutions have changed, so have economist's ideas, theories, assumptions, and ideologies. In different times and spaces, economists have differed. And in the *same* time and space, economists still disagree. Perhaps one way of clarifying this is to examine ideology.

E. K. Hunt, in *Property and Prophets,* defines an ideology as a set of:

> ... ideas and beliefs that tend to justify morally a society's social and economic relationships. Most members of a society internalize the ideology and thus believe their functional role as well as those of others are morally correct and that the method by which society divides its produce is fair. This common belief gives society its cohesiveness and vitality. Lack of it creates turmoil and strife—and ultimately revolution, if the differences are deep enough.

Thus at different times different ideologies may be dominant. At one time, Confucianism was the ideology of China. Now the dominant ideology in China is Maoism and socialism. Catholicism and a concern with the next world once dominated Western Europe; later individualism and materialism held sway.

Additionally, different ideologies concerning the goals of a society and an economic system may conflict. One convenient way of illustrating this is to note that there are three broad groups of Western economists today. Each group has its own ideas, theories, and ideologies. *Liberal economists,* in a liberal Western world, accept the main structures of the economic system but recognize its weaknesses and limitations. They offer reforms to alleviate the problems of capitalism. *Conservative economists* either favor the status quo or argue for a return to more laissez-faire types of capitalism; they are in favor of minimizing the role of the State in the economy. *Radical economists* are more critical of the existing system. They say that the problems are endemic to the system itself; thus, solutions require systemic change. They offer new ideas and new institutions; they are in favor of revolutionary changes. Adam Smith, in his day, was a radical. Karl Marx was a radical. John Maynard Keynes offered a liberal solution to the 1930s crisis of capitalism. Milton Friedman of the University of Chicago, who writes a column on the economy in *Newsweek,* is a contemporary conservative.

---

4. What is your ideology?

5. Compare and contrast Hunt's definition of ideology with that of Joan Robinson.

6. Which set of economic ideas do you think is dominant in the U.S. today?

In the following piece by radical economist David Gordon, excerpted from his book, *Problems in Political Economy,* some of the essential elements of liberal, conservative and radical economics are summarized.

RADICAL, LIBERAL, AND CONSERVATIVE ECONOMICS
DAVID GORDON

"Normal science" means research firmly based upon one or more past scientific achievements, achievements that some particular scientific community acknowledges for a time as supplying the foundation for its further practice.... [Such achievements can be called] "paradigms."... In the absence of a paradigm or some candidate for paradigm, all of the facts that could possibly pertain to the development of a given science are likely to seem equally relevant.... To be accepted as a paradigm, a theory must seem better than its competitors....

—Thomas S. Kuhn

When we asked whether or not we are Marxist, our position is the same as that of a physicist or a biologist when asked if he is a "Newtonian" or if he is a "Pasteurian."

There are truths so evident, so much a part of people's knowledge, that it is now useless to discuss them. One ought to be "Marxist" with the same naturalness with which one is "Newtonian" in physics, or "Pasteurian" in biology.... The advances in social and political science, as in other fields, belong to a long historical process whose links are connecting, adding up, molding and constantly perfecting themselves.

—Ernesto "Che" Guevara

... I concentrate on three general social perspectives: radical, liberal, and conservative.... I agree with Paul Sweezy about the appropriate basis for choosing among alternative paradigms: "It seems to me that from a scientific point of view the question of choosing between ... approaches ... can be answered quite simply. Which more accurately reflects the fundamental characteristics of social reality which is under analysis?"

THE RADICAL VIEW

A modern radical analysis of society draws from, but does not depend exclusively on, the seminal nineteenth-century work of Karl Marx. Marx's analysis of society made original theoretical contributions on both substantive and methodological levels. In his methodological discussions, he insisted that general theories or analytic views of society cannot remain aloof from the course of history, somehow eternally fixed above the evolutions and revolutions of society below. As society

Reprinted by permission of the publisher, from David Gordon, *Problems in Political Economy,* 2nd ed. (Lexington, Mass.: D.C. Heath and Company, 1977).

changes, so must theories about its nature change. Analysis of society should reflect a dynamic synthesis of theory and reality.

... In sketching the basic features of a radical analysis of American society, I have built from recent radical writings more than from Marx, and from recent historical events more than from the events which Marx perceived.

The underlying analytic framework of the radical "paradigm" involves seven basic clusters of hypotheses about society.

1. The analysis argues that the structure and evolution of any society depend principally on the society's dominant mode of economic production.... As Robert Tucker elaborates, "In every instance ... the mode of productive activity has been the definitive fact of the social epoch, the determinant of the character of society in all of its superstructural expressions: political, legal, intellectual, [and] religious."

2. The most important and most distinctive feature of the mode of production in capitalist societies is its organization of labor by means of the wage-contract.

3. This method of organizing production involves two fundamental and connected economic features—one involving production and the other distribution.

First, *production* itself brings together *workers*—with nothing to offer but their capacity to do work—and *capitalists*—who need laborers to set in motion the means of production that they own.

... Second, since people cannot produce for themselves, they must buy products in the market place.

... These two characteristics are integrated through the structure and motion of the whole capitalist system. Workers depend on jobs to support themselves. Their jobs depend on whether or not capitalists can make profits through production. The capitalists cannot realize their profits unless they sell their goods. So they campaign to sell their goods, luring more and more people into the web of market transactions. And as people become more and more dependent on the market, they are less and less able to support themselves. Which means that they must work to support their families. Which replenishes the labor force, keeping wages low and helping maintain the basis for capitalist profits. Around and around these circuits, the system extends itself and deepens its control.

4. This set of connections between production and distribution helps determine the principal dynamic characteristic of the system: the unceasing attempt by owners of capital to increase continuously their stocks of wealth. It is not that capitalists are greedy (although they may be). Capitalists "are driven to expand profits not only because they *want* to," as Richard Edwards has put it, "but also because if they are to remain capitalists, the market *forces* them to do so."

5. With these tendencies, the capitalist system tends more and more to create an opposition between two distinct classes. As people lose control over their own property, they must become workers in order to survive. And as the accumulation of capital leads to an increasing concentration and centralization of wealth, a few capitalists—through their corporations—dominate more and more of our social existence.

6. The dynamics of the system tend to generate some basic contradictions with fundamental impact on its further development.

• The continuing development of production leads to continuing mechanization. The division of labor breeds the minute fragmentation of tasks.

... But people have always sought historically, in the radical view, to increase their control over nature and their own destinies.

- Capitalism leads more and more to the "objective socialisation of production." People no longer work individually, producing for their own needs. The division of labor under capitalism effects a complete interdependence among people as producers.

. . . But at the same time, capitalism depends on and enforces a totally private, frequently ruthless competition among people.

- In similar ways, vast increases in productive capacity establish for the first time in history the fundamental irrationality of class conflict in society. Class conflicts have always existed. With the very early precapitalist development of social cooperation in production and with primitive technological innovations, individuals first became capable of producing more with their own labor than was necessary to sustain their own existence—to feed, house, and clothe them and their families.

But capitalism depends on the private ownership of property and the ability of owners of capital constantly to (try to) accumulate more and more of "surplus product." Some members of society continue to obtain enormous shares of wealth and leisure, while others continue to support both themselves and others with their labor. Class conflicts inevitably continue in capitalist societies.

7. Finally, these basic forces defining and driving capitalist societies produce a constantly changing set of social institutions. These institutions largely determine the nature and content of daily life in capitalist societies, as well as the ways in which the basic forces driving capitalist societies are manifested. Given these institutions, the analysis involves three basic hypotheses about them: first, that the nature and structure of these institutions directly determine the nature of social relations in society; second, that these institutions determine the distribution of power among groups and individuals and therefore determine the specific historical resolutions of class conflicts; and, third, that the most important institutions ultimately benefit those directly included in, or associated with, the capitalist class.

The State, in the radical view, operates ultimately to serve the interests of the controlling class in a class society. Since the "capitalist class" fundamentally controls capitalist societies, the State functions in those societies to serve that class. It does so either directly, by providing services only to members of that class, or indirectly, by helping preserve the system of institutions supporting and maintaining the power of that class.

In general, radicals envision that socialism can provide a better basis than capitalism for transition toward an "ideal" society in which people could be free to develop themselves as human beings and at the same time to cooperate with others in developing their potential together. This movement would become manifest in many different ways:

- People could become more and more free from the "whip of hunger," liberating themselves from the insecurity and occasional starvation that plague people in capitalist societies.

- People could become more and more free from exploitation by more powerful classes. Socialist development would promote *even* development, with growing equality, rather than the uneven development and sharp inequalities dominating capitalist societies.

- People could become freer from the tyranny of the detailed division of labor. Rather than reducing workers to "fragments of their former selves," socialism could begin to develop everyone's potential to do more and more creative work.

- People could become more and more free to contribute positively to the welfare of fellow members of their communities. In capitalism, radicals argue, people are forced to compete with each other. In the process of socialist transition, they could be free to begin building a better society together.

The radical analysis of capitalism and this sense of socialist direction cannot be separated. Radicals argue that theory and practice cannot be divorced. Our knowledge of capitalism helps inform our efforts to change it. And our efforts to change it improve our knowledge. One cannot understand the processes of change in the real world, in this view, without participating in that change. As Mao Tse-tung put it:

> *If you want knowledge, you must take part in the practice of changing reality. If you want to know the taste of a pear, you must change the pear by eating it yourself. . . . If you want to know the theory and methods of revolution, you must take part in revolution. All genuine knowledge originates in direct experience.*

THE LIBERAL AND CONSERVATIVE VIEWS

This section briefly surveys the liberal and conservative perspectives. I summarize these paradigms for comparative purposes.

. . . I will summarize the basic points of the liberal and conservative analyses together, for they begin with the same fundamental hypotheses about social reality. I will discuss their views of the State separately, and their normative predispositions separately, for the two perspectives differ more widely on those levels.

Both liberal and conservative analyses of social problems begin from an underlying view of the society, formulated most rigorously in orthodox economic analysis. This underlying view abstracts from the specific social relations and institutions of a society, taking the existing system of institutions for granted. It then builds from some basic postulates about the behavior of individual decision-making units—like households, workers, or firms—and the ways in which they adjust to the given institutional framework. The analysis postulates specifically that individual units act rationally and are free rationally to maximize their welfare subject to the simplest of constraints. For example, it presumes that consumers are free to choose whatever goods will maximize their welfare, subject to the simple constraint that their expenses not exceed their income. The analysis does not explore the ways in which institutions predetermine the range of goods from which individuals can choose. In political analysis, it tends to imply that voters are free to choose rationally among wide varieties of public alternatives—whether candidates in elections or government programs through representatives. From that beginning, the postulates imply a simple conclusion: final decisions made by individuals accurately reflect their real preferences, about cars or congressmen, for instance, without regard to the institutional context in which those choices are made. The postulates imply that a wide variety of alternative government decisions is possible.

In terms of aggregate social behavior, the liberal and conservative analysis assumes that individual actions combine (or "aggregate," in the technical terms of economics) to produce stable, harmonious social equilibria. This basic postulate involves three separate elements. First, it implies that there is such a thing as an equilibrium in social terms—a conjunction of social forces and relations such that movements away from it will tend to produce countermovements reestablishing the equilibrium. This basic notion dominates economics, where the concept of equilibrium pervades orthodox analysis; sociology, especially in modern applications of "structural-functional" analysis; and much of political science, with its emphases on the stability of political systems. Second, the notion of equilibrium implies that society is relatively free from conflict, that individuals acting privately and independently are capable of combining socially to produce "harmonious" social situations with which few are basically discontented, from which few would like to move. And, third, it tends to imply, more dynamically, that changes in society come gradually, if at all, moving slowly from one harmonious equilibrium to the next.

Given those basic postulates, the two perspectives begin to diverge. Each admits that social problems or difficulties occasionally develop. Each perspective admits, for instance, that the market produces an income distribution in which some earn too little to live, and that, therefore, some way should be found to assist the poorest in society. And each insists that problems develop from minor imperfections in the basic social mechanisms, principally from inadequate information or shortsightedness among individuals. But the two perspectives differ sharply on what should be done about such problems.

And this difference draws essentially from their respective analyses of the State. In the liberal view, the State in a modern democracy adequately reflects individual wishes through group representatives. The government is justified in acting, essentially, because it incorporates the preferences of all individuals and because it seeks to advance the interests of all individuals.

In the liberal analysis, there are three principal kinds of government action that society both prefers and requires. First, the government should redistribute income. Second, the government should act when private market mechanisms cannot satisfy consumer preferences effectively. Third, the government should act to provide certain goods that the market mechanism is incapable of providing, like national defense. Armed with these principles, the liberal perspective has motivated and justified a vast increase in government responsibilities in the United States during the twentieth century. Programs have developed to overcome market inefficiencies in housing, for instance, from public construction of low-cost housing to public provision of financial subsidies for those too poor to afford decent housing.

In the conservative view, the role of the State should be much more limited. Conservatives tend to have greater faith than liberals in the efficiency and optimality of the private market mechanism, and to have greater fear than liberals do of both government inefficiency and government infringement on personal liberties. Friedman elaborates these points clearly.

Despite these differences, however, the two perspectives agree on one central disagreement with the radical view of the State. In neither the liberal nor the conservative perspective does the State serve the interests only of one class, as radicals argue. To conservatives it can barely serve anyone's interest, and to liberals it can effectively serve the interests of all.

The liberal and conservative perspectives also differ sharply with each other on normative grounds, although the differences seem more precisely disagreements of temperament than of basic principle. Conservatives tend to place the highest priority on individual freedom and social order, while liberals tend to place their highest priority on individual equality and social justice. Liberals seem more willing to countenance both rapid social change and extensive government involvement in the private sector. Both differ completely from the radical perspective in one important respect: each tends to regard capitalism as the "best" economic mode of production because it affords, they argue, the maximum feasible individual freedom. Each perspective envisions as its "ideal" society a perfectly functioning capitalist democracy. Each imagines that we can come extremely close to that ideal without major changes in current capitalist institutions (although conservatives would certainly prefer a much less powerful government than we have in the United States).

7. Critically evaluate each of the different perspectives with respect to the statement that: "It seems to me that from a scientific point of view the question of choosing between approaches can be answered quite simply. Which more accurately reflects the fundamental characteristics of social reality which is under analysis?" How are your answers affected by your own beliefs?

8. What is the difference between theory and ideology?

Having seen that there are many different branches of economics, that economists do many different things, and that there is a substantial amount of disagreement among economists on many different issues, in the next Part of this book we will briefly examine the history and development of economic thought.

KEY CONCEPTS

economics
political economy
economic theory
the role of assumptions
ideology
paradigm

orthodox economics
Marxian economics
liberal economists
conservative economists
radical economists

REVIEW QUESTIONS

1. What is economics? Is that what you thought economics was (or should be)?

2. Why do economists disagree?

3. What is a paradigm? In your life have you ever replaced one paradigm with another?

4. What are the main differences among conservative, liberal, and radical economists?

SUGGESTED READINGS

E. Ray Canterbury, 1976. *The Making of Economics,* Wadsworth Publishing Company. An insightful book on the development of economics: "what [it] has been and what it is becoming."

Richard Edwards, Michael Reich, and Thomas E. Weisskopf (eds.), 1978. *The Capitalist System* (2nd ed.), Prentice-Hall. A radical analysis of the American economic system, its institutions, its laws of motion, and its problems by over 20 members of the Union of Radical Political Economics.

Milton Friedman, 1964. *Capitalism and Freedom,* University of Chicago Press. A conservative defense of the capitalist system and market theory by a Nobel Prize winner.

John Kenneth Galbraith, 1977. *The Age of Uncertainty,* Houghton Mifflin. The "text" accompanying Galbraith's recent BBC series on the development of modern economic ideas and institutions.

Robert Heilbroner, 1961. *The Worldly Philosophers,* Simon and Schuster. A classic elementary treatment of the ideas and personal lives of past economic thinkers.

Robert Lekachman, 1976. *Economists at Bay,* McGraw-Hill. A critical study of the state of economics today: its inability to explain and deal with combined unemployment and inflation as well as other problems. Lekachman also presents what he thinks must be the new direction for economics.

David Mermelstein (ed.), 1976. *Economics: Mainstream Readings and Radical Critiques,* (3rd ed.), Random House. Contrasting views of specific economic problems and issues are presented in this reader.

THE DEVELOPMENT OF MODERN ECONOMIC THOUGHT

PART II

Modern economic thinking has been influenced by many economists, among them Adam Smith, Thomas Malthus, David Ricardo, J. B. Say, John Stuart Mill, W. S. Jevons, Alfred Marshall, John Maynard Keynes, P. J. Proudhon, Thorstein Veblen, and Karl Marx. Many of the economists who contributed to the growing body of economic knowledge were British. Britain's emergence as one of the first capitalist powers, through the spread of its colonial empire and the coming of the Industrial Revolution, account for this influence. We can trace many of our theories and ideas about the economy back to these early economists.

This book cannot study all of the ideas of all of the economists who have made significant contributions to the history of modern economic thought; but, in this part, we will focus on the development of a few selected and persistent ways of thinking about an economy. We will concentrate on some *fundamental economic concepts,* many of which we sometimes don't give much thought to. What gives products *value?* Where did *private property* come from? What is the role of the *division of labor* in the wealth of nations? How is the *distribution* of goods and services determined? What role does *laissez-faire* play in economic activity? What is the basis of the *Marxian critique* of capitalism? There are many other important concepts that we could focus on, including capital, entrepreneurship, poverty, efficiency, and so on. We will touch on these in this part and elsewhere in the text, but here we will focus on a limited number of concepts and how they have been treated by some economists in the past. Your own understanding of the economy may become clearer as you agree, or disagree, with the ideas formulated by past economists.

By examining the ideas of these economists as they developed, we can gain some insights on economic concepts and changing economic institutions, ideas, and theories. Some of this will help us directly in understanding our current economic reality. And some will give us perspective on how the thoughts of past economists have influenced the development of economic systems as well as our understanding of the economy today.

THE SETTING—WHAT IS PROPERTY?

CHAPTER 3

INTRODUCTION

All forms of life are sustained by the world, but the world is owned by only some of the people. Who or what institution determines who owns the world, and why do they have the authority to define property rights? Who settles disputes over ownership? Who disputes ownership? Why are some people defined as outlaws? Individuals may evaluate identical economic situations in different ways because they have different perceptions of the situation and different personal interests.

As population increases and requires increasing productivity from the land, the land becomes relatively scarce and property rights become more important to owners. The distribution of property ownership is a significant determinant of the relative size of income received by the inhabitants of countries that stress the sanctity of private property rights.

Kilgore Trout once wrote a story called "This Means You." It was set in the Hawaiian Islands, the place where the lucky winners of Dwayne Hoover's contest in Midland City were supposed to go. Every bit of land on the islands was owned by only about forty people, and, in the story, Trout had those people decide to exercise their property rights to the full. They put up no trespassing signs on everything.

This created terrible problems for the million other people on the islands. The law of gravity required that they stick somewhere on the surface. Either that, or they could go out into the water and bob offshore.

But then the Federal Government came through with an emergency program. It gave a big balloon full of helium to every man, woman, and child who didn't own property.

There was a cable with a harness on it dangling from each balloon. With the help of the balloons, Hawaiians could go on inhabiting the islands without always sticking to things other people owned. . . .

The Governor of New York, Nelson Rockefeller, shook Trout's hand in a Cohoes grocery store one time. Trout had no idea who he was. As a science-fiction writer, he should have been flabbergasted to come so close to such a man. Rockefeller wasn't merely Governor. Because of the peculiar laws in that part of the planet, Rockefeller was allowed to own vast areas of Earth's surface, and the petroleum and other valuable minerals underneath the surface, as well. He owned or con-

Rockefeller Center. (Photograph by Tom Riddell.)

trolled more of the planet than many nations. This had been his destiny since infancy. He had been born into that cockamamie proprietorship.

"How's it going, fella?" Governor Rockefeller asked him.

"About the same," said Kilgore Trout.

Excerpted from *Breakfast of Champions* by Kurt Vonnegut, Jr. Copyright © 1973 by Kurt Vonnegut, Jr. Reprinted by permission of Delacorte Press/Seymour Lawrence.

---

1. As "the law of gravity required that they stick somewhere on the surface," what are your ideas about how all the people might best arrange their affairs to ensure themselves of a place to stick?

THE DEVELOPMENT OF PROPERTY IN ENGLAND

Great Britain, as all of you know, is an island with a total area (England, Wales, and Scotland) less than the area of Pennsylvania and New York. Celts occupied early Britain followed by the Romans who arrived in 55 B.C. and departed about A.D 410. Anglo-Saxons and Jutes arrived in the 5th century.

In 1066 William the Conqueror, with the approval of the pope, invaded England. He, with his Norman followers, slew King Harold at the Battle of Hastings, burned houses, and destroyed crops and cattle.

William and the Normans confiscated all the land, and William became the chief lord. He redistributed land titles to his favorite subjects, reorganized the church, and substituted his selection of foreign prelates for the English bishops.

Hereward is the name of one individual who resisted William's land grab. His story is known as the *Gesta Herewardi*. Here is what happened when he heard about the Norman's takeover.

... he finally arrived one evening at his ancestral home of Bourne, and, not yet revealing his identity, entered the house of one Osred, who had been his father's knight and who now offered him his hospitality. He found the household in deep mourning. Only the day before a Norman lord and his men had come to the village, to demand from Hereward's mother the land and all that belonged to his family. Hereward's younger brother was there, and when two of them laid rough hands on her he slew them, whereon he was surrounded and killed; they had cut off his head and placed it over the door of his own home in token of their revenge. Hereward heard the news in silence, still concealing his own identity; as he went to bed, however, he caught sounds of singing and shouting from somewhere in the village. Wrapping himself in a cloak and taking his servant with him, he went out to investigate. It was the Normans celebrating their victory in his own house. As he entered he took down the head of his brother, which he kissed and wrapped in a cloth. Penetrating further, he found his enemies; they had been feasting and were now all drunk. They had brought in some of the women of the village, in whose arms they lay, while a dancer amused them, singing insultingly songs about the English and imitating their crude manners. Hereward remained unobserved in the shadows; soon one of the girls, whose spirit had been roused by the jester's insults, protested. "If our lord's other son Hereward were here," she cried, "You'd have changed your tune before tomorrow morning." The Norman lord silenced her; "That particular rogue," he said, "is not likely at the moment to show his face this side of the Alps." The jester took up his words, and began his songs again, but at this moment Hereward leapt into the room and cut him down with a single blow of his sword. Then he began to lay about him; the Normans were too drunk to resist; some he killed himself, others his servant, whom he had left at the door, cut down as they tried to escape. No one was left alive. In the morning their fourteen heads grinned down in the place of his brother's at the doorway. The other Normans who had come to the district took warning and fled.

Reprinted with permission from Maurice Keen, *The Outlaws of Medieval Legend,* University of Toronto Press, 1961, and Routledge & Kegan Paul, Ltd., London.

William the Conqueror was displeased. Hereward became an outlaw. He took to the "recesses of the marshes and the woods" along with some other outlaws, and they continued to make William and the Normans uncomfortable.

About 1085-1086 William ordered a detailed survey of every piece of land in England that was to include information about the rights by which it was held by the holders. This survey is the *Domesday Book*. William planned to use this information for tax purposes.

Almost two centuries later in 1215 the barons (landholders), who felt threatened by the Crown, compelled King John to sign the Magna Carta that would ensure the barons' rights from the encroaching authority of the king. This was a rebellion of feudal lords. The peasants and artisans were not rebelling, and the Magna Carta neither improved nor protected their rights.

The Wizard of Id by permission of Johnny Hart and Field Enterprises, Inc.

Robert Jordon, in commenting about these times on the BBC, recently said

A pattern of building was part of *the system* or, as we would call it, the Establishment. It began when William of Normandy parcelled out England to his Norman subjects. It was confirmed by King John at Runnymede—Magna Carta being not the bastion of our liberties, only a landowner's guarantee.

A few centuries later, Henry VIII (1491-1547) established the Church of England. He closed the Catholic monasteries and abbeys, took all of their land, and appointed his own church officers. As British historian Maurice Keen notes in *The Outlaws of Medieval Legend*:

> ... after that the way was clear for the biggest event in our agrarian history—the distribution of all monastery lands to the Tudor millionaires. These landowners—merchants now rather than barons or earls—built themselves ... superb mansions. ...

2. In what ways might these events help shape the kind of economic system that developed in Britain?
3. What is a property right? What determines a property right?

THOSE WITHOUT PROPERTY—THE PEASANTS

During the early Middle Ages, the serfs on the feudal manors seem to have been accepting of their lot in life. There was security and certainty to their lives, if there was also hard work and poverty. What complaining there was seems to have been confined to individual peasants or manors. However, in the later centuries of the Middle Ages as feudal institutions began to undergo change and to be replaced by emergent capitalist institutions, the peasants began to actively and widely oppose their rulers.

Beginning in the late 14th century and continuing through the 16th century, peasant revolts sprang up all over Western Europe. In most cases, the peasants were resisting change and attempting to secure their places in the feudal order of things. They opposed increasing mechanization of agricultural work, the consolidation of plots, the enclosure movement, the seizure of lands, and many of the other changes which signaled the rise of the landed gentry—and the demise of the peasants' rights to land and protection. All of these rebellions were brutally put down by the well-armed nobility. The peasants were leaderless, unorganized, and poorly armed. Their actions, however, did reflect a deep sense of outrage at the costs borne by them as a result of fundamental changes in the economic, political, and social order of their day. Out of this history came the legends of Robin Hood and other outlaws of the Middle Ages. Maurice Keen, in his *The Outlaws of Medieval Legend,* has noted the attraction of these stories at the time:

> But though these risings were doomed to failure before they started, they do reveal just that background of widespread popular unrest which would make men listen, and admire the stories of an outlaw whose defiance of the law was more successful than their own.
>
> Modern historians who have examined the causes of these revolts have diagnosed them in economic terms. But because the rebels were medieval men living in an age which tended to see everything in terms of law, their demands were largely legal, which is what we would expect from the outlaw poems with their persistent bitterness against the men of law.

46   The Setting—What Is Property?

The legal demands of the peasants, however, were primarily concerned with the ownership and the usage of property.

The Wizard of Id by permission of Johnny Hart and Field Enterprises, Inc.

---

4. "Modern historians who have examined the causes of these revolts have diagnosed them in economic terms." What were the economic roots of the peasant rebellions?

During this period, British people in rural England were totally dependent on the productivity of the land. Those who lived in villages used common land to raise their crops, keep their bees, graze their livestock, and gather their firewood. Without access to land they would be without any means to sustain their lives.

Over an extended period of time a series of parliamentary acts converted many of the commons into private property. Whole villages were deserted; people who were independent when they could use the common lands became either vagrants or dependent for employment on those who owned the land. English historian Raymond Williams describes this change and its implications in *The Country and the City:*

There is no reason to deny the critical importance of the period of parliamentary enclosures, from the second quarter of the eighteenth century to the first quarter of the nineteenth century. By nearly four thousand Acts, more than six million acres of land were appropriated, mainly by the politically dominant landowners: about a quarter of all cultivated acreage. But it is then necessary to see the essential continuity of this appropriation, both with earlier and with later phases. It is necessary to stress, for example, how much of the country had already been enclosed, before this change of method in the mid-eighteenth century to a parliamentary act. The process had been going on since at least the thirteenth century, and had reached a first peak in the fifteenth and sixteenth centuries. Indeed in history it is continuous from the long process of conquest and seizure: the land gained by killing, by repression, by political bargains.

Again, as the economy develops, enclosure can never really be isolated from the mainstream of land improvements, of changes in methods of production, of price-movements, and of those more general changes in property relationships which were all flowing in the same direction: an extension of cultivated land but also a concentration of ownership into the hands of a minority.

The parliamentary procedure for enclosure made this process at once more public and more recorded. In this sense it was directly related to the quickening pace of agricultural improvement in the late eighteenth and early nineteenth centuries.... The social importance of enclosures is then not that they introduced a wholly new element in the social structure, but that in getting rid of the surviving open-field villages and common rights, in some of the most populous and prosperous parts of the country, they complemented and were indeed often caused by the general economic pressure on small owners and especially small tenants. No reliable figures are now available, but it can be reasonably argued that as many people were driven from the land, and from some independent status in relation to it, by the continuing processes of rack-renting and short-lease policies, and by the associated need for greater capital to survive in an increasingly competitive market, as by explicit enclosure.

The number of landless, before this period of enclosure, was in any event high: in 1690, five landless labourers to every three occupiers, as compared with a proportion of five to two in 1831. Most of the peasantry, in another sense—the classical sense of the small owner-occupiers under social and political obligations—had been bought and forced out in the period of the building of large estates in the late seventeenth and early eighteenth centuries....

By the eighteenth century, nearly half of the cultivated land was owned by some five thousand families. As a central form of this predominance, four hundred families, in a population of some seven or eight million people, owned nearly a quarter of cultivated land. Beneath this domination, there was no longer, in any classical sense a peasantry, but an increasingly regular structure of tenant farmers and wage-labourers: the social relationships that we can properly call those of agrarian capitalism. The regulation of production was increasingly in terms of an organized market.

From *The Country and the City* by Raymond Williams. Copyright © 1973 by Raymond Williams. Reprinted by permission of Oxford University Press, Inc.

---

5. What are the "social relationships" of agrarian capitalism?

6. "The regulation of production was increasingly in terms of an organized market." What does this mean?

7. What would you predict happened to the distribution of income in England as a result of these changes in property ownership?

CONCLUSION

The formation of truly private property can be traced to this early history of England. It is one of the fundamental prerequisites of capitalism. The notion of property in England as feudalism faded at the end of the Middle Ages was defined in legal terms. Laws conferred or acknowledged the right of ownership and protected the control over the use of property by the owner. From the perspective of the owner, such property rights and legal protection allowed for maximum earnings from the land and ensured their dominant position in society. From the perspective of the peasants, on the other hand, control of the land was torn from them out of their own adversity and weakness through violent conquest and legal manipulation. This ensured their position at the bottom of society. Out of this sense of frustration, peasants revolted against the emergence of private property throughout the late Middle Ages. Control of the land was a dominant concern in England's emerging capitalist economy. Economic ideas were implicit in the struggle for control of the land.

However, as capitalism moved into its adolescent stage with the coming of the Industrial Revolution in the 18th century, economic thinking became significantly more sophisticated.

KEY CONCEPTS

ownership
property rights
relative scarcity of land
economic perceptions and opinions
enclosure acts

REVIEW QUESTIONS

1. What is property? Why is it important?
2. Who or what defines an outlaw?
3. Why is it important to know something about the history of economic thought?

SUGGESTED READINGS

Maurice Keen, 1961. *The Outlaws of Medieval Legend,* The University of Toronto Press. Traces the stories of early opposition to the emergence of modern private property.

Karl Polanyi, 1957. *The Great Transformation,* Beacon Press. A classic treatment of the emergence of private property in Western Europe along with the development of early capitalism.

Raymond Williams, 1973. *The Country and the City,* Oxford University Press. Highlights the relationship between urban and rural areas in England as capitalist institutions developed.

THE COMING OF ADAM SMITH—
THE DIVISION OF LABOR

CHAPTER 4

INTRODUCTION

How did we happen to organize work in the way that we have? People didn't always have the same sense of mechanistic time with which we are obsessed. Does anybody really know what time it is? Assembly lines have existed for less than 100 years. And clocks to control the hours of work are not all that much older. Could we have the same division of labor and specialization without assembly lines and clocks? Is the way in which labor is divided desirable from the viewpoint of the worker? Does it lead us away from democracy into an aristocracy?

    Much of our current thinking about specialization and the division of labor has been influenced by the writings of Adam Smith (1723–1790). In turn, many modern productive methods, including the assembly line, were derived from the early development of capitalism during the Industrial Revolution—the time when Adam Smith wrote his famous *Wealth of Nations*.

The line, the goddamn line. Fifty-five cars an hour, 440 cars a shift . . . two shifts a day, 4400 cars a week . . . 44 assembly plants, 9 million cars a year . . . lights, machinery, noise . . . hundreds of hustling workers, arms moving, legs moving . . . tightening bolts, fastening cables . . . using big electric wrenches and drills, the hoses stretched out behind them . . . and the colors, the brilliant goddamn colors . . . aqua, grabber lime, pewter, pinto red, sassy grass green, rosewood, ascot blue, Nevada silver, cottonwood green, in-violet, curious yellow, burgundy fire, glacial blue, Tor-Red, amber sherwood, formal black, sunflower, sandalwood, cranberry, Sno White, Bahama yellow, true blue, rallye red, yellow gold . . . The Workers, 700,000 of them across the country, 200,000 of them in the Detroit area . . . men and women, whites and blacks . . . big blacks with Afros and young dudes with processes, paunchy whites, paunchy blacks, rednecks, fathers, husbands, suburbanites . . . women, tight-skinned, almost never pretty, with hair teased in the fashion of ten years ago . . . 8 hours a day, not counting a half hour off for lunch . . . 46 minutes of relief time, when a fellow can sit down or use the toilet or have a smoke or get a Coke or a Mallo-Cup . . . workers sanding gray metal and rough spots on painted metal after the cars have come from the bake oven . . . taking windshields from a pile, slopping glue on and attaching a rubber sleeve . . . a worker attaching the windshield to a hydraulic lift with suction cups and swinging it onto the line . . . workers swinging the engine onto the line . . . workers swinging

Worker's Power/cpf

the rear axle in and laying the rear springs on the line ... the body now automatically dropped over the rear axle, the springs, the drive shaft ... tires inflated by machine and workers taking them off conveyors and putting them on the wheels ... workers bolting the tires down ... workers in the pits underneath the assembly line, like slit trenches, standing all day at Ford or GM, sitting at Chrysler ... installing wires, fastening bolts, 8 hours a day, their arms over their heads ... workers beating on latches with rubber mallets to make the hoods fit ... 8 hours a day, 48 weeks a year, $9000 or so a year, $130 to $150 a week in take-home pay ... The Line, The Finest Product of American Inventiveness ... 350 models to choose from ... fascinating, absolutely fascinating, how the engines, tires, fenders, hoods are fed onto the line at the right time, a 429 CID V-8 or a 200 CID Six, the right-size tires, the right-color fenders and hood, the system run by teletype and computer ... A Wonder Of The World ... a few days from the time the iron ore is dug in the Mesabi Range in Minnesota, the coal in West Virginia, Pennsylvania, and Kentucky, the limestone in northern Michigan, the tires manufactured in Akron, Ohio ... the ore hauled to Gary, Cleveland, Pittsburgh, or Detroit, smelted into steel ... rolled into sheet steel at 2300 feet per minute ... stamped into side panels, inner panels, outer panels, fenders, roofs, hoods, decks, floor pans ... the iron cast into engines, steel forged into axles, rolled into frames ... the body welded together ... painted with zinc phosphate ... painted with two coats of primer, wet-sanded, painted with three coats of acrylic enamel, baked for one hour at 250 degrees ... dollied onto the line ... the doors and deck hung ... dropped over the engine and transmission ... windshield, instrument panel, and upholstery installed ... then down the final line ... rear axle, rear springs, drive shaft, gas line, tires, fenders ... six gallons of gasoline injected into the gas tank ... battery hooked up ... a worker gets in, moving fast, turns the key, and this tremendous noise ... rrrrrrRRRRRRRRRrrrrRRRR ... the car starts up ... Mustangs, Cougars, Torinos, Dusters, Bonnevilles, GTO's, Firebirds, Caprices, Mavericks, Pintos, Montereys, Imperials, Furys, El Dorados, Galaxies, LTD's, Thunderbirds, Challengers, Darts, Barracudas, Valiants, New Yorkers, Chevelles, Novas ... off the line ... lights aligned, acceleration and brakes tested ... washed ... waxed ... and onto haulaway trucks or railroad cars, 15 to the car, and hauled across America.

Copyright © 1971 by William Serrin, Reprinted from *The Company and the Union*, by William Serrin, by permission of Alfred A. Knopf, Inc.

1. Do you see working on an "assembly line" in your own future?
2. How did it happen? Why did it happen? Was it intentional? Is it good?

ADAM SMITH AND THE DIVISION OF LABOR

The year of 1776 is significant in our history (recorded time) because Adam Smith's great—in size and fame—book *An Inquiry into the Nature and Causes of the Wealth of Nations* was published. It was the first comprehensive treatise about economics. There had been many books and essays about economic matters before Adam Smith, and he used ideas from them in his book. He brought them all together and created a fairly complete picture of his understanding about the way an economy behaved and why it behaved that way in 1776.

The following article from the March 9, 1976, *New York Times,* marking the 200th anniversary of *The Wealth of Nations,* suggests its importance in economic history and economic thought:

ADAM SMITH LED 1776 REVOLUTION IN ECONOMICS

SOMA GOLDEN

Two revolutions were begun in 1776.

One was by an outraged group of upstart colonists, armed for battle with Britain and determined to win political freedom. The other was by a lone Scottish scholar, Adam Smith, aged 53, armed only with ideas. This revolution, too, was about freedom—but economic, rather than political.

On March 9, 1776, four months before the Americans fired their Declaration of Independence at the British establishment, Adam Smith fired his own salvo—a gigantic work entitled, *An Inquiry into the Nature and Causes of the Wealth of Nations.* It was the 1097-page fruit of a decade's constant labor and a lifetime of study, a book that has shaped economic thinking from that day until this.

Although the American Revolution has generated a hurricane of activity this year, the bicentennial of the publication of "The Wealth of Nations" is a more subdued affair, the subject of a few scholarly lectures and articles in the United States and somewhat more elaborate academic festivities later this year in Britain.

Copyright © 1976 by The New York Times Company. Reprinted by permission.

Adam Smith, 1723-1790.

SLOWER-PACED EVENT

But at another level, the ideas of Adam Smith—known as the ideologist of laissez-faire capitalism, the apostle of the industrial revolution, and the first economic philosopher—are enjoying something of a revival in the United States this election year.

The campaigns of President Ford, of former Gov. Ronald Reagan of California and of the Democratic former Governor of Georgia, Jimmy Carter, are Smithian at their core—calling for less interference by Washington in the lives of the citizens and the operations of business.

For "The Wealth of Nations," in its perceptive and exhaustive examination of late 18th Century socioeconomic life, also is, at its core, a critique of the heavy hand of government regulations and a paean to the power of economic freedom, checked by competition, to generate maximum wealth of nations and of individuals.

"In a simplistic way, Adam Smith's ideas are near those of the Ford Administration," said Paul A. Samuelson, a Nobel Prize winner in economics and professor at Massachusetts Institute of Technology.

Although the notion of reducing governmental power may sound conservative, rather than radical, in the late 20th century, 200 years ago, the idea was far to the left of center. "Adam Smith was a radical, not a reactionary," says Robert Lekachman, economic historian and professor at Lehman College of the City University of New York.

"The book is a revolutionary one," wrote another economic historian, Robert L. Heilbroner, professor at the New School of Social Research, in his popular volume, *The Worldly Philosophers.*

In the entire history of economic thought, there is only one other book that seems to match Smith's in its reach and its grasp. Ironically, that is *Das Kapital,* the ideological handbook of communism, written by Karl Marx, which appeared a century after Smith's ideological handbook of capitalism.

Only Marx, Professor Heilbroner writes in a forthcoming magazine article, compares with Smith "in breadth, depth, and brilliance."

However, the dust of history and hyperbole have done much to hide the fine lines of Smith's radicalism from today's generation. More often than not, the doctrines of the Scottish thinker are unfurled to defend the freedom of big business rather than the freedom of all individuals.

"In 1976," Professor Lekachman wrote in his recent book, *Economists at Bay,* "the natural heirs of Adam Smith are not the presidents of giant corporations who speak on public occasions in favor of competition which they have done their best to suppress."

Economists find it difficult to summarize in a few pithy thoughts the vast and complex tapestry that Smith wove into *The Wealth of Nations.* The book is no abstruse textbook only for economists to absorb. It is a rich, theoretical and political discussion, aimed at statesmen and kings in the fading days of British mercantilism, at the dawn of the industrial revolution.

The book debunks the mercantilist notion that the wealth of a nation, such as Britain, could only grow at the expense of other nations, through stringent limits on Britain's imports, forced-growth of her exports, and the resulting accumulation of hoards of gold.

To Smith, wealth depended not on a mountain of rare metals piled up in the British Treasury, but on efficiency and productive power of the nation. He explains how that kind of wealth could be generated to a maximum by nations freely trading together to the economic betterment of all.

SCHOLARLY REFERENCES

The book's carefully written pages are weighted with scholarly references to ancient empires, theology, history, morality and much more. . . .

Smith first gained fame as a professor of moral philosophy at Glasgow University. . . .

Smith's fundamental idea—which still has enormous force among politicians and economists—is that a democratic society, driven by the self-interest of its people competing against one another, can generate more wealth than the same society, ruled by a government that tries to regulate the minute details of economic life.

Britain's mercantilist government had bent the entire economy to the state's needs, weaving a tight web around individual economic activity—tighter, historians say, than anything the West has seen since then, except during the wartime. But the people had begun to writhe against the endless regulation of wages, apprenticeship rules, state monopolies, import duties and the like.

And Smith, looking over the entire jumbled scene from the quiet beach of Kirkcaldy, fit the pieces of the past and present together like a giant puzzle and offered a rationale for unraveling the mercantilist system and an ideology for the rising business class that would dominate the next century.

The hatchet that Smith used to chop away at the British system was reason, not rhetoric. Mercantilism, he said, was undoing the natural order of things, interfering with progress for the nation and the people, stifling initiative and hobbling growth.

"It is Adam Smith's greatest contribution," said Professor Samuelson, "that he recognized in the social world of economics, what Isaac Newton had recognized in the physical world of the heavens: a self-regulating natured order." The famous metaphor that Smith used to denote that order—mentioned only once in the book's many pages—is the "invisible hand."

Politicians apparently did not take long to get the message. Some members of Parliament came to Scotland to consult the famed author. Others soon quoted him in chamber.

Economists, too, were quick to note Smith's work inasmuch as *The Wealth of Nations* presents a vast spectrum of economic theory, some well-developed, some in germ, some the product of the author's own intelligence, some the refined product of an earlier, lesser-known theorist.

Tucked away in its pages are explanations of capital as a store of wealth; of labor as a source of value; of the productivity to be gained by economies of scale and the division of labor, illustrated by the famous example of the pin factory. Smith also explored the idea of external economies, supply and demand, price determination, worker alienation, comparative advantage, free trade, and even modern equilibrium theory.

Being a pragmatist as well as a theorist, Smith filled his book with policy prescriptions derived from his more abstract thoughts including a recommendation, somewhat tardy, that Britain peacefully sever its colonialist ties with America. He scorned the exclusive trading arrangement that Britain had forced on the colonies and said the mother country derived "nothing but loss" from the relationship.

After 200 years, much of Smith is still surprisingly relevant. Although Smith's professional progeny have criticized him for the sins of superficiality, omission or error, economists generally applaud him for his masterly exposition of the logic and virtues of laissez-faire capitalism in a competitive world.

The loudest applause, perhaps, comes from the so-called Chicago school of economics, which orbits around the University of Chicago, where many of the laissez-faire prescriptions of the 18th-century philosopher are viewed as suitable for the 20th century economy.

"There have been thousands of minor improvements on Smith, but no one has damaged the validity of his central thought," said George J. Stigler, a Chicago professor and noted expert on the history of economic thought. "We are still basically in a Smithian age," he said.

This proposition, however, is challenged by some economists today who think Smith's description of the market is brilliant in theory, but obsolete in practice. Smith, they say, did not anticipate the proliferation of giant private companies that now dominate the skyline of modern American industry.

Thus he saw no need for an activist government antitrust policy. The giant state-backed trading companies that held monopoly power in his day, Smith thought, would be eliminated if the state merely stopped offering them protection.

Another side of Smith that today's liberals cite, is the scholar's worry about the future of the capitalism he championed. Smith did not entirely trust the budding businessmen to compete rather than collude behind closed doors. And he worried about the moral deterioration and alienation of workers that could result from the division of labor he viewed as necessary for economic growth.

In a strongly worded passage, Smith seems to worry that even democracy itself could be undermined by the advent of the modern factory system, where workers would be forced to repeat a simple mind-numbing operation from dawn to dusk.

The "torpor" of the worker's mind, Smith wrote, makes such a man incapable of "forming any just judgment concerning many even of the ordinary duties of private life. Of the great and extensive interests of his country he is altogether incapable of judging."

The rock upon which Smith builds his entire scheme is the desire of all individuals—workers, businessmen, and statesmen—to pursue their competing economic self-interests or, in his words "to truck, barter and exchange one thing for another."

Walter Bagehot, the British economist wrote long ago that Smith seemed to imagine each infant born with a tiny Scotsman inside to direct him along the proper path. Even economists who criticize Smith today concede, in the words of one, that "there's a little Adam Smith inside us all."

Smith begins *The Wealth of Nations* with this classic description "Of the Division of Labour":

The greatest improvement in the productive powers of labour, and the greater part of the skill, dexterity, and judgment with which it is any where directed, or applied, seem to have been the effects of the division of labour.

The effects of the division of labour, in the general business of society, will be more easily understood, by considering in what manner it operates in some particular manufactures. . . .

To take an example from a very trifling manufacture: but one in which the division of labour has been very often taken notice of, the trade of the pin-maker; a workman not educated to this business (which the division of labour has rendered a distinct trade), nor acquainted with the use of the machinery employed in it (to the invention of which the same division of labour has probably given occasion), could scarce, perhaps, with his utmost industry, make one pin in a day, and certainly could not make twenty. But in the way in which this business is now carried on, not only the whole work is a peculiar trade, but it is divided into a number of branches, of which the greater part are likewise peculiar trades. One man draws out the wire, another straights it, a third cuts it, a fourth points it, a fifth grinds it at the top for receiving the head; to make the head requires two or three distinct operations; to put it on, is a peculiar business, to whiten the pins is another; it is even a trade by itself to put them into the paper; and the important business of making a pin is, in this manner, divided into about eighteen distinct operations, which, in some manufactories, are all performed by distinct hands, though in others the same man will sometimes perform two or three of them. I have seen a small manufactory of this kind where ten men only were employed, and where some of them consequently performed two or three distinct operations. But though they were very poor, and therefore but indifferently accommodated with the necessary machinery, they could, when they exerted themselves, make among them about twelve pounds of pins in a day. There are in a pound upwards of four thousand pins of a middling size. Those ten persons, therefore, could make among them upwards of forty-eight thousand pins in a day. Each person, therefore, making a tenth part of forty-eight thousand pins, might be considered as making four thousand eight hundred pins in a day. But if they had all wrought separately and independently, and without any of them having been educated to this peculiar business, they certainly could not each of them have made twenty, perhaps not one pin in a day; that is, certainly, not the two hundred and fortieth, perhaps not the four thousand eight hundredth part of what they are at present capable of performing, in consequence of a proper division and combination of their different operations.

Catchpenny Prints

---

3. Were Adam Smith's perceptions conditioned by time when he wrote this part of the book?

With this description of the division of labor, Adam Smith highlighted the role of specialization in significantly increasing productive potential. He attributed this great increase in productivity to three factors. "First, the improvement of the dexterity of the workman necessarily increases the quantity of work he can perform; and the division of labor, by reducing every man's business to some one simple operation, and by making this operation the sole employment of his life, necessarily increases very much the dexterity of the workman." Second, the worker would gain time that used to be lost in moving from one type of work to another. And, third, labor would be made more productive by the application of machinery that would facilitate the division of labor.

An important result of this increase in output accompanying the division of labor was that each worker "has a great quantity of his own work to dispose of beyond what he himself has occasion for." Since every worker is in the same position, exchange will take place. Smith puts it this way: "He supplies them abundantly with what they have occasion for, and they accommodate him as amply with what he has occasion for, and a general plenty diffuses itself through all the different ranks of the society." Through the division of labor, economic output will increase; and the existence of exchange will facilitate and further encourage this growth in output.

---

4. "... and the division of labor, by reducing every man's business to some one simple operation, and by making this operation the sole employment of his life, necessarily increases very much the dexterity of the workman."
   a) How do you feel about having one simple operation made the sole employment of your life?
   b) Would the people on the "assembly line" agree with your answer?

Smith traces the emergence of the division of labor in production to the fact that people do exchange goods and services. "It is the necessary, though very slow and gradual, consequence of a propensity in human nature which has in view no such extensive utility: the propensity to truck, barter, and exchange one thing for another." Because there is a tendency for exchange, people will begin to specialize in what they do best and to trade with others for the other things that they need. Through this process, the division of labor will proceed and economic output will increase. Historically, the rapidly spreading and more sophisticated markets in Western Europe tremendously accelerated the development of the division of labor.

Adam Smith further argued that all of this great economic progress derived from the seeking of self-interest by individuals. Individuals entered markets for exchange to benefit themselves. But out of this quest for self-gain, a general good developed in the form of increasing prosperity for all.

But man has almost constant occasion for the help of his brethren, and it is in vain for him to expect it from their benevolence only. He will be more likely to prevail if he can interest their self-love in his favour, and shew them that it is for their own advantage to do for him what he requires of them. Whoever offers to another a bargain of any kind, proposes to do this. Give me that which I want, and you shall have this which you want, is the meaning of every such offer; and it is in this manner that we obtain from one another the far greater part of those good offices which we stand in need of. It is not from the benevolence of the butcher, the brewer, or the baker, that we expect our dinner, but from their regard to their own interest. We address ourselves, not to their humanity but to their self-love, and never talk to them of our own necessities out of their advantages.

General prosperity, economic growth, the wealth of the nation, resulted from the pursuit of self-interest.

---

5. Adam Smith thought that the division of labor derived from people's "propensity to truck, barter, and exchange one thing for another." Do you agree with Smith's reasoning here? Why or why not?

6. "But man has almost constant occasion for the help of his brethren, and it is in vain for him to expect it from their benevolence only. He will be more likely to prevail if he can interest their self-love in his favour, and show them that it is for their own advantage to do for him what he requires of them."
   a) Do you agree with Smith's assumption about the nature of people's behavior? How did Smith arrive at this conclusion?
   b) If it is an accurate assumption about present behavior, do people have *any choice* about behaving in any other way?

SIDE EFFECTS OF THE DIVISION OF LABOR

Adam Smith focused on the relation of the division of labor, specialization, exchange, and markets to the wealth of nations. He also showed sensitivity to some side effects of the division of labor. The first of these is a problem that we still experience today in the alienation and boredom of manual labor and the assembly line. Smith wrote about this problem bluntly and graphically in this passage from *The Wealth of Nations*:

In the progress of the division of labour, the employment of the far greater part of those who live by labour, that is, of the great body of the people, comes to be confined to a few very simple operations, frequently to one or two. But the understandings of the greater part of men are necessarily formed by their ordinary employments. The man whose whole life is spent in performing a few simple operations, of which the effects too are, perhaps, always the same, or very nearly the same, has no occasion to exert his understanding, or to exercise his invention in finding out expedients for removing difficulties which never occur. He naturally loses, therefore, the habit of such exertion, and generally becomes as stupid and ignorant as it is possible for a human creature to become. The torpor of his mind renders him not only incapable of relishing or bearing a part in any rational conversation, but of conceiving any generous, noble, or tender sentiment, and consequently of forming any just judgment concerning many even of the ordinary duties of private life.

His dexterity at his own particular trade seems, in this manner, to be acquired at the expence of his intellectual, social, and martial virtues. But in every improved and civilized society this is the state into which the labouring poor, that is, the great body of the people, must necessarily fall, unless government takes some pains to prevent it.

An additional consequence of this tendency is that the guidance of society must be left to the few, the elite, those who are not stupefied by the repetitiveness of their labors. This effectively splits society into classes—the educated elite and the "great body of the people."

Others began to have doubts about some of these possible consequences of the division of labor and the direction in which capitalist society seemed to be headed. Alexis de Tocqueville (1805-1859), a French politician and writer, questioned the future of America if it continued along these lines in his famous book, *Democracy in America*, published in 1835 and 1840.

When a workman is unceasingly and exclusively engaged in the fabrication of one thing, he ultimately does his work with singular dexterity; but, at the same time, he loses the general faculty of applying his mind to the direction of the work. He every day becomes more adroit and less industrious; so that it may be said of him, that, in proportion as the workman improves, the man is degraded. What can be expected of a man who has spent twenty years of his life in making heads for pins? and to what can that mighty human intelligence, which has so often stirred the world, be applied in him, except it be to investigate the best method of making pins' heads? When a workman has spent a considerable portion of his existence in this manner, his thoughts are forever set upon the object of his daily toil; his body has contracted certain fixed habits, which it can never shake off; in a word, he no longer belongs to himself, but to the calling which he has chosen. It is in vain that laws and manners have been at pains to level all the barriers round such a man, and to open to him on every side a thousand different paths to fortune; a theory of manu-

The division of labor. (Photograph by Carol Ingald.)

factures more powerful than manners and laws binds him to a craft, and frequently to a spot, which he cannot leave: it assigns to him a certain place in society, beyond which he cannot go; in the midst of universal movement, it has rendered him stationary.

In proportion as the principle of the division of labor is more extensively applied, the workman becomes more weak, more narrow-minded, and more dependent. The art advances, the artisan recedes. On the other hand, in proportion as it becomes more manifest that the productions of manufactures are by so much the cheaper and better as the manufacture is larger, and the amount of capital employed more considerable, wealthy and educated men come forward to embark in manufactures, which were heretofore abandoned to poor or ignorant handicraftsmen. The magnitude of the efforts required, and the importance of the results to be obtained, attract them. Thus, at the very time at which the science of manufactures lowers the class of workmen, it raises the class of masters.

While the workman concentrates his faculties more and more upon the study of a single detail, the master surveys an extensive whole, and the mind of the latter is enlarged in proportion as that of the former is narrowed. In a short time, the one will require nothing but physical strength without intelligence; the other stands in need of science, and almost of genius, to insure success. This man resembles more and more the administrator of a vast empire—that man, a brute.

The master and the workman have then here no similarity, and their differences increase every day. They are only connected as the two rings at the extremities of a long chain. Each of them fills the station which is made for him, and which he does not leave; the one is continually, closely, and necessarily dependent upon the other, and seems as much born to obey, as the other is to command. What is this but aristocracy?

---

7. Do you think that Alexis de Tocqueville's predictions have proved accurate in America? Do we have a manufacturing aristocracy?

CONCLUSION

The division of labor which Adam Smith saw developing in the new and larger factories in late 18th-century England was another prerequisite in the development of capitalism. It entailed a new method of production which allowed for large increases in production per worker. Adam Smith saw this process in operation and theorized about its benefits. He also, in turn, advocated the use of the division of labor to promote "the wealth of nations." However, other changes in economic institutions supported, and were required by, the spread of specialization resulting from the division of labor. Exchange and markets were needed so people could trade for what they did not produce. As capitalism developed further, all of these institutions—the division of labor, specialization, exchange and markets—matured and contributed to further development and growth.

Smith also noted that there were some drawbacks to the introduction of the division of labor. These concerned the effects on workers. Boredom from dull, specialized work and limitations on the ability to function as a full member of society were to be expected. Such results pointed to possible future problems in the development of capitalism. De Tocqueville thought that in America it would result in a manufacturing aristocracy.

What other kinds of economic thoughts did Adam Smith and other economists who followed him offer? And what other kinds of economic concepts did they analyze? In the next chapter, we will examine some of their thoughts on value.

KEY CONCEPTS

worker's response to the production line
division of labor
specialization
exchange and markets
Smith's assumption about trucking
Smith's assumption about self-interest
manufacturing aristocracy

REVIEW QUESTIONS

1. Would production activity in the U.S. be as advanced as it is without assembly lines and the division of labor?

2. Does specialization normally result in workers who are "as stupid and ignorant as it is possible for a human creature to become"? How was this statement of Smith's conditioned by time? Do you agree with it? Why or why not?

SUGGESTED READINGS

Robert Heilbroner, 1961. *The Worldly Philosophers,* Simon and Schuster, Chapter 3. A nice concise chapter on the development of Smith's economic thought as well as some interesting biographical information.

Adam Smith, 1937. *The Wealth of Nations,* Modern Library Edition, Random House. Go straight to the original and read the classic treatise on how economic progress takes place. Despite its length, it makes fascinating reading; Smith was a real scholar!

CREATING VALUE—PRODUCING GOODS AND SERVICES

CHAPTER 5

INTRODUCTION

What is value? Why do goods and services have value? What determines *how much value* a good or a service possesses? How is value created? Value is a complicated economic, and philosophical, concept. But it is one that economists have been concerned with because it motivates the economic activities of production and consumption.

Some people think that value is created by labor; others think that value is determined by the utility of the product to the consumer. The problem is further complicated by the use of capital in production—in addition to direct labor.

1. Before you read through this chapter, think carefully about what you mean when you say that an object has value. Select an object that has value—a table, a chair, a desk, a pair of shoes, a hamburger, a book, a dormitory, a sweater, a gallon of gasoline—and explain as clearly as you can why it has value. What gives it value?

SMITH AND RICARDO ON VALUE

When economics was first being developed as a body of thought (which was not really so long ago), attention was directed to the concept of value. This became a special problem as exchange and markets became more complex. Goods were exchanged for money and had prices. Did price reflect value?

We will begin our consideration of value with Adam Smith and the labor theory of value from *The Wealth of Nations*:

The value of any commodity, therefore, to the person who possesses it, and who means not to use or consume it himself, but to exchange it for other commodities, is equal to the quantity of labour which it enables him to purchase or command. Labour, therefore, is the real measure of the exchangeable value of all commodities...

Labour, therefore, it appears evidently, is the only universal, as well as the only accurate measure of value, or the only standard by which we can compare the

Shakespeare's value. (Photograph by Robert Bostwick.)

values of different commodities at all times and at all places. We cannot estimate, it is allowed, the real value of different commodities from century to century by the quantities of silver which were given for them. We cannot estimate it from year to year by the quantities of corn. By the quantities of labour we can, with the greatest accuracy, estimate it both from century to century and from year to year.

2. In your own words, state your understanding of what Adam Smith said about value.

The labor theory of value seemed simple enough: the value of a good depended on the amount of labor used in producing it. However, Smith also noted that the concept of value can be slippery. Specifically, there are two different meanings to value. We can measure exchange value by the labor content of a good. These goods have *value in exchange*. But there is another group of goods which have *value in use*. The problem is that, while use values may or may not require labor, some cannot be exchanged for other goods. Smith gave the following example:

The things which have the greatest value in use have frequently little or no value in exchange; and on the contrary, those which have the greatest value in exchange have frequently little or no value in use. Nothing is more useful than water: but it will purchase scarce any thing; scarce any thing can be had in exchange for it. A diamond, on the contrary, has scarce any value in use; but a very great quantity of other goods may frequently be had in exchange for it.

Consequently, some goods that have use values may not have exchange values. The problem is further complicated by the fact that some goods with use values (and without exchange values) may also be produced by labor. Do these goods have value then? Obviously, *most* goods in a market system have *both* use and exchange values.

3. Can you explain why a diamond seems to have a very high exchange value? *Could* water have a high exchange value?

4. Can you think of a good that has use value, requires labor, but has no exchange value?

David Ricardo (1772-1823), another Englishman who was a major contributor to economic thought, read Adam Smith's ideas on value and decided to try to clarify them. The following passage is from his *Principles of Political Economy and Taxation*, published in 1817:

It has been observed by Adam Smith that "the word Value has two different meanings, and sometimes expresses the utility of some particular object, and sometimes the power of purchasing other goods which the possession of that object conveys. The one may be called value in use; the other value in exchange. The things," he continues, "which have the greatest value in use, have frequently little or no value in exchange; and, on the contrary, those which have the greatest value in exchange, have little or no value in use." Water and air are abundantly useful; they are indeed indispensable to existence, yet, under ordinary circumstances, nothing can be obtained in exchange for them. Gold, on the contrary, though of little use compared with air or water, will exchange for a great quantity of other goods.

Utility then is not the measure of exchangeable value, although it is absolutely essential to it. If a commodity were in no way useful—in other words, if it could in no way contribute to our gratification—it would be destitute of exchangeable value, however scarce it might be, or whatever quantity of labour might be necessary to procure it. Possessing utility, commodities derive their *exchangeable value* from two sources: from their scarcity, and from the quantity of labour required to obtain them.

There are some commodities, the value of which is determined by their scarcity alone. No labour can increase the quantity of such goods, and therefore their value cannot be lowered by an increased supply. Some rare statues and pictures, scarce books and coins, wines of a peculiar quality, which can be made only from grapes grown on a particular soil, of which there is a very limited quantity, are all of this description. Their value is wholly independent of the quantity of labour originally necessary to produce them, and varies with the varying wealth and inclinations of those who are desirous to possess them.

These commodities, however, form a very small part of the mass of commodities daily exchanged in the market. *By far the greatest part of those goods which are the objects of desire are procured by labour*; [Emphasis added] and they may be multiplied, not in one country alone, but in many, almost without any assignable limit, if we are disposed to bestow the labour necessary to obtain them.

Once we have delimited those goods which have exchange value, we can proceed to examine the economic laws governing their exchange in markets. This represents the vast majority of goods and the ones that we are most interested in as we examine economic activity. Prices ultimately reflect relative exchange values, and hence labor content, among different goods. Ricardo makes this point as follows:

In speaking, then, of commodities, of their exchangeable value, and of the laws which regulate their relative prices, we mean always such commodities only as can be increased in quantity by the exertion of human industry, and on the production of which competition operates without restraint. . . .

If, among a nation of hunters, for example, it usually cost twice the labour to kill a beaver which it does to kill a deer, one beaver should naturally exchange for, or be worth, two deer. It is natural that what is usually the produce of two days' or two hours' labour should be worth double of what is usually the produce of one day's or one hour's labour.

That this is really the foundation of the exchangeable value of all things, excepting those which cannot be increased by human industry, is a doctrine of the utmost importance in political economy; for from no source do so many errors, and so much difference of opinion in that science proceed, as from the vague ideas which are attached to the word value.

If the quantity of labour realised in commodities regulate their exchangeable value, every increase of the quantity of labour must augment the value of that commodity on which it is exercised, as every diminution must lower it.

5. Do Ricardo's ideas differ from those of Smith?
6. Does your family pay a water bill? Why or why not?

If we think only a little about labor as a theory of value, we will recognize the oversimplification of the deer and beaver illustration. Our definition of value isn't so simple. What about three men who might be trimming equal amounts of a hedge; one has a pair of hand scissors, the second has a manual hedge trimmer, and the third has an electric hedge trimmer. We know who will trim the hedge in the shortest time—with significantly less labor. Here we have introduced a complication that seems to limit the applicability of the labor theory of value. Is having your hedge trimmed by hand scissors more valuable than having it done with an electric hedge trimmer because it takes more labor? Not so fast, says David Ricardo, the value of implements is accounted for in the labor theory of value:

All the implements necessary to kill the beaver and deer might belong to one class of men, and the labour employed in their destruction might be furnished by another class; still, their comparative prices would be in proportion to the actual labour bestowed, both on the formation of the *capital* and on the destruction of the animals. Under different circumstances of plenty or scarcity of capital, as compared with labour, under different circumstances of plenty or scarcity of the food and necessaries essential to the support of men, those who furnished an equal value of capital for either one employment or for the other might have a half, a fourth, or an eighth of the produce obtained, the remainder being paid as wages to those who furnished the labour; yet this division could not affect the relative value of these commodities, since whether the profits of capital were greater or less, whether they were 50, 20, or 10 per cent, or whether the wages of labour were high or low, they would operate equally on both employments.

If we suppose the occupations of the society extended, that some provide canoes and tackle necessary for fishing, others the seed and rude machinery first used in agriculture, still the same principle would hold true, that the exchangeable value of the commodities produced would be in proportion to the labour bestowed on their production; not on their immediate production only, but on all those implements or machines required to give effect to the particular labour to which they were applied.

Ricardo introduced the notion that the value of capital depends on its labor content. He defined *capital* to be "that part of the wealth of a country which is employed in production, and consists of food, clothing, tools, raw materials, machinery, etc., necessary to give effect to labor." According to Ricardo's definition, then, the labor theory of value explains the exchange value of all goods. Everything that is used in production requires labor; and, consequently, the value of a good will reflect its labor content. Therefore, goods will exchange for one another based on their labor content.

7. What does Ricardo mean by "required to give effect to . . . labour"?

8. Is the house your family owns a form of capital?
9. Are the clothes you are wearing capital?

JOHN STUART MILL ON SMITH AND RICARDO

John Stuart Mill (1806–1873), a later English economist, accepted Smith and Ricardo's ideas on value. He restated the ideas, however, in a refreshing way that emphasized the complicated problem of precisely estimating the exact contribution of any one worker to production. In the following, from his *Principles of Political Economy* (1848), he is concerned with the value of a loaf of bread.

The labour which terminates in the production of an article fitted for some human use, is either employed directly about the thing, or in previous operations destined to facilitate, perhaps essential to the possibility of, the subsequent ones. In making bread, for example, the labour employed about the thing itself is that of the baker; but the labour of the miller, though employed directly in the production not of bread but of flour, is equally part of the aggregate sum of labour by which the bread is produced; as is also the labour of the sower, and of the reaper. Some may think that all these persons ought to be considered as employing their labour directly about the thing; the corn, the flour, and the bread being one substance in three different states. Without disputing about this question of mere language, there is still the ploughman, who prepared the ground for the seed, and whose labour never came in contact with the substance in any of its states; and the ploughmaker, whose share in the result was still more remote. All these persons ultimately derive the remuneration of their labour from the bread, or its price: the ploughmaker as much as the rest; for since ploughs are of no use except for tilling the soil, no one would make or use ploughs for any other reason than because the increased returns, thereby obtained from the ground, afforded a source from which an adequate equivalent could be assigned for the labour of the ploughmaker. If the produce is to be used or consumed in the form of bread, it is from the bread that this equivalent must come. The bread must suffice to remunerate all these labours, and several others; such as the carpenters and bricklayers who erected the farm buildings; the hedgers and ditchers who made the fences necessary for the protection of the crop; the miners and smelters who extracted or prepared the iron of which the plough and other implements were made. These, however, and the ploughmaker, do not depend for their remuneration upon the bread made from the produce of a single harvest, but upon that made from the produce of all the harvests which are successively gathered until the plough, or the buildings and fences, are worn out. We must add yet another kind of labour; that of transporting the produce from the place of its production to the place of its destined use: the labour of carrying the corn to market, and from market to the miller's, the flour from the miller's to the baker's, and the bread from the baker's to the place of its final consumption. This labour is sometimes very considerable: flour is transported to England from beyond the Atlantic, corn from the heart of Russia; and in addition to the labourers immediately employed, the waggoners and sailors, there are also costly instruments, such as ships, in the construction of which much labour has been expended: that labour, however, not depending for its whole remuneration upon the bread, but for a part only; ships being usually, during the course of their existence, employed in the transport of many different kinds of commodities.

To estimate, therefore, the labour of which any given commodity is the result, is far from a simple operation. The items in the calculation are very numerous—as it may seem to some persons, infinitely so; for if, as a part of the labour employed in making bread, we count the labour of the blacksmith who made the plough, why not also (it may be asked) the labour of making the tools used by the blacksmith, and the tools used in making those tools, and so back to the origin of things? But after mounting one or two steps in this ascending scale, we come into a region of fractions too minute for calculation. Suppose, for instance, that the same plough will last, before being worn out, a dozen years. Only one twelfth of the labour of making the plough must be placed to the account of each year's harvest. A twelfth part of the labour of making a plough is an appreciable quantity. But the same set of tools, perhaps, suffice to the ploughmaker for forging a hundred ploughs, which serve during the twelve years of their existence to prepare the soil of as many different farms. A twelve hundredth part of the labour of making the tools, is as much, therefore, as has been expended in procuring one year's harvest of a single farm: and when this fraction comes to be further apportioned among the various sacks of corn and loaves of bread, it is seen at once that such quantities are not worth taking into the account for any practical purpose connected with the commodity. It is true that if the toolmaker had not laboured, the corn and bread never would have been produced; but they will not be sold a tenth part of a farthing dearer in consideration of his labour.

We are thus left with the labor theory of value intact as the explanation for the determination of relative values of goods. The labor content that goes into the production of goods, both directly and indirectly, determines their exchange values. However, it is no easy matter to measure that value because of the complexity of the total productive process. Theoretically, though, Smith, Ricardo, and Mill thought that relative prices for goods reflected their relative labor contents.

10. If value is as complicated as Mill indicates, is it possible to determine what anyone's share of production should be if we adopt the principle that income should be directly related to personal contributions to production?

11. If we don't adopt that principle, what principle can we use to determine a person's share of income?

THE CONTRIBUTION OF JEVONS

The second half of the 19th century brought a change in emphasis in regard to developing an explanation or theory of value. One of the early contributors to the change was William Stanley Jevons, 1835-1882. His writing and thinking moved in the direction of abstractions, in contrast to descriptions of real life examples used by Adam Smith or John Stuart Mill. Jevons was obsessed with statistical information. He withdrew himself from social relations and plotted his collection of quantified facts, always searching for their explanation of past, present, and future (or probable) behavior. This was the period of neoclassical economics.

In another way we might think about Jevons as a contributor to a materialistic and hedonistic psychological behavior theory of economics. This followed in the tradition of philosopher Jeremy Bentham's utilitarianism. Jevons was not alone in this revised approach. Economists in other parts of Europe and America were working in the same direction using similar methods—quantitative abstractions and mathematical analysis—in developing economic theory.

In his theory of value, Jevons emphasized the value of a *commodity* as perceived by the consumer, as opposed to the value of a product contributed by the producers. In the following passage from his *The Theory of Political Economy* (1871), he presents his theory of value:

Pleasure and pain are undoubtedly the ultimate objects of the Calculus of Economy. To satisfy our wants to the utmost with the least effort to procure the greatest amount of what is desirable at the expense of the least that is undesirable—in other words, to maximise comfort and pleasure, is the problem of Economy. But it is convenient to transfer our attention as soon as possible to the physical objects or actions which are the source to us of pleasures or pains. A very large part of the labour of any community is spent upon the production of the ordinary necessaries and conveniences of life, food, clothing, buildings, utensils, furniture, ornaments, & c.; and the aggregate of these objects constitute, therefore, the immediate object of our attention.

By a commodity we shall understand any object, or, it may be, any action or service, which can afford pleasure or ward off pain. The name was originally abstract, and denoted the quality of anything by which it was capable of serving man. Having acquired, by a common process of confusion, a concrete signification, it will be well to retain it entirely for that signification, and employ the word *utility* to denote the abstract quality whereby an object serves our purposes, and becomes entitled to rank as a commodity. Whatever can produce pleasure or prevent pain may possess utility.

But it is surely obvious that Political Economy does rest upon the laws of human enjoyment; and that, if those laws are developed by no other science, they must be developed by economists. We labour to produce with the sole object of consuming, and the kinds and amounts of goods produced must be governed entirely by our requirements. Every manufacturer knows and feels how closely he must anticipate the tastes and needs of his customers: his whole success depends upon it; and, in like manner, the whole theory of Economy depends upon a correct theory of consumption.

---

12. "Whatever can produce pleasure or prevent pain may possess utility." Is this true for you in regard to a T-shirt? Coca-Cola? cigarettes? beer? a chair? a car?

13. What does Jevons mean when he says he will "employ the word utility to denote the abstract quality" as opposed to its "concrete signification"?

Thorstein Veblen on the Theory of Utility

The psychological and anthropological preconceptions of the economists have been those which were accepted by the psychological and social sciences some generations ago. The hedonistic conception of man is that of a lightning calculator of pleasures and pains, who oscillates like a homogeneous globule of desire of happiness under the impulse of stimuli that shift him about the area, but leave him intact. He has neither antecedent nor consequent. He is an isolated, definitive human datum, in stable equilibrium except for the buffets of the impinging forces that displace him in one direction or another. Self-imposed in elemental space, he spins symmetrically about his own spiritual axis until the parallelogram of forces bears down upon him, whereupon he follows the line of the resultant. When the force of the impact is spent, he comes to rest, a self-contained globule of desire as before. Spiritually, the hedonistic man is not a prime mover. He is not the seat of a process of living, except in the sense that he is subject to a series of permutations enforced upon him by circumstances external and alien to him.

Thorstein Veblen, The Theory of the Leisure Class.

CONCLUSION

We can see how elusive the quality of value has become. With the contribution of Jevons, we have moved from the realm of labor content in production to abstract notions of utility in consumption. The focus of attention and analysis of economists who followed Jevons's work centered on consumption; this focus was based on his conception of value. This approach, therefore, dismissed from concern the labor theory of value derived from the exploration of productive activity. (Karl Marx, however, as we shall see in Chapter 8, accepted the labor theory of value and continued to examine the productive sphere of economic activity.) This change, which relied very heavily on abstraction, signaled the emergence of neoclassical economics. This branch of economics utilized mathematics, statistics, and abstraction to refine economic theory during the latter part of the 19th century and the beginning of the 20th century.

In the next chapter, we will explore ideas concerning the distribution of values that were produced and were to be consumed.

KEY CONCEPTS

value
labor theory of value
value in exchange
value in utility
capital

verbal descriptions of reality
abstract qualities
calculus of economy
commodity

REVIEW QUESTIONS

1. How does the neoclassical conception of value differ from those of the early British economists?
2. What is the relationship between the value of a good or a service and its price?
3. What is the source of value?

SUGGESTED READINGS

E. K. Hunt and Howard J. Sherman, 1978. *Economics* (3rd ed.), Harper & Row. An introductory economics textbook with a very good chapter (Chapter 16) on the labor theory of value.

Joan Robinson, 1962. *Economic Philosophy*, Anchor Books. The first three chapters deal with the early development of economic thought and ideas on value and utility.

DIVIDING VALUE—INCOME DISTRIBUTION

CHAPTER 6

INTRODUCTION

Economists are always attempting to explain why national products are divided as they are among people. Early economists, such as Smith, who were beginning to think of economics as a social science, defined and classified income receivers as they appeared to them in their time.

In their explanations of the shares received by each factor of production, economists offer reasons for relating the distribution of income to contributions to production.

DISTRIBUTING THE GOODS

Chapter 5 directed your attention to the creation of value—especially for commodities. Later modifications in economic thought would include the value of services in addition to the commodities, so we can think about a large number of goods and services being produced every day by the people throughout the world. Usually economists think about counting all of these goods and services within the political boundaries of a nation during any selected period of time—a day, a month, or a year. Imagine the huge pile of goods—and services—that are created within the United States during a year: cars, houses, planes, schools, clothes, food, drinks, drugs, books, oil products, doctors' services, bombs, highways, lawnmowers, paper, and miscellaneous junk.

1. How would you divide the yearly national production of goods and services among the people: To those who produced according to their contribution? Large shares to those who have the most and smaller shares to those who have the least? Let everyone grab what he or she can? More to people who have been good and less to people who have been bad? Let the President decide? Some other way?

Economists have thought about how to divide these goods and services, and although they have never been in complete agreement—even though they have been very scientific—they have classified the receivers of the shares of output into categories. The receivers are: (1) laborers, (2) landowners, (3) investors of capital, and (4) entrepreneurs. Economists have also named the shares of income that each receives:

1. Labor receives *wages*.
2. Landowners receive *rent*.
3. Investors receive *interest*.
4. Entrepreneurs receive *profits*.

Each of these shares is received in money, but the money is only a claim for the real goods and services and would have no value if there were not those goods and services to claim as the money holder's share. Thus income distribution determines the distribution of products.

2. There was a time long ago before there were economists with their neat categories. (Maybe it was about the time of the Garden of Eden.) In what order were each of these categories imagined and named? Which developed first, second, third, and fourth and why did they?

3. Another way of thinking about money in relation to claims on the shares of production is to imagine each dollar in the hands of the income receivers (labor, landowners, investors, and entrepreneurs) as a draft on people's labor. Are there dollars drafts on your labor? Can you refuse to be drafted? Who might be exempt from the dollar draft? If drafted, when do you have to perform your service?

SMITH ON INCOME DISTRIBUTION

Adam Smith wrote about the division of the shares of the national product. You will remember Smith was writing at the beginning of the industrial revolution in England. The source of the quotations below is *The Wealth of Nations* (1776).

Smith begins by contrasting distribution before and after the introduction of private property:

But this original state of things, in which the labourer enjoyed the whole produce of his own labour, could not last beyond the first introduction of the appropriation of land and the accumulation of stock. It was at an end, therefore, long before the most considerable improvements were made in the productive powers of labour, and it would be to no purpose to trace further what might have been its effect upon the recompense or wages of labour. As soon as land becomes private property, the landlord demands a share of almost all the produce which the labourer can either raise, or collect from it. His *rent* makes the first deduction from the produce of the labour which is employed upon land.

4. Why, in your opinion, did the landlord receive a share of the products in the form of rent?

5. What determined the size of the share received by the landlord?

Adam Smith elaborated on the nature of this payment to the landowner as follows:

Rent, considered as the price paid for the use of land, is naturally the highest which the tenant can afford to pay in the actual circumstances of the land. In adjusting the terms of the lease, the landlord endeavours to leave him no greater share of the produce than what is sufficient to keep up the stock from which he furnishes the seed, pays the labour, and purchases and maintains the cattle and other instruments of husbandry, together with the ordinary profits of farming stock in the neighbourhood. This is evidently the smallest share with which the tenant can content himself without being a loser, and the landlord seldom means to leave him any more. Whatever part of the produce, or, what is the same thing, whatever part of its price, is over and above this share, he naturally endeavours to reserve to himself as the rent of his land, which is evidently the highest the tenant can afford to pay in the actual circumstances of the land.

6. Why did the tenant pay rent to the landlord? What would have happened if he refused?

7. What did the landlord contribute personally to the nation's production?

Smith calls the next receiver of income the "master." He may be the master of a farm or of a manufacturing firm. He owns the "stock," or what we have defined as the capital. The control of capital earned *profit* for the master. This form of income emerged with the advance of the division of labor. As Smith explained, the specialization of production required that *stocks* of goods and raw materials be maintained to support people in their productive activities. People were dependent on others for the things which they no longer directly produced. This accounts for the share of the product which goes to the "master":

It seldom happens that the person who tills the ground has wherewithal to maintain himself till he reaps the harvest. His maintenance is generally advanced to him from the stock of a master, the farmer who employs him, and who would have no interest to employ him, unless he was to share in the produce of his labour, or unless his stock was to be replaced to him with a profit. This profit makes a second deduction from the produce of the labour which is employed upon land.

The produce of almost all other labour is liable to the like deduction of profit. In all arts and manufactures the greater part of the workmen stand in need of a master to advance them the materials of their work, and their wages and maintenance till it be completed. He shares in the produce of their labour, or in the value which it adds to the materials upon which it is bestowed; and in this share consists his profit.

---

8. Why is the following the case: "It seldom happens that the person who tills the ground has wherewithal to maintain himself till he reaps the harvest"? Who has the "wherewithal"? Where did the one who has the "wherewithal" get it?

Finally Smith takes us to the third party who shares in the national product. By this time you have guessed who it is; it is the laborer. Smith wants to have labor receive an adequate share now that the landlord and capital owner have had a cut of the pie because it is good for society.

No society can surely be flourishing and happy, of which the far greater part of the members are poor and miserable. It is but equity, besides, that they who feed, clothe and lodge the whole body of the people, should have such a share of the produce of their own labour as to be themselves tolerably well fed, clothed and lodged.

What the share will be depends upon the amount which is agreed upon by the parties—the master (capital owner) and the laborer. As Smith says:

... in every part of Europe, twenty workmen serve under a master for one that is independent; and the wages of labour are every where understood to be, what they usually are, when the labour is one person, and the owner of the stock which employs him another.

Smith is quite specific about what this means:

What are the common wages of labour depends every where upon the contract usually made between those two parties, whose interests are by no means the same. The workmen desire to get as much, the masters to give as little as possible. The former are disposed to combine in order to raise, the latter in order to lower the wages of labour.

It is not, however, difficult to foresee which of the two parties must, upon all ordinary occasions, have the advantage in the dispute, and force the other into a compliance with their terms. The masters, being fewer in number, can combine much more easily; and the law, besides, authorises, or at least does not prohibit their combinations, while it prohibits those of the workmen. We have no acts of parliament against combining to lower the price of work; but many against combining to raise it. In all such disputes the masters can hold out much longer. A landlord, a farmer, a master manufacturer, or merchant, though they did not employ a single workman, could generally live a year or two upon the stocks which they have already acquired. Many workmen could not subsist a week, few could subsist a month, and scarce any a year without employment. In the long run the workman may be as necessary to his master as his master is to him, but the necessity is not so immediate.

If we suggested to Smith that this division of the national product into shares must bring about some harsh conflicts among the three groups of share receivers, he would tell us:

Envy, malice, or resentment, are the only passions which can prompt one man to injure another in his person or reputation. But the greater part of men are not very frequently under the influence of those passions; and the very worst men are so only occasionally. As their gratification too, how agreeable soever it may be to certain characters, is not attended with any real or permanent advantage, it is in the greater part of men commonly restrained by prudential considerations. Men may live together in society with some tolerable degree of security, though there is no civil magistrate to protect them from the injustice of those passions. But avarice and ambition in the rich, in the poor the hatred of labour and the love of present ease and enjoyment, are the passions which prompt to invade property, passions much more steady in their operation, and much more universal in their influence. Wherever there is great property, there is great inequality. For one very rich man, there must be at least five hundred poor, and the affluence of the few supposes the indigence of the many. The affluence of the rich excites the indignation of the poor, who are often both driven by want, and prompted by envy, to invade his possessions. It is only under the shelter of the civil magistrate that the owner of that valuable property, which is acquired by the labour of many years, or perhaps of many successive generations, can sleep a single night in security. The acquisition of valuable and extensive property, therefore, necessarily requires the establishment of civil government.

The shares of the national product, then, are distributed unequally—primarily because of the unequal distribution of private property (land and capital). While this may lead to conflicts among the different groups of share receivers, because each wants to maximize its own share, the government protects private property and, hence, its share of the output.

---

9. "The acquisition of valuable and extensive property, therefore, necessarily requires the establishment of civil government." Is the purpose of government to protect the rich from the poor?

In addition to the role played by the state in minimizing the conflict over the division of national output, the operation of markets also resolves the conflict. Each group is out to maximize its position, its own share of production. However, all economic transactions take place in markets for goods and services and, as a result, are regulated by the operation of competition. A worker will not work for a lower wage when he knows that he can get a higher wage from another master. A person will not buy a product at a price greater than that of another seller. Smith explains this in the following passage on the "invisible hand":

Every individual is continually exerting himself to find out the most advantageous employment for whatever capital he can command. It is his own advantage, indeed, and not that of the society, which he has in view. But the study of his own advantage naturally, or rather necessarily leads him to prefer that employment which is most advantageous to the society.

But the annual revenue of every society is always precisely equal to the exchangeable value of the whole annual produce of its industry, or rather is precisely the same thing with that exchangeable value. As every individual, therefore, endeavours as much as he can both to employ his capital in the support of domestic industry, and so to direct that industry that its produce may be of the greatest value; every individual necessarily labours to render the annual revenue of the society as great as he can. He generally, indeed, neither intends to promote the public interest, nor knows how much he is promoting it. By preferring the support of domestic to that of foreign industry, he intends only his own security; and by directing that industry in such a manner as its produce may be of the greatest value, he intends only his own gain, and he is in this, as in many other cases, led by *an invisible hand* to promote an end which was no part of his intention. Nor is it always the worse for the society that it was no part of it. By pursuing his own interest he frequently promotes that of the society more effectually than when he really intends to promote it. I have never known much good done by those who affected to trade for the public good. It is an affectation, indeed, not very common among merchants, and very few words need be employed in dissuading them from it.

Despite the apparent conflict and the motivation of self-gain, the operation of the economic system produces the greatest good for the greatest number. A social good results even though "society was no part" of directing the activity. Rather it results from everyone seeking his or her own advantage.

10. What does Smith mean when he says "...he is in this, as in many other cases, led by an *invisible hand*"? What is an "invisible hand"?

11. Do you agree with Smith when he says "But the study of his own advantage naturally, or rather necessarily leads him to prefer that employment which is most advantageous to the society"?

We have now identified three receivers of shares in the national output. The fourth share receiver becomes influential in the economy in the latter half of the 19th century.

VEBLEN ON ENTREPRENEURS

Thorstein Veblen (1857–1929), an American economist, thought and wrote about economics from the 1880s through the 1920s. This was the formative period of giant business corporations in the U.S.

Veblen writes about the fourth share receiver in his book, *Absentee Ownership and Business Enterprise,* published in 1923. This fourth share receiver is a person who is able to organize the resources of the community *to meet the needs of the community*, or at least *to make the public believe this was the case.*

A man of workmanlike force and creative insight into the community's needs, who stood out on a footing of self-help, took large chances for large ideals, and came in for his gains as a due reward for work well done in the service of the common good, in designing and working out a more effective organisation of industrial forces and in creating and testing out new and better processes of production. It is by no means easy at this distance to make out how much of popular myth-making went to set up this genial conception of the Captain in the popular mind, or how much more of the same engaging conceit was contributed toward the same preconception by the many-sided self-esteem of many substantial business men who had grown great by "buying in" and "sitting tight," and who would like to believe that they had done something to merit their gains. But however the balance may lie, between workmanship and salesmanship, in the make-up of the common run of those early leaders of industrial enterprise, it seems that there will have been enough of the master-workman in a sufficient number of them, and enough of adventure and initiative in a sufficient number of the undertakings, to enable the popular fancy to set up and hold fast this genial belief in the typical captain of industry as a creative factor in the advance of the industrial arts; at the same time that the economists were able presently to set him up, under the name of "Entrepreneur," as a fourth factor of production, along with Land, Labour, and Capital.

In making this distinction, economists transformed Smith's categories slightly by making interest the payment to capital for its participation in the productive process. By lending capital to production, the capital owner earns interest. The entrepreneur, the Captain of Industry in Veblen's words, through organization and ownership of the means of production earned profits.

CONCLUSION

We now have the four share receivers, who are also perceived by economists as the factors of production. In theory they receive their shares because of their contribution to production.

Factors of Production	*Shares Received*
Labor	Wages
Land	Rent
Capital	Interest
Entrepreneur MANAGEMENT	Profits

In the next chapter, we will examine the development of another concept introduced by the early economists: laissez-faire.

KEY CONCEPTS

income distribution
labor
landlords
investors

rent
interest
profits
national product

entrepreneurs
wages
subsistence

stock
factors of production
"invisible hand"

REVIEW QUESTIONS

1. Why is income in the U.S. distributed unequally?
2. Should income be distributed more equally? Why or why not?

SUGGESTED READINGS

Maurice Dobb, 1973. *Theories of Value and Distribution since Adam Smith,* Cambridge University Press. A somewhat difficult book on difficult subjects.

Lester C. Thurow, 1975. *Generating Inequality*, Basic Books. A recent study of income distribution in the U.S.

THE RISE AND FALL OF LAISSEZ-FAIRE

CHAPTER 7

INTRODUCTION

Laissez-faire, free-market ideas were promulgated at the end of the 18th century by a new school of economists who wished to transfer control of their national economies from the aristocratic ruling classes to the direction of a self-equilibrating free-market system. Such a policy, it was argued, would produce rapid economic progress. As *laissez-faire* ideas were adopted, growth did take place; but it was accompanied by poverty and business cycles.

J. B. Say assured economists in 1803 that if markets were left free, there could only be temporary and minor problems of unemployment. This was because production always created its own demand, and demand created production. Known as Say's law, this doctrine was widely accepted by most economists throughout the 19th century.

However, some economists attempted to call attention to continuing unemployment problems and suggested various ideas about ways to respond to the problems. These socialistic economists were either ignored or viewed as dangerous radicals by the dominant school of economists in the universities and the ruling classes.

By 1926 John Maynard Keynes was convinced that *laissez-faire* was no longer an appropriate way of thinking about unemployment. Others had noticed this from 50 to 100 years earlier. But it was Keynes's contribution that ultimately signaled the fall of *laissez-faire*.

THE FLOW OF ECONOMIC ACTIVITY

We have seen that four factors of production are combined to create the national product. Each receives a share of the total product transformed conveniently into money. The money is used to claim output by each of the controllers of the four productive factors—landlords, laborers, capital owners, and entrepreneurs. Some classical economists of the 19th century claimed that the demand for the product would always be equal to the supply. The reason seemed self-evident. Each of the four factors of production receives a claim on a share for everything they supply in the production process. These claims become the demand for part of the total prod-

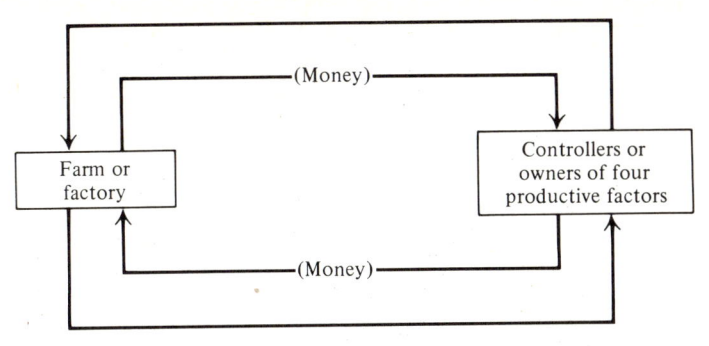

```
                    ←――――――――(Money)―――――――――┐
                    │                          │
                    ↓                          ↓
            ┌──────────────┐          ┌──────────────────┐
            │  Farm or     │          │  Controllers or   │
            │  factory     │          │  owners of four   │
            │              │          │ productive factors│
            └──────────────┘          └──────────────────┘
                    │                          │
                    └―――――――――(Money)―――――――――→
```

FIG. 7.1 Label the outside connecting lines with the following words: "land," "labor," "supply of products," "capital," "enterprise." Use all of the words. Label the inside lines with the appropriate words: "demand for products," "rent," "interest," "wages," "profits." Use all of the words.

uct. Therefore, demand for the products is created in the process of supplying the product.

J. B. SAY AND GLUTS

Jean Baptiste Say, 1767–1832, a French economist who studied, modified, and amplified the ideas of Adam Smith, stated this idea in *A Treatise on Political Economy* (1803):

It is worthwhile to remark that a product is no sooner created, than it, from that instant, affords a market for other products to the full extent of its own value. When the producer has put the finishing hand to his product, he is most anxious to sell it immediately, lest its value should vanish in his hands. Nor is he less anxious to dispose of the money he may get for it; for the value of money is also perishable. But the only way of getting rid of money is in the purchase of some product or other. Thus, the mere circumstance of the creation of one product immediately opens a vent for other products.

However, a few economists were concerned about unemployment resulting from more production than people might demand. What if some wrong products are produced, and they are not all purchased? Won't there be unemployment because of insufficient demand in those industries? What if there is more production generally than the people are able to purchase? Economists called this situation a "glut" in the market. These gluts create unemployment and poverty that lead to terrifying social conditions and great suffering. Wouldn't that be of concern to economists?

Thomas Robert Malthus (1766–1834), British economist, was one of the few economists concerned about these possible "gluts." In his *Principles of Political Economy* he says:

It has been thought by some very able writers, that although there may easily be a glut of particular commodities, there cannot possibly be a glut of commodities in general; because, according to their view of the subject, commodities being always exchanged for commodities, one half will furnish a market for the other half, and production being thus the sole source of demand, an excess in the supply of one article merely proves a deficiency in the supply of some other, and a general excess is impossible. M. Say, in his distinguished work on political economy, has indeed gone so far as to state that the consumption of a commodity by taking it out of the market diminishes demand, and the production of a product proportionably increases it.

This doctrine, however, as generally applied, appears to me to be utterly unfounded, and completely to contradict the great principles which regulate supply and demand.

It is by no means true, as a matter of fact, that commodities are always exchanged for commodities. An immense mass of commodities is exchanged directly, either for productive labour, or personal services: and it is quite obvious, that this mass of commodities, compared with the labour with which it is to be exchanged, may fall in value from a glut just as any one commodity falls in value from an excess of supply, compared either with labour or money.

In the case supposed there would evidently be an unusual quantity of commodities of all kinds in the market, owing to those who had been before engaged in personal services having been converted, by the accumulation of capital, into productive labourers; while the number of labourers altogether being the same, and the power and will to purchase for consumption among landlords and capitalists being by supposition diminished, commodities would necessarily fall in value compared with labour, so as very greatly to lower profits, and to check for a time further production.

But this is precisely what is meant by the term glut, which, in this case, is evidently general, not partial.

---

1. Why has demand decreased according to Malthus?

Say and others countered the argument set forth by Malthus by claiming that whenever a glut of a particular product emerged, markets would immediately adjust through price changes and the reallocation of resources. If one product was overproduced, its price would fall and resources would go elsewhere. Activity would shift to those products "most in request." Consequently, gluts would soon be eliminated through the operation of the market system. This reasoning supported the idea of laissez-faire.

LAISSEZ-FAIRE

J. B. Say won the argument with Thomas Malthus. There were significant reasons for this victory in spite of the prevalence of repeated "gluts," unemployment, poverty, and economic depressions in capitalist nations.

Economists and businessmen were convinced that the self-adjusting qualities of the economy, free from government controls, was the best system for generating profits and growth. This was Smith's concept of an "invisible hand" directing a free economy to prosperity at work. The idea of "laissez-faire" (from the Physiocrats in France) was similar to this "invisible hand." *Laissez-faire* meaning "let it happen," or "let it be." Businessmen wanted to run their own affairs without—well almost without—government interference.

The *"laissez-faire"* idea is to permit market forces *under competitive conditions* to operate unhindered. Economists said that if the market were permitted to work on its own, it would be most efficient and most advantageous to society. People will demand the products that they want as they spend their income. This will determine which products will be produced. Doesn't that seem to be better than having an individual or group of powerful people decide which products will be produced?

Laissez-faire, said the economists, has additional benefits: All of the owners of the factors of production will be directed into the most effective use of the factors of production by the market. It will be to their greatest advantage to produce the products for which there is a demand in the marketplace. If the owners of the productive factors use them to produce only what they themselves want, no one will purchase the products. There will be no shares given in the national pie of products to those productive factor owners who don't follow market demand.

Therefore let the market be, *laissez-faire*; don't interfere with it. It is controlled by an "invisible hand." It will regulate itself.

All of this is based upon the assumption that people will work for their own self-interest. We have already been assured by Adam Smith about the validity of this assumption.

2. What is your evaluation of the *laissez-faire* idea?

3. What are your assumptions about people's behavior? Are they consistently selfish? Are they consistently altruistic? (Altruism: Regard for others as a principle of action.) Which are you? Were you born selfish or altruistic? Have you been educated to be selfish or altruistic?

4. Would Adam Smith think it is more patriotic to be selfish or altruistic?

As mercantilist policies were abandoned and laissez-faire policies were adopted in England, the Industrial Revolution and the emergence of capitalist institutions proceeded. Essentially it was a period in which business sought freedom from state control, and prospered. However, not everyone was happy with the course of events, as this passage from Thomas Fleming's *1776, Year of Illusions* suggests:

There was a constant fear of the uneasy, often resentful poor. Workmen regularly smashed up new machines in the manufacturing towns. In 1765, the pitmen of the Tyne went on violent strike, wrecking the mining machinery and settng fire to the coal under ground. A few years later, riots swept Lancashire as the poor attacked spinning jennies and other machinery that they thought were depriving them of jobs. In 1773, the sailors of Liverpool staged something very close to a revolution, training their cannon on the town's stock exchange, wrecking and looting the houses of prominent shipowners, and even hoisting a "bloody flag."

On July 10, 1776, a mob marched on the town of Shepton Mallet to destroy some new weaving machines. Three justices of the peace ordered the crowd to disperse. They refused, and when two of the justices went home, the mob attacked the poorhouse where the machines had been operating, destroyed the machines, and all but wrecked the building. The remaining justice called out the local regiment of the army, and five ringleaders were arrested. The mob rioted as they were being led to jail. The troops, after firing two rounds over the heads of the mob, let it have a full volley, killing one man and seriously wounding six others. The coroner ruled the death "accidental."

When parliament convened in the fall of 1775, a pamphlet urged the people of London to rise and prevent the corrupt members from continuing to defraud them. The government rushed additional troops into the city. Protesting the American war had nothing to do with this threatened uprising. America was too far away and the grievances of the poor in the city of London too real and immediate to make the Americans a primary concern for most Englishmen in the early days of 1776.

Reprinted with permission from Thomas Fleming, *1776, Year of Illusions*, W. W. Norton & Co., Inc., 1975.

---

5. If you were a member of Parliament during 1776, what kinds of legislation would you have introduced and supported? Would you have been an advocate of *"laissez-faire"*?

It was probably in response to the situation in England that Adam Smith decided it would be better to remove control of the economy from the ruling class to individual self-interest as expressed in the marketplace. His preference for nontraditional direction led him to perceive the market as an impartial control of resource allocation and income distribution. He hoped the market was impartial, but was it? Smith was aware of the difficulties in his solution. He knew about the ability of combinations of employers to overwhelm the bargaining power of workers, but he continued to support markets free from government controls, *laissez-faire*.

What he may have not fully perceived was that the transfer of market controls from the self-interest of the ruling class to the self-interest of those who had the control of the largest quantities of productive resources was not necessarily the ideal solution for a sick economy. But it may have been an improvement in 1776.

Adam Smith thought it would be when he wrote in *The Wealth of Nations* about the allocation of capital by an individual.

What is the species of domestic industry which his capital can employ, and of which the produce is likely to be of the greatest value, every individual, it is evident, can, in his local situation, judge much better than any statesman or lawgiver can do for him. The statesman, who should attempt to direct private people in what manner they ought to employ their capitals, would not only load himself with a most unnecessary attention, but assume an authority which could safely be trusted, not only to no single person, but to no council or senate whatever, and which would nowhere be so dangerous as in the hands of a man who had folly and presumption enough to fancy himself fit to exercise it.

LAISSEZ-FAIRE AND THE POOR: THE SOCIALIST CRITIQUE

The conditions of some members of the economy were improving with *laissez-faire*, while the fate of some others was extreme poverty. Why weren't conditions for the poor improving as well?

Pierre Joseph Proudhon (1809–1865), a French economist, came to a conclusion about the continuing situation of low income that he stated forcefully in his essay "What Is Property?" (1840).

If I were asked to answer the following question: *What is slavery?* and I should answer in one word, *It is murder,* my meaning would be understood at once. No extended argument would be required to show that the power to take from a man his thought, his will, his personality, is a power of life and death; and that to enslave a man is to kill him. Why, then, to this other question: *What is property?* may I not likewise answer, *It is robbery,* without the certainty of being misunderstood; the second proposition being no other than a transformation of the first?

Reader, calm yourself: I am no agent of discord, no firebrand of sedition. I anticipate history by a few days; I disclose a truth whose development we may try in vain to arrest; I write the preamble of our future constitution. This proposition which seems to you blasphemous—*property is robbery*—would, if our prejudices allowed us to consider it, be recognized as the lightning-rod to shield us from the coming thunderbolt; but too many interests stand in the way . . . ! Alas! philosophy will not change the course of events; destiny will fulfill itself regardless of prophecy. Besides, must not justice be done and our education be finished?

The proprietor, the robber, the hero, the sovereign—for all these titles are synonymous—imposes his will as law, and suffers neither contradiction nor control; that is, he pretends to be the legislative and executive power at once. Accordingly, the substitution of the scientific and true law for the royal will be accomplished only by a terrible struggle; and this constant substitution is, after property, the most potent element in history, the most prolific source of political disturbances. Examples are too numerous and too striking to require enumeration.

---

6. "What is property?" "It is robbery." True or false?

Proudhon is careful to differentiate "property" from "possessions." He has no quarrel with people owning *personal* possessions—homes, farms, tools, livestock, furniture, or any of the things we might own and use. He protests the ownership of *impersonal* property that is not used by the owner except to collect rents on land and interest and profits on capital that are produced by others. There is an important difference in "property" and "possessions" to many socialist authors. Here is Proudhon's statement about the difference:

Individual possession is the condition of social life; five thousand years of property demonstrate it. Property is the suicide of society. Possession is a right; property is against right. Suppress property while maintaining possession, and, by this simple modification of the principle, you will revolutionize law, government, economy, and institutions; you will drive evil from the face of the earth.

---

7. To demonstrate your understanding of Proudhon's definition, write five currently familiar examples of "possessions" and five of "property."

Proudhon was only one of many who were sufficiently uncomfortable with economic conditions to want to try something entirely different. America seemed to be a country in which some of these dissatisfied people could experiment. A proliferation of various utopian communities developed in America. After all, wasn't America envisioned as a country for people with hopeful spirits? These people were seeking new forms of a social and political paradise. These communities practiced everything from communism to fascism, from celibacy to communal sexual intercourse and selective human breeding, and from anarchistic decentralization to dictatorial centralization. But what they had in common was a vision of a political and economic situation preferable to that which they were experiencing.

Not all of the discontented people emigrated to America. Many participated in political action to change their home economies and governments. There were general strikes with all workers striking at the same time, revolutions, and political education activities working toward evolutionary change.

John Stuart Mill in his *Principles of Political Economy* envisioned a different kind of economy from the one in which he was writing in England of 1848.

The form of association, however, which if mankind continue to improve, must be expected in the end to predominate, is not that which can exist between a capitalist as chief, and workpeople without a voice in the management, but the association of the labourers themselves on terms of equality, collectively owning the capital with which they carry on their operations, and working under managers elected and removable by themselves.

---

8. How would you evaluate these mid-19th-century comments of John Stuart Mill?

The socialist critique of 19th-century capitalism was developed further in a piece also published in 1848. In this year Karl Marx (1818–1883) and Friedrich Engels (1820–1895) wrote *The Communist Manifesto* for the Communist League, an association of working people in Germany. Marx and Engels argued forcefully that the capitalist system itself was the source of poverty and instability experienced by the growing working class. They urged workers to organize themselves for their own protection and to fight for socialism. We will explore Marx's ideas in more detail in the next chapter.

DOONESBURY   by Garry Trudeau

Copyright © 1975, G. B. Trudeau/Distributed by Universal Press Syndicate.

THE FLOWERING OF LAISSEZ-FAIRE

Despite the conditions of the poor and the socialist critique, laissez-faire capitalism flourished in 19th-century England and throughout Western Europe.

Queen Victoria reigned from 1837 to 1901 and gave her name to the "Victorian Age," an "Age" that is more than a simple designation of time in history. This was the age of increasing commercial dominance over formal and informal institutions that affected social values and behavior. Transportation and communication were revolutionized by railway expansion and the telegraph thereby quickening the pace of life. People began to illuminate their homes with electricity. The first cars were on the roads. The Carnegies, Vanderbilts, and Rockefellers were accumulating their enormous wealth. Coal and oil displaced animals and waterpower as sources of energy.

As the pace quickened, production increased, and more people attempted to be successful in business. A few individuals began to wonder about where all of this movement might lead. In 1864 John Ruskin questioned the "ideal of human life" in an essay named "Traffic," in which he describes the worshippers of the "Goddess of Getting-on." Ruskin was one of the great thinkers and writers in the Victorian Age. His works about art, architecture, and political economy have continuing relevance today.

Your ideal of human life then is, I think, that it should be passed in a pleasant undulating world, with iron and coal everywhere underneath it. On each pleasant bank of this world is to be a beautiful mansion, with two wings; and stables, and coach-houses; a moderately-sized park; a large garden and hot-houses; and pleasant carriage drives through the shrubberies. In this mansion are to live the favoured votaries of the Goddess; the English gentleman, with his gracious wife, and his beautiful family; he always able to have the boudoir and the jewels for the wife, and the beautiful ball dresses for the daughters, and hunters for the sons, and a shooting in the Highlands for himself. At the bottom of the bank is to be the mill; not less than a quarter of a mile long, with one steam engine at each end, and two in the middle and a chimney three hundred free high. In this mill are to be in constant employment from eight hundred to a thousand workers, who never drink, never strike, always go to church on Sunday, and always express themselves in respectful language.

9. Write a paragraph about your ideal of human life in which you discuss the same kinds of subjects mentioned by Ruskin: houses, environment, transportation, recreation, family, and industry.

The majority of the people in England didn't share the same dream. You may remember Eliza Doolittle's dream in *My Fair Lady,* the musical version of George Bernard Shaw's *Pygmalion,* was

All I want is a room somewhere,
Far away from the cold night air,
With one enormous chair.*

Poor people were still around all through the Victorian Age, and the people in the mansions were uneasy about their presence.

Walter E. Houghton published an illuminating book *The Victorian Frame of Mind* in 1957 that helps us understand this period. His book has become an essential work for people who are interested in the opinions and ideas of the 19th century.

To think it strange that the great age of optimism was also an age of anxiety is to overlook the ambivalent reaction which the main social and intellectual tendencies of the period provoked. Expanding business, scientific development, the growth of democracy, and the decline of Christianity were sources of distress as well as of satisfaction. But since optimism was expressed more often than anxiety (partly

*Copyright © 1956 by Alan Jay Lerner and Frederich Loewe. Chappell and Company, Inc., owner of the publication and allied rights throughout the world. International copyright secured. ALL RIGHTS RESERVED. Used by permission.

because it was more widely felt, and partly because any pessimistic attitude toward the human situation was considered weak or unmanly), we are still unaware of the degree to which the Victorian consciousness—and especially the subconsciousness—was haunted by fear and worry, by guilt and frustration and loneliness.

Bertrand Russell tells us that his grandfather, lying on his deathbed in 1869, "heard a loud noise in the street and thought it was the revolution breaking out." The incident is symbolic. For all its solid and imposing strength, Victorian society, particularly in the period before 1850, was shot through, from top to bottom, with the dread of some wild outbreak of the masses that would overthrow the established order and confiscate private property.

The possibility that it might happen here was abundantly supported, a priori, by the spread of radical propaganda, both political and religious, among the working classes. The two most influential books, Tom Paine's *The Rights of Man* and *The Age of Reason,* hardly seem dangerous now, for the former did not go beyond democracy nor the latter beyond deism. But democracy, to consider that first, carried connotations much like those of communism today.

Another source of alarm came from quite a different quarter. The decline of Christianity and the prospect of atheism had social implications which now seem curious (though they may have more bearing on our contemporary situation than we suppose). It was then assumed, in spite of rationalist denials, that any collapse of faith would destroy the sanctions of morality; and morality gone, society would disintegrate. Mill described the age as one in which the opinion that religious belief was necessary for moral and social purposes was universal, and yet real belief was feeble and precarious—a situation well calculated to arouse anxiety. But just such doubts were being raised on every side. Even so honest and courageous a thinker as Henry Sidgwick was reluctant to publish his skeptical views about immorality because the loss of such a hope, "from the minds of average human beings as now constituted, would be an evil of which I cannot pretend to measure the extent,"—if not the actual "dissolution of the existing social order," at least the increased danger of such a catastrophe.

What gave edge to these general speculations on the causal relationship of disbelief and disorder was their particular application to the lower classes. For "everyone" agreed that any discarding of the Christian sanctions of duty, obedience, patience under suffering, and brotherly love was obviously "fraught with grievous danger to property and the State." Nothing could illustrate that assumption more tellingly than the reviews of *The Descent of Man* (1871) in the most important newspapers, where Darwin was severely censured for "revealing his zoological [anti-Christian] conclusions to the general public at a moment when the sky of Paris was red with the incendiary flames of the Commune."

Reprinted with permission from Walter E. Houghton, *The Victorian Frame of Mind,* Yale University Press, 1957.

---

10. Are wealthy people in the U.S. today worried about democracy? Why or why not?

11. Would the wealthy people in America today be alarmed if the poorer people abandoned religion? Why or why not?

THE SITUATION IN THE UNITED STATES

In the U.S. at the end of the Victorian Age, economic crisis, panics, unemployment, and poverty had not been eliminated. Industrial trusts were increasing, but labor unions were kept weak by the courts' interpretation of property rights. Antitrust legislation, designed to control monopolistic business practices of the trusts, was used by the courts to eliminate union bargaining power.

Edward Bellamy (1850-1898), an American socialist author, published *Looking Backward, 2000-1887* in 1888. His book tells the story of a world in the year 2000 when the United States has turned to state socialism. More than a million copies were sold within a few years. "Nationalist" clubs were formed around America to discuss Bellamy's ideas.

In 1897 Bellamy published *Equality,* a sequel to *Looking Backward.* One of the chapters tells, in the form of a parable, about the reasons for the recurrence of economic fluctuations.

THE PARABLE OF THE WATER TANK
EDWARD BELLAMY

There was a certain very dry land, the people whereof were in sore need of water. And they did nothing but to seek after water from morning until night, and many perished because they could not find it.

Howbeit, there were certain men in that land who were more crafty and diligent than the rest, and these had gathered stores of water where others could find none, and the name of these men was called capitalists. And it came to pass that the people of the land came unto the capitalists and prayed them that they would give them of the water they had gathered that they might drink, for their need was sore. But the capitalists answered them and said:

"Go to, ye silly people! Why should we give you of the water which we have gathered, for then we should become even as ye are, and perish with you? But behold what we will do unto you. Be ye our servants and ye shall have water."

And the people said, "Only give us to drink and we will be your servants, we and our children." And it was so.

Now, the capitalists were men of understanding, and wise in their generation. They ordered the people who were their servants in bands with captains and officers, and some they put at the springs to dip, and others did they make to carry the water, and others did they cause to seek for new springs. And all the water was brought together in one place, and there did the capitalists make a great tank for to hold it, and the tank was called the Market, for it was here that the people, even the servants of the capitalists, came to get water. And the capitalists said unto the people:

"For every bucket of water that ye bring to us, that we may pour it into the tank, which is the Market, behold! we will give you a penny, but for every bucket that we shall draw forth to give unto you that ye may drink of it, ye and your wives and your children, ye shall give to us two pennies, and the difference shall be our profit, seeing that if it were not for this profit we would not do this thing for you, but ye should all perish."

And it was good in the people's eyes, for they were dull of understanding, and they diligently brought water into the tank for many days, and for every bucket which they did bring the capitalists gave them every man a penny, but for every bucket that the capitalists drew forth from the tank to give again unto the people, behold! the people rendered to the capitalists two pennies.

And after many days the water tank, which was the Market, overflowed at the top, seeing that for every bucket the people poured in they received only so much as would buy again half of a bucket. And because of the excess that was left of every bucket, did the tank overflow, for the people were many but the capitalists were few, and could drink no more than others. Therefore did the tank overflow.

And when the capitalists saw that the water overflowed, they said to the people:

"See ye not the tank, which is the Market, doth overflow? Sit ye down, therefore, and be patient, for ye shall bring us no more water till the tank be empty."

But when the people no more received the pennies of the capitalists for the water they brought, they could buy no more water from the capitalists, having naught wherewith to buy. And when the capitalists saw that they had no more profit because no man brought water of them, they were troubled. And they sent forth men in the highways, and byways, and the hedges, crying, "If any thirst let him come to the tank and buy water of us, for it doth overflow." For they said among themselves, "Behold, the times are dull; we must advertise."

But the people answered, saying: "How can we buy unless ye hire us, for how else shall we have wherewithal to buy? Hire ye us, therefore, as before, and we will gladly buy water, for we thirst, and ye will have no need to advertise." But the capitalists said to the people: "Shall we hire you to bring water when the tank, which is the Market, doth already overflow? Buy ye, therefore, first water, and when the tank is empty, through your buying, will we hire you again." And so it was because the capitalists hired them no more to bring water that the people could not buy the water they had brought already, and because the people could not buy the water they had brought already, the capitalists no more hired them to bring water. And the saying went abroad, "It is a crisis."

And the thirst of the people was great, for it was not now as it had been in the days of their fathers, when the land was open before them, for everyone to seek water for himself, seeing that the capitalists had taken all the springs, and the wells, and the water wheels, and the vessels and the buckets, so that no man might come by water save from the tank, which was the Market. And the people murmured against the capitalists and said: "Behold, the tank runneth over, and we die of thirst. Give us, therefore, of the water, that we perish not."

But the capitalists answered: "Not so. The water is ours. Ye shall not drink thereof unless ye buy it of us with pennies." And they confirmed it with an oath, saying, after their manner, "Business is business."

But the capitalists were disquieted that the people bought no more water, whereby they had no more any profits, and they spake one to another, saying: "It seemeth that our profits have stopped our profits, and by reason of the profits we have made, we can make no more profits. How is it that our profits are become unprofitable to us, and our gains do make us poor? Let us therefore send for the soothsayers, that they may interpret this thing unto us," and they sent for them.

Now, the soothsayers were men learned in dark sayings, who joined themselves to the capitalists by reason of the water of the capitalists, that they might have thereof and live, they and their children. And they spake for the capitalists unto the people, and did their embassies for them, seeing that the capitalists were not a folk quick of understanding neither ready of speech.

And the capitalists demanded of the soothsayers that they should interpret this thing unto them, wherefore it was that the people bought no more water of them, although the tank was full. And certain of the soothsayers answered and said, "It is by reason of overproduction," and some said, "It is glut"; but the signification of the two words is the same. And others said "Nay, but this thing is by reason of the spots on the sun." And yet others answered, saying, "It is neither by reason of glut, nor yet of spots on the sun that this evil hath come to pass, but because of lack of confidence."

And while the soothsayers contended among themselves, according to their manner, the men of profit did slumber and sleep, and when they awoke they said to the soothsayers: "It is enough. Ye have spoken comfortably unto us. Now go ye forth and speak comfortably likewise unto this people, so that they be at rest and leave us also in peace."

But the soothsayers, even the men of the dismal science—for so they were named of some—were loath to go forth to the people lest they should be stoned, for the people loved them not. And they said to the capitalists:

"Masters, it is a mystery of our craft that if men be full and thirst not but be at rest, then shall they find comfort in our speech even as ye. Yet if they thirst and be empty, find they no comfort therein but rather mock us, for it seemeth that unless a man be full, our wisdom appeareth unto him but emptiness." But the capitalists said: "Go ye forth. Are ye not our men to do our embassies?"

And the soothsayers went forth to the people and expounded to them the mystery of overproduction, and how it was that they must needs perish of thirst because there was overmuch water, and how there could not be enough because there was too much. And likewise spoke they unto the people concerning the sun spots, and also wherefore it was that these things had come upon them by reason of lack of confidence. And it was even as the soothsayers had said, for to the people their wisdom seemed emptiness. And the people reviled them, saying: "Go up, ye bald-heads! Will ye mock us? Doth plenty breed famine? Doth nothing come out of much?" And they took up stones to stone them.

And when the capitalists saw that the people still murmured and would not give ear to the soothsayers, and because also they feared lest they should come upon the tank and take of the water by force, they brought forth to them certain holy men (but they were false priests), who spake unto the people that they should be quiet and trouble not the capitalists because they thirsted. And these holy men, who were false priests, testified to the people that this affliction was sent to them of God for the healing of their souls, and if they should bear it in patience and lust not after the water neither trouble the capitalists, it would come to pass that after they had given up the ghost they would come to a country where there should be no capitalists but an abundance of water. Howbeit, there were certain true prophets of God also, and these had compassion on the people and would not prophesy for the capitalists, but rather spake constantly against them.

Now, when the capitalists saw that the people still murmured and would not be still, neither for the words of the soothsayers nor of the false priests, they came forth themselves unto them and put the ends of their fingers in the water that overflowed in the tank and wet the tips thereof, and they scattered the drops from the tips of their fingers abroad upon the people who thronged the tank, and the name of the drops of water was charity, and they were exceeding bitter.

And when the capitalists saw yet again that neither for the words of the soothsayers, nor of the holy men who were false priests, nor yet for the drops that were called charity, would the people be still, but raged the more, and crowded upon the tank as if they would take it by force, then took they counsel together and sent men privily forth among the people. And these men sought out the mightiest among the people and all who had skill in war, and took them apart and spake craftily with them, saying:

"Come, now, why cast ye not your lot in with the capitalists? If ye will be their men and serve them against the people, that they break not in upon the tank, then shall ye have abundance of water, that ye perish not, ye and your children."

And the mighty men and they who were skilled in war harkened unto this speech and suffered themselves to be persuaded, for their thirst constrained them, and they went within unto the capitalists and became their men, and staves and swords were put in their hands and they became a defense unto the capitalists and smote the people when they thronged upon the tank.

And after many days the water was low in the tank, for the capitalists did make fountains and fish ponds of the water thereof, and did bathe therein, they and their wives and their children, and did waste the water for their pleasure.

And when the capitalists saw that the tank was empty, they said, "The crisis is ended"; and they sent forth and hired the people that they should bring water to fill it again. And for the water that the people brought to the tank they received for every bucket a penny, but for the water which the capitalists drew forth from the tank to give again to the people they received two pennies, that they might have their profit. And after a time did the tank again overflow even as before.

And now, when many times the people had filled that tank until it overflowed and had thirsted till the water therein had been wasted by the capitalists, it came to pass that there arose in the land certain men who were called agitators, for that they did stir up the people. And they spake to the people, saying that they should associate, and then would they have no need to be servants of the capitalists and should thirst no more for water. And in the eyes of the capitalists were the agitators pestilent fellows, and they would fain have crucified them, but durst not for fear of the people.

And the words of the agitators which they spake to the people were on this wise:

"Ye foolish people, how long will ye be deceived by a lie and believe to your hurt that which is not? For behold all these things that have been said unto you by the capitalists and by the soothsayers are cunningly devised fables. And likewise the holy men, who say that it is the will of God that ye should always be poor and miserable and athirst, behold! they do blaspheme God and are liars, whom he will bitterly judge though he forgive all others. How cometh it that ye may not come by the water in the tank? Is it not because ye have no money? And why have ye no money? Is it not because ye receive but one penny for every bucket that ye bring to the tank, which is the Market, but must render two pennies for every bucket ye take out, so that the capitalists may have their profit? See ye not how by this means the tank must overflow, being filled by that ye lack and made to abound out of your emptiness? See ye not also that the harder ye toil and the more diligently ye seek and bring the water, the worse and not the better it shall be for you by reason of the profit, and that forever?"

After this manner spake the agitators for many days unto the people, and none heeded them, but it was so that after a time the people harkened. And they answered and said unto the agitators:

"Ye say truth. It is because of the capitalists and of their profits that we want, seeing that by reason of them and their profits we may by no means come by the fruit of our labor, so that our labor is in vain, and the more we toil to fill the tank the sooner doth it overflow, and we may receive nothing because there is too much, according to the words of the soothsayers. But behold, the capitalists are hard men and their tender mercies are cruel. Tell us if ye know any way whereby we may deliver ourselves out of our bondage unto them. But if you know of no certain way of deliverance we beseech you to hold your peace and let us alone, that we may forget our misery."

And the agitators answered and said, "We know a way."

And the people said: "Deceive us not, for this thing hath been from the beginning, and none hath found a way of deliverance until now, though many have sought it carefully with tears. But if ye know a way, speak unto us quickly."

Then the agitators spake unto the people of the way. And they said:

"Behold, what need have ye at all of these capitalists, that ye should yield them profits upon your labor? What great thing do they wherefore ye render them this tribute? Lo! it is only because they do order you in bands and lead you out and in and set your tasks and afterward give you a little of the water yourselves have brought and not they. Now, behold the way out of this bondage! Do ye for yourselves that which is done by the capitalists—namely, the ordering of your labor, and the marshaling of your bands, and the dividing of your tasks. So shall ye have no need at all of the capitalists and no more yield to them any profit, but all the fruit of your labor shall ye share as brethren, every one having the same; and so shall the tank never overflow until every man is full, and would not wag the tongue for more, and afterward shall ye with the overflow make pleasant fountains and fish ponds to delight yourselves withal even as did the capitalists; but these shall be for the delight of all."

And the people answered, "How shall we go about to do this thing, for it seemeth good to us?"

And the agitators answered: "Choose ye discreet men to go in and out before you and to marshal your bands and order your labor, and these men shall be as the capitalists were, but, behold, they shall not be your masters as the capitalists are, but your brethren and officers who do your will, and they shall not take any profits, but every man his share like the others, that there may be no more masters and servants among you, but brethren only. And from time to time, as ye see fit, ye shall choose other discreet men in place of the first to order the labor."

And the people harkened, and the thing was very good to them. Likewise seemed it not a hard thing. And with one voice they cried out, "So let it be as ye have said, for we will do it!"

And the capitalists heard the noise of the shouting and what the people said, and the soothsayers heard it also, and likewise the false priests and the mighty men of war, who were a defense unto the capitalists; and when they heard they trembled exceedingly, so that their knees smote together, and they said one to another, "It is the end of us!"

Howbeit, there were certain true priests of the living God who would not prophesy for the capitalists, but had compassion on the people; and when they heard the shouting of the people and what they said, they rejoiced with exceeding great joy, and gave thanks to God because of the deliverance.

And the people went and did all the things that were told them of the agitators to do. And it came to pass as the agitators had said, even according to all their words. And there was no more any thirst in that land, neither any that was ahungered, nor naked, nor cold, nor in any manner of want; and every man said unto his fellow, "My brother," and every woman said unto her companion, "My sister," for so were they with one another as brethren and sisters which do dwell together in unity. And the blessing of God rested upon that land forever.

---

12. What would Adam Smith say about Bellamy's essay? J. B. Say? J. P. Proudhon?

The classical economists of Bellamy's time believed the economy would always restore itself through the market. But Bellamy was not the only skeptic.

THE KEYNESIAN CRITIQUE OF LAISSEZ-FAIRE

John Maynard Keynes (1883–1946), the British economist, followed the classical tradition, but in 1926 he began to write about his departure from classical ideas held by most economists. By 1929, he was advising the British government to spend freely on public works programs to promote employment. President Franklin Roosevelt, confronted by millions of families without any income because *laissez-faire* capitalism was unable to provide employment in the 1930s, increased the influence of government in the American economy.

During the prosperous 1920s, Keynes wrote about "The End of Laissez-faire." The following are selected excerpts from his essay:

THE END OF LAISSEZ-FAIRE

JOHN MAYNARD KEYNES

Let us clear from the ground the metaphysical or general principles upon which, from time to time, *laissez-faire* has been founded. It is *not* true that individuals possess a prescriptive "natural liberty" in their economic activities. There is *no* "compact" conferring perpetual rights on those who Have or on those who Acquire. The world is *not* so governed from above that private and social interest always coincide. It is *not* so managed here below that in practice they coincide. It is *not* a correct deduction from the Principles of Economics that enlightened self-interest always operates in the public interest. Nor is it true that self-interest generally *is* enlightened; more often individuals acting separately to promote their own ends are too ignorant or too weak to attain even these. Experience does *not* show that individuals, when they make up a social unit, are always less clearsighted than when they act separately.

(1) I believe that in many cases the ideal size for the unit of control and organisation lies somewhere between the individual and the modern State. I suggest, therefore, that progress lies in the growth and the recognition of semi-autonomous bodies within the State—bodies whose criterion of action within their own field is solely the public good as they understand it, and from whose deliberations motives of private advantage are excluded....

(2) I come next to a criterion of *Agenda* which is particularly relevant to what it is urgent and desirable to do in the near future. We must aim at separating those services which are *technically social* from those which are *technically individual*. The most important *Agenda* of the State relate not to those activities which private individuals are already fulfilling, but to those functions which fall outside the sphere of the individuals, to those decisions which are made by *no one* if the State does not make them. The important thing for Government is not to do things which individuals are doing already, and to do them a little better or a little worse; but to do those things which at present are not done at all....

Confusion of thought and feeling leads to confusion of speech. Many people, who are really objecting to Capitalism as a way of life, argue as though they were objecting to it on the ground of its inefficiency in attaining its own objects. Contrariwise, devotees of Capitalism are often unduly conservative, and reject reforms in its technique, which might really strengthen and preserve it, for fear that they may prove to be first steps away from Capitalism itself. Nevertheless a time may be coming when we shall get clearer than at present as to when we are talking about Capitalism as an efficient or inefficient technique, and when we are talking about it as desirable or objectionable in itself. For my part, I think that Capitalism, wisely managed, can probably be made more efficient for attaining economic ends than any alternative system yet in sight, but that in itself it is in many ways extremely objectionable. Our problem is to work out a social organisation which shall be as efficient as possible without offending our notions of a satisfactory way of life.

Keynes thus began to explore the idea that laissez-faire did not always and necessarily result in the greatest social good. He argued, in fact, that the State should take an active part in certain economic matters. This emerging argument and the Great Depression of the 1930s signaled the end of laissez-faire. Keynes, while accepting capitalism as an economic system, rejected the classical notion of laissez-faire. His primary argument in reaching this conclusion was that the laissez-faire capitalist economic system could easily result in chronic unemployment and instability, just as Malthus had argued more than 100 years earlier. In Part IV we will examine in more detail the Keynesian body of thought on instability and the proper role for the State in the economy.

---

13. What would Adam Smith think about Keynes's argument?

KEY CONCEPTS

laissez-faire
Say's law
glut
altruism

self-interest
difference between "possessions" and "property"
socialist critique of laissez-faire
Keynesian critique of laissez-faire

REVIEW QUESTIONS

1. What are the strengths of laissez-faire capitalism both in theory and in practice?

2. What have been the major shortcomings in the operation of laissez-faire capitalism?

SUGGESTED READINGS

E. Ray Canterbury, 1976. *The Making of Economics,* Wadsworth. See Chapter 7 on Keynes.

Robert Heilbroner, 1961. *The Worldly Philosophers,* Simon and Schuster. See Chapter 7 on the Victorian World and Chapter 9 on Keynes.

E. K. Hunt, 1975. *Property and Prophets,* Harper & Row. See Chapter 5 on early socialist critics of capitalism.

THE MARXIAN CRITIQUE OF CAPITALISM

CHAPTER 8

INTRODUCTION

As capitalism developed in Western Europe and the United States, a critique of some of its results began to emerge. As we have seen in Chapter 7, some economists and historians noted the spread of poverty and the recurrence of depressions while others theorized on these problems. One of the first systematic analyses and critiques of capitalism was made by Karl Marx (1818-1883) in the mid and late 1800s. Marx's system provides a comprehensive and consistent framework for understanding, evaluating, and criticizing the development of capitalism. For that reason alone, it would be important to summarize Marx's system of thought concerning capitalism. In addition, Marxian economics has been important to the development of economic thought; and Marxism as a political movement has become increasingly widespread in the modern era.

John Gurley of Stanford University has said the following about why it is important for us to study Marxism:

Many Americans . . . are unaware of Marxism as a philosophical world-outlook, a useful framework for understanding much of what is going on in the world. In a way, this is strange, inasmuch as hundreds of millions of people around the world know and use Marxism, at least to some degree; it is probably the most prevalent set of ideas in the world today. A study of Marxism is not only useful for understanding the robustness of the continuing attacks on capitalism and the Western way of life, but it is also helpful, almost indispensable, for understanding capitalism itself. Marxism offers new and surprising insights into this subject.

John Gurley, *Challengers to Capitalism,* San Francisco Book Company, 1975.

We will encounter Marxist analysis elsewhere in this book. This chapter will provide a brief introduction to Marxist analysis.

KARL MARX: POLITICAL ECONOMIST AND REVOLUTIONARY

Marx was born in 1818 in Trier in what is now West Germany. His father was a successful lawyer and Marx began his college career in legal studies. However, he soon switched to philosophy in which he earned a Ph.D. at the age of 23. Having already become a radical in his student days, he was unable to secure a teaching position. Instead he became the editor of the *Rheinische Zeitung,* in Cologne. However, this journal was suppressed by the Prussian government in 1843; and Marx with his new wife, Jenny von Westphalen, moved to Paris. In Paris, Marx was active in left-wing journalism and in the workers' movement. It was here that he met Friedrich Engels and first began to study political economy and capitalism.

Over the last half of the 1840s Marx's radicalism continually got him in trouble with governments. In 1845, he was expelled from France and moved to Brussels. Here he wrote *The German Ideology* and *The Communist Manifesto* with Engels. In 1848-1849 several workers' revolutions occurred in Europe; and Belgium sent Marx packing. He first went to Paris and then to Germany. He was soon kicked out of Germany and then France, again. Finally, in 1849 his family settled in London, where he was to remain for the rest of his life.

In London, Marx devoted himself to studying political economy and writing. His years there were spent in constant poverty, but he received substantial support from his friend, Engels, who had a family interest in a manufacturing firm in Manchester. Marx developed into one of the most profound and widely known critics of capitalism in mid-19th-century Europe. His work had two basic elements: one was his study and writing and the other was his political activism. He was a correspondent for the *New York Daily Tribune* and published numerous books, the most famous of which is *Capital*. His political activism was as a socialist and Communist in the worker's movement. He helped organize the International Working Men's Association—the First International—and was active in workers' struggles throughout the rest of his life.

MARX'S GENERAL SYSTEM OF THOUGHT

Marx's political activism and his analysis of capitalism were both based on his general system of social development. This system amounted to a theory of history and of social change. As he put it in *The Communist Manifesto,* "The history of all hitherto existing society is the history of class struggles." This expressed his "materialist conception of history" that emphasized the role of the economic aspects of life in social development. This conception is central to Marx's system of thought and his analysis of capitalism, and we will explore it briefly here.

Dialectics

Marx's general system was based on two philosophical notions: dialectics and materialism. Dialectics was borrowed by Marx from the German philosopher Hegel (1770-1831). It emphasizes the idea that all things change and that all things contain not only themselves but their opposites. Dialectics is the study of the contradictions within the essence of things. A rock is a rock; but it is also, at the same time, "not a rock" because it could become a million grains of sand. And, consequently, development becomes the struggle of opposites—things becoming other things. Capitalists cannot be capitalists without their opposites, the workers (and vice versa); and both capitalists and workers will develop as they interact and influence each other. Out of this struggle of opposites comes change in which both elements, capitalists and workers, and the thing itself, capitalism, are transformed into something else. Ultimately, Marx thought that capitalism would develop into socialism and then communism. Dialectics, then, emphasizes change, contradiction, and the struggle of opposites. It thus constitutes a challenge to formal logic that concentrates on things as they are and their interrelationships. Marx wrote the following in his Preface to *Capital:*

Dialectic . . . in its rational form is a scandal and abomination to bourgeoisdom and its doctrinaire professors, because it includes in its comprehension and affirmative recognition of the existing state of things, at the same time, also, the recognition of the negation of that state, of its inevitable breaking up; because it regards every historically developed social form as in fluid movement, and therefore takes into account its transient nature not less than its momentary existence; because it lets nothing impose upon it, and is in its essence critical and revolutionary.

---

1. **Develop your own example which emphasizes the dialectical nature of some thing or process.**
2. **Why is dialectic "critical and revolutionary"?**

Materialism

Materialism concerns the notion that what is basic to the real life of human beings is their activity in the world. To understand the world, we must focus on real people and their day-to-day activities—especially those that are concerned with production for continued survival in this world. To Marx, materialism concerns "real, active men, and on the basis of their real life-process demonstrates the development of the ideological reflexes and echoes of this life-process." To know the world we must study things and their development. In addition, we must study the interrelationships of *things:* ". . . things come into being, change and pass out of being, not as separate individual units, but in essential relation and inter-connection, so that they cannot be understood each separately and by itself but only in their relation and inter-connection." To know the U.S., we must study its productive process and how that relates to its laws, beliefs, social classes, patterns of consumption, and so on. Additionally, we must study the history of how all these elements have changed over time and developed. Materialism contrasts with the notion that change takes place through the development of *ideas.* For Marx, the source of change rests, ultimately, in actual productive activity.

---

3. **How else could we "know" our world other than through its material aspects?**

The Materialist Conception of History, or Historical Materialism

From these two philosophical bases, Marx developed his theory of history—*the materialist conception of history,* or *historical materialism.* Productive activity is fundamental to human beings and to their societies. Consequently, the organization of production, the economic structure, forms the basis of all societies. All other social institutions and ideas are derived from the economic structure of the society. If the economic structure changes, all other aspects of the society will also change.

Marx formalized his analysis in the following way. The economic structure, or base, was the *mode of production* and consisted of the *forces of production* and the *relations of production.* The *forces of production* included all of the things that were necessary to produce goods and services: tools, machines, factories, means of transportation, raw materials, human labor, science, technology, skills, and knowledge. Over time, obviously, the forces of production changed. The *relations of production* were determined by the relationship of people to the productive process. When the forces of production are organized in a certain way, there will be different classes of people defined by their relationship to production. The relations of production, therefore, will be determined by patterns of ownership of productive resources, the nature of property relations and the division of labor. These will determine a class structure of society. A certain mode of production, then, consists of specific forces of production and specific relations of production (that is, a specific *class structure).* In addition, the mode of production determines the *superstructure* of society. The superstructure consists of the ideas, institutions and ideologies of the society, including laws, politics, culture, ethics, religion, morals, esthetics, art, philosophy, and so on. The purpose of the superstructure is to support the economic base of society. For example, feudalism organized production with certain methods and institutions and it had its own class structure and superstructure.

Within this framework is Marx's theory of historical change. When the forces of production change, the relations of production—social classes—will also change; this brings about a new mode of production that will, in turn, develop its own specific superstructure. It is in this context that class struggle takes place; different classes have different interests and visions and thus will do battle over the organization of production and, hence, society. The "old" classes will fight to preserve the old mode of production; and the new will fight for change. One of the most fundamental aspects of this "materialist conception of history" is that men, through acting on the forces of production, create their own history. Marx sums up his historical materialism in this passage from the *Critique of Political Economy:*

In the social production which men carry on they enter into definite relations that are indispensable and independent of their will; these relations of production correspond to a definite stage of development of their material powers of production. The sum total of these relations of production constitutes the economic structure of society—the real foundation on which rise legal and political superstructures and to which correspond definite forms of social consciousness. The mode of production in material life determines the general character of the social, political, and spiritual processes of life. It is not the consciousness of men that determines their existence, but, on the contrary, their social existence determines their consciousness. At a certain stage of their development, the material forces of production in society come into conflict with the existing relations of production, or—what is but a legal expression for the same thing—with the property relations within which they had been at work before. From forms of development of the forces of production these relations turn into their fetters. Then comes the period of social revolution. With the change of economic foundation the entire immense superstructure is more or less rapidly transformed. In considering such transformations the distinction should always be made between the material transformation of the economic conditions of production which can be determined with the precision of natural science, and the legal, political, religious, aesthetic, or philosophic—in short ideological forms in which men become conscious of this conflict and fight it out.

4. Apply the "materialist conception of history" (historical materialism) to the transition from feudalism to capitalism.

5. "It is not the consciousness of men that determines their existence, but, on the contrary, their social existence determines their consciousness." What does this mean? And how does it mean that men create their own history?

Mode of production:

    Forces of production
       (Instruments of production:
       tools, machinery, human labor, raw
       materials, science, technology, etc.)

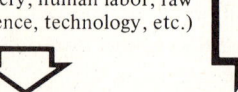

    Superstructure:
       (Institutions, ideologies, laws,
       politics, art, esthetics, culture,
       morals, religion, etc.)

    Relations of production
       (Class structure, ownership, property
       relations, division of labor)

FIG. 8.1 Marx's model of social development and change. One should be careful not to oversimplify this model and the direction of change. Dialectics and materialism are concerned with the contradictory interrelationships of things. Consequently, while the primary direction of change is from the forces of production to the relations of production to the superstructure, both the superstructure and the relations of production also affect the development of the forces of production.

THE MARXIAN ANALYSIS OF CAPITALISM

It was from this view of social change and history that Marx proceeded to develop his analysis and critique of capitalism. His conclusion was a condemnation of capitalism and its results, as well as a scientific appraisal of its likely future development and eventual replacement by socialism. Here, we will very briefly review Marx's theory of capitalist development.

Capitalism uses advanced methods of production including factories, transportation, and technology and, as it expands, has access to greater supplies of raw materials. Accompanying this mode of production are its own relations of production Basically, according to Marx, with the advance of the division of labor and private property, there were two social classes in capitalism. They were defined by their relationship to the productive process. First of all, there were the capitalists, or the bourgeoisie, who owned the means of production, controlled productive activity and earned profits. Secondly, there were the workers, the proletariat, who had nothing to sell in markets but their own labor power and, as a result, had to work for wages to survive. The history of capitalism, then, can be seen as the history of the struggle between these two classes. Marx condemned capitalism because it reduced social relations to impersonal market relations, or the "cash nexus." As he and Engels argued in *The Communist Manifesto:*

It has pitilessly torn asunder the motley feudal ties that bound man to his "natural superiors," and has left remaining no other nexus between man and man than naked self-interest, than callous "cash payment." It has drowned the most heavenly ecstasies of religious fervour, of chivalrous enthusiasm, of philistine sentimentalism, in the icy water of egotistical calculation. It has resolved personal worth into exchange value, and in place of the numberless indefeasible chartered freedoms, has set up that single, unconscionable freedom—Free Trade. In one word, for exploitation, veiled by religious and political illusions, it has substituted naked, shameless, direct, brutal exploitation.

Additionally, since workers were forced to work for capitalists for wages and since the capitalists controlled production, capitalism produced *alienation*. The following is from one of Marx's early critical works, *The Economic and Philosophic Manuscripts of 1844:*

What, then, constitutes the alienation of labour? First, the fact that labour is external to the worker, i.e., it does not belong to his essential being; that in his work, therefore, he does not affirm himself but denies himself, does not feel content but unhappy, does not develop freely his physical and mental energy but mortifies his body and ruins his mind. The worker therefore only feels himself outside his work, and in his work feels outside himself. He is at home when he is not working, and when he is working he is not at home. His labour is therefore not voluntary but coerced; it is *forced labour*. It is therefore not the satisfaction of a need; it is merely a *means* to satisfy needs external to it. Its alien character emerges clearly in the fact that as soon as no physical or other compulsion exists, labour is shunned like the plague. External labour, labour in which man alienates himself, is a labour of self-sacrifice, or mortification. Lastly, the external character of labour for the worker appears in the fact that it is not his own, but someone else's, that it does not belong to him, that in it he belongs, not to himself, but to another.... As a result, therefore, man (the worker) no longer feels himself to be freely active in any but his animal functions—eating, drinking, procreating, or at most in his dwelling and in dressing up, etc.; and in his human functions he no longer feels himself to be anything but an animal. What is animal becomes human and what is human becomes animal.

6. Did Marx deplore the "cash nexus" because it destroyed feudal relationships?

7. According to Marx, why is labor alienated?

From this early condemnation of capitalism, Marx went on to develop a detailed and lengthy analysis of capitalism in such works as *Wage Labour and Capital, The Grundrisse, Theories of Surplus Value,* and *Capital.*

Marx accepted *the labor theory of value* as it was developed by Smith and Ricardo, but turned it to his own purposes. For Marx it became a way of demonstrating the opposition of capitalists and workers and the exploitation of labor in capitalism. Marx contended that the value of all goods and services was a function of the labor (both direct and indirect) that went into them. Labor, in turn, was paid by capitalists to produce goods and services. However, since the capitalists controlled the productive process and the final output, they could earn *surplus value.* The trick was that the exchange value of goods and services, or what the capitalist sold, could be greater than the exchange value of labor power, or what the capitalist bought from the workers. The difference between these values was surplus value (the source of profit) that was appropriated by the capitalist. The exchange value of labor power, because of the existence of a mass of unemployed workers, *the industrial reserve army* of the unemployed, would always hover around "subsistence" (the value of the goods and services necessary for continued survival and the reproduction of the working class). Workers could produce enough value in only part of the working day to cover their subsistence needs. The rest of the day they labored to produce surplus value for the capitalist. As a result, the very structure of capitalism and its social relations produced *exploitation of labor.* Labor accounted for the value of all goods and services, but it received in return only a portion of that value because it did not own productive assets or control the production process.

Since capitalists derive surplus value and profits from production and since they operate in a competitive environment in which other capitalists also attempt to earn profits from the same type of activity, they are forced to accumulate capital. *Capital accumulation* is the driving force of capitalism. Profit is used to increase the capital, and hence the productive activity, of capitalists. This capital accumulation results in additional profits which, in turn, will be reinvested in more capital. Capitalists, if they wish to stay in business, have no choice about this. If they do not reinvest their profits in new and better forms of capital, they will be driven out of business by their competitors.

This process of capital accumulation forms the basis of Marx's understanding of *capitalist instability.* Capital accumulation produces economic growth, but it does so in cycles with periods of prosperity followed by depression. When production is expanding, capitalists will buy more machines and raw materials and other forms of capital. But this also requires them to hire more workers. This depletes the reserve army of the unemployed and consequently begins to drive up wages. This, however, tends to reduce profits. Consequently, capitalists would introduce new methods of production that would save on the use of labor; more capital intensive production allowed them to produce more with less labor (substitution of capital for labor). In addition, workers would lose jobs and the wage would go down as the reserve army was replenished.

This course of action was not without its own contradictions. With more workers out of jobs and with lower wages, it was more difficult to sell what was produced. This tended to reduce capitalists' profits. In addition, with more capital intensive methods of production, the capitalists reduced relatively the source of profits in production, surplus value generated by labor. This also tended to produce a declining rate of profits. With profits reduced, capital accumulation would slow down. All of these effects combined to produce depressions in economic activity as goods went unsold, profits decreased, workers lost jobs, and capital accumulation slowed. In true dialectical fashion, the expansion out of its own internal workings turns into its opposite, a depression. With wage rates depressed, though, capitalists will eventually rehire workers because they can once again produce surplus value and profits for the capitalists. And out of the depression comes an expansion of economic activity. Capitalism, Marx argued, grew in starts and spurts. The great mass of the people under capitalism, the working class, was dependent upon this unstable process for its livelihood and subsistence.

In addition to this cyclical instability, Marx thought that there were secular tendencies that would exacerbate the opposition between the capitalist class and the working class. Due to competition, *economic concentration* tended to occur as capitalists bought each other out or went bankrupt during depressions. The strong survived and came to dominate certain industries. As this occurred, the capitalist class became relatively smaller, as well as relatively more wealthy. Meanwhile, the working class became relatively larger and relatively poorer, as it remained near "subsistence." Marx called this *immiserization* of the proletariat. And, all the while, the capitalist retains control and the workers are powerless. Ultimately, as a result of continuing instability and these secular tendencies, which reinforce the class structure of capitalist society, the workers will organize for their own class interests and overthrow the capitalist system.

The political requirement for workers in the Socialist and Communist movement was described by Marx and Engels as follows at the end of *The Communist Manifesto:*

In short, the Communists everywhere support every revolutionary movement against the existing social and political order of things.

In all these movements they bring to the front, as the leading question in each, the property question, no matter what its degree of development at the time.

Finally, they labour everywhere for the union and agreement of the democratic parties of all countries.

The Communists disdain to conceal their views and aims. They openly declare that their ends can be attained only by the forcible overthrow of all existing social conditions. Let the ruling class tremble at a Communistic revolution. The proletarians have nothing to lose but their chains. They have a world to win.

However, this social revolution would not be easy. As Marx emphasized from his general system of social development, capitalism supports itself with its superstructure. The institutions, ideologies, and beliefs of the society defend capitalist economic institutions and social relations. Perhaps most important in this connection is the State. The State, according to Marxian analysis, serves as the "executive committee of the ruling class." The State protects private property and property rights and, thereby, the class structure of the system. It is in the camp of the capitalists and will actively oppose the worker's movement with all the resources at its command.

8. Evaluate Marx's analysis of capitalism. Does it describe economic reality and the historical development of capitalism? Does it help you understand how capitalism works?

9. Why do you suppose Marx kept getting kicked out of European countries?

SOCIAL REVOLUTION

Marx argued that workers would be exploited, alienated, and condemned to subsistence standards of living under capitalism. He further argued that in their association at work and in their communities, they would be able to objectively analyze their reality and the reasons for their oppression. Consequently, they would organize themselves and transform the whole capitalist system. (Indeed Marx spent much of his time in political activity with workers.) In *Capital,* he describes the process of social revolution as follows:

Along with the constantly diminishing number of magnates of capital, who usurp and monopolize all advantages of this process of transformation, grows the mass of misery, oppression, slavery, degradation, exploitation; but with this too grows the revolt of the working class, a class always increasing in numbers, and disciplined, united, organized by the very mechanism of the process of capitalist production itself. The monopoly of capital becomes a fetter upon the mode of production, which has sprung up and flourished along with, and under it. Centralization of the means of production and socialization of labour at last reach a point where they become incompatible with their capitalist integument. This integument is burst asunder. The knell of capitalist private property sounds. The expropriators are expropriated.

Once the death knell of capitalism sounded, what would the Socialists, Communists, and workers create? What would they do? While Marx never wrote extensively on this question, a hint at the answer is contained in *The Communist Manifesto:*

The distinguishing feature of Communism is not the abolition of property generally, but the abolition of bourgeois property. But modern bourgeois private property is the final and most complete expression of the system of producing and appropriating products, that is based on class antagonisms, on the exploitation of the many by the few.

Copyright © (1974) by Noah's Ark, Inc. (for Ramparts Magazine) reprinted by permission.

In this sense, the theory of the Communists may be summed up in the single sentence: Abolition of private property.

We Communists have been reproached with the desire of abolishing the right of personally acquiring property as the fruit of a man's own labour, which property is alleged to be the groundwork of all personal freedom, activity and independence.

Hard-won, self-acquired, self-earned property! Do you mean the property of the petty artisan and of the small peasant, a form of property that preceded the bourgeois form? There is no need to abolish that: the development of industry has to a great extent already destroyed it, and is still destroying it daily.

Or do you mean modern bourgeois private property?

The proletariat will use its political supremacy to wrest, by degrees, all capital from the bourgeoisie, to centralise all instruments of production in the hands of the State, *i.e.*, of the proletariat organised as the ruling class; and to increase the total of productive forces as rapidly as possible.

Of course, in the beginning, this cannot be effected except by means of despotic inroads on the rights of property, and on the conditions of bourgeois production; by means of measures, therefore, which appear economically insufficient and untenable, but which, in the course of the movement, outstrip themselves, necessitate further inroads upon the old social order, and are unavoidable as a means of entirely revolutionising the mode of production.

These measures will of course be different in different countries.

Nevertheless in the most advanced countries, the following will be pretty generally applicable.

1. Abolition of property in land and application of all rents of land to public purposes.
2. A heavy progressive or graduated income tax.
3. Abolition of all rights of inheritance.
4. Confiscation of the property of all emigrants and rebels.
5. Centralisation of credit in the hands of the State, by means of a national bank with State capital and an exclusive monopoly.
6. Centralisation of the means of communication and transport in the hands of the State.
7. Extension of factories and instruments of production owned by the State; the

bringing into cultivation of wastelands, and the improvement of the soil generally in accordance with a common plan.
8. Equal liability of all to labour. Establishment of industrial armies, especially for agriculture.
9. Combination of agriculture and manufacturing industries; gradual abolition of the distinction between town and country, by a more equable distribution of the population over the country.
10. Free education for all children in public schools. Abolition of children's factory labour in its present form. Combination of education with industrial production, &c., &c.

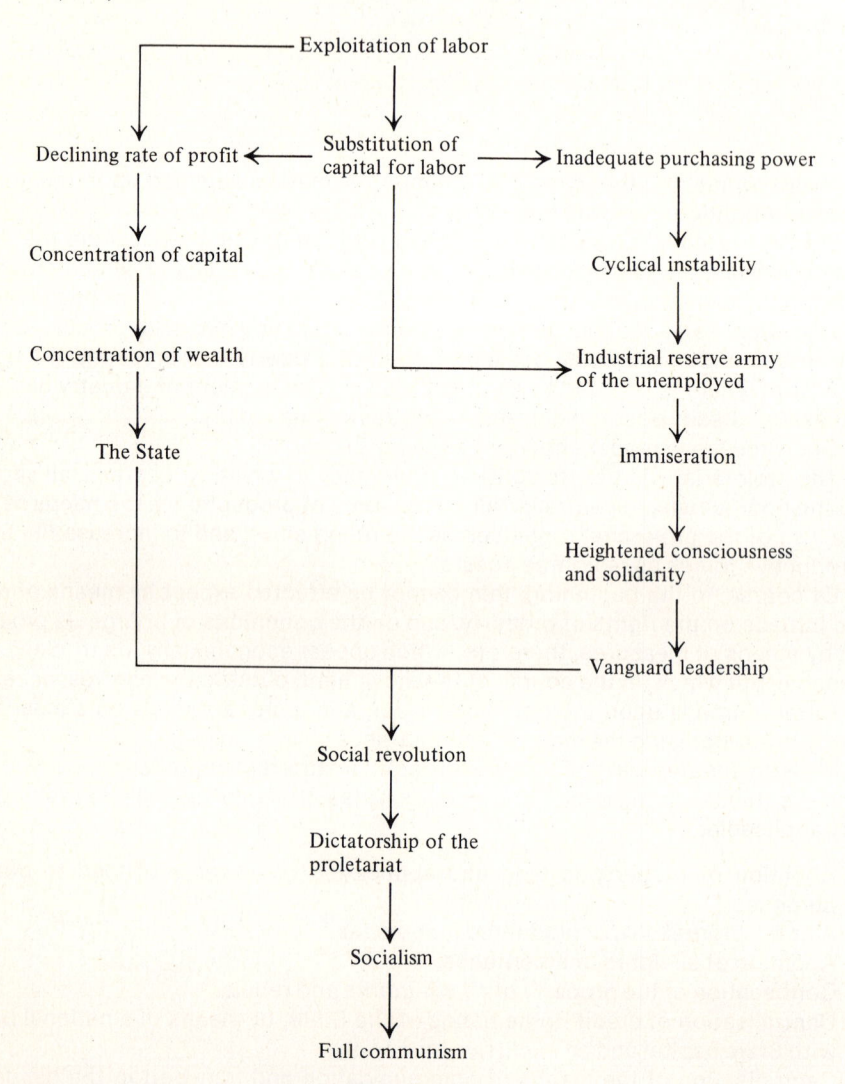

```
                    ┌──── Exploitation of labor
                    │            │
                    │            ▼
                    │      Substitution of
 Declining rate of profit ◄── capital for labor ──► Inadequate purchasing power
         │                       │                          │
         ▼                       │                          ▼
 Concentration of capital        │                   Cyclical instability
         │                       │                          │
         ▼                       │                          ▼
 Concentration of wealth         └─────────────► Industrial reserve army
         │                                         of the unemployed
         ▼                                                  │
     The State                                              ▼
         │                                            Immiseration
         │                                                  │
         │                                                  ▼
         │                                        Heightened consciousness
         │                                           and solidarity
         │                                                  │
         │                                                  ▼
         └────────────────────────────────── Vanguard leadership
                                 │
                                 ▼
                          Social revolution
                                 │
                                 ▼
                       Dictatorship of the
                           proletariat
                                 │
                                 ▼
                             Socialism
                                 │
                                 ▼
                         Full communism
```

FIG. 8.2. **Marx's model of social revolution.**

10. Would the Communists take your personal possessions away from you? What kinds of property would they "wrest" away?

11. In Marx and Engels' ten-point program, which are accepted in the U.S.? which are partially accepted? which are rejected?

CONCLUSION

In this chapter we have briefly presented Marx's system of thought—his "materialist conception of history" and his analysis of capitalism. We have not tried to apply it strictly to the actual historical development of capitalism in Western Europe and the U.S. Nor have we traced its theoretical and political development by the followers of Marx. Nor have we examined the arguments of its critics. However, its strength and validity must ultimately be tested by its ability to help us understand the world and by its congruence with actual economic and social events.

KEY CONCEPTS

historical materialism
the mode of production
the forces of production
the relations of production
class
superstructure
surplus value

alienation
exploitation
capital accumulation
Marxian theory of instability
economic concentration
immiserization
social revolution

REVIEW QUESTIONS

1. Why do people in the U.S. tend to reject Marxism?

2. Why is it that an increasing number of newly independent countries in the world have Marxist governments (i.e., politicians and leaders who rely on Marxist analysis)?

3. What do you feel is the weakest part of the Marxist argument?

4. What do you feel is the strongest part of the Marxist argument?

5. What is the purpose of Marxist economics?

SUGGESTED READINGS

E. K. Hunt, 1975. *Property and Prophets,* Harper & Row. See Chapter 6 on Marxian economics.

John Gurley, 1976. *Challengers to Capitalism,* San Francisco Book Company. Chapters 2 and 3 contain very readable treatments of Marx's theory of history and analysis of capitalism.

Karl Marx and Friedrich Engels, 1848. *The Communist Manifesto,* China Books and Periodicals. A classic piece of Marxist analysis and propaganda.

David McClellan, 1975. *Karl Marx,* Penguin Books. A short biography of Marx.

Robert C. Tucker, 1978. *The Marx–Engels Reader,* Norton (2nd ed.). An excellent selection of writings by Marx and Engels, including *The Communist Manifesto,* parts of *Capital* and *The Critique of the Gotha Program* in which Marx briefly discusses postcapitalist society.

MICROECONOMICS

PART III

As we have seen in our account of the transition from feudalism to capitalism, markets have emerged in the Western world as a method of organizing society's production. *Markets* exist for all of the factors of production and for final consumption goods. Through the information transmitted by markets, producers make decisions about what factors of production to use and consumers decide what to consume. The information appears in the form of *prices*. Based on these decisions made by various economic agents in the society, resources will be used in certain ways to produce certain goods and services.

Microeconomics is concerned with describing how the economic system operates to allocate resources and to organize production. Consequently, it focuses on the decision makers—the firms, the consumers, the government—who determine how resources will be used. Microeconomics is fundamentally concerned with the major problem of all economies: that there are not enough resources available to satisfy all the desires of all the economic agents. *Scarcity* is the supreme economic fact of life. Given scarcity, microeconomics also concentrates on how the market system allocates resources by valuing them. Therefore, it examines the operation of markets and price determination. Finally, microeconomics is concerned with *evaluating how well* society allocates its scarce resources. *Ideally, society should use resources efficiently. Efficiency* means minimizing the use of scarce resources to achieve that mix of output most highly valued by society.

In this Part, we will begin with a consideration of the basic microeconomic problem and develop some economic concepts useful in helping us to understand the consequences of scarcity. In Chapter 10 we will examine the microeconomic theory of competitive markets. In Chapters 11 and 12 we will introduce the economic reality that many productive units in our economic system are not competitive; and we will consider the theoretical results of this economic fact. In Chapter 13 we will concentrate on a more institutional examination of the dominant productive unit in the American economy, the corporation.

Now that we are about to begin studying modern economic theory, we might pause to ask ourselves what economic theory should do. Ideally, it should have *explanatory value* to help us understand how economic forces work, *predictive power* to help us understand what might happen in the future, and *relevance* so that it helps us to solve the economic problems that we face. Keep these criteria in mind as you learn economic theory.

SCARCITY: "YOU CAN'T ALWAYS GET WHAT YOU WANT"

CHAPTER 9

STUDY FORECASTS MAJOR SHORTAGES

Scientists report the world faces future of dwindling oil and mineral supplies

HAROLD M. SCHMECK

WASHINGTON, Feb. 11—The world faces a future plagued by shortages in those resources vital to modern industrial civilization, according to a major study made public today by the National Academy of Sciences.

"Many face the prospect of a series of shocks by varying severity as shortages occur in one material after another, with the first real shortages perhaps only a matter of a few years away," said the report, titled "Mineral Resources and the Environment."

The report concluded that it was "essentially impossible" for United States oil production to rise enough in the next decade to make the nation independent of foreign supplies. . . .

The report predicted that most of the world's oil supplies would be used up within 50 years and that the "enormous" reserves in the Middle East would be gone in 30 years at the present and prospective rates of use.

WHAT KIND OF CULTURE?

. . . The central conclusion of the report, which was released today . . . was that the United States must emphasize conservation of energy and other resources to a degree hitherto unparalleled. Indeed, . . . it should become almost a religion. In answer to questions at the news conference . . . there was little evidence that the government was pursuing the conservation goal as vigorously as would be necessary.

© 1975 by The New York Times Company. Reprinted by permission.

ENERGY AND RESOURCES

"Because of the limits to natural resources as well as to means for alleviating these limits," the report said, "it is recommended that the federal government proclaim and deliberately pursue a national policy of conservation of material, energy and environmental resources, informing the public and the private sectors fully about the needs and techniques for reducing energy consumption, the development of substitute materials, increasing the durability and maintainability of products, and reclamation and recycling."

The committee recommended a national policy of stockpiling critical materials to sustain both civilian and military needs in case of emergencies. It also said better ways of making long-range demand forecasts should be developed.

"THREATENED LIST"

Although the report did not predict which material resources would be in short supply first, it did list several on a "threatened list." Among those it cited asbestos, helium and mercury because they have vital industrial uses and special properties that are not duplicated by any other substances. Tin was on the list because of a "potential general worldwide shortage."

Although the study noted that the United States had abundant copper reserves it predicted that the nation would not be able to depend entirely on domestic supplies much longer. It recommended developing means of obtaining copper from metallic nodules that occur naturally on the ocean bottom.

The report also said it was no longer safe to assume that technology could solve every problem of material shortage.

The committee said the report should not be viewed as a counsel of despair. It said the United States had abundant resources that should insure it a continued strong position in the world.

But the report said efforts to increase supplies should be made concurrently with policy aimed at decreasing demand, that progress in substitution and recycling should be stimulated along with, not independently of, encouragement of the conservation ethic.

The committee said United States and world dependence on coal would increase the years ahead and that the United States had huge reserves of this valuable resource. The report continued, however, that the mining and burning of huge amounts of coal could have serious environmental and health consequences that must be taken into account.

---

1. Why are there shortages? What factors play a role in creating shortages?
2. What sorts of actions could be taken to alleviate these projected shortages?

SCARCITY: THE FUNDAMENTAL ECONOMIC FACT OF LIFE

Scarcity is the fundamental economic fact of life. All societies must develop methods and institutions to produce goods and services and to distribute them to people for consumption. However difficult that task is, it is further complicated by

Scarcity: The Fundamental Economic Fact of Life

the overriding reality of scarce resources and unlimited human wants and needs. Human societies, and the individual people within them, have certain physical needs for short-run and long-run survival. Food, shelter, and clothing must be provided. With the desire to live beyond subsistence and to experience a richer life, the wants of a society are subject to constant expansion.

But the physical and mental resources that can be used to provide for material needs are not subject to constant expansion. This limitation is especially true if we concentrate on the short-run—the present and the immediate future. The mental capabilities of humans are at a certain stage of development. Physical resources are at a fixed level. There are just so many people who can labor. There is just so much wheat, or corn, or coal, or gas, or bauxite, or copper, etc. Even in the long run, though, the problem of scarcity governs the decisions that must be made; society must still concern itself with using its possibly expanding resource base in the best way possible to meet its needs.

The problem for society then becomes using the resources that are available in the best way possible to meet as many of the needs and wants of its people as it can. This is an incredibly difficult and complicated task. How much of our resources should be used to develop nuclear energy? Should we devote more or less to exploring the possibilities of solar energy? Should more resources go to housing or to transportation? Should we build automobiles for private transportation or buses for public transportation? Because of scarcity, *we must make choices*. Society must, in addition to deciding how to organize itself for production and distribution, develop mechanisms and institutions for making *economic decisions* about how best to use the resources that are available to it. How can we make sure that resources are allocated in the best way possible?

In our largely private economic system, many of these decisions are made through markets. Cars are produced because people demand them and are willing to buy them for the prices charged by producers. The prices reflect the costs to the producers for the resources that are used in production. Based on price information and individual tastes and preferences, people make decisions about what to spend money on. We will examine the workings of markets in a bit more detail in Chapters 10 and 11 to see how they allocate resources.

Public choices must also be made about the use of resources. For example, every society desires to protect itself from foreign enemies. Some countries do this through the establishment of a military force; the threat of physical reaction is intended to forestall aggressive actions by others. In the event of attack or hostile action, military force can be used to protect the interests and possessions of the society. The construction of a military force, however, requires the use of resources. Resources devoted to the production of a military potential are automatically unavailable for other uses. The *opportunity cost* of using resources to produce guns, tanks, planes, etc. is that those resources cannot be used for other purposes. Society must make a choice, then, about how much of its resources to devote to producing military goods and services, with the realization that the cost of doing so is forgoing the opportunity to use resources in the production of nonmilitary goods and services. Obviously, different societies have made different choices about the size of their military establishments, and thus over how to use their scarce resources.

THE PRODUCTION POSSIBILITIES CURVE

The *production possibilities* curve is a device developed by economists to illustrate the concepts of scarcity and opportunity cost. Economic choices, necessitated by scarcity, have costs. The following presentation concentrates on the public choice between military and civilian goods. This same analysis could also be applied to other public choices about how to use tax moneys: should we build more highways? Should we overhaul the railroad system? Should we increase welfare spending? And so on. It can also be applied to analyzing the results of decisions usually made in the private sector: should we produce more big cars? or more little cars? Should we produce Screaming Yellow Zonkers? or pet rocks? or more housing? The point is that choices must be made—and all choices to use resources in any way means that they can't be used for other purposes.

---

3. What is the opportunity cost of not using resources for a particular purpose?

Every society possesses resources and uses those resources to produce goods and services. But a society *cannot* have all of the goods and services it desires because resources are *scarce*. The production possibilities curve is a useful way of illustrating this concept. We will make the following *assumptions*:

1. The economy is experiencing full employment of all its resources.
2. The supplies of the factors of production are fixed at one point in time.
3. Technology is constant (again, at one point in time).

We will make one further assumption. The economy produces consumer goods and military goods (or "butter and guns"), and the resources can be used to produce both types of goods (although some will be better at producing one type of goods than the other).

Here is the problem. With our resources (and our assumptions) we can make only limited amounts of both types of goods. We must then make a choice about how much of each type of good to produce. Since our resources are fully employed and limited, we can produce more of one type of good only by producing less of the other. That is, if we decide to produce more military goods, we can do it only by taking resources away from the production of civilian goods and thus produce fewer consumer goods. The *opportunity cost* of producing more military goods is that we will have fewer civilian goods.

This is shown graphically in Fig. 9.1. If we produce *only* military goods (using all our resources to do so), we can have M_1 of them. On the other hand, if we produce only consumer goods, we can have C_1 of them. Let's assume that the economy is at A. Then we produce C_2 of consumer goods and M_2 of military goods. However, there is a whole range of different *combinations* of military goods and

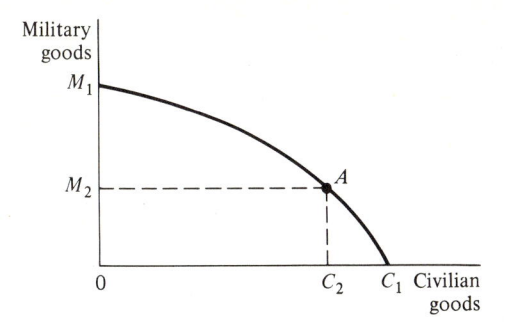

FIG. 9.1 The production possibilities curve.

consumer goods that we *could* have. The locus of all of those possible combinations gives us a production possibilities curve. The important point here is that, at a given moment in time, whenever a society chooses to have more of one type of good, it must sacrifice some of the other type of good. To have more military goods (moving toward M_1) means that the society will have fewer resources to devote to the production of civilian goods.

This problem, obviously, can be alleviated over time somewhat by the discovery of new resources or by the institution of new technology that allows us to get more production from our resources. In either case, the entire curve would move outward.

---

4. Can you show graphically, and explain why the production possibilities curve will move outward with (1) more resources available or (2) an improvement in technology that increases *efficiency*?

GRAPHS, EQUATIONS, AND WORDS

Economists like to use graphical representations. The production possibilities curve is one example of this pedagogical technique, and you will encounter many others in this book. Economic theory seeks to establish relationships among economic variables. Economists often use three different techniques to explain these relationships. First, they use words. Second, they use graphical illustrations to show the relationships. And, finally, they sometimes utilize mathematical equations. In our production possibilities curve, we have discussed in words the notion of the opportunity costs between military goods and civilian goods. We have also illustrated this same relationship on a graph. If we wanted to proceed we could write an equation, $M_x = f(C_x)$, showing that, given our assumptions, the amount of military goods (M_x) the society has will depend on the amount of civilian goods, (C_x) it has (*given* all of our assumptions).

On the graph, the amount of military goods is measured on the vertical axis and the amount of civilian goods on the horizontal axis. Thus any point on the graph represents a single combination of civilian goods and military goods. And every point represents a *different* combination.

---

5. Explain what it would mean if society were at a point inside its production possibilities curve.

The production possibilities curve is shaped the way it is (concave to the origin) because resources are not completely adaptable to other uses. For example, the more consumer goods we sacrifice (moving toward M_1), the fewer and fewer military goods we will be able to *add* to military production (for each marginal loss of consumer goods). (Can you show this on the graph?) This is because some resources are best suited for producing consumer goods and not suited for military production (e.g., pacifists). As more of these resources are transferred to military production, the *addition* to military goods will decline. (The reverse is true, too. If we disarmed, some generals might not be too good at producing consumer goods.)

DEFENSE VS. CIVILIAN PRIORITIES

A particularly controversial example of the problem of scarcity in recent years has been the debate about national priorities. Perhaps the sharpest focus of this debate has been on defense spending vs. spending on civilian priorities. Proponents of defense spending want more resources for producing military goods. They argue that more is needed because of the potential military capabilities of our enemies and because they feel that military power is the best way to assure national security. Critics of defense spending argue that too many of our resources are devoted to defense (more than $1.3 *trillion* since World War II!) and that defense spending deprives us of the use of resources for domestic purposes (e.g., education, health, etc.).

The arguments on both sides, over the years, have become more sophisticated and complex; but at the heart of the matter is an economic choice about how best to use scarce resources. In this public issue obviously, though, it is not simply an economic question. It is also a question concerned with philosophy (how best to resolve conflicts?) and with international and domestic politics. The following selections indicate the richness and complexity of this public decision about how to use our resources.

In the following article, Donald Neff reports on the state of the arms race between the Soviet Union and the U.S. as of 1977. At that time, each of the major military superpowers was spending well in excess of $100 billion a year for defense. In addition, at that time, the consensus of American intelligence was that the U.S. maintained superiority in the strategic balance.*

---

*Drew Middleton, U.S. held to maintain lead over Soviet in strategic arms. *New York Times,* October 3, 1977.

THIS SIDE OF DOOMSDAY
DONALD NEFF

Five years after the U.S. and the Soviet Union signed the widely hailed SALT I pact (Strategic Arms Limitation Agreement), and two-and-a-half years after the broad goals of SALT II were agreed upon, the world—in the words of a Rand researcher—is "up to its ass in nukes." The United States' bulging nuclear arsenal today includes 8500 nuclear warheads, Russia's 3500. And those are only the biggies—the so-called strategic forces; another *20,000* tactical (shorter range) nuclear weapons are held by both sides. Yet, as sure as mushrooms follow a rain, both sides will add thousands more strategic warheads to their stockpiles, regardless of whether or not President Carter has his way and SALT II is finally signed this fall.

The reason is simple: after nine years, the SALT talks still have not progressed to the point where they are concerned with actual disarmament. Rather, they have been talks about how much more each side can go on adding to its nuclear force. SALT I, signed in May 1972, froze the number of strategic launchers allowed by both sides. But the real armaments action, then and now, was not in the quantity of launchers, but in the quality and quantity of warheads. In one of those euphemisms so dear to the Strangelovian set, that meant multiple independently targetable re-entry vehicles—MIRVs. With MIRVs, a theoretically infinite number of warheads could be placed atop one missile. That was an opportunity no warrior could pass up, and none did. By the time the SALT talks started, the U.S. was already busy MIRVing its missiles, and Russia was not far behind.

When President Ford and Chairman Brezhnev decided to set general limits on MIRVs as well as launchers at Vladivostok in November 1974, the number of warheads possessed by each country had grown fantastically. Yet the two leaders set the MIRV limits so high (1320) that neither side had yet reached that point. Naturally, the race to MIRV continued, and continues. All indications are that Washington and Moscow will use the Vladivostok figures when they sign SALT II, even though neither side has yet MIRVed that many missiles—and won't have for years.

Small wonder that while Henry Kissinger called the Vladivostok formula one that can "be justly described as a major breakthrough," former presidential science adviser Dr. George B. Kistiakowsky said that it "protects the arms race for the next ten years from interference by the arms controllers."

Indeed, the arms race remains unchecked, and the pace is faster than ever. Despite SALT, both sides are looking to the future as though there is no doubt there will be one. In the U.S. (and Russia has similar programs underway), production is going ahead on a new submarine, the Trident, which will become operational next year at an estimated cost of $949 million for each of the 11 on order. It will carry 24 missiles, each with 10 to 14 MIRVs or MARVs (MIRVs that can be maneuvered onto a target for pinpoint accuracy). Although President Carter has halted production of a fleet of B-1 bombers (each capable of carrying a 25,000-pound payload), a handfull

Reprinted from *New Times*, August 5, 1977 by permission of the author and *New Times*.

will nonetheless be built as possible chips in the armaments game. And, naturally, there is a stylish new missle for the eighties under study. Called the MX, it would carry 15 MIRVs, roll around on a railroad track so it could not be hit, and cost $34 billion for a network of 300. Finally, there is the long-range cruise missile, now being tested, that can buzz over land or sea at low altitudes for 1500 miles, then dump a 200-kiloton nuke on target. Costing just under $1 million each, the cruise is considered a bargain.

There is really no need for such added overkill. As the reliable Stockholm International Peace Research Institute notes: "The nuclear arsenals of the USA and the USSR contain intercontinental ballistic missiles, medium-range ballistic missiles, intermediate-range ballistic missiles, short-range ballistic missiles, submarine-launched ballistic missiles, depressed-trajectory ballistic missiles, fractional-orbital bombardment systems, free-fall tactical bombs, free-fall strategic bombs, air-to-surface missiles, air-to-surface standoff missiles, air-to-air missiles, army artillery shells, naval artillery shells, howitzer projectiles, torpedoes, rocket torpedoes, depth charges, demolition devices, land mines, sea mines, antiballistic missiles, and so on."

This awesome array of killing machines has put the superpowers in a strategic position felicitously called Mutual Assured Destruction. It would take Lewis Carroll to do it justice, but an adequate definition was once provided by Dr. Herbert York, dean of the UCLA physics department and a private consultant to Secretary of Defense Brown. "For now and the foreseeable future," he said, "a nuclear exchange would result in the destruction of the two principals as nations, regardless of who strikes first."

Understandably, the acronym MAD has been coined by opponents of the strategy.

The actual achievement of SALT to date has been to preserve the state of MAD in which the superpowers find themselves. MAD becomes threatened if either side believes it can survive attack. That means that the development of an effective defense against nuclear attack is now as threatening to peace as the development of new offensive weapons. In the upside-down world of MAD, the most dangerous weapon of all is one that would save lives. As author John Newhouse explains in his book on SALT, *Cold Dawn*, "defending people is the most troublesome of all strategic options, for stability demands that each of the two societies stand wholly exposed to the destructive power of the other. . . ."

. . . Modern weapons are not cheap. Worldwide expenditures on "defense" budgets last year totaled $334 billion. (In terms of 1970 constant dollars, that compares with $65 billion in 1948 and less than $10 billion in 1900). The Pentagon's proposed budget for next year is $120.4 billion. The Soviet annual arms budget is probably well above $130 billion, according to CIA estimates.

Just as the two superpowers spend most of the world's defense funds, they also provide most of the world's weapons. The U.S. last year sold $10 billion worth of arms; that is half of the $20 billion annual world trade in weaponry, and it makes America the world's largest arms dealer. Before the mid-1960s, the U.S. was extremely discriminating in the sale of weapons outside of the country and usually gave away only surplus arms. Western Europe and such old treaty partners as Turkey, Iran, Greece, Korea, Taiwan, and the Philippines were all favored buyers.

But then the Johnson administration and later, at an accelerating pace, the Nixon–Kissinger administration, discovered that diplomacy-by-arms-give-aways was easier than traditional diplomacy and began offering allies (and would-be allies) the very latest hardware.

To assure that more and more new weapons are developed each year, the industrial nations, mainly the U.S. and the USSR, spend annually $20 billion of their defense budgets on research. The efforts of about 400,000 scientists and engineers are devoted to this dark crusade throughout the world.

The focusing of so much money and brainpower on weapons research means that the entire arms industry is in a constant state of almost instant obsolescence. While it took from the beginning of mankind to the 14th century to discover the cannon, and from then until World War II to discover a family of "better" weapons like rockets, it took only about 30 years to develop electronic warfare.

As historian Carroll Quigley has observed, "weapons will continue to be expensive and complex. This means that they will increasingly be the tools of professionalized, if not mercenary, forces. All of past history shows that the shift from a mass army of citizen-soldiers to a smaller army of professional fighters leads, in the long run, to a decline of democracy. . . . The weapons obtainable by the state today are far beyond the pocketbook, understanding, or competence of the ordinary citizen."

Unless SALT can start focusing on real disarmament, and parallel talks are begun to hold down the equally dangerous race in conventional weapons, a decrease in democracy could soon be the least of our worries. On the day the nukes start flying and the death rays flashing, we will have no worries at all.

---

6. According to the Neff article, what are the opportunity costs of spending vast sums of money on defense? Are there additional ones that you can think of?

7. What is national security? What determines whether a nation is secure or not?

Throughout the 1960s and 1970s, the defense budget in general and some weapons systems in particular have been debated. In the early 1970s, largely as a result of public pressure and opinion, defense budgets were restricted by Congress. In 1968, the antiballistic missile system (ABM) was approved by a single vote in the Senate. This program, however, was later scrapped after about $5 billion had been spent constructing ABM sites in the upper Midwest. More recently, in 1977, the B-1 bomber program was halted by President Carter. Nevertheless, the defense budget as a whole has begun expanding again, with projections calling for annual increases of about 10 percent in the defense budget; and many new weapons are being developed. The following editorial from *The Progressive* magazine discusses this trend and argues that the opportunity costs of such spending are too large. They urge support for efforts to halt the increase in defense spending and the arms race.

MOBILIZING FOR SURVIVAL

THE EDITORS OF *THE PROGRESSIVE*

Peace activists who waged a vigorous three-year campaign against the B-1 bomber won a hollow victory on June 30, when President Carter announced he was abandoning the B-1—except for continuing research and development work—as "a very expensive weapons system" that is not necessary to the national defense. In the same breath the President raised the nuclear arms race to a new and even more dangerous level by giving the green light to the cruise missile.

The B-1 would, indeed, have been "very expensive"; the cost of the 224-plane fleet sought by the Air Force would have approached and eventually surpassed $100 billion, and no persuasive rationale for the bomber has ever been advanced—except that it would gratify the egos of Air Force generals and fatten the profits of aerospace manufacturers.

The cruise missile, on the other hand, is an "attractive" weapon—relatively inexpensive and easy to produce, and capable of being launched from the air, ground, or sea. Equipped with nuclear warheads, it can vastly increase the Pentagon's overkill capacity, and neither the quantity of missiles nor their range is readily verifiable under an arms control agreement.

In their perfectly understandable initial euphoria over the B-1 victory—it was, after all, the first major weapons system to be canceled in at least a decade and a half—the peace forces almost ignored the frightening implications of the cruise missile decision. But they had, in fact, been stuck with the short end of a lopsided trade-off: The taxpayers will be spared the burden of another enormously expensive but ineffective toy. The Pentagon will gain an inexpensive but enormously effective weapon. Like the equally "attractive" neutron bomb and the new strategic missiles soon to be deployed . . . the cruise missile takes us a long step closer to doomsday.

What are the lessons of the B-1 victory?

First, that President Carter—like all of his predecessors since we entered the nuclear age—is trapped in the mentality of an arms race without end.

Millions of human beings found new hope for peace when Jimmy Carter addressed these words to the Democratic Party's platform committee on June 16, 1976:

"The core of detente is the reduction of arms. We should negotiate to reduce the present SALT ceilings on offensive weapons before both sides start a new arms race to reach the current maximums and before new missile systems are tested or committed for production."

That statement and the President's subsequent rhetoric about his yearnings for disarmament have been rendered meaningless by the cruise missile decision and by his calm assertion that "I think we should have the option" to build and deploy the neutron bomb.

Second, that we can not look to a Democratic Congress to oppose the steps toward nuclear escalation proposed by a Democratic Administration. . . .

Reprinted by permission from *The Progressive,* 408 West Gorham Street, Madison, Wisconsin 53703. Copyright © 1977, The Progressive, Inc.,

... Ironically, some of the most eloquent opposition is being voiced by Republicans—Senator Mark Hatfield of Oregon, who says the neutron bomb is "in the realm of the unconscionable," and Senator H. John Heinz of Pennsylvania, who calls it "even more repugnant than usual" and "literally dehumanizing."

Third and most important, that those of us who are determined to halt the mad momentum toward a nuclear holocaust can no longer afford to squander our energies on opposition to one or another weapons system or on campaigns to trim a few million dollars from the military budget here and there. What must be relentlessly attacked is the whole lunatic rationale of the arms race. In our own country and around the world, people must be mobilized around the understanding that more weapons do not bring us closer to some ephemeral "security," but to the final catastrophe of nuclear devastation.

Fortunately, the vehicle for such a campaign is at hand. Formation of the new Mobilization for Survival is being announced as this issue of *The Progressive* goes to press. . . .

The Mobilization's stated aims are: "to reawaken public awareness of the scale of the threat which faces us all; to channel this awareness into dramatic and effective actions; to take the initiative from those with a vested interest in the arms race; to build a truly massive movement which can change the policies and direction of the nation, and to achieve a transformation of consciousness on the international level, in cooperation with groups active in Europe, Asia, and the Third World."

To achieve those aims, the Mobilization will mount a series of teach-ins and speak-outs this fall on campuses and in communities around the nation. Early next year, it plans to organize local protests against the arms race and for more attention to domestic needs. And next spring, when the U.N. Special Assembly on Disarmament is scheduled to convene, the Mobilization will sponsor internationally coordinated demonstrations in major cities.

More information on the Mobilization's aims and activities is available from the national headquarters: 1213 Race Street, Philadelphia, Pennsylvania 19107. The telephone number is (215) 563-1512. The cause is one that deserves the total support and participation of everyone who cares about the future of this planet.

"We Will Shake the Foundation. . . ."

We are frightened to realize how little chance there is that our children will live to see the year 2001. We are frightened at the determination of military leaders in all nations to press ahead with weapons systems. We are horrified that *our* money, the product of *our* labor is drained away from human needs and invested in machinery of unspeakable destruction.

We are angry that Government leaders have thought us such fools that they believed they could buy our silence with words about disarmament. We will educate ourselves. We will raise the consciousness of our communities. We will move into the streets. We will shake the foundation of any institution which tries to turn our future into a radioactive zone.

From the "Call to Action" of the Mobilization for Survival

124   Scarcity: "You Can't Always Get What You Want"

It's not a war toy, Madam. It's a cease fire toy.

Joe Mirachi, copyright © 1976, the *Wall Street Journal*.

8. What are the opportunity costs of increased defense spending according to *The Progressive*?

9. What alternative uses of resources do they suggest in place of defense spending?

10. What would be the opportunity costs of a significant reduction in defense spending in the U.S.? (George McGovern, when he ran for President in 1972, proposed a 33 percent reduction in defense spending.)

11. How do you feel about this general debate concerning the use of our society's scarce resources? Try to focus your response on the economic ramifications of the various choices.

APPLYING THE CONCEPT OF CHOICE TO PERSONAL DECISIONS

As is implicit in all of the foregoing, when making decisions about using society's resources, what we do is to compare the costs and the benefits of a particular use of resources. Included in the costs are the opportunities forgone by not using resources for alternatives. This balancing of costs vs. benefits also occurs in the economic decisions made by individuals. These include choices about work vs. leisure, type of work, consumption, and so on. Consumers will weigh the benefits of buying a particular good (say, a new car) vs. the opportunity costs of not buying other goods (what else could have been bought for the same price as the car). Based on such judgments, consumers make decisions about what to consume. An example of one such personal decision is whether to go to college or not.

In making such a decision, an individual must weigh the benefits of going to college against the opportunity costs of doing so. The Doonesbury cartoons which

Applying the Concept of Choice to Personal Decisions

follow and the article from *U.S. News and World Report* reflect different aspects of this personal decision. The article from the *New York Times*, July 20, 1977, provides some recent data that suggest that going to college, on the average, is a rational economic decision.

DOONESBURY by Garry Trudeau

Copyright © 1973, G. B. Trudeau/Distributed by Universal Press Syndicate.

Copyright © 1973, G. B. Trudeau/Distributed by Universal Press Syndicate.

VALUE OF A COLLEGE DIPLOMA: CENTER OF GROWING DEBATE

REPRINTED FROM "U.S. NEWS & WORLD REPORT."

At a time when many college graduates are finding it difficult to get a worthwhile job, faith in the value of a degree—intellectual or monetary—is slipping badly.

More and more young people are proclaiming their disdain for a four-year course of study, especially in liberal arts.

Junior colleges are packed with students taking two-year vocational courses. So are schools specializing in electronics, secretarial work, and mechanical repairs.

Educators themselves concede that the value of a college degree may have been oversold.

In an article entitled "The Declining Value of College Going," in the September issue of *Change* magazine, Profs. Richard Freeman and J. Herbert Hollomon write: "By all relevant measures, the economic status of college graduates is deteriorating with employment prospects for the young declining exceptionally sharply. In the brief span of about five years, the college job market has gone from a major boom to a major bust." They cite these statistics:

In 1958, only 1 percent of the college graduating class was unemployed. In 1972, it was 9.3 percent—compared with 7.7 percent for high-school graduates of the same age and 5.6 percent for all workers. Of all those with college degrees, fewer than 1 percent were unemployed in 1969. In 1974, it was 2 percent.

CONTINUING SLIDE

Bureau of Labor Statistics figures show that, at present, unemployment among all holders of college degrees has risen further—to 2.9 percent. And a College Placement Council survey reported in August that the hiring of college graduates by industry was off this year by 24 percent.

Selling briskly, and soon to appear in paperback, is the recently published book "The Case against College," by Caroline Bird, a feminist and herself a college lecturer.

The book contains iconoclastic statements such as:

"We may now be systematically damaging 18-year-olds by insisting that their proper place is in college."

"In strictly financial terms, college is the dumbest investment a young man can make."

"The most charitable conclusion is probably correct: College has very little, if any, effect on people and things at all."

Such judgments are producing angry denials and counterarguments from educators. Large numbers still retain the historic faith of Americans in education's benefits in providing for a better and happier life as well as more hard cash. They cite arguments to prove that college is still a good way to "get ahead."

They point out that the current 2.9 percent unemployment among holders of college degrees is considerably below the 9.1 percent for high-school graduates,

---

Reprinted from *U.S. News & World Report*, October 13, 1975. Copyright © 1975 by U.S. News & World Report, Inc.

the 9.2 percent for the nation's work force as a whole, and 15.2 percent among those who did not graduate from high school.

Also seen are long-range employment trends that favor college graduates.

Department of Labor estimates are that about 20 percent of all jobs in this decade will require a college degree, while only 15.7 percent of the people in the labor force are college graduates now. . . .

NARROWING GAP

What seems clear is that the salary differential between college graduates and other Americans is narrowing. Professors Freeman and Hollomon report:

"From 1969, the last good year in the college job market, to 1975, the starting salaries of male graduates in industry, having increased rapidly in the previous decade, dropped sharply, both in real terms and relative to the earnings of other workers. College Placement Council data show a decrease of 23 percent in the real starting pay for men with social science or humanities degrees; a fall of 21 percent in the real pay for beginning mathematics majors; and of 17 percent for beginning electrical engineers with doctorates.

"The ratio of college-graduate to high-school-graduate incomes—quite stable since World War II—also dropped in the early 1970s. In 1969, full-time male workers with four years of college earned 53 percent more than male workers with four years of high school; in 1973, 40 percent more."

Defenders of college training do not deny that its relative monetary value has lately been decreasing. But they point out that male workers with four years of college still earn 40 percent more than those with four years of high school, which translates into nearly $300,000 over a lifetime.

While Ms. Bird argues that family status—not eduation—is the biggest single source of income differences among males, Prof. David Featherman of the University of Wisconsin says:

"We are moving toward a more meritocratic society—with increased returns for eduational advancement, and a decrease in the effects of social origins on occupational status and earnings."

Increased cost of college, coupled with decreased financial rewards in many instances, raises the question of the value of college as a long-term financial investment.

Here again, opinions differ. Professors Freeman and Hollomon find that "according to one set of estimates, the return on college investment dropped from 11 to 12 percent in 1969 to 7 to 8 percent in 1974. A decrease of this magnitude is unprecedented." . . .

THE INTANGIBLES

Lately the controversy over education's worth has moved beyond its monetary benefits to less-tangible areas. Defenders of liberal-arts college education point out that jobs which require a college degree often carry such nonmonetary benefits as greater stimulation, less fatigue, and a cleaner and more healthful environment. Even more important, they say, are a multitude of off-the-job gains for degree holders.

A typical comment comes from Thomas Bonner, president of Union College in Schenectady, N.Y.: "Whoever said life was a matter of bread alone? No educated person would argue seriously that the study of history, literature, art, or philosophy is irrelevant to a satisfactory life or the enduring values of a citizen. What of the quality of a graduate's life, the realization of one's own goals, success as a parent or marriage partner, or one's contributions as a citizen?"

Skeptics remain unimpressed by such arguments. Says Ms. Bird: "College doesn't make people intelligent, ambitious, happy, liberal, or quick to learn new things. Colleges can't claim much credit for the learning experiences that really change students while they are there. Jobs, friends, history, and most of all the sheer passage of time have as big an impact as anything even indirectly related to the campus."

How young people themselves are being affected by the arguments and counterarguments in this debate is hard to measure.

In absolute figures, college enrollment this fall is at an all-time high—nearly 4 percent above last year. But the percentage of young people who choose to go to college seems to be declining.

Professors Freeman and Hollomon report that the proportion of 18- to 19-year-old men enrolled in higher education declined from 44 percent in 1969 to 33.4 percent in 1974.

WHY THE FALL-OFF?

The question arising, however, is this: Does the decline result chiefly from the rising cost of college or from disillusionment with higher education?

The growing controversy on the value of going to college could have far-reaching consequences.

Professors Freeman and Hollomon speculate that large numbers of young people, for the first time, are likely to obtain less schooling and potentially lower occupational status than their parents.

Ms. Bird advocates shifting money now used to subsidize college education to such alternatives as job apprenticeships and national-service jobs.

In this controversy, one thing is emerging clearly: Americans, in growing numbers, are turning a hard look on the assumption, once taken for granted, that a college degree is the gilt-edged passport to success in life.

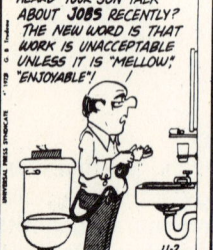

DOONESBURY by Garry Trudeau

Copyright © 1973, G. B. Trudeau/Distributed by Universal Press Syndicate.

A COLLEGE DEGREE STILL MAINTAINS ITS AURA
EDWARD B. FISKE

Despite published research and widespread anecdotal evidence to the contrary, a college degree is still a solid economic investment, according to a new study by the Conference Board.

The analysis, based on Federal labor and census figures, acknowledges that the income advantages of recent college graduates over their noncollege peers has been blunted in recent years. It argues, however, that figures shaped by "the recession experience of the past 10 years" should not be used as a basis for longterm projections.

"Measured by the likelihood of becoming unemployed, by earnings, or by the increases in earning with age and experience," it concludes, "college graduates continue to make up an economically favored group."

The Conference Board is a nonprofit, Manhattan-based organization that conducts research in the areas of economics and management. The analysis published in its monthly magazine, *Across the Board*, was written by Leonard A. Lecht, director of special projects research.

JOBLESS GRADUATES

Questions about whether a college education is worth the investment of time and money have frequently been raised in the wake of stories of college graduates who cannot find jobs or who have been forced to accept blue-collar jobs that do not make use of their education....

... In the Conference Board study, Mr. Lecht acknowledged the decline in income differentials for college graduates. "Males age 25 and over with four or more years of college who worked a full year in 1969 received, on an average, 46 percent more income than their high school counterparts," he said. "By 1974 the differentials had shrunk to something more than a third, 36 percent."

Copyright © 1977 by The New York Times Company. Reprinted by permission.

I don't really think college would be right for me, Dad. Could I just have the $6000 a year in CASH instead?

Reprinted by permission of Randy J. Glasbergen

BASED ON UNIQUE PERIOD

The "pessimistic analysis of the status of college graduates in the labor market," he said, is based on a unique period in which the proportion of young people in the population was high and the supply of graduates substantially outstripped the growth of new jobs.

Nevertheless, the income differential for the average college graduate over the age of 25 was still $4500, he stated, and there are some good reasons not to project the decline into the future.

From 1960 to 1970 degree-credit enrollment rose from 3.4 percent to 7.5 percent, an increase of 117 percent. Employment in the professional and technical fields that normally draw college graduates grew by 49 percent during the same period. While this was more than double the 20 percent increase in total employment, he said, "it was less than half the corresponding increase in the higher education enrollments in the same period."

Mr. Lecht suggested that the supply side of the job squeeze is likely to ease up in the coming years for several reasons. For one thing, fewer people will be entering the labor market because of declining birth rates. For another, the growth in college enrollment is slowing down. "As a consequence," he said, "there will be fewer people, college-educated or otherwise, competing for entry-level jobs in the next decade."

Another change that is likely to give an economic advantage to the college graduate, said the Conference Board report, is a broadening of the definition of "white-collar" occupations. "The graduate who becomes a management trainee rather than a professor, the engineering student who enters technical sales work, or the would-be elementary school teacher who becomes an administrative assistant are more typical than those who have become unemployed or have turned to unskilled work," he stated.

Mr. Lecht estimated that from 1974 to 1985 approximately 2.1 million jobs will have opened up for college graduates because of "educational upgrading" in fields such as physician's assistant and legal paraprofessional. In addition, he said, traditional professional and technical employment is expected to continue to grow more rapidly than total employment.

The report said that any consideration of the value of an investment in a college education must also take into account the facts that college graduates are three times less likely than noncollege graduates to become unemployed and that "income progression" is greater for men with a college diploma. Whereas the income of male college graduates 45 to 54 years old was 133 percent more than that of 18- to 24-year-olds with college degrees, the income of older high school graduates was only 83 percent above their younger counterparts.

The author also argued that, while comprehensive figures are not available, "it is likely that they would show that the college group was also less exposed to occupational accidents and illnesses, and that graduates were typically employed in positions involving more generous fringe benefits—such as paid vacations or retirement benefits—than were generally available."

The Conference Board study also noted that the available data "refers exclusively to males" and that differentials between college and high school educated women have narrowed at only half the rate for men.

"Recent graduates, at least for the next few years, will probably face more difficult problems in finding suitable jobs than their predecessors in the 'golden age' for graduates in the 1960s," Mr. Lecht concluded. "But the evidence also underscores a continuing and substantial economic advantage from attending college. It does, for most people, literally pay off."

12. What are the benefits of going to college?

13. What are the costs (and opportunity costs) of going to college?

14. Did you make the right decision about going to college? Why or why not?

> I shall be telling this with a sigh
> Somewhere ages and ages hence:
> Two roads diverged in a wood, and I—
> I took the one less traveled by,
> And that has made all
> the difference.
>
> —Robert Frost, "The Road Not Taken"

CONCLUSION

Scarcity requires choices in both public and private matters. This fundamental economic fact requires societies and individuals to develop institutions and procedures for making hard decisions. Most individuals don't have enough income to buy everything they might want. Governments don't have enough tax money to do everything that their constituents would like them to do. In addition, sometimes decisions mean that someone or some group will benefit, while others suffer losses. The costs and benefits must be weighed in reaching decisions that maximize the use of scarce resources.

One of the most important institutions in a private economy for facilitating such decisions is the market. Markets determine *prices* for goods and resources. With this information, economic agents can make decisions comparing alternative courses of action. Producers can decide what to produce and what resources to use. Consumers can decide what goods to purchase. (Oftentimes government decisions operate "outside" of market forces because there is no profit objective; nevertheless government cost–benefit studies of alternatives must use price data for the resources involved).

In the next chapter, we will examine the economic theory of markets—how they operate and how prices are determined.

132 Scarcity: "You Can't Always Get What You Want"

DOONESBURY   by Garry Trudeau

Copyright © 1973, G. B. Trudeau/Distributed by Universal Press Syndicate.

KEY CONCEPTS

scarcity	the production possibilities curve
economic choice	prices
allocation of resources	microeconomics
opportunity cost	efficiency

REVIEW QUESTIONS

1. From your own experiences and lifetime, do you think that scarcity is really a problem for the U.S.?

2. What is the difference between wants and needs?

3. Are wants and needs really unlimited? If they are, why?

4. How does the concept of opportunity cost help societies and individuals to make choices?

5. Why do economic choices have to be made?

6. Think of examples from your own life when the concepts of scarcity and opportunity cost have influenced your decisions.

SUGGESTED READINGS

The daily newspaper for innumerable examples of choices on private and public issues!

Caroline Bird, 1975. *The Case against College,* D. McKay. On why you made a mistake by going to college!

Robert Heilbroner, 1974. *An Inquiry into the Human Prospect,* Norton. One view of possible global scarcity and the results.

Seymour Melman, 1974. *The Permanent War Economy,* Simon and Schuster. On the adverse economic effects (the opportunity costs) of massive military spending since World War II in the U.S.

THE THEORY OF MARKETS

CHAPTER 10

INTRODUCTION

We intimated in Chapter 9 that markets guide decisions about resource allocation, that is, how society decides to use its scarce resources. How exactly do markets accomplish this? The purpose of this chapter is to develop the economic analysis of markets so that we might begin to get some insight into the relationship between markets and resource allocation.

As we saw in Part I, markets emerged as one of the first and most fundamental institutions of capitalism. Markets replaced tradition and feudal authority as the principal organizers of economic activity. Markets exist in capitalism for all consumer goods and productive resources. *Markets* are the places in which buyers and sellers exchange goods and services. Usually, in our economy, goods and services are exchanged for money. All goods and services, then, must have prices that reflect their values and that govern their exchange. It is these *prices* that end up guiding production and resource allocation. Producers and consumers use prices as basic information in making decisions about which resources to use and which products to purchase. Consequently, to see how markets allocate scarce resources, it is essential to understand *how markets determine prices*.

MARKETS AND PRICE DETERMINATION: SUPPLY-AND-DEMAND ANALYSIS

In order to highlight the economic analysis of markets, we will use as an example the market for a college education in the U.S. In the last chapter, we examined the decision about going to college as an example of a personal choice about the use of scarce resources. How much does it cost? What else could one do with the money? Why should (or why shouldn't) one go to college? What does one sacrifice by going to college for four years? Does it make more sense to enter the labor force right after high school? What are the benefits of a college education? Obviously, one crucial element in making such an important decision is the dollar cost of going to college.

In the following analysis, we will try to isolate the factors that determine the price of a college education. Hopefully, our analysis will help us to gain some insights into and understanding of how this market operates—how its price is deter-

An example of a market. (Photograph by Bill Weibel.)

mined and what implications there are for resource allocation. We will develop a method of analysis, *the theory of supply and demand*, that should assist us in understanding generally the functioning of markets in our capitalist economy.

Before we begin our analysis, however, as in all economic theory, we will have to make some assumptions to simplify our model of the market. Despite these simplifying assumptions, our theory should provide us with some tools for understanding the functioning of real markets in the economy. It should also help us to understand why market prices change over time. And it might also help us to develop some possible solutions to economic problems.

---

1. Why has the price of a college education been continually increasing over the past ten years? What can be done about this problem?

Now for the assumptions. We will begin with one fundamental assumption of microeconomics: that economic agents are rational calculators and are motivated by self-interest. We assume that consumers are rational with respect to their purchases and that they try to maximize their own welfare through consumption, given their available spending power (that, through calculations and trial and error, consumers seek to maximize their satisfaction). Generally, we assume that producers calculate costs and revenues and try to maximize their profits from production. In the supply-and-demand analysis of markets, we also usually assume *a competitive market*, one in which there are a large number of buyers and sellers.

For our particular example of the market for a college education, there are some additional assumptions and qualifications that we should make clear at the outset. The first is that we will assume that there is, in some sense, a homogeneous product. In other words, we will concentrate on *a* college education as a good that is exchanged in a market of buyers and sellers. That is, we will assume away the differences between a Harvard education and a Bucknell education or between a private university and a public university. Obviously, these differences do exist; and they will account in part for the differences in cost among these different possibilities. However, for the moment, we wish to simplify and to concentrate on *one* price for a college education. Once the model of supply and demand is developed, we should be able to use it to account for differences in cost at different institutions of higher learning. We also will assume away the admissions problem (the product is not necessarily available to any buyer who might wish to purchase it) and the graduation problem (actually getting the product in hand is not merely a matter of paying the costs to the cashier). Finally, in this case, the producer of the product is not (presumably) a profit-making institution. However, colleges and universities must take their costs and revenues into account, utilize scarce resources efficiently, and charge prices that reflect their costs.

We will begin by examining each side of this market in isolation from the other. For the buyer's side of the market, we will focus on demand; for the seller's side of the market, we will focus on supply. Then we will put supply and demand together to see how the market price is determined.

DEMAND

First of all, let's isolate and examine the buyer's side of the market. We will call this the *demand* for the product. What determines the demand for any product? In our example, there are many factors that would influence the demand for a college education. The essential factor behind the demand for any product obviously is that it is useful to the buyer; it satisfies some want or desire or need. Beyond this, we can list some other influences on the demand for a product.

Tastes and Preferences

Consumers' tastes and preferences guide their demand for different goods. Tastes and preferences are influenced by social, political, and cultural forces, as well as by the physical, psychological, and mental requirements of daily survival in the world. Obviously, over time, in any given society, tastes and preferences will change and will, in turn, influence changing patterns of consumer demand for different goods and services. Tastes and preferences will also be different in different countries.

Throughout the history of the U.S., a college education has been a valued "product." Presumably, it helps to better prepare people for coping with the world, it broadens people's horizons and perspectives, it prepares people for professional positions in society, and it paves the way for further education. It may even help people to gain entry to the labor force.

In recent years, the demand for a college education has been substantial, primarily because people perceive that it is an almost certain necessity for obtaining specific types of employment. Indeed, the realities of the labor market suggest that a college education is extremely valuable in this regard. Consumers' tastes and preferences thus influence the demand for a college education. Throughout the 1960s the percentage of high school graduates who went on to college steadily increased; however, in the 1970s the percentage has leveled off.

2. Why do you suppose that tastes and preferences have changed to cause a leveling off in the percentage of high school graduates who go on to college? *Did* tastes and preferences change?

Income

How much consumers can demand of the products they prefer depends on their incomes, how much they have to spend. And who consumes what products depends on the distribution of income in the society. Since we have assumed that consumers try to maximize their satisfaction and that they derive it from goods because they are useful, we conclude that with more money consumers will purchase larger quantities of goods and services. During the 1960s, the U.S. experienced one of its longest periods of prosperity. The real income of the average American family increased throughout this period. This increasing income certainly provided the resources for an increasing percentage of American youth to attend college. In the early 1970s, however, the increase in average real incomes began to slow down. This, in part, probably accounts for some of the "leveling off" in college attendance. (Here, families with lower incomes will no longer be able to afford the "good.")

Prices of Related Goods

Consumers are very sensitive to the prices of goods they consider to be substitutes, goods that satisfy the same need. In this case, if some nonprofessional training schools lowered their prices, then that might reduce the demand for college educations, as some people substituted that educational experience for that of college. On the other hand, there may be some goods that are complementary, i.e., go together or are consumed together. For example, if the price of law school increased, that might dissuade some people (who had planned on being or hoped to be lawyers) from going to college. The point is that the demand for a college education may be sensitive to (and influenced by) the prices of related products.

Number of Demanders

The total demand for a product is obviously affected by the number of people who desire to consume it. During the 1960s and 1970s, the number of college-age people in the U.S. has been steadily expanding. In the 1960s, with an increasing percentage of youths attending college, there was a dramatic increase in the total number of "demanders" in the market. Recently, the increase in the numbers has been less dramatic, although older people are now increasing their attendance in college. In the 1980s, based on population projections of fewer college-age people, experts predict that the total number of people who go to college will actually decrease. This has serious implications for the market for a college education in the U.S.

Expectations of Future Prices

If consumers expect the price of a product to change, oftentimes this will affect their demand for that product. For example, if high school graduates expect that the price of attending college is going to continue to increase in the future, this may cause many of them to attend college right away rather than wait. Price expectations, then, will tend to influence consumers' demands for a product. (Notice the constant use in economics of the words "tend to." The conclusions of economists tend to be tentative because they are usually based on assumptions and expectations of normal behavior on the part of the economic agents and variables the economists are examining. In your own thinking, try to replicate this word usage; the conclusions of economists are not carved on stone and should not be accepted as gospel. Economic theory deals with assumptions and tendencies; if "this" happens, probably "that" will happen.)

Miscellaneous Factors

Other factors may also influence consumers' demands for products. In the 1960s the federal government and several state governments significantly increased their support of higher education in the U.S. This increased concern with the benefits to the country of higher education by itself probably influenced the demand for a college education. In addition, however, this support made it easier for more high school graduates to attend college. It also opened up the college experience to a class of people that historically had not had access to higher education in the U.S. by significantly expanding public universities and community colleges throughout the country.

---

3. **What other factor(s) would influence the demand for a college education?** *Remember* we are considering so far *only* the demand side of the market.

CETERIS PARIBUS AND THE DEMAND CURVE

If you answered "the *price* of a college education" to the question above, you are on your way to becoming an economist (for what that's worth). Economists attempt to isolate the effect of *price* on the demand for a product. In analyzing the demand for a product, they acknowledge that all of the factors above do influence demand. But sometimes simplification helps analysis. Therefore, economists concentrate on the relationship between price and the quantity demanded of a good. To do this, they assume that at one moment of time all of the other factors are given; then only price will affect the quantity demanded. The other factors are considered to be in a *ceteris paribus* category, all other things being equal.

==Demand is concerned with the relationship between price and quantity demanded, all other things constant.==

It's Mrs. Hawthorne. She wants to know what sirloin opened at today.

Copyright © 1976. Reprinted by permission of the *Wall Street Journal* and Brenda Burbank.

So let's make that rather large assumption and see what happens. What *is* the effect of price on the *quantity demanded* of a college education? At one moment in time, assuming (again) that there is some one average type of college education, there is only one price for this product. In 1977, the College Entrance Examination Board estimated that the annual average cost of a private college education was $4905—and $3005 for a public college. So $4000 was around the average cost. However, we can hypothesize about what would happen to the quantity demanded if the price were different, higher or lower. In fact, we would guess *if* the price were lower, people would consume more—the quantity demanded would increase—and that *if* the price were higher, people would consume less—the quantity demanded would decrease. This is true for almost all goods and services: if the price is lowered, the quantity demanded will increase and if the price is increased, the quantity demanded will decrease. Price and *quantity demanded* are inversely related.

Well, we've done it in words. Now how about numbers? A demand equation, generally, would show that the quantity of college education demanded, C_d, is a function of the price of a college education, P_c, given all of the *ceteris paribus* conditions. Or, $C_d = f(P_c)$, *ceteris paribus*. We can construct a hypothetical demand schedule (Table 10.1) showing different possible prices and the quantities demanded at those prices. Let's hypothesize about the national market for college educations for a year (again assuming that there is some average education).

TABLE 10.1 The Demand Schedule

P_c (Cost in Thousands Per Year, Tuition, Room and Board, and Fees)	C_d (Numbers of Students in Millions)
$10	5
8	6
6	8
4	10
2	16

If the price were $4000 (which is about what the national average cost was in 1977), then about 10 million people would be enrolled in the nation's colleges and universities as full-time students. *If*, however, the cost went up to $10,000 per year, then the quantity demanded would be cut back to 5 million. What are the other possibilities?

Not surprisingly, we can also describe the relationship between price and quantity demanded graphically. We will call this a *demand curve*. On the vertical scale we will measure price, and on the horizontal scale we will measure quantity demanded. Any point on the graph then represents a certain price–quantity demanded combination. Let's take the information from our demand schedule and transfer it to the graph.

At a price of $2000, the quantity demanded will be 16 million. At $4000, it will be 10 million. And so on. See Fig. 10.1

If we connect all the price-quantity demanded points, we get our demand curve for a college education during one year in the U.S. It shows, hypothetically, all of the possible prices for a college education and the respective quantities demanded. It has a negative slope reflecting the inverse relationship between price and quantity demanded. At lower prices, the quantity demanded is greater and at higher prices, the quantity demanded is lower. Normally, for convenience, we draw demand curves as straight lines.

The demand curve illustrates the buyers' side of the market. Now let's turn our attention to the seller's side of the market and consider it in isolation. After that, we will put the two sides of the market together in our model and get a market price for a college education.

140 The Theory of Markets

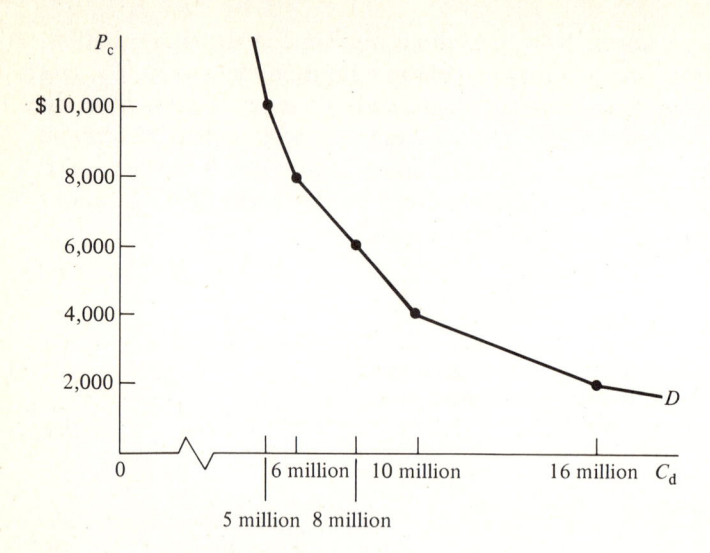

FIG. 10.1 Demand curve.

SUPPLY

Here we will focus on the sellers' side of the market. What influences the quantity supplied of a product? What factors determine the numbers of students that colleges and universities can allow to enroll? Obviously the price that they can get from students has a lot to do with it. But, for the moment, let's try to list other influences.

Resource Prices

The costs of producing goods and services weigh heavily on the ability of sellers to supply to the market. Thus resource prices will help determine the supply of any product offered for sale. In supplying college educations, if the salaries of professors and other staff increase, it will tend to reduce the supply offered or to make a college education more expensive. With the inflation of the late 1960s and the 1970s, the labor resource costs of running universities has skyrocketed as employees have demanded commensurate increases in their incomes. As a result, the cost of supplying a college education has also increased. Increasing food, construction, and energy prices will also increase the costs of providing a college education.

Technology

The techniques of production influence supply. If computers and television sets were used to teach students, to grade their work, and to write letters of recommendation for students, it would probably allow colleges and universities to greatly increase the numbers of students to whom they could supply a college education. (Of course, that might make the process of getting an education a little bit less attractive. But that is a *demand* factor.) For the time being, however, the technology of education still relies heavily on human beings.

Prices of Related Goods and Resources

The ability of suppliers to supply any product to the market will also be affected by the prices of other products and resources. If a college or a university could make a better go of it by operating as a summer camp rather than by offering summer sessions, then maybe it would decide to supply that product instead. In the same way, if resource prices change, it might influence the decisions of how to provide an education, as well as how much education to offer. For example, if construction costs were to decrease, then a college or a university might be influenced to build some large lecture halls to accommodate more students.

Sellers' Expectations

Sellers' expectations about the future will condition their supply of a product to the market. If colleges and universities expect lower enrollments in the future, they might be inclined to try to offer more students the chance to go to college now (that is, increase the supply of the product now). They might do this to better prepare themselves for the foreseen lean days ahead.

Numbers of Sellers in the Market

If the number of sellers in the market decreases, it will tend to decrease the supply of the product. And, if the number of sellers increased, it would tend to increase the supply. In 1977, almost 10 colleges and universities in the U.S. closed their doors. The predictions are that this trend will continue into the future.

---

4. **Of the five factors above that influence supply, which, in your opinion, is the most influential in determining the supply of a product?**
5. **What sorts of factors influence sellers' expectations about their markets?**

CETERIS PARIBUS AND THE SUPPLY CURVE

As for the demand curve, we will hold all of these nonprice influences on supply constant. They constitute the *ceteris paribus* conditions for supply. As a result, we will concentrate on the effect of price on the *quantity supplied* of a product. At one moment in time, we assume that all of the *ceteris paribus* factors are given and then consider in isolation the effect of price. *Supply is concerned with the relationship between price and quantity supplied, all other things constant.*

Again, there is probably only one price in existence. But we can hypothesize different possible prices and examine the effects on quantity supplied. If the price were higher, we would expect that sellers would increase the quantity supplied; if they are offered a higher price, they will be willing to supply more. If they are offered a lower price, we would expect them to reduce the quantity supplied. For supply, price and quantity supplied are directly related.

In equation form, $C_s = f(P_c)$, *ceteris paribus*. With all other determinants of supply held constant, the quantity supplied of a college education, C_s, is a function of the price offered for a college education, P_c. As before for demand, we can construct a hypothetical *supply schedule* (Table 10.2), showing different possible prices and the quantities that would be supplied at those prices. The following schedule hypothesizes about the total national supply of a college education:

TABLE 10.2 The Supply Schedule

P_c (in Thousands)	C_s (in Millions)
$10	20
8	18
6	14
4	10
2	6

If the price were only $2000, then colleges and universities would offer places for only 6 million students. *If* the price were $10,000, on the other hand, then colleges and universities would be willing to offer places to 20 million students. What are the other possibilities?

Again, we can show the supply relationship graphically. We measure price on the vertical scale and quantity supplied on the horizontal scale. Each point in Fig. 10.2 then represents a certain price-quantity supplied combination. If we connect the five combinations from the schedule above, then we get a supply curve for a college education. It shows, hypothetically, all the possible prices for a college education and the respective quantities supplied. It has a positive slope showing the direct relationship between price and quantity supplied; at higher prices, greater quantities will be supplied and, at lower prices, lower quantities will be supplied. Usually we draw supply curves as straight lines for convenience.

The supply curve illustrates the sellers' side of the market. The demand curve shows the buyers' side. Let's see what happens when we put them together to look at both sides of the market.

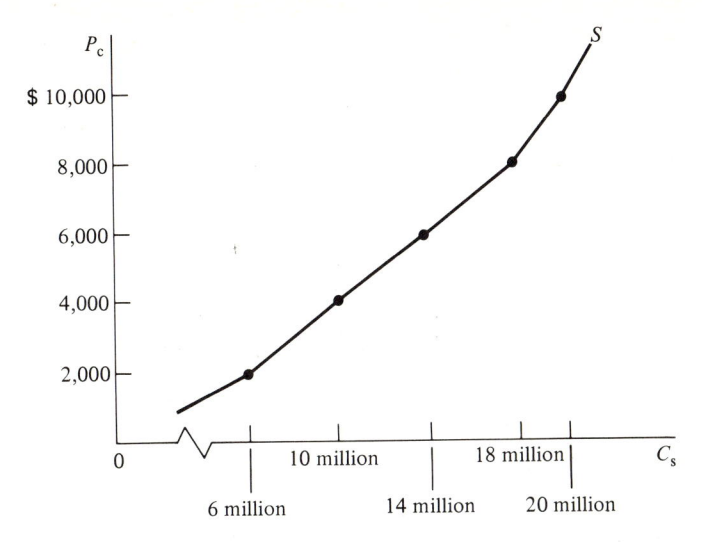

FIG. 10.2 Supply curve.

THE MARKET AND EQUILIBRIUM PRICE

First of all, let's put the supply-and-demand schedules together as shown in Table 10.3:

TABLE 10.3 The Supply Schedule Combined with the Demand Schedule

P_c (in Thousands)	C_d (in Millions)	C_s (in Millions)
$10	5	20
8	6	18
6	8	14
4	10	10
2	16	6

And then the supply curve and the demand curve together (Fig. 10.3) give us a hypothetical picture of the market. The conclusion of our analysis, when we put supply and demand together, is that the supply and the demand for a product determine a market price. It is an *equilibrium price*. Equilibrium connotes a situation in which the tendency is towards a certain state; and once that state is achieved, in the absence of outside disturbances, it will be maintained.

In our example, a price of $4000 is the equilibrium price. At this price, the desires of buyers and sellers are consistent. Buyers want to buy 10 million places at

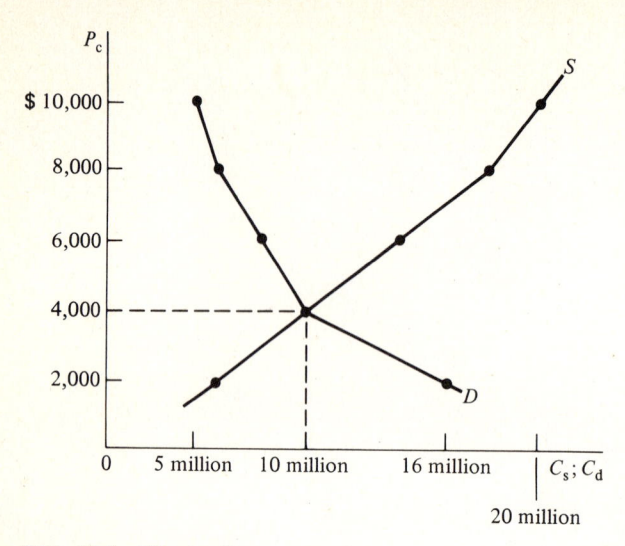

FIG. 10.3 The market.

colleges and universities, and sellers are willing to offer 10 million places. The quantity demanded equals the quantity supplied. At $P_c = \$4000$, $C_s = C_d$. The equilibrium price and quantity exchanged are the point at which the supply and demand curves intersect. At any other price, C_s does not equal C_d; and there will be a tendency for the price to change because buyers' and sellers' desires are *not* consistent.

For example, at $P_c = \$8000$, $C_s = 18$ million and $C_d = 6$ million. *If* the price were $8000, there would be an oversupply, or a *surplus*. That is, 18 million places would be available, but only 6 million students would want to go to college at that price. In this case, sellers would lower their prices to eliminate the excess supply. This has a two-fold effect: it reduces the quantity supplied and increases the quantity demanded. We can see this by examining what happens at a price of $6000. At this price, C_s still exceeds C_d (14 million > 8 million). Suppliers will then lower prices again. This process will continue until $C_s = C_d$. This occurs at a price of $4000. Thus price changes will eliminate a surplus in the market until the equilibrium price is reached. See Fig. 10.4.

In the same way, *if* the price were below $4000, there will be a tendency to move toward the $4000 price. If the price were $2000, then $C_d = 16$ million and $C_s = 6$ million. In this case, the quantity demanded exceeds the quantity supplied (16 million > 6 million); and a *shortage* of places at colleges exists. Here, purchasers, facing a shortage, would begin to bid up the price. Again, this causes a two-fold effect; it increases the quantity supplied but decreases the quantity demanded. This will continue until the desires of buyers and sellers are consistent at one price where $C_s = C_d$. See Fig. 10.5.

Supply-and-demand analysis has shown us how markets determine equilibrium prices! There is a tendency to establish, to move toward, the equilibrium price. And,

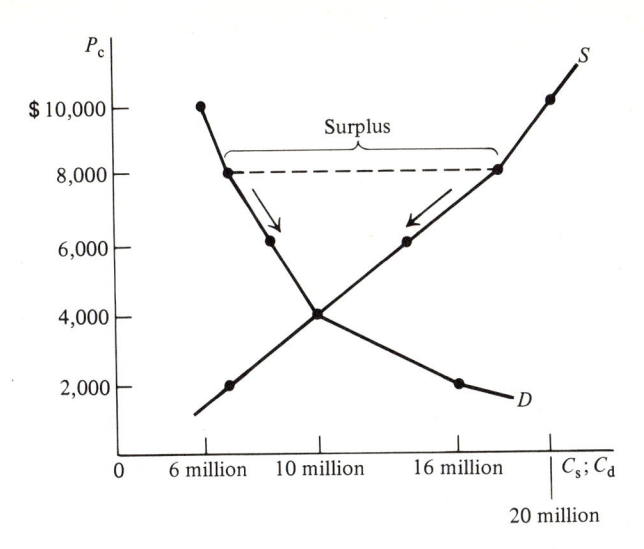

FIG. 10.4 Surplus eliminated by price decreases.

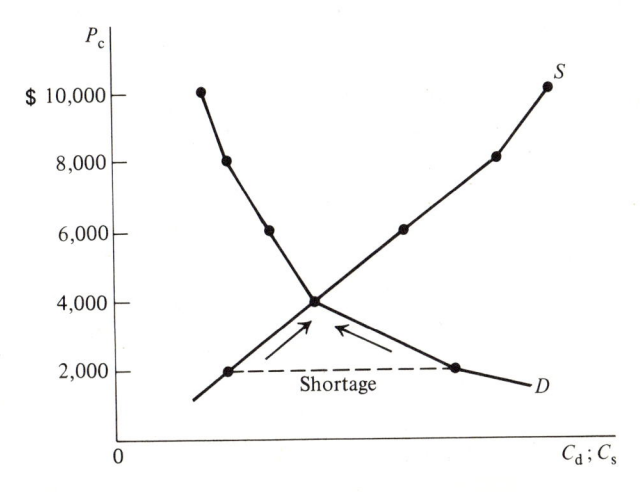

FIG. 10.5 Shortage eliminated by price increases.

once there, with buyers' and sellers' desires consistent (when the quantity supplied equals the quantity demanded) and no outside disturbances, that price will tend to be maintained.

6. *Why* do sellers lower price when there is a surplus?
7. *Why* do buyers bid up the price when there is a shortage?

A TINGE OF REALITY: IT'S NOT A *CETERIS PARIBUS* WORLD

Our supply-and-demand model so far has included the rather strict assumptions involved in our *ceteris paribus* conditions on both sides of the market. However, one of the most beautiful aspects of this model is that we can use it to accommodate for changes in the *ceteris paribus* conditions. It is useful because obviously in a changing world these other determinants of supply and demand do change. A couple of examples will suffice to illustrate the richness of this approach and the ability of the supply-and-demand model to explain changes in market conditions and prices.

First, let's take a change in the demand conditions. We will call this a *change in demand*, and it will cause the whole demand curve to shift. Any of the determinants could change, or all of them could change. They could move in the same direction (causing an increase or a decrease in demand), or they could influence demand in opposite directions. Go back and consider the various determinants of demand (the *ceteris paribus* conditions) and consider the complexity of factors that are behind a demand curve.

Let's just examine one possibility. Assume that in the late 1960s and early 1970s, for whatever reasons, a college degree is perceived as being more attractive to students. This represents a change in tastes and preferences. What will it do to demand? What effect will it have on the market for a college education?

First of all, it will cause a shift in the demand curve. It causes an increase in demand; the demand curve will shift out to the right. At every possible price, the quantity demanded will have increased and we thus get a new demand curve. The demand curve for a college education shifts from D_1 to D_2 as shown in Fig. 10.6.

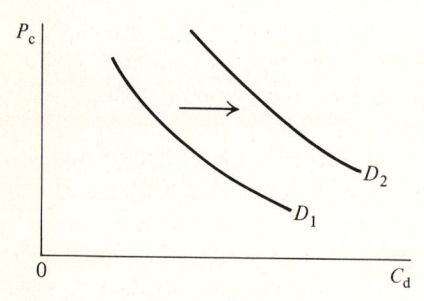

FIG. 10.6 Change in demand.

---

8. What other changes in demand might cause an increase in demand, a shift of the curve to the right?

9. What would cause a shift back to the left, a decrease in demand?

What happens in the market? Here we must look at supply and demand together as shown in Fig. 10.7.

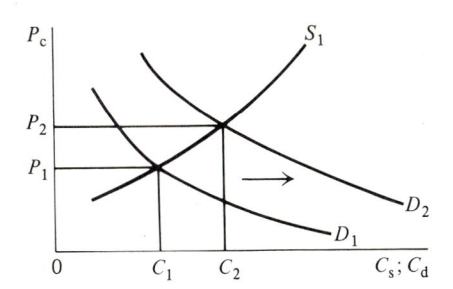

FIG. 10.7 Change in demand: the market.

With the new demand curve, D_2, we get a new equilibrium price, P_2, and a new equilibrium quantity exchanged, C_2, where $C_s = C_d$. With an increase in demand, we get a new higher price in the market. *This analysis suggests to us that one place to look for an explanation of increasing prices in a market is in the dynamic changes in the determinants of demand.* The market price of a college education tended to increase in the late 1960s and early 1970s as the demand for the product increased due to a change in the public's tastes and preferences. Also the amount exchanged by buyers and sellers has increased in our example. A word of caution, however, is in order here. Tastes and preferences were not the only determinant of demand that was changing during this period of time (and, in addition, the determinants of supply were probably also changing). For example, the increased number of youths in the U.S. of college age as a result of the postwar baby boom also contributed to the shift in demand. We can conclude, though, that the change in preferences was, in part, responsible for the increase in demand and for the increase in price.

Our final example involves a *change in supply*. Here we allow the determinants of supply to change. Again, any or all could change, in the same direction or opposite directions. Reexamine the determinants of supply (the *ceteris paribus* conditions).

Assume that in the late 1960s and early 1970s the prices of the resources used in providing college educations were increasing. As a result, there would be a change in supply. Suppliers would tend to require higher prices for every different quantity supplied (or, they would be willing to offer lower quantities supplied at every possible price). There would be a decrease in supply; the supply curve would shift back to the left. The supply curve for a college education shifts from S_1 to S_2 as shown in Fig. 10.8.

---

10. **What other forces might cause a shift to the left in the supply curve?**

11. **What would cause a shift to the right in the supply curve?**

What will this do in the market? Assume demand conditions are unaltered. Figure 10.9 puts supply and demand together. (We assume that D_1 remains unchanged.) With the new supply curve, S_2, we get a new equilibrium price, P_2, and

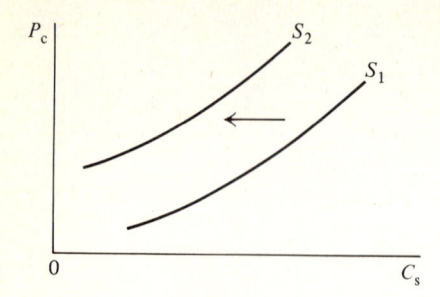

FIG. 10.8 Change in supply.

a new equilibrium quantity exchanged, C_2, where $C_s = C_d$. With this decrease in supply we get a new higher market price and a lower quantity exchanged. Again, *this analysis may help us to explain price increases by examining what happens to the determinants of supply*. If forces are creating decreases in supply for a particular product, that will help to explain the emergence of higher prices for it.

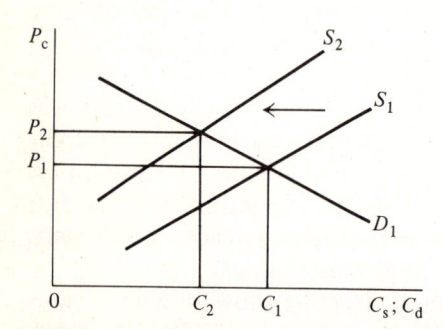

FIG. 10.9 Change in supply: the market.

---

12. What happens if we put both of our examples together, an increase in demand and a decrease in supply? Show this result in your own graphical illustration.

Now you are familiar enough with the supply and demand model to apply it to some real world examples.

YOU ARE WHAT YOU EAT, AND YOU PAY FOR IT

Agricultural prices have always been one of the best applications for supply and demand analysis. This is primarily because agriculture is a relatively competitive sector of our economy. There are lots of farmers and lots of consumers of food in the U.S. As a result, agriculture is a useful area to try to utilize our supply-and-demand analysis to analyze why prices change and what goes on in markets.

Even if a market is not competitive, and in Chapter 12 we will discover that many markets in the U.S. are not, supply-and-demand analysis is still very useful because it provides a framework for focusing on key variables and determinants. It also helps us to understand the relationships between the two sides of the market.

Agriculture, as a matter of fact, does have many noncompetitive aspects. Agribusiness, or corporate farming, is on the increase in the U.S.—especially in California. There is much economic concentration and power in the intermediary areas between the farmer and the consumer. At the supermarket level there is also a *lack* of competition—in the sense of lots of sellers (we will define competition much more precisely in the next chapter). Nevertheless, agricultural prices are a good example to use in applying supply-and-demand analysis.

In the following article, Seth S. King focuses on some recent trends in agricultural markets and the effects on supply, demand, and prices.

HARD ECONOMICS THE KEY TO WORLD LIVESTOCK SUPPLY

SETH S. KING

CHICAGO, Feb. 7—American farmers who have been fattening cattle, hogs and poultry with corn and soybeans are now cutting back on their feeding operations more sharply than in any period since the 1950s.

These deliberate reductions in the production of feed grains—and thus of livestock, America's prime source of protein—are not moral responses to appeals for Americans to eat less meat and free the unused grains for the world's hungry.

Nor is this country, the world's largest producer and consumer of animal protein, nearing the point where it cannot raise any more animals.

The reason, rather, is purely economic. After last summer's drought, the world's supply of feed grains is now at the lowest point since World War II. The costs of feeding livestock and poultry have soared above the prices these animals bring in the market.

To dilute their losses, American farmers are reducing their feeding operations. By reducing supply, they hope to force meat prices higher. Meanwhile, they are waiting for a bumper grain crop next fall to push feed costs down and bring them a profit.

There are now 133-million head of beef cattle on American ranges, the largest number in this century. In Australia the beef herds are at record levels. The European Common Market countries have a beef surplus that they are having difficulty selling.

When it is once again more profitable to raise and fatten hogs, poultry and feed-lot cattle in this country, the food forecasters are confident that all meat supplies will increase again.

The more optimistic of these experts believe that for the rest of this century, if weather patterns are normal, supplies of animal protein in the affluent nations can be increased faster than the population is growing.

If the underdeveloped countries can somehow find the money to acquire feed grains and create transportation systems for distributing meat, these forecasters

© 1975 by The New York Times Company. Reprinted by permission.

also believe, enough can be produced to increase the animal protein in these countries and improve the diets of their people.

Like most forecasts involving the global food situation, these are predicated on "ifs" that could turn out much less favorably than is expected by the optimists. In the view of some experts, it would be foolish to assume that weather will be consistently normal and that supplies of fertilizer and fuel will always be adequate.

Recent suggestions of climatic shifts and the volatility of international politics, for example, could drastically reduce the supplies of rainwater, fertilizer and oil.

Another assumption that some food experts would hesitate to make is that the poor countries will be able to find financing for their expensive import needs.

If the assumptions by the optimists should prove wrong, the supplies, not only of animal protein but of all food resources, could be seriously jeopardized.

World Meat Production

Includes beef and veal, pork, lamb, mutton, goatmeat and horsemeat; excludes rabbit, poultry meat and miscellaneous.

Thousands of metric tons
One metric ton = 2,200 lbs.

	1964-68 average	1972	1973*	Per cent change 1973 from 1964-68	1973 from 1972
North America	17,488.4	19,799.7	18,806.5	+8	-5
South America	6,448.6	7,119.6	7,491.9	+16	+5
Western Europe	14,272.8	16,251.5	16,379.4	+11	-1
Eastern Europe	4,289.2	5,048.2	5,185.5	+21	+3
Total Europe	18,562.0	21,299.7	21,564.9	+16	+1
Soviet Union	7,956.0	10,012.7	9,952.0	+25	-1
Africa and Asia	3,311.6	4,294.1	4,458.8	+35	+4
Oceania	2,547.4	3,424.5	3,323.6	+30	-3
Total world	56,314.4	65,950.4	65,597.7	+16	-1

*Preliminary   Note: Totals may not add due to rounding

Average Per-Capita Meat Consumption in Various Countries

(In kilograms—2.2 pounds)

Continent and country	Average 1965-69	1969	1970	1971	1972	1973*
NORTH AMERICA						
Canada	69	72	73	74	74	71
Costa Rica	14	13	14	15	14	15
Dominican Republic	8	8	9	10	10	10
El Salvador	11	9	9	9	8	9
Guatemala	10	10	10	10	10	9
Honduras	9	8	8	10	9	8
Mexico	17	17	18	18	18	19
Nicaragua	20	22	21	23	22	22
Panama	25	26	27	29	28	29
United States	80	83	84	87	86	80
SOUTH AMERICA						
Argentina	97	107	96	82	76	81
Brazil	25	27	26	24	25	30
Chile	26	26	26	25	24	21
Colombia	22	23	23	25	22	19
Paraguay	40	39	41	32	29	21
Peru	15	16	15	15	12	11
Uruguay	97	78	89	93	71	66
Venezuela	24	26	23	24	23	23
WESTERN EUROPE						
European Community						
Belgium-Luxembourg	57	60	64	63	68	70
Denmark	58	56	61	56	58	63
France	62	63	63	64	64	63
West Germany	58	60	63	66	66	53
Ireland	57	55	59	61	61	55
Italy	32	37	41	42	42	46
Netherlands	48	46	47	50	48	46
Britain	63	62	63	66	63	59
Average	53	55	57	59	59	58
Austria	57	59	60	61	62	63
Finland	38	40	43	44	46	50
Greece	32	35	38	41	39	45
Norway	38	39	37	39	39	39
Portugal	20	23	23	25	27	28
Spain	26	28	31	29	31	35
Sweden	45	46	48	47	45	46
Switzerland	55	58	60	61	60	62
EASTERN EUROPE						
Bulgaria	37	35	34	36	40	39
Czechoslovakia	49	50	53	58	60	60
Hungary	40	39	42	41	46	45
Poland	40	41	41	44	46	49
Yugoslavia	30	29	30	36	32	33
SOVIET UNION	36	37	38	40	41	40
AFRICA						
South Africa	34	35	37	37	34	33
ASIA						
Taiwan	21	22	24	25	24	28
Iran	9	10	9	9	9	9
Israel	19	20	20	20	11	8
Japan	8	9	12	12	15	16
Philippines	13	14	12	12	12	11
Turkey	14	14	15	15	12	13
OCEANIA						
Australia	94	93	94	99	96	90
New Zealand	102	88	93	81	96	89

*Preliminary

AFFLUENCE AND RELIGION

The rest of the world, like the United States, derives its animal protein from the same sources: beef, poultry and eggs, pork, and dairy products. The numbers of these animals and the amount of meat eaten vary in direct proportion to affluence and religious beliefs rather than to human populations.

Most of the world's meat and dairy supplies are now concentrated in North America, the Soviet Union, Western Europe, and parts of South America. Last year North America and Western Europe produced more red meat—beef, pork and mutton—than all the rest of the world. Australia and New Zealand, with their tiny populations, produced almost as much as Asia, with its millions, and Africa combined.

The world's champion red meat consumers are the Australians and New Zealanders, who eat nearly 198 pounds per person each year. The Americans and Argentinians are close behind at 177 pounds each. In 1973 the Western Europeans consumed 128 pounds each, while the Russians ate only 88 pounds per citizen.

But in most of Asia and Africa, red meat consumption was only a fraction of the leader's. The affluent Japanese, despite a national effort to increase meat consumption, ate only 35 pounds each and the Filipinos consumed only 24.

Hogs and poultry can be raised almost anywhere in the world in a minimum of space. Thousands of chickens, confined from birth to slaughter in tiny pens, can be raised each year in an area no larger than a supermarket parking lot. Hundreds of hogs can be handled at one time on a few acres. And in most modern dairy operations the cows are kept in small feed yards and milked in sheds no larger than a small house.

But beef cattle and sheep need rangeland or pasture on which to graze, and the number of animals an acre will sustain varies with the amount and quality of the forage on it.

Thus the world's capacity for raising hogs and poultry is limited, in theory, only by the amount of feed grains that can be grown for them. Hogs and poultry compete with humans for cereal grains in the sense that humans can, and to varying degrees do, eat the same wheat, corn, soybeans, and sorghum grains.

Virtually all of the American wheat crop is now used for human foods. But more than 90 per cent of the American corn and sorghum crops and virtually all of the soybean meal, after the edible oil is removed, are fed to livestock.

The United States exports two-thirds of its wheat crop, almost half of its soybeans, and about 20 percent of its corn. Foreign buyers of American corn and soybean meal use virtually all of it for livestock feeding, mostly for hogs and poultry.

But cattle and sheep are ruminants. Their digestive systems convert forage, which humans cannot eat, directly to meat protein.

The soybean meal and feed grains now fed sheep and beef and dairy cattle put extra fat on them, making their meat tender and juicy or increasing their daily yield.

A beef steer or heifer fed only on forage can attain a choice grade weight, with its meat almost as flavorful as a grain-fed animal's, if the forage is abundant. But it takes nearly twice as long to fatten an animal on forage as it does on grain.

A NEW PRACTICE

Fattening beef cattle on grains is a relatively new practice in the United States and still relatively rare in other countries. Since 1952 the percentage of American beef cattle fed on grain rose from 45 to 78 percent, though it is declining slightly now as more grass-fed animals are going directly to the packing houses.

The burgeoning of grain-fed beef has been caused by economics and eating taste. From the end of World War II until 1973, when the Russians and Japanese began buying tons of American grain in a deliberate effort to increase their own livestock production. This country had towering surpluses of feed grains. Stuffing them into livestock was the only profitable way to use them.

At the same time, take home pay of Americans rose and so did their preference for beef and their ability to buy it.

In the last decade beef production in the United States has jumped 36 percent. Broiler production has increased 58 percent. But pork production increased only 10 percent and there has been an actual drop of 23 percent in lamb and mutton slaughter. Americans preferred more beef and poultry and more money could be made raising them.

The world's population is growing by more than 2 percent, or about 75-million persons, each year. Among the questions pondered constantly by the farm and food experts is whether the production of livestock and poultry can keep pace with this human growth and whether the current high animal protein diets of the more affluent countries can be continued into the next century without more of the poor starving.

KEY IS RISING GRAIN OUTPUT

Although most of these experts agree that much more grain can be grown in the United States and some other parts of the world in the next decade if the weather is normal, there is no consensus on how much.

They agree that if grain production can be increased sharply, then poultry, pork, and dairy production can be increased as well in most of the world. But the chances of the underfed sharing in these increases will depend more than anything else on their achieving the means to pay for it.

Dr. Leroy Quance, program leader of the Agriculture Department's Economic Research Service foresees the possibility that, given average weather and continuing supplies of fertilizer and fuel, the world's capacity for growing cereal grains could increase faster than consumption in the next decade.

His study envisages the opportunity, if the money is available, of adding about 30-million acres of cropland to the roughly 350-million now being cultivated in the United States.

Assuming that the 1 to 1.5 percent annual yield increases of the last 20 years will continue—an assumption questioned by some private forecasters—American farmers could produce by 1984 a corn crop of 9.1-billion bushels. This would compare to the 6-billion bushel crop expected in 1974 had the weather been normal. The Quance projection also foresees American soybean crops by 1985 increasing nearly 40 percent, and a jump of 42 percent in grain sorghums.

With these sharp increases in feed grains, the study also predicts a 33 percent rise in American beef supplies, and a 13 percent increase in pork production by 1985. Broiler production could rise 36 percent and the egg supply could be increased by 2 percent. The projections point to an increase of only 2 percent in dairy supplies and a huge decline of 65 percent in sheep production, based on projected demand and not capacity.

The National Academy of Sciences, in a lengthy analysis of agricultural efficiency published in mid-January, was more conservative. The academy agreed that increases in per-acre corn yields would probably continue in the coming decade. It also foresaw a continuing improvement in broiler feeding efficiency.

But the academy warned that progress in increasing efficiency in feeding livestock was not as likely as some experts believe.

"Advances in animal production have not kept pace with those for crops," the academy declared. "It seems clear that nothing as dramatic as the increase in corn yields, nor even as the increase in broiler meat production per unit of feed, has occurred with beef, pork and lamb."

The greatest potential for a quantum leap in red meat supplies, some food experts believe, is on the grazing lands. With better management of herds and the use of now idle grassland, they believe that additional thousands of cattle and sheep could be raised with little new demand on the grain supply.

Today there are a record 133-million beef cattle and calves in the United States. Range experts with the American National Cattlemen's Association believe Western ranges, as they are now used, are at near capacity for beef cattle without being overgrazed.

But there are thousands of acres of grassland in the Southeastern and Eastern states that are now idle because there has been little economic incentive to graze cattle or sheep on them.

In the last decade alone, the number of beef cattle in the Southeast has increased by nearly 700,000. Part of the land they graze on was once in cotton and tobacco. Most of these animals now go into fattening pens. But they could be marketed at grass fed weights if Americans again accept leaner beef.

Citing Agriculture Department studies published earlier last year, the Council for Agricultural Sciences and Technology notes that 63 percent of America's total land area is classified as grazing land. Currently, these grazing areas, most of them in the West, produce about 213-million animal-unit-months of grazing for domestic livestock. This means they have the forage required to keep a mature, calf-producing cow for a month. The study estimates that if more fully developed and intensively managed, this country's total forage lands could reach 1.7-billion animal-unit-months.

While this might sound wildly optimistic to the more cautious, the council cites other recent studies showing that in many parts of the West and Southwest, ranges would actually yield greater amounts of usable forage if sheep and cattle were allowed to graze together. This offers the possibility of increasing the red meat supply by including sheep with the cattle.

Australia, the largest exporter of beef, could, if the economic incentives developed, increase its cattle herds from the current 30-million head to at least 50-million with the forage the country now has.

SUBSTITUTES FOR GRAIN

The American Forage and Grassland Council cites an assessment made this summer by W. F. Wedin, H. J. Hodgson, and N. L. Jacobsen, plant and livestock specialists, in which they foresee increased grain production barely keeping even with increasing demand for livestock if these animals get the same amount of grain as they do now.

"But the fact remains that there are tremendous acreages in the United States and in the world where the only chance for having high quality protein food available is through conversion [of forage] by ruminant livestock [cattle and sheep]", the assessment states.

Dr. Paul Putnam, assistant director of the Agriculture Department's Beltsville, Md., research center, points to the availability of many livestock and poultry feeds that can now be substituted for grain.

These have not been fully utilized, Dr. Putnam said, because there have always been cheaper feed grains available.

These substitutes include sugar beet tops, citrus pulp, "tankage" matter left from slaughtered animals, grain mash left from distilling alcohol, apple pomace, whey left from making butter and cheese, high nitrate animal wastes, and even cellulose fibers from wood pulp, newsprint, and sawdust.

The Wedin-Hodgson-Jacobson study notes that in the United States enough rough forage is left largely unused on 75-million acres of corn and sorghum stalks, after the grain is harvested, to maintain between 12-million and 30-million additional head of beef cows annually.

Looking toward the future, Dr. James Smith, chairman of the Animal Physiology and Genetics Institute at Beltsville, said recently:

"If economic incentives are great enough, we believe the world's farmers have the capacity to breed and feed livestock and poultry in numbers great enough to keep pace with the population increase and provide a better diet for the hungry—certainly during the rest of this century."

---

13. Why has the percentage of American beef cattle fed on grain increased in the last 20 years? Cite one reason on the demand side of the market and one on the supply side.

14. Grain-fed animals compete with humans for cereal grains. What effect does this have on grain prices? Why? And what effect does this have on the pattern of world meat consumption? Why?

15. What would be the effect on grain prices of an increase in the use of grazing land to raise cattle? What happens to the supply curve for beef? What happens to the demand curve for grain? What assumptions did you make?

In this chapter we have developed a theoretical model of markets to explain how markets determine prices. We have focused on demand and supply, how they are determined, and how they interact in markets. In the next chapter, we will explore the theoretical implications that this has for resource allocation.

KEY CONCEPTS

markets
prices
demand (schedule, curve)
supply (schedule, curve)
price (equilibrium)

shift in demand (change in)
shift in supply (change in)
surpluses
shortages

REVIEW QUESTIONS

1. Use supply-and-demand analysis to explain why your school's tuition and overall charges have been continually increasing in the past few years. Address yourself to demand factors first, supply factors second, and then put them together.

2. How are tastes and preferences for goods and services determined in the U.S.?

3. Markets and prices for different products are interrelated. Why is that? Can you give some examples?

4. Examine recent issues of newspapers to see how prices of certain products are changing. Use supply-and-demand analysis to explain these changes.

5. *How* do prices influence resource allocation? Use examples.

SUGGESTED READINGS

Any introductory textbook intended for a two-semester course will provide a more extensive treatment of the supply-and-demand model. Try Paul Samuelson's *Economics* (McGraw-Hill), Campbell R. McConnell's *Economics* (McGraw-Hill), or Daniel Fusfeld's *Economics* (D. C. Heath).

Samuel Bowles and Herbert Gintis, 1977. *Schooling in Capitalist America,* Harper Colophon Books. A political economic analysis of education in the U.S. that goes beyond (and behind) supply-and-demand analysis of the market for a college education.

Douglass C. North and Roger Leroy Miller, 1971. *The Economics of Public Issues*, Harper & Row. The model applied to several issues, e.g., marijuana.

WHEREIN PROFIT MAXIMIZATION AND COMPETITION PRODUCE CONSUMER SOVEREIGNTY, EFFICIENCY, AND THE "INVISIBLE HAND"

CHAPTER 11

INTRODUCTION

Microeconomics assumes that consumers, in demanding goods, attempt to maximize their satisfaction. Firms, furthermore, are assumed, in supplying goods, to be concerned with *maximizing profits*. In Chapter 10 we saw how supply and demand for a good will determine a market price, *given* certain conditions (i.e., *a* supply curve and *a* demand curve). If either or both the demand curve and the supply curve shift, we will tend to get a new equilibrium price in that market.

In this chapter we will examine how profit maximization *and* competition, using supply-and-demand analysis and some new tools of economics, theoretically produce Adam Smith's "invisible hand" and *consumer sovereignty*. That is, we will discover how competitive markets operate to allocate resources *efficiently*.

I'm pleased to tell you, gentlemen, that in addition to serving the public, helping find answers to some of the world's problems, improving the quality of life in America, and providing new and better products for the consumer, this quarter we made a bundle.

Reproduced by permission; copyright © James Stevenson. Originally in *Saturday Review*.

PROFIT MAXIMIZATION AND THE COMPETITIVE FIRM

In the following we will examine a particular market and what happens in it over time; we will concentrate our attention on the *firm*. This is a theoretical market—so we will state some definitions and make some assumptions. Our market will be the national market for pocket calculators.

The *consumer* is the economic unit that demands goods and/or services because they serve some purpose and give the consumer some satisfaction. Our consumers in this example include accountants, housewives, elementary school students, college students, and so on who have a particular need for instant calculation. In the U.S., with the recent invention and development of transistors and miniaturized circuits, there has been a boom in the market for pocket calculators. There is a wide variety of calculators designed to accomplish a whole range of mathematical and statistical operations. In our example, we will assume that there is some average type of calculator and concentrate our attention on that market.

The *firm* is the economic unit that brings goods to the market. It takes raw materials and other resources and transforms them into final consumer goods. Its motivation, or goal, is to maximize its profits. In our example, the firm would be any company that produces and sells pocket calculators.

If we put the firms and the consumers (sellers and buyers) together, we have a market for pocket calculators. We will assume that this is a competitive market, that is, one characterized by *competition*. This means that:

1. The product is homogeneous.
2. There is a large number of buyers and sellers in the market.
3. No *one* buyer or seller can influence the price of the product (a seller can't raise his or her price because buyers can go to a competitor and buy).
4. There is free entry into the market (anyone can be a buyer or a seller).
5. There is no need for advertising (since every seller has the same product and charges the same price).

Thus there is a *market equilibrium price*. Can you illustrate this market graphically?

---

1. Are any of these theoretical characteristics absent in our real world example of the market for pocket calculators in the U.S.? Why?

Let's return to the firm. The firm raises *revenues* by selling its product. The more it sells, the greater are its revenues. The greater the number of pocket calculators the firm sells, the more money it receives. In producing calculators and bringing them to market, the firm also has certain costs—labor, raw materials, depreciation, rent, interest payments on loans, and the firm's *opportunity cost*. We define the firm's opportunity cost as being the amount of money that the firm could earn by using its facilities and its resources to produce something else (like fire alarms or CB radios, etc.) The firm has some expectation of a "normal profit" from doing business. Therefore, the firm has as one of its *costs* of doing business that opportun-

In competition, firms don't need to advertise. (Photograph by John Herrlin.)

ity cost. Stated slightly differently, the producer of pocket calculators must earn at least its opportunity cost (a normal profit) to stay in the business of making calculators. Anything above that is economic *profit*. Profit equals the difference between the firm's total revenues and its total costs. Or, profit equals TR − TC, where TR equals total revenues and TC equals total costs. If the firm's revenues are just sufficient to cover all of its costs for raw materials, labor, etc. *and* its opportunity cost, then the firm will earn no profits. If revenues exceed costs, then there will be economic profits. That is, the firm will earn a return over and above its opportunity cost.

Based on these definitions and assumptions, we will now proceed to examine the behavior of the firm in a competitive market. Profits, revenues, and costs for the firm will vary with the amounts of calculators produced and sold. Total revenue is equal to the quantity sold times the price of the product; or, TR = $P \times Q$. For a firm in a competitive market, the price is determined by the market and will not vary with the number of units that the firm sells (see the third characteristic of a competitive market above). Consequently, total revenue increases at a constant rate as more pocket calculators are sold. Total cost also increases as more calculators are produced. It costs more to produce more. Total cost is usually considered to increase at a decreasing rate and, then, beyond some level of output, to increase at an increasing rate. (We will explore the reasons for this momentarily.) In Fig. 11.1, *profit* is the difference between TR and TC. We measure amounts of calculators on the horizontal axis and money (costs and revenues) on the vertical axis. Profit is at a maximum when the difference between TR and TC is greatest.

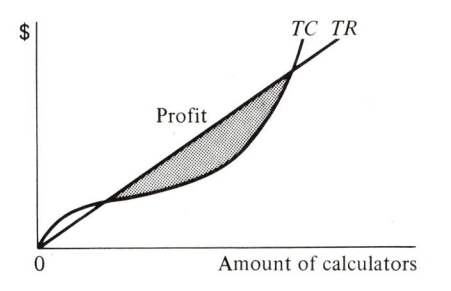

FIG. 11.1 Total revenue and total cost.

A DIGRESSION ON TOTAL COST AND THE LAW OF DIMINISHING RETURNS

Before we proceed with our analysis, it is useful to pause for a bit to explain the shape of the total cost curve above. The total cost curve increases slowly at first with increasing output; but then, beyond some point, as output increases, total costs increase by greater and greater amounts. The reason for this is the *law of diminishing returns*.

Output requires the use of inputs. In production, there are certain physical relationships between these inputs and the output. Let's construct a simplified example to illustrate the law of diminishing returns. Assume that a farmer has one acre of land on which he grows wheat. We will hold constant the land used as an input and the amount of seed used. The only variable resource, then, will be the amount of labor that the farmer uses as an input to produce wheat. At first, with increasing amounts of labor, the farmer will be able to produce increasing amounts of wheat. With each additional worker the farmer is able to add larger and larger amounts of wheat. Each worker adds more to total output than the last worker. However, beyond some point, when the farmer adds more workers, although they may continue to add to output, the marginal contributions of the last workers are less than the contributions of the previously added workers. The problem is essentially that there is not enough space for all the workers to work together well. They get in each other's way, etc. In fact, the farmer might add so many workers to the land that the marginal contributions of the last added worker to total output might be negative; that is, the last worker added might cause total output to decrease. (See the boxed material.) This simplified example is extended by economists to describe what happens in any productive activity in which there are fixed and variable resources. In the case of a calculator producer, the fixed resource might be the plant and the equipment used in production and the variable resources would be the raw materials and the labor utilized.

We have just illustrated *the law of diminishing returns!* As more and more of a variable resource is added to the production process, given fixed amounts of other

For those who like numbers:

Input of land	Input of labor	Total output (bushels of wheat)	Marginal contribution of last unit of labor
1	1	100	
1	2	110	10
1	3	130	20
1	4	160	30
1	5	180	20
1	6	190	10
1	7	185	−5

resources, the marginal contribution of the variable resource will eventually diminish. Total output would continue to increase but by a smaller and smaller amount as more of the variable resource is added. In our example, as we added more labor eventually the continued use of labor resulted in diminishing returns in terms of output. So much of a variable resource could be added that the marginal contribution of the last unit might be negative. That is, with the addition of one more unit of a resource total output actually decreases.

So now that we know what the law of diminishing returns is, what does this have to do with the shape of the total cost curve? The cost curve compares total costs with increasing output. If we assume that the law of diminishing returns holds for *all* variable resources, it follows that there will be some point in increasing output where costs will begin to increase at an increasing rate. If resources have diminishing returns, then it means that more and more resources must be added to get equivalent increases in output. But to use more resources costs more. And when diminishing returns set in, the total costs will increase at an increasing rate. To produce an additional unit of output will cost more than the last additional unit of output because more resources will be required. Because of the law of diminishing returns, the total cost curve, beyond some level of output, will increase at an increasing rate.

2. **Why does the total cost curve increase at a *decreasing* rate at relatively low levels of output?**

PROFIT MAXIMIZATION

Let's return to Fig. 11.1 on total costs and total revenue. This illustration shows us a very important relationship. As the amount of pocket calculators brought to market and sold changes, so do costs and revenues. Costs and revenues both vary with output. In fact, for every *additional* calculator produced and sold, there is a marginal addition to revenue and to cost. We call these marginal revenue (MR) and marginal cost (MC). *MR* equals the addition to total revenue from selling one more unit of the output. In competition, this marginal addition to revenue equals the price of the product (MR = P). This is so since the price of a calculator is determined by the whole market, and any seller can produce as many as he or she wants at that price. The addition to total revenue from selling one more calculator will always be equal to the market price (in competition). *MC* equals the addition to total cost from producing and bringing to market one more unit of the product. Since we have said that total costs begin increasing at a slow rate and then begin increasing at an increasing rate, MC will at first decrease and then increase. That is, after some level of output, it will cost successively more and more to bring each additional calculator to market (given a fixed plant and the application of additional variable resources).

---

3. *Explain* how the law of diminishing returns will cause MC to be increasing.

We can illustrate MC and MR as shown in Fig. 11.2.

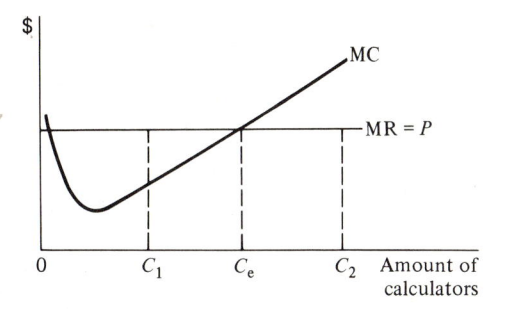

FIG 11.2 Marginal cost and marginal revenue.

MR is constant for every different amount of calculators brought to market by the producer. Remember we have assumed in a competitive market that no one producer can affect market price. The price is determined by the market of buyers and sellers. So the amount of additional revenue the producer gets for each additional calculator sold is equal to the market price. MC after very low levels of production is increasing; it costs the producer more and more to bring each successive calculator to market.

What quantity of calculators will the producer decide to bring to market? Remember we have assumed that the producer's goal is to maximize profit (which is the difference between TR and TC). We have also assumed that the firm has a fixed plant, certain production techniques available and access to certain resources with fixed prices. The answer to the question above is that the producer will produce and sell that quantity of calculators where MR equals MC. *When the marginal cost of producing a unit of output is just equal to the marginal revenue from selling it, profits for the firm are maximized.* This is at C_e in Fig. 11.2. Perhaps by referring to this graph we can see why this level of output will maximize profits.

If the producer were to bring C_1 to market, the MR of the last unit sold would be above the MC of producing it. In this case, the addition to revenues from selling the last calculator is greater than the addition to costs, on the margin. As a result, total revenue will have increased more than total costs (since MR > MC); and thus profits will go up. The addition to revenue was greater than the addition to cost from producing and selling the last calculator and so profits will increase. In fact, as long as MR is greater than MC, the producer will increase profits by bringing additional amounts to market (the marginal revenues from doing so exceed the marginal costs). These marginal additions to profit stop when the producer reaches that level of output where MC = MR. If additional amounts of calculators are brought to market, the MC of doing so will exceed the MR from doing so. As a result, additional costs will exceed additional revenues and profits will decrease. For example, at C_2, marginal cost is greater than marginal revenue; the addition to total costs from producing the last unit of output to get to C_2 is greater than the added revenue from doing so. As a result, profits will be decreased. Profits would be increased by moving to lower levels of production. Profits are at a maximum at C_e, where MC = MR.

4. Explain why profits will *increase* by moving to lower levels of production from C_2.
5. What is the relationship between the firm's total profits at C_e and total profits at C_2?
6. Go back to Fig. 11.1. When does the firm suffer losses (i.e., "negative profits")? What is the relationship between MC and MR at these points?

AVERAGE COSTS AND PROFITS

It will enrich our continuing analysis of the firm if we identify something called *average cost* as well as total cost and marginal cost. Average cost is the cost *per unit* of producing any level of output. It is equal to the total cost of producing any level of output divided by the number of units of output. For example, if it costs $40 to produce four pocket calculators, then the average cost is $10 per calculator. The total cost is $40 and includes all costs of production (including opportunity costs). The average cost is $10. (And we don't know what the marginal cost was of producing the fourth unit.) Average cost will vary with the level of output. Generally, the average cost curve, relating average cost to different levels of output, will look as follows in Fig. 11.3.

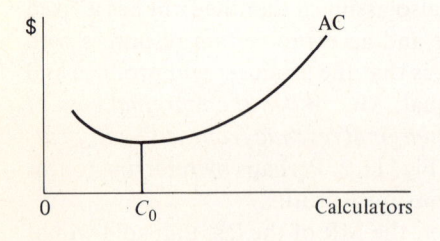

FIG. 11.3 Average cost.

Average Costs and Profits

The average cost curve is U-shaped. At first, over a range of output, average cost decreases; then it reaches a minimum, at C_o, and begins to increase for levels of output beyond C_o. The reason behind this is, again, the law of diminishing returns. At first, when there are increasing returns to the use of variable resources (here we assume a plant size, a physical location, as a fixed resource) the per unit cost of production will decrease as output increases. The per unit amount of resources needed to produce increasing levels of output decreases. However, beyond some level of output, average costs begin to increase as *each* unit of output requires the use of more resources. It is useful to relate the MC curve to the AC curve and both to profits.

Figure 11.4 relates marginal cost to average cost. We will not go into a lengthy description or proof of their relationship. Suffice it to say that if MC is below AC, then AC must be decreasing (if the cost of producing the last unit of added output is below per unit cost, then per unit cost will decrease!). So from output levels 0 to C_o, MC is below AC. If MC is above AC, then AC must be increasing. (Why?) So beyond output C_o, AC is increasing. Then at output C_o, where AC is at a minimum (where the per unit costs of production are minimized), MC = AC. This point is worth further comment. The level of output that minimizes the average cost of production is the most efficient level of output because it means that society is minimizing the cost of using its resources with respect to the production of the good. C_o in Fig. 11.4 represents an optimum level of output because it minimizes the per unit cost of producing the good. Raising or lowering output would increase per unit costs.

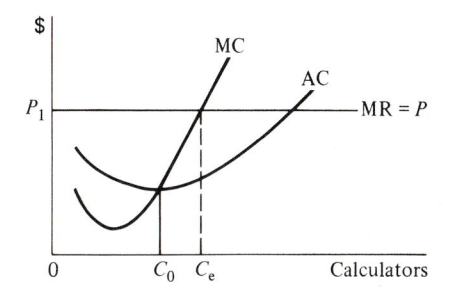

FIG. 11.4 Average cost, marginal cost, and profit.

Note, however, that the firm in Fig. 11.4 will choose to produce and sell C_e of calculators, since, with a price of P_1, it's at this level where MC = MR. At C_e, profits are maximized for the firm. At C_e, AC is larger than it is at C_o; by increasing output beyond C_o the firm experiences increasing average costs. However, for the firm, since MC = MR, this is the point of maximum profit. And, even though AC is increasing, the price per unit (P_1 = MR) is greater than AC. So the firm makes a profit per unit on every unit produced and sold. For the firm, as long as P is above AC, there will be profits. See the box for a summary.

> For those who like numbers, the following data summarize our discussion thus far:
>
> | Output | Total cost | Marginal cost | Average cost |
> |--------|-----------|---------------|--------------|
> | 1 | 10 | | 10.0 |
> | 2 | 18 | 8 | 9.0 |
> | 3 | 24 | 6 | 8.0 |
> | 4 | 32 | 8 | 8.0 |
> | 5 | 42 | 10 | 8.4 |
> | 6 | 54 | 12 | 9.0 |
> | 7 | 70 | 16 | 10.0 |
> | 8 | 88 | 18 | 11.0 |
> | 9 | 112 | 24 | 13.6 |
> | 10 | 142 | 30 | 14.2 |
>
> | Total revenue | Average revenue and marginal revenue | Profit (or loss) |
> |---------------|--------------------------------------|------------------|
> | 12 | 12 | +2 |
> | 24 | 12 | +6 |
> | 36 | 12 | +12 |
> | 48 | 12 | +16 |
> | 60 | 12 | +18 |
> | 72 | 12 | +18 |
> | 84 | 12 | +14 |
> | 96 | 12 | +8 |
> | 108 | 12 | −4 |
> | 120 | 12 | −22 |
>
> Profit maximization occurs between five and six units of output, where MC = MR. At what level of output is average cost at a minimum?

7. What is the profit per unit at C_e for the firm illustrated in Fig. 11.4? What are total profits then?

8. What would the firm do if the price of calculators were such that it passed through the point where MC = AC. What level of output would it produce? What would profits be? Would this firm be getting its opportunity costs?

THE "INVISIBLE HAND" AND CONSUMER SOVEREIGNTY

What does all of this have to do with the *"invisible hand"* and *consumer sovereignty*? Markets and prices indicate to potential producers where profits can be made in the economy. If a producer can produce a product at a lower average cost than the price at which he or she can sell it, then a profit can be earned. In addition, producers will attempt to maximize their profits. We can immediately see, then, that producers will probably try to lower their costs—because that will increase their profits. Consumers will also benefit from this because the price of the product will eventually be lowered because of the cost reduction. This may not be intuitively obvious, so let's examine this theoretical conclusion in more detail.

Say we have a calculator producer who has an MC and MR graph that looks like Fig. 11.5. MC_1 represents the firm's costs and MR is determined by the market price for calculators. This firm then discovers a new and cheaper method of making its calculators. As a result, MC falls from MC_1 to MC_2 (each successive calculator can now be brought to market for a lower marginal cost).

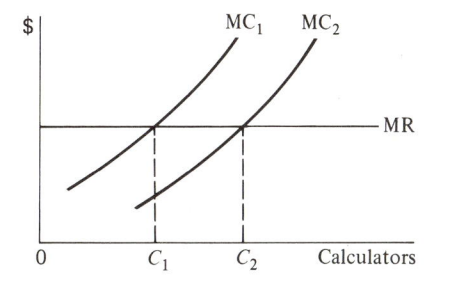

FIG 11.5   Change in cost.

With the change in costs, the firm makes a new decision about the level of output to produce. Originally, profits were maximized at C_1; with the new marginal cost curve, the profit maximizing level of production increases to C_2. (Since average costs also decrease, the firm also will make larger profits since price is still the same and the firm is now producing more.) At first, the price stays the same; the firm is so small in relation to the market that the additional amount brought to market is not noticeable and has no effect on market price. However, the firm does have larger profits.

Eventually, other participants in the market notice the improvement made by this firm and the extra profits that are being earned as a result. These other suppliers begin to attempt to utilize the same or similar cost-reducing methods of production. In addition, the lure of profits (a return to the firm over and above opportunity costs, remember) may induce some new firms to enter the market as sellers. (Again, a characteristic of a competitive market is free entry.) What does this do to market supply? It increases it; more calculators will be brought to market. Graphically, in Fig. 11.6, we get a new supply curve, S_2; more pocket calculators are brought to market at each possible price.

Consequently (*note* we have assumed that D stays the same), the market price will decrease from P_1 to P_2. The cost reduction ended up also reducing the market price! This was brought about through the market and by competition. The market showed that profits could be made, and competition allowed new firms to enter the market. (Note that each producer's profits are lowered due to the price decrease; although each producer will still bring to market that amount that maximizes its profits. *Show this using MR and MC curves.*)

166 Profit Maximization and Competition

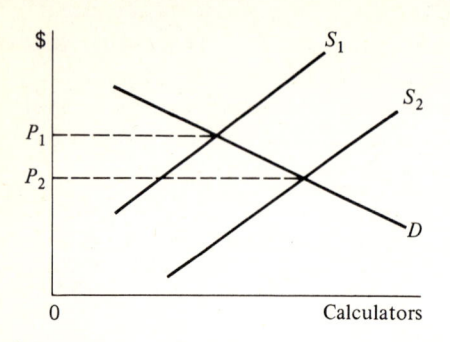

FIG. 11.6 Change in supply.

Despite the fact that each producer (firm) is out to maximize its own profits, the market and competition have brought about a situation in which there is an incentive to lower costs and whereby prices are reduced also when costs are. Consumers benefit as a result; they get their product for a lower price. The "invisible hand" lives (at least theoretically)! (Go back to Chapter 4 and read what Adam Smith had to say about the "invisible hand.")

In addition, the market will respond to consumers' demands. This is referred to as *consumer sovereignty*. For example, let's assume that calculators become regarded as necessities by college students, accounting majors, engineers, even economics students! This change in tastes and preferences will tend to increase the demand for pocket calculators. What effect will this tend to have on the market price for calculators? Use diagrams to show that the price of calculators will tend to increase. What assumption did you make?

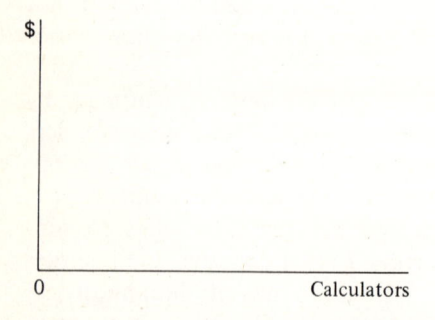

FIG. 11.7 Change in demand.

With this increased price, the profits of calculator producers should increase; and they will produce increasing amounts of calculators. Consequently, the desires of consumers show up in the market and indicate to producers what to do with respect to production. If consumers want more calculators, the market will indicate that and producers will respond by producing more. This is *consumer sovereignty*. (By extension, this process also has implications for resource usage in the economy. For when production of any good or service is expanded or contracted, then the usage of resources for that purpose will also increase or decrease.)

COMPETITION AND EFFICIENCY

One other theoretical result of competition is worth noting. Besides ensuring consumer sovereignty and the operation of the invisible hand, competition ensures *efficiency*. That is, competition tends to encourage production at lowest average cost. We have already developed the tools to show this. Assume that one of our calculator producers is in a position similar to Fig. 11.4. C_e units of calculators are produced and sold, since MC = MR at this point and profits are maximized. And, since P is greater than AC, we know that profits do exist. Furthermore, AC at C_e is above minimum AC (at C_0).

But since this is a competitive market and since profits exist, *entry* into the market will occur. New firms will enter to try to earn profits. But this just causes market supply to increase and market price to decrease. Each firm in the market will reduce its production to a lower level where the new MR equals MC. However, as long as P is above AC, profits continue to exist, entry will continue, and P will continue to decrease. This process will continue until P = AC. Figure 11.8 shows this situation for the firm and the market, in comparison to the original situation depicted in Fig. 11.4.

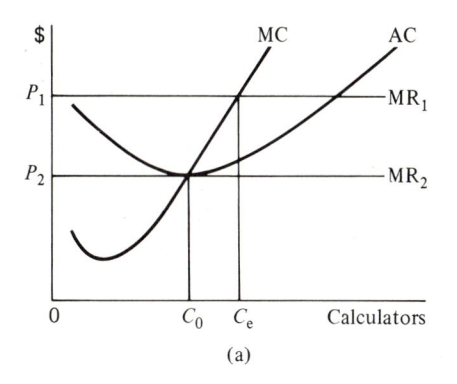

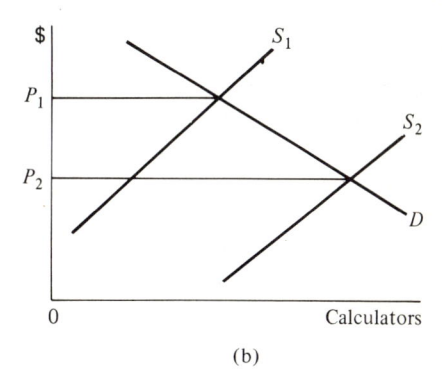

FIG. 11.8 Competition and efficiency.

At the market price of P_1, the firm chooses a level of output, C_e, where MR = MC. Since P is above AC, profits are earned. Entry occurs, pushing the market supply curve out to the right, and market price decreases. When market price falls to P_2, entry will cease. For the firm, MR = MC at C_o (so profits are "maximized," the firm does the best it can given the circumstances); and there are no profits, since AC = P! The cost per unit produced is equal to the price the firm gets per unit sold. Revenues just cover costs. However, remember that costs include opportunity cost for the firm! Even though no economic profits are earned at this level of output, the firm still gets enough revenue to cover its opportunity costs (normal profit). So the firm will remain in business.

But note what has happened. Due to competition and free entry, the firm has been forced to produce at that level of output that mimimizes average cost! Competition, consequently, through the forces that we have analyzed, *tends* to result in efficient production. Firms tend to produce at the optimum level of output, minimizing the per unit cost of production. So competition tends to produce *efficiency*.

What assumptions have we made? We assumed that D stayed constant. And we assumed that the cost curves did not change. With these simplifying assumptions, our analysis showed the tendency towards efficiency. Obviously, the real world would involve more change that would make our analysis a bit more complicated; but the essential conclusion remains: competitive markets tend to result in efficiency.

---

9. Explain and show in an illustration what happens in our competitive market when market prices goes below P_2. What happens to profits? What do the firms in the industry do? What happens to market supply?

CONCLUSION

The competitive market model thus has some attractive properties. It will register the desires of consumers and these desires will guide production. It will force production at lowest average cost (i.e., efficiency). In addition, the invisible hand will bring about cost and price reductions for the consumer. All of this occurs because of the existence of markets and of competition. Competition and markets guide resource allocation. *If* every market were competitive (remember our definition of what that means), then the whole economy would be characterized by efficiency, the invisible hand, and consumer sovereignty. Stated differently, the *theory* of the competitive market model produces efficiency, consumer sovereignty, and the invisible hand. As a result, there is no need for the government to be involved in the economy (except for the purposes outlined by Adam Smith). If the competitive markets are allowed to operate freely and individuals allowed to follow their maximizing opportunities, the best economic results are achieved. The competitive model, then, justifies a policy of *laissez-faire*.

In the next chapter, we will examine some other market structures that describe markets that are not competitive—monopoly, oligopoly, and monopolistic competition. Given the existence of these market structures in the real economy, we are less likely to get the operation of the invisible hand and consumer sovereignty as described in the competitive market and model.

KEY CONCEPTS

profit maximization	MC
competition	MR
costs	average cost
revenues	consumer sovereignty
law of diminishing returns	invisible hand
profits	efficiency

REVIEW QUESTIONS

1. How accurate is this competitive model with respect to the current U.S. economy? Are its conclusions applicable to our economy?

2. Why are profits maximized when MR = MC? Can you explain this logically?

3. Do you think firms really *do* try to maximize their profits? Do they have other goals? Which is most important?

4. Give some examples of the law of diminishing returns in production. Specify what resource is variable and which ones are fixed.

5. Explain why profits cease to exist in competition (as a tendency). What is the implication of this? Why do firms stay in a market in which there are no profits?

SUGGESTED READINGS

Any of the introductory books suggested in Chapter 10 will provide a more detailed treatment of this theory.

Adam Smith, *The Wealth of Nations*, represents an even fuller and classic treatment of these theories expanded to almost 1000 pages! (Especially see Book I, Chapters 5 through 7.)

THE MARXIAN THEORY OF PROFIT

APPENDIX 11A

In Chapter 11, we have examined the orthodox, neoclassical theory of the firm in a competitive market. In the long run, the results suggest that competition produces maximum social welfare (efficiency, consumer sovereignty, and the invisible hand) and that firms earn only "normal" profits. From a Marxian perspective, the operation of competitive capitalism is shown to have results that are much less attractive. Marx concludes that there is inherent conflict between capital and labor, that the source of profits lies in the exploitation of labor, and, furthermore, that the orthodox analysis hides the source of profits and the social relationships in capitalist production.

In the following, we will present a very brief treatment of Marxian microeconomics. (For those who might be interested in pursuing this further, please see the suggested readings at the end of this appendix.)

Marx's analysis focuses on the process of *production* within the capitalist mode of production. According to Marx, the *value* of all goods and services is determined by their labor content—both the direct labor of active labor power by workers and the embodied labor of past labor power in raw materials and capital goods. Consequently, Marx's interpretation of the behavior of firms has its roots in the *labor theory of value*. In addition, Marx assumes that firms are in business to earn profits through the process of capital accumulation (indeed, competition forces firms to seek profits). Finally, productive activity within capitalism has inherent in it certain social relations of production—specifically, there are two basic classes of people: capitalists who own and control the means of production and workers who must sell their labor power to capitalists to earn a living.

Given this Marxian framework of analysis, we can proceed to examine the behavior of firms. Our analysis will concentrate on the source of capitalist profits, the determinants of the prices of products, and the relationships between capitalists and workers.

The capitalist owns the means of production and the capital necessary for the organization of production. There are two forms of this capital: *constant capital* and *variable capital*. *Constant capital* refers to those "factors of production" that have embodied labor in them, e.g., the factory itself, the machinery and equipment in it, and the raw materials used in production. Theoretically, it is possible to place a value on this constant capital. For example, for purposes of simplifying the analysis, let us assume that we can determine the value of one unit of labor power at $5. This assumes that we can value all labor in terms of some abstract unit of average labor. As a result, then, this $5 price for one unit of labor represents the value of the commodities necessary (at least) for the sustenance and the reproduction of this one unit of labor power. Let's assume that the constant capital (machines, raw materials, etc.) has embodied in it six units of abstract labor; therefore, the constant capital is valued at $30 in our example. *Variable capital* refers to the capitalist's outlay of money for the purchase of active labor required, along with constant capital, to produce his or her product. It is variable in the sense that workers can work more or less hours and more or less hard during the working day. Let's assume that the capitalist hires 14 units of living labor to engage in production; therefore, the variable capital (labor) is valued at $70.

What about the capitalist's share? This enters the picture via Marx's concept of *surplus value*. Capitalists hire labor to put into motion constant capital and the production process. Capitalists must pay both constant and variable capital according to the value of the labor embodied in them and required to enable them to work respectively. However, in the process of production, additional value is created. The ultimate value of the product will depend upon the amount of labor contained in it. Capitalists must be able to organize production in such a way that the value of the final product *exceeds* the value of constant and variable capital. This occurs as a natural result of the operation of capitalist production. The capitalist controls production and, specifically, the length of the working day. Let's assume that the working day is ten hours long. During the working day, workers can produce value equivalent to the value of their abstract labor power in six hours. During the remaining four hours, the workers produce value over and above the value necessary for the purchase of their labor power. This is surplus value which derives from surplus labor that is unpaid. Consequently, the 14 units of labor power are used to produce commodities embodying more than 14 units of labor power. Only six hours of labor power are required to produce commodities necessary to cover the costs of the value of the labor power itself. The remaining four hours of labor power produce surplus value. The proceeds from the surplus value go to the capitalists when they sell the products for the value contained in them. The six hours of labor power produce commodities with a value of $70 (the value of variable capital). The four hours of "surplus labor power produce commodities with a value of $46⅔ (the value of surplus value—$70 × ⅔).

The 14 units of living labor power produce commodities embodying 14 units of labor power (the value of variable capital) *and* commodities embodying 9⅓ units of labor power (the value of surplus value—46⅔ ÷ 5). The six units of labor embodied in the constant capital produced commodities with six units of labor embodied in them.

What is revealed in this analysis (which is quite simplified compared with the complexity of Marx's original contribution) is that the source of profits for the capitalists, surplus value, results from the capitalists' control of the production process and their ability to pay living labor (variable capital) less than the full value of what it produces. Hence, labor is exploited, since it has little control over the production process (the essence of which is human labor) and since it does not receive compensation commensurate with what it adds to the value of social production. What's more, it is obvious that inherent in this mode of production is *conflict* between capitalists and workers. Workers will prefer to work fewer hours, less hard, and for money; while capitalists would prefer workers to work longer, harder, and for less money. Capitalists and workers will struggle with each other over the length of the working day, the intensity of work, and the division of the fruits of variable capital (the return to variable capital vs. surplus value). The operation of the capitalist system in Marx's view thus involves differing class interests. In fact, the source of capitalists' profits is the exploitation of labor. This is hardly Smith's picture of the invisible hand, which leads to the greatest social welfare for all.

We can formalize this analysis as follows. The objective of capitalist production is to earn profits and to accumulate capital. The capitalist begins with money, transforms that money into constant and variable capital, utilizes the production process to produce commodities, and then finally transforms those commodities into a larger amount of money. The source of profits is production (which requires human labor) and surplus value. We can characterize this process as follows: $M \rightarrow C \rightarrow M'$, where M = money, C = commodities, and $M' - M$ = profits. In the next round, the capitalist can use profits to accumulate more capital and earn additional profits.

Furthermore, we can express the total value of any product as being equal to the sum of the various forms of embodied labor in it. Total value = constant capital + variable capital + surplus value. For example, from our analysis above:

29⅓ units of labor = 6 units of labor + 14 units of labor + 9⅓ units of labor.

If the value for one unit of labor power is $5, then

$$\$146\tfrac{2}{3} = \$30 + \$70 + \$46\tfrac{2}{3}.$$

From an orthodox perspective, we can view this as:

Price = costs of fixed resources and variable resources (excluding labor) + costs of labor + profits.

Or from the Marxian perspective:

Price = constant capital + variable capital + surplus value. ($P = C \times V \times S$.)

From this information, we can define and calculate:

$$\text{the rate of exploitation} = \frac{\text{surplus value}}{\text{variable capital}} = \frac{\text{profits}}{\text{costs of labor}} = \frac{46\tfrac{2}{3}}{70}$$

$$= 66\ 2/3\%$$

$$\text{and the rate of profit} = \frac{\text{surplus value}}{\text{variable capital} + \text{constant capital}}$$

$$= \frac{\text{profits}}{\text{costs of resources} + \text{costs of labor}}$$

$$= \frac{46\tfrac{2}{3}}{30 + 70} = 46\tfrac{2}{3}\%.$$

The greater the rate of exploitation, the greater will be the rate of profit.

We will conclude our presentation of the Marxian theory of profits by noting that there is one other ratio that affects the rate of profit. The *organic composition of capital* is the ratio of constant capital to variable capital. It will rise whenever capitalists substitute capital for labor in the production process. They may be inclined to do this if labor is battling for higher wages and thus limiting profits. However, the increase in the organic composition of capital will impair the capitalists' ability to earn profits from the surplus value produced by labor. These possibilities suggest, once again, from the Marxian perspective, the inherent instability of capitalist production. Over time, the rate of profit will tend to be equalized through competition (the rate of profit in this sense is comparable to the "normal" profits we identified in Chapter 11). However, Marx preferred to emphasize the tendency toward instability as profits rose and fell in the process of capitalist accumulation and production.

One last aspect of Marx's analysis of the operation of the firm that is worth pointing out is the tendency towards economic concentration that results from long-term capital accumulation and the pursuit of profit. Historically, this theoretical tendency has accounted for the disappearance of competitive markets in capitalist systems.

Postscript: One of the strengths of the Marxist analysis of capitalism is its integration of the micro and macro aspects of economic activity. Profits flow from the organization and control of the capitalist mode of production. The process of capital accumulation and the production of surplus value, in turn, provides the framework within which economic crises are engendered under capitalism.

KEY CONCEPTS

capitalist mode of production
capitalist relations of production
constant capital
variable capital
surplus value

labor theory of value
$P = C + V + S$
rate of profit
rate of exploitation

REVIEW QUESTIONS

1. Is the labor theory of value valid? Why or why not?

2. Marx's theories were originated about 100 years ago. Was labor exploited then? now? Why or why not?

3. Obviously, in the U.S. *most* people are not living on "subsistence" wages. What is the source of the increased wages for variable capital in many industries in the U.S.?

4. What is the *source* of profits according to the Marxian interpretation? Critique this explanation.

5. Given the production of surplus value in the production process, capitalists cannot realize profits unless they sell their products for more than the value of constant and variable capital. In fact, sometimes capitalists will experience losses. What kinds of behavior will capitalists pursue in order to assure the realization of profits?

SUGGESTED READINGS

John Gurley, 1976. *Challengers to Capitalism*, San Francisco Book Company. Chapter 3 provides a relatively simplified introduction to the Marxist analysis of capitalist production and the theory of profit.

Karl Marx, "Wage Labour and Capital," in Robert C. Tucker (ed.), 1978. *The Marx-Engels Reader* (2nd ed.), Norton. One of Marx's early attempts to develop and outline the extended analysis of capitalist production in *Capital*.

Joan Robinson, 1942. *An Essay on Marxian Economics*, Macmillan. An attempt by a leading English economist to summarize Marx's analysis of the distribution of income between labor and capital and to connect that analysis with the causes of economic crises.

Paul Sweezy, 1942. *The Theory of Capitalist Development*, Monthly Review Press. Part I on value and surplus value represents an attempt by a leading American Marxist to explain the labor theory of value and surplus value.

WHEREIN NONCOMPETITIVE MARKET STRUCTURES DISTURB ADAM SMITH'S PERFECT WORLD

CHAPTER 12

INTRODUCTION

One of the things we have learned so far in this Part is that, according to neoclassical theory, competitive markets tend to produce consumer sovereignty, to provide for the operation of the invisible hand, and to lead to economic efficiency. However, if markets are *not* competitive, i.e., do not have all of the characteristics of competition, then these results are less likely. In fact, in noncompetitive markets there is likely to be some amount of *producer sovereignty*, the existence of "monopoly" profits (i.e., profits will not be reduced by competition), and some amount of inefficiency. In this chapter, we will define some other models of market structure and examine their results.

NONCOMPETITIVE MARKET STRUCTURES

The competitive market model gives us a standard by which to judge *real* economic markets and other models of market structures. Chapter 11 defined a competitive market and examined its workings and results. In what follows, we will define some other models of market structures and briefly examine their workings and results. With these additional models we will have a more complete theoretical system for understanding the behavior of firms in the economy and for evaluating their performance.

Before we examine monopoly, oligopoly, and monopolistic competition, we ought to point out that the competitive model is a *model* and that it roughly describes only about 10 percent of the total private economic activity in the U.S. The best examples of competitive markets are those of raw agricultural products—which are homogeneous, are not advertised, have large numbers of buyers and sellers, and can be entered by almost anyone.

MONOPOLY

Monopoly is a market structure in which there is only *one seller* of a good or service. The firm is the industry. Many monopolies are legalized due to the confusion that competition would create. (At the same time, their prices are usually regulated by public authority.) Examples of legal monopolies are local gas, electric, and water companies, AT&T and long-distance telephone lines and equipment, and local telephone companies. F. M. Scherer, an industrial economist, has estimated that about 6 to 7 percent of private economic output originates in monopolies.

AT&T is the biggest monopoly of them all. It has a monopoly on all interstate telephone service and equipment. It owns all or part of several regional and state Bell Systems that monopolize telephone service in those areas. It buys all of its equipment from Western Electric, which is another of its subsidiaries (Western Electric has a monopoly with AT&T). In 1977 it had assets of almost $100 billion, more than GM and Exxon combined. It employed close to a million people.

The characteristics of monopoly markets include the following:

1. There is one seller of a good or service.
2. The product is unique, there are no close substitutes; buyers must buy the good or service from the monopolist.
3. The monopoly can control the price of the good/service, since it supplies the total quantity of the good/service. This is opposed to the competitive firm whose price is determined by the market; the competitor has no influence on the price of its product.
4. Monopolies usually exist because there are barriers to entry into the market; no other firm can supply the product due to legal, technological, or geographical barriers.
5. The monopoly may or may not advertise.

The theoretical results of monopoly markets are that they tend to restrict output and tend to charge higher prices than they could if there were competition in the market for that monopoly's product. As a result, they are less beneficial to consumers who would prefer to have more of the product at a lower price. Monopolies, also, as a result, interfere with efficient resource allocation. Monopoly power allows a firm to remain immune from competition and to retain monopoly profits. (For these reasons, most monopolies in the U.S. are regulated.) Monopoly thus is less desirable than competition. The theoretical analysis that demonstrates these results is not too terribly complicated, so let's try to follow it through.

The monopolist faces the entire demand curve for a product, since there are not any competitors. Thus to sell more, the monopolist must lower price. Or if the monopolist raises price, less will be demanded. As a result of this, the monopolist's marginal revenue curve will be below the demand. Since price must be lowered to sell more, the marginal addition to revenue will always be below the price. (See the boxed material.) This is shown in Fig. 12.1. If we assume that the monopoly buys its resources in competitive markets, its MC and AC curves will look like the ones we derived in Chapter 11. These are also shown in Fig. 12.1.

For those who like numbers:

Output	Price	Total revenue	Marginal revenue
1	10	10	
2	9	18	8
3	8	24	6
4	7	28	4

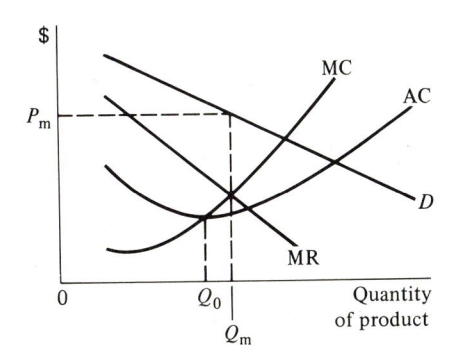

FIG. 12.1 The monopoly.

What level of output will the monopoly choose to produce? It will produce Q_m, where MC = MR, because that level of output maximizes its profits. It will charge a price of P_m for that amount of output, because that is the price the market is willing to pay for that quantity. The monopoly is earning profits since P is well above AC. And the monopoly is producing at a rate of output that does not minimize average costs (Q_o is where AC is at a minimum).

However, in a monopoly, when profits are being earned, there is no entry into the market, because there are no competitors. We can examine the theoretical results of this by focusing on the market, shown in Fig. 12.2.

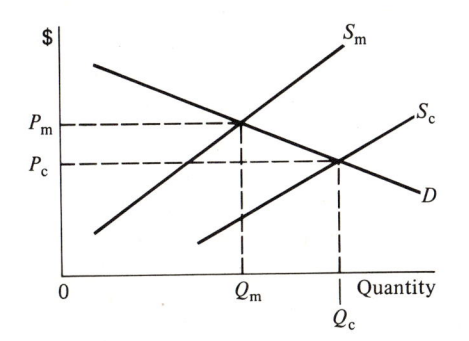

FIG. 12.2 Monopoly—output restriction and high price.

If there were competition in the market, new firms would enter, market supply would increase to S_c, and market price would decrease to P_c. Thus, monopoly restricts output, since $Q_m < Q_c$. And monopoly charges higher prices, since $P_m > P_c$. Finally, monopolies earn monopoly profits.

An important conclusion that can be drawn from the monopoly model is that the existence of market power (ability to control supply and price) tends to prevent the occurrence of consumer sovereignty, the attainment of economic efficiency, and the operation of the invisible hand. The monopoly benefits at the expense of the society. This says nothing at all about the further problem of the relationship of economic power to political power. Monopolies, through their economic power and resources, may come to wield undue political power. Monopolies, as a result, may also tend to disrupt democracy. As Henry Simons, an economist who taught at the University of Chicago, noted ". . . political liberty can survive only within the effectively competitive economic system. Thus, the great enemy of democracy is monopoly. . . ." Any economic unit tending towards monopoly power, consequently, tends toward these same results.

1. What's so bad about monopolies? What can we do if they exist?
2. Analyze Henry Simons's comment above. Do you agree or disagree? Why?
3. AT&T is a monopoly, but it advertises. Why?

OLIGOPOLY AND MONOPOLISTIC COMPETITION

Oligopoly and monopolistic competition are the other two market structure models that economists have developed to roughly approximate economic reality. Somewhere around 80 percent of private economic production comes from firms with oligopoly or monopolistic competition elements. (In *Economics and the Public Purpose,* John Kenneth Galbraith estimates that about 50 percent of private production originates in industries that are competitive or monopolistically competitive and the remainder comes from firms that are monopolies or oligopolies.)

Oligopoly markets have the following characteristics:

1. A *few* firms produce most of the output in an industry. Examples are automobiles, aluminum, cigarettes, steel, chewing gum, etc.,
2. The product may be differentiated or homogeneous. Usually raw materials (e.g., copper) are homogeneous. Final goods (e.g., cars) may be differentiated to gain the consumer's attention and to distinguish them from the products of a rival firm.
3. There may be technological reasons for a few firms dominating an industry. Costs may be reduced in large-scale operations. Firms may also have grown large through mergers. *Entry*, as a result, into such a market *is difficult*. A firm must be *large* to enter. How many firms have entered the auto industry recently and can "compete" with the Big Three?

4. The firms in an oligopoly industry are *interdependent*. Their pricing and other decisions all affect the other firms in the industry. For example, the auto companies and the steel companies follow each other pretty closely on price changes. Despite this interdependence, oligopolies do have some control over price and quantity produced.
5. They usually have a good bit of nonprice competition, e.g., differentiating goods and *advertising*.

Copyright 1973, G. B. Trudeau/Distributed by Universal Press Syndicate.

The results of oligopoly are similar to the results of monopoly. Since there is no real competition (only a limited number of firms are of importance in the market), oligopolies earn oligopoly profits. They are not competed away by entry into the market. As a result, they also tend to charge higher prices and restrict output, although not as severely as a monopoly would. Consequently, oligopolies tend not to be efficient, are not subject to consumer sovereignty, and are not guided by the invisible hand. Again, the standard of comparison is what happens in a competitive market.

Monopolistic competition is characterized by:

1. A large number of buyers and sellers in the market.
2. Products are differentiated by quality differences, advertising, and psychological appeal.

3. Firms have limited control over price, because they are small in relation to the market but sell a differentiated product (which hooks some consumers).
4. Entry into the market is easy, but initial advertising costs could be large.
5. Lots of nonprice competition (differentiation and advertising).

Since monopolistically competitive firms have some market power, their results are not as good as those of a competitive market. However, there is enough competition to force firms to pay substantial attention to consumers, to achieve near maximum economic efficiency and to be close to the invisible hand's "dictates." The results of the model of monopolistic competition are the closest to the competitive model. Examples include toothpaste, aspirin, clothing, and retail stores in metropolitan areas.

THE IMPORTANCE OF NONCOMPETITIVE MARKETS IN THE AMERICAN ECONOMY

That noncompetitive market structures should be of interest to us in attempting to develop a model of the productive units in the American economy can be seen in the following statistics. In 1963, the 100 largest manufacturing corporations accounted for:

25% of all domestic manufacturing employees
32% of domestic manufacturing payrolls
33% of value-added in manufacturing
43% of after-tax profits in manufacturing
34% of domestic manufacturing sales
36% of domestic manufacturing assets.

In 1974, the 500 largest industrial corporations accounted for:

almost 60% of final sales in the entire economy
45% of total profits in the economy
about 20% of employment in the whole economy.

Furthermore, all of these statistics have been increasing steadily throughout the 20th century. In the next chapter, we will explore the dimensions and implications of the corporate sector in a bit more detail.

The following tables show the concentration ratios in various American industries. The concentration ratio shows what percentage of total sales in an industry is accounted for by a specific number of firms. Usually, if the ratio is above 50 percent for the four largest firms in an industry, we call it an oligopoly. If one firm had 100 percent, it would be a monopoly. If the eight largest firms had less than 10 percent of industry sales (and there were lots of other firms in the industry), we'd say that it was close to being a competitive market. From these tables, the importance of concentration in the American economy should be apparent. Most of the leading sectors of the U.S. economy are heavily concentrated.

TABLE 12.1 Percentage of Output* Produced by Firms in Selected Low-Concentration Manufacturing Industries, 1970

Industry	Four Largest Firms	Eight Largest Firms	Twenty Largest Firms
Plywood	30%	44%	50%
Costume jewelry	26	36	43
Men's and boys' suits and coats	19	27	43
Metal house furniture	16	28	40
Wood furniture	14	23	29
Upholstered furniture	13	20	31
Paperboard boxes	12	19	32
Women's and misses' suits and coats	10	14	22
Fur goods	6	10	15
Concrete block and brick	5	7	13

*As measured by value of shipments. Data are for 1970.
Source: Bureau of the Census, *Annual Survey of Manufacturers, 1970.*

TABLE 12.2 Percentage of Output* Produced by Firms in Selected High-Concentration Manufacturing Industries, 1970.

Industry	Percent of Industry Output Produced by Largest Four Firms
Primary aluminum	100
Locomotives and parts	97
Telephone and telegraph equipment	94
Electric lamps (bulbs)	92
Motor vehicles	91
Synthetic fibers	86
Cigarettes	84
Typewriters	81
Sewing machines	80
Gypsum products	79
Steam engines and turbines	77
Metal cans	72
Tires and inner tubes	72
Soap and detergents	70
Phonograph records	62
Distilled liquor	47

*As measured by value of shipments. Data are for 1970.
Source: Bureau of the Census, *Annual Survey of Manufacturers, 1970.*

SOURCES OF CONCENTRATION IN THE ECONOMY

The following factors have contributed to increasing concentration and centralization in the economy over the last century.

1. Legislation and government policy have promoted both competition and monopoly. Governments have granted legal monopolies. In addition, the government has provided support and assistance to several industries with a high degree of concentration—e.g., railroads, airlines, defense, automobiles, etc. On the other hand, *antitrust legislation* and some regulatory legislation are designed to promote competition. These laws are based on economic arguments; our theory has demonstrated that competitive markets tend to produce efficiency, consumer sovereignty, and the invisible hand and that noncompetitive markets, with market power and economic concentration, do not operate as well.

---

4. Articulate the reasons why the government ought to promote competition and prevent extreme economic concentration and market power.

One could argue over how well the antitrust laws have been enforced and whether they have prevented the accumulation of economic power by many of our industries and large firms.

2. Business policies and practices, including trusts, pools, holding companies, and mergers, have tended towards the creation of monopolies and/or oligopolies. Many firms have amassed substantial economic power in their markets and in the economy at large. The elimination of cutthroat competition through bankruptcy and merger, etc. has decreased the number of competitors in many industries. The auto industry used to have over 100 companies in the late 1920s. There have been several merger waves in American economic history that have produced increased economic concentration.

3. Technology has developed in some industries to the point where large-scale operations are necessary for efficiency. This promotes large firms and oligopoly. Technology allows some firms to outpace their competitors who then fall by the wayside. An argument in favor of oligopoly, in fact, is that it can use some of its oligopoly profits to finance research to further advance technology (and presumably its own oligopoly power!).

4. Capitalism's economic freedom of enterprise is permissive of the growth of private corporations. With a motive of profit making and a laissez-faire attitude by government, the creation of economic power was tolerated (and even lauded by some) in our economic history.

Whatever the reasons for noncompetitive markets, we can still conclude that they are theoretically inferior to competitive markets in terms of consumers' and society's preferences. Resources *are* allocated throughout the noncompetitive sectors of the American economy; but noncompetitive markets and prices do not produce the ideals of the invisible hand, consumer sovereignty, and efficiency, as do competitive markets (theoretically). Adam Smith, where are you?

SOME CASES OF NONCOMPETITIVE MARKET STRUCTURES

Case 1—You Can't Eat Automobiles

The following news article appeared in the *New York Times* on August 3, 1976.

Representative James O'Hara, Democrat of Michigan, wants the Big Three automakers to cut prices saying the move would stimulate jobs. In telegrams to the three companies, Mr. O'Hara said:
 "The all-time record profits announced [last] week by General Motors, Ford and Chrysler amounting to more than $1.5 billion for the April-to-June quarter offers a once-in-a-lifetime opportunity for these companies to demonstrate their commitment to our American economic system in its time of great need."
 He suggested that "significant price cuts in their 1977 model year cars," might cause millions of potential car buyers who deferred purchases because of "year-after-year price increases" to buy them at this time.
 In turn, he continued, this would result "in increased production and many additional jobs in the auto companies, plus those generated by parts firms and the thousands of suppliers who rely on a healthy auto industry for their lifeblood."

---

5. Is it very likely that the automobile companies took Congressman O'Hara's advice? Why or why not?

6. Did O'Hara represent the Detroit area? How could you find out?

7. What kind of market structure does the automobile industry have?

The following two articles appeared almost exactly one year earlier than the article above. These two, in fact, were in the paper on the same day, August 14, 1975.

AUTO SALES DOWN 28.9% AUG. 1 TO 10
Drop exceeds forecasts—results worst in 14 years

DETROIT, Aug. 13—The United States auto industry reported 131,218 new-car sales in the Aug. 1–10 period, off 28.9 percent from a year ago and a sharper decline than had been expected by analysts.
 The results were the worst for the period in 14 years and sent the annual selling rate for domestic cars down to about a 6.8 million level in August against 7.4 million in all of July.

© 1975 by The New York Times Company. Reprinted by permission.

The sales figures for this month contrasted with the 207,624 cars sold at this point last year when buyers were rushing to get 1974 models in advance of predicted 10 percent price rises on the 1975 models.

This year, manufacturers have announced or predicted increases of 4 to 6 percent on the 1976 models but this has not caused a similar buying surge of the 1975 cars. Today, the General Motors Corporation announced a retail increase on 1975 models averaging 4.4 percent.

Sales in the period were off 33 percent from the full month of July while the normal falloff is 27 percent. So, said one analyst, "this was a relatively soft period; but I don't know if there is anything significant about it."

All four domestic manufacturers reported sharp declines in sales this month from a year ago.

34.3 PERCENT G.M. DROP

General Motors reported a 34.3 percent sale drop, the Chrysler Corporation a 28 percent decline, the Ford Motor Company a 20.3 percent slide and the American Motors Corporation a 10.3 percent drop.

Following are sales reported by the four car makers for the Aug. 1-10 period:

	1975	1974
G.M.	70,529	120,717
Ford	39,088	55,189
Chrysler	14,984	23,420
A.M.C.	6,617	8,298
Totals	131,218	207,624

For the year, industry sales are off 16.3 percent. Chrysler sales are off 26.5 percent, Ford's are down 20 percent, A.M.C.'s are off 16 percent and G.M.'s are down 11 percent.

Following are sales reported thus far this year:

	1975	1974
G.M.	2,116,760	2,379,162
Ford	1,114,515	1,400,074
Chrysler	596,987	816,487
A.M.C.	200,600	240,471
Totals	4,028,862	4,836,194

8. What was the reason for this decrease in auto sales? What would you expect to happen to automobile prices as a result?

GENERAL MOTORS RAISES '76 PRICES OF CARS BY 4.4%
Increase, average of $206, smaller than forecast—others likely to follow
U.S. approval is seen
Acting director of stability council says rises won't match higher costs

DETROIT, Aug. 13—The General Motors Corporation said today it was raising prices on its 1976-model cars by an average of $206, or 4.4 percent, a smaller increase than had been forecast by industry analysts.

General Motors, the world's largest automobile manufacturer and the traditional price leader in the industry, was the first of the four United States auto makers to announce its prices for the coming model year. Analysts said the other companies could be expected to announce prices similar to those set by G.M.

United States car prices already have risen by an average of about $1,000 since the 1974 models were introduced in the fall of 1973. Increases on the 1974 models totaled more than $500 and those on the 1975 models introduced last fall were more than $400.

SHIPPING CHARGES RAISED

While there were no later general increases during the course of the 1975-model year, some auto makers did increase shipping charges and optional-equipment prices on selected models. The latest increase of more than $200 will mean the total average price rise in the last two years will be about $1,100 to $1,200.

The General Motors price increase apparently will be accepted by Federal wage-price officials. In Washington, George Eads, acting director of the Council of Wage and Price Stability, said the agency believed G.M.'s increase was "tailored to the current realities of the automobile market place."

He said the price increases would not recover the costs incurred by the auto maker since the 1975-model run began last fall. The company said in its statement that, since then, costs had gone up an average of $375 a car.

G.M. added that its price increases took into account rises in steel costs. Steel makers have announced average price rises of 3.8 percent.

WARNING BY ANALYSTS

General Motors' chairman, Thomas A. Murphy, said that an increase that was higher than the one the company posted today might hurt future sales. He thus seemed to agree with some auto analysts who had warned that if the industry went ahead and set the 6 percent tentative price rise, it would jeopardize sales gains.

© 1975 by The New York Times Company. Reprinted by permission.

They warned that such an increase would result in a sales slump like the one they said was set off last year by an increase averaging 8 percent or $400 a car.

Because of the sales slump the industry was forced to institute price rebates early this year to lower the record backlog of unsold cars. Chrysler is still continuing the rebates but the other auto makers have stopped the practice.

LOSSES AND DECLINES

The auto industry has been hit with losses and sharp declines in profits over the last year.

AFRAID OF A BACKLASH

A.M.C.'s chairman, Roy D. Chapin Jr., in a view similar to those of other auto executives, said manufacturers need more than a 6 percent raise on the new models but were afraid of a backlash if the increase was higher than consumers could take. Domestic sales so far this year are off 16 percent from last year's already depressed levels.

G.M.'s pricing statement served notice that dealers will have to absorb a portion of the added costs. That is, their discount is being cut. This is the margin between the price they pay for the car from the manufacturer and the suggested retail selling price.

The margin has been as high as 26 percent on some big cars but in recent years, as the industry has brought out more smaller models that carry smaller price tags, the auto companies have trimmed the dealers' margin on these cars.

Mr. Murphy said: "We are increasing our wholesale prices to our dealers on a 1976 base car with comparable standard equipment by an average of $216, or 5.4 percent—only a little more than half our cost increases.

"At the same time, we are adjusting our suggested dealer markups so that retail sticker prices will increase an average of only $206, or 4.4 percent.

"This increase is well below the recent increases in the Consumer Price Index."

EQUIPMENT MADE OPTIONAL

Mr. Murphy also said prices of some models have been cut because standard equipment has been removed and made optional. He said steel-belted radial tires had been taken off as a standard item on compact cars and power brakes on sub-compacts. He explained this was "to achieve the lowest possible retail price on the base model and to give the customer wider latitude in equipping the car."

---

9. Given the concurrent decrease in demand for cars, how can you explain GM's decision to *raise* prices?

Case 2—And You Can't Drink Petroleum

As we have mentioned above, one way to attempt to preserve competition and its beneficial results and to prevent market power and economic concentration is through governmental antitrust legislation. The goal is to control the adverse results of market power by splitting up companies, preventing mergers, prosecuting price setting and other noncompetitive activities, and regulating monopolies. A current debate raging over antitrust legislation is whether to break up the oil companies or not. Proponents of the legislation argue that the industry is too concentrated and that making it more competitive would benefit consumers and the economy. Opponents, primarily the oil companies themselves, argue that the industry is not all that concentrated and that breaking up the oil companies would hurt consumers and the economy.

In the following we have reproduced several pieces about this debate. The first article from the *New York Times* summarizes the debate.

BREAKUP OF OIL INDUSTRY STIRS DISPUTE IN CAPITAL

WILLIAM D. SMITH

The American oil industry has grown to world dominance under a structure in which the major companies control all their operations from production through marketing. But in recent months a question raised with growing intensity is whether the consumer is best served by such an arrangement.

Divestiture, as the breakup of the present oil industry structure is called, has thus become one of the hottest and most controversial issues in Washington.

It is an issue in which ideology, politics and economics have mixed in an election year to make an already complex issue even more difficult.

More than 30 separate bills have been introduced in Congress to break up the oil companies in one way or another. Almost half the Senate has gone on record at some time in favor of a major structural change in the industry.

The issue has broad implications since oil is the commodity next to food in importance to most Americans. Energy is the vital spark that drives industrial economics. No place is this more evident than in the United States, where 6 percent of the world's population consumes a third of its energy.

The Senate Judiciary Committee is scheduled today to vote on a bill titled the Petroleum Industry Competition Act. The bill, drafted by Senator Birch Bayh, Democrat of Indiana, calls for vertical divestiture, that is, a breakup of the large oil companies along functional lines into separate production, transportation, refining and marketing units.

An amendment introduced by Senator Philip A. Hart, Democrat of Michigan, calls for a three-part breakup allowing the companies to keep their refining and marketing operations intact as one unit. The Hart version extends from three to five years the period the companies have to divest themselves and creates a divestiture court to handle the substantial volume of litigation likely to accompany any breakup. The bill would break up the nation's 18 largest energy companies.

In addition to vertical divestiture, a number of bills call for horizontal divestiture, or the breaking off from the oil companies of nonoil and gas energy operations such as coal, uranium, shale and solar.

© 1976 by The New York Times Company. Reprinted by permission.

What would oil industry dismemberment do? It could hurt you five ways.

Senate Bill 2387, which recently squeaked through the Judiciary Committee on an 8-to-7 vote, proposes to break up the 18 major U.S. oil companies. If that happens, here are five likely results:

1. It would hurt the consumer. Says economics professor Neil H. Jacoby of U.C.L.A.: "Prices of petroleum products would rise, product improvements would diminish, and services would shrink. Consumers would suffer, and the social consequences would be adverse as well." Says Don Paarlberg, economist for the Department of Agriculture: "Disruption caused by divestiture would impact not only at the farm level, but on through the economy."

2. It might raise taxes. Listen to banker Raymond B. Gary of Morgan Stanley & Co.: "The price for enacting such legislation will have to be paid by someone—if not by the consumer...then certainly by the taxpayer: either prices will have to be raised...or the Federal Government will have to step in, with programs of guarantees, insurance, or even direct subsidies."

3. It would help foreign producing countries at U.S. expense. A *New York Times* editorial explains why: "Breaking up the largest oil companies—and the long period of uncertainty through which the industry would have to pass—would probably cause a major cutback in investment in new energy resources, both in the United States and abroad (including non-OPEC areas). This would strengthen market domination by OPEC [Organization of Petroleum Exporting Countries] by contracting other sources of supply."

4. It could cost jobs. That's the prediction of John Winger of the Chase Manhattan Bank: "...if a lack of energy prevented any further growth in the GNP, we could, by 1985, expect unemployment that would exceed that of the 1930s."

5. It would weaken America's security. Our authority for that? Roger E. Shields, Deputy Assistant Secretary of Defense, who says: "...the bill would be highly detrimental to the nation's security and its defense...."

Isn't it time for the Senators who are trying to break up a vital industry to listen to voices of reason? Including the experts'. Including, we hope, *yours*. Write your Senators. Let them know that you think divestiture is bad news for America.

Mobil

BACKGROUND

Oil, probably more than any other industry in the nation during this century, has been an object of public attention and political interest.

While petroleum is an international commodity, it has had a distinctly American character since the first well in the United States was drilled by Edwin Drake in 1859 in Titusville, Pa. This country developed its oil industry before any other, and petroleum has been one of the chief reasons for the emergence of the United States as a world power in this century.

Five of the world's seven largest oil companies are American. The United States is conceded technological leadership in petroleum by every nation. Even the Soviet Union and China are eager to obtain American help to develop their hydrocarbon resources.

Nonetheless, the average American's opinion of the industry and oilmen has seldom been favorable. While the industry's competence is generally conceded, critics through the years have said that its skills are used for self-serving purposes rather than the public good.

According to some industry observers, much of the distrust of the oil industry dates to John D. Rockefeller, Sr. and the Standard Oil Trust he put together. The senior Rockefeller managed to monopolize not only most of the American trade in petroleum products but also world trade before the trust was broken up in 1911. The move to this day is considered the nation's most significant antitrust action.

Oil has become the nation's and world's largest industry other than agriculture. The large companies, the objects of the divestiture bills, usually started in one respect of the business and integrated forward or backward into the other segments. Indeed, one of the basic questions in the whole divestiture issue is whether vertical integration is the natural structure of the oil business or whether it came about in an effort to obtain unfair advantage.

Issues such as the depletion allowance, which permitted tax benefits for oil-producing companies, have kept the oil business in the public arena. During the 1940s, 50s and early 60s, the oil industry had considerable support among the Washington hierarchy, including Sam Rayburn and Lyndon Johnson of Texas. During the late 1960s, Washington leadership switched to other sections of the country, such as the Northeast, where both constituent politics and ideology often put it in direct opposition to the oil industry.

Disputes over oil-import quotas and a refinery at Machiasport, Me., further alienated Northeastern Congressional delegations in particular and liberals in general.

The Arab oil embargo of 1973 and the fivefold increase in world oil prices that followed sharply increased the number of citizens and politicians suspicious of oil company motives and actions.

The question of whether the structure of the oil industry should be altered has been discussed in Congress for at least 11 years by critics but was not considered a serious possibility and had been low on the Congressional priority list of even most breakup advocates.

The issue became a major question last Oct. 8, when the Senate rejected by a 54 to 45 margin an amendment to a natural gas pricing bill that would have broken up the nation's 22 largest integrated oil companies.

Both supporters and opponents were shocked by the closeness of the vote. Proponents set out to get more support, while the industry started a counterattack involving a budget of several million dollars.

On April 1, the bill passed the Senate Antitrust and Monopoly subcommittee by a 4 to 3 vote, leaving as the next step today's vote by the full Judiciary Committee.

The supporters of divestiture include liberal members of Congress and the traditional anti-oil forces. Breakup measures are also supported by some economists, as well as some environmentalist and consumer organizations. The most active group has been the recently formed Energy Action Committee, which includes Paul Newman, the actor.

"Our goal is to provide and to sustain competition in the domestic oil industry," Senator Bayh said in introducing his bill. "Moreover, only a major step such as requiring vertical divestiture, can bring competition to the oil industry."

To support their contentions, proponents point out that oil companies are huge compared with most other concerns, noting that half the nation's 10 largest industrial corporations are oil companies.

They point out that the 20 largest oil concerns accounted for 76.3 percent of the crude oil produced in the United States in 1973 and that the same 20 companies accounted for about 93.5 percent of the country's reserves in 1970.

In transportation, the 16 largest oil companies control pipelines that received 92 percent of the crude oil flowing into all pipelines. And as of 1973, the 20 largest companies maintained 82.9 percent of the total United States refining capacity.

In marketing the top 20 companies controlled 77.2 percent of gasoline sales in 1973.

Critics contend that, beyond the actual measurements of market concentration, the major oil companies are interlocked in a complex network of joint ventures that makes the industry far less competitive than numbers indicate.

The fine tuning of this network, according to divestiture supporters, enables the large integrated companies to manipulate supplies and prices, giving preferential treatment to their own subsidiaries while discriminating against the industry's independent segments. The companies are also accused of making large and excessive profits.

An argument in favor of divestiture that has gained prominence recently is that an industry broken into separate production, marketing and refining units would be better able to deal with Organization of Petroleum Exporting Countries, the producing nations' cartel.

Supporters of this position contend that integrated companies have a vested interest in "playing ball" with the producing nations, while a marketing and refining company without producing interests would bargain harder for lower prices.

Supporters of divestiture, while conceding that the process will be complicated legally and logistically, argue that it will be nowhere near as difficult as opponents of the measure contend.

Supporters of horizontal divestiture say that the oil companies are gaining increasing control of other energy resources, which could lead to higher prices for all energy because of lack of competition between various energy forms.

OPPONENTS

Besides the major oil companies that are actually threatened with divestiture, the smaller companies in all segments of the industry also oppose the measure. Some other industries and business groups have also come out against the measure as the first step toward elimination of the free-enterprise system, a notion the bill's sponsors emphatically deny.

Among a number of economists who oppose the bill, is Prof. Neil H. Jacoby of the University of California at Los Angeles. He contends that a forced breakup of the industry "would lead to higher-priced petroleum products, would increase dependence on foreign energy, would strengthen and prolong the effectiveness of the OPEC cartel and paradoxically, would probably make for a less competitive structure of the industry."

In recent weeks the [Ford] Administration has come out strongly against divestiture, with the heads of a number of government agencies testifying against it at hearings.

Opponents of the bill argue that the oil industry is less, rather than more, concentrated than most industries.

They note that the domestic oil industry has 10,000 companies exploring and producing oil, 131 companies operating refineries, 15,000 wholesalers and 190,000 retailers of gasoline. They contend that, in terms of market share of the top eight and top four companies, petroleum is 26th and 27th on the list of all United States manufacturering industries. In the average manufacturing industry, the top four companies have 40 percent of the market while the top eight have 60 percent.

The four largest oil companies have only 26 percent of crude oil and natural gas production, 28.6 percent of refinery capacity and 29.8 percent of the gasoline market. The eight largest oil companies have 42.1 percent of production, 51 percent of refining and 51.8 percent of the gasoline market.

In addition, no single company has as much as 11 percent of the business in any single category and no single company is the largest in all three.

Industry supporters agree that the companies are massive noting that vast amounts of capital are needed to do the job. They cite the billions of dollars needed to develop the North Slope of Alaska and the North Sea.

The industry contends that its profits are roughly equal to those for business in general, being slightly below average in the 1960's and slightly above average in the 10 years ended in 1974.

Antidivestiture forces suggest that if breakup measures were enacted, the resulting legal, international and logical chaos would take 10 to 20 years to straighten out, while the nation's energy independence would suffer.

Rather than a weakening of OPEC, opponents of divestiture say that the companies divested would be less able to strike a bargain with producing nations.

Regarding horizontal divestiture, opponents contend that, rather than reduce competition in other energy fields, the entry of the oil companies has increased competition and injected new and needed capital.

Opponents of divestiture have also challenged the proponents to demonstrate how breaking up the industry would reduce prices to consumers or increase energy supplies. . . .

10. Are you an opponent or a proponent? Why?

DEBUNKING MADISON AVENUE

LEONARD ARROW

The oil companies are nervous. For the first time since the Standard Oil trust was broken up in 1911, the oil industry faces a major threat to its monopoly control.

It all began rather quietly. Last October during the debate on deregulating natural gas prices, some U.S. senators offered an amendment which proposed prohibiting any company from engaging in more than one of the four functions of the oil industry (production, refining, transporting and marketing). Normally the amendment would have been greeted with a big yawn. Similar proposals have usually managed to persuade all of 15 senators out of the total 100.

The amendment received the usual listless debate. The oil industry didn't take it seriously, the press didn't take it seriously and some of the senators were bored as well. But to the wonder of even its supporters, 45 senators voted for the proposed divestiture. No longer was breaking up the oil companies a laughing matter.

Reprinted from *Environmental Action*, the biweekly magazine of Environmental Action, Inc., 1346 Connecticut Avenue, Washington, D.C. 20036. A one-year subscription is $15.

The industry, its honor impugned, responded. The president of Exxon testified about the tragedy that would befall the nation if Exxon were forced to become four little Exxons (each unit would still remain among the top 50 corporations in the country). Advertising designed to make you think of oil companies as good neighbors, just like the Joneses across the street, increased in volume and stridency. Mobil continues its chatty sweet nothings on the Op-Ed page of the *New York Times,* Exxon shows an oil rigger fishing from an offshore oil platform. Shell offers the "Bicentennial (That's the way it was—200 years ago today) Minute" and Texaco says "Trust us."

The latest addition to this "good neighbor" campaign is an ad from Texaco which makes only two substantive claims.* The first is that divestiture would increase prices by imposing a costly layer of "middlemen." Is this true?

The oil companies would like you to believe it is, but when their money is at stake, they tell a different story. Senator Ernest Hollings (D-S.C.) learned that Exxon was repudiating the "no middleman" argument in a South Carolina tax court. Here is how Senator Philip Hart (D-Mich.), who is chairman of the Subcommittee on Antitrust and Monopoly, described the discovery:

> What originally aroused Senator Holling's curiosity was a lawsuit filed by Exxon for a tax refund on the grounds that its South Carolina marketing activity was unconnected with its refining and crude production elsewhere in the country. This is a fairly startling proposition for anyone who has not been in a monastery for the past six months.

A similar suit was also initiated by Exxon in Wisconsin on the same grounds.

What Exxon was admitting was that the company is arranged in a decentralized manner. When products move from one segment of the company to another, it is the same as if they are being bought and sold among separate companies. Each segment of the company is responsible for earning its own profits. According to an Exxon vice president the objective of this "functional independence" is "to provide a basis of valuing transfers which would approximate the same results as if one separate independent company has negotiated with another separate independent company." The middlemen and their costs are already included in the price of Exxon's products.

But is Texaco's corporate structure the same as Exxon's? An Exxon witness, the head of the Houston office of a major accounting firm, testified that other oil companies are financially arranged the same way—and he specifically mentioned Texaco. Further, the Texaco ad speaks of "the more than 50 integrated oil companies" and "the industry" in making its argument.

The ad's second assertion is that a breakup would endanger the corporation's "ability to raise capital, particularly for purposes of new exploration;" job security would be endangered and technical advances slowed down as a result. The claim is

---

*The Texaco ad referred to, "If They Break Up the Oil Companies, You'll Pay through the Hose," appeared in the May 15th, 1976 issue of *Saturday Review* on page 9. The ad argues that oil industry divestiture would increase the cost of gasoline to consumers, increase the difficulty of raising needed capital for the industry, endanger oil-industry related jobs, reduce technical advances, and increase our dependency on foreign oil. We encourage you to go to the library and read the ad for yourself.

made (implicitly in the ad, explicitly elsewhere) that a divested company could not compete with other corporations for investment capital. But the separate units of the oil companies already compete for capital within the corporation. Exxon, for instance, is set up so that each segment is "in competition with each other ... which results, of course, in competition for the available funds for investment in the business activities of each of these operating functions." Senator Hart answers the ad's claim this way:

> *Divestiture would eliminate the intermediate capital distribution now performed at the corporate management level. The capital market itself will be able to measure the performance of each functional entity and allocate capital accordingly. Such a result could hardly lead to the economic collapse of the republic. In fact there are some that might argue that free markets allocate goods, services, and even capital more efficiently than do bureaucrats, even corporate bureaucrats.... Moreover, it should be remembered that functional units of the major companies are large by any standard. Exxon's crude producing unit, after being severed, would be the fourth largest corporation in the United States, behind only General Motors, Ford, and IBM.*

Perhaps you are wondering what antitrust legislation and economic policy have to do with the environment; at first glance the two don't appear to be related. But environmentalists, delving into the reasons for environmental degradation and skewed government policies regarding natural resources, soon learned that issues they had thought of as limited to the economic sphere actually had crucial ramifications for the environment. Railroad regulatory reform, for instance, has become an environmental issue because of the inefficiency of our transportation system, its overdependence on automobiles and trucks, and built-in discrimination against transporting recyclable materials.

The structure of the large integrated companies is similarly important. Because they set the price of their products with little regard for free market forces, they control the petroleum market, and can price oil to their own advantage. Thus they can make other energy sources "uneconomic" in comparison.

Less than two decades ago oil corporations could not have cared less about coal. Oil was so cheap, by comparison, that coal simply could not compete. But when they became worried about future shortages of oil, industry leaders began to worry about coal again, fearing that they were losing the freedom to price oil as they wished. If the price of oil got out of control, coal would again become an economically attractive alternative. The oil companies began to buy coal corporations.

The power to control the price of all fossil fuels affects the ability to develop other sources of energy. Consider solar energy. There is no resource to be mined, marketed, and controlled through a tight network. The technology for harnessing solar energy is small scale and thus does not require the enormous capital reserves needed to purchase mineral concessions and exploit them. So corporations with no interest in fossil fuels are entering the solar field, interested not in protecting the energy industry but in selling their rapidly developing technology.

But in order to be successful, solar technology will have to compete—at least for the next 50 to 100 years—with fossil fuels. And if the energy industry can price fossil fuels without regard to market conditions, then it can always set a price just high enough to return sufficient revenues for profits and new investment, but not high enough to allow solar energy (and other potential competition) to advance. I can easily imagine the oil companies deliberately lowering their prices in order to halt the development of alternative energy sources. Everyone would breathe a sigh of relief that gas station prices had come down. But a rational energy policy, based on allowing each potential energy source to compete on an equal footing for markets, would be devastated.

The present structure also prevents serious energy conservation. If the oil companies are going to refrain from increasing prices—because they fear competition from other energy producers—they will try to increase profits by selling more oil and gas. This, in turn, increases the pressure to drill offshore, to push shale oil production, etc.—all in an effort to maintain the proper price for energy products and to maintain the profit margin of big oil.

Government's attempt to monitor the oil monopoly, traditionally through regulation, has several problems. The first is that regulatory bureaucracies almost inevitably come to believe that the large corporations they monitor are truly efficient. But there is no solid evidence that large corporate bureaucracies are normally any more efficient than large government bureaucracies (if you want to hear how inefficient government is, ask an oil company executive). The second problem is that of choosing the regulators. If drawn from the oil industry, they are likely to accept and advance industry views. If drawn from elsewhere, they may know little about the industry they presume to control in the public interest.

A better alternative, I suggest, is antitrust. I concede that present antitrust laws and enforcement mechanisms are inadequate. But the attempt to break up the oil companies (and other oligarchies) by legislation is far more promising than is current litigation. This year, after 11 years of waiting in the wings, members of the Senate Judiciary Committee have pledged to shake an oil divestiture bill out of the moribund committee and onto the Senate floor for a direct vote. And with three defenders of business interests retiring from Judiciary this year, further action can be expected in 1977 and 1978. Even Jimmy Carter, if he is elected President, may be forced by the rest of the Democratic party to push for divestiture.

You can see why the oil companies are nervous. Their profits are at stake and the only arguments they have are the weak ones of the Texaco ad.

---

11. *Now are you an opponent or a proponent of breaking up the oil companies? Did you change your mind or not? Why?*

KEY CONCEPTS

monopoly
oligopoly
monopolistic competition

market power
concentration (ratio)
antitrust

REVIEW QUESTIONS

1. What are the theoretically adverse results of monopoly markets?

2. What benefits might be derived from oligopoly to offset its inefficiencies and higher prices? Can you give some examples?

3. Why do you think that the automobile industry is not competitive, according to our model of competition? What evidence can you cite to show its noncompetitiveness and inefficiency?

4. Why is AT&T a monopoly? What would happen if it weren't?

5. What would happen to the marijuana "industry" if it were legalized in the U.S.? What kind of market is it now?

SUGGESTED READINGS

Walter Adams (ed.), 1977. *The Structure of American Industry* (5th ed.), Macmillan. Case studies of some noncompetitive industries in the U.S., e.g., steel, telephone, automobiles, and beer.

John M. Blair, 1972. *Economic Concentration,* Harcourt Brace Jovanovich. A wealth of information on economic concentration, as well as some economic theory explaining it.

John Kenneth Galbraith, 1967. *The New Industrial State,* and 1973, *Economics and the Public Purpose,* Houghton Mifflin. Two well-written treatments of the sources and implications of economic concentration in the American economy.

THE CORPORATION

CHAPTER 13

INTRODUCTION

Now that we have examined the economic theory of the competitive and noncompetitive market structures and explored the results of different types of firms, it is worthwhile to conclude with a more "realistic" approach to the *firm*. The corporation, as a productive unit in the American economic system, has become a dominant institution. In Chapter 12 we saw some statistics that showed the impact of the 100 and 500 largest industrial corporations on several economic categories—manufacturing employment, manufacturing assets, etc. American corporations stand out for consideration in any discussion of production and how resources are allocated in the U.S. Therefore, this chapter will concentrate on American corporations: a description of what they are, the economic power they have, *and* an analysis of what that power implies.

THE CORPORATION

Corporations are legal entities that engage in the provision of goods and services for the public. They have legal authority to enter into contracts with other parties. The characteristic of corporations that distinguishes them from other productive units—e.g., partnerships, proprietorships, etc.—is that the individuals who own the corporation, the stockholders, have *limited liability*. Stockholders are liable to the corporation's creditors only to the extent of the value of their stock. They can not be sued by creditors. This differs from other forms of business in which individuals who operate them *are personally liable* to creditors. This gives the corporation a great advantage in amassing financial resources to underwrite production. Issues of corporate stock can raise capital, and this capital base can be used to raise further capital through bank loans, etc. Corporations have used this ability to form large productive operations—large plants, nationwide productive and distributive facilities, and even worldwide networks. In addition, the technological advances of the Industrial Revolution spurred the development of larger and larger corporations.

Through these legal advantages and historical developments, many American corporations have grown to be quite large in terms of assets, profits, employees, and economic (and political) power.

How many corporations are there in the U.S.? And just how large have they grown? The following tables should help us to answer these questions. Table 13.1 presents information on the types and numbers of business firms in the U.S. in 1973.

TABLE 13.1 Types of U.S. Business Firms

Type of Business Organization	Number of Firms In Thousands	Percent of Total	Total Receipts In Billions	Percent of Total	Net Profits (In Billions)
Proprietorships	10,648	78.3	$ 311	10.4	$ 47
Partnerships	1,039	7.6	124	4.1	9
Corporations	1,905	14.1	2,558	85.5	120
Totals	13,592	100.0	2,993	100.0	176

Source: *Statistical Abstract of the U.S., 1976.*

In 1973, there were almost 2 million corporations in the U.S.; they constituted 14.1 percent of businesses but had 85.5 percent of all business receipts. So corporations handle the vast majority of business transactions in the U.S.

Which corporations are the biggest and how big are they? Table 13.2 shows the ten largest industrial corporations in the U.S. in 1976 ranked by sales. It also shows total assets, number of employees, and net income for each.

TABLE 13.2 Ten Largest Industrial U.S. Corporations

Rank	Company	Sales	Assets	Net Income	Employees
		(in Millions of Dollars)			
1	Exxon	$48,631	$36,331	$2,641	126,000
2	General Motors	47,181	24,442	2,903	748,000
3	Ford	28,840	15,768	983	443,917
4	Texaco	26,452	18,194	870	72,766
5	Mobil	26,063	18,767	943	199,500
6	Standard Oil of California	19,434	13,765	880	38,397
7	Gulf Oil	16,451	13,449	816	53,300
8	IBM	16,304	17,723	2,398	291,977
9	General Electric	15,697	12,050	931	380,000
10	Chrysler	15,538	7,074	423	244,865

Source: *Fortune,* May 1977.

Table 13.3 presents data on the top 750 largest industrial, banking, insurance, retailing, transportation, and utility corporations for 1973.

TABLE 13.3 The Assets, Sales, Income, and Employees of the 750 Largest Industrials, Banks, Insurance Companies, Retailing Companies, Transportation Companies, and Utilities

	Assets ($000)	Sales ($000)	Income ($000)	Employees
500 largest industrials	555,462,284	667,105,712	38,680,461	15,531,683
50 largest commercial banks	459,027,367	364,704,942*	2,401,867	427,412
50 largest life insurance	204,848,629	31,860,578†	1,075,471	410,918
50 largest retailing	44,318,645	100,493,724	2,113,727	2,683,337
50 largest transportation	48,153,394	30,602,389	856,368	924,314
50 largest utilities	181,203,583	55,795,040	7,248,364	1,275,943
Total	1,493,013,902	1,250,562,385	52,376,258	21,253,607

*Deposits.
†Premium and annuity income.
Source: *Fortune,* May 1974.

Note that these 750 companies, which constitute less than 1 percent of all corporations, accounted for almost 25 percent of *all* employment in the U.S. in 1973.

Some American corporations have grown very large indeed and dominate certain sectors of our economy. So what? The question is a good one, and the answers to it will differ among those of us in the U.S. who are affected by corporations. Some will argue that the large size and dominance of corporations is necessary to organize production, to provide employment, and to produce goods and services efficiently. Others might use economic arguments pointing out that almost all large corporations are in concentrated industries and are thus likely to be theoretically deficient due to their economic power. (If it were a perfectly competitive economy, there would be a lot more companies and none would be so dominant.) Others might be less theoretical and say that corporations are only out to make a buck, have too much economic power, and sometimes do things to the detriment of society.

1. How do you feel about corporations?
2. Would you like to work for one? Why or why not?
3. How would you like to work for GM, where you would be one of almost one million employees?
4. Why are some American corporations so big?

The following selections are intended to reflect the flavor of the debate about this modern American institution that is so much a part of our economic system.

THE ROLE OF PROFITS IN THE CORPORATE SYSTEM

The Chairman of GM in 1974 put it succinctly: ". . . our future depends on the profitability of free enterprise." And he goes on, in the following selection, to argue that corporate profits and social progress go hand in hand.

The Role of Profits in the Corporate System

Not everyone in the U.S., as Richard C. Gerstenberg admits (and complains about), would agree with his conclusions. At one level, he is correct: given corporate concentration and economic power, we are dependent on corporate profitability for our jobs, our products, capital accumulation, technological change, and so on. However, there is another side to the coin; and that is what else is involved in the earning of profits by the corporate world. The following list of complaints of corporate wrongdoing and questionable behavior is a long one and *not* exhaustive: pollution for decades without cost to the corporation, exploitation of workers—minorities, women, children, aliens, etc., three-martini lunches charged off as business expenses, corporate bribery of foreign officials, illegal corporate political campaign contributions, food additives that destroy our health, disproportionate economic and political power, misleading advertising. And so on. All to make a buck. . . .

However, there is the other side to the story, from the perspective of the corporations themselves. The following selections are from two corporate leaders in the U.S.—John T. Connor, Chairman of Allied Chemical (and a former Secretary of Commerce), and Richard C. Gerstenberg, former Chairman of GM.

Profits Are For People...

As essential as profits are to the survival of our way of life, I know of few subjects so universally misunderstood. And a recent nationwide survey indicated that misconceptions about profits are increasing. Obviously, business is not getting the message through. The time is long overdue for some old-fashioned plain talk.

By putting profits to work, companies build new factories, modernize existing facilities, enable Americans to compete with manufacturers abroad and—most critical—create jobs for our people and opportunities for future generations. The company that doesn't make a consistent profit year in and year out withers and disappears, and so do the jobs of its employees.

Most experts agree that our economy will need at least $4 trillion in new capital during the next 10 years. Unless we plan to convert to socialism—and we certainly don't want to do that—a good part of it will have to come from corporate profits. Yet, contrary to what most Americans think, corporate profits have been shrinking. Today, the rate of profit by U.S. corporations is about 5% on sales, less than it was a decade ago. If profitability continues to shrink, we can look forward to an era of diminished economic growth and fewer jobs.

And when there is less profit to tax, our federal, state and local governments cannot obtain the revenues needed to carry out public programs, and the goals we have set for our society will be seriously threatened.

Our company—Allied Chemical—is a good example of profits at work. From 1970 to 1974, we earned net profits of $436 million and plowed back $258 million into business expansion and job-creating activities. That's about 62¢ of every dollar we earn. But this creative reinvestment of profits is only part of the story. Businesses that are profitable provide much of the support for public spending. During this same period, our company paid more than $382 million in taxes. Our employees paid taxes from their wages, and our stockholders paid taxes on their dividends. So, profits are continually recycled for everyone's benefit.

In newspapers and magazines during the past few months we have been talking publicly about corporate profits because we are convinced that an understanding of this subject by our people is vital to protect America's quality of life. We are pleased to report that the points of view conveyed in the series have drawn overwhelmingly favorable support from readers of these publications.

John T. Connor
Chairman

Allied Chemical

© 1976 Allied Chemical Corporation   P.O. Box 2245R, Morristown, New Jersey 07960.

THE PROFIT SYSTEM AND AMERICA'S GROWTH

RICHARD C. GERSTENBERG

WARREN, Mich.—As a nation we have launched ourselves on a most ambitious social agenda. We want to achieve even higher standards of education, health, and well-being for all our people. We want to abolish poverty. We want to rebuild our cities. We want to preserve and restore the beauty of our great resources: our land, our waters, and our skies. We want to give every American—of whatever color, religion, or background—an equal opportunity to become all he is capable of becoming. We aim for full employment, and even more—the full opportunity for everyone to participate in all that America has to offer.

These tasks are inherent and they are right—right for our country and for our time. But they are formidable, and sustained achievement will require a full committal of our moral and mental resources. Right now the hard fact is that the material resources essential to this task will simply not be available unless our economy stays healthy, and this is possible only if business remains profitable. Not one of our grand national goals—not one—can be accomplished unless business prospers. Profits, from which come all wages, taxes, and dividends, fuel the growth of our nation, and our future depends on the profitability of free enterprise.

Yet we are daily confronted with evidence that not enough Americans understand this. To them, the word "profit" has a grubby, selfish sound. The Vice President, Gerald Ford, noted recently, that many Americans consider a legitimate profit as a "rip-off, something that the bad guys steal from the good guys."

My concern today is heightened because so many of the most pressing issues confronting our nation are economic in nature. There are dollars-and-cents considerations, hard questions of profit and loss, in the energy situation, in housing, the deterioration of public transit, in the economic inequities between the races. Yet most of our people are ill-equipped to recognize the economics in these issues, much less to recommend the economic remedies. This lack of public understanding seriously threatens the continuation of our competitive private enterprise system.

In America, public understanding is fundamental. The public still have the ultimate power. Nothing endures—not on Capitol Hill, not in Detroit, and not anywhere in our nation—except by the will and vote of the American people, however unwieldy, however imperfect, however capricious the democratic system may seem. In the last analysis, the people determine what regulations will govern our economy and the conduct of our business.

Remember when we used to say, "Fifty million Frenchmen can't be wrong." Now 200 million Americans can be wrong on balance if a growing number of them believe, as they seem to, that profits are too high, that more regulation is needed, and that big business is getting too big.

The opinion polls present a grim arithmetic. According to a recent survey, only 3 percent of the American people think business as a whole is not making enough profit, while 35 percent—or more than ten times as many—think business is mak-

© 1974 by The New York Times Company. Reprinted by permission.

ing too much profit. The latest public estimate of the average manufacturer's after-tax profit is 28 cents on the dollar, whereas actually he earns in the neighborhood of a nickel.

For the first time since World War II, a majority of Americans no longer thinks that companies should be allowed to make all the profits they can. The trend instead shows a growing public support for a government ceiling on profits. And it may be significant that this study was taken before the energy situation was brought to the forefront of public attention by the oil embargo.

The public is wrong. Dangerously wrong, because the typical corporation is not the insensitive, unchanging inaccessible giant that so many picture it to be. On the contrary, it is one of the most flexible and responsive of man's creations. It takes on the character of its times.

We in General Motors know there is no conflict between corporate profits and social progress. We know that each is necessary for the other. We expect that the American corporation will continue to be one of the most effective and efficient assets to society that man has devised to achieve his social and economic goals.

In addition to our efforts at General Motors to earn a profit, and largely because of our success in those efforts, we are helping to create a better balanced system of transportation in this country and throughout the world; to explore space; to cleanse our air and water; to develop new materials and means of manufacture; to recruit, hire, and advance minority employees and women; to foster minority enterprise; to support education and a wide range of other community and civic programs. In short, to help do what must be done if our country and the world are to become all that we want them to be.

In such ways a corporation—and remember that there are more than 1.6 million of them in the country today—can help swell the tide of social and economic advancement for all the people of this country, even as they seek a profit.

We make these contributions today because the people—that is, the society we serve—expect us to. In that light, these contributions make good business sense, indeed, the times allow no alternative. And we will continue to make such contributions for as long as our business remains profitable.

In the minds of many people, these social contributions are no longer understood as ancillary to a corporation's basic purpose; they are judged to be basic—responsibilities whose performance is even more essential, or at least more praiseworthy, than providing value for the customer, wages for employees, and a fair return on the stockholder's investment.

In many popular trends of thought, basics have been turned upside down. A private corporation is being confused with a public, tax-supported agency. Profits are not applauded; they are scorned. Business is not encouraged; it is regulated. Enterprise is not rewarded; it is questioned and regarded with suspicion.

This is a road down which we dare not travel. It is a road darkened by a lack of public appreciation of what makes a person willing to risk his capital or to work harder than the next fellow. It is a road which leads to the dead end of excessive and irrational government regulation—and ultimately to the end of private enterprise.

This, I know is not what the American people want. But this is what we will all get unless more understanding is gained of the importance of profit. Somehow, we must convince people, more people than we have already, that a corporation—or any business for that matter—must first do well before it can do good. Better understanding of our institutions won't just happen. We must make it a goal, make it "happen."

---

5. What's your analysis of Gerstenberg's argument?
6. "The public is wrong." Do you agree or disagree?
7. "Profits are continually recycled for everyone's benefit." Do you agree? Why or why not?

FREE ENTERPRISE VS. THE GOVERNMENT

A perennial issue surrounding corporate power concerns the relationship between corporations and the federal government. Corporate officials constantly complain of governmental regulation of and interference with their business, e.g., occupational health and safety legislation, environmental protection legislation, etc. They argue that this restriction on their business hampers their initiative and independence in bringing the goods to the American consumer. Sometimes they even imply that continued regulation will dry up their profits, and hence their corporations. This view sees corporations and the government as adversaries.

Critics of this position argue that, if anything, regulation and governmental controls over business merely increase the costs of business—that the corporations then succeed, through market power, in passing on to consumers. Beyond that, a more fundamental criticism is offered. In most cases, governmental regulation is designed to *protect* corporations from competition. An often-cited example is the protection the railroad and trucking industries receive from the ICC. The government, rather than being an adversary, is an ally of business. Also, in many cases, the government has provided direct assistance such as loans to troubled corporations like Lockheed and the Penn Central. This symbiotic relationship has its roots in common goals shared by business and government such as economic growth, profits, employment, technological advance, and defense. Furthermore, it can be argued, corporations have substantial political power in the government through lobbying, indirect campaign contributions, and corporate representatives in all branches of the government.

Two lighthearted, but nevertheless serious, treatments of this issue follow.

Free Enterprise vs. the Government   203

The Modern Little Red Hen.

Once upon a time, there was a little red hen who scratched about the barnyard until she uncovered some grains of wheat. She called her neighbors and said, "If we plant this wheat, we shall have bread to eat. Who will help me plant it?"

"Not I," said the cow.
"Not I," said the duck.
"Not I," said the pig.
"Not I," said the goose.

"Then I will," said the little red hen. And she did. The wheat grew tall and ripened into golden grain. "Who will help me reap my wheat?" asked the little red hen.

"Not I," said the duck.
"Out of my classification," said the pig.
"I'd lose my seniority," said the cow.
"I'd lose my unemployment compensation," said the goose.

"Then I will," said the little red hen, and she did.

At last it came time to bake the bread. "Who will help me bake the bread?" asked the little red hen.

"That would be overtime for me," said the cow.
"I'd lose my welfare benefits," said the duck.
"I'm a dropout and never learned how," said the pig.
"If I'm to be the only helper, that's discrimination," said the goose.

"Then I will," said the little red hen.

She baked five loaves and held them up for her neighbors to see.

They all wanted some and, in fact, demanded a share. But the little red hen said, "No, I can eat the five loaves myself."

"Excess profits!" cried the cow.
"Capitalist leech!" screamed the duck.
"I demand equal rights!" yelled the goose.

And the pig just grunted. And they painted "unfair" picket signs and marched round and round the little red hen, shouting obscenities.

When the government agent came, he said to the little red hen, "You must not be greedy."

"But I earned the bread," said the little red hen.

"Exactly," said the agent. "That is the wonderful free enterprise system. Anyone in the barnyard can earn as much as he wants. But under our modern government regulations, the productive workers must divide their product with the idle."

And they lived happily ever after, including the little red hen, who smiled and clucked, "I am grateful. I am grateful."

But her neighbors wondered why she never again baked any more bread.

At the conclusion of the required business of the 1975 Pennwalt Annual Meeting, Chairman and President William P. Drake, commenting on the state of the company in today's economy, read this, his own adaptation of a modern version of the well-known fable of The Little Red Hen.

For 125 years we've been making things people need – including profits.

PENNWALT
CORPORATION
Three Parkway, Philadelphia, Pa. 19102
Chemicals • Health Products • Specialized Equipment

---

8. Do you think Mr. Drake has engaged in hyperbole? Why? Why not? What is his point?

THE FABLE, AMENDED
This is what *really* happened to the Little Red Hen
BRUCE R. MOODY

Vice President in Charge of Corporate Mythology
Pennwalt Corporation
Three Parkway
Philadelphia, PA 19102

Dear Sir (or Madam):

    The advertisement entitled "The *Modern* Little Red Hen" was most entertaining, but certain documents that have recently come into my possession suggest certain inaccuracies. Just for the record, here's what really happened.
    Once upon a time there was a little red hen who got a tip from a friendly rat that there was a sizable quantity of wheat in a grain elevator in New Orleans that had been illegally diverted from its rightful owners and thus could be had for a song.
    Thanks to a family trust set up by Grandfather rooster, which provided the little red hen with bundles of tax-free income, she was able to take such a flyer with ease, and so she did.
    "Now that I own all this grain," she said, "what should I do with it?"
    "I happen to know of a bakery that is having tax problems," answered a duck who made a nice living advising the little red hen and other well-to-do animals on such matters. "With a little nudge from my friends in Washington I can see that the IRS puts the screws to them and thus soften them up for a deal."
    "Dandy!" cried the little red hen, tossing half a dozen tons of grain to the duck. And half an hour and three phone calls later, the thing was done.
    When the grain had been milled and baked into bread, all the animals crowded around to see what it would taste like. The little red hen took the first bite.
    "Goodness," she coughed, "this is the strangest-tasting bread I ever ate. What could be wrong with it?"
    "It's moldy," said a mouse, who was an expert in such matters. "You got stuck with a shipload of moldy grain."
    "But what do I do now?" wailed the little red hen.
    Once again, it was the duck who had the answer. "Very simple," he winked, "just dose the next batch with a little diflourinated oxylactidaze. It doesn't exactly stop mold, but it does paralyze the taste buds so the customer doesn't know what he's eating."
    Now the cow spoke up for the first time. "But wasn't I reading that diflourinated oxylactidaze makes people's hair fall out?"
    "Never mind," said the duck, "leave everything to me."
    But for good measure, it was decided to mount a million-dollar advertising

---

Reprinted by permission from *The Progressive*, 408 West Gorham Street, Madison, Wisconsin 53703. Copyright © 1976, The Progressive, Inc.

campaign pointing out that the new bread was not only tasty and nutritious, but was also an effective depilatory. And the sales curves went off the chart.

Now it so happens that about this time the animals were experiencing great financial distress, largely because of the elaborate and costly missile system that had been set up around the barnyard to guard against chicken hawks. A few of the more intelligent animals had argued that since chicken hawks attack only chickens, it was unfair to make the pigs, cows, and horses pay for this system. But the duck had masterminded an expensive but effective campaign to replace the term "chicken hawk" with the term "animal hawk," a huge and rapacious creature that carried off animals as big as a horse and ate them. This effectively silenced the grumblers, who no longer dared open their mouths for fear of being called anti-animal.

But the money problem still existed, and was in fact made worse because the little red hen, who had insisted upon the missiles in the first place, did not, as was mentioned earlier, pay any taxes at all.

"I'm getting awfully hungry," said the pig. "Remember how you used to creep into my pen to sleep when you got cold?"

"I'm starved," said the goose. "Remember how I used to sit on your eggs when you went shopping?"

"Me too," said the horse. "Remember how I used to carry you around on my back when you were a little baby chick?"

"Buzz off!" cried the little red hen. "You're not going to sponge off of me! If you want bread, steal your own grain, grab your own bakery, and bribe your own inspectors. You're nothing but a bunch of cheats and parasites!"

And so saying, she sat down to count her bags of grain for the hundredth time, breathing thanks that she still lived under a system in which diligence and enterprise are justly rewarded.

Moral: So bemused and bewildered is the public at large by tax-free corporate advertising, public relations experts, lobbyists, and bought politicians that an accurate account of the facts seems bizarre, tendentious, and even subversive.

You have my permission to make use of the fable as amended in any way you see fit.

Sincerely,
Bruce R. Moody

---

9. Who wins? Mr. Drake or Mr. Moody? What is Moody's point?

AMERICAN CORPORATIONS GO GLOBAL

No treatment of the modern American corporation would be complete without some reference to one of the dominant corporate trends in the post-World War II period. This is the increasing multinationalization of American corporations. We will explore this issue in some more detail in Part V on International Economics.

The piece that follows serves as an introduction to the issues and problems raised by the emergence of the multinational corporation.

A modern multinational corporation. (Photograph by Tom Riddell.)

COPING WITH THE NATION-STATE: MULTINATIONALS AT BAY

GURNEY BRECKENFELD

The old law of physics that every action produces an equal and opposite reaction has lately seemed to apply with sardonic irony to multinational corporations. Last year that eloquent defender of the American position, Daniel P. Moynihan, now U.S. ambassador to the United Nations, singled out the multinational corporation as an example of the "enormous recent achievements" in international liberalism. "Combining modern management with liberal trade policies," he declared, "it is arguably the most creative international institution of the 20th century." That proposition once met with little argument. Five years ago multinationals, about half of them American, were expanding lustily across most non-Communist parts of the world, increasing their sales, profits, and penetration of foreign markets so rapidly that they already were producing about a sixth of the world's goods and services. Direct foreign investment, mainly and increasingly by multinationals, had already replaced trade as the most important ingredient of international economics. Some respectable authorities calculated that 300 giant companies might account for half the world's economic activity well before the end of the century.

© Saturday Review, 1976. All rights reserved.

Today the multinationals are bigger than ever but are under attack at home and abroad—their image tarnished, their prospects imperiled, their leaders dismayed. Consumer groups, the media, and academia are increasingly critical. Organized labor in the United States is demanding legislation to prevent the multinationals from "exporting jobs." Congress has taken away a few of their alleged tax advantages and may hit them with severe, even crippling, new restrictions. Many foreign governments are imposing tough new conditions on their operations, cutting into their profits and incentive to invest. The United Nations is moving on several fronts toward measures that may impede the future growth of multinationals. And the disclosures of bribery and political manipulations, which have seriously damaged their public reputation, are also fanning demands for "codes of conduct" that may impose onerous and perhaps unnecessary burdens. . . .

Stuart Leeds.

FOGGY STATISTICS

For a perspective on the pros and cons of the intensifying debate about multinational enterprises, it helps to begin by looking at some economic fundamentals. U.S. investment in factories and similar facilities abroad, most of it by big multinational concerns, has now reached the impressive total of $110 billion, according to treasury officials. That is nearly five times the foreign direct investment in the United States, and it brought the nation an equally impressive $17.6 billion income in 1974.

Until recently, U.S.-based multinationals had been expanding their overseas investment at the rate of about 10 percent a year. Investment abroad—$7.3 billion last year—is still rising, but the pace has slowed. Some bankers find the decline in American investment in Europe especially marked, and a study conducted last summer by the Department of Commerce provides supporting evidence. After surveying some 350 American companies and their 5000 majority-owned foreign affiliates, the department reported that outlays for property, plant, and equipment abroad would increase by only 4 percent in 1975, a huge drop from the 25 percent rise the year before. In short, the global row about global companies is reaching a crescendo as their expansion rate wanes.

Changing political and economic circumstances underlie the slowdown. In the Fifties U.S. companies pushed abroad to get around high tariffs and other barriers to American exports. In the Sixties they did so to cut production costs with cheaper labor. At the same time, an overvalued dollar made it cheap to buy assets abroad, the world economy was expanding at a brisk pace, prices were stable, and most foreign countries were quite receptive toward U.S. private companies. Not one of those conditions prevails today. Dollar devaluations have made our exports more competitive in world markets, lessening the need to produce overseas. Labor costs are rising faster abroad, especially in Europe, so that it is more attractive to expand factories at home.

These changes, in turn, have set others in motion. As U.S. exports boom, Japanese and European multinational companies feel the effects in their own foreign sales. So multinationals from all three continents are shifting more and more production into the Third World, once chiefly a source of raw materials and domestic exports....

HOW THINGS FELL APART

With hindsight, it is now clear that the great turning point for the fortunes of the multinationals came in 1971, the year when the Organization of Petroleum-Exporting Countries (OPEC) first showed that it could impose its own terms for oil on industrialized Western nations of far greater economic and military strength. In the wake of that confrontation, which was followed by an extortionate price increase in 1973 and the outright nationalization of most Western oil company holdings in OPEC countries, other underdeveloped nations felt emboldened to impose tougher rules and higher taxes on foreign enterprises.

Another 1971 event, a book tellingly titled *Sovereignty at Bay* by Harvard Prof. Raymond Vernon, sounded a central theme, which critics of multinationals have been embellishing ever since. Vernon argued that "sovereign states are feeling naked." He contended that the great size, the financial strength, and the superior technology and organization of vast international enterprises set them beyond the effective control of individual nation-states, which needed their jobs and money too much to resist whatever came along in the bargain.

By now, a whole body of literature has appeared about multinational companies; some of it is factual, much of it a beguiling mixture of insight and fantasy. The American public is entitled to feel confused by the polemics, for many of the issues do not yield easily to simplification or sweeping generalization. In this cascade of words, the book with the mightiest impact is *Global Reach*, by political scientist Richard J. Barnet and economist Ronald E. Müller....

The authors' thesis is that "the structural transformation of the world economy through the globalization of Big Business is undermining the power of the nation-state to maintain economic and political stability within its territory." However plausible, that theory itself bestirs controversy. For it overlooks the powers that all governments possess. Idaho Democrat Frank Church, chairman of the Senate subcommittee that has been investigating multinational corporations, once put the matter in perspective. Noting that the spread of multinationals had helped to promote a "new nationalism" among the proliferating new nations of the post-World War II era, he remarked that a witness had likened the "developing confrontation" between the two groups to the dispute eight centuries ago between King Henry II and Thomas a Becket, archbishop of Canterbury—a contest that ended with murder in the cathedral. "It is possible that murder could occur again," said Church, "this time the murder of the multinationals. For despite their enormous growth and wealth it is still an unequal contest. Armies march for governments, whether large or small, and each of these governments possesses, in its sovereign right, the power to tax, to restrict, to discriminate against, or to nationalize foreign-owned businesses, or indeed to confiscate their properties."

No armies have recently marched against a multinational company, but a recent U.N. study found that nationalizations by developing countries doubled from an average of 45 a year during the Sixties to 93 annually in the Seventies. And host countries, especially in Latin America, have become increasingly successful at extracting benefits for their economies from foreign investors. Mexico, for example, is forcing foreign-based automakers to export more of their Mexican output and will eventually require them to sell as much abroad as in the local market. Colombia is placing branches of foreign banks under majority Colombian control. Iran is insisting that many foreign-based industrial companies sell 49 percent of their already limited equity to employees or to the general public.

Industrially advanced countries are also demanding a bigger share of profits, jobs, technology, and management in their dealings with multinationals. Several European nations, including even West Germany, which has had a particularly liberal attitude toward foreign investment, are starting to look closely at foreign investments for the national benefits involved. Last year Canada imposed a set of formal criteria on foreign-controlled companies, including a requirement that a majority of their boards of directors be composed of Canadians. The province of Saskatchewan decided to nationalize its huge potash-mining industry; of the 12 companies affected, seven are American or American-controlled.

FIVE ISSUES, PRO AND CON

In the debate about multinationals, at least five major questions deserve close scrutiny:

(1) *Are multinational companies exporting U.S. jobs?*

PRO: thousands of jobs in such industries as apparel, radios, and bicycles have been lost to American workers because U.S. companies have shifted manufacturing or the production of component parts to such places as Taiwan, Singapore, or Korea, where labor costs are far lower. Between 1966 and 1969, 500,000 U.S. jobs were exported by such arrangements, says the AFL-CIO.

CON: the charges are correct in general but misrepresent the total situation. When companies moved production abroad, the usual alternative was to lose sales—perhaps even in the domestic market—to foreign competitors. Says Reginald Jones, the chairman of General Electric: "As the last company in the United States to give up the manufacture of radios, we know exactly how tough the foreign competition has been." Moreover, U.S. multinationals export so much to their overseas affiliates that the net effect is that more jobs are created than are lost (but not necessarily in the same occupations or cities). Robert S. Stobaugh, professor of business administration at Harvard Business School, found in a recent study "using every bit of information available" that on balance U.S. corporate operations abroad add 700,000 jobs to the domestic economy and add an income of $7 billion a year to the nation's balance of payments. Some other studies have put the figures much higher.

(2) *Do multinationals create "export platforms" abroad to ship back cheaply made goods to the United States?*

PRO: one need only consider where TV sets and radios are being made nowadays. Companies shift manufacturing overseas to exploit cheap labor, to circumvent antipollution laws, and to avoid taxes.

CON: again, the balance runs in the other direction. Less than 10 percent of the products manufactured by overseas affiliates of U.S. companies are imported into the United States. But nearly a third of all U.S.-manufactured exports go to foreign affiliates of American companies. The Department of Commerce, in its latest study of the matter, found that in 1972 majority-owned foreign affiliates of American companies sold 72 percent of their goods and services in the country where they were produced. Another 22 percent of their sales went to other foreign countries; only 7 percent was exported to the United States, an increase from 6 percent in 1966.

(3) *Are multinationals the villains of currency crises?*

PRO: companies have shifted "hot money" out of weak currencies and into strong ones in such massive amounts that past efforts to stabilize the dollar were weakened. By so doing, it has been argued by Andrew Biemiller, the AFL-CIO's chief lobbyist, that "corporations and banks put profits ahead of patriotism." Sometimes they do so to protect their holdings against anticipated exchange-rate changes and sometimes to engage in outright speculation.

CON: since the major currencies have been "floating"—that is, allowed by governments to fluctuate in value day by day in the international money market—the complaint is partly moot. After a long study, the U.S. Tariff Commission concluded in 1973 that while multinationals do have the "capacity for disruptive movements" of funds, few of them use it. The commission found that "only a small fraction" of corporate treasurers and bank vice-presidents speculate in currencies. (When ITT tried to hedge against currency fluctuations in 1974, it miscalculated and lost more than $25 million.) The real cause of currency crises, as research economist Edward M. Bernstein told a U.N. inquiry, was the failure of governments to raise or lower the value of their currencies until long after it became clear to the world's financial experts that they must do so.

Stuart Leeds.

(4) Do multinationals exploit the economies of underdeveloped countries?

PRO: critics, mostly from academia, complain that even when multinational companies have accelerated economic development, as, for instance, in Brazil and (in the late Sixties) Pakistan, the poor remain as poor as ever. Sometimes the multinationals preempt scarce local resources. Barnet and Müller contend that between 1957 and 1965 U.S.-based companies financed more than four-fifths of their operations in Latin America with local capital or reinvested earnings.

CON: governments, not multinational corporations, set the policies that determine whether all classes in a given country will share in economic advances. The poor of most newly rich Arab oildoms have received little of much of their countries' larger slice of the petroleum pie. Peru has been busy expropriating U.S. subsidiaries in the name of controlling its own economy, but there has been no transformation of class structure or the power of the elite. It is probable that some siphoning off of local capital did occur, though host governments could have prevented it at the time. In any case, it is becoming much more difficult to do so.

(5) Do multinationals evade taxes abroad by rigging prices?

PRO: in buying or selling goods within the confines of a company, but across national borders, companies manipulate prices so that they can avoid taxable profits in high-tax countries and inflate profits in low-tax countries. According to a U.N. study, such intracorporate trade within multinational companies accounts for nearly a quarter of the world's foreign trade in goods. It is concentrated in a few industries, including chemicals and autos. Some studies contend that overpricing in underdeveloped countries has ranged from 30 percent to 8,000 percent; underpricing, from 40 percent to 60 percent.

CON: some of this activity undoubtedly does, or at least did, go on. But most big companies require "arm's length" pricing of sales between subsidiaries or divisions. In the United States and Europe, tax collectors are zealous about auditing corporate books to prevent such practices. Apparently few executives would object if governments reached an international agreement setting uniform rules for tax purposes on all transfer pricing.

ZEROING IN ON BRIBERY

The issue that may really cause trouble for U.S. companies, and not just for multinationals, is bribery and political manipulation. Companies can't condone the practice. Responsible executives are right to insist that it shouldn't happen. Many companies insist that they have strict rules prohibiting it. Oddly, Americans seem much more upset over such ethical problems than over the economic nitty-gritty that concerns rulers and power elites abroad. . . .

The sequence of revelations dates all the way back to March 1972, when columnist Jack Anderson exposed U.S. government and corporate intervention by ITT in Chilean elections. Chile asked for a U.N. investigation, thus setting in motion the chain of events that has created wide demand at home, abroad, and in several international forums for stricter regulation of multinationals. The United Nations named a 20-member Group of Eminent Persons to make a far-reaching inquiry into the activities of multinational companies. Its report, rendered in June 1974, was largely critical. The only two Americans on the panel, Sen. Jacob Javits, a New York Republican, and J. Irwin Miller, chairman of Cummins Engine Company, filed dissenting opinions.

Without waiting for that report, the U.N. General Assembly in April 1974 adopted its controversially one-sided proposal calling for a "new international economic order." Among many other things, it demanded "regulation and supervision of the activities of transnational corporations" but said nothing about whether such controls should be non-discriminatory or conform to the norms of international law. (The resolution also asserted all states' rights to nationalize economic activities without mentioning any duty to pay compensation.)

In December 1974 the United Nations went still farther in adopting, by a vote of 120 to 6 in the General Assembly, a Charter of Economic Rights and Duties of States. Article 2 provides that if a country expropriates a foreign-owned company, any disagreements about the compensation shall be settled "under domestic law of the nationalizing country" and "by its tribunals." Fortunately for the future of international investment, the charter is only a recommendatory resolution, lacking the force of law. Otherwise, it might preclude an investor and a foreign state from effectively contracting in advance to submit disputes to international arbitration. And it certainly would prevent companies from suing in courts of another country, as Kennecott Copper and British Petroleum did in European courts after expropriations in Chile and Libya. State Department officials have labeled the charter "a step backward."

Considering the composition of the United Nations, dominated by an irresponsible majority of anti-Western Third World dictatorships, U.S. officials never had much chance of deflecting its attack. Anticipating that the United Nations would write just such an unfair, one-sided "code of conduct" as it seems about to do, the United States supported a similar effort by the Organization for Economic Cooperation and Development. Since the OECD's 24 member states are drawn largely from Europe, American strategists figured that the result would be more evenhanded and might even help sway the United Nations toward a more moderate stand. The tactic backfired. A draft code issued last fall by the OECD is "much worse than anything we contemplated," says one U.S. source close to the situation. The code proposed, among other things, that companies be required to divulge confidential financial data about their operations and taxes, country by country. The proposal would be, as one pained businessman puts it, "an open invitation to the world's tax collectors to raise taxes everywhere."

Worst of all, although the proposed code would place tough restrictions on private multinational corporations, it is silent about government-owned enterprises and private national enterprises. With strong support from the business community, the United States is pressing for a parallel code of conduct for governments in dealing with multinational companies.

SORTING OUT THE ISSUES

In their fight to keep the United Nations and foreign countries from hamstringing multinational companies, U.S. businessmen have found an ally in Secretary of State Henry Kissinger. Addressing the U.N. General Assembly last fall, he praised multinational companies as "one of the most effective engines of development" and added that "the controversy over their role and conduct is itself an obstacle to development."

Somewhat similar views come from the Manhattan-based National Foreign Trade Council, a private, non-profit, non-partisan business association. "The major problem today," said the council in a policy declaration last November, "is not how to further restrict or leash the multinational enterprise but . . . how to encourage [it] to continue performing its essential international economic role."

A large element of socialist philosophy runs through the efforts to curb the multinational corporation. Jacques G. Maisonrouge, chairman of IBM World Trade Corporation, recently defined the struggle as "the latest manifestation of the long tug-of-war between the private and collective control of property." Many other businessmen would agree, but the conflict is not quite that simple.

The fragility of the multinationals' arrangements for doing business abroad has legal underpinnings derived from the Napoleonic code, which holds that if changing circumstances make a contract impracticable for either party it should be revised. (In contrast, the U.S. Constitution explicitly prohibits states from passing any law "impairing the obligation of contracts.") The French doctrine has given rise to the notion that a sovereign state can override all commercial commitments. British economist Paul Frankel once observed that "this has downgraded international intercourse to the level of the jungle." In any case, the "new economic order" means that nowhere in the world is private foreign investment safe from the xenophobic pressures of nationalism. What began in oil is spreading throughout the world.

The recent surge of nationalistic fervor contains other seeds of evil. It is precisely because multinational companies can, and do, rise above the parochial interests of sovereign states that we ought to applaud their growth in the interests of world prosperity and, ultimately, abiding peace. Northcote Parkinson, the British historian, put the case well in his book *Big Business*:

> *If we are to save our civilization from tragedy, it will be through applying to politics the trained intelligence and methodical thought that we have already applied to science and technology. But even that will not be enough if we fail to apply the lessons of big business: the lessons of organization and control and, above all, of the international approach. . . . The whole idea of nationality rests upon divergent interests and mutual suspicion, sharply drawn frontiers, and ill-concealed fear. Set quite apart from the blood-stained arena of nationalism is the new world of big business, a world where the jealousies of the nation-states are actually forgotten. If we are to have a prosperous future, we shall owe it to men who have already learned how to cooperate and see the world as one.*

The trouble with Professor Parkinson's vision of a world stripped of quarreling nation-states—many with selfish oligarchical elites and dictatorial rulers—is that nobody knows how to get from here to there. That is, to be sure, a depressing prospect. For nation-states and the fervid nationalism that they all too often inspire are surely one of the worst conceivable arrangements for the governance of a small planet. Yet, as Professor Vernon points out, the nation-state "is the only legitimate political process we've got, so the people of the world use it to do things for themselves. It's a terrible system, but everything else is worse." The practical probability is that both multinational corporations and nation-states are going to be around for quite a long time to come, and the frictions between the two will continue, if not increase.

Many businessmen insist that the great growth of multinational companies is ending, if not already over. However, an upturn in global prosperity could give such predictions a short life span. It does seem likely that multinationals and governments will be able to compose their differences sooner in industrial countries than in the Third World, if only because nationhood is more important to the elite of underdeveloped countries than it is in industrial states. From today's perspective, multinational companies and the Third World are moving on a collision course that might, at the extreme, simply dry up much foreign investment. Still, as executive vice-president Wylie Robson of Eastman Kodak observes, "The more time that elapses, the more chance for cooling off." The economic interdependence of the world's 140 nations rises year by year. The great question is whether enough politicians and rulers will recognize the mutual benefits of cooperation before the increasingly global economy suffers serious damage.

TABLE 13.4 The Top 15 Multinational Companies

Company	Total 1971 Sales ($ Billions)	Foreign Sales as a Percentage of Total	Number of Countries in Which Subsidiaries Are Located
General Motors	28.3	19	21
Exxon	18.7	50	25
Ford	16.4	26	30
Royal Dutch/Shell	12.7	79	43
General Electric	9.4	16	32
IBM	8.3	39	80
Mobil Oil	8.2	45	62
Chrysler	8.0	24	26
Texaco	7.5	40	30
Unilever	7.5	80	31
ITT	7.3	42	40
Gulf Oil	5.9	45	61
British Petroleum	5.2	88	52
Philips Gloulampenfabrieken	5.2	N.A.	29
Standard Oil (California)	5.1	45	26

Source: "The U.N. Sizes Up the Global Giants," *Business Week*, p. 26, August 18, 1973.

10. Are you pro or con? Why? (What is Breckenfeld's position on MNC's?)

CONCLUSION

Much of the analysis in Part III on Microeconomics is directly derived from classical and neoclassical economics. In the realm of the market and the firm, its analysis is helpful, although slightly qualified by the historical emergence of noncompetitive market structures and the corporation. We are no longer in the ideal and competitive world of Adam Smith. However, supply-and-demand analysis can still help us in understanding how markets work to determine prices and allocate resources. And the focus of microeconomics on the firm has caused economists to pay increasing attention to the modern corporation.

In the realm of the total economy, though, classical theory has had more severe problems. It contended that the market system would produce growth and full employment. However, this theoretical result conflicted with historical experience. As a result, Keynesian theory emerged to provide an alternative understanding of the macroeconomy. It is this theory which we will explore in Part IV on Macroeconomics.

KEY CONCEPTS

the corporation
economic concentration
the role of profits

laissez-faire vs. government regulation
the free enterprise system
multinational corporations

REVIEW QUESTIONS

1. Why is the corporation a dominant institution in the American economic system?

2. Is the relationship between big business and big government adversarial? or symbiotic?

3. Why have corporations gone global? What are some of the implications of this trend?

SUGGESTED READINGS

Council on Economic Priorities, 1974. *Guide to Corporations: A Social Perspective*, Swallow. Essays on the role of the corporation in American society and profiles of individual corporations.

Fletcher Knebel, 1975. *The Bottom Line,* Pocket Books. A novel on the modern corporation.

One of the topics we have not covered in our treatment of microeconomics is labor economics and labor unions. For those interested in this subject, we recommend William H. Miernyk, *The Economics of Labor and Collective Bargaining*, D. C. Heath, 1973, for an orthodox treatment of the subject, and Harry Braverman, *Labor and Monopoly Capital*, Monthly Review Press, 1974, for a Marxist analysis.

MACROECONOMICS
PART IV

As we learned in Part III, *microeconomics* analyzes the behavior of consumers and firms in our economic system. We focused on topics such as consumer behavior, the behavior of markets, the different types of market structures, efficiency, scarcity, and last, the nature of the modern corporation.

We will now supplement this microeconomic theory with macroeconomic theory and policy. What is macroeconomics and what does it attempt to explain? *Macroeconomics* is the body of economic theory that attempts to analyze the behavior and performance of the whole economy. It describes and explains the dynamics of the institutional and governmental framework of our economic system by focusing on *the total or aggregate performance* of the economy. This usually begins with an exposition of income-expenditures theory. This theory explains the performance of the economy in terms of *employment, income, output,* and *price levels.* A macroeconomic perspective further requires that we explore the relationship between the monetary system and the aggregate performance of the whole economy. We can then utilize our understanding of *monetary theory and policy* and the role of governmental *fiscal policy* (government spending and taxation) to focus on how best to achieve the major *macroeconomic goals of full employment, economic growth, and price stability.*

Chapter 14 identifies and describes some of our most important macroeconomic issues and problems. The appendix to Chapter 14 treats the method of calculating Gross National Product (National Income Accounting). Chapter 15, explores the theoretical roots of modern macroeconomics. Chapter 16 describes the Keynesian model using graphical analysis and simple algebraic formulas. Chapter 17 focuses on the role of government in making fiscal policy. Chapter 18 introduces the concept of money, its role and its institutions, in the macroeconomy. Chapter 19 explores the major macro problems we face today—unemployment, inflation, and declining economic growth. This last chapter also integrates, summarizes, and critically reflects on the past and present efficacy of contemporary macroeconomics in the United States. (In addition, Chapter 24, following a treatment of International Economics in Part V, presents a broadened consideration and critique of modern macroeconomic theory and policy.)

MACROECONOMICS: ISSUES AND PROBLEMS

CHAPTER 14

GOALS OF THE UNITED STATES ECONOMY

In the early 1950s the U.S. government accepted as its responsibility three basic macroeconomic goals. These were (1) maximum employment, (2) economic growth, and (3) price stability. The government was expected to utilize economic theory to analyze the economy and to apply macroeconomic policy to produce the desired results. The primary macro tools are monetary and fiscal policy. Let's examine each of these separately.

The government through the Federal Reserve System manages, coordinates, and controls the monetary system of the U.S. economy. Proper management of this system makes available the quantity of money necessary for desired economic growth at interest rates capable of inducing the desired levels of investment and spending. In this way, *monetary policy* tools administered by the Federal Reserve System manage the money system to promote the desired economic performance. Thus monetary policy is used to achieve and promote economic growth, maximum employment, and price stability.

Fiscal policy is administered by the executive and legislative branches of government and is combined and coordinated with monetary policy to achieve the same desired objectives. With fiscal policy, the government manipulates government expenditures and taxation to attain the basic macroeconomic objectives.

This briefly is the essence of contemporary macroeconomic policy as it has developed over the last score of years. There are several important issues and problems associated with this theory and policy. We shall examine a few of these in this chapter.

PROBLEMS AND ISSUES—FROM THE 1930s TO THE 1970s

Economic Growth

One of the primary features of the Keynesian macro model is the emphasis on *economic growth*. We have as a consequence adopted a general attitude as a nation that economic growth is not only necessary and good but more and more growth is better. Economic growth, after all, creates employment, income, and greater output of goods and services. In our preoccupation with economic growth we have developed very sophisticated tools by which we measure the performance of the economy and its annual rate of real economic growth. By using a method of National Income Accounting (see the appendix to this chapter), we have been able to calculate and monitor the rates of growth of *Gross National Product*—the total dollar value of all goods and services produced in a given year. Our obsession with economic growth is somewhat symbolized by a "GNP clock," built by the Nixon administration in the early 1970s at a cost of one million dollars, that in early 1978 ticked off $2 trillion—officially registering the fact that the U.S. has the world's largest GNP.

In recent years, the basic assumptions concerning economic growth have been challenged by critics. Some have argued that more growth does not necessarily mean that our standard of living has improved. Others charge that GNP as a statistical measurement is becoming more and more meaningless. It can as a measure quantify the performance of the economy, but it does not reflect nor include the "qualitative" dimension that considers the question "What is the real societal value and/or cost of increased GNP growth?" Much of this criticism stems from a consideration of the environmental aspects of increasing economic growth. A growing ecological awareness in the context of our emergent energy crisis has made us examine our values, attitudes, goals, and economic assumptions more intensely. The current economic growth controversy has also raised the critical issues of the distribution of income in the U.S. If economic growth increases from year to year, does this mean that the increased output is being distributed more equally or equitably? Empirical data supports the claim that despite the tremendous increases in GNP since World War II, the distribution of income in the U.S. has not changed significantly. In addition, this period of unprecedented economic growth has not evolved in a stable pattern. We have experienced six major recessions in this time period. The instability characterized by the fluctuations of the business cycle has been a primary characteristic of the postwar era.

The following article by Barbara Miner, from the radical publication, *The Guardian*, highlights some of the remaining weakness in an economy that has, through economic growth, attained one of the highest average standards of living in the world. Her focus is upon the relationship between poverty and children's lives.

POVERTY, DEPRIVATION, HAUNT MILLIONS OF KIDS

BARBARA MINER

What is the most serious threat to the well-being of this country's most valuable resource—its children?

According to a recent report released by the Carnegie Council on Children, it is not the child molester walking the street, the parent who lashes out in anger and batters children or even the breakdown of an educational system that leaves millions of high school graduates functionally illiterate.

Reprinted by permission of The Guardian. The Guardian, November 9, 1977.

At issue is something far more basic, according to the council: jobs for their parents at a living wage.

"The single most important factor that stacks the deck against tens of millions of American children is poverty," states the council report, titled, "All Our Children."

"We estimate that a quarter to a third of all American children are born into families with financial strains so great that their children will suffer basic deprivations.

"Of all age groups in America, children are the most likely to be poor," the report continues. "In 1974, more than 17 million children were living below our [poverty] figure."

The council's report, authored by Kenneth Keniston, chairman of the council and professor of human development at the Massachusetts Institute of Technology, is the result of a five-year, 221-page study by council members. It offers a plethora of facts on the traps of poverty: the one-fifth of poor and minority children who have not seen a doctor in two years although they are four times as likely to need medical help than children from families with a decent income; the thousands of children removed from their homes and institutionalized "based on the parents' inability to provide a child with necessities due to poverty"; poor children who are five times less likely to attend college as well-off children.

And though the council doesn't provide the individual cases that transform its statistics into concrete human terms, such cases are not hard to find. Take the following examples:

In Chicago, Dwight Battles, 25, was unemployed. He was unable to keep up with the bills and the lights and gas were turned off. His two children, Stephanie, 3, and Audrey, 2, became nervous, hungry and upset. "They started crying. For two days they cried for something to eat," reported the Chicago Daily Defender, the city's black newspaper.

Finally, a drunken Battles allegedly beat the two young girls to death in an effort to stop their crying. He was charged with murder.

In Harlem, New York City, thousands of young children have turned to drug running to supplement the meager incomes of their families. "I was spending my money to help my family," said Janet P., who was arrested when she was 15 for selling drugs. "I started cutting dope on the kitchen table of my family's apartment when I was 13.

"Mom didn't care if I ever went back to school so long as I brought in the money," Janet explained. "I got her a washing machine, bought clothes for my sisters and brothers."

In Philadelphia, Thomas Pankowitz, 54, attempted to care for his 14-year-old daughter Helena. Stricken with cerebral palsy, she cannot walk, talk, or care for herself.

On Oct. 26, authorities found a malnourished Helena on a urine-soaked mattress in Pankowitz' living room. She weighed only 24½ pounds. Pankowitz was arrested and charged with child neglect.

"He [Pankowitz] would never do anything intentional to hurt her," said Joann Sireci, a neighbor. "It's just that none [of the family] seemed to know how to take care of her."

In all these cases, a typical reaction would be to blame the parents—a reaction strongly attacked by the council.

"Blaming parents and giving them advice both spring from the assumption that the problems of individuals can be solved by the individuals who have the problems," the council's report states.

"Families are not now, nor were they ever, the self-sufficient building blocks of society, exclusively responsible, praise-worthy and blamable for their own destiny," the report continues. "They are deeply influenced by broad social and economic forces over which they have little control."

Although blaming the victim and lack of decent-paying jobs are two of the major themes of the report, there is a third, equally important point stressed by the council: in all areas, the crisis of poverty hits hardest at minority children.

"Here the statistics become truly chilling," the report warns. "Children in black families are four times more likely to be poor than white children; native American children suffer even more terrible odds. In large metropolitan areas and in the rural South, the infant mortality rate for minority children is almost double that of whites. Nutritional deficiencies are over three times more common among black children (32.7 percent overall) than among white children. Native American children are ten times more likely to be placed in foster care than other children. Where other types of data are available, they show the same trends."

And what of education, the often-cited panacea for minorities? While important, the council cautions against viewing this as the overall solution, citing statistics that "Blacks with the same education consistently earn far less than whites."

Children do not read these statistics, the council explains, "but they don't have to. The most crucial facts for them are daily experience. And when daily experience shows a black, Mexican-American, Puerto Rican or native American child that the adults with whom he lives, no matter how capable, have difficulty in gaining education and work, what can he conclude about his own future? Why should he remember what he learns in school when the process has no real use for him? Concepts like 'unequal access,' 'job discrimination,' and 'promotion ceilings' filter down to become the stuff of daily life for children who have never heard the abstract terms."

1. What is your immediate reaction to this article? Do you think that this analysis is valid? What was your own experience as a child?

Unemployment

The attainment of maximum employment has been one of our nation's primary macro goals since the *Employment Act of 1946*. Thus far, however, we have come close to this objective only during periods of war. We have not been able to achieve full employment in peacetime. One great problem associated with *unemployment* is the economic (opportunity) cost. We know that for every 1 percent of the labor force unemployed today we lose about $60 billion in potential GNP. In addition, we are learning more and more about the social and psychological cost associated with unemployment—crime, family disintegration, and increasing mental health problems, to name a few. An examination of the nature of unemployment in the U.S. also reveals an identifiable institutionalized process of discrimination according to one's race, sex, and age. This is becoming more and more evident as unprecedented numbers of minorities, women, and teenagers enter the labor force. When we see a national unemployment rate of 7 percent unchanged for the last several years, a 14 percent unemployment rate for minorities and women, and a 40 percent unemployment rate for black teenagers, the charges of discrimination have more validity. Critics also claim that the national measures of unemployment actually understate the real rate of unemployment. They argue that a different definition and measurement technique would reveal a national *under*employment rate of 14 to 17 percent.

A last consideration related to unemployment is poverty and welfare, previously addressed in the Miner article. Almost ten million Americans who work full time or part time are earning less than the U.S. government's poverty level of income of $5800 per year (1976) for a metropolitan family of four. For the citizens of the U.S. who are neither employed nor receiving any form of income from unemployment compensation, social security, or disability, being on welfare is the only choice in terms of survival needs. Welfare has become a very costly, cumbersome, degrading, inefficient, and unmanageable government program presently in need of drastic reform.

Inflation

The rate of *inflation* (a general increase in the prices of goods and services over time) during the 1950s and the early 1960s was moderate and stable. Monetary and fiscal policy combined to control the money supply, the level of government spending, and taxes to produce this moderate inflation of 1 to 3 percent. By the late 1960s and early 1970s, the rate of inflation began to increase substantially and evidenced wide fluctuations. Part of this was due to the economic stimulus from the Vietnam War. Another factor was the 1973 OPEC oil embargo and subsequent quadrupling of the price of oil. Increasing energy costs since 1973 have become a permanent feature of our modern inflationary economy. We have, also, become more aware of the power of organized labor to demand and receive higher wages thus increasing the inflationary pressures in the economy. Last, we have become aware of the ability of firms in the corporate sector in particular to use their market power to artificially increase (or administer) prices thereby contributing to the growing institutionalized or structural inflation we are experiencing.

These then are the basic macroeconomic issues and problems we will be examining in this section. In addition to these primary issues and problems, there are several others which merit our attention. What are they?

Tax Reform The inequality of income distribution and the inability of the U.S. tax system to reduce this inequality has recently brought forward demands for wholesale *tax reform*. Such tax reform would eliminate the many "loopholes" that allow for differences between what people should pay and what they do in fact pay. This would make the tax system more progressive and equitable, thereby possibly reducing income inequalities.

National Debt   The U.S. government has a *national debt* of over $700 billion. This debt has been growing greater and greater over the years. As large government annual deficits continue to exist, this debt will mount rapidly. For example, the annual deficit for 1977 was $45 billion; and 1978's deficit is estimated to be at least $58 billion, while 1979's estimated deficit will be about $40 billion. The government is forced to pay over $42 billion a year just in "interest" alone on this debt, or about one-tenth of our total federal budget.

Stagflation   The U.S. during the 1960s typically had a choice (in making macroeconomic policy) between unemployment and inflation. A British economist named Phillips empirically validated this relationship and illustrated it in what has become known as the Phillips Curve. Since 1970, the U.S. economy has been plagued both by high rates of inflation and by unemployment. This condition commonly referred to as *"Stagflation"* (meaning slow economic growth, high unemployment, and high inflation) has called into question the ability of current macroeconomic theory to resolve the apparent dilemma.

Energy Crisis   Since the OPEC embargo of 1973, the U.S. has been forced to carefully assess and analyze its use and availability of *energy resources*. The quadrupling of the price of oil has forced us to develop an Energy Program that will accomplish at least the following: (1) conservation of our energy resources, (2) reduction of our dependency on imported foreign oil, (3) expansion and development of our domestic energy production, and (4) development of alternative forms of renewable energy resources.

These are just a few additional problems and issues that have become more and more critical in the 1970s.

ECONOMIC THEORY VERSUS ECONOMIC REALITY: THE FUTURE?

With this brief overview of macroeconomic problems and issues, it is important that we study this material with one basic question in mind—To what extent does contemporary macroeconomic theory adequately explain our current economic reality? To be able to answer this question, we will need to begin at the beginning. So let us embark upon this voyage through macroeconomics by first learning what the theory is in the context of its historical roots.

The following article, "High Price of Prodding the Economy" by William C. Freund appeared in the *New York Times* on October 23, 1977. A careful reading of this article will be useful as a first exercise and exposure to the use of macroeconomic ideas, terms, and concepts. Pay attention to the language and relationships between terms. This article touches upon almost everything that we will be attempting to learn and understand in this section. Do not be frustrated or confused if you do not totally understand the content of the article. You will in several weeks!

HIGH PRICE OF PRODDING THE ECONOMY
WILLIAM C. FREUND

Unemployment remains stuck at around 7 percent of the labor force, considerably above the 5 to 6 percent that most economists define as full employment. For all teenagers, the rate is 17.5 percent and for nonwhite teeagers, 40.4 percent. By any measure, too many willing persons are still deprived of the opportunity to work.

A recent study by the Council on Children concluded that family stability requires dedicated federal programs to guarantee full employment. The council urged the highest priority for full employment programs to ensure that no child suffers because his parents cannot find work. Every person is entitled to the dignity of a job. Even risking inflation, according to this report, is not too high a price to avoid the damage of unemployment on families and children.

Unemployment is indeed a very serious economic ailment. But simply blowing up government spending, or giving large tax rebates (as opposed to longer-range tax reform), or flooding the nation's money supply will not solve the problem. All these might have been appropriate federal policies in the Great Depression of the 1930s; they are not today.

For the new insight of economists is that loose Federal fiscal and monetary policies can cause inflation which, in the longer run, is likely to kill off the very jobs the federal policies were designed to create. Going after unemployment with broad brush economic policies, as occurred in 1973–1974, will produce not only more inflation, but in the end more unemployment.

Back in the Depression of the 1930s, when Lord Keynes was writing his General Theory, there was little reason to worry about inflation. With over 25 percent of the labor force out of work, with a shameful excess of productive capacity, there was no inflation push either from higher wages or rising levels of demand.

The General Theory advocated government stimulation of demand and output, primarily through easier fiscal policies—that is, more government spending and less taxing. Keynes believed that the system of private enterprise could be preserved only if government pumped up aggregate demand and created desperately needed jobs. In the midst of depression, worry about any trade-off between employment and inflation was unrealistic.

Keynes was right in counseling against concern about inflation in the economic environment of the 1930s. To provide a conceptual or theoretical foundation for his policy prescriptions, Keynes developed his well known "bottleneck" theory of inflation, which states that inflation begins to become a problem only in the vicinity of full employment.

The economy has the shape of a bottle with a broad base below and a tapering as it nears the top. Think of a beer bottle with a neck. The beer will flow less freely as it nears the narrowing at the top. The neck constricts the flow and puts the beer under greater pressure. That was the analogy Keynes had in mind when he wrote about bottleneck inflation.

William C. Freund, senior vice president and chief economist for the New York Stock Exchange, is also professor of economics and finance at the Pace University Graduate School. © 1977 by The New York Times Company. Reprinted by permission.

In the vicinity of full employment, inflation pressures intensify as economic activity passes through the narrowing neck of capacity limitations. Near full employment, demand pulls up prices at the same time as wages and other costs begin to respond to selected shortages. But in the depth of a depression, when the economy is operating at the broad base of the bottle, increased employment will not cause increased inflation.

The Keynesian lesson was learned well, perhaps too much so. The Depression and World War II demonstrated that government spending can stimulate employment and provide jobs by the millions. Confidence grew that our economy need never—and shall never—incur the personal suffering and the loss of output occasioned by deep depression. Increasingly, economists talked not only about obliterating depressions but "fine tuning" activity to ensure a perpetual state of full employment.

But Keynes was right. Near the bottleneck, indeed some distance before reaching it, rising employment will generate rising inflation. The recognition of this trade-off was formulated most explicitly by the British economist A. W. Phillips. He constructed a curve purporting to show the trade-off between employment and inflation: more employment yields more inflation and vice versa.

Endless scholarly debate ensued. The relationship between unemployment and inflation is undoubtedly a rather loose proposition; but the tendency is clearly there.

The existence of the unemployment-inflation trade-off has been a factor in the decision of the Carter administration to resist an all-out, no-holds-barred full employment program, even though unemployment remains stuck around 7 percent of the labor force.

On taking office, President Carter did not undertake massive new federal spending, or a quickie tax cut, or a loosening of the monetary spigot to bring unemployment down quickly. That would have been good depression economics. But the administration, like most of us, has vivid memories of 1973, when total spending surged (with Vietnam still an element), and when unemployment did fall to 4.9 percent. But we also remember the 14 percent per annum inflation which followed in early 1974 (partly as a result of the oil embargo and the shortage of grains) and the big recession that put in an appearance shortly thereafter.

Much as a full employment program is desirable in alleviating human suffering, a quick fix through government action can give inflation a big push, especially now when rock-bottom inflation hovers around 6 percent a year. That, of course, is the Phillips Curve conclusion: less unemployment will mean more inflation. But then some people might simply shrug their shoulders. Like the Council on Children, they man conclude that inflation is the lesser evil.

The trouble with that notion is that a new and longer run trade-off has been identified. rising inflation hurts jobs. Inflation undermines the incentive to invest and spend and therefore decreases the number of jobs available. We shall call this new economic theory the Greenspan Thesis, after Alan Greenspan, chief economic adviser to President Ford. It has been gaining considerable ground among other economists.

Mr. Greenspan has argued that in the short run the Phillips Curve may portray correctly the trade-off between employment and inflation. But in the longer run, over a period of several years, nothing destroys job opportunities more than inflation. True, we seemed to lick unemployment in 1973 and early 1974 through large increases in overall spending. And inflation accelerated, just as the Phillips Curve would predict. But look at the repercussions thereafter.

Inflation systematically destroyed business and consumer confidence as purchasing power ebbed away. Spending dropped. To control inflation, the Federal Reserve stepped on the credit brakes. The economy was sent into a tailspin, resulting in the deepest recession since World War II. Boom and full employment gave way to bust. In the end, inflation did come down (6 percent today), but unemployment was back up again. To this day, we suffer from the excesses of that period. The failure of business confidence to sustain rising capital expenditures today remains one of the legacies of the 1973–1974 trauma.

The Greenspan Thesis makes the ironic point that in the longer run inflation destroys jobs. Indeed, the government policies that were designed to bring on full employment produce inflation and a boom-bust cycle that destroy the very jobs the original policies were intended to create. Inflation breeds caution, inadequate investment, slower economic growth and unemployment. Only with greater price stability can full employment be reached in the longer run in a free market setting. That has been the experience both in the United States and abroad.

Federal monetary policies aimed at unemployment can in the long run cost jobs, Keynes's "bottleneck theory" notwithstanding.　　　　　　　　　　Eugene Mihaesco

How then can we reconcile the short run trade-off between employment and inflation and the longer run trade-off between inflation and unemployment? That is the fundamental challenge for economists and policymakers today, not only in the United States but in the entire industrialized world. We need a new Keynes. Unfortunately, he has not appeared.

The best answer is to keep inflation down through creating conditions that give full expression to the free market forces of competition. We need to end artificial restrictions that limit worker output and productivity. There are still untold "firemen on diesel engines" throughout American industries. Such artificial practices bloat wage bills, restrict wage competition and inflict higher costs on consumers. On the business side oligopolistic pricing practices are equally culpable. Business protectionism, both domestic and international, limit our ability to keep inflation down.

But what about jobs at a time when unemployment remains a national problem? When the economy is only a stone's throw from the Keynesian bottleneck, a general program of inflating aggregate demand should be avoided lest it lead first to the Phillips and then the Greenspan trade-off. Instead specific programs are needed to deal with the concentrated pockets of unemployment, where they exist. It is the proverbial rifle-versus-shotgun approach.

Ways can be found to provide jobs for the young, the minorities and women, whose unemployment rate is particularly high. Perhaps the minimum wage should be considered less than sacrosanct if we really want to provide jobs for our young people who often are unskilled and whose productivity does not justify the minimum. Training in improving skills (primarily manual) is necessary. Government contracts can be directed to areas of highest unemployment without increasing total spending. The structure of taxes can provide incentives for job creation. In short, we can concentrate our efforts on the specific worker categories, geographic areas, and industries where joblessness is highest.

In today's world, broad policies to puff up overall demand will only lead to more inflation, and in the longer run, to another ride on the boom-bust rollercoaster.

---

2. Do you agree or disagree with the Greenspan thesis? Why?

3. Should we focus on limiting inflation or on ending unemployment? Why?

4. What causes the "bottleneck" problem?

KEY CONCEPTS

macroeconomics
macro goals and objectives
John Maynard Keynes
Gross National Product
Employment Act of 1946
monetary policy

fiscal policy
economic growth
unemployment
inflation
public debt
stagflation

QUESTION FOR REVIEW

Examine a daily newspaper (e.g., the *New York Times*) for a few days and see how many articles there are that address macroeconomic issues and problems. Make a list of the macroeconomic terms, concepts, and issues that you find.

SUGGESTED READINGS

Michael Best and William Connolly, 1976. *The Politicized Economy*, D. C. Heath. See Chapters 1, 2, and 3 for an excellent introduction to our major macroeconomic issues and problems.

Robert Lekachman, 1973. *Inflation: The Permanent Problem of Boom and Bust*, Vintage. A good primer on the modern sources of inflation and on the economic problems of economic growth, unemployment, and economic instability.

MEASURING GNP

APPENDIX 14A

GNP, NNP, PI, DI. . . .

People, and economists are no exception, have been measuring things—or at least trying to—since the beginning of time. Though many of us are still not convinced that metrics is magnificent or any better than our conventional foot, we nonetheless will measure with it—to compare the size or the value of things. When one speaks of the product of a nation, one speaks in terms of GNP or Gross National Product. This mystical number for the U.S. is given to us in quarterly reports issued by the Department of Commerce. Wily reporters seemingly hover over the Commerce Department for days and then give us the verdict as to whether GNP is up or down. Then, one finds that the results are most often qualified—GNP was up 3 percent over last quarter *but* the rate of inflation has been increasing at a 4-percent rate at the same time.

Perhaps we *should* spend an appendix looking at the ins and outs (or rather the ups and downs) of the GNP—an area better known in economics jargon as the *National Income Accounts*.

There are *two* basic ways of arriving at final figures for the various accounts. There is the *goods flow* approach and the *income flow* approach. These may be seen in the circular flow diagram in Fig. 14A.1. One can measure either the *top* or the bottom of the circular flow and measure national income.

The following definitions, relations and data in Tables 14A.1 and 14A.2 show the derivation of GNP. If you start from the top, you quickly arrive at GNP = C + I + G + (X − M) via the goods flow. Starting from the bottom takes longer—but you will eventually arrive at GNP via the income flow approach as well.

PROBLEMS WITH NATIONAL INCOME ACCOUNTING

In these definitional relationships, many difficult and rather perplexing problems are ignored. First, there is the problem of the measuring rod, money. And a very flexible yardstick it is, too—dollars being worth more or less as time passes (usually

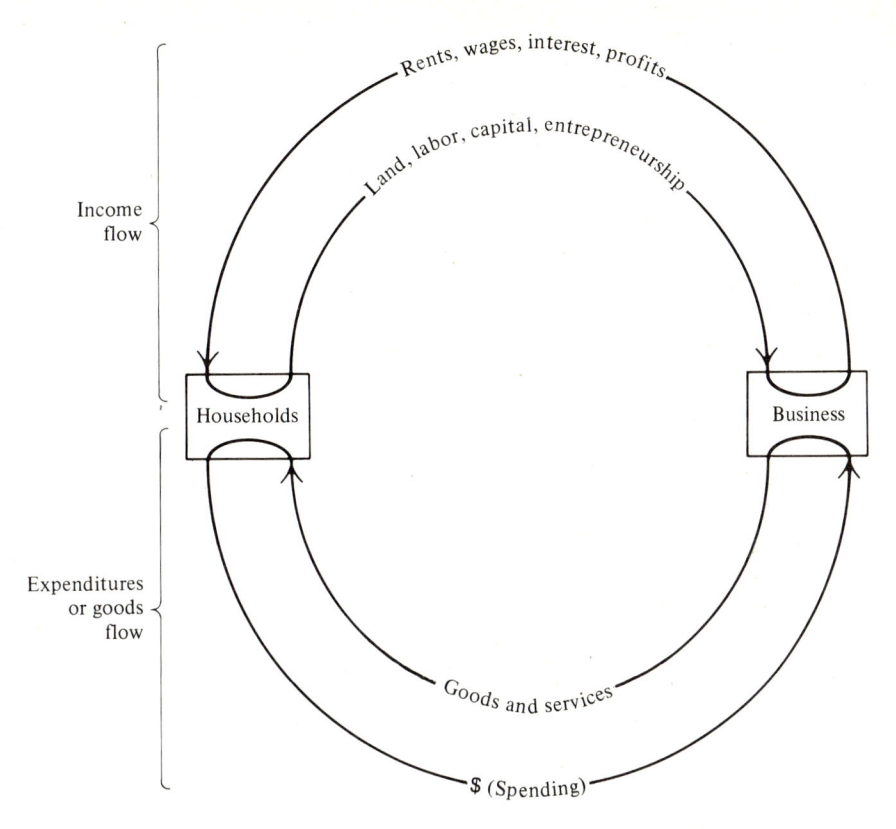

FIG. 14A.1 The income and spending flows.

less). In order to solve the flexibility dilemma, index numbers are used in which "market baskets" of goods and services in one accounting period are compared with a similar basket in some base accounting period—thus statisticians can avoid the perils of price instability by inflating or deflating accordingly. This device allows us to remove the effects of price changes from GNP, so that we can measure the changes in *real* output, the actual physical volume. The GNP deflator is a systematized equation that has been shown to be a "reasonable" indicator of how much the national product has gained or lost due to recession or inflation. For example, in 1975 GNP went up by 7.3 percent, but prices went up by 7 percent; so real GNP increased by only 0.3 percent. Figure 14A.2 shows what has happened to the GNP since 1940 in both current dollars and "real" 1972 dollars.

A second problem in the national income accounts is the actual counting process. One can either count the final products produced or sum each of the values added by each phase of the production process. Both methods should yield the same result, but there is often a chance of double counting in the final product method.

TABLE 14A.1 Relation of Gross National Product, Net National Product, National Income, Personal Income, and Disposable Income

(Millions of Dollars)

		1973	1974	1975	1976
Expenditure flow	The sum of Personal consumption expenditures (C)	809,885	889,603	980,409	1,093,950
	Gross private domestic investment (I_d)	212,999	214,589	189,112	243,339
	Government purchases of goods and services (G)	269,527	302,657	338,935	361,352
	Net exports of goods and services (X—M)	7,143	6,040	20,366	7,820
Equals:	Gross national product ....(GNP)	1,306,554	1,412,889	1,528,822	1,706,461
Less:	Capital consumption allowances with capital consumption adjustment	117,652	137,651	162,531	179,038
Equals:	Net national product ....(NNP)	1,188,902	1,275,238	1,366,291	1,527,423
Less:	Indirect business tax and nontax liability	120,193	128,582	138,701	150,477
	Business transfer payments	5,375	5,886	7,008	8,091
	Statistical discrepancy	2,629	5,763	5,862	5,509
Plus:	Subsidies less current surplus of government enterprises	3,872	952	2,264	767

Problems with National Income Accounting 233

Equals:	National income.................(NI)	1,064,577	1,135,959	1,216,984	1,364,113
Less:	Corporate profits with inventory valuation and capital consumption adjustments	99,064	83,553	99,264	128,058
	Net interest	52,334	68,998	79,063	88,395
	Contributions for social insurance	91,524	103,805	110,120	123,849
	Wage accruals less disbursements	−56	−530	0	0
Plus:	Government transfer payments to persons	113,511	134,940	169,825	184,741
	Personal interest income	84,051	103,014	115,598	130,299
	Net interest	52,334	68,998	79,063	88,395
	Interest paid by government to persons and business	25,626	29,283	33,299	39,297
	Less: Interest received by government	14,111	17,618	19,651	22,388
	Interest paid by consumers to business	20,202	22,351	22,887	24,995
	Dividends	27,792	30,963	32,399	35,756
	Business transfer payments	5,375	5,886	7,008	8,091
Equals:	Personal income.................(PI)	1,052,440	1,154,936	1,253,367	1,382,698
Less:	Personal tax payments	193,012	218,001	219,367	252,120
Equals:	Disposable personal income.......(DPI)	901,663	984,627	1,084,359	1,185,824
Less:	Personal outlays	831,339	912,974	1,004,200	1,119,893
	Personal consumption expenditures......(C)	809,885	889,603	980,409	1,093,950
	Interest paid by consumers	20,202	22,351	22,887	24,995
	Personal transfer payments to foreigners	1,252	1,020	904	948
Equals:	Personal saving..................(S_p)	70,324	71,653	80,159	65,931

Income* flow

*Note that indirect business taxes and business transfers and capital consumption allowances must be added to national income to arrive at GNP via the income flow approach.
Source: *Survey of Current Business*, July 1977.

234 **Measuring GNP**

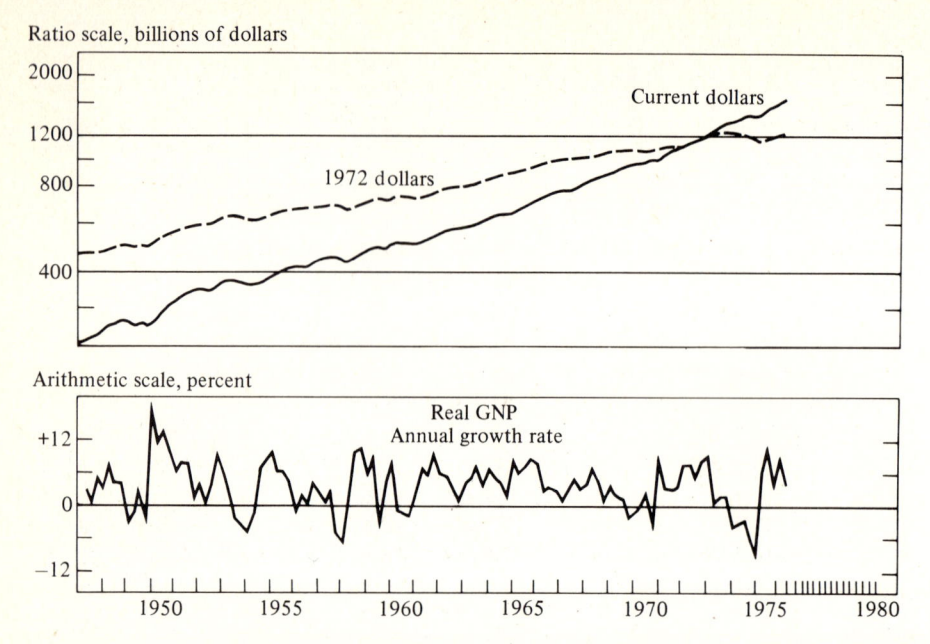

FIG. 14A.2 Gross National Product (GNP). Seasonally adjusted annual rates, quarterly. (From *Historical Chartbook,* **Board of Governors of the Federal Reserve System, 1972, p. 12.**)

The most recent criticism involves the significance of the accounts—or the lack of it. Lots of market transactions are excluded from the accounts (an estimated $80 billion of Mafia money for example) as well as capital gains and losses—and lots of nonmarket transactions are included. Imputed values are added for owner-occupied homes, room and board for services exchanged, etc. And imagine what would happen to the accounts if housewives simply traded homes with their neighbors each day and paid one another $48 a day (the estimated market worth of housewives' services.) The activities of these women are productive, they are services, but they are not included in the national income accounts.

Another misleading characteristic of the national product accounts involves the social costs, that, rather than being subtracted from, are added to the nation's GNP. As we spend more and more to clean up pollution, the spending *adds* to our national product. As cigarette sales increase, GNP increases. As hospital costs for increased numbers of cases of lung cancer and emphysema occur, the GNP increases. GNP, in other words, is not a measure of overall welfare. Recently economists and other social scientists have been attempting to gather together a qualitative index that measures social welfare. Thus far the index is quite crude, but shows significantly that nations with the highest GNP don't necessarily have the highest social welfare ratings, while a few countries with extremely low GNPs have *relatively* high standings on the social welfare index.

TABLE 14A.2 Definitions

The sum of:

1. *Personal consumption expenditures* (C) consists of the market value of purchases of goods and services by individuals and nonprofit institutions and the value of food, clothing, housing, and financial services received by them as income in kind.
2. *Gross private domestic investment* (I) consists of acquisitions of newly produced capital goods by private business and nonprofit institutions and of the value of the change in the volume of inventories held by business. It covers all private new dwellings.
3. *Government purchases of goods and services* (G) consists of government expenditures for compensation of employees, purchases from business, net foreign purchases and contributions, and the gross investment of government enterprises. It excludes transfer payments, government interest, and subsidies.
4. *Net foreign investment* (X − M) measures the excess of (1) domestic output sold abroad over purchases of foreign output, (2) production abroad credited to U.S.-owned resources over production at home credited to foreign-owned resources, and (3) cash gifts and contributions received from abroad over cash gifts and contributions to foreigners.

Equals

5. *Gross national product* (GNP) = the market value of the newly produced goods and services that are not resold in any form during the accounting period (usually one year).

Less

6. *Capital consumption allowances* is an allowance for capital goods that have been consumed in the process of producing this year's GNP. Consists of depreciation, capital outlays charged to current expense, and accidental damage.

Equals

7. *Net national product* (NNP) is the net creation of new wealth resulting from the productive activity of the economy during the accounting period.

Less

8. *Indirect business tax* consists primarily of sales and excise taxes, customs duties on imported goods, and business property taxes. These taxes are collected from business and are chargeable to their current costs.

Equals

9. *National income* (NI) = the total income of factors from participation in the current productive process.

Less

10. *Social Security contributions* consists of payments by both employees and the self-employed.
11. *Corporate income taxes* comprises federal and state taxes levied on corporate earnings.
12. *Undistributed corporate profits* is what remains of corporate profits after both corporate income taxes and dividends have been paid.

Plus

13. *Transfer payments* (government and business) consist of monetary income receipts of individuals from government and business (other than government interest) for which no services are rendered currently.

Equals

14. *Personal income* (PI) = income received by households—as opposed to income earned by households.

Less

15. *Personal taxes* consist of the taxes levied against individuals, their income, and their property that are not deductible as expenses of business operations.

Equals

16. *Disposable income* (DI) is the income remaining to persons after deduction of personal tax and nontax payments to general government.

Less

17. *Personal consumption expenditures* (C) (Same as 1)

Equals

18. *Personal saving* (S) may be in such forms as changes in cash and deposits, security holdings, and private pension, health, welfare, and trust funds.

---

1. Why is it important to collect data on all of these different macroeconomic variables?

THE CLASSICAL AND KEYNESIAN MODELS AND THE GREAT DEPRESSION

CHAPTER 15

INTRODUCTION

The tenets of classical macroeconomic theory, formed by Adam Smith, David Ricardo, John S. Mill, and others, were carried pretty much intact through the 19th century. Economists in the latter part of that era concentrated more on the microeconomic elements of utility and production rather than the total economy. This chapter will sort out the three major parts of the classical doctrine, illustrate their use, and then examine the Keynesian critique of classical macro-theory and its inability to deal with the depression-plagued world of the 1930s. The logic of the Keynesian argument will then be formulated.

Keynes's theory challenged the longstanding economic traditions, and his efforts were criticized as heresy before he was knighted for his genius. Some view the Keynesian contribution as a new paradigm, while others view it as simply a major revision of classical theory. It might be noted that the classical model discussed here was never formally set up as such by any of the classical economists. Rather, Keynes drew together the foundations from the writings of the classical economists and constructed the model primarily as a "strawman." He then proceeded to break the model down a part at a time in *The General Theory*.

THE CLASSICAL SYSTEM

MV = PQ **or the Quantity Theory of Money**

One of the three major tenets of classical economic theory was the *Quantity Theory of Money*. Most often this is expressed by the following *"equation of exchange"*:

$$M \cdot V = P \cdot Q,$$

where M is the money stock in the economy, V is the income *velocity* of money or the rate of turnover of money, P is the price level, and Q is the level of real national income. This equation appears simple enough—perhaps too simple, for when it is examined carefully, it becomes an obvious tautology. It is true because it is by definition true. It is redundant because of the definition of velocity—the rate at which money moves through the economy during a given period, or the number of times a piece of money gets spent,

$$V = \frac{P \cdot Q}{M}.$$

Since national income is a measure of all output (Q) in a country for a year multiplied by the price (P) of each good or service, V is equal in effect to national income in a given year divided by the total amount of money available (on the average) during that year.

The classical economists elaborated further on each of the variables in the "equation of exchange." They expressed the belief that each of the variables in the equation was affected by a variety of external and internal forces. Q, or national output, was determined primarily by real factors that changed slowly over time, such as capital, technology, resource availability, and labor. The quantity of money (M) would not influence these variables in "any significant way." The classical economists argued that the income velocity of money (V), on the other hand, was determined by institutional factors that were also independent of any change in the money stock (M). Some of these institutional factors accounting for changes in V or payment habits of the public were population density, custom, transportation factors, the state of the art of banking, wage payments and practices, and so on. With Q and V unaffected by changes in the supply of money, only P or the level of prices is left to have some relation to changes in the quantity of money (M).

According to the classical economists, only the price level was determined in the money market. Since Q and V were relatively constant, this meant that changes in the quantity of money produced nearly proportional changes in the price level. Thus if the quantity of money in the economy is doubled, the price level is likely to double as well. In terms, then, of output and employment in the economy, money didn't matter very much; but in terms of wages and prices, it mattered a lot.

In the world of the classical economists, *money* was considered to be *neutral* in that it satisfied no direct utility or want and merely reflected real activity in the economy. It served as a veil behind which the real action of economic forces such as the growth of the national product and employment were concealed. Yet, money was viewed as a lubricant for the economy, keeping it well oiled so that it (the economy) was able to run smoothly and effectively.

The Goods Market in Classical Economics

On the goods or real side of the classical scheme, equilibrium output was determined by the demand for and the supply of labor. Increases in the demand for labor increased output (Q) while decreases in the supply of labor decreased output. The level of output was determined by the full employment level in the classical system. The equilibrium real wage defined the level of full employment in the labor force. Anyone willing to work at the prevailing equilibrium wage would be employed—the quantity supplied of labor would equal the quantity demanded of labor. Anyone unwilling to work at that wage was regarded as not desiring to work (i.e., they were not classified as unemployed). As long as wages were flexible (both upward and downward) in the classical world, no conflict arose. Full employment, as they defined it, was the norm.

Say's Law

The third major foundation of classical macroeconomic theory was Say's law, named for the French economist Jean Baptiste Say (1767–1832) who popularized the principle. In its overly simplified form, the "law" states that *supply creates its own demand*. In other words, no matter what the level of output (supply), the income created in the process of its production must create an amount of spending sufficient to purchase those goods and services produced. For every dollar of product produced, there is a dollar of income created and spent.

Say's law gives rise to the *circular flow* diagram, shown in Fig. 15.1, that is very important to the discussion of both the Keynesian and classical models. The crude circular flow of the classics shows: (1) the movement of goods from the business sector of the economy to the household sector in return for spent income *and* (2) the transfer of the services of land, labor, and capital from households to business for use in the production of goods and services in exchange for rents, wages, and interest.

The *aggregate supply*, or output, that "creates its own demand," is the goods and services that are produced by the firms or businesses. The factors of production (land, labor, capital, and entrepreneurship) receive returns of rents, wages and salaries, and interest and profits for their part in the production process. Higher income levels in the household sector create more demand for goods and services, thus *aggregate demand* increases. This income in the household sector is then spent on the goods and services that have been produced, and create an income stream, through spending, for the business sector. The result is that the aggregate demand for goods and services of the household sector will equal the aggregate supply of those goods and services produced by the business sector. Equilibrium, then, occurs where aggregate supply or income equals aggregate demand or spending.

THE FLAWS IN THE CLASSICAL SYSTEM

Between 1860 and 1929 the United States economy was growing rapidly. The phases of growth tended to be cyclical with upswings in economic activity accompanied by downswings, but, with an overall upward secular trend in economic activity *averaging* about 2 percent per year. Many explanations were offered to account for the waves in the *business cycle*. These ranged from increases in sunspot activity to overconsumption/underinvestment, to monetary expansion and contraction and to innovation. Indeed, compelling arguments have been made for each of these in explaining the pattern of growth.

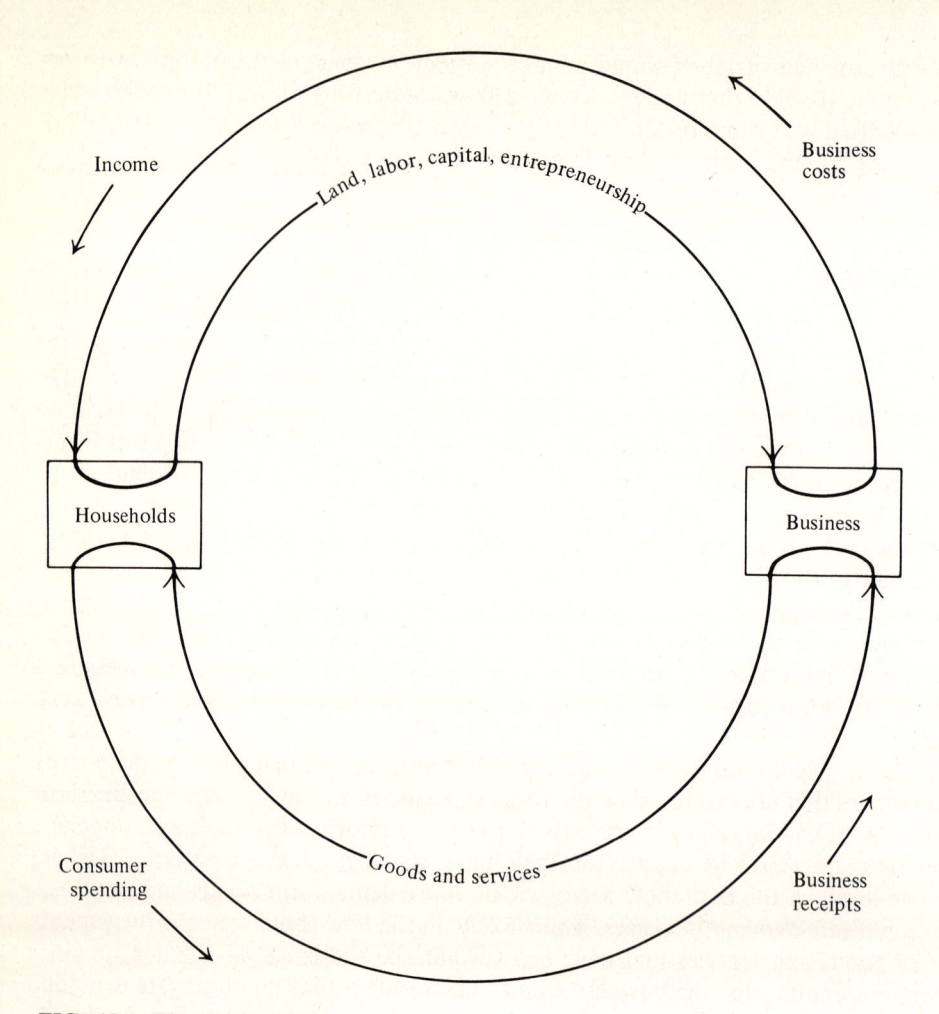

FIG. 15.1 The circular flow.

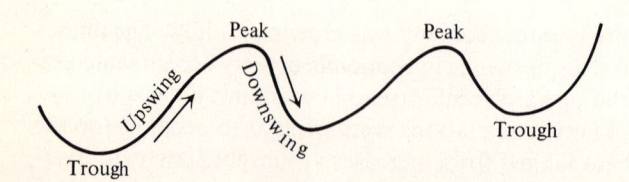

FIG. 15.2 Business cycle.

1. **What argument might you use to convince your roommate that the level of business cycle activity was the result of sunspots? the result of overconsumption followed by underinvestment?**

When economic conditions were in the downswing or trough of the cycle as in the 1930s, classical economic theory explained the resulting levels of unemployment by insisting that those out of work were simply voluntarily unemployed. They believed that more employment opportunities could be made by reducing the prevailing wage rate. As wages fell, there would be an increase in the demand for labor. According to classical theory, these unemployed workers would be more than happy to work as long as their wages were above zero. However, during the Great Depression, as wages dropped lower, even more people were out of work—not fewer.

THE GREAT DEPRESSION

The Great Depression was a result of many different phenomena that seemed to culminate all at once. Some people who are interested in business cycles believe that short-, medium-, and long-run cycles all reached bottom at the same time. Nonetheless, we should explore some of the causes of this depression that lasted for ten years and left enduring imprints on millions of Americans.

It took more than just the 1929 stock market crash to sustain the Depression for such a long period. Despite the robustness of the stock market before its fall, several sectors of the economy were essentially weak. The agriculture and manufacturing sectors were perhaps the most important sectors contributing to the duration of the Depression.

As the country had grown in the first few decades of the century, the agriculture sector had dwindled. Hurt by the exploitation of the rail and storage bosses, and burned by their own speculative activities in land, more and more farmers were leaving or selling out to join the urban migration or to become tenants. The number of independent farms had dropped by 40 percent during the 1920s. Output, however, was increasing and the inelastic demand for farm production did little to help the agriculture sector. Unlike the other sectors of the economy in which greater supplies meant lower prices and increased demand, demand was not forthcoming to the lower priced agricultural products. In addition, the European export market was lost as Europe restored its ability to produce for itself following World War I.

In manufacturing concerns, conditions were mixed. Many people in business foresaw a time of weakness ahead and, although sales and prices and output were at an all-time high, employment had been cut back substantially, especially in the mines and mills. Only in the service and construction industry did employment levels hold their own—for this was an area in which men and women could not yet be displaced by technology. Prosperity increased throughout the 1920s. But workers were no better off than before. Wages and employment levels simply did not increase. Profits on the other hand swelled rapidly as did the concentration of economic power. Profits in 1929 were three times those of 1920. But firms were not reinvesting. This was partially due to the fact that demand was unable to keep up with supply.

The weaknesses in these two sectors are directly linked to other causes of the Depression: the lopsided distribution of income and the lack of new investments by the business sector. In addition, a somewhat shaky banking system, defaults by European governments on U.S. loans, and a "balanced budget" philosophy in Congress helped to make a bad situation even worse.

All of this suggests that the U.S. economy was fundamentally unsound at the time of the stock market crash. From the widespread prosperity of the early 1920s, the lack of capital formation, the overproduction of goods and services, an agricultural glut, in addition to international disequilibrium and deep-seated psychological effects from the crash all led to the prolonged instability.

Between 1929 and 1932 the following occurred: (1) 85,000 businesses failed; (2) 5000 banks closed; (3) stock values decreased from $87 billion to $19 billion; (4) unemployment increased to 12 million or 25 percent of the labor force; (5) farm income decreased by 50 percent; and (6) manufacturing output decreased by 50 percent. By 1933, GNP had declined from $104 billion in 1929 to $56 billion with unemployment firmly at 25 percent.

The Depression—In Human Terms

The Depression of the 1930s is the example most people reflect upon as a time of severe unemployment and poverty for the men, women, and children who suffered and endured through it. Ask your grandparents sometime about the era. Over a third of the nation was unemployed or in poverty. And conditions were abysmal for all but a few well-to-do. The middle class suffered and the poor starved. The following excerpt illustrates the reality of the Depression.

When the breadwinner is out of a job he usually exhausts his savings if he has any. Then, if he has an insurance policy, he probably borrows to the limit of its cash value. He borrows from his friends and from his relatives until they can stand the burden no longer. He gets credit from the corner grocery store and the butcher shop, and the landlord forgoes collecting the rent until interest and taxes have to be paid and something has to be done. All of these resources are finally exhausted over a period of time, and it becomes necessary for these people, who have never before been in want, to ask for assistance. The specter of starvation faces millions of people who have never before known what it was to be out of a job for any considerable period of time and who certainly have never known what it was to be absolutely up against it.

Lester V. Chandler, *America's Greatest Depression.* New York: Harper & Row, 1970, pp. 41–42.

ENTER JOHN MAYNARD KEYNES—STAGE RIGHT . . . MOVING LEFT

John Maynard Keynes (1883-1946) was born into a prosperous Victorian setting at the turn of the century. He watched the economic importance of his native Britain wane with the rapid growth of the United States and continental Western Europe.

Certainly one of the most illustrious and eccentric of all economists, Keynes's interests were centered in the "Bloomsbury Group," comprised of such people as Leonard and Virginia Woolf, Clive Bell, Sidney and Beatrice Potter Webb who, along with the brightest economists of Cambridge, served as the sounding board for all of Keynes's work.

Keynes's ideas and his critique of the classical model were developed slowly, and over a rather lengthy period of time. Much of his writing was highly critical of the British authorities. He was one of the first to recognize the implausibility of the British attachment to the gold standard and to object to the Versailles Peace Treaty. (He felt that it would be impossible for Germany to meet the reparations called for by the treaty.) His work came at a time when the classical model was most under fire because of its inability to account for continued and worldwide depression in the 1930s.

The major question being asked in each world capital was what to do? According to the classical doctrine, the simple remedy was a wage reduction. But wages *were* falling, and more unemployment resulted, not less. Say's law was being violated. Supply was not creating its own demand. The circular flow was not working right. Classical theory and classical economists were in a quandary.

KEYNES TO THE RESCUE

Keynes and a few other economists recognized that there were leakages from the income and spending flows as well as injections to them. *Leakages* included savings, taxes, and the purchases of goods and services from foreign nations (imports). With each of these actions, income would flow out of the circle in the circular flow diagram of the classical economists. Saving and hoards remove money from the spending stream and occur when households decide that future consumption is better than present consumption and put their money into savings and time accounts at financial intermediaries, into the stock market or under their mattresses. Taxes leave the spending stream of the household and business sectors and are turned over to the government. Imported goods and services from other nations increase the goods and services received by households but reduce the total domestic spending since these dollars now go abroad to pay for the goods and services received.

On the other hand, Keynes noted that there were *injections* that could be and were made to the income and spending system. Government spending, investment, and the purchase of goods by foreign nations (exports) added to the flow. Government spending, like consumer spending, increases the income received by the business sector, since purchases are made of business products. Government spending may also go directly to the household sector in the form of transfer payments or income supplements, which in turn will increase spending as well. Investment occurs when the business sector creates new capital in the form of new plants, or additions to equipment or the buildup of existing inventories—or stocks of goods and services that are in their warehouses. Investment is, in effect, business spending. Exports create an injection into the income stream since businesses have a new market for their products and receive income in return. (Figure 15.3 illustrates the dynamics of these flows.)

For the economy to be in equilibrium then, the injections had to be equal to the leakages. As a result, aggregate demand for goods and services in the economy would be equal to the aggregate supply. This would establish an equilibrium level of income and output that might or might not be at full employment. According to Keynes, an

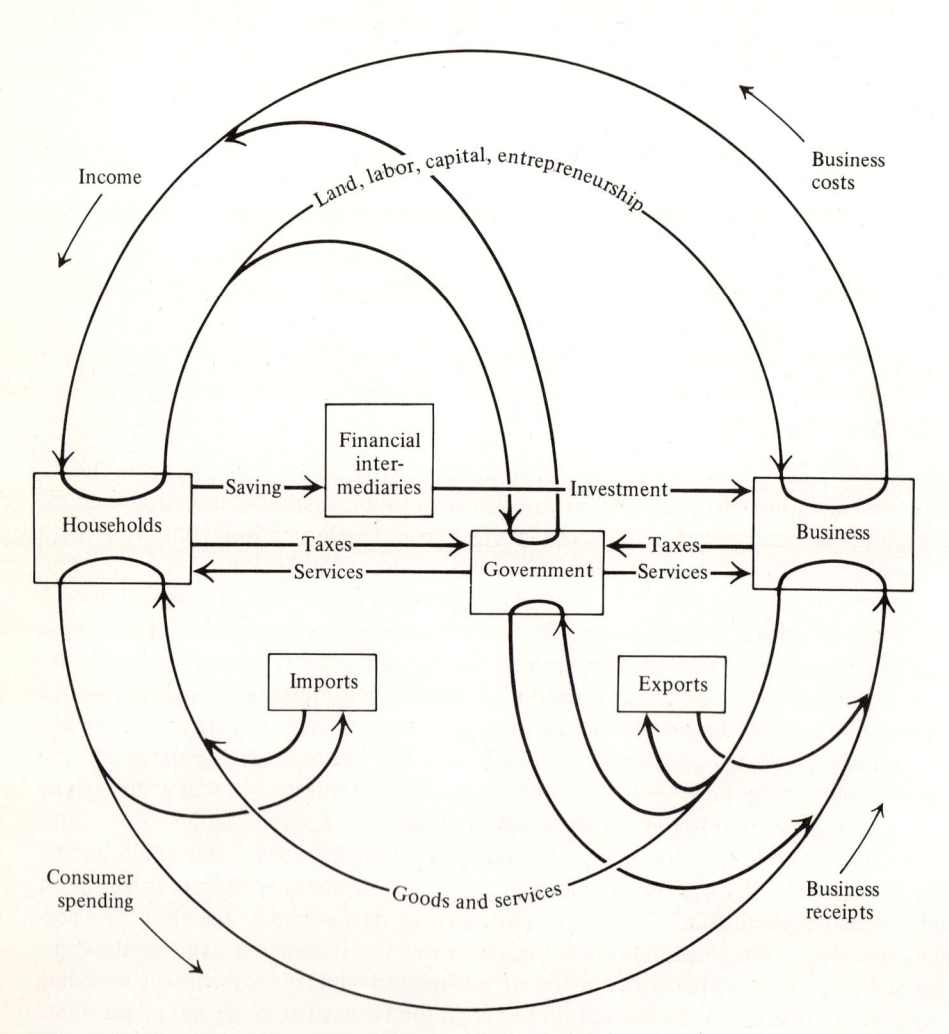

FIG. 15.3 The circular flow with leakages and injections.

infinite number of equilibrium positions could exist in an economy but only one was at full employment. The classical economists, however, saw one and only one equilibrium—the one that existed at full employment.

According to Keynesian theory, equilibrium would be inevitable since self-adjusting mechanisms would be at work within the economy to restore equilibrium. In the following, we will abstract and concentrate on the savings leakage and the investment injection ignoring taxes and government spending and imports and exports. If a situation of disequilibrium existed where injections were not equal to leakages, there would be a "natural" tendency for readjustment.

As the economy grew, each increase in investment would lead to even higher levels of income in the economy through a multiplier effect. As incomes increased, Keynes predicted that savings would increase since individuals with higher incomes saved proportionally more (and consumed proportionally less) than individuals with low incomes. For the economy to continue to grow and for business to expand profits, investment must grow over time to keep pace. Investment funds could be borrowed from households' savings funds. This most likely was facilitated by some financial intermediary such as a commercial bank.

If the planned savings of the household sector exceeded the investment levels planned by the business sector, a disequilibrium would result. With planned savings greater than planned investment, consumers simply would not be purchasing sufficient goods and services to keep pace with investment. The leakage from the spending flow would cause inventories to build up (aggregate supply would exceed aggregate demand). As consumption decreases, producers would alter their investment decisions. Since inventories would be accumulating in the warehouses, businesses would begin to cut back on output. This could decrease the level of production, income, and, finally, saving. At some point, reduced planned saving would equal planned investment.

---

2. What would happen if planned investment were greater than planned saving?

In the case of a depression, this circle of causation simply feeds upon itself. As a firm sees income decreasing and becomes even more myopic, it plans even lower levels of investment. Again with saving greater than investment, consumption falls lower, inventories increase more so the cutback of firms is even greater resulting in more unemployment and incomes lower than ever. (Note however, that the economy is still in equilibrium since as income drops, savings will drop to the level at which $S = I$.) Is there no end to this process during a recession?

As we've stated before, the classical economists believed that wages simply weren't low enough. Keynes, on the other hand, viewed wages as inflexible downward and saw relief from the downward spiral with new injections into the economy in the form of increases in government spending rather than through the normal investment channels that could not be relied upon when business expenditures were low. With the government employing people in public works, social service, the military complex or whatever, the cycle could be broken and full employment restored. Keynes was unconcerned about the form this spending took as we see in this passage from *The General Theory:*

> If the Treasury were to fill old bottles with banknotes, bury them at suitable depths in disused coalmines which are then filled up to the surface with town rubbish, and leave it to private enterprise on well-tried principles of *laissez-faire* to dig the notes up again (the right to do so being obtained, of course, by tendering for leases of the note-bearing territory), there need be no more unemployment and, with the help of the repercussions, the real income of the community, and its capital wealth also, would probably become a good deal greater than it actually is. It would, indeed, be more sensible to build houses and the like; but if there are political and practical difficulties in the way of this, the above would be better than nothing.

Excerpted from *The General Theory of Employment, Interest, and Money*, by John Maynard Keynes. Reprinted by permission of Harcourt Brace Jovanovich, Inc.

---

3. Does it make any difference what the government might spend money on? Why or why not?

And so it was that the Keynesian solution and analysis eventually captured the minds and hearts of economists throughout the world. And how very simple. Increased government spending would increase the levels of income, employment, and output. Using government spending policies to operate counter to the business cycle, a full range of economic maladies could be cured.

KEY CONCEPTS

$M \cdot V = P \cdot Q$
quantity theory of money
equation of exchange
velocity of money
money as neutral
Say's Law

circular flow
business cycle
injections
leakages
aggregate supply
aggregate demand

REVIEW QUESTIONS

1. Why might Keynes's theory be called a "depression theory"? Can you make a few arguments as to why it might command a more general usage?

2. Why would the classical economists distinguish among the variables in the equation of exchange being determined by real factors or monetary factors? What is the implication of prices increasing as the quantity of money increases?

3. What is the logical flaw in Say's law?

4. Why must leakages equal injections in the Keynesian world for an equilibrium level of income to exist?

5. If depressions become self-fulfilling prophecy, can inflationary periods be likewise? What would you expect the Keynesian prescription to recommend in such a case?

6. In your experience are wages sticky in a downward direction? Was Keynes "right" in assuming this inflexibility? How sticky are wages when they are going up?

SUGGESTED READINGS

Joan Robinson, 1962. *Economic Philosophy,* Aldine Publishing Company. The second chapter gives a good summary of the work of the classical economists. Chapter IV is devoted to Keynes.

Robert L. Heilbroner, 1953. *The Worldly Philosophers,* Simon and Schuster. A well-written and humorous account of the lives of classical economists through Keynes—and then some.

John Kenneth Galbraith, 1954. *The Great Crash 1929,* Houghton Mifflin. An interesting and readable account of the Depression.

Robert Lekachman, 1966. *The Age of Keynes,* Random House. This work provides an interesting biography of Keynes and an analysis of his work.

"We are all Keynesians now." *Time,* December 31, 1965. A short readable essay on the Keynesian influence.

KEYNES IN WORDS AND PICTURES

CHAPTER 16

INTRODUCTION

The Keynesian model has remained the prevailing economic paradigm for the past 40 years. Originating in the depression-plagued world of the 1930s, Keynesian economic theory has persisted through the slow-moving 1950s, the inflationary 1960s as well as the unstable 1970s. It has not always been successful, as economists have bent its rules and principles and redefined the priorities to fit the current circumstance; but it still solidly remains *the* economic theory of the age. Monetarist Milton Friedman perhaps stated it best when he said, "We are all Keynesians now." This chapter will describe and explore in detail the assumptions, methods, and the implications of the full Keynesian *model*. Both verbal and graphical analyses will be used to illustrate the theory since, to many, a picture is indeed worth a thousand words. Several examples will follow illustrating the use of Keynesian Theory.

CONSUMPTION

The very best place to start is, of course, the beginning; and though it is sometimes difficult to distinguish the beginning from the middle or the end in Keynesian theory, this examination will start with the consumption function and the assumptions and hypotheses that underlie one of America's favorite pastimes. *Consumption* is the purchasing of goods and services, the spending of income for necessities and luxuries. It is perhaps intuitive that consumption depends on many things. Some of these are income, interest rates, price levels, and expectations along with the other financial assets the consumer might possess. But, as one might well expect, consumption is primarily a function of income. This can be expressed by the following functional notation:

$$C = f(Y),$$

where C is the consumption of individuals over some period of time, Y is income, and f indicates the functional notation. Keynes in his "fundamental psychological law" states: "Men are disposed, as a rule and on the average, to increase their consumption as their income increases." In other words, as your income increases (perhaps upon graduation and securing a job), your expenditures will rise as well: but, says Keynes, not by as much. This relationship may be expressed graphically with consumption (C) on the vertical axis and income (Y) on the horizontal axis. Since consumption is an increasing function of income (Y), as Y increases, C will also increase.

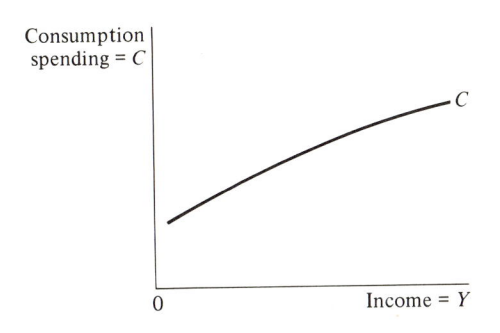

FIG. 16.1 The consumption function.

What will be done with the income *not* spent on consumption? Simple! It will be saved. Saving is any part of income that is not spent on consumption. There is nothing left to do with it. (Burning it isn't rational—and Keynes assumes after all that we are all rational.) In equations, our relationship is:

$$Y = C + S.$$

Again, Y is income, C is personal consumption expenditures, and S is personal saving. Saving is, in effect, a residual of consumption. Saving occurs when individuals defer present consumption or spending and keep the funds for future use. People save for many different reasons. It may be for precaution or fear of what might lie ahead. It may be for a desire to become "financially independent" some time in the future. Or it may be for pride or avarice. For whatever reasons, saving does occur; and, like consumption, it too is a function of income [$S = f(Y)$].

Before proceeding further in the analysis of consumption and saving, it is important to establish a reference position (or helping line) so that the relation of the level of consumption to the level of income may be more easily discussed. This helping line (sometimes called an aggregate supply line*) is a 45° line from the origin of the Consumption-Income axis. (See Fig. 16.2.)

According to high school geometry, the 45° line bisects the 90° angle and, at any point on the line, income will be equal to consumption. For example at point A, both Y and C are equal to $4000 while at point B, $Y = C = 5000. If the consumption curve is now superimposed upon this 45° line, it will allow an examination of the relationship of consumption to the actual level of income in the economy.

---

*At each level of income (Y), firms desire to sell a maximum amount of their products. Each point on the 45° line represents a level of business receipts (consumer spending) just equal to the corresponding level of national income (Y). Thus points on the 45° line form the desired aggregate supply curve for firms.

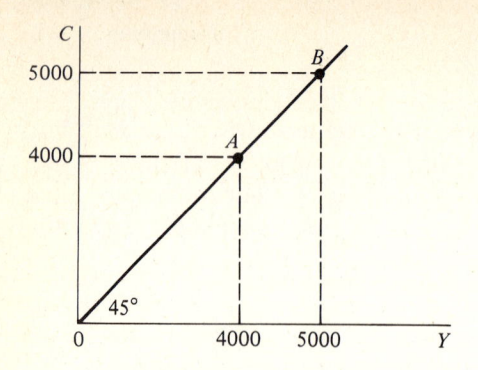

FIG. 16.2 The 45° line (aggregate supply).

In Fig. 16.3 at point A, consumption and income are equal since the consumption curve passes through the 45° line at that point. Point A is called the *breakeven level of income* as Y = C = $4000. Savings equal zero. At point D, however, consumption is less than income indicating that some amount of saving must be taking place. Since income is $5000 and consumption is only $4500, $500 must be saved. At point B, consumption is greater than income. Income is $3000, but consumption spending is $3500. "Dissaving" is taking place to allow the desired level of consumption to occur. Dissaving consists of borrowing or drawing down other financial assets in order to purchase products for consumption purposes. Individuals on low fixed incomes frequently dissave. So do young people starting families or households. (Note that even when income is zero, there is some amount of consumption spending.)

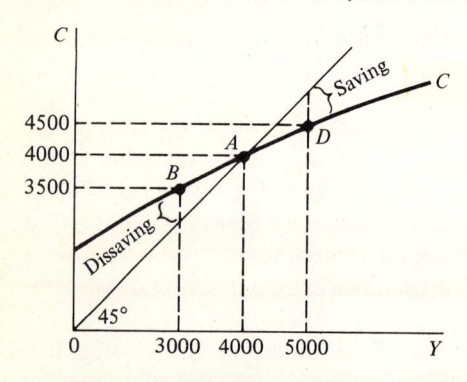

FIG. 16.3 The consumption function and the 45° line.

---

1. Do you dissave now? Do you expect to dissave in the next year or two? Draw a curve on the graph in Fig. 16.4 indicating what you expect your consumption pattern to look like for the rest of your life. At what periods do you think you might be dissaving?

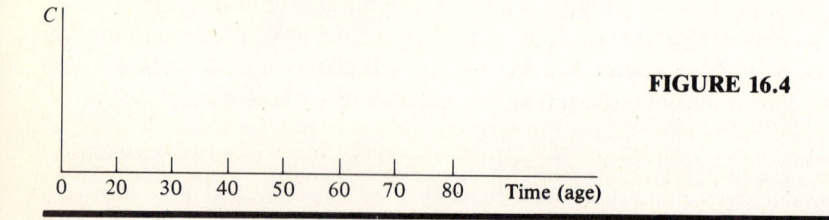

FIGURE 16.4

Average and Marginal Propensity to Consume

The average consumption-income ratio can be determined by the information given thus far. This ratio is simply C/Y. At point A in Fig. 16.3, the average consumption-income ratio, the *average propensity to consume* or the *APC*, is $C/Y = \$4000/\$4000$, or 1. At point D, it is $C/Y = \$4500/\$5000 = 0.9$; and at point B, $APC = C/Y = \$3500/\$3000 = 1.167$. The APC is one of the two fundamental ratios that are derived from the consumption function. The second of these ratios, and perhaps the more important, is the *marginal propensity to consume,* or the *MPC*. The MPC is the ratio between the *change* that occurs in consumption with some given change in income. This may be expressed as $\Delta C/\Delta Y$, where Δ is a symbol for change, C is consumption, and Y is income. If income increases from $4000 to $5000, we find consumption increases from $4000 to $4500. The change in income is $5000 - $4000, or $1000; while the change in consumption is $4500 - $4000, or $500. The MPC then is $\Delta C/\Delta Y = \$500/\$1000$, or 0.5. This means that for every additional dollar of income $0.50 will be used for consumption and the remaining $0.50 will be saved.

---

2. **What is the MPC when we move from point B to point A?**

The MPC or $\Delta C/\Delta Y$ relationship is also the slope of the consumption function. (See Fig. 16.5.) It should be noted that the consumption function will be a straight line only when the MPC is constant at all levels of income. This will seldom occur since each individual as well as each income earning group reacts differently to changes in income. However, for ease of analysis, in most cases we will assume a constant MPC (and thus a straight-line consumption function).

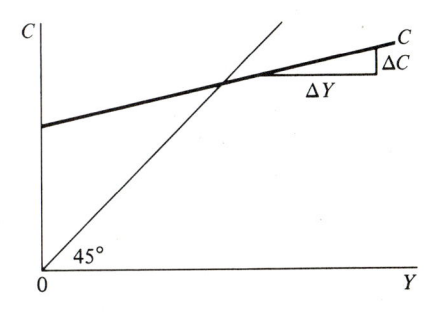

FIG. 16.5 The marginal propensity of production.

---

3. **How might your reaction to a change in income be different from that of Nelson Rockefeller? from that of a poor person?**

Table 16.1 summarizes our data thus far:

TABLE 16.1

Y	C	APC	MPC
$3000	$3500	1.17	
4000	4000	1.00	0.5
5000	4500	0.90	0.5

SAVINGS

Earlier we established that the savings function is a residual of consumption. Whatever income is not spent for consumption purposes is saved. ($Y = C + S$, so $S = Y - C$). An analysis similar to the one developed for the consumption function can be developed for the savings function. Data for a savings function is derived in Table 16.2.

TABLE 16.2

Y	C	S = Y - C
$3000	$3500	-$500
4000	4000	0
5000	4500	500

This information also can be expressed graphically as it is in Fig. 16.6.

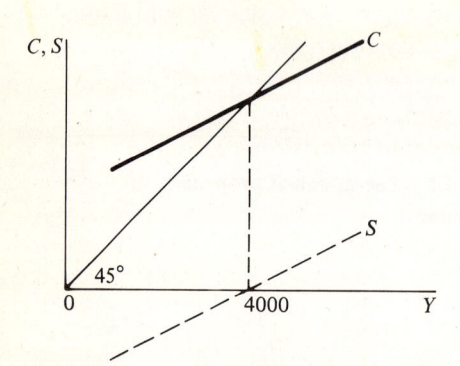

FIG. 16.6 The savings function.

The Average and Marginal Propensity to Save

The ratio of savings to income S/Y, or the *average propensity to save* (APS), can also be found; as can the *marginal propensity to save* (MPS), which is the ratio between the change in saving to any change in income, $\Delta S / \Delta Y$. Our information thus far is summarized in Table 16.3.

TABLE 16.3

Y	C	S	APS = S/Y	MPS = $\Delta S/\Delta Y$
$3000	$3500	−$500	−0.167	
4000	4000	0	0	0.5
5000	4500	500	0.1	0.5

It might be noted that MPS + MPC = 1. This must be true since the change in C and the change in S must add to the whole of every new dollar of income.*

INVESTMENT AND THE TWO-SECTOR MODEL

The simplest Keynesian model consists of an analysis of two sectors in the economy. The household and business sectors will be examined first—in a model that has no government and no foreign sectors. Total income from these two sectors in the economy then must be:

$$Y = C + I,$$

where Y is income, C is consumption, and I is investment. This relationship is derived from the national income accounts that were examined in the Appendix 14A, as well as from the circular flow diagram, where Y comes from the production of goods and services (aggregate supply). Consumption represents spending by households on consumer goods and services. Investment is the spending by businesses for inventories and capital goods. Together they make up the aggregate demand for goods and services produced. From the preceding section we know that $C = f(Y)$. But we know little about investment. *Investment* consists of additions to plant, equipment, and inventories in the business sector. Inventories may be goods of any type, from raw material inputs to intermediate and finished products. In this simple two-sector model, we will assume that investment is an exogeneous variable determined outside of the model itself. For example, if General Motors decides to invest $1000, it is a decision made without considering the variables included in this model. Expected profits, interest costs, or business confidence might be more important to investment decisions than income and consumption levels.† Graphically, then investment would be constant at all levels of income as in Fig. 16.7.

---

*$Y = C + S$
$\Delta Y = \Delta C + \Delta S$
$\Delta Y/\Delta Y = \Delta C/\Delta Y + \Delta S/\Delta Y$, and 1 = MPC + MPS.

†Investment in a more sophisticated model is a function of income, since as income in the economy increases, businesses will more than likely increase their level of investment. For simplicity, however, we will use the less complex model and assume that investment decisions are exogeneous to the system.

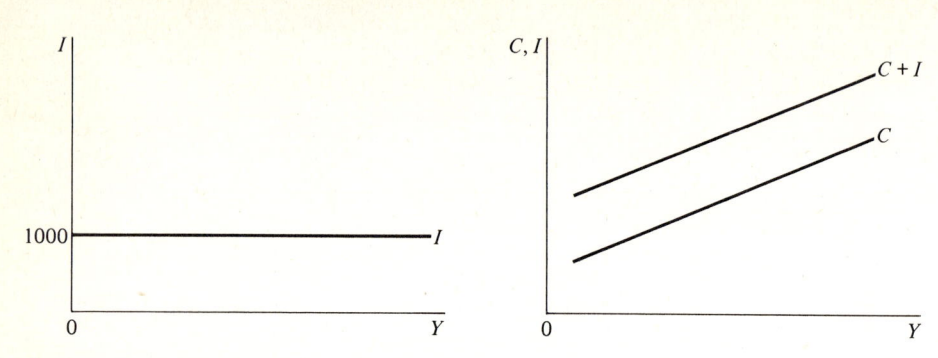

FIG. 16.7 The investment function.

In the two-sector model, it is known that:

$$Y = C + I$$

and that

$$Y = C + S.$$

Putting these two equations together tells us that in the two-sector Keynesian model the only leakage from the system, savings, must be equal to the only injection, investment. This describes the equilibrium condition for the model; when aggregate supply ($Y = C + S$) equals aggregate demand ($Y = C + I$), then $S = I$.

$$\cancel{C} + S = \cancel{C} + I$$

$$S = I.$$

Several important factors should be noted in the $S = I$ relationship. First, savings and investment are done by two different groups of people for totally different reasons. The second point is that realized, or actual, savings must equal realized, or actual, investment. There is no guarantee that the dollar amount of investment *planned* by the business sector will be the same as the savings planned in the household sector. Using the data in Table 16.4 with planned investment spending of $1000, we can graphically and logically view the following problem. I^p equals planned investment and I^a equals actual investment.

TABLE 16.4

Y	C	S	I^p	I^a
5000	4000	1000	1000	1000
6000	4500	1500	1000	1500

Figure 16.8 shows that the equilibrium income level of the two-sector model is at point A where the $C + I$ line intersects the 45° reference line. This point is some-

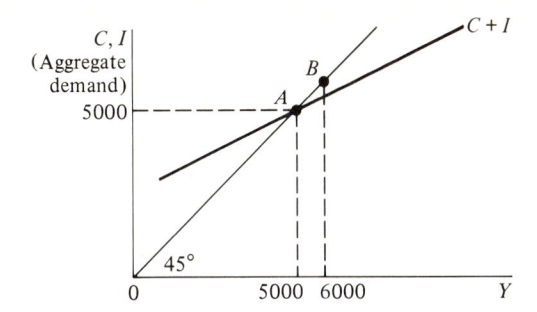

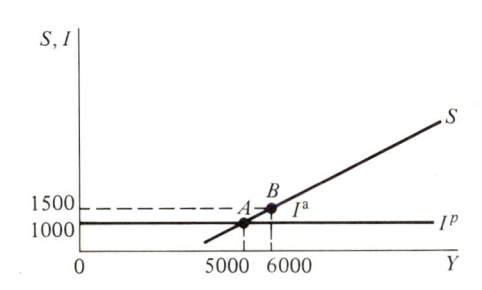

FIG. 16.8 The equilibrium level of income.

times referred to as the "Keynesian cross." Here, $Y = C + I$; $Y = \$5000$, $C = \$4000$, and $I = \$1000$. All higher and lower levels of income are not at equilibrium. At those points, $S \neq I$ and aggregate demand $\neq$ aggregate supply. At $Y = \$5000$, $C + I = C + S$, and aggregate demand equals aggregate supply. Only when income and output are at $\$5000$ does *planned I = actual I*.

One can examine the disequilibrium position B, where $C = \$4500$, $S = \$1500$, and $Y = \$6000$. Here, intended savings are greater than intended investment, since savings are $\$1500$ and investment is only $\$1000$. With planned I at $\$1000$, there will be an unplanned increase in inventories since some of the goods produced will not be sold because consumers desire to increase their savings balances. At $Y = \$6000$, $C + I =$ (only) $\$5500$ (and $C + S = \$6000$). Aggregate supply is greater than aggregate demand. Total output is $\$6000$, but total spending is only $\$5500$. Therefore, inventories increase by $\$500$. Since the increase in inventories is counted as investment, *actual I* will increase to $\$1500$. Actual savings equal actual investment.

---

4. **In the next time period with an increased supply of inventories already accumulated, what do you expect the planned *I* response of business would be? What would this do to the equilibrium level of income?**

However, since planned S is greater than planned I, this is not an equilibrium position. With increased inventories, which were unplanned, producers will reduce output; and hence income will also be reduced. As income is reduced, both C and S will decrease. This movement will continue until an equilibrium is reached where aggregate demand equals aggregate supply. This occurs at point A, where

$C+S=C+I$, and where planned S of $1000 equals planned I of $1000. This equilibrium may be or may not be at full employment. Unlike the classical model, the Keynesian model may have equilibrium conditions at greater than, less than, or equal to full employment.

CHANGES IN INVESTMENT AND THE KEYNESIAN MULTIPLIER

Once equilibrium has been reached in the two-sector model, there will be no tendency for the system to change until some exogenous disturbance occurs—such as a change in the level of investment. Suppose investment increases from $1000 to $3000 for a *change* of $2000. This is represented graphically in Fig. 16.9.

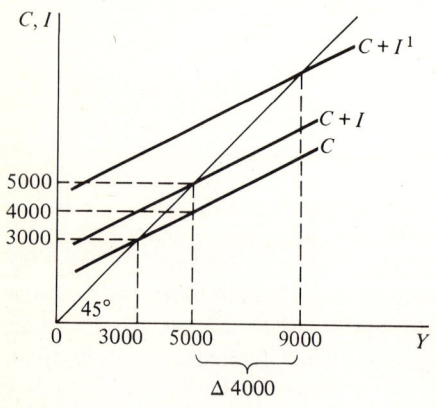

FIG. 16.9 An increase in investment spending.

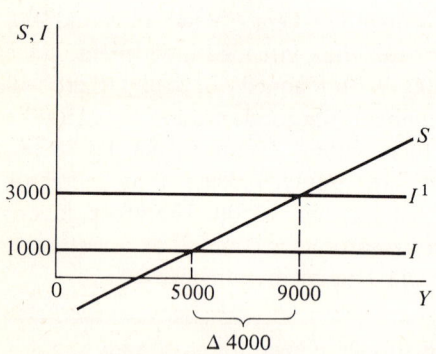

How much will income increase as a result of this $2000 increase in investment? What is the new equilibrium level of income? It is here that the infamous Keynesian *multiplier* has its effect. When additional investment enters into the model, a response occurs that increases the equilibrium level of income by some multiple of the change in investment. This multiple (called the Keynesian multiplier) is equal to 1/1−MPC, and is equal to the ratio between the change in income and the change in investment or $\Delta Y/\Delta I$.

A Simple Derivation of the Multiplier

We know that in the Keynesian system $\Delta I = \Delta S$. If both sides of this identity are divided by ΔY, the right side of the equation becomes the MPS:

$$\frac{\Delta I}{\Delta Y} = \frac{\Delta S}{\Delta Y} = MPS = \frac{1}{\text{the multiplier}}.$$

If we invert the equation we get:

$$k = \text{the multiplier} = \frac{\Delta Y}{\Delta I} = \frac{\Delta Y}{\Delta S} = \frac{1}{MPS}.$$

Since

$$MPC + MPS = 1,$$

Then

$$\frac{\Delta Y}{\Delta I} = \frac{1}{1 - MPC} = \text{the multiplier} = k.$$

Example: Given MPC = 0.75

$$k = \frac{\Delta Y}{\Delta I} = \frac{1}{1 - 0.75} = \frac{1}{0.25} = 4.0$$

so for each ΔI, income will increase by $4 \times \Delta I$.

An example of this multiplier process is seen if a nursery decides to expand by adding a greenhouse that costs $20,000. The first round of spending, then, is $20,000 that is added to the income stream. The contractor who built the greenhouse now has the $20,000 (as income) and will respend it according to the MPC formulation. If the MPC is 1/2 or 0.5, the contractor will spend $10,000 (perhaps on sand, gravel and a CB for the rig) and save the remaining $10,000. The $10,000 then enters the income stream (as other people's income), and one-half of that will be spent and one-half saved in the third round. Table 16.5 illustrates this process.

TABLE 16.5

Expenditure	ΔY	$\Delta C = 1/2\, \Delta Y$	$\Delta S = 1/2\, \Delta Y$
Greenhouse = round 1	$20,000	$10,000	$10,000
Sand and sound = round 2	10,000	5,000	5,000
round 3	5,000	2,500	2,500
round 4	2,500	1,250	1,250
round 5	1,250	625	625
round 6	625	312.50	312.50
etc.			
Total*	$40,000	$20,000	$20,000

*Until $20,000 $\cdot$ (1/1 − 0.5) = $20,000 $\cdot$ 2 = $40,000 is generated in new income. The initial increase in spending is multiplied through the economy.

Thus $40,000 of new income will be generated by the $20,000 increase in investment, given an MPC of 0.5 (a multiplier of 2). We are assuming that one can "generalize" an MPC for the whole economy at some point in time in consistently using MPC = 0.5. In Fig. 16.9, an increase in I of $2000 will produce a new equilibrium level of $Y = \$9000$ (with an additional "multiplied" increase in Y of $4000).

Believe me, the whole economy profits. We rob somebody of five grand. Then we buy some stuff from a fence. He gives his cut to the mob. They pay off the cops. . . .

Reprinted by permission of Sidney Harris.

---

5. What is the new level of consumption in Fig. 16.9 at Y = $9000? Also, what is the level of savings?

THE THREE-SECTOR MODEL

To add a bit more realism to the model, the government sector will now be added to the simple two-sector Keynesian model. The government enters into this analysis, like investment, as an exogenous variable,

$$G = G_o.$$

This indicates that there will be a given level of *government spending* for goods and services at all levels of income as shown in Fig. 16.10.

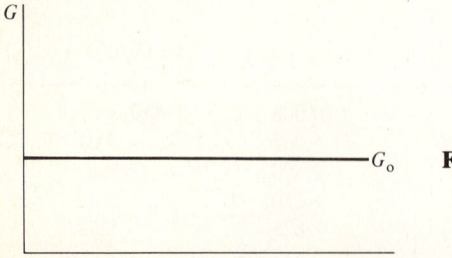

FIG. 16.10 The government spending function.

Once government spending is added to the two-sector model, the income identity, or aggregate demand, becomes that shown in Fig. 16.11.

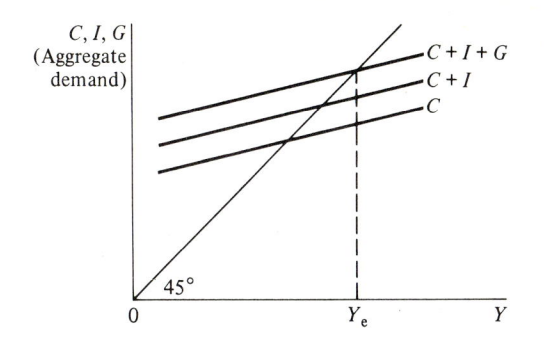

FIG. 16.11 The Keynesian model with C, I, and G spending.

The aggregate supply or aggregate income line is again represented by the 45° line. Expenditures are now made by consumers, investors, and the government creating the aggregate demand curve for the economy. The equilibrium level of income is Y_e. $Y_e = C + I + G$. At any other level of income $Y \neq C + I + G$.

Shifts may also occur in government expenditures. Indeed, the government may make decisions that will effect the level of income in the economy. These expenditures are often aimed at *directly* changing the level of income—perhaps a level of income *not* at full employment to a new equilibrium level of income *at* full employment. Government expenditures for goods and services work through the Keynesian multiplier process just as investments do. Government spending becomes income that enters the spending flow as recipients consume and save at levels reflected by their MPC and MPS. Any increase in G will increase Y by an amount equal to $\Delta G \cdot 1/1 - MPC$.

The results of government spending may be analyzed if we look at a purchase of 750,000 typewriter ribbons by the Government Services Administration (GSA) at a total cost of $500,000. Graphically in Fig. 16.12 we see that aggregate demand has increased from its equilibrium position at $10 million (where $Y = C + I + G$). If the marginal propensity to consume remains at 0.5, the multiplier is 2. The increase in income that results from the purchase of typewriter ribbons is $2 \cdot \$500,000$

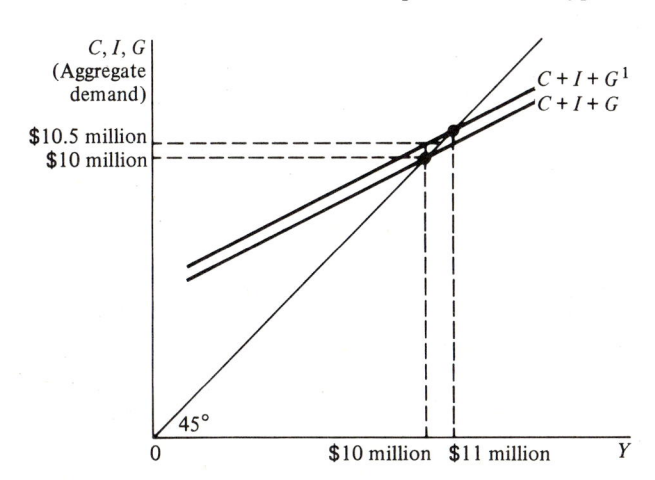

FIG. 16.12 The effects of increased government spending on the equilibrium level of income.

($k \cdot \Delta G$), or $1 million. The new equilibrium level of income is $11 million ($10m + $1m).

An increase in defense spending by the government will have the effect of stimulating the economies of Wichita, Seattle, and Los Angeles, while more research money spent for the space shuttle will boost the economies of Huntsville, Alabama, and Houston, Texas, as well as increasing the enrollments in aerospace engineering next year.

6. What kinds of government spending programs would stimulate growth in your area of the world? What are a few government spending programs that would help us all?

THE FOUR-SECTOR MODEL

We could extend the model even further to include the international sector, and we will—briefly. Here aggregate demand would be equal to consumption, investment, government spending, and the net addition of export income (or exports-imports).

$$Y = C + I + G + (X - M).$$

The equilibrium level of income would be at the point at which this expanded aggregate demand intersects the aggregate supply or income line.

7. Would you expect the international sector to have a multiplier effect like investment and government spending? Why or why not?

CONCLUSION

The Keynesian *model* thus gives us a theoretical framework within which to analyze how the aggregate economy operates and to examine the sorts of macroeconomic problems one might expect to encounter. If aggregate supply is greater than aggregate demand, we can expect a lower level of national income. On the other hand, if aggregate demand is greater than aggregate supply, we would expect an expansion of economic activity and a higher equilibrium level of national income. An equilibrium level is where aggregate supply (Y) equals aggregate demand ($C + I + G$).

KEY CONCEPTS

consumption
marginal propensity to consume (MPC)
average propensity of consume (APC)
marginal propensity to save (MPS)
average propensity of save (APS)
saving
dissaving

investment
two-sector model
planned investment/saving
actual investment/saving
multiplier
government spending
breakeven point

REVIEW QUESTIONS

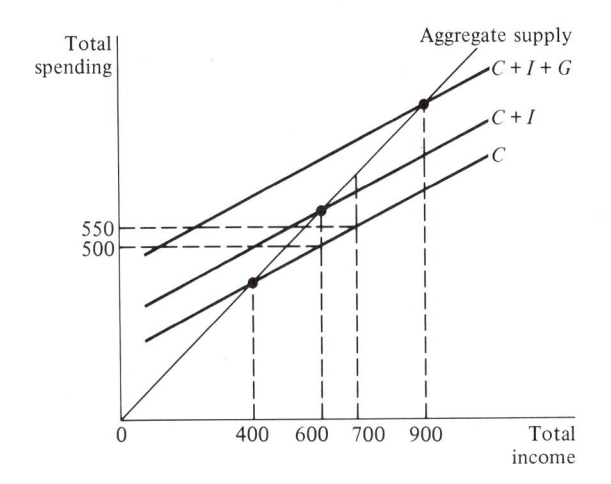

FIG. 16.13 A problem on the Keynesian model. The intersection of aggregate supply and $C+I+G$ = 900.

Use the information in Fig. 16.13 to answer the following:

1. Explain in words why the equilibrium level of income would be 400 if there were no savings or investment. What would be the level of output at this income level?

2. Why would the consumption function (if extended) intersect the spending axis at a positive value? What does this mean? Is it realistic?

3. The slope of the consumption function tells us that as income increases, consumption (increases/decreases) but at a (slower/faster) rate. Is this realistic?

4. What assumptions are required to draw an investment function parallel to the consumption function? How realistic are these assumptions? What is the amount of desired investment in Fig. 16.13?

5. What is the level of saving at income of 600? What is the level of desired investment at income of 600? Why is income of 600 an equilibrium level of income (with $C+I$)?

6. What would be the level of savings if the income were at 700? What is the level of desired investment at this income level? What forces are at work at an income of 700? What will be the equilibrium level of income?

7. What is the MPC in Fig. 16.13?

8. Assume that income is at 600 but that it takes an income of 900 to generate enough jobs for full employment. What level of government spending will be necessary to achieve full employment?

SUGGESTED READINGS

Gardner Ackley, 1961. *Macroeconomics,* Macmillan. This is a major restatement of Keynes. Graph upon graph of *C*'s, *I*'s, and *G*'s.

Alvin Hansen, 1953. *A Guide to Keynes,* McGraw-Hill. More graphs and an explanation of the Keynesian system. Hansen's book helped popularize Keynesian economics in the U.S. in the postwar period.

E. K. Hunt, 1975. *Property and Prophets* (2nd ed.), Harper & Row. Chapter 10 has a simple verbal description of Keynes's economics.

John Kenneth Galbraith, 1958. *The Affluent Society,* Houghton Mifflin. Gives a good view of the consumer and the consumption ethic in a growing affluent society.

FISCAL POLICY: GOVERNMENT SPENDING AND TAXATION

CHAPTER 17

INTRODUCTION

The federal government has been officially committed to maintaining employment, price stability, and output since the passage of the Employment Act of 1946. This act states:

The Congress hereby declares that it is the continuing policy and responsibility of the Federal Government to use all practicable means consistent with its needs and obligations and other essential considerations of national policy, with assistance and cooperation of industry, agriculture, labor and state and local governments, to coordinate and utilize all its plans, functions, and resources for the purpose of creating and maintaining, in a manner calculated to foster and promote free competitive enterprise and the general welfare, conditions under which there will be afforded useful employment opportunities, including self-employment, for those able, willing, and seeking to work and to promote maximum employment, production, and purchasing power.

It is within the framework of these economic objectives that government *fiscal policy* tries to operate.

According to Keynesian theory, when the economy gets out of kilter for any one of a variety of reasons, governments possess an arsenal of tools with which to fight the economic enemies, inflation and unemployment. While normally we think of the federal government as the major spending and taxing authority, state and local governments are very active in the process as well. In some cases, however, we find that state and local governments actually exacerbate economic problems (pursuing cyclical rather than countercyclical measures).

In addition to governments, at the state and local as well as at the federal level, many groups and organizations within these governmental organizations are involved in the making of fiscal policy.

The President receives advice on fiscal policy from his *Council of Economic Advisors* (CEA). Some of the advice is accepted and successfully makes its way through the bureaucratic channels. But other advice does not. In addition to advice from the CEA, the President receives advice from the Office of Management and Budget. Meanwhile, the "Hill" has its own Joint Economic Committee and Con-

Congress plays a role in determining the macroeconomic performance of the U.S. (Photograph by Tom Riddell.)

gressional Budget Office to assist in legislative decisions on government spending and taxation. Policy studies in all these bodies are constantly ongoing. Often the dynamics of these public offices, plus the host of private organizations engaged in economic research, lead to a profusion of mixed analysis and advice.

When poverty and unemployment arise or inflation rages, the government has tools to deal with each. Unemployment and poverty suggest that government spending and/or transfers are necessary. These may be in the form of unemployment and welfare benefits, food stamps, medicaid or a variety of other payments or through purchases of goods and services. Other remedies that might be suggested are increases in employment opportunities and decreased tax levels. The government may try to stimulate employment by directly adding programs that put people back to work. Or it may try to induce business to increase its investment and employment levels. This may be done through a series of tax credits or advantages for those firms increasing employment and investment.

To combat inflation, fiscal policy commands spending reductions or tax increases. Cutbacks of all types and tax increases are urged to restrict household and business spending.

This chapter will explore how each type of fiscal action works. We will deal with the shortcomings as well as the advantages of using fiscal policy.

FISCAL POLICY

Fiscal policy concerns actions of taxation or government spending that are designed to change the level of income. These actions may be made with respect to a *particular* situation, or they may occur automatically with a given change in economic conditions. The former are *discretionary*—the latter are automatic. These automatic actions are known as *nondiscretionary* forms of fiscal policy or "built-in stabilizers." Examples of built-in stabilizers include the progressive income tax system, unemployment insurance, and all other compensatory programs that come into effect when income levels are low and that are shut off when income levels are high. As economic activity decreases during a recession, income is lost. This threatens additional decreases in economic activity. However, as unemployment increases, unemployment compensation *automatically* "increases" income and spending to prevent a cumulative decrease in economic activity.

1. If income is increasing at a highly inflationary rate, how do income taxes help to stabilize the economy automatically?

Government Spending

Policy positions are often made when employment levels are not deemed adequate by politicians and public opinion; for example, if the full employment level of income is thought to be at $1.7 trillion and income is currently $1.1 trillion. In this situation, there will probably be a substantial amount of unemployment and the government can opt for fiscal action that will increase the level of employment and the level of income by $0.6 trillion.* In its arsenal of policies are spending, taxing authority, and the ability to issue transfer payments. Transfer payments are income supplements paid to individuals. These payments are not for current productive services and thus are not included in the yearly national product accounts. In some sense, they were "earned" previously. Transfers include social security, welfare, and veterans benefits among others, and are a part of the personal income tally. (Thus, they enter the income-spending flow.)

Government spending (on defense, on space, on buildings, etc.) will have the largest expansionary impact on income in the economy *since the full amount of spending enters the economy in the first round*. In the case of transfer payments and tax reductions, some of the impact in the first round is "leaked" into savings.

If the MPC in the economy is $\frac{2}{3}$ we can easily find that the multiplier is 3, given the formula $k = 1/1(1 - MPC)$.† To discover the amount of government spending that is necessary to increase the level of income by $0.6 trillion, one need only know these two variables since $Y = k \cdot \Delta G$. We know the desired ΔY to be $0.6 trillion and k to be 3, so $0.6 trillion $= 3 \cdot \Delta G$, and $G = \$0.2$ trillion.

Our policy recommendation then is that the government build a (big) dam at a price of $0.2 trillion to increase income by $0.6 trillion to $1.7 trillion (the full employment level of income). Graphically, this is shown in Fig. 17.1.

Tax Cuts

If the government decides that the way to accomplish the desired increase in Y of $0.6 trillion is by a cut in taxes, the same question is raised. How much of a tax reduction is needed to generate new increases in income equal to the $0.6 trillion?

The answer is not as easily found as before since tax cuts have a different channel of operation through the economy. The crucial difference is during the first round of spending. Rather than $0.2 trillion being directly spent on our dam, the $0.2 trillion in tax cuts goes into the pocketbooks and bank accounts of the taxpayers. According to our marginal propensities, we will save part of the $0.2 trillion and spend the remainder. Again, with an MPC of ⅔ and a tax cut equal to $0.2 trillion or $200 billion, the first action is to consume ⅔ of $200 billion or $133 billion and save $66 billion. So that in the initial round of spending, only $133 billion enters the total income steam rather than the $200 billion (or $0.2 trillion) that entered in the case of government spending.

---

*Conversely, we could establish an example in which inflation was the primary problem with income being *above* the full employment level. For example, income could be at $1.7 trillion with the full employment level at $1.1 trillion. In that case, the policy measures would be the opposite of those we discuss in the following sections.

†$k = \dfrac{1}{1-MPC}$; $k = \dfrac{1}{1-2/3}$; $k = \dfrac{1}{1/3}$; $k = 3$.

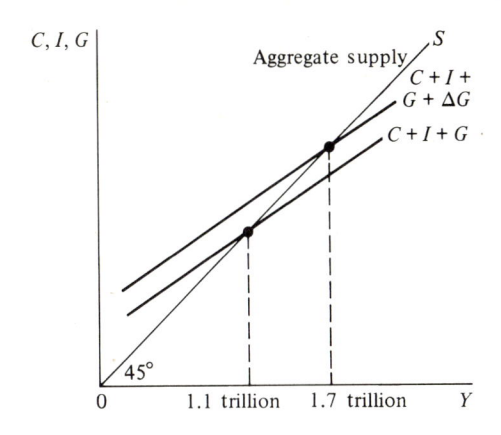

FIG. 17.1 The effect of increased government spending.

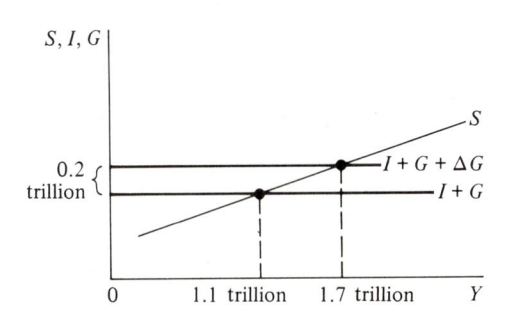

This indicates that the *tax multiplier* is less than the *spending multiplier,* in fact one less, $k - 1 = k_{tx}$ or $k_{tx} = -MPC/(1 - MPC)$.* (Note the minus sign since a tax *cut* will increase income). Using our previous example, to get an increase in income of $0.6 trillion with a tax multiplier of 2 (3 − 1 = 2), the decrease in taxes which must occur is:

$$\Delta Y = k_{tx} \cdot \Delta T_x$$
$$\$0.6t = 2 \cdot \Delta T_x, \text{ and } \Delta T_x = 0.3t.$$

Or, taxes must be reduced by $0.3 trillion to increase Y by $0.6 trillion.

Transfer Payments

Transfer payments work essentially the same way as tax cuts in their impact on the economy. Again, the income of households will increase in the first round—instead

---

*This can be derived as follows:
$$-k_{tx} = \frac{1}{1-MPC} - 1$$
$$= \frac{1}{1-MPC} - \frac{1-MPC}{1-MPC} = \frac{MPC}{1-MPC}$$
$$k_{tx} = -\frac{MPC}{1-MPC}.$$

of having a direct expenditure on goods by the government. The *transfer multiplier* "like" the tax multiplier is $k - 1 = k_{tr}$ (only it is positive since an increase in transfers increases income). Transfer expenditures worth $0.3 trillion would be necessary to raise income by $0.6 trillion.

More realistically, we might try to examine the impact of an increase in social security payments of $4 billion.

---

2. If the MPC were 0.9, how much of an impact would this transfer package have on the economy?

3. What complications might you run into in trying to estimate the total income effect of this policy? (Hint: *Part* of the $4 billion is in the form of transfers.)

The government, of course, might choose one or any combination of these three alternatives. It also might decide to pass legislation to encourage new consumer and/or investment spending. Tax credits and incentives have been utilized in recent years to stimulate certain industries that might be suffering more than others in the economy. The 5-percent housing tax credit of 1974 was a fine example of such a policy. Many newly constructed homes provided a 5-percent credit on the purchaser's income taxes. The measure was designed to pick up a depressed housing industry, as well as to stimulate economic activity in general.

The Balanced Budget Multiplier

The notion of a balanced budget (by 1985!?) has been an exceedingly popular campaign device and easily gains a large public following (despite Keynes's put-down). Logically if family budgets should balance (before creditors start beating at the door), why shouldn't the federal government balance its budget? Balancing the budget means essentially taking in amounts equal to those spent. For example, if the government decides to spend some $0.3 trillion it should collect $0.3 trillion in additional taxes so that the budget will balance. Exactly what are the implications of this? Again, using the Keynesian multiplier analysis (given an MPC = ⅔ so that $k = 3$ and $-k_{tx} = 2$), the $0.3 trillion increase in government spending would increase income by $0.9 trillion ($\Delta Y = k \cdot \Delta G$ or $3 \cdot \$0.3 = \$0.9$), while the $0.3 trillion *increase* in taxes would decrease income by $0.6 trillion ($\Delta Y = k_{tx} \cdot \Delta T_x = -2 \cdot \$0.3T = -\$0.6T$). The *net* result of a balanced budget in this case is an *increase* in income of $0.3 trillion. In case you hadn't noticed, the balanced budget multiplier is 1:

$$(\Delta Y = k_{BB} \cdot \Delta \text{Budget}; \quad k_{BB} = \frac{\Delta Y}{\Delta \text{Budget}} = \frac{0.3T}{0.3T} = 1).$$

---

4. What would be the effect on income of a decrease in government spending of $0.3 trillion and a tax cut of $0.3 trillion? Is this a balanced budget?

LAGS, LAGS, AND MORE LAGS

From the discussion thus far, it seems that all that is needed for full employment in the economy is a mighty snap of the government purse strings. Several rather sticky problems emerge in the deployment of these strings, however. One problem encountered early on is the one of simple recognition of the fact that a problem exists—in effect a *recognition lag*. Another is trying to estimate the MPC and thus the multiplier effect that each expenditure might have on the economy. Some types of spending tend to generate larger stimulative and investment effects than others. For example, estimates have placed the defense spending multiplier somewhat lower than that of other forms of government spending.

---

5. Why might defense spending have a smaller multiplier?

Another problem with government spending is that it tends to be lumpy. Projects are normally large and are generally confined to a reasonably small geographical area. A dam in Lewisburg, Pa. (where?) will hardly help unemployment in Dubuque or Detroit. (Perhaps that's why the Army Corps of Engineers wants to build a dam on every square inch of the earth—to spread the impact of the dollar as well as of the water.)

Next, log rolling, a delightful game perfected by politicians, is played after the corps is convinced that a dam is desperately needed for a congressional area. "I'll most certainly vote for a dam in your district if you'll vote for a highway in mine," the dialogue goes. As these games continue, unemployment levels may be skyrocketing.

Legislation tends to move slowly through Congress. By the time funds are allocated, new and different problems might emerge (inflation), and the expenditure of government funds would only add fuel to the flames of inflation. Though tax policies effect every individual in the nation, they also take time before enactment. The favorite example of economists is the 1964 tax cut, and this is an example of Keynesian economics well thought out and used! The cut was proposed in 1963 and, after more than a year of hearings, was finally approved. (Our loyal members of Congress were unconvinced that the cut would be remembered by their constituents—but they were sure that a tax increase would be necessary at some later point in time—so why bother to cut taxes now?) Oftentimes it is a conflict between the President and the Congress that leads to bitter policy debates. These problems are oftentimes referred to as the *legislative lag*.

Execution presents another delay in transferring the legislation into action. Tax policies tend to be faster and more efficient after passage, while spending packages may be hung up in a bidding and allocation process for months. This has been called the *implementation lag*.

Yet, once the legislation for government spending is enacted and executed, it is effective. Empirical results from the Federal Reserve-M.I.T.-Penn (FMP) econometric model show that one year after a government expenditure of $1 billion has taken place, GNP increases by about $3 billion. (The monetarist's model at the St. Louis Fed estimates that there is no effect after one year—but we'll discuss the implications of this model in the chapter on monetary policy.)

COUNTER-COUNTERCYCLICAL POLICY

In the introduction to this chapter we suggested that state and local governments have their own fiscal policy. They are active in spending and taxing as well as in issuing transfers. Often, however, these tools are used at the "wrong time." Fiscal policy is designed to counter inflationary and recessionary trends in economic activity. Yet local spending is often done when "good times" prevail. It is much easier to get a school or a library or a park issue through the polls in boom periods; and so construction projects add to the boom.

---

6. What does Keynesian theory tell you about this kind of policy? What would be the economic effects?

7. Is there any salvation to the procyclical policies of state and local governments? (What happens when bond isues are passed?)

In the same vein, when times are hard, it is often difficult for state and local governments to finance new spending projects that might stimulate the economy.

THE DEBT

The national debt is one of the great conversation pieces of Americana. Make sure that your instructor covers this section before Thanksgiving recess, since it always makes for interesting turkey table talk. (In fact your parents may decide not to send you back to school to learn any more of this "propaganda.") All forms of debt have increased dramatically since World War II. Corporate debt has increased by more than 1500 percent. State and local debt has increased by about 1250 percent, while consumer debt has increased by 2500 percent! During this period the debt of the federal government has increased by about "only" 1000 percent.

Why is the debt so worrisome to so many of our fellow citizens? Probably because it is so large. By the end of 1977, the national debt stood at about $700 billion or $3256 per person.* The debt could be eliminated fairly easily, though a bit painfully. Taxes could have simply been increased by $3256 for every man, woman, and child in the next year.

But there are other more important facets of the debt that need to be examined. Looking at Table 17.1 one can see that most of the national debt was accumulated during the war years: World War II and Vietnam. Debt as a percentage of our

---

*The national debt is the debt of the federal government. It is brought about by deficits in the federal budget. These deficits are financed through borrowing from the public (treasury bills, treasury bonds, and savings bonds).

national income has fallen yearly. Since GNP is increasing at a rate faster than the debt, why is there concern?

The three areas which are most troublesome are (1) who owns the debt, (2) who pays the interest, and (3) who does the debt compete with for dollars.

The obvious concern over who owns the debt arises when the thought of repayment occurs. It is one thing to repay the interest to ourselves and quite another to owe it to someone else. About 6 percent of the debt is owned by foreign individuals and governments, while the remaining 94 percent is held internally. The share of the debt held by the foreign sector rose considerably during the 1972–1975 period.

8. Why has the foreign-held debt increased? Will it continue to do so?

It would be naive to assume that of the $700 billion of the debt (government bonds) held by the U.S. public that all of us own some. Obviously some of us own a lot more of the debt than others, and the richer we are, the more debt we are likely to own (or bonds we hold); while the poorer among us hold few if any bonds.

This brings us to the second problem of the interest payments on the debt. Our $700-billion debt costs us each year some $40 billion in interest payments. Where do these funds come from? Right again—from our tax returns. Perhaps you can see how this interest payment/ownership phenomenon leads to a redistribution of income in the economy—from bottom to top. Everyone pays taxes—some of which are used to pay the interest on the debt—but only individuals with higher incomes receive these interest payments. This is a cause of concern for some economists and politicians.

9. Does it concern you? Why or why not?

The final area of concern with the debt lies in the realm of alternative sources for the financing of government expenditures. The government can increase taxes or borrow. In either case, spending potential of another sector is reduced. In the case of tax increases, the spending power of the consumer is reduced. Borrowing, or creating a larger debt, will force interest rates up because the government bond issues will have to be offered with a higher yield. Most of these bond issues will be sold to financial intermediaries so that government spending will tend to take place at the expense of investment (instead of consumption) since financial intermediaries would normally lend to corporations for investment purposes rather than buying bonds. All of this assumes that the economy is operating at close to full capacity. If there were severe levels of unemployment and excess capacity, it would probably be unnecessary for interest rates to rise with the new bond issues; and in times of recession businesses are reluctant to invest anyway.

The national debt, then, must be discussed carefully rather than with the emotion it normally generates. Historically, the debt has financed wars and higher levels of employment and income, and inflation. Some, however, argue that the results are a bargain at $3256 per person.

TABLE 17.1   Net Public and Private Debt, 1929–1975

[Billions of dollars]

End of Year	Gross National Product	Public — Federal Government	Public — Federally Sponsored Credit Agencies	Public — State and Local Governments	Private Total	Corporate	Individual and noncorporate Total	Farm	Nonfarm Total	Nonfarm Mortgage	Nonfarm Commercial and Financial	Consumer
1929	103.4	16.5	———	13.6	161.8	88.9	72.9	12.2	60.7	31.2	22.4	7.1
1933	55.8	24.3	———	16.3	127.9	76.9	51.0	9.1	41.9	26.3	11.7	3.9
1939	90.8	42.6	———	16.4	124.3	73.5	50.8	8.8	42.0	25.0	9.8	7.2
1940	100.0	44.8	———	16.4	128.6	75.6	53.0	9.1	43.9	26.1	9.5	8.3
1941	124.9	56.3	———	16.1	139.0	83.4	55.6	9.3	46.3	27.1	10.0	9.2
1942	158.3	101.7	———	15.4	141.5	91.6	49.9	9.0	40.9	26.8	8.1	6.0
1943	192.0	154.4	———	14.5	144.3	95.5	48.8	8.2	40.5	26.1	9.5	4.9
1944	210.5	211.9	———	13.9	144.8	94.1	50.7	7.7	42.9	26.0	11.8	5.1
1945	212.3	252.5	———	13.4	140.0	85.3	54.7	7.3	47.4	27.0	14.7	5.7
1946	209.6	229.5	———	13.7	153.4	93.5	59.9	7.6	52.3	31.8	12.1	8.4
1947	232.8	221.7	0.7	15.0	178.3	108.9	69.4	8.6	60.7	37.2	11.9	11.6
1948	259.1	215.3	.6	17.0	198.4	117.8	80.6	10.8	69.7	42.4	12.9	14.4
1949	258.0	217.6	.7	19.1	208.4	118.0	90.4	12.0	78.4	47.1	13.9	17.4
1950	286.2	217.4	.7	21.7	246.4	142.1	104.3	12.3	92.0	54.8	15.8	21.5
1951	330.2	216.9	1.3	24.2	276.8	162.5	114.3	13.7	100.6	61.7	16.2	22.7
1952	347.2	221.5	1.3	27.0	300.4	171.0	129.4	15.2	114.2	68.9	17.8	27.5
1953	366.1	226.8	1.4	30.7	322.7	179.5	143.2	16.8	126.4	76.7	18.4	31.4
1954	366.3	229.1	1.3	35.5	340.0	182.8	157.2	17.5	139.7	86.4	20.8	32.5

1955	399.3	229.6	2.9	41.1	392.2	212.1	180.1	18.7	161.4	98.7	24.0	38.8
1956	420.7	224.3	2.4	44.5	427.2	231.7	195.5	19.4	176.1	109.4	24.4	42.3
1957	442.8	223.0	2.4	48.6	454.3	246.7	207.6	20.2	187.4	118.1	24.3	45.0
1958	448.9	231.0	2.5	53.7	482.4	259.5	222.9	23.2	199.7	128.1	26.5	45.1
1959	486.5	241.4	3.7	59.6	528.3	283.3	245.0	23.8	221.2	141.0	28.7	51.5
1960	506.0	239.8	3.5	64.9	566.1	302.8	263.3	25.1	238.2	151.3	30.8	56.1
1961	523.3	246.7	4.0	70.5	609.1	324.3	284.8	27.5	257.3	164.5	34.8	58.0
1962	563.8	253.6	5.3	77.0	660.1	348.2	311.9	30.2	281.7	180.3	37.6	63.8
1963	594.7	257.5	7.2	83.9	722.3	376.4	345.8	33.2	312.6	198.6	42.3	71.7
1964	635.7	264.0	7.5	90.4	789.7	409.6	380.1	36.0	344.1	218.9	45.0	80.3
1965	688.1	266.4	8.9	98.3	871.4	454.3	417.1	39.3	377.8	236.8	51.1	89.9
1966	753.0	271.8	11.2	104.7	952.1	506.6	445.5	42.2	403.3	251.6	55.4	96.2
1967	796.3	286.4	9.0	112.8	1,031.5	553.6	477.9	47.9	429.9	267.0	62.2	100.8
1968	868.5	291.9	21.5	122.7	1,147.4	631.5	515.9	51.7	464.2	284.9	68.5	110.8
1969	935.5	289.3	30.6	133.3	1,284.4	734.2	550.2	55.2	495.0	303.9	70.0	121.1
1970	982.4	301.1	38.8	144.8	1,384.9	797.3	587.7	57.8	529.8	332.4	70.3	127.2
1971	1,063.4	325.9	39.9	162.8	1,522.1	871.3	650.8	62.5	588.3	372.6	76.5	139.1
1972	1,171.1	341.2	41.4	176.9	1,716.5	975.3	741.2	68.2	673.0	426.2	88.9	157.9
1973	1,306.6	349.1	59.8	189.5	1,933.7	1,106.7	827.0	79.0	748.1	482.8	84.5	180.8
1974	1,413.0	360.8	76.4	206.4	2,124.9	1,239.0	885.9	89.2	796.6	523.7	81.5	191.5
1975	1,516.0	446.3	78.8	216.1	2,255.9	1,306.2	949.7	98.0	851.7	566.1	88.8	196.7

Source: *Economic Report of the President, 1977*, p. 265.

AN ISSUE IN FISCAL POLICY–URBAN POLICY

In Table 17.2 one can see just where the federal government gets its funds and how those funds are allocated.

TABLE 17.2 Federal Budget Receipts by Source and Outlays by Function 1975–1977

Description	Actual 1975	Estimate 1976	Estimate 1977
Receipts by source			
Individual income taxes	122.4	130.8	153.6
Corporation income taxes	40.6	40.1	49.5
Social insurance taxes and contributions	86.4	92.6	113.1
Excise taxes	16.6	16.9	17.8
Estate and gift taxes	4.6	5.1	5.8
Customs duties	3.7	3.8	4.3
Miscellaneous receipts	6.7	8.3	7.2
Total receipts	**281.0**	**297.5**	**351.3**
Outlays by function			
National defense[1]	86.6	92.8	101.1
International affairs	4.4	5.7	6.8
General science, space, and technology	4.0	4.3	4.5
Natural resources, environment, and energy	9.5	11.8	13.8
Agriculture	1.7	2.9	1.7
Commerce and transportation	16.0	17.8	16.5
Community and regional development	4.4	5.8	5.5
Education, training, employment, and social services	15.2	18.9	16.6
Health	27.6	32.1	34.4
Income security	108.6	128.5	137.1
Veterans benefits and services	16.6	19.0	17.2
Law enforcement and justice	2.9	3.4	3.4
General government	3.1	3.5	3.4
Revenue sharing and general purpose fiscal assistance	7.0	7.2	7.4
Interest	31.0	34.8	41.3
Allowances[2]	....	.2	2.3
Undistributed offsetting receipts	–14.1	–15.2	–18.8
Total outlays	**324.6**	**373.5**	**394.2**

[1] Includes civilian and military pay raises for the Department of Defense.
[2] Includes allowances for civilian agency pay raises and contingencies for relatively uncontrollable programs and other requirements.
Source: *U.S. Budget in Brief—Fiscal Year 1977*, p. 57.

---

10. What was the impact on the economy over these three years? What has happened to the national debt?

In March of 1978, President Carter presented his "Urban Policy" to Congress. This *new* Urban Policy is based upon a unique combination of government spending and taxation policies and tools.

In the excerpt from his statement that follows, attempt to understand how President Carter is using fiscal policy to solve urban problems and what the impact will be of these proposed policies if enacted.

EXCERPTS FROM THE PRESIDENT'S MESSAGE TO CONGRESS OUTLINING HIS URBAN POLICY

March 27, 1978—I submit today my proposals for a comprehensive national urban policy. These proposals set a policy framework for actions my Administration has already taken, for proposed new initiatives and for our efforts to assist America's communities and their residents in the years to come. The policy represents a comprehensive, long-term commitment to the Nation's urban areas.

The urban policy I am announcing today will build a New Partnership involving all levels of government, the private sector and neighborhood and voluntary organizations in a major effort to make America's cities better places in which to live and work. It is a comprehensive policy aimed both at making cities more healthy and improving the lives of the people who live in them.

The major proposals will:

Improve the effectiveness of existing Federal programs by coordinating these programs, simplifying planning requirements, reorienting resources and reducing paperwork. And the proposals will make Federal actions more supportive of the urban policy effort and develop a process for analyzing the urban and community impact of all major Federal initiatives.

Provide employment opportunities, primarily in the private sector, to the long-term unemployed and the disadvantaged in cities. This will be done through a labor-intensive public works program and tax and other incentives for business to hire the long-term unemployed.

Provide fiscal relief to the most hard-pressed communities.

Provide strong incentives to attract private investment to distressed communities, including the creation of a National Development Bank, expanded grant programs and targeted tax incentives.

Encourage states to become partners in assisting urban areas through a new incentive grant program.

Stimulate greater involvement by neighborhood organizations and voluntary associations through funding neighborhood development projects and by creating an urban volunteer corps. These efforts will be undertaken with the approval of local elected officials.

Increase access to opportunity for those disadvantaged by economic circumstance or a history of discrimination.

Provide additional social and health services to disadvantaged people in cities and communities.

Improve the urban physical environment and the cultural and esthetic aspects of urban life by providing additional assistance for housing rehabilitation, mass transit, the arts, culture parks and recreation facilities. . . .

276 Fiscal Policy: Government Spending and Taxation

The need for a New Partnership is clear from the record of the last 15 years. During the 1960s, the Federal Government took a strong leadership role in responding to the problems of the cities. The Federal Government attempted to identify the problems, develop the solutions and implement the programs. State and local governments and the private sector were not sufficiently involved. While many of these programs were successful, we learned an important lesson: that the Federal Government alone has neither the resources nor the knowledge to solve all urban problems.

An equally important lesson emerged from the experience of the early 1970's. During this period, the Federal Government retreated from its responsibilities, leaving states and localities with insufficient resources, interest or leadership to accomplish all that needed to be done. We learned that states and localities cannot solve the problems by themselves. . . .

These initiatives require $4.4 billion in budget authority, $1.7 billion in new tax incentives, and $2.2 billion in guaranteed loan authority in fiscal year 1979. For fiscal year 1980 the budget authority will be $6.1 billion, the tax incentives $1.7 billion and the guaranteed loan authority $3.8 billion.

---

11. What are the trade-offs that Carter had to deal with in establishing his urban policy? What other choices did he have? Would you have dealt with the problem differently? How?

Urban America. (Photograph by Steve Stamos.)

12. What will be the impact of this policy on the economy? on the budget? on the deficit?
13. Do you think Carter's policy will be successful? Why or why not?

CONCLUSION

This chapter has highlighted the process and ways in which fiscal policy works through the tax, transfer, and spending multipliers. We've noted that fiscal policy isn't always efficient for a wide variety of reasons, but it is most often effective—at least when estimated by Keynesian models. Chapter 18 introduces money into the Keynesian economy, which gives us yet another set of tools to use to achieve our policy objectives.

KEY CONCEPTS

fiscal policy
Employment Act of 1946
Council of Economic Advisers
tax multiplier
transfer multiplier

balanced budget multiplier
lags in fiscal policy
countercyclical policy
procyclical policy
debt

REVIEW QUESTIONS

1. Most of the examples in this chapter have dealt with policy designed to combat unemployment and recession. What fiscal measures would you recommend if the economy were in the midst of a prolonged period of inflation? (Use an MPC = 0.8 for the economy as a whole.)

2. Do you favor a taxing policy over a curb in government spending? Why or why not?

3. What might be the end result of your policy? How long do you expect the lags to be before it will be enacted?

4. Would you ever recommend a balanced budget for the federal government? Why or why not? If so, when?

5. Would you make any recommendations to alleviate some of the lags involved with fiscal actions? Are these delays "healthy"?

SUGGESTED READINGS

E. Ray Canterbery, 1968. *Economics on a New Frontier,* Wadsworth. This interesting and readable account details the first Presidential administration employing Keynesian theory in the deployment of fiscal policy.

Milton Friedman, 1972. *An Economist's Protest,* Thomas Horton. See Chapter 4, in which the leading monetarist critiques fiscal policy during the Nixon era.

Walter W. Heller, 1976. *The Economy, Old Myths, and New Realities,* W. W. Norton. Heller focuses on the economic problems that occurred in the mid-1970s and the effect of many of the fiscal measures in this period of instability.

Walter W. Heller, 1966. *New Dimensions of Political Economy,* Harvard University Press. The CEA Chairman under Kennedy and Johnson recounts the changes taking place in economic policy.

The new debt economy. *Business Week,* October 16, 1978. The most recent analysis of the total debt structure in the U.S. and its implications.

Leonard Silk, 1972. *Nixonomics,* Praeger. A play by play of Nixon's economic policies by the economics editor of the *New York Times.*

George P. Schultz and Kenneth W. Dam, 1977. *Economic Policy beyond the Headlines,* Norton. A behind-the-scenes view of fiscal policy in the works—the pressures, demands, and formal and informal promises that lie at the heart of policymaking.

THE ROLE OF MONEY AND FINANCIAL INTERMEDIARIES

CHAPTER 18

INTRODUCTION

Money, and its role in the economy, has been one of the most debated issues among the last generation of economists. Obviously everyone knows all there is to know about money. We need more and we want more of it. Money is a growth industry. Financial intermediaries (FIs) have developed as the country has grown, providing the services that are demanded by the consumers in a changing society. Commercial banks are the oldest and still the most important of all FIs. The late 1800s saw the rise of savings banks and insurance companies while the 20th century has given us credit unions, real estate trusts, investment banks, bank holding companies, and finance companies. Financial intermediaries all facilitate the exchange of money. Unlike other FIs, commercial banks have the power to "create money"; but many economists are beginning to share the view that other financial intermediaries have an impact on the money supply similar to that of commercial banks.

We shall first look at the utility of money and the demand for it in our examination of money and FIs. Then we shall turn our attention to the mystique of the money supply, examining how money is "created" and what it really is. Finally, we shall examine money in the Keynesian model.

THE USES OF MONEY

Why is money so important? Because of its uses. Money is as money does. Few individuals hold dollars for the sheer joy of counting and stacking them. Money is valued for the goods and services that it buys—for its use as a *medium of exchange*. It is commonly accepted in payment for goods and services. Before money was institutionalized, barter was the rule of the day. One simply exchanged goods and services. Of course problems would arise when one couldn't agree upon objects to trade—or there was no double coincidence of wants. Perhaps one trader desired shoes and had only nuts to offer while the shoemaker wanted only leather in exchange for shoes. Larger problems would arise if one was trading a horse.

A second use for money, implicit in its medium of exchange function, is that it serves as a measuring rod for the value of each good or service. It is, in essence, a *unit of account*. A pound of nuts may be valued at $1.69, a pair of shoes at $20.24, and a horse and buggy at $2753. Since all goods are measured by a dollar amount, this accounting function has become extremely important for measuring the national income accounts of GNP and NNP as well as accounting for the flow of goods and services in an individual firm. Only money fills the medium of exchange and unit of account functions.

These, however, are not the only two uses of money. Money may serve as a *store of value* and as a *standard of deferred payment*. To be a store of value, an asset must hold its value into the future. Other assets that serve this function are stocks and bonds and diamonds and property. As a standard of deferred payment, other individuals must be willing to accept "it" for future payment. Again, assets besides money adequately serve this function.

---

1. What assets would you be willing to accept in the future?

DEMANDS FOR MONEY

These four uses are associated with the three demands people have for money. The classical economists recognized only the *transactions demand*, which is similar to the medium of exchange function, that indicates the amount of money balances that individuals desire for transactions (purchasing) purposes. Most often this demand will be constant, given a level of income and a pattern of consumption expenditures.

A second demand for money balances is the *precautionary demand*. This demand was first separated into a category of its own by John Maynard Keynes in *The General Theory*. Given the norm of cataclysmic catastrophes that always occur at the same time, one has a propensity to save—to accumulate a nest egg while waiting for the next unfortunate event or cycle. (The car breaks down the week the kids are sick and the dog bites the mail carrier and the washing machine floods the basement, etc.)

---

2. Divide your demands for money into transactions and precautionary balances. What percentage of your money balances do you hold for each?

Like the transactions demand, people at certain income levels will tend to save or keep a relatively fixed proportion of their income for precautionary purposes. A demand curve for the transactions and precautionary balances is plotted on a price-quantity axis in Fig. 18.1 to further illustrate (and to add money to the array of goods and services for which there is a demand—and later, of course, a supply). The quantity of money (M) is on the horizontal axis and the price of money—represented by the interest rate (r)* is on the vertical axis. The vertical line M_d in Fig. 18.1

---

*The price of money is the rate of interest since when one buys or borrows money, one pays for it at the prevailing rate of interest. It should be recognized that there is a wide array of interest rates in the economy at any one time depending on such factors as risk and time to maturity of the asset. We will, however, focus on *an* interest rate—assuming that all of them will behave in a similar manner.

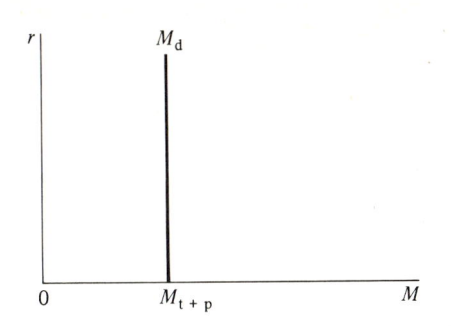

FIG. 18.1 The transactions and precautionary demands for money.

indicates that at all rates of interest the precautionary and transactions demand will be constant for a given individual at a given income level.

The third demand for money recognized by Keynes is the *speculative demand* or, as he called it, the *liquidity preference*.* This demand rises from the desire of people to maximize their returns on the funds left over after their transactions and precautionary demands have been satisfied. The speculative demand for funds is inversely related to the rate of interest in the economy. If the rate of interest is high, people will hold relatively few speculative or liquid balances. They will be holding stocks and bonds or goods instead of money balances. If, on the other hand, the rate of interest is low, individuals may decide to simply "wait and see" what happens to interest rates in the future. If interest rates rise, people want to avoid being "locked in" to low yielding assets—thus they prefer to hold (speculative) cash or money balances. One may plot the speculative demand for money with respect to interest and the quantity of money since $M_{spec} = f(r)$ as shown in Fig. 18.2

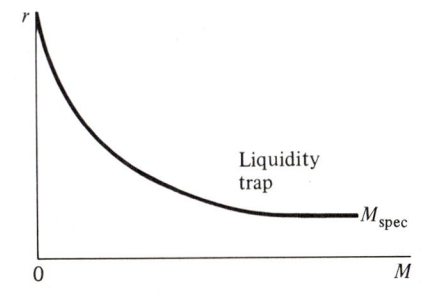

FIG. 18.2 The speculative demand for money.

At extremely high rates of interest, the speculative demand for money balances approaches zero, while at very low rates of interest, people will desire to hold only money balances. This low-interest range in which the demand for money is perfectly elastic has been dubbed the *Keynesian liquidity trap*. Keynes pointed out that at extremely low rates of interest people feel that interest rates can go no lower and can only rise. To buy bonds would be courting disaster, so people hold on to their cash.

---

*Liquidity is the degree of "moneyness." One-hundred percent liquid suggests that all of one's assets are in cash and/or demand deposits. Stocks and bonds and property denote somewhat lesser levels of liquidity.

This trap area becomes important in discussing various aspects of monetary policy and will be taken up later in the chapter.

If all three demands for money are combined, the total demand for money curve can be plotted as in Fig 18.3.

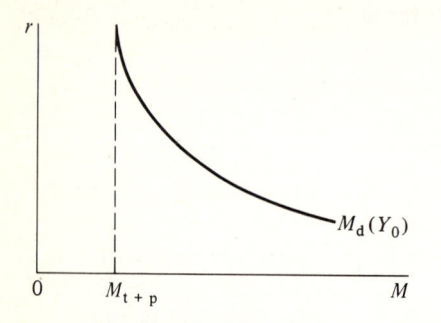

FIG. 18.3   The demand for money.

This demand curve for money indicates that, like all demand curves, the quantity demanded varies inversely with price. It also indicates that as the interest rate rises, fewer money balances will be held—though enough will always be held to meet transactions and precautionary demands.

Changes in the Demand for Money

Like other demand curves, the demand for money curve can shift. Shifts or changes in demand are primarily caused by a change in the level of income. For example, if an individual's income increases from $10,000 a year to $15,000 a year, there will more than likely be an increase in that person's demand for money. This is explained by the increase in the demand for precautionary and transactions balances as income increases. Changes in income, as they affect the demand for money, are shown in Fig. 18.4.

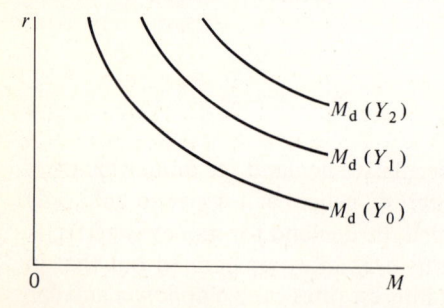

FIG. 18.4   The effect of changes in income on the demand for money.

SUPPLY OF MONEY

Unlike the supply of most goods and services, the total supply of money is controlled not by individual firms as such but by the Federal Reserve System—more commonly and affectionately known as the Fed.

The Fed

The *Federal Reserve System* was established by the Federal Reserve Act of 1913 to help mend an ailing National Banking System. The Fed is an *independent* agency of the government established by an act of Congress to centralize control over the banking system and the money supply. The "basic" structure of the Federal Reserve System may be seen in Fig. 18.5.

```
                    ┌──────────────────────────┐
            ┌──────▶│  Board of Governors of the│◀──────┐
            │       │  Federal Reserve System   │       │
            │       │      (seven members)      │       │
            │       └──────────────────────────┘       │
            │                    │                      │
    ┌───────┴────────┐           │            ┌────────┴────────┐
    │ Federal Open   │           │            │                  │
    │ Market Committee│          │            │ Federal Advisory │
    │   (FOMC)       │           │            │ Council (12 Members)│
    │ (Board of Governors and five│           │                  │
    │ regional bank presidents)  │            └──────────────────┘
    └────────────────┘           │
                                 ▼
                    ┌──────────────────────────┐
                    │  Federal Reserve Banks   │
                    │ (12 banks with 24 branch banks)│
                    └──────────────────────────┘
                                 │
                                 ▼
                    ┌──────────────────────────┐
                    │ Commercial banks 5726 members│
                    └──────────────────────────┘
```

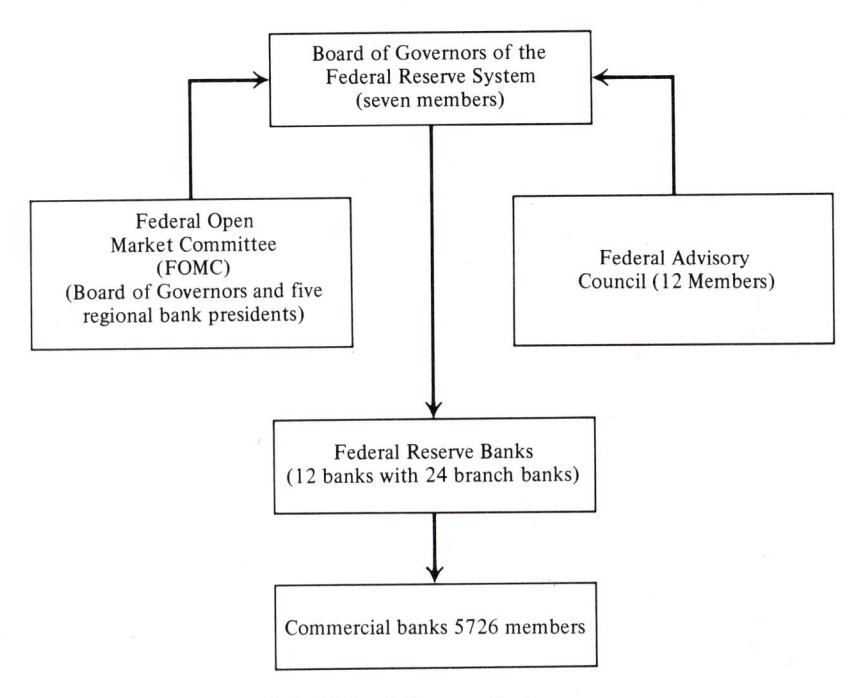

FIG. 18.5 Elements of the Federal Reserve System.

The Board of Governors of the Federal Reserve System are appointed by the President with Congressional approval to coordinate and regulate the money supply in the U.S. The chairperson of the Board of Governors acts as spokesperson for the entire System. The Federal Open Market Committee directs Fed bond sales and purchases in their directives and the Federal Advisory Council exists mostly for show.

The twelve regional Federal Reserve Banks and their 24 branches are scattered throughout the country and oversee operations of the member commercial banks in their districts. The locations of these can be seen in Fig. 18.6.

Though there are over 14,600 commercial banks in the country, only 5726 are members of the Federal Reserve System. Each year has witnessed a flow of banks out of the system (due to the high cost of membership), yet control over the money supply is maintained since the member banks (40 percent of the total) control the majority of deposits in the nation (75 percent).

The Federal Reserve System
Boundaries of Federal Reserve Districts and Their Branch Territories

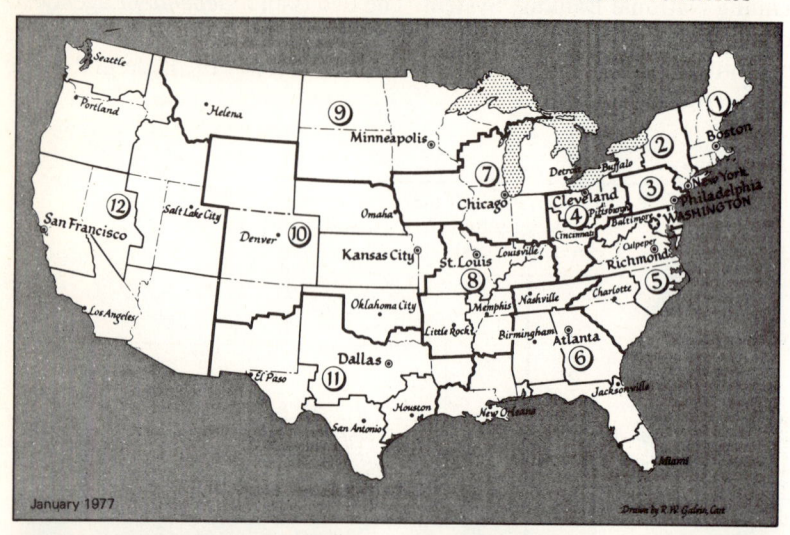

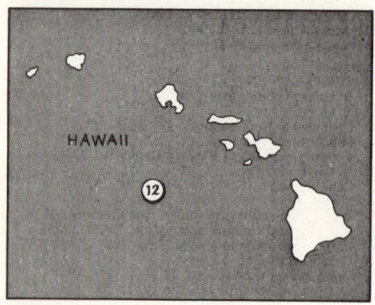

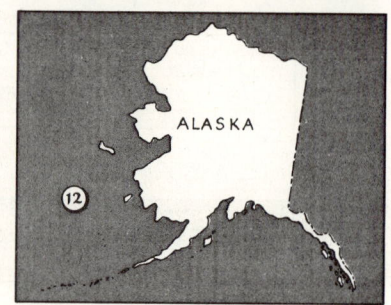

LEGEND

— Boundaries of Federal Reserve Districts
— Boundaries of Federal Reserve Branch Territories
★ Board of Governors of the Federal Reserve System
⊙ Federal Reserve Bank Cities
• Federal Reserve Branch Cities
· Federal Reserve Bank Facility

FIG. 18.6 The Federal Reserve System. Boundaries of Federal Reserve Districts and their branch territories.

---

3. Why was the Federal Reserve established by Congress as an independent agency of the federal government (that is, outside of the operational control of the Congress or the President)?

4. Who is the current chairperson of the Fed?

The Suppliers of Money

The Fed controls the amount of credit in the banking system. One is always tempted to say the Fed controls the money supply—but then the question of what the money supply is is sure to arise. This is a question to which each economist has a different answer. Generally, economics texts, like this one, define the money supply as being coin and currency plus demand deposits held by the public, or M_1 in economics jargon. In 1977, currency and coins accounted for about 26 percent of the money supply, and demand deposits (which are checking accounts) for 74 percent. The total money supply stood at $312 billion at the end of 1976, and it tends to grow at an annual rate of around 5 or 6 percent. Some economists prefer an expanded definition of the money supply that includes time and savings deposits at commercial banks (M_2). Milton Friedman is a leading proponent of this definition of the money supply. If time and savings accounts are included, the money supply at the end of 1976 would have been $739 billion—more than double the M_1 value. Friedman and others feel that the use of the M_2 definition better explains consumption and other decisions made in the economy. Additional definitions exist for M_3 through M_5. Yet, some economists believe that the Federal Reserve—when reflecting on policy actions that will result in changes in the money supply—really look at the availability of credit in the economy rather than any M_1 or M_5 definition. For example, if the Fed feels credit is too tight, it will take measures to increase credit availability by increasing the supply of money in the economy.

Though the Fed is responsible for initiating changes in the money supply, individual banks allocate the money to the public, and to a large extent their allocation reflects the rates of interest in the economy. If interest rates are low, banks are reluctant to lend large quantities of money and to risk being locked into a low-yielding asset. On the other hand, if interest rates are high, the banks will be more willing to lend money *if it is available to them* (or if the Fed has allocated additional moneys by increasing the money supply). Constructing a money supply curve then can be quite simple, by again placing the price of money, or the rate of interest, on the vertical axis and the quantity of money on the horizontal axis as in Fig. 18.7.

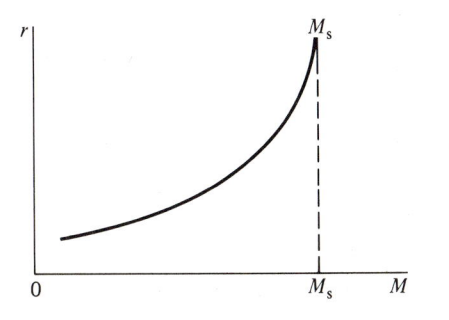

FIG. 18.7 The money supply function.

One should notice that the supply of money curve, M_s, becomes vertical (inelastic) at very high levels of r since the total quantity of money in the economy is fixed by the Fed.

The supply-and-demand curves for money can be illustrated together with the intersection of the two curves signifying equilibrium in the money market, as they are shown in Fig. 18.8.

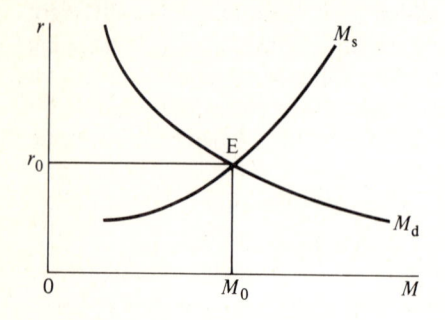

FIG. 18.8 Equilibrium in the money market.

At point E the quantity demanded for money is equal to the quantity supplied at an interest rate of r_0. There is no excess demand or supply in equilibrium.

If the Fed allows the money supply to increase, then the M_{s_0} curve will shift to the right (M_{s_1}) resulting in a lower rate of interest (r_1) in the economy as in Fig. 18.9.

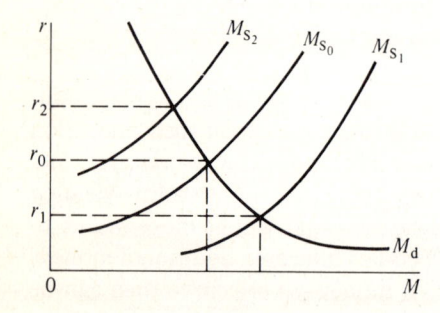

FIG. 18.9 A change in the money supply.

A decrease in the money supply will shift M_{s_0} to the left (M_{s_2}) and increase the interest rate (r_2). We will look at the tools with which the Fed changes the money supply after examining the process by which commercial banks "create money" and how this money works within the Keynesian model.

THE MYTH AND MYSTIQUE OF MONEY

In the following excerpt from "Commercial Banks as Creators of Money," Yale economist James Tobin tries to "steal our thunder" in explaining the multiple money creation process in a principles text.

Perhaps the greatest moment of triumph for the elementary economics teacher is his exposition of the multiple creation of bank credit and bank deposits. Before the admiring eyes of freshmen he puts to rout the practical banker who is so sure that he "lends only the money depositors entrust to him." The banker is shown to have a worm's-eye view, and his error stands as an introductory object lesson in the fallacy of composition. From the Olympian vantage of the teacher and the textbook it appears that the banker's dictum must be reversed: depositors entrust to bankers whatever amounts the bankers lend. To be sure, this is not true of a single bank; one bank's loan may wind up as another bank's deposit. But it is, as the arithmetic of successive rounds of deposit creation makes clear, true of the banking system as a whole. Whatever their other errors, a long line of financial heretics have been right in speaking of "fountain pen money"—money created by the stroke of the bank president's pen when he approves a loan and credits the proceeds to the borrower's checking account.

In this time-honored exposition two characteristics of commercial banks—both of which are alleged to differentiate them sharply from other financial intermediaries—are intertwined. One is that their liabilities—well, at least their demand deposit liabilities—serve as widely acceptable means of payment. Thus, they count, along with coin and currency in public circulation, as "money." The other is that the preferences of the public normally play no role in determining the total volume of deposits or the total quantity of money. For it is the beginning of wisdom in monetary economics to observe that money is like the "hot potato" of a children's game: one individual may pass it to another, but the group as a whole cannot get rid of it. If the economy and the supply of money are out of adjustment, it is the economy that must do the adjusting. This is as true, evidently, of money created by bankers' fountain pens as of money created by public printing presses. On the other hand, financial intermediaries other than banks do not create money, and the scale of their assets is limited by their liabilities, i.e., by the savings the public entrusts to them. They cannot count on receiving "deposits" to match every extension of their lending.

The commercial banks and only the commercial banks, in other words, possess the widow's cruse.* And because they possess this key to unlimited expansion, they have to be restrained by reserve requirements.

Tobin, J., "Commercial Banks as Creators of Money," in *Banking and Monetary Studies*, D. Carson, ed. (Homewood, Ill.: Richard D. Irwin, 1963©). Reprinted by permission of the publisher.

Commercial banks create money based upon a *fractional reserve system* of deposit balances. The Fed (or a state agency if the bank is not a member of the Fed) requires that every bank hold a certain percentage of its total deposits in its vault or in the nearest Federal Reserve Bank to ensure safety and an ability to meet deposit withdrawals. These *reserve requirements* vary according to the size of the banks' assets and the exact percentage to be held may be changed by the Fed at any time. The limits within which the Fed can set reserve requirements were specified most recently by Congress in 1973 and are as follows:

Time (Savings) Accounts . . . . min. 3 percent—max. 10 percent
Banks with DD's>$400M . . . . min. 10 percent—max. 22 percent
Banks with DD's<$400M . . . . min. 7 percent—max. 14 percent

---
*The widow's cruse implies an unending supply.

As of mid-1977, the following reserve requirement rates were in effect.

TABLE 18.1 Recent Reserve Requirements

Type of Deposit	Reserve Requirements (Percentage)
Demand deposit (in millions)	
The 1st $2	7
From $2—10	9.5
From $10—100	11.75
From $100—400	12.75
Over $400	16.25
Time Deposit	
Savings	3
Other time	
0 to 5 million	
Maturing 30–179 days	3
180 days–4 years	2.5
4 years or more	1
Over $5 million	
Maturing 30–179 days	6
180 days–4 years	2.5
4 year or longer	1

Source: *Federal Reserve Bulletin,* May 1977, Table A-9.

5. Why isn't there a 100 percent reserve requirement?

An example of the money-creation process should aid in clarifying what happens to a deposit in a commercial bank. For simplicity's sake, we shall use a 10 percent reserve requirement for demand deposits and begin with a $1000 deposit. New deposits in the banking system increase by $1000 and required reserves increase by $100. This, then, leaves the bank with $1000 minus $100 or $900. The prudent (profit maximizing) banker would undoubtedly make use of the $900 by generating loans and investments of an equal amount. Perhaps you are in the market for a $900 loan. If our friendly, neighborhood banker decides you are credit worthy, you may receive the "extra" $900. If you spend the $900 on new stereo components, there is a pretty good chance that the full $900 will enter the banking system when the *Stereo Shack* deposits its daily balances. The banking system then has another deposit. This time one of $900. So, 10 percent of $900 or $90 must be held as the reserve requirement on the *new* $900 deposit. Total new deposits are now $1900 and total new reserves are $190 in the banking system. And what will happen to the $900 minus $90 or $810 left in the bank? Of course, potential increases in loans and investments. The final result of the initial $1000 demand deposit can be seen in Table 18.2.

TABLE 18.2 Money Creation

Position of Bank	New Demand Deposits	New Loans and Investments	New Reserves
Original bank	$ 1000.00	$ 900.00	$ 100.00
2nd bank	900.00	810.00	90.00
3rd bank	810.00	729.00	81.00
4th bank	729.00	656.10	72.90
5th bank	656.10	590.49	65.61
6th bank	590.49	531.44	59.05
7th bank	531.44	478.30	53.14
8th bank	478.30	430.47	47.83
9th bank	430.47	387.42	43.05
10th bank	387.42	348.68	38.74
11th bank	348.68	313.81	34.87
12th bank	313.81	282.43	31.38
Sum of 12 banks	$ 7175.71	6458.14	$ 717.61
Sum of remaining banks	2824.29	2541.86	282.39
Total for system as a whole	$10,000.000	$9000.00	$1000.00

(Totals may not be accurate due to rounding.)

Rather than carrying this process to its final result as above, the total amount of money "created" can more easily be found by the following formula:

$$\Delta R \times \frac{1}{r_{dd}} = \Delta DD,$$

where ΔR is the original change in reserves, r_{dd} is the reserve requirement on demand deposits and ΔDD is the total change in demand deposits. In our example, this becomes:

$$\$1000 \times \frac{1}{1/10} = \Delta DD$$

$$\$1000 \times 10 = \$10,000$$

$$\Delta DD = \$10,000.$$

From $1000 with the stroke of the pen, as Tobin says, banks can "make" $10,000—$9000 of new money. There are, however, several things that must be pointed out before accepting this fountain pen magic. The first is that an individual bank acting alone cannot create money. The process must operate through the whole banking system. This is perhaps more easily understood by looking at a single bank that might try to expand or create money on its own. For example, if the first bank tried to make loans of $9000 based on the $1000 increase in its reserves with the $1000 deposit—what happens to that bank when someone comes to "withdraw" or use the funds the bank has just lent? As one might imagine, many problems can result—one being the bank's inability to maintain its reserve requirement.

6. What other difficulties might this bank run into?

So now we too have triumphantly explained the multiple creation process. What else makes the process not quite so grand as it seems? A second point to remember is that the multiple creation process "works" only if there are no leakages in the system. Leakages may occur in several places. Individuals may decide to place their funds elsewhere—either outside of the banking system or in hoards. If the funds are not redeposited, then there is no "new money" to expand upon. Some funds may be placed in time accounts by consumers. This will lead to an even greater expansion of the money supply, since there is a lower reserve requirement placed on these funds and thus a larger money multiplier.

Another leakage might appear within the banking system itself. Bankers may decide that greater profits are to be made in asset holdings other than those of a loan—investment variety. Perhaps bankers feel their liquidity is too low—and desire to place their remaining funds (or excess reserves) in more short-term types of assets (such as government bonds). In either case, there is a leakage of funds, funds that do not reenter the demand deposit flow for an indefinite period of time. Indeed, the percentage of assets that banks hold in loans or investments is approximately 36 percent of their total portfolio. So caution should be the byword when examining the money creation process. Nevertheless, the process does suggest that the commercial banking system does have the ability to expand the money supply by "creating" demand deposits. In addition, the simple formula, $\Delta R \times r_{dd} = \Delta DD$, approximates the amount of money that can be created from a new deposit in the banking system.

7. What happens to the money supply when people take $1000 out of their bank deposits?

But is it just money creation? Are commercial banks the only intermediary that "creates money"? James Tobin continues in his article, "Commercial Banks as Creators of Money," with the conclusion that other nonbank intermediaries aren't very different from commercial banks and may affect credit expansion and contraction as well.

8. How do savings banks enter into this process? What about a life insurance company?

MONEY AND THE KEYNESIAN SYSTEM

Money can be an integral part of the Keynesian system, as it was developed by Keynes and as it has been extended by post-Keynesian economists. You will recall from the last chapter that the "general gist" of the Keynesian system is that changes in consumption, investment, and government spending may be effectively used to expand or lower the level of income in the economy. Money can and most often does work within the Keynesian sphere to allow income changes as well. Changes in the money supply often directly influence both the business and household sectors in their investment and consumption decisions.

We know from our earlier discussion that an increase in the supply of money will lower the rate of interest (Fig. 18.10), just as (ceteris paribus) any increase in supply will decrease the price of a product. As money becomes "cheaper," investors will reconsider their present levels of investment.

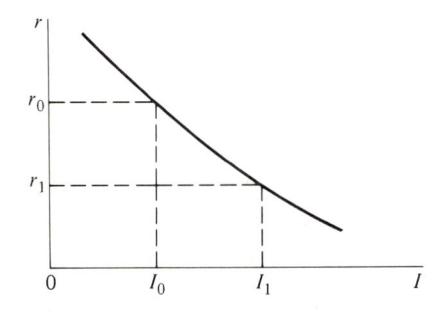

FIG. 18.10 The interest–investment relationship.

Low interest rates will encourage businesses to borrow from banks and to spend these funds on new plants and equipment (i.e., investment); high rates on the other hand deter investment decisions. This is expressed graphically in Fig. 18.10 as an indirect relationship between the rate of interest (r) and the level of investment (I) or $I = f(r)$.

From the Keynesian model developed in the last chapter, let's look at the effect of an increase in investment, this time stimulated by a reduction in the rate of interest which resulted from an increase in the money supply. (See Fig. 18.11.)

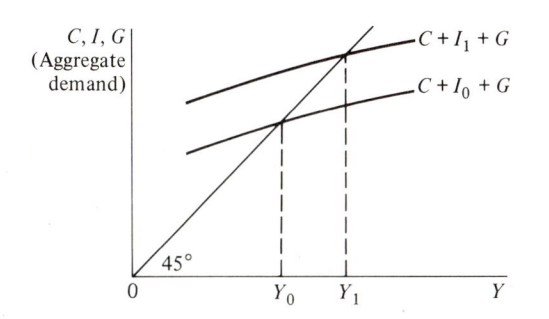

FIG. 18.11 Income response to a change in investment.

We find that as the money supply is increased from M_{s_0} to M_{s_1} as in Fig. 18.9, the interest rate decreases from r_0 to r_1 and, as this occurs, investment is increased from I_0 to I_1 (Fig. 18.10) and finally this increased investment working through the multiplier generates a new higher income level Y_1 as in Fig. 18.11. (Remember $I_1 - I_0 = \Delta I$, $Y_1 - Y_0 = \Delta Y$ and the $\Delta Y = k \cdot \Delta I$.

9. What happens when the Fed decreases the money supply? What happens to interest rates? the level of investment? the level of income? employment?

Keynes relied more on fiscal policy for the stimulation of aggregate demand in *The General Theory*. This was because he felt that during times of depression the economy would operate in the area of the liquidity trap. In this area no matter how much the money supply was increased, the rate of interest would fall no lower. And, due to grim expectations of the future, the business community would not be tempted to further its investment activity, even with low rates of interest. The analogy is often made that increasing the money stock in this situation is much like pushing on a string.

Since severe depressions have not been the dominant feature of our economy, we should examine the tools with which the Fed can and does alter the supply of money so that the Fed can attempt to change the level of income in the economy.

MONETARY POLICY—TOOLS OF THE TRADE

The Fed has at hand several policies that may be used to affect the level of income in the economy. The tools the Fed uses are (1) *reserve requirement changes*, (2) *open-market operations*, and (3) *discount rate changes*. These, along with the Fed's Regulation Q that sets the legal limit on the rate of interest that can be paid by commercial banks, are the major tools. During World War II several *selective credit controls* on home mortgages and consumer credit were implemented by the Fed. The only credit control still in effect is the margin requirement for stocks that stipulates the percent of payment that must be in cash on any security purchase.

Reserve Requirements

Required reserve levels may be changed at any time the Board of Governors deems it necessary that they be changed. In general, the central bank views reserve requirements as its most powerful tool and uses it with utmost discretion. Critics claim that it works like an axe, rather than a scalpel. Since only a one percent change in reserve requirements alters the monetary situation geometrically, changes in reserve requirements tend to be infrequent. This tool has been used since 1935 and has been altered only a few times in the Federal Reserve history. One can see why this tool is unpopular with bankers in the following example. Assume that the Fed wishes to restrict economic activity by reducing the money supply (e.g., to fight inflation). If banking assets are at $400 billion with 10 percent reserve requirements, some $40 billion are being held as reserves. If reserve requirements are increased by one percent to 11 percent, some $44 billion must be held. This takes $4 billion out of the banking system immediately as loans and investments are called in to increase reserves to this proper level.

10. In the example above what might happen to interest rates? Why?

11. What would happen if reserve requirements were lowered by one percent? How much would member banks be required to hold? What would happen to the "extra" money (or excess reserves)?

An increase in reserve requirements can absorb large changes in *excess reserves* such as those that occurred during the 1930s when substantial amounts of gold flowed into the country. A reserve requirement reduction may offset a large loss in reserves. In either case, a change in reserve requirements announces a change in Fed policy to the public as well as to the banks. Critics of the Fed suggest that other means are more appropriate for the announcement of policy changes.

Open-market Operations

The Fed is engaged daily in *open-market operations* through the activities of the Federal Reserve Open Market Committee. Activities in the open market involve the actual *purchases and sales* of government bonds, bills and notes at the New York Fed. These actions will affect the money supply as well as interest rates. To increase the money supply (and economic activity, e.g., to combat recession) the Fed will

The Fed is responsible for the nation's monetary policy. (Photograph by Robert Bostwick.)

actively *buy* bonds (Treasury issues). Buying bonds takes them out of the hands of the banks and the public, and exchanges them for money (a check or cash from the Fed); thus increasing the money supply. If, on the other hand, the Fed desires to draw down the money stock, they will step up bond *sales* to commercial banks and other financial intermediaries, this time increasing the stock of bonds at commercial banks and decreasing their stock of money.

The effect on interest rates by these bonds sales and purchases is inversely related to the money supply. When the money stock is reduced by bond sales, interest rates must increase in order to attract businesses as well as households to purchase the bond offerings. Otherwise, these funds would be invested or saved in something other than bonds. Bond sales then encourage interest rates upward as they compete with other assets for the public's cash balances. The interest rate will also rise due to the shortage of money—once the bond sales have been made.

Open-market operations are the Fed's most important and powerful tool. They take place on a day-to-day basis, and the Fed's Open Market Committee meets regularly to decide what impact they want open-market operations to have on the money supply and interest rates.

---

12. How do bond purchases affect the interest rates in the economy? Why?

The Discount Rate

The *discount rate* is the rate at which a member bank can borrow from the Federal Reserve. Banks often borrow from the Fed to protect their reserve position. Most often collateral of bonds is presented by the banks and they are discounted by the Fed for short-term borrowing purposes. To increase the money supply (and economic activity), the Fed should lower the discount rate, making borrowing more attractive for the commercial banks. The banks can then pass the funds along to households and businesses by increasing the availability of loans. The discount rate should be increased when the Fed desires tight money—making the discount window available only when it is absolutely essential. As a tool for the adjustment of the money supply, the discount rate is pretty much antiquated, yet it is still used in "emergency" situations with the Fed serving as "the lender of the last resort." The Fed sometimes uses changes in the discount rate to signal its concern about economic activity. For example, if it were concerned about inflation and excess economic activity, it might increase the discount rate to discourage continued expansion of the money supply and economic activity.

Lags in Monetary Policy

Like fiscal policy, lags and delays are inherent in monetary actions as well. These lags have been classified by economists into two major types, the *inside lag* and the *outside lag*. The inside lag is comprised of the *recognition lag* and the *action lag*. The time that it takes for the Federal Reserve authorities to recognize that there is indeed a problem in the economy has been dubbed the recognition lag. Between that time and the time some policy is implemented is the action lag. These lags are usually a function of measurement and forecasting. After the action takes place, there is a lag before impact (either partial or total) is felt in the economy. The length of these impact lags is a subject of dispute among economists and economic models. Monetarists argue that the impact lag with monetary actions is much shorter than their Keynesian (fiscal) counterparts. Several econometric models have been used to estimate the effectiveness of policy actions. According to the St. Louis Fed economic model, monetary policy is significantly felt in the economy four months after action, while the Fed–M.I.T.–Penn model indicates that a much longer period is needed for the impact to be felt. To more fully examine the differences in these two models, we should explore the world of the Monetarists.

MONETARISM

The Monetarists trace their roots directly to the classical economists and to the quantity theory of money. This relationship, which was discussed in Chapter 15, is the identity, $M \cdot V = P \cdot Q$, where M is the quantity of money; V, the velocity; P, the price level; and Q, the volume of physical output. In the equation of exchange the relationship between M and P was of primary concern. Unlike the Keynesians, the Monetarists see the money stock as the major stimulus for economic activity. Though their model is more sophisticated than the one of the classical economists, today's Monetarists still use the velocity of money as the major link between money and the GNP (or output). They have found "direct and reliable links" between the two as well as evidence indicating the stability of the velocity of money over time. The Monetarists agree that the velocity of money has changed over time as one can see in Table 18.3. As income has increased since 1950, people have chosen to hold less money *relative* to their incomes. From 1880 through 1950, however, velocity declined steadily. The Monetarists believe that there are long-run trends and short-

TABLE 18.3 The Income Velocity of Money

Year	(1) Gross National Product, GNP (in Billions)	(2) Money Supply, M (in Billions)	(3) Velocity, GNP/M, [(1)/(2)]
1947	$ 232.8	$113.1	2.05
1950	286.2	116.2	2.46
1955	399.3	135.2	2.95
1960	506.0	144.2	3.51
1965	688.1	171.3	4.02
1970	982.4	219.8	4.47
1975	1,516.3	294.8	5.14

Source: *Economic Report of the President, 1977.*

run lags for which velocity must be adjusted. Once these adjustments are made, the relationship between GNP and the money held by the public (GNP/M) is stable. It is stable enough to predict changes in aggregate demand with given changes in the money supply, according to the Monetarist argument.

With the relation $M \cdot V = P \cdot Q = $ GNP or $MV = $ GNP, $V = $ GNP/M, Monetarists believe that the $V = $ GNP/M ratio will stabilize to the same ratio with increases or decreases in the money supply. The value of V then changes as the money supply is altered, but will readjust to its former level. The transmission mechanism, then, is velocity, not the rate of interest, as it is in the Keynesian system.

The Monetarists argue that the only fiscal actions that have any impact at all on the economy are those financed by the creation of new money or by Treasury borrowing from the Federal Reserve. They argue that any other means of financing, such as borrowing from the public through deficit financing, merely takes money from one sector and gives it to another.

The Friedman Rule

The leading Monetarist, Milton Friedman, has severely criticized the Fed in its "erratic" policy towards money creation. Friedman argues that more problems have been created by the discretionary actions of the monetary authorities—pumping money into and pulling money out of the economy—than a monetary rule would have created. Friedman's rule would inject a constant percentage of money into the economy yearly and would eliminate the need for a Federal Reserve. According to Friedman, periods of inflation would be eliminated since the money supply would not be permitted to grow at a rate that would fuel the fires of inflation. Recession would be averted because a guaranteed supply of money would be available for investment purposes at all times, and businesses could be confident that the economy would not be tightened intentionally.

THE EFFECTIVENESS OF MONETARY POLICY

It was noted earlier that the FMP econometric model developed by the Fed, M.I.T., and the University of Pennsylvania indicates that in one year a $1-billion government expenditure is worth $3-billion of GNP. The same model also predicts that in one year a $1-billion increase in the money supply will lead to a $2.5-billion increase in the GNP. The St. Louis Federal Reserve model, on the other hand, shows that a $1-billion increase in government spending has *no* effect on GNP at the end of one year. (Some increase in GNP is seen within six months after the spending increase, but is entirely wiped out by the end of the year.) At the same time, the St. Louis model predicts a $5-billion increase in GNP with a mere $1-billion addition to the money stock.

These models give such different results because of the underlying assumptions each uses. The Monetarists emphasize velocity as the mode of transmission, and the Keynesians, the rate of interest. Monetarists assume that there can be no effective fiscal policy unless it is accompanied by an increase in the money supply. Why is this? The government *must* finance its expenditures with increases in taxes or by debt issue. In either case, money is being transferred from one sector of the economy to another. As government spending proceeds and GNP increases, if there has not been an increase in the money supply, consumers and investors will find themselves short of cash and will begin to try to increase their liquidity by selling their financial holdings. This will have the effect of increasing bond sales even further, driving the price down and the interest rate up. As the interest increases, business investors are crowded out of financial markets by the government so that GNP doesn't change. Spending is just transferred from one sector to another.

Keynesians, however, would argue that the reason for government spending was to stimulate an economy where neither business *nor* households *were* spending—so that the government at least got the process started. This would encourage spending by these sectors in the future.

Shortcomings of Monetary Policy

There are several additional factors which can prohibit monetary policy from being totally successful in its efforts to regulate and stimulate the economy. Six of these factors are as follows:

1. *Private offsets.* Policy can be thwarted by the actions of banks, specialized financial institutions, and private corporations by outwitting Fed policy. Such things as borrowing from the Eurodollar market have caused disruptions in the past.

2. *Cyclical asymmetry.* Policy can be victimized by changing conditions in the economy. This is a problem of timing. A policy is designed to treat a specific condition but when the policy does take effect, the problem may be totally different. This is a problem of "lags" and policy backfiring.

3. *Velocity.* Monetary policy is often frustrated by the tendency of changes in velocity to jeopardize targeted goals of the money supply.

4. *Treasury goals.* Quite often the Treasury may desire conditions in the money and credit markets that are contradictory to the stated policy objectives of the Federal Reserve. This situation creates a conflict that can obstruct the success of the Fed's desired policy.

5. *Cost-push inflation.* Monetary policy does not effectively affect the causes of inflation that lie on the cost or supply side of the market.

6. *Investment impact.* Some argue that the Fed's policies have a marginal impact upon consumer spending. Others argue that the impact of Fed policy on the investment process is overstated since many corporations finance their investments internally.

AN ISSUE IN MONETARY POLICY—INDEPENDENCE OF THE FED

The Federal Reserve System has a number of critics. Monetarists feel that the discretionary powers of the Fed should be revoked and instead the money supply should grow at some fixed rate. Others, however, suggest that more coordination between the monetary and fiscal authorities is needed. Some even argue that since the executive branch is responsible for national economic policy and since monetary policy is an integral part of the larger national economic policy, it should (along with fiscal policy) be coordinated by the President. In the following article, former Chairman of the Board of Governors of the Federal Reserve System, Arthur Burns, discusses the importance of maintaining an independent Fed despite shortcomings in the past.

THE INDEPENDENCE OF THE FEDERAL RESERVE SYSTEM
ARTHUR BURNS

WASHINGTON—Industrial nations, including our own, nowadays rely heavily on monetary policy to promote expansion of production and employment, to limit any decline that may occur in overall economic activity, or to blunt the forces of inflation.

There are two major reasons for the emphasis on monetary policy. First, manipulation of governmental expenditures has proved to be a rather clumsy device for dealing with rapidly changing economic developments. Second, the process of reaching a consensus on needed tax changes often turns out to be too time-consuming to be of much value in moderating fluctuations in business activity.

Fortunately, monetary policy is relatively free of these shortcomings. Changes in the course of monetary policy can be made promptly and—if need be—frequently. Under our scheme of governmental organization, the Federal Reserve can make the hard decisions that might be avoided by decision makers subject to the day-to-day pressures of political life.

Our system of monetary management, I believe, is working in the way the founders of the Federal Reserve intended. Nonetheless, there are some well-meaning individuals who believe that the authority of the Federal Reserve to make decisions about monetary policy should be circumscribed. The specific proposals that have been put forth differ greatly, but they usually have had one feature in common—namely, control by the executive branch over the monetary authority.

Such a step would create a potential for political mischief or abuse on a larger scale than we have yet seen. If the spending propensities of federal officials, whether in the executive or the Congress, were given freer rein, the inflationary tendency that weakened our economy over much of the past decade would in all likelihood be aggravated.

The need for a strong monetary authority to discipline the inflationary tendency inherent in modern economies is evident from the experience of nations around the world. Among the major industrial countries, West Germany and the United States appear to have achieved the greatest success—albeit woefully insufficient success—in resisting inflationary pressures in the period since World

© 1976 by The New York Times Company. Reprinted by permission.

War II. It is no accident that both countries have strong central banks. In some other countries, where the monetary authority is dominated by the executive or the legislature, inflationary financial policies have brought economic chaos and extinguished political freedom.

Over the past year, the Congress has been exercising its vital oversight function through a new and more systematic procedure, spelled out in House Concurrent Resolution No. 133. That resolution requires the Federal Reserve to report to the Congress at quarterly intervals on the course of monetary policy, and to project ranges of growth in the major monetary and credit aggregates for the year ahead.

Such a course of policy, I believe, is the only option open to us if we as a nation are to have any hope of regaining price stability and maintaining a robust economy. Economic, social and political trends of the past several decades have released powerful forces of inflation that threaten the vitality of our economy and the freedom of our people.

Defeating the forces of inflation requires determined action. Greater discipline is needed in fiscal affairs, and structural reforms are required to improve the functioning of labor and product markets. But all such reforms would come to naught in the absence of a prudent monetary policy. At this critical time in our history, any interference with the ability of the Federal Reserve to stick to a moderate rate of monetary expansion could have grave consequences for the economic and political future of our country.

13. What is the Fed doing today to "defeat the forces of inflation? Is policy being coordinated with the executive branch?

14. What kinds of "political mischief" might Burns be thinking of if the monetary authority were controlled by the executive branch?

MONETARY AND FISCAL POLICY—A SUMMARY

Thus far we have surveyed the major macroeconomic issues and problems, examined the theoretical basis for the Keynesian system and studied the framework and behavior of the U.S. banking system. We have also devoted special attention to fiscal and monetary policy. All of this can be reviewed and summarized in the schematic outline in Fig. 18.12.

KEY CONCEPTS

money
money supply
M_1
M_2
transactions demand
speculative demand
precautionary demand
Federal Reserve System

reserve requirements
open-market operations
discount rate
lags
Monetarism
monetary policy
money creation

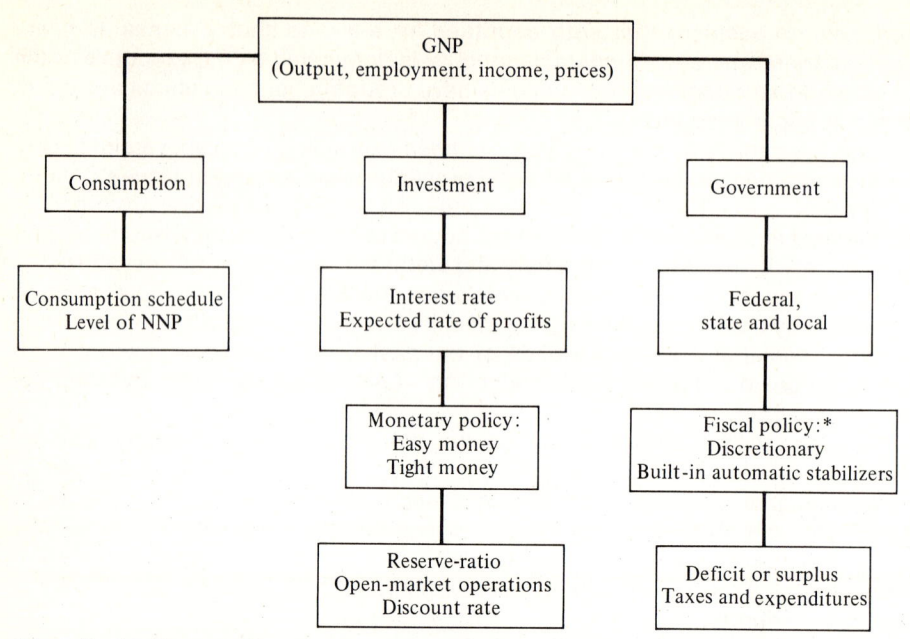

```
                    ┌─────────────────────────────┐
                    │           GNP               │
                    │ (Output, employment,        │
                    │   income, prices)           │
                    └─────────────────────────────┘
         ┌─────────────────┼──────────────────┐
  ┌────────────┐    ┌────────────┐    ┌────────────┐
  │ Consumption│    │ Investment │    │ Government │
  └────────────┘    └────────────┘    └────────────┘
         │                 │                  │
  ┌────────────┐    ┌────────────┐    ┌────────────┐
  │Consumption │    │Interest    │    │Federal,    │
  │schedule    │    │rate        │    │state and   │
  │Level of NNP│    │Expected    │    │local       │
  │            │    │rate of     │    │            │
  │            │    │profits     │    │            │
  └────────────┘    └────────────┘    └────────────┘
                           │                  │
                    ┌────────────┐    ┌──────────────────┐
                    │Monetary    │    │Fiscal policy:*   │
                    │policy:     │    │Discretionary     │
                    │Easy money  │    │Built-in automatic│
                    │Tight money │    │stabilizers       │
                    └────────────┘    └──────────────────┘
                           │                  │
                    ┌────────────┐    ┌──────────────────┐
                    │Reserve-    │    │Deficit or surplus│
                    │ratio       │    │Taxes and         │
                    │Open-market │    │expenditures      │
                    │operations  │    │                  │
                    │Discount    │    │                  │
                    │rate        │    │                  │
                    └────────────┘    └──────────────────┘
```

*Note: fiscal policy can affect all types of spending—*C, I,* and *G*.

FIG. 18.12 Monetary and fiscal policy.

REVIEW QUESTIONS

1. How do the demands for money relate to Keynesian income and employment theory?

2. What are the basic differences between a Monetarist and a Keynesian?

3. Of the basic monetary policy tools the Federal Reserve can utilize, which do you think is the most effective? Why?

4. What are some of the factors that inhibit the successful implementation of monetary policy?

5. Do you think the Fed ought to be "independent"?

6. What would be some of the complications of finding the proper mix of monetary and fiscal policy?

7. If the economy were experiencing high unemployment and moderate inflation, what would be the appropriate monetary policy? Why?

SUGGESTED READINGS

Milton Friedman, *An Economist's Protest,* 1972. Thomas Horton. Chapter 3 is a repeat of *Newsweek* articles of the Nixon era on Fed actions.

John Kenneth Galbraith, 1975. *Money: Whence It Came and Where It Went,* Houghton Mifflin. For Galbraith addicts. An account of money throughout history—from the beginning to Keynes to now.

George Goodman (alias Adam Smith), 1972. *Supermoney,* Random House. Maybe even better than *The Money Game.* Goodman amusingly tells how "big money" operates and of the grim world of cocoa futures.

Martin Mayer, 1974. *The Bankers,* Ballantine Books. A "bestseller" that's really informative. It gives interesting behind-the-scene accounts of banking happenings.

Thomas Mayer, 1968. *Monetary Policy in the United States,* Random House. Mayer discusses the advantages and the disadvantages of monetary policy as a tool for economic stabilization.

J. Huston McCulloch, 1975. *Money and Inflation: A Monetarist Approach,* Academic Press. More complex than the others mentioned, it is by no means too difficult for those seeking more on the Monetarists' methods.

Lawrence S. Ritter and William L. Silber, 1970. *Money,* Basic Books. An excellent *and* amusing account of how money works in the economy.

Adam Smith (alias George Goodman), 1967. *The Money Game,* Random House. A very well-written and readable account of how money works on Wall Street, and more importantly an insight into the human side of money.

UNEMPLOYMENT, INFLATION, AND STABILITY

CHAPTER 19

INTRODUCTION

The previous chapters dealing with macroeconomic theory and policy have touched only slightly on the controversy that surrounds most problems in policy decisions. Only hints have been made that there is some problem between the Monetarists and the Keynesians about solving the problems and that there might be some trade-offs between the macro goals. Conservatives, liberals, and radicals see different sorts of problems and different sets of solutions. One of the most heavily debated issues that we shall focus on here is the trade-off problem between unemployment and inflation. An even more problematical situation results when inflation and unemployment occur at the same time resulting in the modern phenomenon of stagflation. (We will leave an extended analysis of stagflation for Chapter 24, after we have introduced international economic considerations, that also impact on domestic inflation and unemployment.)

THE TRADE-OFFS: UNEMPLOYMENT AND INFLATION

If you've learned your Keynesian lessons well, and we presume that you have, you should recognize a flaw within the system. Given the economic goals of price stability, full employment, and growth, Keynesian policy prescriptions tell us that increased spending is necessary to attain full employment. This will increase income, employment, and encourage more spending. This will have the result of forcing prices upward—resulting, perhaps, in inflation. On the other hand, if inflation is to be attacked using Keynesian measures, income will be reduced—but so will employment. We seem to be between a rock and a hard spot. But an even more difficult problem emerges when the economy develops high inflation as well as high unemployment rates.

There was a time when economists believed they had a rather simple answer to questions dealing with the trade-off between full employment and price stability. A British economist, A. W. Phillips, had studied the British economy over the past century and found that a rather stable relationship existed between increases in the wage rate and the rate of unemployment. High rates of unemployment were associated with low wage increases and since there also appeared to be a relationship between wage increases and the general rate of inflation, people began to conclude that inflation and unemployment were inversely related. High rates of inflation were associated with low unemployment rates and vice versa. This relationship came to be known as the *Phillips curve*. If the Phillips curve were a valid concept, then the matter of priorities seemed to be rather straightforward. Economists could present a menu of the various trade-offs that were possible: 4 percent inflation with 5 percent unemployment, 2 percent inflation with 6 percent unemployment—the democratic process would then be utilized to determine which combination the electorate desired and the policymakers would "fine tune" the economy to obtain this trade-off. If the economy had 5 percent inflation and 4 percent unemployment but the electorate and policy makers desired 4 by 4.5 percent, then economic policy should be ever so slightly more restrictive.

Those were heady days and during the 1960s things seemed to be working according to this approach. (See Table 19.1 and Fig. 19.1) We had our longest period of uninterrupted economic growth during the Vietnam War, inflation was kept to an average of around 2 percent (although accelerating to over 5 percent by the late 1960s) and the unemployment rate went from 6.7 percent in 1961 to 3.5 percent in 1969. But the 1970s seemed to destroy all of this. In 1971, the unemployment rate moved to above 6 percent while the inflation rate rose to nearly 5 percent. By

TABLE 19.1
Phillips Curve and United States Economy, 1960-1976

	Percent Change in Consumer Price Index	*Percent Official Unemployment*
1960	1.6	5.5
1961	1.0	6.7
1962	1.1	5.5
1963	1.2	5.7
1964	1.3	5.2
1965	1.7	4.5
1966	2.9	3.8
1967	2.9	3.8
1968	4.2	3.6
1969	5.4	3.5
1970	5.9	4.9
1971	4.3	5.9
1972	3.3	5.6
1973	6.2	4.9
1974	11.0	5.6
1975	9.1	8.5
1976 (est.)	7.2	7.8

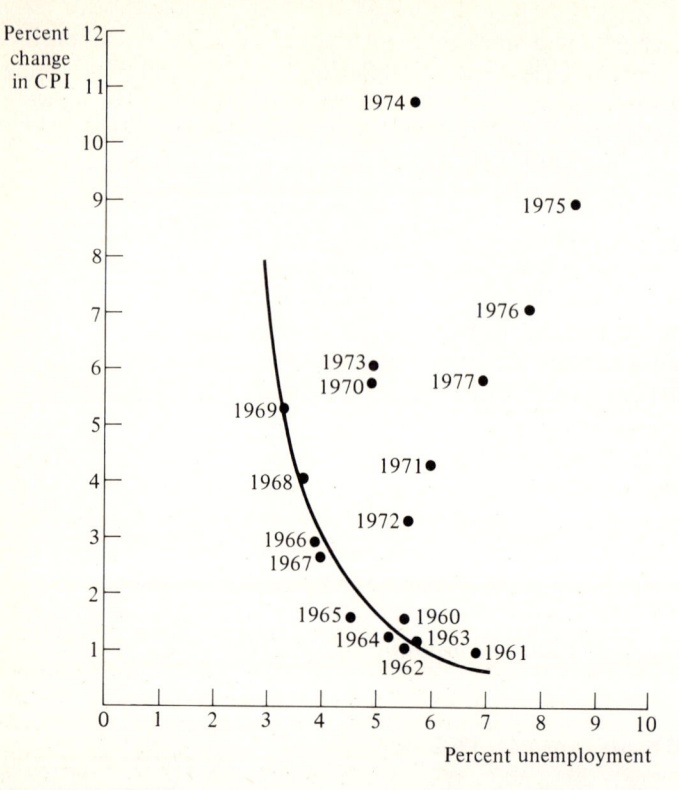

FIG. 19.1 Phillips curve and the United States economy, 1960–1976.

1975 the unemployment rate was over 8 percent and inflation over 9 percent. The concept of a simple trade-off between inflation and unemployment had broken down.* The world seemed to have grown more complex. Before looking at the trade-off controversy that rages, perhaps we should examine the evidence and the characteristics of inflation and unemployment.

INFLATION

Inflation may be defined as a rise in the general price level. One expects some increase in prices to accompany a growing, viable economy, but at some point the increase gets out of hand. It no longer accounts for productivity increases or growth in real output, and is simply inflationary. During the past two decades there have been two prevailing theories of inflation. They are demand–pull inflation and cost–push, or supply, inflation.

---

*Most economists would hold that inflation and unemployment are still inversely related: as the rate of unemployment decreases, price pressures will tend to increase; and, conversely, as unemployment increases, price pressures will tend to abate. What seems to have happened, though, for a variety of reasons, is that the whole curve has shifted out. The "trade-off" has worsened.

The *demand-pull* explanation of inflation is very compatible with Keynesian economic analysis. If it was a flabby aggregate demand that created unemployment and recession, then an excessive aggregate demand was surely responsible for inflation. One can look at this view graphically in Fig. 19.2, where S represents aggregate supply, D represents different levels of aggregate demand, Q represents real output, and P represents the general price level.

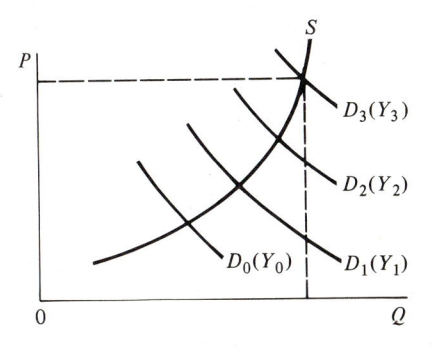

FIG. 19.2 Demand-pull inflation.

As income levels increase in the economy, the demand for goods and services will increase. Normally this will increase output and prices. But what happens when the increase in the demand for goods and services, raw materials, and labor exceeds the capacity to generate new output? Prices rise but output does not—or it increases at a slower rate. The old saying "too much money chasing too few goods" proves to be true. In our Keynesian cross diagram this will present us with an *inflationary gap*. In Fig. 19.3, with AD_1 (that is, if spending were at AD_1) an inflationary gap exists at E^1. There is an equilibrium at an inflationary level of income (Y_{infl}). If the optimum level of income is Y_{FN}, or at full employment (E), there must be a reduction in government spending and transfers, or an increase in taxes or a reduction in the money supply. Similarly, E^2 represents a *recessionary gap* with AD_2; in this case, to reach Y_{FN} requires increased spending or transfers, or a decrease in taxes, or an increase in the money supply.

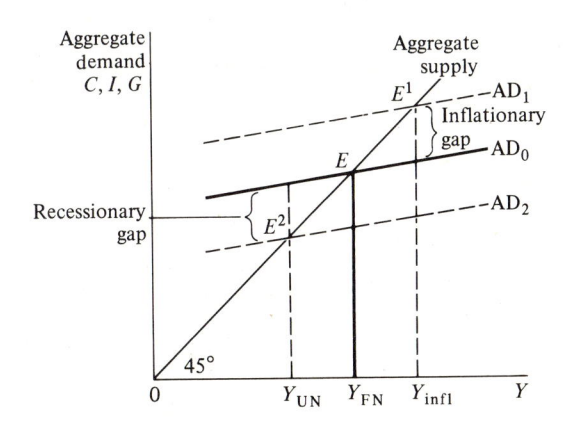

FIG. 19.3 Inflationary and recessionary gaps.

Cost-push or supply inflation puts the responsibility for the price increases on the costs of production that push prices up. You might recall from the analysis of demand and supply in Chapter 10 that as costs increased in the production process, the supply curve would shift to the left—leading to higher prices. (Wages, raw material prices, interest rates, and profits are a few of the cost factors that might cause a shift in the supply function.) We see from the graph in Fig. 19.4 not only increases in price as a result of higher costs but also a reduction in output. Cost increases can, of course, come from many places. One of the earliest groups to be blamed for such increases were unions because their collective bargaining abilities gained wage increases for their members. It should be remembered that wage increases are inflationary only when the increase in output falls behind the increase in wages. There is, in addition to this *wage-push,* a *profit-push* from the entrepreneur. As market structures have become more concentrated, it has become easier for large corporations to increase or *administer prices* for their own benefit—which in most cases means to increase profits.

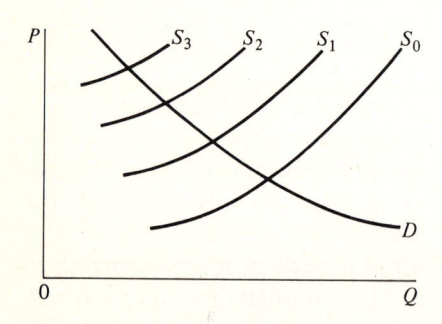

FIG. 19.4 Cost-push inflation.

In recent years we have seen resource shortages send the prices of some goods upward. The lack of supply creates a bottleneck in the production process with very little of the raw materials forthcoming—even at higher costs. For aggregate demand inflation, the simple remedy was to cut back—on spending and on the money supply. For cost-push or supply inflation there, unfortunately, is no very simple remedy. Resource shortages are difficult to prevent. Cartels that withhold raw materials are hard to bargain with. Wage and price controls or some other types of incomes policy don't seem to work very well—when viewed in a historical context. Indeed, controls often lead to contrived shortages themselves, as suppliers hesitate to continue production when costs, which can not be recouped, increase.

Demand-pull and cost-push inflation can also work together and form a *wage price spiral.* As spending and wages increase, so does demand for goods and services —which increase prices—which results in demand for even higher wages. Expectations of the public have added a psychological theory to the group of causes. This theory suggests that people expect higher prices in the future and so they spend now —which leads to higher prices in the future. Nonetheless, inflation does affect us all —and some more than others. Those on fixed incomes are hurt, as are creditors. Borrowers generally are helped.

1. How is a person who borrows money helped by inflation? Is this always the case? Do you know of any banks losing money? Which ones? Why?
2. What effect will "bottlenecks" have on the trade-off between inflation and unemployment? For example, when unemployment is increasing?

Economists believe that wage earners lose and profit earners gain from inflation since there is a lag in the adjustment of wages to the price increases.

Tables 19.2 and 19.3 indicate what has happened to prices in the past quarter of a century. Note the rates of inflation in recent years.

3. On the average, how much would something that cost $200 in 1967 cost in 1975? How much inflation has there been since you were born?
4. Does any information in the table surprise you? Which category affects you most? Is it higher or lower than average?

The following article, "Inflation: A Tale of Two Decades," presents some historical perspective, as well as an additional view on recent inflation problems.

INFLATION: A TALE OF TWO DECADES

Over the past 25 years, prices have doubled in the U.S. Does this process indicate a permanent inflationary tendency in our economy? Where does inflation come from, and why has it been so severe in recent years?

Inflation, a general rise in prices, was relatively modest from 1960 to 1965. Prices rose on the order of 1 percent to 2 percent annually. Beginning in 1965, however, these rates of increase accelerated to 3 percent to 5 percent annually. This increase was directly connected to the large increase in government spending to fight the war in Vietnam.

INFLATION AND THE WAR

As the war developed, federal expenditures jumped between 1965 and 1968 from $123.8 billion to $180.6 billion, with military expenditures leading the climb. This expansion of government spending increased the demand for goods and services, and, because of the widespread opposition to the war, the government was not able to restrain private demand by either a compensating tax increase, rationing or wage-price controls. With the government caught in a political straitjacket, its spending meant a large net addition to total demand.

It is not always inflationary when the government increases demand. If there is a great deal of unemployment and idle factories, the added demand can create jobs

Reprinted with permission from *Dollars & Sense* (May 1976), a Socialist Monthly Bulletin of Economic Affairs, 324 Somerville Ave., Somerville, MA 02143.

TABLE 19.2
Consumer Price Indexes* by Expenditure Classes, 1948–1977 for Urban Wage Earners and Clerical Workers (1967 = 100)

Year or Month	All Items	Food	Housing Total	Housing Rent	Apparel and Upkeep	Transportation	Medical Care	Personal Care	Reading and Recreation	Other Goods and Services
1948	72.1	76.6	69.8	65.1	83.3	61.8	51.1	68.5	72.2	66.8
1949	71.4	73.5	70.9	68.0	80.1	66.4	52.7	68.3	74.9	68.7
1950	72.1	74.5	72.8	70.4	79.0	68.2	53.7	68.3	74.4	69.9
1951	77.8	82.8	77.2	73.2	86.1	72.5	56.3	74.7	76.6	72.8
1952	79.5	84.3	78.7	76.2	85.3	77.3	59.3	75.6	75.9	76.6
1953	80.1	83.0	80.8	80.3	84.6	79.5	61.4	76.3	77.7	78.5
1954	80.5	82.8	81.7	83.2	84.5	78.3	63.4	76.6	76.9	79.8
1955	80.2	81.6	82.3	84.3	84.1	77.4	64.8	77.9	76.7	79.8
1956	81.4	82.2	83.6	85.9	85.8	78.8	67.2	81.1	77.8	81.0
1957	84.3	84.9	86.2	87.5	87.3	83.3	69.9	84.1	80.7	83.3
1958	86.6	88.5	87.7	89.1	87.5	86.0	73.2	86.9	83.9	84.4
1959	87.3	87.1	88.6	90.4	88.2	89.6	76.4	88.7	85.3	86.1
1960	88.7	88.0	90.2	91.7	89.6	89.6	79.1	90.1	87.3	87.8
1961	89.6	89.1	90.9	92.9	90.4	90.6	81.4	90.6	89.3	88.5
1962	90.6	89.9	91.7	94.0	90.9	92.5	83.5	92.2	91.3	89.1
1963	91.7	91.2	92.7	95.0	91.9	93.0	85.6	93.4	92.8	90.6
1964	92.9	92.4	93.8	95.9	92.7	94.3	87.3	94.5	95.0	92.0
1965	94.5	94.4	94.9	96.9	93.7	95.9	89.5	95.2	95.9	94.2
1966	97.2	99.1	97.2	98.2	96.1	97.2	93.4	97.1	97.5	97.2
1967	100.0	100.0	100.0	100.0	100.0	100.0	100.0	100.0	100.0	100.0
1968	104.2	103.6	104.2	102.4	105.4	103.2	106.1	104.2	104.7	104.6
1969	109.8	108.9	110.8	105.7	111.5	107.2	113.4	109.3	108.7	109.1
1970	116.3	114.9	118.9	110.1	116.1	112.7	120.6	113.2	113.4	116.0
1971	121.3	118.4	124.3	115.2	119.8	118.6	128.4	116.8	119.3	120.9
1972	125.3	123.5	129.2	119.2	122.3	119.9	132.5	119.8	122.8	125.5
1973	133.1	141.4	135.0	124.3	126.8	123.8	137.7	125.2	125.9	129.0
1974	147.7	161.7	150.6	130.6	136.2	137.7	150.5	137.3	133.8	137.2
1975	161.2	175.4	166.8	137.3	142.3	150.6	168.6	150.7	144.4	147.4
1976	170.5	180.8	177.2	144.7	147.6	165.5	184.7	160.5	151.2	153.3
1977	181.5	192.2	189.6	153.5	154.2	177.2	202.4	170.9	157.9	159.2

*The Consumer Price Index (CPI) measures changes in the "cost of living."

TABLE 19.3 Percent Changes in Consumer Price Indexes, Major Groups

Year	All Items Dec. to Dec.	All Items Year to Year	Food Dec. to Dec.	Food Year to Year	Commodities Less Food Dec. to Dec.	Commodities Less Food Year to Year	Services Dec. to Dec.	Services Year to Year
1948	2.7	7.8	−0.8	8.5	5.3	7.7	6.1	6.3
1949	−1.8	−1.0	−3.7	−4.0	−4.8	−1.5	3.6	4.8
1950	5.8	1.0	9.6	1.4	5.7	−.1	3.6	3.2
1951	5.0	7.9	7.4	11.1	4.6	7.5	5.2	5.3
1952	.9	2.2	−1.1	1.8	−.5	.9	4.6	4.4
1953	.6	.8	−1.3	−1.5	.2	.2	4.2	4.3
1954	−.5	.5	−1.6	−.2	−1.4	−1.1	1.9	3.3
1955	.4	−.4	−.9	−1.4	0	−.7	2.3	2.0
1956	2.9	1.5	3.1	.7	2.5	1.0	3.1	2.5
1957	3.0	3.6	2.8	3.3	2.2	3.1	4.5	4.0
1958	1.8	2.7	2.2	4.2	.8	1.1	2.7	3.8
1959	1.5	.8	−.8	−1.6	1.5	1.3	3.7	2.9
1960	1.5	1.6	3.1	1.0	−.3	.4	2.7	3.3
1961	.7	1.0	−.9	1.3	.6	.3	1.9	2.0
1962	1.2	1.1	1.5	.9	.7	.7	1.7	1.9
1963	1.6	1.2	1.9	1.4	1.2	.7	2.3	2.0
1964	1.2	1.3	1.4	1.3	.4	.8	1.8	1.9
1965	1.9	1.7	3.4	2.2	.7	.6	2.6	2.2
1966	3.4	2.9	3.9	5.0	1.9	1.4	4.9	3.9
1967	3.0	2.9	1.2	.9	3.1	2.6	4.0	4.4
1968	4.7	4.2	4.3	3.6	3.7	3.7	6.1	5.2
1969	6.1	5.4	7.2	5.1	4.5	4.2	7.4	6.9
1970	5.5	5.9	2.2	5.5	4.8	4.1	8.2	8.1
1971	3.4	4.3	4.3	3.0	2.3	3.8	4.1	5.6
1972	3.4	3.3	4.7	4.0	2.5	2.2	3.6	3.8
1973	8.8	6.2	20.1	14.5	5.0	3.4	6.2	4.4
1974	12.2	11.0	12.2	14.4	13.2	10.6	11.3	9.3
1975	7.0	9.1	6.5	8.5	6.2	9.2	8.1	9.5
1976	4.8	5.8	.6	3.1	5.1	5.0	7.3	8.3
1977	6.8	6.5	8.0	6.3	4.9	5.4	7.9	7.7

Source for Tables 19.2 and 19.3: *Economic Report of the President*, 1977, pp. 241, 246; 1978, pp. 314, 318.

and provide the basis for expansion with stable prices. But in 1965, unemployment was down near 4 percent and plants were operating near capacity, so employment and output could not be readily expanded to meet the increased demand. Inflation was therefore generated in two ways.

First, as government spending rapidly increased overall demand, and supply could not quickly respond, businesses were able to sell goods at higher prices. In a sense, the government was competing with firms and consumers for a larger share of output, and business could raise prices by selling to the highest bidder.

INFLATION AND CLASS STRUGGLE

Second, as the increase in government spending pushed the economy to full speed operation, unemployment dropped. For the four years 1966 through 1969, the unemployment rate was below 4 percent, an experience unparalleled except in other war years. Low unemployment rates strengthened the power of working people, and they were able both to claim a larger share of national income as their own and to resist speed-up and other forms of on-the-job oppression.

The power of workers is reflected in the strike data of the period. On average, twice as many workers were involved in strikes during the second half of the 1960s as during the first half of the decade. While the price increases of the period cut away individual wage gains, more people with jobs meant that working people as a group, and especially the poor, experienced a rapid increase in income.

Business, of course, does not sit idle in the face of rising labor militancy. Among its chief weapons of counterattack were price increases, justified with pious statements of how the price increases were forced by workers' "unreasonable" wage demands. Blame might be laid instead at the door of business for making "unreasonable" profit demands. In fact, however, this type of inflation seems best understood as reflecting an intensification of class conflict.

The new two-dollar bill. Today it buys no more than $1.16 did in 1966, the last time two-dollar bills were issued.

RECESSION, SPIRALS, AND MONOPOLY

In any case, the experience of the late 1960s did hurt profits, and business, using another of its weapons, cut back on investment spending. Combined with government cutbacks, business's action created the recession of 1969–1970, and unemployment rates rose above 6 percent. While demand declined and workers' strength was undermined, inflation did not stop.

Inflation has a self-perpetuating nature. Past price increases make people anticipate future increases. Consumers buy more goods sooner, workers include projected price hikes in their wage demands, and businesses set prices to compensate for cost increases. Thus an inflationary spiral can continue on after its original impetus has been eliminated. Such was the case in the 1970 recession.

Moreover, the falling demand during an inflation will have an *immediate* impact on businesses and force them to stop raising prices only if they are competitive. Monopolies are much less sensitive, raising prices more rapidly than other firms in recessions and less rapidly in expansions. And in the U.S., where 78 giant corporations own 43 percent of all manufacturing assets and get 49 percent of all manufacturing profits, monopoly is the name of the game.

Thus, in 1969, as the recession developed, prices in competitive industries declined by 3 percent while those in monopoly industries rose 6 percent. And, more recently, automobile prices rose 5 percent in 1974 while auto sales declined 20 percent.

Sorry, Buster. Fixed income, you know.

Reprinted by permission of the *National Enquirer* and Mel Yauk.

POWER LOSS: PRICES RISE

While prices did not stop rising during the recession, the increase was peanuts compared with the double-digit inflation of 1973–1974. Wage-price controls had reduced the inflation rate for a two-year period. But with remnants of the late 1960s inflation still hanging on, heavy government expenditures, undertaken to halt the 1969–1970 recession, triggered a new round of price increases.

In addition, losing in Vietnam, the U.S. began to lose power in world economic affairs as well. For 25 years, that power had assured the U.S. of cheap resources—most importantly oil, but other basic materials as well. In the early 1970s, all that began to change. The U.S. was less able to discipline the poor countries and less able to impose policy on the other rich countries. The result was a whole set of price hikes.

U.S. business then needed to sell more abroad to finance its more expensive imports. Accordingly, as one policy, the government pushed agricultural exports, the value of which tripled between 1970 and 1974. This attempt by the government to adjust to the new international situation had predictable results: selling more abroad meant less was available at home. And with food monopolies taking advantage of this situation, food prices rose 30 percent between 1972-1974.

With food and oil prices leading the way, inflation was bombing along at an annual rate of 15 percent at the end of 1974's summer, and the current recession began to blossom.

What about Money?

Inflation is sometimes described as a result of too much money being in circulation. If the amount of money is increased too rapidly, the value of each dollar declines, which is to say that prices go up. ("Money" or the "money supply" includes the value of checking accounts as well as cash in circulation.)

It's true that in the first half of the 1960s, when inflation was slight, the money supply rose by only 14 percent. It rose by 27 percent in the latter half of the 1960s and by 36 percent in the first half of the 1970s, times of greater inflation. But the question that needs to be answered is, why was the money supply increased in this manner?

Probably the best answer is that the government increased the money supply to finance the war expenditures of the late 1960s, the counter-recessionary expenditures of the early 1970s, and the high import costs in the more recent period. In other words, the money supply was manipulated to deal with certain economic problems—the same problems that can be directly tied to inflation.

WHERE IS IT GOING?

What does all this history mean for the future? The severity of the current recession has had a greater downward impact on inflation than did the 1969-1970 recession. Prices rose at an annual rate of only 3.6 percent from November to February. But there are good reasons to think the lower inflation is temporary.

The current lull in inflation is largely the result of declines in food and energy prices, but without stability in international affairs new increases are likely. Any major gains by labor in key negotiations (trucking, rubber, auto, construction) will be countered by business with price increases. Finally, in an effort to overcome the recession, the government has been spending heavily and, if the economy heats up too quickly, this will induce more inflation.

While it is anyone's guess what this year's inflation rate will be, it will take more than the usual mumbo-jumbo of government and business economists to make the problems go away. In the meantime, the dollar of 1967 is worth 60 cents today.

---

5. What do you think the rate of inflation will be this year? Explain.

6. If one accepts the view of inflation in the article above, then what stabilization policies should monetary and fiscal policy follow? Are any other policies needed?

UNEMPLOYMENT

The Department of Labor defines those people who are over the age of 16 and actively seeking work as unemployed if they do not have a job. A little less than half of the population is in the labor force; and it is on this base that the unemployment estimates are made. By 1977 almost 100 million of the 215 million people in the U.S. were in the labor force.

---

7. From Fig. 19.3 can you explain a recessionary gap?

Economists have defined five basic types of unemployment.

1. *Frictional unemployment* is caused by the temporary mismatching of people with jobs due to the facts that workers change jobs, employers are constantly seeking new workers, and new people are entering the labor market. All labor markets have such frictional unemployment; for even during World War II when there existed a severe labor shortage, unemployment was still about 2 percent.

2. *Seasonal unemployment,* as the name implies, results from changing seasonal demand and supply for labor. Students seeking jobs in the summer, farm workers laid off in the winter are both part of this seasonal unemployment.

3. *Structural unemployment* presents a more serious problem than the previous types of unemployment. It is the unemployment which results from permanent displacements of workers due to shifting product demand and/or technological changes that require new labor skills. The shift in demand from natural to synthetic fibers created problems of structural unemployment for places like Fall River, Mass. The mechanical picking of tomatoes has caused many migrant workers to become structurally unemployed. Such unemployment is a function of geographic, as well as job skill level, mobility.

4. *Cyclical unemployment* is due to the decreased demand for labor which is a result of the business cycle. The high unemployment of the 1930s was basically a problem of cyclical unemployment.

5. *Hidden unemployment* is probably the hardest concept to both define and measure. There is growing evidence that many people would like a job if they thought one was available, but many have become so discouraged by their past failures to find employment that they have literally given up trying. Technically, such people are outside of the labor force, but in fact they are unemployed. One sign that such hidden unemployment exists can be seen from the fact that in the early stages of economic recovery, the labor participation rate (i.e., the proportion of the total population which is seeking a job) rises. More people seek jobs as the number of jobs increases and the question arises as to why they were not part of the labor force when the unemployment rate was higher. In addition, there are many people who work part time but would prefer to work full time. These people are now counted as being employed. (We might also add a group of people that work but earn a lower than poverty level of income.)

Table 19.4 shows selected unemployment rates for workers from 1948 to 1977.

TABLE 19.4 Selected Unemployment Rates, 1960–1977.

	By Sex and Age			By Color			By Selected Groups			
Year	All Workers	Both Sexes 16–19 Years	Males 20 Years and Over	Females 20 Years and Over	White	Black and Other	Experienced Wage and Salary Workers	Household Heads	Married Men	Full-Time Workers	Blue-Collar Workers
1948	3.8	9.2	3.2	3.6	3.5	5.9	4.3	....	....	....	4.2
1949	5.9	13.4	5.4	5.3	5.6	8.9	6.8	....	3.5	5.4	8.0
1950	5.3	12.2	4.7	5.1	4.9	9.0	6.0	....	4.6	5.0	7.2
1951	3.3	8.2	2.5	4.0	3.1	5.3	3.7	....	1.5	2.6	3.9
1952	3.0	8.5	2.4	3.2	2.8	5.4	3.3	....	1.4	2.5	3.6
1953	2.9	7.6	2.5	2.9	2.7	4.5	3.2	....	1.7	....	3.4
1954	5.5	12.6	4.9	5.5	5.0	9.9	6.2	....	4.0	5.2	7.2
1955	4.4	11.0	3.8	4.4	3.9	8.7	4.8	....	2.8	3.8	5.8
1956	4.1	11.1	3.4	4.2	3.6	8.3	4.4	....	2.6	3.7	5.1
1957	4.3	11.6	3.6	4.1	3.8	7.9	4.6	....	2.8	4.0	6.2
1958	6.8	15.9	6.2	6.1	6.1	12.6	7.2	....	5.1	7.2	10.2
1959	5.5	14.6	4.7	5.2	4.8	10.7	5.7	....	5.6	....	7.6

Table 19.4 continued

1960	5.5	14.7	4.7	5.1	4.9	10.2	5.7	...	3.7	...	7.8
1961	6.7	16.8	5.7	6.3	6.0	12.4	6.8	...	4.6	6.7	9.2
1962	5.5	14.7	4.6	5.4	4.9	10.9	5.6	...	3.6	...	7.4
1963	5.7	17.2	4.5	5.4	5.0	10.8	5.5	3.7	3.4	5.5	7.3
1964	5.2	16.2	3.9	5.2	4.6	9.6	5.0	3.2	2.8	4.9	6.3
1965	4.5	14.8	3.2	4.5	4.1	8.1	4.3	2.7	2.4	4.2	5.3
1966	3.8	12.8	2.5	3.8	3.4	7.3	3.5	2.2	1.9	3.5	4.2
1967	3.8	12.8	2.3	4.2	3.4	7.4	3.6	2.1	1.8	3.4	4.4
1968	3.6	12.7	2.2	3.8	3.2	6.7	3.4	1.9	1.6	3.1	4.1
1969	3.5	12.2	2.1	3.7	3.1	6.4	3.3	1.8	1.5	3.1	3.9
1970	4.9	15.2	3.5	4.8	4.5	8.2	4.8	2.9	2.6	4.5	6.2
1971	5.9	16.9	4.4	5.7	5.4	9.9	5.7	3.6	3.2	5.5	7.4
1972	5.6	16.2	4.0	5.4	5.0	10.0	5.3	3.3	2.8	5.1	6.5
1973	4.9	14.5	3.2	4.8	4.3	8.9	4.5	2.9	2.3	4.3	5.3
1974	5.6	16.0	3.8	5.5	5.0	9.9	5.3	3.3	2.7	5.1	6.7
1975	8.5	19.9	6.7	8.0	7.8	13.9	8.2	5.8	5.1	8.1	11.7
1976	7.7	19.0	5.9	7.4	7.0	13.1	7.3	5.1	4.2	7.3	9.4
1977	7.0	17.7	5.2	7.0	6.2	13.1	6.6	4.5	3.6	6.5	8.1

Source: *Economic Report of the President*, 1977, p. 221; 1978, pp. 291–292.

8. Does it surprise you that married men typically have the lowest unemployment rates? Why or why not?

In 1975 more than 7.5 million people in the U.S. were unemployed. The fact of unemployment is an economic problem—both for the individual and for society. Beyond that, however, there are also problems in even counting and defining the unemployed in our economy.

Counting the Unemployed

Many economists are now beginning to use a new method of calculating the level of unemployment in the U.S. David Gordon from the New School of Social Research has proposed that we focus on *underemployment* rather than our traditional notion of unemployment in order to arrive at a more *realistic* and *meaningful* statistic. This statistic would give us better information and would be more instructive to policy-makers trying to combat high rates of underemployment. How is this concept different from the one presently utilized?

Gordon defines underemployment as the statistic which calculates the number of people who fall into the following four categories:

1. *Unemployed* people who are actively looking for work but unable to find a job.
2. *Discouraged workers* are unemployed and wanting work but have given up in frustration because they believe no jobs are available.
3. *Involuntary part-time* people working part time who actually want fulltime work but are unable to find it.
4. *Underemployed* people are working *full time* but earning *less* than the poverty level of income as specified by the Bureau of Labor Statistics (1977–an urban family of four, $5800/yr.) (A person working full time at the minimum wage will earn approximately $5000/yr.)*

With this definition, Gordon calculated 1975 underemployment to be as shown in Table 19.5.

TABLE 19.5 Counting the Underemployed, 1975

(All Numbers in Thousands)	Low Estimate Number	%	Middle Estimate Number	%	High Estimate Number	%
Expanded labor force	93,695	100.0	95,232	100.0	97,809	100.0
1. Unemployed	7,830	8.4	7,830	8.2	7,830	8.0
2. Discouraged workers	1,082	1.2	2,619	2.7	5,196	5.3
3. Involuntary part time	3,748	4.0	3,748	3.9	3,748	3.8
4. The working poor	3,234	3.5	7,146	7.5	15,274	15.6
Total underemployment	15,894	17.0	21,343	22.4	32,048	32.8

*David M. Gordon, *Problems in Political Economy* (Second Edition), D.C. Heath, 1977, see pp. 70–75.

With the low estimate, Gordon's level of underemployment of 17 percent is far greater than the "official" figure of 8.4 percent.

9. Do you anticipate unemployment in your future? Why or why not? What are your "odds"?
10. Does it make any difference for economic policy how we count the unemployed?

Economic realities often have direct social consequences. "The Hidden Costs of Unemployment" looks at the family problems unemployment creates in black society and the vicious cycle that results.

THE HIDDEN COSTS OF UNEMPLOYMENT

JAMES P. COMER

NEW HAVEN—The most recent report shows that 15 percent of the black work force is unemployed. Many are heads of households with young children. In fact, the highest rate of unemployment, up to 50 percent, is among black teenagers and young adults.

These people have the youngest children who are in the most crucial stages of development. Unemployed people are more likely to have social and psychological problems and are often unable to rear their children in a way which promotes healthy development. Thus we will lose too many of two more generations of black people to drugs, crime, undereducation, and underachievement.

Most are the victims of a monetary policy designed to cool off inflation by deliberately creating an economic recession with resultant unemployment. In every recession, regardless of the cause, blacks have paid first, most, and the longest and many have never recovered.

Unemployment, marginal and/or periodic, is a way of life for many. Family problems are more often severe and persistent in such cases. Many people who father children, and nowadays, mother children, do not stay around to face the embarrassing situation of not being able to care for them. This further decreases the possibility of healthy child development.

A remarkable number of black people have always found, and even now will find, a way to family stability and will rear healthy children without a job or without a steady "living wage" job. But it is difficult and too many people and communities will be badly hurt by the situation.

What is the effect of unemployment on parent and child relationships? Our most accepted principles of child development tell us that preparation for adult-

© 1975 by The New York Times Company. Reprinted by permission.

hood does not begin with the 18-year old, the 10-year old, not even entirely with the infant. It begins with the parents, their hopes, plans, sense of belonging in the community and society, their sense of personal adequacy and specific child-rearing skills.

Nothing speaks louder to their sense of belonging and adequacy, nothing shapes their hopes and dreams and plans, and nothing enables them to exercise their child-rearing skills more than their ability to find and hold a job and meet the major responsibility that society charges them with—that of taking care of their families.

Jobless people are under great stress. Society condemns them for not being able to care for themselves and accepting "handouts." Parents are unable to feel good about themselves. They often take their bad feelings out on each other—parent on parent, parent on child, and children on parents. Homes of unemployed, frequently unemployed, and marginally employed people are more often chaotic and filled with high conflict than those of people who are regularly and well employed. Family break-up and movement from place to place in search of a better situation or "just in front of the rent man" is more likely.

Communities of yesterday's unemployed and marginally employed are the places where many of the children of today's unemployed parents will grow up and prepare for adulthood. These communities, schools, decaying buildings and street gangs, are often seething with hopelessness and despair, anger and alienation, apathy, and disruptive behavior.

What is learned is not likely to lead to success and good citizenship but to the problems which are paralyzing and destroying our urban areas today. Worst of all, blacks will be blamed for this predicament and not the policymakers who made it all possible.

It has always amazed me that we ask why young people who grew up in such homes and communities often can't go out and have a successful college career, learn a trade, hold a job, care for a family, find joy and happiness in leisure time, and be all-around good citizens.

Yet we know very well that preparation to do these things begins with the stability and security of their parents in the home—a security made possible by a job and a living wage.

But what is the value of good child development and work skills if there is no work? The motivation for good cannot be sustained, at least not in this society in which work so directly determines one's self-worth and is the basis of personal organization. Without job opportunities hundreds of educational programs preparing one for work have little meaning. The uncertainty and sense of apathy we see in so many training and educational programs, even at the graduate and professional school level, are in part an outcome of the bleak employment picture.

11. Can economists deal with social ills? Is it their job?

And sometimes, middle-aged white men find themselves unemployed, with special problems all their own.

THE FEAR, THE NUMBING FEAR

EDWARD B. FUREY

BRIGHTWATERS, N.Y.—Let me tell you what it's like for one guy to be 52 years old and jobless in America in 1975.

As a recently fired middle-management executive of a division of one of America's top 500 companies, I have sent out over 150 résumés. Less than 10 percent have drawn a response of any kind. Five percent drew requests for additional information, while less than 4 percent resulted in a personal interview. None resulted in a job.

As an infantry veteran of World War II in the South Pacific, I've had some experience with fear, and how men deal with it. I like to feel that I don't scare any easier than the next guy, but to be 52 years old and jobless is to be frightened—frightened to the marrow of your bones. Your days start with it, and end with it. It's all pervasive. It's numbing. It's mind-boggling.

Things you've always taken for granted fall apart. You can no longer maintain your hospitalization insurance, and for the first time in 28 years you and your family are unprotected against a medical emergency. You are unable to meet the payments on your life insurance. The bank holding your mortgage warns that foreclosure is being considered. Bills to the utilities are overdue and you're keeping vital services only through partial payments, aware of the fact that time is running out.

It's to tell a fine 14-year old son that you haven't got the five bucks you owe him for the great report card he brought home.

It's to pass local merchants on the street and feel embarrassment, wondering when you'll be able to pay them what you owe them.

To feel the disintegration of your confidence as a man, and your ability to protect your family from economic disaster.

It's to envy just about everybody who has a job, any job.

It's to see the doubt on the faces of your children about what's going on in their house, when so many of their friends are unaffected.

It's to add a crushing dimension to the natural self-doubts that are part of the process of growing older.

It's to stand silently on unemployment lines with other surplus members of America's work force, waiting to sign for your unemployment check.

It's to see what the neighborhood looks like at 10:30 on a Tuesday morning.

It's to feel embarrassed to answer the ring of the telephone at the same hour.

It's to watch assorted politicians in dialogues with fat-cat television interviewers in an atmosphere replete with camaraderie, purporting to discuss America's problems, where the right questions are not asked, and the unchallenged responses consist mostly of noncommittal and vacuous banalities.

It's to realize the simple stunning fact that you are without meaningful representation in this society.

And in the late evening when your household is quiet and you switch off the bedroom light it's to be alone, alone like you've never been before. To lie there looking at the darkness and wonder if you're going to lose the home that you've worked

© 1975 by The New York Times Company. Reprinted by permission.

all your life for, the home that represents the only equity you've been able to accumulate in 30 years of working and raising a family.

It's to realize that for many Americans the problem you are facing for the first time has become a way of life.

The carnage is strewn about America for anyone with eyes to see. In our mental hospitals, in our drug-abuse centers, in the alcoholic wards of our hospitals, in our juvenile shelters, in our prisons, and on the streets of our cities.

And finally, it's to lie sleepless in bed waiting for the dawn of a new day and realize that something is terribly wrong in America.

12. Why might Edward Furey be unemployed at age 52? Would you hire him?

13. If you were unemployed, what do you think your attitude would be?

14. What are the economic and noneconomic costs of unemployment?

Can you type?

Copyright © 1976. Reprinted by permission of the *Wall Street Journal* and Brenda Burbank.

ON POST-POST-KEYNESIANISM

A growing number of people are becoming disillusioned with the basic Keynesian approach because they feel that it ignores (and thus can't deal with) many of the major problems, like unemployment and inflation, that exist in both the U.S. and the rest of the world. These and other objections to the post-Keynesian synthesis are discussed by Daniel Fusfeld, an economist at the University of Michigan, in "The Shattered Synthesis," which appeared in 1972 in the *Saturday Review*.

POST-POST-KEYNES: THE SHATTERED SYNTHESIS
DANIEL R. FUSFELD

Within the theoretical and political framework of the post-Keynesian synthesis, solutions seemed to be present for all of the great economic problems of the postwar world. Liberals and reformers flocked to embrace it. Yet, underneath the sur-

Copyright © 1972 by Saturday Review Co. First published in *Saturday Review*. Reprinted by permission. All rights reserved.

face it was the economics of the status quo, of anticommunism and the Cold War, of reform around the edges of the social and economic order.

The post-Keynesian synthesis, in fact, reflected and provided justification for the concentration of power in American society in the years after World War II. The locus of governmental power had shifted to the federal government, and within the federal government to the executive branch. With world power came further concentration within the executive branch itself, into the hands of the national security managers. This growing concentration of political power was paralleled by an increasing concentration of economic power in the business community. A recent Federal Trade Commission study showed that in 1968 the 100 largest manufacturing corporations held a larger share of manufacturing assets than the 200 largest in 1950 and that the 200 largest in 1968 controlled a share equal to that of the 1000 largest in 1941.

Big business and big government have been coming together in an increasingly symbiotic relationship. Big government needs big business because the giant corporation has become the key to effective functioning of the economy—witness the Penn Central and Lockheed rescue operations—and because big business is the source of the weaponry on which national power rests. Government, in turn, provides the environment of economic growth within which the large corporation flourishes, educates the managers and technicians that big enterprises need, maintains the framework for settlement of labor disputes, and seeks to maintain a system of world order conducive to the growth of international corporations. Concentrated economic and political power are allies.

Sustained full employment and economic growth, emphasized by the post-Keynesian synthesis, became the twin keystones of an understanding between those who held and exercised power and those who did not. The levers of power remained in the hands of those who managed big business and big government. In exchange for allowing them a relatively free rein, the great middle-income majority obtained the material benefits that accrued from a quarter century of economic expansion.

How smoothly indeed the post-Keynesian synthesis seemed to be working, both in theory and in practice. Then, in the 1960s, at the height of its influence, the synthesis began to be faced with a group of problems that it could not handle effectively.

Inflation was the first to appear. The monetary and fiscal policies designed to achieve full employment and economic growth seemed to generate rising prices when full employment neared. Even during substantially slack economic periods, price levels showed an upward creep.

An incomes policy—government control of wages and prices—was never envisaged in the post-Keynesian synthesis, for one of its chief points is the idea that management of the economy need not extend into the microeconomic domain of wages, prices, profits, and incomes generally. But, of course, an incomes policy has come to us full force with the phases of the Nixon controls—an acknowledgment by a Republican administration that the private sector alone cannot be relied on to achieve stabilizing results in these areas.

Closely related to the problem of domestic inflation is a second problem: the continuing crisis in the international monetary system. The U.S. deficit in its balance of international payments, sustained since 1950 with the exception of the Suez crisis years, 1957–1958, finally wrecked the system established at Bretton

Woods in 1944. The immediate cause of the problem was U.S. private investment and military expenditures abroad on a scale too great to be financed by a favorable balance of trade. When our favorable trade balance fell victim to domestic inflation at the same time that military spending was vastly increased, the end quickly came. A historic devaluation of the dollar has resulted.

A deeper issue lurks beneath these events. A nation's domestic economic policies influence its balance of international payments, and its balance of payments limits the freedom it has in pursuing domestic economic goals. Moreover, the balance of payments of the United States, as the dominant nation in world trade and finance, affects the balance of payments of other nations, which affects their domestic economic policies and limits the alternatives among which they can choose. In this way, our domestic economic policies ultimately weigh on those of other nations. These are worldwide economic relationships that the post-Keynesian synthesis had hardly considered and for which it has almost no policy prescriptions.

A third problem to emerge in the 1960s concerned the underdeveloped countries. Growth of the advanced economies was supposed to generate capital resources that could be channeled into the less-developed economies, getting them started on the path to self-sustained growth. It didn't work out that way. Economic growth was spotty and, as Gunnar Myrdal and others pointed out, in many areas there was a reverse drain of capital and skilled manpower out of the underdeveloped areas and into the advanced international economy. Meanwhile, the public health technology of the advanced countries was imported into the backward nations, causing declining death rates and rapid population growth that literally ate up the gains from economic growth. The gap between the rich and poor nations tended to widen rather than narrow, which is just the opposite of the results suggested by economic orthodoxy.

These three issues—inflation, the international financial system, and underdeveloped nations—were serious problems, but they did not involve the implicit values and goals of the post-Keynesian synthesis. In recent years, however, a series of issues which do just that has come to the fore: economic growth, the environment, the racial problem, and militarism. The discussions of these issues did not center on the theoretical basis of the post-Keynesian synthesis. Rather, its implicit policy goals were questioned, along with the social and economic institutions it sought to explain.

The once sacrosanct goal of economic growth was the first to be criticized, with the onslaught being led in this country by John Kenneth Galbraith and in England by E. J. Mishan. Galbraith pointed out that an economy dominated by private decisions about consumption and production tends to starve its public sector. This is especially true when motivations center on individual gains in income and wealth. Private spending on luxuries and entertainment expands while such foundations of the future as education and basic science are slighted. Furthermore, modern marketing and advertising techniques are used by business firms to mold consumer spending to their needs as producers, instead of adjusting production to match a pristine pattern of consumer wants. The system as a whole operates for the benefit of producers rather than consumers, if Galbraith's analysis is reasonably correct, and its goal is the aggrandizement of business wealth instead of the individual welfare.

Mishan went even further, arguing that a materialistic society interested primarily in piling up more and more material goods was destructive of humane values and pursued goals antithetical to human happiness. The important point about Mishan's argument is not its novelty—his views are even older than the science of economics itself—but in its popularity. It struck a note that many were eager to hear.

The views expressed by Galbraith and Mishan were echoed by a new generation of youth disenchanted with the materialism of middle-income America, by workers dissatisfied with the monotony of their jobs and the limited horizons of their lives, and by blacks and Latins condemned to low wages, poverty, and welfare. Disenchantment, hostility, and alienation became facts of life for the economist as well as the psychiatrist to consider.

The growing militarism of American life raised further questions about economic goals. In the 1950s and 1960s, the greatest industrial nation in the world was using between 10 and 15 percent of its huge and increasing output for military and related purposes. The obvious question arose: What is the advantage of economic growth if a large portion of the gain is used for wasteful or destructive purposes? But underlying that was an even more basic question: What is it about the economic system that drives it (or allows it to be driven) to such ends? Had military expenditures created such strong vested interests in the "military-industrial complex" that there was no going back to a humane economy? If these questions generated breezes of doubt before 1965, after the war in Southeast Asia escalated to high levels, they brought storms of dissent.

An equally fundamental issue arose as many people became aware of the potential environmental crisis the industrial nations seemed to be heading for. A growing economy produces increasing amounts of waste, and one in which high consumption levels are a major feature contributes even more. Modern industrial technology, furthermore, was not developed with compatibility with the natural environment in mind. Would continued economic growth destroy the ecological base not only of the economy but of human life as well? The economics of the post-Keynesian synthesis had no answer to that question, and the ameliorative measures suggested were only partial responses to a huge problem.

Finally, the persistence of poverty and the emergence of the urban-racial crisis in the United States in the late 1960s pointed up the fact that a large portion of the American people was not participating adequately in the affluence achieved by many. A devastating social and economic conflict emerged in the midst of what should have been a society with reduced conflict—because of growing affluence. It became clear that the benefits of affluence were *not* being so widely diffused as to strengthen the social fabric.

By now, even the orthodox post-Keynesian economist has good reason to doubt that the private-enterprise, market-oriented economy can resolve its problems effectively. A high-pressure economy has brought new strains on the social fabric and exposed intractable problems. Growth is now seen as potentially unbalanced, misdirected, or destructive. Inflation, a succession of international financial crises, problems of the Third World, cities torn by conflict, an endangered natural environment, militarism, the persistence of poverty, and growing alienation—instead of increased well-being, there is a crisis of confidence.

The tacit agreement between the haves and the have-nots has broken up. The war in Southeast Asia laid bare the shift in the locus of power to a relatively small group whose control over the decision-making process is supplemented by careful manipulation of public opinion and political process. The gains from economic growth stopped as the costs of the war escalated. Many young people saw, perhaps more clearly than their elders, the essential polity compromise that traded affluence for power and refused to accept it. Blacks and other minority groups, segregated in their urban ghettos and developing a racial and political consciousness, refused to accept their continued status as second-class citizens. The whole system of polity broke down. Along with it went the orthodox post-Keynesian synthesis of theory and policy. The paradigm of a smoothly adjusting system of largely competitive markets that produces what consumers want, provides rewards appropriate to effort, and is assured of stable economic growth through Keynesian macroeconomics policies lost its credibility. A growing radical movement sees the economic and political systems as essentially malign rather than benign, antagonistic to humane values rather than supportive of them. Contemporary economics is in crisis because the social order is in crisis, unable to go back to the old and unwilling to strike boldly toward the new.

The problems of the present indicate the path to the future. A reconstruction of economics—a new synthesis and a new paradigm—will have to move toward greater concern for humane values, toward a humane economy on a worldwide scale.

A humane economy requires more than prosperity and economic growth, more than efficient allocation of resources. It demands changes in the framework of economic institutions to achieve greater equality and freedom. It requires dispersal of the economic power and governmental authority that support the present disposition of income, wealth, and power. It requires a social environment that brings a sense of community and fellowship into human relationships. It demands compatibility among man, his technology, and the natural environment. And all of these things must be done on a worldwide scale. These are the goals of the future, to which economists and everyone else will have to devote their energies.

---

15. Fusfeld argues that the post-Keynesian synthesis has been shattered. What is the basis of his argument? Do you agree with him? Why or why not?

In a lighter vein, Liane Ellison Norman has a somewhat different analysis and remedy to the unemployment–inflation dilemma. It reflects indirectly on the strengths and weaknesses of the economy itself.

LIVE A LITTLE

LIANE ELLISON NORMAN

PITTSBURGH—The recession has spread the pain of unemployment, but neither generously or evenhandedly. For an astonishing proportion of our society, unemployment is nothing new.

© 1976 by The New York Time Company. Reprinted by permission.

The political scientist Andrew Hacker wrote recently that "at full employment, the American economy wants the services of [only] about 43 percent of the work-age population." The other 57 percent are college students (not counting younger children), housewives, early retirees, and the permanently poor. Our economy, he said, defines "a portion of the population as extraneous to its own well-being."

Work is what we esteem. It is therefore unconscionable that over half the adult population, even in the best of times, is excluded from any part in it. Indeed, employment is a monopoly, one badly in need of being broken up.

Part of the problem is unemployment, the estrangement of well over half of us from what gives lives personal significance and public value. We pay a high price for this. Jails, schools, welfare and wars all keep the unemployed out of the way.

The other part of the problem, over-employment, is less obvious because the overemployed define the norm. We respect those who do too much. Ulcers and full calendars are marks of distinction. Officials boast how busy they are, how hard they work. Professionals are rushed to distraction. The most unfortunate dig coal, mend roads and dump garbage, but earn little honor and no repose. No wonder they are jealous for their jobs. It's all or nothing, exhaustion, solaced by beer and the tube— or unemployment!

But how essential overworkers feel! How self-righteous! How they pity and despise the poor souls who can't get work, proving their inferiority. And over their jobs, like legendary dragons on hoards of gold, the overworkers crouch, protecting their prestige along with their incomes.

If some people have too much work and others none at all, why not spread the work around? Nothing so alarms the work monopolists.

I am a reformed overworker. When I taught full time, I was fueled by nervous energy, conscientious to the point of obsession, sure I was indispensable. My family, less compelling than the demands of the job, occupied the mere periphery of my attention.

So I quit and now teach part time. I now work more carefully, explore more byways, think more calmly, less compulsively. Institutions have learned to stand without my efforts. Work and home are integrated. As professional conscientiousness has slackened, human conscientiousness has grown. We have less money and more pleasure.

My full-time colleagues teach more than they adequately can, run to more meetings and events than they can contribute to or absorb. They are absentee family members, leaving children and home fires to someone else. They firmly believe in overemployment, and their graduated students cannot find jobs.

The ideal would be employment for everyone, but not too much for anyone. In other words, part-time work all around. Imagine. . . .

No one would be extraneous to the production of what we need. Every one would have standing to help decide what we *do* need. Workers could rejoin families, and the nature of need would be clearer. (If you spend eight to 16 hours a day making aerosol-spray cans, it is easy to forget the children at home.)

Ambition would be scarcer; fewer people would walk over their grandmothers to please the boss. Incomes would be smaller, but affluence serves mainly the acquisition of goods that need dusting but do not satisfy the desire for warmth and purpose.

Fewer people would be dirt poor. More time saved from the bottomless pit of work would be more time to make more compassionate communities. Even the excitements of war might pale if homely connections ran deeper.

People would do their work with love because they could afford to. Old people would not go to the glue factories of early retirement. Women would share in the world's work outside the home, and men would come home to share the domestic part of the world's work. Economic growth would slow down, saving resources, cooling the furnaces of empire.

The imagination rejoices. Think of a President more intent on his family's happiness than the nation's prestige! Think of a Secretary of State or corporation chairman sharing their jobs with two or three persons each!

Monopolies mean power, and overworkers will not happily yield theirs up. But the secret weapon the rest of us have is to look at overwork not as nobility, but as a selfish usurpation, an unwarranted pre-emption. We can simply stop admiring those who have too much work at the expense of those who have none.

---

16. What is your reaction to Norman's proposal? Is it realistic? Why or why not?

CONCLUSION

This chapter completes our discussion of macroeconomics. We have seen that the Keynesian approach to economic policy has carried us a long way from the classical approach. And yet problems still exist and new approaches may be needed to deal with future problems. Indeed, many of these issues are increasing our attention towards microeconomics and the functioning of specific markets. Traditional macroeconomic policies for controlling inflation and achieving full employment do not seem to be working. Indeed, the two have coexisted throughout the 1970s and have been, as we mentioned earlier, dubbed stagflation. It has been a failure in Keynesian economics to deal with this phenomenon. We will discuss this problem in significant depth in Chapter 24, but, before we do, we need to first broaden our perspective and see what is happening in international economics, since an understanding of this arena is necessary to appreciate the complexity of the problem. As you might have guessed, if you think the problems we've been dealing with so far are complicated, "you ain't seen nothing yet."

KEY CONCEPTS

trade-offs
Phillips Curve
inflationary gap
demand-pull
cost-push
wage-push

underemployment
profit-push
administered prices
types of unemployment
stagflation
post-Keynesian synthesis

REVIEW QUESTIONS

1. Do you think fighting inflation is more important than fighting unemployment? Why or why not?

2. Are conventional economic policies capable of dealing with the current situation of high levels of both inflation and unemployment? Why or why not?

3. What *structural* elements in the economy limit the effectiveness of fiscal and monetary policies?

4. How does avoiding a boom avoid a recession? What is the resultant impact on inflation? (Go back to Chapter 14 and read Freund's article.)

SUGGESTED READINGS

Michael H. Best and William E. Connolly, 1976. *The Politicized Economy*, D. C. Heath. An attempt to suggest the problems for economic theory in the modern context and a prescription for the future.

Robert Aaron Gordon, 1974. *Economic Instability and Growth,* Harper & Row. An economic history of the recent, postwar performance of the American economy, focusing on macroeconomic goals and policy.

Walter Heller, 1976. *The Economy*, Norton. A leading liberal economist's attempt to lead us out of the woods.

Robert Lekachman, 1976. *Economists at Bay*, McGraw-Hill. An interesting and easy-to-read account of the failure of modern economists to adequately deal with economic issues.

Robert Lekachman, 1973. *Inflation*, Vintage Books. This is an interesting and well-written examination of the process and causes of inflation. Lekachman also gives five solutions to the dilemma.

Abba P. Lerner, 1973. *Flation*, Penguin Books. Lerner examines many of the complexities involved with the inflation–deflation problem.

Howard Sherman, 1976. *Stagflation: A Radical Theory of Unemployment and Inflation*, Harper & Row. One radical's attempt to explain the modern phenomenon of stagflation.

INTERNATIONAL ECONOMICS

PART V

In this part on international economics we will be examining some of the following issues and questions: (1) Why does it matter if the U.S. trade deficit is $26 billion this year and the value of our currency is declining? (2) Why does it matter that Third World nations have a combined debt of $180 billion? (3) Why are most nations utilizing floating exchange rates as opposed to fixed exchange rates? (4) Will the sluggish recovery from the deep recession of 1973-1975 result in widespread "protectionism" among the major Western industrial nations? (5) Why are developing nations demanding commodity price stabilization agreements with the advanced nations? (6) What role will the International Monetary Fund play in the years ahead? (7) Will the OPEC cartel continue to exert leverage and control in the international economic and financial arena? (8) How important are food and arms

Pounds, pounds . . . nothing but pounds. Haven't you got any deutsche marks?

Copyright ©, the *Philadelphia Inquirer*. The Washington Post Writers Group. Reprinted by permission of Tony Auth.

sales to the U.S. in terms of export earnings to improve our balance of payments position and strengthen our currency? (9) Will the demand of developing nations for a "New International Economic Order" receive an affirmative response from the developed world? (10) What kinds of economic systems will we see in the future as developing nations attempt to create their own development models and strategies?

To analyze these questions, we will focus upon the following general areas of study in the next four chapters (1) international economic interdependence, (2) international trade, (3) international finance, and (4) economic problems of developing nations.

INTERNATIONAL ECONOMIC INTERDEPENDENCE

CHAPTER 20

INTRODUCTION

Interdependence among nations is a major feature of the modern world economy. This interdependence will be a salient theme throughout the remainder of this book. It is necessary for us to be more specific about this concept if we are to understand it properly and apply it to the crucial problems we will be examining.

By the term *economic interdependence* we mean simply that all countries are affected by the events of an economic nature that occur in many other countries. For example, many industrialized nations rely on the developing nations for basic food and raw materials needs. And, in turn, many developing nations import manufactured finished goods from industrialized nations. The degree of interdependence is, of course, different for each and every nation. For example, Japan is severely affected by OPEC price increases yet relatively unaffected by Costa Rica's decision to increase banana prices. On the other hand, Costa Rica, also strongly affected by an OPEC price increase, has the flexibility to shift her imports of television sets from the U.S. to Japan. As we have defined this concept, it is a purely economic concept. It is meant to be descriptive of the complex international flow of goods, services *and* capital among nations.

The nature of this contemporary interdependence has been discussed by Richard N. Cooper (Undersecretary of State for International Economic Affairs in the Carter Administration):

Actions in one country are transmitted ever more quickly and sometimes irritatingly to other countries. Economic relationships are no longer confined to the traditional exchange of manufactures for food and raw materials, although much of that remains. Rather, economic transactions have increasingly become exchanges of manufactures for manufactures (an enterprise in which the mutual benefits of an international division of labor are far less intuitively evident), financial capital movements between countries, transfers of technology, and, not least, direct investment abroad, with ownership of an establishment lying outside the country in which it is located. These developments reflect a growing mobility in factors of production, and this greater mobility in turn implies less natural insulation between national economies.

Richard N. Cooper (ed.), *A Reordered World,* "Interdependence in the Modern World," Potomac Associates, 1973.

1. What will happen to "national sovereignty" as this process of increasing interdependence unfolds?

With an understanding of this concept—economic interdependence—let us now raise two key questions and then develop an economic tool to help us answer these questions. First, what is the nature of this interdependence in the contemporary world? And, second, how has this interdependence evolved historically, especially since 1945?

In order to handle these questions with any degree of sophistication, we need to develop an understanding of what is referred to by economists as the *balance of payments*. It is a tool of economics that will help us to understand international interdependence.

THE BALANCE OF PAYMENTS

All nations must eventually adjust their national economic policies to meet the demands of the international trading and financial system. The mechanism commonly used by a nation for keeping track of these demands is the balance-of-payments accounting system. A balance-of-payments account is a statement of a nation's aggregate international economic transactions over a period of time, usually one year. It helps a government keep track of and to some extent control the flow of goods and services between its country and the rest of the world. In this accounting statement, all international economic and financial transactions must have either a positive or a negative effect on a nation's balance of payments accounts. For example, Fig. 20.1 shows how this occurs in five selected categories.

Positive credits (+)	*Negative debits* (−)
1. Any *receipt* of foreign money	1. Any *payment* to a foreign country
2. Any *earnings* on an investment in a foreign country	2. Any *investment* in a foreign country
3. Any sale of goods or services abroad *(export)*	3. Any purchase of goods and services from abroad *(imports)*
4. Any gift or aid *from* a foreign country	4. Any gift or aid *given* abroad
5. Any *sale* of stocks or bonds abroad	5. Any *purchases* of stocks or bonds from abroad

FIG. 20.1 Balance of credit and debts.

The balance-of-payments accounting statement is divided into *three* major classifications: (1) the current account, (2) the capital account, and (3) the reserve asset account. Let us examine each of these carefully. (We will be discussing these in the context of Tables 20.1 and 20.2 so please refer to them as we discuss each category.)

The *current account* includes the import and export of all goods and services during a year. Exports of goods create a receipt of income, while imports of goods command payments abroad thus resulting in an outflow of income. Payments subtracted from receipts are noted under the balance column of Table 20.1. Besides merchandise trade, the current account records services of various types. For example, military services payments include the hiring of foreign employees at U.S. military bases, construction and maintenance of installations abroad, and military aid.

Military receipts would include, for example, sales of surplus weapons to another country. From 1974 to 1977, the U.S. annually exported over $10 billion worth of military weapons. (These are recorded under trade receipts.) Investment income is the return on investment made abroad in past years. If Pepsico earned $4 million on its investments in the Soviet Union and brought this income back into the U.S., this $4 million is reported in the current account as a receipt. If Saudi Arabian

TABLE 20.1 U.S. Balance of Payments, 1975 (in Billions of Dollars).

Transactions	*Receipts*	*Payments*	*Balance*
Current account	147.6	135.3	12.3
Merchandise trade (goods)	107.2	98.1	9.1
Services	40.2	32.7	7.5
Military	4.0	4.8	−.8
Investment income	17.8	11.8	6.0
Travel and transportation	11.6	13.5	−1.9
Other services	6.8	2.6	4.2
Transfer payments	0.0	4.5	−4.5
Private	0.0	1.0	−1.0
Government (foreign aid)	0.0	3.5	−3.5
Capital account	13.7	30.0	−16.3
Private long-term	11.7	14.5	−2.8
Direct investment	1.9	5.7	−3.8
Portfolio investment	3.4	6.3	−2.9
Bank and other loans (net)	6.4	2.5	3.9
Private short-term	0.0	12.0	−12.0
Government loans (net)	1.8	3.5	−1.7
Errors and omissions	4.6	0.0	4.6
Balance on current and capital accounts	165.9	165.3	0.6
Transactions in U.S. Official reserve assets (gold, SDRs, and convertible currencies)	0.0	0.6	−0.6
Total dollar flows	16.9	16.9	0.0

Source: *Survey of Current Business,* March 1976.

TABLE 20.2 U.S. Balance of Payments (in Billions of Dollars), 1970-1975.

Transactions	1970	1971	1972	1973	1974	1975
Current account	0.5	-2.8	-9.8	0.4	-3.4	12.3
Merchandise trade (goods)	2.1	-2.7	-7.0	1.0	-5.3	9.1
Services	1.5	3.5	0.9	3.2	8.0	7.5
Military	-3.3	-2.9	-3.6	-2.3	-2.2	-0.8
Investment income	6.2	8.0	4.5	5.2	10.1	6.0
Travel and transportation	-2.0	-2.3	-3.1	-2.9	-2.7	-1.9
Other services	0.6	0.7	3.1	3.2	3.8	4.2
Transfer payments	-3.1	-3.6	-3.8	-3.8	-7.2	-4.5
Private	-1.4	-1.6	-1.6	-1.9	-1.7	-1.0
Government (foreign aid)	-1.7	-2.0	-2.2	-1.9	-5.5	-3.5
Capital account	-2.6	-6.1	-7.3	-5.8	-22.7	-16.3
Private long-term	-0.1	-1.5	-4.4	-0.2	-8.5	-2.8
Direct investment	-3.5	-5.1	-3.1	-2.3	-5.2	-3.8
Portfolio investment	1.1	1.3	3.9	3.2	-1.3	-2.9
Bank and other loans (net)	1.0	1.0	-0.7	-0.9	-1.9	+3.9
Private short-term loans	-0.5	-2.3	-1.5	-4.2	-12.9	-12.0
Government loans (net)	-2.0	-2.3	-1.4	-1.4	-1.2	-1.7
Miscellaneous (Errors and omissions, SDR allocations)	0.2	-10.0	-1.0	-2.4	4.7	4.6
Balance on current, capital, and miscellaneous accounts	-3.3	-18.9	-18.1	-7.8	-21.4	0.6
Transactions in U.S. Official reserve assets (gold, SDRs, and convertible currencies) (net)	2.5	2.3	0.0	0.2	-1.4	-0.6
Total dollar flows	-0.8	-16.6	-18.1	-7.6	-22.8	0.0

Note: Figures may not add due to rounding.
Source: *Survey of Current Business,* March 1976.

oil sheiks invest in the U.S., their earnings remitted abroad would be recorded as payments in the current account. Travel and transportation charges are also included in the current account. U.S. dollars spent by Americans traveling abroad are payments in the current account, while money spent by foreign tourists coming to the U.S. from abroad will result in current account receipts. And, finally, there are private and governmental gifts, grants, and aid in the form of transfers between nations. If the U.S. gives foreign aid, this results in a payment in the current account. If we receive a gift from another country, this would be a receipt.

The *capital account* includes all *capital flows* other than investment income, which is included in the current account. Private long-term direct investment by

American multinational corporations is included in the capital account as a payment, while OPEC petrodollars that are invested in the U.S. are counted as receipts. Portfolio investment includes the purchase and sale, by U.S. residents, of all stocks and bonds issued by foreigners. These transactions are recorded as payments. On the other hand, Saudi Arabian direct or portfolio investment in this country represents receipts for the U.S.

---

2. If investment by Saudi Arabia in the U.S. results in a "receipt" or positive effect on our balance of payments in the capital account, does this mean that it is necessarily good for the U.S. to have this investment? Why or why not?

3. What would be an example of a government loan payment? a government loan receipt?

The *errors and omissions account* is not what it first appears to be—something someone forgot about. It is primarily short-term capital movements, which are speculative in nature. Note that in 1971 (see Table 20.2), a year of international economic crisis, there was a massive shift of some $10 billion out of the U.S. As a currency is perceived to be "weak," holders of that currency will sell it for other "stronger" currencies. In 1971, many multinational corporations found themselves with excess cash holdings. Dollar holdings were extremely risky so the MNCs spread their excess dollar holdings into Eurodollar and other currency markets. This caused a flow of dollars out of the U.S.

When we take the sum of these items—the current account, the capital account, and errors and omissions—we have the balance on current and capital accounts. This is simply a net sum of all of the international transactions by U.S. citizens, corporations, and the government during a specific year. The balance of payments always "balances" because whatever surplus (net inflow) or deficit (net outflow) these transactions generate, it is offset by the use of *official reserve assets*—gold, special drawing rights (SDRs), and convertible currencies.

For example, if there is a deficit in the balance on current and capital accounts, foreigners will either hold dollars abroad (represented in the item Total dollar flows) or they will return them to the U.S. through their central banks in which case there would be an outflow of gold, or other currencies held by the U.S. or special drawing rights (SDRs), to compensate the holders of dollars. As shown in Table 20.2, most of our balance-of-payments deficits have been settled by outflows of dollars. This is reflective of the fact that the dollar is widely used and accepted as a means of payment around the world.

Further Notes on the Balance of Payments

When reporters, economists, and politicians speak of balance-of-payments "deficits" (outflows of dollars) and "surpluses" (inflows of dollars), they are referring only to the transactions in the current and capital accounts—and not in the balancing cash, gold, or bond accounts. Often, this is referred to as the *basic balance* and includes the balance on the current account added to the long-term capital movements. This basic balance will normally show a payments deficit (payments >receipts) or surplus (receipts >payments).

If one looks only at the merchandise balance in the current account, which is called the *balance of trade*, one finds that historically for the U.S. this "balance" has been a surplus. In other words, exports were greater than imports for every year from 1893 until 1971.

The prices of oil and other raw materials have increased the value of our imports in the last several years, but note in Table 20.2 the current account surpluses in 1973 and 1975. This was due to the worldwide shortage of wheat and other grains and the resultant price increases. Our sales of grains offset the higher prices of oil imports. Our grain exports rose from $3.5 billion in 1972 to $8.5 billion in 1973 and $10.3 billion in 1974, while imports of petroleum rose during those years from $4.3 billion to $7.6 billion to $24.2 billion, respectively.

The recent deficits that have been reported have come from the basic balance. Here we find that annually, capital account payments are greater than receipts. If the capital account deficit is greater than the current account surplus, then a deficit is recorded in the basic balance. (Or, if there's a deficit in *both*, then there will be a deficit in the basic balance.)

One of the problems that a nation encounters in trade, just as in life, is that one must pay for the goods and services received. In your own case, you can either use cash or an IOU. In the international sphere there are several alternatives. Payments are accepted in cash (dollars), gold, or SDRs (more on Special Drawing Right later). If your country's exports exceed its imports, it will have attained a balance-of-payments surplus. The reward for this is increased employment and income at home. The penalty is higher prices. Why is this? As we export more and more of our goods and services, income (Y), and hence GNP, increases. As income increases, consumption increases. (Remember your basic macro model?) As consumption increases, more dollars are competing for fewer domestic goods and prices will tend to rise.

A payments *deficit* (where imports are greater than exports) earns your nation's economic and political leaders severe criticism. Contrary to popular opinion, great bolts of lightning will not be fired down from above, but deficits do have their disadvantages. Strains are placed on a nation's gold supply and on its currency with respect to the other currencies. If these strains become too severe, the country's currency will depreciate (be worth less) with respect to other stronger currencies. This means that imported goods will cost more, but that exports will become more attractive to foreign nations.

It might be worthwhile to note that as of May 1976 the U.S. government announced that it will no longer publish any measures of the "overall" United States balance of payments because they are "no longer meaningful." It was also recommended that "the words 'surplus' and 'deficit' be avoided insofar as possible. These words are frequently taken to mean that the developments are 'good' or 'bad,' respectively. Since that interpretation is often incorrect, the terms may be widely misunderstood and used in lieu of analysis."

---

4. Why, do you think, did this announcement come in May 1976?

One final comment should be made on the balance-of-payments statement. It should not be thought that since a particular item is "big," a deficit would be done away with if we removed or reduced that item. For example, opponents of foreign aid have argued that this expenditure was the reason for deficits in the basic trade balance for so many years. This is not true. Over 80 percent of foreign aid is "tied," that is, it must be spent on goods produced in the U.S. So if we cut foreign aid by $1 billion, our exports would be reduced by $800 million! The gain would be very small indeed. Many of the items in the balance of payments are related to other items in this way.

It is, however, legitimate to note that since a particular item is in surplus, the country has the freedom to run up a deficit in some other item without creating pressure against its currency. This sort of situation can be created in either of two ways: (1) there may be items that in the working out of "basic economic forces" generate a surplus, or (2) other countries in the world economy may "allow" deficits to exist without exerting pressure for policy measures that would reduce them. An example of the former is the flow of investment income into the U.S. The net income on U.S. investments abroad allows the U.S. to, among other things, increase its ownership of factories and mines in other countries and finance military expenditures abroad.

The following article from *Dollars & Sense,* a monthly bulletin of economic affairs, summarizes much of this discussion of the balance of payments mechanism in its analysis of the recent decline in the value of the dollar.

THE DECLINE OF THE DOLLAR

At the beginning of March, the U.S. dollar fell in value to the point where it could buy less than two German marks. While the dollar received considerable publicity as it crossed the two mark line, the event itself was no particular surprise.

In terms of the currencies of most other advanced capitalist nations, the value of the dollar has been falling steadily since early 1977. And this recent deterioration of its international exchange value is only the latest phase in the dollar's long-run drop which has been going on throughout the 1970s.

The decline of the dollar reflects some serious problems in the U.S. economy. But it also reflects the general turmoil of international capitalism in the 1970s, marked by the failure of the leading capitalist nations to establish policies assuring a stable expansion of trade and investment activities worldwide.

Reprinted with permission from *Dollars & Sense* (April 1978), a Socialist Monthly Bulletin of Economic Affairs, 324 Somerville Ave., Somerville, MA 02143.

The 1950s and 1960s were an era of rapid growth for the economies of the U.S., Western Europe, and Japan; international trade grew along with each country's domestic production and spending. Since the international economic pie, so to speak, was getting bigger, the competition over the size of the slices was not so intense. The biggest slice still went to the U.S. by virtue of the economic and political muscle with which it emerged from World War II.

In the 1970s, however, the economies of all the advanced capitalist nations have begun to sputter, and the pie has stopped growing so fast. The competition for slices has grown fiercer. At the same time, several countries—particularly West Germany and Japan—have challenged the leading role of the U.S.

The changing values of these countries' currencies (dollars, marks, yen, etc.) represent adjustments to their changing positions of power. As Germany has grown stronger with respect to the U.S., the mark has come to be worth more dollars. But in the short run, when the value of the dollar drops, the U.S. gains some advantages in its attempts to increase its share of the pie. This occurs in the competition over trade, which will be discussed below.

WHY CURRENCIES CHANGE VALUE

The value (or price) of a nation's currency rises or falls according to supply and demand like that of any other good. Four main factors determine currency supply and demand.

One is trade: if a German company wants to buy some steel in the U.S., it needs to acquire some dollars; if an American company wants German steel, it needs to acquire some marks. A second factor is what is known as "real productive investment"; if a U.S. company wants to build a steel plant in Germany, it needs marks to pay for machinery, construction, and workers. Two other factors are investment in foreign stocks and bonds, and decisions by companies, banks, and money speculators to switch their liquid cash from a currency that seems to be dropping in value to one that seems to be rising.

The marketplace where currencies are bought and sold is the foreign exchange departments of banks. If a country's products are not in demand and it does not appear to be a profitable place to invest, many corporations and other holders of that country's currency will want to get rid of it and get a more useful currency instead. Thus banks may end up with a large supply of (for instance) dollars, with few customers coming in seeking them.

At this point, major banks may decide they won't take any more dollars unless they can get them more cheaply. For instance, German banks would pay out fewer marks per dollar. The value of the dollar falls.

The most significant factor in the dollar's decline in the 1970s has been trade. The U.S. has spent more dollars buying goods to import from many other countries than the businesses, people, and institutions of those countries have acquired in order to buy goods for export from the U.S.

In 1977, the U.S. trade deficit (imports minus exports) was $31.4 billion, and in January and February of this year the deficit continued to run at roughly the same rate. This is by far the largest trade deficit in U.S. history. In fact, in this century up to 1971, the U.S. continually ran a trade surplus (exports greater than imports). Since then, only 1975 has shown a large trade surplus, and in 1976 the deficit rose to $9.3 billion. Then came 1977.

THE DOLLAR'S VALUE IN MARKS

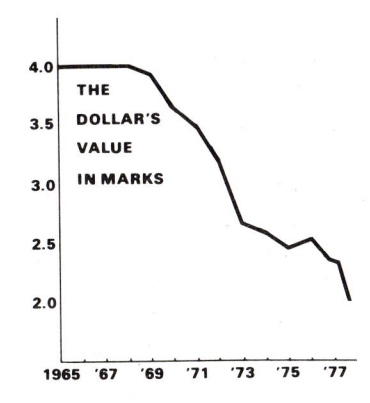

Note: The decline with respect to the yen has been similar though not quite so steady or severe. Annual figures through 1976, quarterly in 1977 and 1978.

Sources: *International Financial Statistics* 5/76, 3/78; *Wall Street Journal* 2/1/78, 3/1/78, 3/23/78.

In and of itself, a trade deficit may be an indication that the U.S. economy has been growing more rapidly than the economies of our major trading partners. Because we are growing rapidly, our demand for our imports is strong. Because they are growing slowly, their demand for our exports is weak.

STRENGTH OR WEAKNESS?

If this were true, the trade deficit would indicate strength not weakness. But then it is unlikely that the decline in the value of the dollar would be so great. For if the trade deficit were a sign of strength, the dollar outflow which it creates would be offset by dollars flowing into this country for investment in securities (stocks and bonds) and productive assets. One component of the demand and supply for dollars would more or less offset another component, and there would be no precipitous decline of the dollar. In early 1977, this appears to have been the case.

But the value of the dollar has declined sharply in recent months, and this is largely due to the fact that foreign and U.S. banks and corporations have been choosing to buy their securities in other countries and to hold their money in the form of other currencies. For example, in the first half of 1977, the increase of private foreign-held securities and bank deposits in the U.S. exceeded the increase of private U.S.-held securities and bank deposits abroad by $2.9 billion; but in the second half of the year, the balance shifted in the other direction, to a $6.6 billion net outflow.

Also, throughout the 1970s central banks, analogous to the Federal Reserve here, of many nations have been shifting their countries' reserves out of dollars and into other currencies. Data on these movements are not public, but according to one very conservative estimate central bank reserves in German marks rose from $700 million worth in 1970 to $7.7 billion in 1976. This process has probably speeded up in recent months.

Data for real productive investment do not show any change for the first three-quarters of 1977 compared to the previous year. Companies don't buy and sell factories as readily as currency and bonds, so this type of investment is not so subject to short-run variation. If the huge 1977 trade deficit were really an indication that the U.S. economy is headed for prosperity, foreign real investment would be on the rise. But, it appears that by cutting back their holdings of U.S. assets, foreigners are reading signs of weakness in the U.S. economy.

U.S. BUSINESS AND THE DOWN DOLLAR

While the devaluation of the dollar reflects weakness in the U.S. economy, it does hold out some possibilities of substantial gains by U.S. business. Most important, the competitive position of U.S. business is strengthened in the world economy.

For example, in order for a U.S. company to get $100 for an export sold in Germany, it need charge only 200 marks. A year ago, it would have been necessary to charge 236 marks. Or today, for a Japanese auto firm to obtain one million yen, it must sell a car in the U.S. for $4300. A year ago it could have obtained one million yen by selling the car for only $3600.

For those industries—particularly steel and electronics—which have been suffering by their inability to compete with imports (let alone compete on export markets), the lower value of the dollar may provide a new lease on life. For U.S. export industries—from farm products to high technology equipment—the cheaper dollar should provide a strong stimulus to demand.

The fact that U.S. business can derive these benefits from a devalued dollar reflects the changes in the international economic situation which have taken place since the boom years of the 1950s and 1960s. In those years, U.S. business sought its profits in the rapidly growing economies in Europe more through investment than through trade. A high value for the dollar was then an advantage because it made the acquisition of foreign assets cheap.

Now, however, the advantages of investment (relative to trade) in Europe have declined. Slower growth means lower returns. Also labor costs in Europe are no longer low, and some governments are not quite so friendly to U.S. companies.

These advantages of a declining dollar apply only to the exchange rates with other advanced capitalist countries, the main competitors of the U.S. in international trade. They do not apply to the poor countries where investment, and often sales back to the U.S. market, are a major source of U.S. business profits. But with respect to the currencies of most of these countries—Brazil, Taiwan, Hong Kong, Mexico, and South Korea, for example—the dollar has remained stable.

THE POLICY LINE ON THE DOLLAR'S DECLINE

The West German and other governments, recognizing the trade advantages for the U.S. from a declining dollar, have urged Washington to borrow foreign currencies, buy dollars with them, and thus keep the demand for the dollar—and the value—from falling so far. But the U.S. has used very few of the maneuvers open to it to protect the dollar. At times during the past year, Treasury Secretary Blumenthal has explicitly favored a lower value for the dollar.

The government must respond to other pressures besides international economic ones, and the do-nothing policy on the dollar is related to domestic political issues and difficulties. The declining dollar, by making U.S. exports cheaper, is expected to offset the inflation in the U.S. economy, which makes them more expensive. If the Administration wanted to protect the dollar, it would need to take harsher steps against inflation, such as cutting spending, raising taxes, or otherwise passing still more of the burden onto workers and consumers, and possibly triggering a new recession as well.

Similarly, the declining dollar's effect on exports removes some of the pressure for an energy program to slow the rise in oil imports. (Oil makes up roughly

30% of U.S. imports, and is the major contributor to the negative trade balance.) Or, to look at it another way, if business did not see benefits resulting from the lowering of the dollar's value, it would have been likely to unify and push the government harder on an anti-oil-import program to slow the outflow of dollars.

A DIFFICULT GAME

On the other hand, the drop in the dollar, the continued inflation, and the delay on oil policy all contribute to the weakness which international investors see in the U.S. The policy has other dangers as well.

The lower value of the dollar means higher prices for imported goods here. It will also raise the prices of goods produced here with foreign materials. And in cases where foreign competition has kept domestic producers' prices down, these will rise also; if the price of a Datsun rises $500, GM is likely to hike the price of a Nova as well.

Also, when foreign companies have trouble selling their now-more-expensive goods here, the effect will be felt in their home economies. That in turn will affect the market for U.S. exports. The consequence could be a general worldwide recession.

The U.S. would like foreign governments to respond by stimulating their own economies through government spending. But instead, they may take actions to protect their industries by restricting imports, further damaging world trade.

U.S. government and business interests are not oblivious to these dangers. But the situation of U.S. business in the world economy and the economic weaknesses at home force them to live with the risks.

---

5. Given the data in this article, what do you expect will happen in the near future to the current account balance for the U.S. vis-à-vis Western Europe? How about its capital account balance with the poor countries?

6. Do you think the value of the dollar will decline or rise in the near future? That is, will our large deficits continue or not? Why?

With the distinction in mind between trade and capital flows among nations, let us now turn back to the concept of international economic interdependence. We will briefly examine the nature of international trade and the process of the internationalization of production to illustrate contemporary interdependence.

TRADE AND THE INTERNATIONALIZATION OF PRODUCTION: ELEMENTS OF ECONOMIC INTERDEPENDENCE

Trade and Interdependence

One of the major ways to examine economic interdependence is by looking at the nature of international trade. By examining relevant trade data and identifying the major trade trends since 1950, we can begin to appreciate the nature of contemporary interdependence.

The following observations and generalizations can be made from these data:

1. Most nations from 1950 to 1970 did not export significantly increasing shares of their respective GNPs. This result challenges the notion that nations tend to increase exports as a percentage of their GNPs as they develop.

2. The developing nations are experiencing a secular decline in export trade as a percentage of their GNPs.

3. The developing nations are not participating in the long-run growth of world trade. The major gains have been registered by the nations of industrial Europe.

4. The U.S. share of total world trade is declining and that trade is still a relatively minor part (approximately 7.2 percent of our GNP).

While these observations do not present a clear indication of the relationship of international trade to national economic health, the one conclusion that we would like to emphasize is that to the extent *trade* is a determinant of international *interdependence*, it is not always due to the *magnitude* of trade between nations, but more often the specialization and composition of trade among nations. This phenomenon has high lighted economic interdependence over the past few decades.

Internationalization of Production and Interdependence

A second major way to examine economic interdependence is to look at the "internationalization of production." This dimension of interdependence can be analyzed by examining the capital flows among nations (rather than the flows of trade). Some of these capital movements have taken the form of foreign investment and have included the process of the internationalization of capital and labor. This process is more readily understood by tracing the history of the operations of multinational corporations. It is these institutions more than any other that have created a new international division of labor on a global scale.

The multinational corporation (MNC) is a feature of this century, having matured in the post-World War II period. A typical U.S. multinational's history might read in the following manner: the corporation begins its initial production for the U.S. market only; next it creates a factory abroad because of inexpensive labor and the accessability of raw materials; and, finally, the new foreign subsidiary's production is distributed in the local economy while some is exported back to the U.S. When a U.S. firm either builds a production facility or takes over an existing facility in another nation, direct investment occurs.

The modern expansion of the operations of MNCs had led to an internationalization of production on a global scale. People in many countries are now dependent on decisions made in boardrooms of corporations in New York, Stuttgart, or Tokyo for their jobs and the products they consume. Individual MNCs based in the U.S. are increasingly dependent on other countries for their labor, resources, and markets to a far greater extent than that suggested by the U.S. export/GNP ratio. As this one major institution internationalizes, so must other institutions—social, economic, political, and cultural. Coincidentally, the call for free trade, tax and legal harmonization, and closer intergovernmental cooperation increases in intensity.

MNC-related capital movements gradually transfer the control of the accumulation and allocation of capital from institutions that are essentially national in character to multinational corporations and banks that are global in their orientation. Each national economy is being more thoroughly integrated into the world market for capital and is therefore increasingly affected in a very direct way by events which take place in other national economies. Hence there is increasing interdependence along with multinationalization. However, people are reluctant to grant so much freedom of operation to one private-sector institution. Calls for protection by nation-states and other political agencies and plans for controlling MNCs abound, from state or provincial governments to the United Nations. People are reluctant to accept the MNCs vision of one, homogenized world of consumers all with similar tastes and life-styles—Coca-Colanization, as it is called. This concern, in fact, is part of the desire of some countries to create a "New International Economic Order."

The next two chapters treat the historical evolution of international trading and financial relations, as well as the major body of theory economists use to examine this interdependence. This chapter should also be kept very much in mind when we examine the problems confronting the developing nations of the Third World and their demand for a "New International Economic Order."

KEY CONCEPTS

economic interdependence
balance of payments
current account
capital account

basic balance
balance of trade
foreign investment
internationalization of production

REVIEW QUESTIONS

1. How has increasing international interdependence since 1945 affected the nature of the relationship between industrial nations and the Third World?

2. If you were the Minister for the Economy in a developing nation, how would you respond to the advice of a development economist from the U.S. that your country's best strategy for economic growth was to "fit itself" into the liberal world economic order?

3. What are the linkages among nations that have been most important in increasing interdependence in the world economy today?

4. When we say that the world economy is characterized by interdependence, does this mean that all nations are equally dependent on other nations, or are some nations more dominant and others more dependent? Why is that so?

SUGGESTED READINGS

David E. Apter and Louis Wolf Goodman, 1976. *The Multinational Corporation and Social Change*, Praeger. An excellent series of essays exploring every facet of MNC behavior. Especially recommended is Chapter 8 "The Multinational Corporation and Development: A Contradiction?" by Harry Magdoff.

Richard J. Barnet and Ronald E. Muller, 1974. *Global Reach*, Simon and Schuster. One of the most authoritative studies on multinational corporations. Part I gives an overview of the historical development of the MNC. Part II treats the impact of the MNC on the Third World. Part III analyzes the impact of the MNC on the U.S. and concludes with some thoughts about how to reform the MNC.

Jagdish N. Bhagwati (ed.), 1972. *Economics and World Order: From the 1970's to the 1990's*, Macmillan. A collection of essays dealing with global interdependence. We recommend the Introduction and Chapter 2, "Global Perspectives." Also, we strongly urge you to look at Chapter 4, "The Multinational Corporation and the Law of Uneven Development."

John Deverell and the Latin American Working Group, 1975. *Falconbridge—Portrait of a Canadian Mining Multinational*, Lorimer. An excellent biography of a MNC.

Anthony Sampson, 1974. *The Sovereign State of ITT*, Fawcett. Another "biography" of a prominent MNC and its effects on economic interdependence.

INTERNATIONAL TRADE AND PROTECTIONISM

CHAPTER 21

INTRODUCTION

International trade is one of the most intensely discussed areas of economics. At times, political parties have justified their existence and relevance on their position for or against free trade. This logic has been one of the most fascinating debates in economics for the past two centuries. It is the question of comparative advantage: how nations have actively pursued specialization in a few lines of production for export, thus imposing on themselves a dependency or absolute reliance on others for products that may be crucial to their style and standard of living. Of course, this has not been done frivolously or out of allegiance to some obscure political philosophy. The theoretical payoff from specialization and exchange among nations is that world output will be maximized and that this maximum output is possible through free unhindered trade. The benefits of free trade were not, however, immediately apparent to people; and once free trade was adopted by England in the latter half of the 19th century, a countermovement toward protection soon developed.

This chapter examines trade theory and presents some of the more convincing arguments for protection. It concludes with a look at the current confrontation between free traders and protectionists.

THE MODERN THEORY OF INTERNATIONAL TRADE

1. **How will you be matched with the work you will do for your working life? What will be your "specialty"?**

The very same question is confronted for the world economy as a whole. How does an individual nation "fit into" the world economy? Why does one nation specialize in production of ground nuts; a second, textiles; a third, aircraft; and a fourth, banking and insurance services? Adam Smith was the first economist to deal with this question meaningfully, and in 1817 David Ricardo refined Smith's ideas. It is this general approach that we still use today. The basic concepts are *absolute* and *comparative advantage*, and the model of trade follows. (Incidentally, this is also a good example of the way in which an economist approaches an issue and reasons it out through an economic model and the development of economic theory.)

Who Trades What? And Why?

Let us begin by making some assumptions that will greatly facilitate matters and that will allow us to deal only with the essentials. In our hypothetical world we have two nations, producing two goods. There is competition everywhere, no transportation costs, and labor cannot move between the two nations. The costs of production in the two nations are assumed to be as follows:

Cost of production in work hours of one unit of

	Wheat	Cloth
U.K.	10	20
France	15	45

The first thing we note is that the U.K. can produce both goods with less cost than can France. So we then say that the U.K. has an *absolute advantage* in producing both wheat and cloth and that France has an absolute disadvantage in each. This does not mean however that the U.K. produces and exports both goods and that France produces and/or exports neither, as any import/export trader will be quick to tell you. The important thing here is to note that *within* the U.K., since one unit of wheat is produced with just one-half the work hours of cloth, one unit of cloth will exchange for two units of wheat. While in France, again because of the relative costs of production, one unit of cloth can be exchanged for three units of wheat.

This gives us the following internal rates of exchange of cloth for wheat:

U.K.	1 cloth = 2 wheat
France	1 cloth = 3 wheat

or

U.K.	½ cloth = 1 wheat
France	⅓ cloth = 1 wheat

Our astute trader would look at this and reason: "If I could buy one unit of wheat in Paris, ship it to London, and exchange it there for cloth, I could get one-half of a unit of cloth; if I exchanged it in France, I would get only one-third of a unit of cloth. My gain from this trade is one-sixth of a unit of cloth. On the other hand, taking one unit of cloth from Paris to London and exchanging it for wheat would bring me only two units of wheat; whereas I could have gotten three units of wheat at home in France. I lose one unit of wheat in the process."

The trader would quickly conclude that France has a *comparative advantage* in the production and export of wheat, even though France has an *absolute* disadvantage in both goods. By similar reasoning, we can conclude that the U.K. has a comparative advantage in cloth only.

---

2. What is the gain from exporting cloth from England to France?

Remember that the important point here is the comparison of the internal rates of exchange between the two commodities in each of the two countries.

The assumptions on which this theory is based are extremely "unreal" given today's world. However, since David Ricardo's time economists have shown that this comparative advantage model is also valid for a world of many nations producing many different goods. Other economists have demonstrated that dropping the assumption of perfect competition and zero transport costs only reduces the gain from specialization and trade but does not invalidate the theory in any way. The only assumption crucial to our results is that of relative labor immobility. If workers migrated freely from country to country, we would have exchanges of labor rather than exchanges of goods.

Total World Output

The next step is to see what happens to total output of wheat and cloth. We can use the concept, developed in microeconomics, of the production possibilities curve here. We don't know the sizes of their labor forces so we can't calculate total output precisely, but it would be consistent with our hypothetical costs and rates of exchange to assume the following:

Total country production

	Wheat		*Cloth*
U.K.	2000	or	1000
France	2400	or	800

If each country has no international trade and uses half of its resources to produce each good to meet its own domestic demands, total world output will be:

Total world output
(without trade)

	Wheat	*Cloth*
U.K.	1000	500
France	1200	400
Total	2200	900

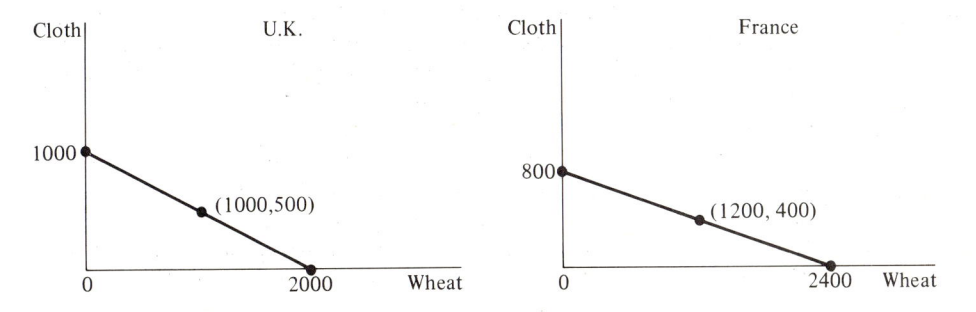

FIG. 21.1 Production possibilities without trade.

But if France specializes in wheat production and the U.K. specializes in cloth, and if each exchanges some of that good for its needs of the other commodity, then world output becomes:

Total world output
(with specialization and trade)

	Wheat	Cloth
U.K.		1000
France	2400	
Total	2400	1000

France produces wheat and uses some for domestic consumption and exports the rest. The U.K. produces cloth and uses some for domestic consumption and exports the rest. After trading, we might get a result like the following:

	Wheat	Cloth
U.K.	1200	500
France	1200	500
Total	2400	1000

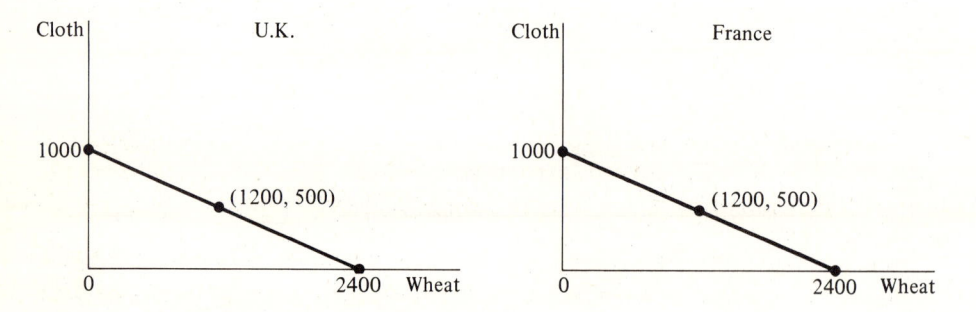

FIG. 21.2 Production possibilities with trade.

3. Who has gained what through specialization and trade?

Thus if each nation specializes in the product in which it has a comparative advantage, world output of both commodities is increased—in this case by 100 units of cloth and 200 units of wheat. If there is a reasonable distribution of this gain from specialization and trade, both countries are better off than they would be in the absence of trade. This is the essence, then, of the argument for free trade.

We now turn to a consideration of free trade theory and then we will examine the case for restricted trade—or protectionism.

CLASSICAL LIBERALISM AND FREE TRADE

The philosophy of *classical liberalism* was the first to advocate international as well as domestic free trade. The classical liberal belief in self-regulating markets was projected to the international level where, again, *laissez-faire* prevailed. The development of this argument, it should be remembered, took place in the context of increasing international economic activity accompanying the emergence of capitalism in Western Europe. Free traders compiled an impressive list of benefits that should accrue to society as a whole if their policy were to be adopted. In general, proponents of free trade argued and *still* argue: (1) that world output will be increased through a more "rational" and "efficient" use of the world's resources and (2) that the increase in production be equitably shared among all who participate in free trade.

RESTRICTIONS TO FREE TRADE—PROTECTIONISM

Free trade exists if there are no barriers to the export and import of goods and services. Though most economists have argued hard and long for some 200 years for free trade, nations have nonetheless felt impelled for just as many years to erect barriers to inhibit free international exchange. There are many types of trade restrictions that a nation might utilize, but the most common have been tariffs and quotas. *Tariffs* are simply *taxes* on the goods imported or exported, while *quotas* are limits on the *quantities* of goods imported or exported.

There are many reasons for establishing tariff and quota barriers between nations. Most often they are designed to protect some interest in the home country. In general, tariffs are successful in their objective—they protect a special interest at the expense of the whole population. In other words, a few people are helped a lot while all citizens are hurt a little as a result of paying higher prices for the goods and services on which tariff duties are imposed.

Special interest groups often appeal to Congress for a protective tariff. The textile industry has asked and received protection from cheaper foreign textile products. These tariffs increase the price of all textiles in the U.S. The U.S. consumers are, in effect, subsidizing an inefficient industry—one in which we do not possess a comparative advantage.

During the Depression, the Smoot-Hawley tariff was levied to keep money in the country and to keep wages and employment levels as high as possible. Would the economy be led to high levels of income and employment and would money remain in the country with the extremely high Smoot-Hawley tariff? Let's see how economists use the Smoot-Hawley era to express their frustration toward protective tariffs. In 1971 several thousand economists signed a petition against the Burke-Hartke Trade Bill. This was an attempt to move the country toward a policy of increased protection for domestic producers. In arguing their case the economists referred to the Smoot-Hawley Tariff of the 1930s.

Forty years ago, in the midst of a growing economic crisis at home and abroad, Congress enacted and the President signed the highest tariff in the nation's history. This curbed the ability of foreign nations to sell to us and hence their ability to buy from us. Our higher tariffs induced other democracies to *retaliate* with higher tariffs against our goods, notably farm products and machinery. Our exports shrivelled, intensifying our unemployment and deepening the Depression. The dollar weakened. The fabric of international cooperation further unraveled. Economic depression spread. Democracy floundered in many parts of the world. These were the seeds of World War II.

The same scenario, they argued, would unfold today if the nation reversed the post-World War II trend of tariff reduction that had by the 1960s alleviated the trade hardships created by the Smoot-Hawley tariff.

But included in the protectionist's argument is another reason for tariff levies—retaliation. Tariffs have been increased many times in response to tariff increases by trading partners. The Smoot-Hawley tariff, for example, set off a worldwide round of tariff increases. This "do unto others as they have done unto you" philosophy has also been used many times simply for the sake of self-esteem. As a result, consumers in both nations pay the higher price. And, at worst, such retaliation can compound recession into worldwide depression.

At times there are proposals that Congress should levy tariffs for the purpose of raising revenue since the proceeds from the tax are collected by the government. This is well and good, but there are many ways of raising revenue that are more effective. Besides, if the tariff prices the imported goods above that of the domestic product, no revenue will be collected since the consumer will be priced out of the import market and will purchase only the domestic product.

Another protectionist argument centers on the need to reduce the competition of cheap foreign labor. In the 1950s, a Houston oil and cotton magnate responded to the free trade argument by stating that:

The only thing that made our country great is the protective tariff to protect us from the cheap labor abroad. Those people haven't developed in two thousand years. They've been letting the flies eat their children's eyes out all that time. If they take our tariff off, it's just a matter of time before the American people will be living like them.

---

4. How do you think the "cheap labor abroad" would respond to this argument? Do you think they might be concerned by the technology exports of the U.S.? Would they, too, argue for protection?

Other arguments on trade policy have run from the rather dry and abstract to the invective. The "national defense" argument falls into both categories. The merchant marine and oil industry have argued for protection since they are essential in times of national emergency. The cotton industry also requested a tariff for these reasons, presumably on the basis that no decent nation could run the risk of having an army forced to fight in the nude for want of good cotton clothing.

5. The oil industry was protected for "defense" reasons by import quotas during the period from 1954 to 1973. How did these protective quotas, designed to encourage U.S. oil production, work during the oil embargo of 1973?

NEOMERCANTILISM

What we are witnessing today is the fundamental clash of national policies which are primarily oriented towards solving domestic political and social problems. . . . Multilateral discussions are at a standstill. There has been a rise in mercantilist sentiment in most of the world. . . .

This neomercantilism is a profoundly disruptive force in international relations. It takes many forms. . . . In the case of the Common Agricultural Policy [of the EEC] for example, the Europeans have taxed imports, thus reducing import sales while gaining revenues. The revenues are used to push domestic surpluses onto world markets, further taxing the exports of competitors by depressing their potential profits elsewhere. All exporters thus end up paying part of the cost of Europe's social program for its rural population. The American textile restriction program has a similar effect. It penalizes Asian exporters and American consumers in order to provide special benefits to Southern mills in areas of low wages and high availability of black labor. Neomercantilism, sector by sector, whether aimed at industry relief or rural poverty, must inevitably repress the interests of other countries, in particular sectors, in particular regions.

Harold B. Malmgren, "Coming Trade Wars?" *Foreign Policy* (Winter): 1970–1971, 115–143.

6. If a nation does encourage free trade, what happens to the "Southern mills," "low wages," and "black labor"?

In the post-World War II period, there has been a marked movement away from the excessive protection of the Depression years. This has been accomplished primarily through international negotiations in organizations such as the General Agreement on Tariffs and Trade (GATT).

There have been, of course, disagreements between nations on goods that should be exempt from tariff reductions and on tariff levels that should be aimed for; and, though the enthusiasm of reductions of the 1960s has given way to protectionist sentiments of the 1970s, noteworthy accomplishments have been made.

The protectionist tendencies were particularly prevalent during 1975 as the impact of a severe recession was felt throughout the world and as countries competed for a shrinking export market. The U.S. steel industry lobbied for protection from imports. So did the automobile industry, tobacco growers, and clothing manufacturers. Other nations also received complaints from their industries along with requests for greater tariff protection. The cry that has been raised is "Let's stop exporting jobs and stop importing products that compete with our industries."

U.S. industries accused nations within the European Common Market of subsidizing steel and other industries by returning the value added tax (a national sales tax) on these items to the producers.

Japanese steel producers were accused of dumping steel in the United States in 1977. "Dumping" occurs when the exporting nation sells the product at a lower price in the importing country than it does in the home or producing country—thus undermining the importing nation's domestic market.

All nations realize that trade wars and retaliation are often the ultimate consequence of increased protectionism, yet when tariffs or quotas are renewed it is always with the hope that there will be no retaliation or destructive trade wars.

Retaliation and trade wars were averted during the 1973–1975 recession when worldwide unemployment rose to the highest levels since the 1930s. Though, as we have just mentioned, unions and industrialists alike argued for tariffs to protect jobs, the Ford administration focused on inflation as the number one enemy. They realized that new tariffs would mean higher prices as well as increased job opportunities, and so worked for the *reduction* of import controls to help fight inflation.

In 1976, however, new import restrictions were initiated by the European Economic Community on "sensitive industries" and the U.S. appeared to be heading toward restraints. In 1977, the Carter administration developed a "trigger" price mechanism to limit steel imports to the U.S. Import controls as well as export subsidies are being used by several of the LDCs to improve their trade position. This trend seemed to be caused by the weakening of inflationary activity and the persistence of high unemployment levels.

In the two articles that follow, we have expressions of protectionist sentiment from opposite sides of the bargaining table. George Meany, President of the AFL-CIO, expresses the fears of organized labor. His reservations are couched in the context of the long-run position of the entire U.S. economy. Meany's article is followed by a *Wall Street Journal* piece that analyzes the prospects for the global trade environment beyond the late 1970s.

A MODERN TRADE POLICY FOR THE SEVENTIES

GEORGE MEANY—PRESIDENT, AFL-CIO

The problem of the rapid deterioration of our country's position in the world economy is a problem of mutual concern to business management and organized labor. It is a problem that affects workers directly and immediately, because it involves the loss of jobs and incomes. I believe it is a problem that also affects American business—in the long run, if not in the short run—because a continuing erosion of industrial payrolls will weaken the consumer markets that are the basis for business prosperity.

In fact, this problem involves all of us, as Americans, because the decline of the U.S. position in international economic relationships is narrowing our country's industrial base and bringing economic troubles to communities in all parts of our nation.

At stake are the American standard of living and America's prospects for remaining an industrial nation with a wide range of industries, products and employment.

The world economy has changed drastically in the past 20 years, and America's position in world trade has been deteriorating rapidly since the early 1960s.

It was reasonable to expect some decline in America's economic position in the world after World War II. That was a time when the war-torn economies of the other industrial countries were reviving with the help of American economic aid. But this decline did not halt at the end of the 1950s, when those industrial nations were back on their feet. Instead America's share in the world's exports of manufactured goods continued to move down rapidly.

In the past dozen years imports have shot up sharply. The rise of exports has lagged. Within a period of only a few years, the U.S. has become a net importer of an increasingly wide variety of products. These include goods for which America was world-famous only five or ten years earlier, such as autos, typewriters, steel, and electrical consumer goods. Even in products of which the U.S. has thus far remained a net exporter, such as machinery for construction and mining, the American share of world exports moved down in the 1960's. . . .

Many imports, of course, do not compete with American products at all. Some imports are obviously necessary.

However, the sharp rise of imports in recent years has been in goods that are directly comparable to U.S.-made products. According to trade experts, such imports accounted for 30 percent to 40 percent of all imports in the 1950s. By 1966, according to a report by George Shultz when he was Secretary of Labor, about 74 percent of the much greater volume of imports were in that category, while the remainder were not produced here or were in short supply. . . .

The problem is concentrated in manufactured products and components. Back in 1960, American exports of manufactured goods were close to twice as great as manufactured imports. By 1972 imports of manufactured goods are running some $3 billion greater than manufactured exports. I think it is a fair guess that about three-quarters of imports today are competing with American-produced goods.

In this process of rapid and drastic change, large parts of entire industries are being wiped out. It is not one industry or two industries, and it is not merely the older industries. Some people talk as if this problem is a textile problem alone, or a garment problem or a glass problem. That is not true at all.

As president of the AFL–CIO, I get reports on conditions in all kinds of industries. I can assure you that the problem is pretty much across the board—in new and sophisticated products, as well as in older industries.

In addition, there is a ripple effect—or a compounding effect—from one industry to another. When the shipbuilding industry was hit, steel production was affected. When the shoe industry was hit, the shoe machinery industry was also hit. The displacement of American auto production has an impact on tires, glass and steel, and on replacement tires and parts. If the American aircraft industry goes down, the aluminum industry cannot escape the effects. It is like a fast-creeping disease.

According to *Fortune*, imports now account for about half of the sales in the U.S. of black and white television sets, 96 percent of portable tape recorders, 100 percent of 35mm still cameras and 80 percent of electronic microscopes.

Estimates are about 15 percent of steel sold in the U.S. is imported; about 20 percent of autos; nearly 60 percent of sewing machines and calculating machines and 35 percent or more of shoes.

Baseball is an American game, but about 90 percent of baseball mitts sold in the U.S. are imports. Similarly, a large percentage of other goods sold in the U.S. are imported, including typewriters and shirts, color TV sets and textiles, pianos and tires, work clothes and glass....

These factors that displace American production also displace American employment. The AFL-CIO staff estimates that the decline of America's position in the world economy resulted in a net loss of about 900,000 job opportunities from 1966 to 1971....

According to the Electronic Industries Association, there was a direct displacement of 122,500 American jobs in radio, TV and electronic component production between 1965 and 1970. Scores of thousands of additional jobs have been wiped out with the shutdown of entire plants and departments in a spreading number of industries. They include skilled and technical jobs, as well as unskilled and semiskilled.

Communities throughout the country are adversely affected. The loss of industrial payrolls means the erosion of the tax base of many communities and the loss of retail sales for local merchants.

There are many causes of this situation. One is that foreign nations have direct and indirect subsidies for their exports, combined with various types of barriers to imports. The result is that foreign products flood American markets and the expansion of American exports is blocked or held down.

Another factor is the export of American technology by American companies to their own foreign subsidiaries or to foreign companies with whom they have license and patent agreements. Connected with the export of technology is the sharp increase of investments of American companies in foreign operations and the rapid spread of multinational companies, most of them based in the U.S.

The result of this combination of developments has been the export of American production facilities, the export of American technology and know-how, the export of American jobs....

A *New York Times* report last April 2 indicated the complex and confusing nature of the realities of America's position in the world economy. It said: "The Chrysler Corporation now imports an English car and calls it a Plymouth Cricket, and a Japanese car and calls it a Dodge Colt. General Motors and Ford import Japanese-made trucks and give them American names. And that American Pinto may carry a German engine and be assembled in Canada."

The sales of American-owned foreign manufacturing subsidiaries in recent years have been more than twice as great as the exports of manufactured goods from the U.S. Some of these products of the foreign subsidiaries of American companies are shipped back to the U.S., in direct competition with U.S.-made goods. Another portion of these sales is in foreign markets, frequently in competition with American exports.

The sales of foreign firms operating with American patents and licenses are also substantial. They compete with U.S.-produced goods both at home and abroad.

A large part of the decline of America's position in the world economy, therefore, is related to the activities of American companies.

I am convinced that much of these activities are short-sighted, even in terms of the interests of American business.

There undoubtedly is a fast buck to be made in foreign-plant operations—or at least there is the hope of a fast buck. With American technology and know-how, such a foreign plant is as efficient or nearly as efficient as a similar plant in the U.S. With wages of 12 cents, 25 cents or even 50 cents an hour, the labor-cost advantage is clear. There are tax advantages, as well.

How can an American worker possibly compete under such conditions? The American factory worker, with an average wage of about $3.80 an hour, can't possibly compete with foreign workers, using the same machinery and know-how and with wages that are 50 percent to 90 percent less.

But workers making 12 cents, 25 cents, or even 50 cents an hour cannot possibly provide much of a market for the sale of TV sets or most other consumer goods that are not immediate necessities.

Where does this leave the company? Its main market—and this is true of almost every American company, even most of the big multinationals—is here at home, in the United States. And that market is based on the American standard of living, on American wages, on the buying power of American consumers.

But the American worker who loses his job is a lost customer for the products of American business. He is also a lost taxpayer. He can't buy much on unemployment insurance payments. When they run out, he may be forced to go on welfare. That adds to the burden of the community.

However, we are not talking of one worker or one plant. We are talking of entire industries and entire communities that are being hit. We are talking of scores of thousands of jobs that are being exported each year.

Here's the way one businessman has described these events of recent years. In an article in the Chemical and Engineering News, Mr. Nathaniel Brenner, the director of marketing of Coates and Weller Corp., stated:

> "For many years our advanced products enabled us to compete in international markets despite high prices (and high wage rates).
> What has happened in the 1960s and continues is that American corporations, via licensing agreements, foreign plant construction and other multinational arrangements, have given away for a very small portion of real cost and value this advanced technology and, with it, the jobs it created. Where a multinational corporation licenses a product abroad, it gives away the technology created by Americans educated at public expense, and the American jobs which produce that product, for the 5 or 10 percent represented by the license fee or return on invested capital. Result—the American worker loses a job, the U.S. loses an export product and becomes an importer of that product, but the corporation still nets 5 or 10 percent. Result—unemployment plus balance of payments problems. Naturally, the foreign producer can sell for less—he hasn't had to invest in the education, the R&D, or the wages which support the American system."

This quotation, I emphasize, is from an American businessman.

By the time the imported product reaches the consumer, it is usually sold at an American price, or close to it. And it is often sold under an American brand-name. So the consumer—who is also a wage or salary earner—typically gets little, if any, benefit in the price of the product, while the worker loses his job. The short-term advantage goes to the increased mark-ups of the companies involved.

The consequences of these trends are the undermining of America's consumer markets. And, in the long run, the fast buck of today will probably result in a lost buck for American business tomorrow or the day after. I think it is a basic truth about our American system that American business generally, cannot prosper in the long run if American consumer markets continue to be undermined.

The basic source of American economic strength is here in the United States—in our people, in our free institutions, in our schools and skills, in our research and development. Yet part of that basic strength is being given away. . . .

The drastic decline of the American merchant marine in the past 25 years is a case in point. It has made this country dependent on foreign-flag shipping and foreign seamen, even for delivery of military equipment. That decline was permitted to occur without government remedy. Its causes were varied—and the blame is not altogether on one side, as against another—but there was no comprehensive government remedy until recently, after more than 20 years of rapid deterioration.

As Americans, concerned about the future of our country and its economy, we should not permit a similar elimination of American industry and the jobs that go with it.

American business, as well as American workers, needs economic growth, not economic stagnation. That means an improving standard of living. That means more jobs, at decent wages, for our growing labor force. That means expanding markets.

That is the objective of American trade unions. I believe it is also the goal of American business. The major differences between American unions and American business are on how to share the benefits of economic efficiency and growth, not on the goal itself.

We in the AFL-CIO are concerned about the deterioration of America's position in the world economy—about the export of American jobs and technology. We do not believe that either business or workers can possibly prosper, in the long run, if America becomes a nation of hamburger stands, hotels, importers and international banks, without the broad base of various types of industries and production. We do not believe that American business, any more than American workers, can prosper over a period of years, if one industry after another goes down the drain.

---

7. **How many of the following traditional arguments for tariffs can you find in Meany's arguments?**

   tariffs for special interest groups
   tariffs for high wages and employment levels
   tariffs for retaliation
   tariffs for revenue
   tariffs to reduce competition from cheap foreign labor
   tariffs for national defense

GLOBAL COMMERCE EXPANDS MORE SLOWLY AS BARRIERS TO IT SPREAD

European Bloc Limits Steel from Japan; Jamaicans Ban All Imports of Autos U.S. Protectionism Is Rising

ALFRED L. MALABRE, JR.   Staff Reporter of the *Wall Street Journal*

World trade shows worrisome signs of a slowdown.

That's the view of many analysts who follow trends in global commerce. Few forecasters anticipate an actual shrinkage of trade in the months just ahead, but most believe that gains will become increasingly difficult. Looking beyond 1977, there's concern that trade expansion could grind nearly to a halt.

"It's entirely possible that we may be entering a prolonged period of substantially slower growth in international commerce," remarks an economist at the International Monetary Fund in Washington. A similar opinion comes from an analyst at Chase Manhattan Bank in New York: "World trade has expanded vigorously in the recent past, but there's a serious question as to whether even moderate expansion is in prospect now."

DEBTS AND OIL BILLS

Various factors are cited. Protectionist measures to limit imports are proliferating. Economic growth in some key industrial lands remains surprisingly sluggish, and expansion in the U.S., relatively brisk in recent months, seems likely to slow as the year unfolds. Huge debts and burdensome oil bills, particularly in poorer countries, are restricting the funds available for less-than-essential imports.

Expanding international trade, of course, has been a main ingredient in the global prosperity marking the past couple of decades. Through the 1960s, for example, the value of goods traded internationally rose at an annual rate of about 9 percent. Many analysts are convinced that free, growing trade between nations is not only desirable politically but also on economic grounds, in that it fosters the most efficient geographic allocation of labor and material resources. Trade-curbing practices are widely blamed for the scope and severity of the economic slump during the 1930s.

Recent data compiled by the International Monetary Fund indicate that the growth of global trade is already diminishing. Last year, the value of goods traded internationally amounted to nearly $1 trillion—a record that exceeded the 1975 total by 11 percent after allowing for inflation. The increase represented a welcome rebound from 1975, when the recession caused world trade to dwindle some 5 percent, the first such drop since 1958. So far this year, however, year-to-year gains have averaged only about 7 percent. Many forecasters expect the gains to continue to narrow in coming months.

Reprinted by permission of the *Wall Street Journal*. © Dow Jones & Company, Inc. 1977. All rights reserved.

BEYOND THIS YEAR

Sharing such a view is Lawrence R. Klein, a University of Pennsylvania economist who keeps tab on world trade trends. For 1977 as a whole, he foresees a 6.5 percent increase in global trade. And looking far down the road, Prof. Klein anticipates a further "slowing down in world trade growth." He now questions whether next year's gain will match the projected 1977 increase; as recently as December, he forecast an 8 percent expansion for 1978.

Many economists note that the recent slowing in trade growth would be still more severe were it not for oil shipments from petroleum-producing nations. Without oil, it's estimated that world trade has risen only some 4 percent so far this year. And if America's soaring imports are also taken out of the picture, analysts say trade expansion would be skimpier still. In recent months, U.S. imports, led by oil, have been running nearly 20 percent higher than in 1976. In the process, the country's trade balance has been registering record monthly deficits.

A major factor underlying the trade slowdown appears to be protectionism, although its impact is impossible to pinpoint.

"There are more and more instances of protectionism around the world, but it's a hard thing to quantify," Prof. Klein says. This view is supported by a recent report from the International Monetary Fund. Issued early this month, the report finds that "a greater proportion of world trade" recently has become subject to such restraints as import surcharges, quotas, trade-limiting pacts and various other nontariff barriers. The trend—ranging from West European restraints on textile imports to Japanese restrictions on silk to Indonesian curbs on iron and steel—marks "an interruption to the reduction of protectionism that had characterized" the policies of most major trading nations, the report says.

A BAN ON AUTOS

Jamaica, a relatively poor island nation wholly dependent on imported oil, provides an extreme illustration of the recent patterns. As oil prices have soared, Jamaica's foreign-exchange reserves, which exceeded $200 million in mid-1974, have shriveled to less than $30 million. Jamaican authorities have had to clamp rigid import controls on a widening assortment of key products. Perhaps the most drastic step was a ban on auto imports, effective last month, even though Jamaica turns out no cars itself.

More-affluent nations also are moving to restrict imports. Early this year, Europe's Common Market imposed duties of up to 20 percent on various industrial bearings imported from Japan. Officials of the trade bloc claimed that some 5,000 workers had lost jobs because of low-priced Japanese bearings.

The European bloc also recently established rigid limits on car and steel imports from Japan. The Japanese agreed to hold car shipments to less than 10 percent of the area's overall auto sales and steel shipments to about 1.2 million tons yearly. Analysts estimate that such agreements could bring an actual contraction of trade between Japan and Western Europe. The agreements have brought angry protests from U.S. manufacturers fearing that more Japanese autos and steel will be diverted to the American marketplace....

Economists agree that a brisk pickup in economic activity in key industrial nations would bring more growth in international commerce and, possibly, a turn away from protectionism. At present, however, the recovery from the last recession, which ended in most countries about two years ago, remains distressingly slow nearly everywhere but the U.S. The Bank of New York estimates that economic growth this year will amount to only 3.9 percent in West Germany, 3 percent in France, 2 percent in Switzerland and 1.1 percent in Britain.

Continuing concern about severe inflation is prompting leaders in many areas to aim for relatively modest economic growth in coming months. The slow growth not only limits import demand in the various countries, but fosters protectionist sentiment, to the extent that unemployment remains high. Joblessness in Britain, France and West Germany recently has been close to post-World War II highs.

A large imponderable in the trade picture, analysts say, is the U.S. economy. America's recovery from the recession has been relatively strong, and this is the major reason that U.S. imports have risen so sharply. However, forecasters generally think that U.S. economic growth will slow substantially in the year's second half, to perhaps an annual rate of 5 percent from about a 7 percent annual pace in recent months. And a further easing in economic growth is foreseen during 1978.

Such a development would tend to reduce the expansion of world trade, analysts say. In addition, however, there is mounting worry that America, with its soaring import bill, also will resort increasingly to trade restrictions.

CARTER'S PUBLIC STAND

The Carter administration is solidly on record against such practices. Last spring, President Carter ordered a study aimed at easing or terminating a system of quotas imposed during the Ford administration on specialty-steel imports. And recently U.S. officials have opted against imposing import curbs on items ranging from Taiwanese mushrooms to Japanese electronic products to South Korean shoes. Nonetheless, analysts question how long U.S. authorities can resist mounting protectionist pressures.

Major labor unions that supported President Carter during his election campaign are plugging harder and harder for import curbs. So are manufacturers in industries such as steel and textiles.

And the public at large apparently has started to view imports as a major economic threat rather than as merely a source of inexpensive goods. A national survey recently found growing public support for trade curbs. Nearly 60 percent of those polled endorsed a cut in imports of color-TV sets from Japan, in the belief that U.S. jobs would be safeguarded. Only 29 percent expressed concern that such a cutback might raise TV prices. Asked whether the U.S. should trade more or less with six key countries, most people opted for less.

U.S. calls for trade restrictions would doubtless be much louder were it not for some recent trade-limiting agreements. The Japanese, for instance, agreed in May to restrict their color TV exports to the U.S. to 1,750,000 sets annually for three years. Last year, Japanese manufacturers shipped a record 2,800,000 color TV sets to American customers.

"While such agreements are preferable to a unilateral imposition of trade restrictions, they nevertheless represent interference with free trade," states an analysis by economists at the Chicago Federal Reserve Bank. It goes on to predict that such agreements "may be expected to lead to higher prices to U.S. consumers for these goods."

Despite mounting pressures in many lands to restrict trade, multinational efforts to expand global commerce and remove restraints go on. Continuing in Geneva, for example, is the latest round of the so-called Multilateral Trade Negotiations, attended by member nations of the General Agreement on Tariffs and Trade. The GATT talks aim at reducing tariff and nontariff barriers to international commerce. [But] these negotiations will prove difficult precisely because of the "numerous" trade curbs recently implemented around the world.

8. Do you see any possibility of a relaxation of protectionist trends in the near future? Why? What would have to occur to bring about such a trend?

9. Should the U.S. steel industry, for example, be protected from foreign imports? Why or why not?

KEY CONCEPTS

free trade	quotas
protectionism	comparative advantage
tariff	General Agreement on Tariffs and Trade (GATT)

REVIEW QUESTIONS

1. What factors other than comparative advantage might induce nations to trade?

2. Are you a believer in free trade or protectionism? Why? For the U.S.? for the world?

3. How would you explain a reduction in tariffs to a textile worker in South Carolina?

4. What is the proper international trade policy for a nation experiencing a deep recession in its domestic economy?

SUGGESTED READINGS

David P. Calleo and Benjamin M. Rowland, 1973. *America and the World Political Economy*, University of Indiana Press. Calleo and Rowland examine the postwar economic growth of Western Europe and Japan and their challenge to U.S. supremacy. They question the viability of the world economic system based on the old liberal order.

Anthony Harrison, 1967. *The Framework of Economic Activity: The International Economy and the Rise of the State in the Twentieth Century*, Macmillan. A history of the international economy from the rise and fall of the gold standard and economic liberalism to the managed world economy of the 1950s and 1960s.

Harry G. Johnson, 1965. *The World Economy at the Crossroads*, Oxford University Press. A renowned international economist deals with the history of trade and monetary and institutional organizations with a special section devoted to the problems of the developing countries.

THE INTERNATIONAL FINANCIAL SYSTEM

CHAPTER 22

INTRODUCTION

Thus far we have considered the theory and the recent history of international trade. We shall now turn our focus to the world of *international finance* that, as its name implies, deals with money flows between nations. These money flows are the consequence of decisions by citizens or institutions of a given nation to lend to or borrow from foreigners and to import or export goods and services. In recent years, these transactions have been referred to as a monetary muddle, maze, and mystery with the implication that the subject is so esoteric that only central bankers and the "gnomes of Zurich" could understand its complexities. International finance has been referred to as a game in which the rules have broken down and have been ignored since 1971. This chapter briefly examines the history of international finance through 1944 when the Bretton Woods System was established. It then examines the Bretton Woods System in order to understand how it functioned until the destruction of the system in the early 1970s. It concludes by examining international finance during the 1970s that has been characterized by floating exchange rates and continuing problems.

THE GOLD STANDARD

Some type of international financial system is required as a result of the "imbalances" in the balance-of-payments positions among nations. If the U.S., for example, has an overall balance-of-payments deficit with the rest of the world, some mechanism must exist for "balancing" that deficit. Throughout the history of modern world capitalism, several different systems have existed for accomplishing this task. The first of these that we will examine is the *gold standard*.

Gold served as the external form of payment in the international system from the Middle Ages until the 20th century. Under a gold standard, a country's currency was convertible into gold at a fixed price. The price of the currency expressed in terms of gold was known as its *parity value*. The mechanism worked in the following way. Both the U.S. and the U.K., for example, defined their currencies in terms of gold. As a result, surpluses and deficits in the balance of payments were equivalent

The Arab nations have recently become more active participants in the international financial system. (Photograph by Bill Weibel.)

to a certain amount of gold. If the U.S. had a surplus in its balance of payments with the U.K., then the U.K.'s deficit would be settled by the shipment of the appropriate amount of gold to the U.S. British pounds, having demanded American goods and services, would have accumulated in the U.S. The U.S. would then convert its "unwanted" pounds into gold from the U.K. In this way, the U.K.'s deficit would be "balanced."

This mechanism was relatively simple and had some other attractive results. The flow of gold from the U.K. would reduce the money supply in the U.K. and increase it in the U.S. As an automatic reaction, prices would fall in the U.K. and rise in the U.S.—since less (more) money would tend to force prices downward (upward) and since gold was a part of the money supply. Consumers in each country would then respond to these price changes—exports of U.S. goods would tend to fall and those of the U.K. would tend to increase. Consequently, the balance-of-payments surplus of the U.S. would tend to decline (all without any intervention of the government!). Thus under the gold standard, where gold flowed freely and was part of the money supply, there was an automatic mechanism for settling balance-of-payments imbalances and, in addition, imbalances would tend to be automatically eliminated.

However, there were some practical problems with the gold standard that eventually led to its replacement and, in the interim, created problems for the operation of the international financial system and, hence, for international trade. Under the gold standard, gold created the liquidity necessary to finance international trade and the resulting deficits for some countries.

The concept of liquidity is vital to trade in that some standards of "moneyness" must be universally accepted for transactions to occur. One must have this liquidity if trade is to take place. If there are not enough gold reserves (or gold mines) to facilitate trade or if output of goods and services outstrips the output of gold, a *liquidity crisis* emerges. In this situation, the health of domestic economies were at the mercy of the ability of the world to produce gold. For example, if the U.K. could not get enough gold to finance its deficit with the U.S., then it could not import goods and services from the U.S. As a result, while the U.S. might have a balance in international accounts with the U.K., domestic production levels would be restricted. The gold standard, then, limited the amount of international trade that could be financed and tended to restrict some domestic economies.

Furthermore, following the turmoil, destruction, and economic havoc of World War I, the gold standard operated in such a way as to depress economic activity in Western Europe as these countries attempted to maintain the parity values of their overvalued currencies. (Overvaluation of a currency tends to limit the ability of a country to export its goods and to enhance its ability to import goods, thus tending to create international payments deficits.)

Feelings of nationalism and the need for *independent national* monetary and fiscal policies relegated the size of international reserves to a secondary position. People were more concerned with internal price, income, and employment levels than they were with the state of the currency on the international market. These along with other pressures of the age left a rather precarious international system to face the events of 1929. The system struggled and eventually failed. The high Smoot–Hawley tariff of 1930 and those made in retaliation to it ensured the demise of the gold standard and a virtual end to international trade for the duration of the Depression. Nations began abandoning gold as sailors might a sinking ship—even first-class seats offered no security. Gold was no longer used as a mechanism to settle balance-of-payments deficits.

Several international conferences led to draft resolutions, but the tremendous instability of *all* currencies permitted no permanent international economic structure to develop during the 1930s. As various agreements were being reached and order was being regained, World War II began and then the system went into chaos once again. This time, however, negotiations were occurring throughout the war years to allow the birth and formation of a new international economic system.

THE INTERNATIONAL MONETARY FUND AND THE BRETTON WOODS SYSTEM

The framework for that system, which forms the official organizational structure for today's international financial negotiations, was formulated in 1944 at a conference in Bretton Woods, New Hampshire. The economic arrangements made then are referred to as the Bretton Woods System. Many different arguments were advanced concerning the shape that the world monetary system was to take at the conclusion of the war. The institutional arrangements made then were to be overseen by a new organization, the *International Monetary Fund* (IMF). The major purposes of the IMF were as follows:

1. The International Monetary Fund itself provided the institutional framework for monetary cooperation and consultation when problems arose. Member nations purchased subscriptions to the fund in accordance with their standing in world production levels. Policy was then heavily influenced by Western nations. In 1944 the U.S. contributed one-third of the Fund's stock of gold and currency and received one-third of the votes in major policy proposals. Today the U.S. annual quota is about 22 percent; and when an 80 percent majority vote is needed on a major policy issue, the U.S. has veto power. The Fund provides the arena for discussions of international monetary problems, although most developed countries have ignored this forum. They have chosen to discuss and solve many of their monetary difficulties among themselves. At one time, this ad hoc arrangement was known as the *Group of Ten*. It consisted of the central bankers of the nations with the most economic strength and clout. This group met monthly to discuss problems and difficulties. One can see the limitations of the Fund as a consulting forum when immediate decisions are made by the more powerful countries to avert crises.

Today, the Group of Ten has been superseded by an expanded Group of Twenty. In addition to problem solving we find that in general these most powerful central bankers have sought to maintain the status quo—promoting their own self-interest while preserving their own power.

2. The second goal of the IMF was to facilitate expansion and balanced growth of trade with high levels of domestic income and employment. A system of *fixed exchange rates* was established to accomplish this goal. Under the fixed exchange system, currencies were defined in terms of one another. Consistency was assured with each nation also defining its currency in terms of gold and the U.S. dollar.

3. To provide stable exchange rates between currencies, the U.S. dollar maintained a passive role because it was chosen to serve as the *key* or *reserve currency* that would be as acceptable as gold in international transactions. Currencies were defined in terms of the dollar, and the dollar became an acceptable means of international payment. Consequently, if the U.S. had a deficit with Italy, this could be financed by Italy's merely maintaining possession of its "excess" dollars. Italy would be inclined to do this because it could use those dollars to settle its deficits with other nations.

4. To guarantee a multilateral payments system, sufficient international liquidity was needed. Under the Bretton Woods System, gold, U.S. dollars, and IMF balances were the major sources of liquidity. A nation could also borrow from the IMF on a short-term basis if additional liquidity was needed. As we shall see shortly, insufficient liquidity became a problem during the 1960s. To provide additional liquidity with which to facilitate world trade, the Fund created *Special Drawing Rights* (SDRs) in 1968. The creation of SDRs had been discussed throughout the 1960s. At their initial creation, they were given the dollar value of gold and could be used to settle international accounts. They were first put into use in 1970 when $10 billion of SDRs were allocated for use between 1970 and 1972. They were distributed to each nation on the basis of IMF quotas or voting rights. SDRs were created to fill two basic voids in the international monetary system. (1) They were to substitute for gold as an ultimate means of settling balance of payments deficits; and (2) they were designed to substitute for dollars as an international reserve currency. The growth in international reserves could now be more stable with this bookkeeping currency. The value of the SDR has been based on the currencies of 16 industrial countries since 1974. The change from the gold value was made to offset world monetary fluctuations. In mid-1976, the SDR was worth about $1.26. Each one-cent increase in its value indicates a weakening of the dollar in the world exchange market.

5. To correct disequilibrium conditions in balance of payments, countries were expected to utilize both monetary and fiscal policy. For example, deficits could be corrected by limiting economic activity and, hence, imports. If this was insufficient for the necessary adjustments, the Bretton Woods System provided for a change in the exchange rates. When a revaluation occurs the currency that goes down in value is said to have *depreciated* while the currency going up has *appreciated*.

---

1. When a country's currency depreciates, it is worth less in terms of other currencies. What effect will this have on that country's exports? its imports? its balance-of-payments position?

If the parity rate has changed in terms of gold (more dollars buying the same amount of gold), the currency is said to have experienced a *devaluation*.

WHAT WENT WRONG? INTERNATIONAL MONETARY CRISIS

The IMF was created and designed to guarantee the working of the Bretton Woods System and so the question that naturally arises is what went wrong? Why are we constantly reading about and hearing of new problems in the world economic arena? It is clear that the system was capable of dealing with many of the financial problems of the past three decades while other problems have sent the scheme into periods of chaos—never quite fulfilling the dreams of its creators.

As we examine the history of the collapse of the Bretton Woods System, we will find the recurrence of two fundamental shortcomings:

1. There was no mechanism designed within the system to *force* countries to change their exchange rates even though they were substantially overvalued or undervalued.

2. There was no *consistency* included in the system. National monetary policies were not necessarily compatible with the exchange rate system that, in turn, was not necessarily compatible with international liquid assets.

THE DOWNFALL OF THE BRETTON WOODS SYSTEM

We can, perhaps chronologically date the process of decay of the Bretton Woods System immediately after its creation. The U.S. dollar was given the role of a "key" or reserve currency. Following the war, it was one of the few currencies that was "fully convertible" or accepted by all nations. Reasonably stable prices within the U.S., the wide circulation of the dollar, and the strength of the growing U.S. economy all accounted for the rise to the key currency position.

The demand for dollars was very high at that time, particularly in Europe. U.S. dollars were needed to purchase the goods and services essential for the postwar rebuilding process, but they were in very short supply at that time. Because the war had left European plants totally devastated, the only country whose economy remained intact was the U.S. Needless to say, the U.S. rose to the occasion supplying dollars where shortages existed. Dollars began pouring into Europe. Some $37 billion had entered during the war under the Lend-Lease program and some $130 billion continued to be shipped in for aid between 1945 and 1967. Perhaps the most politically and economically significant program was the Marshall Plan, initiated in 1948. Under this act $10 billion was designated for European "recovery." This program was significant to the self-interest of the U.S. After all, what good was the U.S. productive capacity if there were no nations with which to trade? If Europe couldn't buy our goods and services, who could? European economic stability, both internally and externally, as well as increased European productivity were necessary for the U.S. to achieve its optimum economic goals.

Part of the program was designed to protect the domestic stability and capitalist structure of Western Europe. The Truman Doctrine, designed to halt the spread of Communism in Greece and Turkey, was extended to ensure political stability within Europe and to "halt" the "Soviet Union's plan for the international takeover of the 'free world'." During the Cold War, the U.S. provided military aid, troops, and bases to various countries. No doubt this encouraged many U.S. firms to invest their funds in these rebuilding nations. Indeed, the returns to investments made in Europe were expected to be much larger than those made in the U.S. because production costs were lower and there was a newly emerging "consumption market" to be tapped. So it was that U.S. dollars flowed into Europe and turned the dollar shortage of the 1940s into the dollar *glut* of the 1960s.

This dollar glut meant that an excess supply of dollars was being held by Europeans and these dollars were not being "recycled" for U.S. goods and services. Several questions emerged from this oversupply situation. First, how many dollars would the Europeans be willing to hold before they stopped accepting them for exchange? New markets were now opening to the Europeans and the demand for U.S. products were decreasing due to their higher prices. A second and more fundamental question concerned the balance-of-payments position of the United States. As the dollar outflows continued and the *balance-of-payments position worsened*, economists wondered about the strength of the U.S. economy relative to nations that were no longer weak but were by now strong, viable, and competitive economies. (For one view of the consequences of these trends, see the reading from *Dollars & Sense* in Chapter 20.) It was in this area that the Bretton Woods System failed. According to the system, exchange rate adjustments should occur in cases of persistent balance-of-payments difficulties—yet because the dollar was the reserve currency and essential for international liquidity, necessary adjustments were avoided. The trouble lay deeper than this, however. There were extremely few realignments in currencies under the Bretton Woods System. Many felt depreciation was a sign of national weakness, while appreciation was viewed not as a sign of strength but as a compromise to a weaker economic position. You can imagine just how out of kilter these exchange rates were since they were essentially the same parity rates in existence right after World War II.

Multinationals and Eurodollars

Dollars continued to flow abroad during the 1950s to purchase the new, relatively cheaper European goods and services and to seek the higher returns from European investments. As these investments spread and U.S. firms began locating business operations in these countries and buying European corporations, new and diversified institutional frameworks were needed. The multinationals required more convenient financial markets within the European host countries to facilitate capital flows. The dollars deposited in European banks by these multinational corporations were soon dubbed Eurodollars. Eurodollars have grown from total obscurity to a position of prominence in both world and national financial affairs during the past decade. The sudden and astounding rise of this market is without precedent in modern financial history. Estimates place the current volume of Eurodollar funds at about $300 billion with large quantities of petro-dollars (from the increased value of oil sales) being recycled into this market. As we mentioned earlier, the Eurodollar market developed as a response to real needs of the international financial community rather than as some freak money market discovery made in trying to decide how funds might be used more profitably. Eurodollars are U.S. dollar-denominated deposits at commercial banks outside the U.S. They derive all of their characteristics from the U.S. dollar. The only difference between dollars and Eurodollars is their geographic location. This geographic difference means that Eurodollars are *not subject to U.S. governmental control*. Eurodollar banks are *not subject to legal reserve requirements*, but are subject to regulation by the country in which they are located.

Eurodollars are created, for example, when a New York investor decides to switch funds from New York to Zurich. To do this, the investor simply writes a check on the New York account. The investor now holds dollar deposits in a bank in Zurich. Another creation occurs when a U.S. firm borrows $1 million from a Zurich bank. Just as in the multiple creation of demand deposits in the U.S., the bank in Zurich has now increased the number of dollars held by increasing the account of the firm by $1 million. Why is there so much banking interest in Eurodollars and other Euro-currencies? Why are U.S. banks interested in establishing branches in foreign countries? Right both times! Profits! There is considerably more interest rate competition in Eurobanking than there is in domestic banking but because costs are lower, profits will be higher. Investors prefer holding Eurodollar deposits because they can receive higher interest on their funds with no higher risk (except perhaps political risk).

U.S. central bankers are concerned about the growing size of the Eurodollar market and their lack of control over it. They become quite frightened at the thought of a $1 million transfer from a U.S. bank to a Swiss bank going through the multiple expansion process and ending up increasing dollar deposits abroad by four- or five-fold. This would obviously reduce the effectiveness of the central bank in controlling the money stock because dollar loans could be obtained from the Eurodollar market—even at a time of strict money policy. Eurodollars, therefore, contribute to worldwide inflation by increasing the availability of money on an international scale.

U.S. Policy in the Crunch

Despite these developments, along with ever-increasing deficits in the balance of payments, U.S. policy remained much the same during the 1960s. During this period the IMF virtually conceded its operations to the Group of Ten. At their meetings they discussed and acted at any indication of weakness in currency operations—but *prompt realignment* of parity rates was not forthcoming! A system of emergency capital flows was used instead, with funds being shuttled from one weak currency to the next. This led only to greater instability within the Bretton Woods System. By

1968 it was readily apparent to most economists that the system was preparing for collapse—but still it hung on.

Early in 1971 there were large movements of "interest sensitive" capital from the United States to Europe. Speculation against the dollar grew and, as more and more dollars were dumped on the foreign exchange markets, more deutsche marks and yen were demanded to take their place in individual and corporate portfolios. In Fig. 22.1, we can see how this affected the U.S. dollar. As the supply of dollars increased in the European markets, their price was driven down in terms of (in this case) deutsche marks.

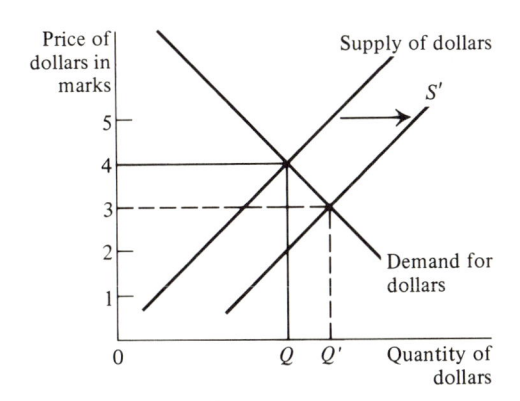

FIG. 22.1 The pressures on the dollar.

Pressure was put on the dollar and it should have been revalued under the Bretton Woods System. But, because the U.S. dollar was a reserve currency, the change was not forthcoming. According to our example, the dollar should have depreciated from four marks per dollar to three marks per dollar thus making the new higher priced German products less attractive as imports while at the same time increasing U.S. exports to Germany because they would be a great deal cheaper than they were before.

To avoid the appreciation of the mark and yen at that time, both the German and Japanese central banks began buying dollars with the hope of absorbing enough to avoid realignment of the two currencies. By doing this, they hoped to keep German and Japanese exports at high levels and thus maintain high levels of employment in the two countries. Figure 22.2 illustrates the short-run results of the action of the two central banks. Because Germany and Japan bought dollars, the demand for dollars was increased from D to D^1, thus keeping the old exchange rates in effect.

2. Would you have bought dollars if you were a central banker in Germany?

3. Why were the German and Japanese bankers so hostile to an appreciation of the mark and the yen in terms of the U.S. dollar? Doesn't appreciation signify strength?

The International Financial System

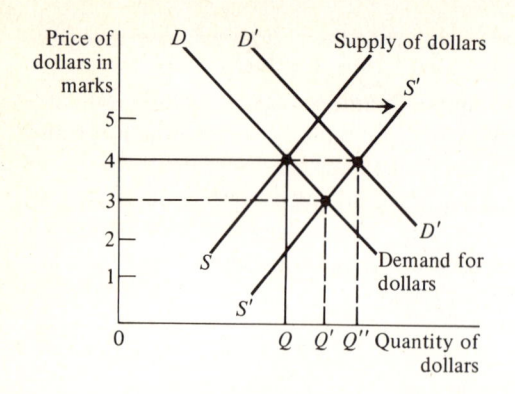

FIG. 22.2 Keeping the value of the dollar up.

By mid-year the German central bank decided that it was spending too many of its valuable marks to support the overvalued dollar and so it stopped dollar purchases and allowed the deutsche mark to *float*. Floating occurs when the exchange rate of the currency is determined strictly by market supply-and-demand factors. This means that the value of the currency could change from day to day.

---

4. What are some factors that might change the demand for the mark? the supply? Refer to Chapter 10 and review the determinants of supply and demand to help you with your answer.

By the time of the German decision to float the deutsche mark, a U.S. Congressional subcommittee reported that the dollar was overvalued and called for a general realignment of exchange rates. Needless to say, this report caused even more speculation against the dollar, driving its value down even further. (The Japanese as well soon abandoned their policy of buying dollars.)

In August of 1971, President Nixon introduced the New Economic Policy (NEP) that, along with domestic wage and price controls, called for a temporary 10-percent surcharge on all imports as well as a "temporary" halt in the convertibility of dollars into gold. (This temporary condition still exists and it is now understood that August 15, 1971, marks the complete end of the gold exchange standard. Though U.S. citizens have not been able to exchange their dollar holdings for gold since 1934, foreign holders could until this suspension.)

After the NEP, chaos existed in the European money markets because there was no coordinated approach to the new developments. Again, rampant speculation against the dollar occurred, and the value of most major trading currencies rose with respect to the dollar.

The September 1971 meeting of the Group of Ten ended in total discord. The U.S. insisted on a revaluation of other currencies, a reduction of trade barriers and a "sharing of the burden" of international defense.

By winter of 1971, pressures on the dollar continued to rise due to the war in Vietnam. Because of the tremendous costs of the war, the U.S. balance of payments deficit was larger and more pressing than it had been at anytime in the nation's history. Both private and government capital flowed into Southeast Asia for investment as well as defense purposes. Though the U.S. balance-of-payments position had been precarious during the 1960s, these new pressures made the condition impossible.

FLOATING EXCHANGE RATES

On December 18, 1971, President Nixon committed what a few years earlier would have been political suicide and devalued the dollar. The "historic" Smithsonian Agreement called for an 8-percent devaluation of the dollar and a realignment of other currencies reflecting the lower value of the dollar. Currencies were then pegged so that the market exchange could fluctuate within a 2.25-percent band (up or down) from the new rates. Again, as in so many times in the past, this solution did not deal with the *structural* problems of the Bretton Woods System. Superficial adjustments were once again made, working within the system to solve the mounting world financial difficulties.

The Float

In 1973, the world became aware that the "band-aid" solutions instituted in 1971 were not working at all well. Speculation pressures were again being brought against the dollar. The result of these new pressures and instability was the abandonment of the fixed rate monetary system associated with both the Bretton Woods and Smithsonian agreements. A system of *floating exchange rates* emerged as a temporary settlement until "a more permanent solution to the chronic problems of the world's monetary system could be developed." The IMF has lost most of the strength and clout it once had in the arena of foreign exchange. Now the monetary systems are joined by a series of floating rates and linked floating rates that are sometimes called "joint floats." An example of this is the Common Market currencies that float together against the world. One sometimes hears of *dirty* or *managed floats* that are encountered when governments intervene in the currency markets to keep the floating currencies within desired bounds.

After 1973, the rules were changed so that de facto depreciation or appreciation could occur without official IMF sanction. It was by such a method that the U.S. "adjusted" the balance-of-payments deficit encountered during and after the OPEC oil embargo. The once overvalued dollar was now allowed to seek its own worth in the somewhat free international currency markets. In the current context, when the U.S. experiences a deficit, this deficit is "settled" through a combination of other countries' holding their dollar balances and some amount of decrease in the value of the dollar.

In the few years since the introduction of floating exchange rates, the international monetary system has found itself adjusting surprisingly well even though the central banks of most major industrial countries have intervened at one time or another to "manage" their exchange rates. Until the early months of 1976, there had been no attempts at competitive depreciation to gain an advantage in product export but, in the spring and summer of 1976, the British pound was allowed to fall to much lower levels than its worth. This increased the demand for British goods throughout the world and boosted tourism to the U.K. Other European countries have also been accused of a bit of competitive devaluation and nations are reminded that if every country devalues, few if any gains are made.

The float has presented special problems for the less developed countries (LDC). Because few of these nations had well-developed currency markets, they simply pegged their currency to that of their major industrial trading partner. An LDC whose currency was pegged to the British pound also found that its currency depreciated by almost 25 percent between May of 1975 and the end of 1976.

These kinds of exchange rate movements can cause severe inflationary pressures in LDCs in which inflation is a persistent problem. Some of the OPEC nations have recently linked their currencies to the SDR to guard against inflation resulting from exchange rate changes.

"Currency jitters" seems to sum up the feeling in the 1970s as there was mounting disarray in the currency markets. Many nations have an inherent fear of floating and are looking for new stability.

The experience of the U.S. dollar in international financial markets during the middle and late 1970s clearly reflected the problems that will continue to plague the Western world throughout the early 1980s. The following article by Clyde Farnsworth summarized this present and future condition.

STABILIZING THE AILING DOLLAR— ACTIVE AND PASSIVE ASPECTS

CLYDE H. FARNSWORTH

WASHINGTON, March 19—Ever since the collapse of the postwar monetary system in the summer of 1971, the dollar has been losing value in the international marketplace. The decline, at times gradual, at times precipitous, has been inexorable. The dollar today buys less than half as many West German marks, Swiss francs and Japanese yen as it did ten years ago.

Should the U.S. do more to support the dollar? There are significant consequences for good and for bad, in the currency's long slide.

American exports are more cheaply priced in world markets meaning additional business for domestic producers and additional jobs for domestic labor. Foreign commerce, directly or indirectly, already employs one out of six American workers.

On the other hand, imports cost more, which means higher price tags for everything from French perfumes to Toyotas and an extra push to an already uncomfortably high rate of inflation in the United States.

© 1978 by The New York Times Company. Reprinted by permission.

And on the international front, there are potentially dangerous implications for the price of oil. Members of the Organization of Petroleum Exporting Countries, its secretariat asserts, are losing between $10 billion and $20 billion a year in purchasing power because the dollars their oil earns no longer buys as many West German machine tools, Japanese compressors, or Belgian machine guns.

Within OPEC, there is talk of changing pricing formula for oil in order to get a bigger return. This could mean a further squeeze on the economies of the industrial nations.

In checking the expansion, or profitability, of exports of such countries as Germany and Japan, the shrinking dollar has contributed to a slowdown in growth internationally. And it has encouraged protectionism as companies press their governments to build walls around markets.

The growing list of disadvantages, not least of which is the psychological effect of the deterioration of a basic store of value, has made the fall of the dollar and what can be done about it a prime policy issue.

THE BACKGROUND

The problem has its roots in the proliferation of dollars to finance both the Vietnam War and American social needs, as well as to keep world economic activity ticking after the depressive effects of the 1973-1974 quadrupling of oil prices.

Dollar-denominated interest bearing assets held by foreigners now total more than $500 billion. They represent some three-quarters of the store of value of holdings of multinational corporations and foreign official agencies such as the Bundesbank, the West German central bank.

To the extent that asset managers perceive that future purchasing power of the dollar will be less than that of Germany, Switzerland and Japan, managers seek to diversify into currencies of those nations, which has put ever greater downward pressure on the dollar.

FOR MORE ACTION

Europeans argue that the United States should be accepting more responsibility to stabilize the dollar's exchange rate by intervening in the free market. They say it should not be difficult for the world's greatest economic power to generate, through borrowing or other methods, the foreign money required to prop up the dollar's rate.

The current position is unfair, they say, because most of the burden of intervention has fallen on their shoulders and it is they who have to accept the inflationary consequences. As they check the appreciation of their currencies, they buy dollars with newly created marks, or yen, or Swiss francs, adding quantities of local currency to the world money supply.

This has already created a "dangerous inflation of both international and national liquidity," says Dr. Otmar Emminger, Governor of the Bundesbank. In fact, the world's monetary reserves soared in 1977 by a record $50 billion, or 20 percent, mainly because of central bank absorption of dollars.

The proponents of action point to a number of things the United States could do. Most frequently discussed is the sale of foreign-currency denominated debt by the United States so as to build a stockpile of marks or Swiss francs, for intervention.

Proponents of such action argue that the bonds would sop up liquidity and indicate to the markets that the United States is ready to move aggressively to defend the dollar. In such a case, they say, the United States might never have to actually use the funds.

Another suggestion is that the United States sell some of its 277 million ounces of gold, thus depressing the gold price, which improves the psychological climate for the dollar, as well as building up a stock of intervention currencies.

Some also say the United States should slow its economic growth rate to redress the deficit in its balance of payments, which is the immediate cause of the dollar's weakness. Reduced energy consumption, either through slower growth or an effective energy conservation policy, would go far towards reducing the deficit.

Another deficit, the persistent budget deficit, also weighs on the dollar. Proponents of change would like to see federal spending cut. They say this would reduce inflationary pressures and thus automatically strengthen the dollar.... Exchange controls of the type introduced in the mid-1960s could also help matters, others say. Similarly, it would help, they add, if countries that receive the dollars would tighten their own controls. Switzerland has already acted and the West Germans are said to be considering such a move.

The basic argument is that the dollar is oversold and is ready to bounce back once a firm commitment is made to defend it.

AGAINST MORE ACTION

Opponents of change do not disagree that the dollar is oversold, but they maintain that most of the actions recommended would simply make matters worse. It would be better, they say, to let the fundamentals of good economic growth, attractive investment opportunities and economic and political stability impress themselves on the market.

Sometime soon, they add, there will be an energy policy that will demonstrate a commitment both to building up domestic supplies and to reducing the oil demand from abroad that is hurting the balance of payments.

What really can be done, ask those for the status quo, against the overhang of more than $500 billion of liquid dollar assets in the world, and perhaps as much as $6000 billion of total assets that can be easily converted into dollars. A few billion dollars worth of intervention is like a bucket of water against the sea, as they explain it.

"We could be swamped, and taxpayers would lose billions," says one official who puts little faith in market intervention.

But the same officials who have been advocating a hands-off policy in the marketplace have been quietly stepping up interventions all the same. They say this is designed to do no more than eliminate disorderly movements, the stated policy since mid-1973. "Disorderly" is officially defined rather imprecisely—too wide a spread between bid and asked quotations in the market.

And to build up currency reserves for the interventions the United States has increased its borrowings of German marks. Last week, the United States added the equivalent of $2.7 billion of marks to its intervention capabilities by doubling its line of credit with the Bundesbank and selling it $700 million worth of Special Drawing Rights on the International Monetary Fund.

The United States also indicated it may be willing to borrow as much as $5 billion of additional foreign currencies from the IMF.

The opponents of further action contend that it would be the height of folly—equivalent to hitting a fly with a sledgehammer—to risk bringing on an American recession to help the dollar. Not only would it create hardships here, but also it might tilt the whole world into a new depression, they say.

Foreign exchange controls are similarly ruled out as regressive. It is said they could encourage the 1930-type withdrawal into economic nationalism that most governments are trying to resist.

THE OUTLOOK

The likehood is that the United States continue to gradually increase its arsenal of foreign currencies, and the next step may well be through the sale of treasury gold, perhaps in foreign market centers such as Zurich or London.

Treasury officials, who resisted earlier sales because they might have driven down the price of gold in Paris on the eve of French elections and damaged the chances of the center-right coalition of President Valéry Giscard d'Estaing, are known to be studying the move.

The United States has sold Treasury gold before, in line with its policy of demonetizing the metal. On the books, the 277 million ounces left in Fort Knox are valued at $12 billion, but at present market levels they are worth nearly five times that amount.

But the real hope for the dollar, and the international economy, is expected to lie in increased international cooperation.

The currency's weakness had strained relationships among the Western industrial countries. With the stakes so high, new efforts were made to increase economic cooperation. And recent agreement on an economic summit this summer means the accent will continue on cooperation.

5. Should the U.S. government more vigorously attempt to keep up the value of the dollar? Why or why not?

6. Should the U.S. sell some of its hoard of gold? What effect would this have on the value of the dollar?

KEY CONCEPTS

international finance
gold standard
parity
liquidity
Bretton Woods System
International Monetary Fund (IMF)
Group of Ten
appreciation

depreciation
devaluation
dollar shortage
dollar glut
multinationals
Eurodollars
float
dirty float

REVIEW QUESTIONS

1. If you had been a Minister of Finance in 1944, would you have encouraged your nation to join the IMF? Explain your reasoning.
2. Is gold useful today—or is it simply a barbaric relic?
3. How did the U.S. finance its post-World War II international deficits?
4. Why do nations hesitate to float? Who gains? Who loses?
5. What impacts have the Arab nations had recently on the international financial system?

SUGGESTED READINGS

Robert A. Aliber, 1976. *The International Money Game,* Basic Books. A witty, yet excellent, discussion of the international money markets and the international financial system.

William Ashworth, 1975. *A Short History of the International Economy since 1850,* Longman. An historical perspective on the evolution of foreign exchange systems, international transactions, and international economic relations.

Robert Triffin, 1968. *Our International Monetary System: Yesterday, Today, and Tomorrow,* Random House. A thorough discussion of the underpinnings of the Bretton Woods System and proposals for international monetary reform.

Paul E. Erdman, 1973. *The Billion Dollar Sure Thing,* Scribner's. A novel of suspense and intrigue surrounding international finance by a former Swiss banker. Erdman has also written *The Silver Bears* and *The Crash of '79.* Be prepared, as well, for a significant amount of sexism.

ECONOMIC PROBLEMS OF DEVELOPING NATIONS

CHAPTER 23

Development processes are both cruel and necessary. They are necessary because all societies must come to terms with new aspirations and irresistible social forces. Yet the choices they face are cruel because development's benefits are obtained only at a great price and because, on balance, it is far from certain that achieving development's benefits makes men happier or freer.

Denis Goulet *The Cruel Choice*

DEVELOPMENT AND UNDERDEVELOPMENT: WHAT'S THE DIFFERENCE? WHY DOES IT MATTER?

The United Nations' world population projections indicate that by the year 2000, world population will be six billion people. Of these six billion human beings, four billion will be living in the less developed nations of the Third World. Two-thirds of humanity will be experiencing a standard of living barely above subsistence. For these people, life at the margin of existence is horribly ugly, agonizing, and destructive. The statistics so often quoted to illustrate the objective poverty of the Third World are themselves cold and empty when juxtaposed with the harsh everyday reality of the struggle for survival.

What does it mean to live in a country in which the following factors characterize a person's daily existence: (1) GNP per capita is less than $500 per year, (2) unemployment in the rural and urban areas is over 35 percent, (3) the annual rate of economic growth is consistently less than 3 percent, (4) population growth rates are 3 percent per year, (5) over 70 percent of the population is engaged in agricultural production, (6) there are few if any schools or hospitals easily accessible to the majority of the population, (7) houses are without running water and other sanitary facilities, (8) infant mortality rates are ten times those in the developed world, (9) life expectancies are 35 years for males and 42 years for females, and (10) millions of children suffering constantly from hunger and malnutrition?

From the following article, we can get some idea of what life is like in the developing world. By examining the life and daily existence of nine-year-old Enrique

Otero, the author allows us to understand the many dimensions of underdevelopment. The setting of Santiago, Chile, is interesting for several reasons. First, it exemplifies the nature of uneven development. Most developing nations have very backward agrarian areas and a few modern developed urban areas. This "dualism" is evidenced in Chile by the modern European atmosphere of Santiago contrasted with the poverty and squalor of the dirty and overcrowded slums on the periphery of the city. The second reason for the importance of Santiago, Chile, is that, in 1973, a military dictatorship overthrew the democratically elected Socialist President, Dr. Salvador Allende Gossens. Since 1973, the military junta has imposed harsh economic policies to counter excessively high rates of inflation. These policies affect all Chileans, especially those like Enrique Otero.

HOW LIFE SUBSISTS IN A CHILEAN SLUM

JONATHAN KANDELL

SANTIAGO, Chile, March 14—Enrique Otero makes his living by looking after the cars that are parked in front of a government ministry and hotel in downtown Santiago.

When a driver gets into his car, Enrique wipes the windshield with a dirty cloth, and thrusts his hand through the window hoping for a few pennies before the owner drives off.

The money is not enough to survive on, so Enrique strolls through the street market a few blocks away where the vendors give him overripe fruits because they know he will steal them anyway.

At night, he sleeps in alleyways or in the parks where the policemen and soldiers ignore him despite the night curfew that has been enforced throughout the country since the overthrow of the Marxist government two and a half years ago.

During these days of economic depression, there is nothing unusual here about Enrique's situation. Not even the fact that he is only nine years old.

For a year now, the right-wing military junta has been putting into effect an economic program it calls a "shock treatment." There have been sharp reductions in public spending and restrictions on bank credits aimed at restraining runaway inflation inherited from the government of the late President Salvador Allende Gossens.

But inflation has not slowed down. Last year it reached 340 percent, the highest in the world, and it climbed another 21 percent during the first two months of 1976.

At the same time, the austerity program has caused industrial production to drop precipitously. Unemployment in the greater Santiago area has risen to almost 20 percent—the highest level in more than 30 years—and malnutrition is widespread in working-class slums.

"My mother doesn't care whether I'm home or not," said Enrique without a trace of sentiment. "There is nothing to eat there anyway."

© 1976 by The New York Times Company. Reprinted by permission.

Home for Enrique is El Duraznal, a sprawling slum of wooden shacks and unpaved alleys much like the other shantytowns where about a fourth of greater Santiago's 3.5 million people live.

His father lost his job in a factory cutback about two years ago. After repeated drunken brawls with his wife and neighbors, Mr. Otero left home and has not been seen in months. Enrique's mother, Margarita Otero, ekes out a living for herself and two infant daughters by selling ice cream downtown.

"COULDN'T CONTROL ENRIQUE"

"I couldn't control Enrique," said Mrs. Otero. "The neighbors complained he was stealing. He was always running away. So I stopped looking for him. I have the other two to take care of."

Since both of the Otero girls are under six, they qualify for a church-sponsored food program for preschool children from working-class families with no steady income. But officials in the church program admit that only a fraction of the neediest families receive food, and that even children receiving the emergency rations continue to suffer from malnutrition.

Children above six years of age are supposed to be fed lunch in school. But in many shantytowns there is not enough food. So, alternately, half the students eat lunch while the rest are served tea and biscuits.

About a fourth of El Duraznal's 580 families have household heads who are unemployed. Some families have moved back to their native farm areas in search of easier access to food. But most have broken their ties with their rural relatives and find it impossible to abandon the city even in these hard times.

Despite the economic deterioration, there is little possibility of popular outburst or other form of protest. After the coup in 1973, the military government swept aside Marxist leaders and community organizations in the urban shantytowns and replaced them with appointed officials considered favorable to the junta.

---

1. In your opinion, what does the future hold for Enrique Otero? Compare your childhood experience at age nine with that of Enrique Otero.

Underdevelopment is truly a shocking phenomena. When one is placed in the midst of this human condition, it is impossible not to be stunned by the poverty, disease, and squalor so prevalent throughout the developing world. Indeed, as Denis Goulet, the author of *The Cruel Choice,* has said, "Chronic poverty is a cruel kind of hell."

Once one confronts the physical and objective conditions of underdevelopment, it is not long before the emotional and psychological factors become evident and imposing. Underdevelopment breeds impotence, hopelessness, and vulnerability. Yet, at the same time, it creates the preconditions for action, hope, and independent self-determination. As we shall see, to move from underdevelopment to development is a revolutionary and dialectical process.

Assuming that we have a general sense of what it means to be underdeveloped, what then does it mean to be developed? Western economists have traditionally preferred to view development strictly in economic terms. Thus a nation able to increase its GNP per capita would be able to improve its standard of living. This requires increasing GNP and curbing population growth. In most cases, economic development would be characterized by an evolutionary process through which the developing nation becomes more and more like the advanced developed nations in the Western world today.

In recent years, this simplistic linear thinking has come under attack. There are several reasons for this questioning of the traditional viewpoint. First, in the developed world today, there is little agreement as to what it means to be developed. In fact, some are putting forth the notion of "overdevelopment" when describing the advanced nations. This is in part related to the issues surrounding the "quality of life" as the material standard of living increases. Second, there is a growing awareness of the multidimensional nature of development. In this context, economic development cannot be viewed as coincident with social development. It is necessary to examine the other institutions and processes of change in order to fully understand and appreciate the development process. We must, also, carefully investigate the political, social, and cultural institutions related to economic development. This point of view is articulated by E. F. Schumacher, a British economist, in the following:

Economic development is something much wider and deeper than economics.... Its roots lie outside the economic sphere, in education, organisation, discipline and, beyond that, in political independence and a national consciousness of self-reliance. It cannot be "produced" by skillful grafting operations carried out by foreign technicians or an indigenous elite that has lost contact with the ordinary people. It can succeed only if it is carried forward as a broad, popular "movement of reconstruction" with primary emphasis on the full utilisation of the drive, enthusiasm, intelligence, and labour power of everyone. Success cannot be obtained by some form of magic produced by scientists, technicians, or economic planners. It can come only through a process of growth involving the education, organisation, and discipline of the whole population. Anything less than this must end in failure.

E. F. Schumacher, 1973. *Small Is Beautiful,* Harper & Row, pp. 192-193.

As we discuss the economic problems of developing nations, let us remember Schumacher's message and the human dimension of the subject. Also let us keep in mind the fact that, although we group the nations of the developing world together for the purpose of generalization, these nations are incredibly diverse. Their diversity is reflected in their geography, language, culture, customs, religion, political and social institutions, history, and natural resource endowments.

THE QUEST FOR ECONOMIC DEVELOPMENT

The quest for economic development by the Third World (Asia, Africa, and Latin America) is, as Goulet suggests, both "cruel and necessary" yet unavoidable. As we have noted, economic development has become synonymous with Western industrialization. For years, particularly during the 1960s (labeled the Development Decade by the United Nations), it was believed by most Western economists that the only way for a developing nation, or underdeveloped nation, to modernize was to follow the development model and experience of the now powerful and industrialized Western nations. The only real alternative to this model was the relatively new, yet impressive, model of socialism as practiced in the Soviet Union. However, the atrocities of Stalinist Russia and subsequent Cold-War tensions made most nations reluctant and skeptical of the Soviet model even though by the mid-1960s the liberalized planning and market system of the Soviet economy had demonstrated its ability to produce rapid industrialization.

Many developing nations by the late 1960s and early 1970s began to realize that their quest for economic development and modernization was beginning in a period quite different from those that produced the success stories of the U.S., Western Europe, and Japan. They have slowly come to the conclusion that this time period calls for a different strategy and a model more closely related to their own particular conditions and needs. It is important to recognize that they did not arrive at this conclusion overnight. It was reached after years of experience filled with trial and error and the failure to develop. Nevertheless, for those developing nations that have come to this conclusion, their present realities make it very difficult to change the course of history in midstream. On the other hand, there are some who are still committed to following the Western industrialized model.

As we saw in the last few chapters, in terms of international trade and finance the developing nations are having their share of problems in constructing a development model and strategy in a very competitive and often hostile interdependent global environment. In order to better understand their plight, let us now consider several crucial questions: (1) What is different about this particular historical epoch for the developing nations? (2) What basic problems and obstacles block them from achieving genuine economic development? (3) What are the basic economic schools of thought used to analyze their problems, and what policy prescriptions emanate from the different economic paradigms?

2. *Why* is it important for the developed world to understand the problems of the developing world?

THE MODERN CONTEXT FOR DEVELOPING

The developing nations are launching their development schemes at a critical historical juncture. The emerging global awareness of resource scarcity, especially with respect to energy, has cast a dark shadow on industrialization dreams in terms of Western affluence. (Of course, oil-exporting developing nations such as Venezuela face a different set of future options.) What is hard to accept is that development requiring high-cost energy and capital-intensive technology is just not possible for every nation. Availability and cost considerations prohibit the continued use of and reliance upon such methods of production in the long-term future. Second, developing nations begin their bid for modernization in a world with great disparities of wealth and power. In the world political economy, the developing nations are weak, fragile, vulnerable, and dependent vis-à-vis the advanced nations. A few nations have some leverage because of their control over scarce natural resources needed by the advanced nations, but most do not have this power. Finally, the developing nations, many of which were once the colonies or possessions of the advanced nations, cannot themselves gain colonies or possessions to supply them with the inexpensive labor and raw materials necessary for their own industrialization.

BASIC ECONOMIC PROBLEMS

Given these qualifying considerations, what then are the most important basic economic problems facing the developing nations? Over the past several years each and every international conference related to this broad topic has inevitably identified *five* areas of concern: (1) population growth and rates of economic growth; (2) the distribution of income; (3) inflation and unemployment; (4) balance of payments difficulties, unequal terms of trade, currency instability, and mounting debt problems; and (5) questions of external control and influence, and human rights. Let us look briefly at each one of these basic problems.

1. Population growth rates alone make the prospect of meaningful economic development difficult. With the population growth rates in many developing nations greater than 3 percent a year, it would require unprecedented rates of economic growth to make any progress whatsoever. For example, it would require a real GNP growth rate of 8 percent to achieve a net growth rate of 5 percent in GNP per capita if population growth were 3 percent a year. At present, many developing nations are experiencing real GNP growth rates of less than 2 percent a year. Against these empirical data, the future is indeed grim. It would appear that a successful population control effort is a must for most nations. The growth of population, in addition to influencing the economic growth rate, also puts great pressure on the cities as the rural-to-urban migration trends continue to result in overcrowded, congested, and polluted urban environments.

2. The distribution of income is a continuing problem for the developing nations. First, there is the problem of the growing gap between the developed and the developing nations in terms of income distribution. A recent U.N. study on the future of the world economy made the following point:

If the minimum targets of growth for the developing countries, as set by the International Development Strategy, were implemented continuously throughout the remaining decades of this century, and if the growth rates prevailing in the developed countries during the past two decades were to be retained in the future, then the gap in per-capita gross product between these two groups of countries, which was 12 to 1 on the average in 1970, would not start diminishing even by the year 2000.

In addition to this growing "gap" between the rich and poor nations, there is the problem of *internal* unequal distribution of income. The economic growth that has taken place has resulted in a highly unequal distribution of income and wealth such that the bottom 60 percent of the population has not benefited at all from this growth. In fact, it is the top 20 percent of the population in most developing nations that accumulates the income and wealth produced.

3. Added to the problems of population and income distribution are the problems of inflation and unemployment. Inflation has resulted in a declining standard of living and currency instability. It is not uncommon to see rates of inflation in developing nations ranging from 25 to 300 percent a year.

Accompanying the high inflation and sluggish growth rates is the problem of unemployment. Unemployment in most developing nations ranges from 15 to 40 percent. This problem is exacerbated by the concentrated nature of the urban population. Thus Mexico City with a population of ten million can have an unemployment rate of 35 percent.

4. The problems of international trade and finance are many. Highly unequal terms of trade and commodity price instability typically result in balance-of-payments difficulties. These balance-of-payments problems then trigger off foreign exchange and currency instability problems. Sooner or later, the developing nation out of desperation is forced to borrow money from any one of a number of sources (International Monetary Fund, World Bank, Agency for International Development, Export–Import Bank, private banks and financial institutions, etc.). This act of borrowing creates a debt burden for the developing nation. This process initiates a "vicious circle" that effectively makes the development effort more and more difficult. With the added burden of the OPEC price increase in 1973, the nations that do not export oil will have increased their combined debt to over $180 billion by 1978. Experts are now debating the possibility and consequences of defaults on these debts on the international financial system.

5. The last of the five basic problems is the issue of external control, influence, and human rights. A truly frustrating and contradictory dilemma exists for any developing nation today. It is impossible to attain economic development in isolation. Like it or not, global interdependence is a reality. Most nations admit that they need help in many ways from other nations. Yet, assistance in whatever form is difficult to receive without also accepting some degree of external control and influence. Ideally, most nations would like to solicit assistance in a form and manner consistent with their goals of independence, autonomy, and self-determination. The reality is certainly far from this ideal. Given the nature of the major international financial institutions, nation-states and their nationalistic behaviors, multinational corporations, global technology, communications systems, etc., the possibility of interacting with others without being controlled and influenced by the others becomes almost impossible. The most recent evidence of this is the "Human Rights" issue. There is great pressure on the major Western nations and their institutions that deal with the developing nations not to grant aid or loans to nations that "vio-

late basic human rights." Some developing nations such as Argentina, Brazil, and Chile have reacted strongly against this kind of political leverage by the Western nations.

These, then, are a few of the major issues and problems currently facing the developing world. How do economists from different schools of thought analyze these problems?

---

3. Given this host of problems, do you think the developing countries will be able to develop? Why or why not?

COMPETING VIEWS OF UNDERDEVELOPMENT: THE DIFFUSION, STRUCTURALIST, AND DEPENDENCY MODELS

The Diffusion Model

The diffusion model most closely represents the orthodox or mainstream economic school of thought. It posits at the outset the following crucial assumptions: (1) progress is related to the spread of modernism to backward, archaic, and traditional areas; (2) the primary catalyst for development is the diffusion of advanced technology and foreign capital from the advanced nations to the developing nations, for example, through MNCs; (3) underdevelopment is a condition that all nations have experienced; (4) traditional cultural and behavioral values need to be transformed into modern cultural and behavioral values; (5) economic development means essentially industrialization and diversification; (6) economic development requires political stability and limited government; and (7) the process of economic development is a gradual evolutionary process.

How does the diffusion model *explain* the phenomenon of underdevelopment? Diffusion theorists maintain that the developing nations are underdeveloped because:

1. They lack sufficient educational systems to provide their citizens with the basic literacy and skills necessary to cope with modern technology.
2. They lack effective systems of contraception and the proper modernized cultural values and behaviors conducive to the mass acceptance and widespread use of birth control methods to limit population growth.
3. They lack efficient government and general administrative systems to efficiently manage and implement proper development programs.
4. They lack the ability to produce the levels of agricultural output necessary to generate a sizeable economic surplus for capital accumulation and investment in order to sponsor the growth of the industrial sector.
5. They lack the proper economic policies that would allow them to solve their problems of slow growth rates, high inflation, high unemployment, balance of payments deficits, currency instability, and debt.
6. They experience too much internal political instability and social unrest.

Basically, the diffusion model claims that the developing nations lack (1) capital, (2) technical knowledge, and (3) the proper cultural perspective. It is usually further argued that the institutions of capitalism—private gain, private property, markets, and individualism—will be best capable of creating economic development.

The Structuralist Model

A second school of thought on development evolved in the 1960s during the United Nations Development Decade. This school was pioneered by Raul Prébisch, an economist with the United Nations' Economic Commission on Latin America.

This model argues that the lack of development in the Third World (particularly Latin America) is due to "structural" deficiencies of the capitalist-oriented economic systems of the developing world. The capitalist diffusion model does not deal with what Prébisch and others felt were the fundamental obstacles to development such as: (1) the inefficient systems of land tenure in the agricultural sector, (2) the excessive reliance on a mono-crop economy, and (3) the concentration of economic wealth and power in the hands of elite classes, resulting in the persistent unequal distribution of income.

The structuralist model rejects the analysis of the diffusion model. For example, as Prébisch points out, the diffusion model implies that specialization and division of labor should form the basis of exchange between nations such that all nations tend to benefit by trading with one another. The question remains, why is it that advanced nations are supplied with raw materials at low prices and, in return, the developing nations receive capital and manufactured goods at high prices. Commodity pricing and the unequal terms of trade are basic issues analyzed in the structuralist model.

The structuralist model also questions the capitalist diffusion model's reliance upon the market system to meet the needs of the developing nation's economy. Given the unequal distribution of income and wealth, the insufficiency of supply compared to demand, and the luxury consumption of the elite classes, the uncritical reliance on the market system to allocate and distribute goods and services equitably is totally incomprehensible. The structuralists argue that the use of the free-market mechanism, given these institutionalized imperfections, becomes irrational in the context of the developing world.

The most important contribution from the structuralist model is that economic theories developed in advanced nations should not be blindly transferred to the developing nations, each of which has its own unique problems.

To conclude, the structuralist model would like to see the capitalist diffusion model reformed. If the structural constraints were removed, then the unfettered diffusion model would be an excellent development strategy for the developing nation. This would require, among other things, major land reform, the redistribution of income and wealth, the diversification of production, commodity price stability and equality, and a variation of orthodox economic policies designed specifically for the needs of the developing nations.

Uneven development: Mexican affluence. (Photograph by Steve Stamos.)

The Dependency Model

By dependence we mean a situation in which the economy of certain countries is conditioned by the development and expansion of another economy to which the former is subjected. The relation of interdependence between two or more economies, and between these and world trade, assumes the form of dependence when some countries (the dominant ones) can expand and can be self-sustaining, while other countries (the dependent ones) can do this only as a reflection of that expansion, which can have either positive or negative effect on their immediate development.

Theotonio Dos Santos

The dependency model was developed out of the analysis of underdevelopment in Latin America. However, its proponents believe that the model also has general applicability for the rest of the developing world. As general dissatisfaction increased over the inability of the "structuralist" school to explain the continuing stagnation and uneven development throughout the 1960s, radical economists developed this model as a modern Marxist model of imperialism. What made this model a more relevant extension of the original imperialist model was the inclusion of a concrete analysis of the multinational corporation and major international financial institutions as the major vehicles of modern imperialism.

The dependency model is based upon a number of essential assumptions and postulates. They are as follows:

1. Underdevelopment is not an original state from which every country begins its quest for development.

2. Contemporary underdevelopment has been "created" by the process of global capitalist development and expansion.

3. The economies of the developing nations have been integrated into and shaped by the needs of the advanced nations' economies, such that the developing nations become "dependent" upon the advanced nations.

4. This dependency is created by foreign penetration of the developing nation's banking system, manufacturing sector, retailing sector, communications system, advertising, and educational sector.

5. The developing nation's economic surplus is systematically drained out of the nation and is transferred to the advanced nations.

6. Foreign investment by the multinational corporation in particular is the primary vehicle for the penetration of the economy and the extraction or appropriation of the economic surplus. Foreign investment may increase the GNP but results in the outward flow of capital, foreign control of the internal economy, and investment decisions made according to the criteria of profitability rather than domestic employment and production needs.

7. As the conditions of uneven development and dependency deepen, the developing nation is forced to seek aid, grants, and loans from international financial institutions, governments, and private lending agencies. This process eventually puts the developing nation into the situation of being controlled by outside institutions while becoming more and more dependent as debts mount because of excessive borrowing to pay off current debts and finance future development projects.

8. Dependency theorists claim that "authentic" development and the elimination of the state of underdevelopment requires the elimination of foreign capital and penetration, and the creation of Democratic Socialism. This will allow for the following: economic sovereignty, production and distribution of basic necessities according to the needs of the people, the production and use of the economic surplus for continued authentic development and social and political equality.*

---

4. **In the light of these brief sketches of the schools of thought on underdevelopment, which seems most helpful to you in understanding underdevelopment? Why?**

---

*See Ron Chilcote and Joel Edelstein, *Latin America: The Struggle with Dependency and Beyond*, Schocken, New York, 1974, Part I.

Uneven development: Mexican poverty. (Photograph by Steve Stamos.)

THE FUTURE OF THE DEVELOPING NATIONS

Making prognostications about the future of the developing world is not an easy task. Certainly, it would be easy either to speak optimistically or to speak of obstacles and impossibilities. We shall for the moment do neither. It is our feeling that some optimism and some skepticism is not only warranted but necessary and healthy in order to develop a rational and mature perspective.

In our minds, we observe a world fraught with complex changes being brought about by a myriad of forces all interacting simultaneously. It is possible to say that the developing nations are fast approaching a truly unique historical watershed. Out of this apparent chaos is emerging a "new awareness" evidenced in recent years by the repeated demands on behalf of the leaders of the developing world for a New International Economic Order. The people of the developing world, while certainly not united in their stands on such issues, nevertheless share a common belief that one day they will have a future characterized by authentic development defined in their own terms. What this future will be and what role a New International Economic Order will play in it is mere conjecture at this time. Nevertheless, the dialogue going on now between the industrialized nations and the Third World must be examined in more detail. It is to this task that we now turn.

The Call for a New International Economic Order (NIEO)

The developing nations have come increasingly to realize that the international economic system based upon the principles of free trade and the international division of labor has resulted in an unequal distribution of total global wealth. They perceive the nature of their present integration into the global economy as being detrimental to their dreams of genuine development. This position of inequality and dependency has been viewed as intolerable and unacceptable. The developing world is no longer willing to acquiesce to a system in which it sees no hope for the future.

The increasing collective consciousness of the nonaligned developing nations in the late 1960s and early 1970s produced extensive debate and dialogue centered on the need for a global restructuring of the international economic and financial systems. These discussions resulted in the Sixth Special Session of the United Nations in April of 1974. At this session of the U.N. General Assembly two resolutions were drafted and adopted. The first called for the establishment of a New International Economic Order. The second resolution outlined a Programme of Action to bring about the creation of the New International Economic Order.

With these actions, the Group of 77 (the developing nations) evidenced a new global posture vis-à-vis the developed world. They substituted "defiance for the deference of the past."

On December 12, 1974, at the regularly scheduled 29th Session of the U.N. General Assembly, the call for an NIEO was reaffirmed in the adoption of the "Charter of Economic Rights and Duties of States." Later in 1975 the U.N. called for the "full and complete economic emancipation" of the developing world.

The following article is the May 1, 1974, "Declaration of the U.N. General Assembly on the Establishment of a New International Economic Order."

DECLARATION ON THE ESTABLISHMENT OF A NEW INTERNATIONAL ECONOMIC ORDER

We, the Members of the United Nations,

Having convened a special session of the General Assembly to study for the first time the problems of raw materials and development, devoted to the consideration of the most important economic problems facing the world community,

Bearing in mind the spirit, purposes and principles of the Charter of the United Nations to promote the economic advancement and social progress of all peoples,

Solemnly proclaim our united determination to work urgently for THE ESTABLISHMENT OF A NEW INTERNATIONAL ECONOMIC ORDER based on equity, sovereign equality, interdependence, common interest and co-operation among all States, irrespective of their economic and social systems which shall correct inequalities and redress existing injustices, make it possible to eliminate the widening gap between the developed and the developing countries and ensure steadily accelerating economic and social development and peace and justice for present and future generations, and, to that end, declare:

1. The greatest and most significant achievement during the last decades has been the independence from colonial and alien domination of a large number of peoples and nations which has enabled them to become members of the community of free peoples. Technological progress has also been made in all spheres of economic activities in the last three decades, thus providing a solid potential for improving the well-being of all peoples. However, the remaining vestiges of alien and colonial domination, foreign occupation, racial discrimination, *apartheid* and neo-colonialism in all its forms continue to be among the greatest obstacles to the full emancipation and progress of the developing countries and all the peoples involved. The benefits of technological progress are not shared equitably by all members of the international community. The developing countries, which constitute 70 percent of the world's population, account for only 30 percent of the world's income. It has proved impossible to achieve an even and balanced development of the international community under the existing international economic order. The gap between the developed and the developing countries continues to widen in a system which was established at a time when most of the developing countries did not even exist as independent States and which perpetuates inequality.

2. The present international economic order is in direct conflict with current developments in international political and economic relations. Since 1970, the world economy has experienced a series of grave crises which have had severe repercussions, especially on the developing countries because of their generally greater vulnerability to external economic impulses. The developing world has become a powerful factor that makes its influence felt in all fields of international activity. These irreversible changes in the relationship of forces in the world necessitate the active, full and equal participation of the developing countries in the formulation and application of all decisions that concern the international community.

3. All these changes have thrust into prominence the reality of interdependence of all the members of the world community. Current events have brought into sharp focus the realization that the interests of the developed countries and those of the developing countries can no longer be isolated from each other, that there is a close interrelationship between the prosperity of the developed countries and the growth and development of the developing countries, and that the prosperity of the international community as a whole depends upon the prosperity of its constituent parts. International co-operation for development is the shared goal and common duty of all countries. Thus the political, economic and social well-being of present and future generations depends more than ever on co-operation between all the members of the international community on the basis of sovereign equality and the removal of the dis-equilibrium that exists between them.

4. The new international economic order should be founded on full respect for the following principles:

(a) Sovereign equality of States, self-determination of all peoples, inadmissibility of the acquisition of territories by force, territorial integrity and non-interference in the internal affairs of other States;

(b) The broadest co-operation of all the States members of the international community, based on equity, whereby the prevailing disparities in the world may be banished and prosperity secured for all;

(c) Full and effective participation on the basis of equality of all countries in the solving of world economic problems in the common interest of all countries, bearing in mind the necessity to ensure the accelerated development of all the developing countries, while devoting particular attention to the adoption of special measures in favour of the least developed, land-locked and island developing countries as well as those developing countries most seriously affected by economic crises and natural calamities, without losing sight of the interests of other developing countries;

(d) The right of every country to adopt the economic and social system that it deems the most appropriate for its own development and not to be subjected to discrimination of any kind as a result;

(e) Full permanent sovereignty of every State over its natural resources and all economic activities. In order to safeguard these resources, each State is entitled to exercise effective control over them and their exploitation with means suitable to its own situation, including the right to nationalization or transfer of ownership to its nationals, this right being an expression of the full permanent sovereignty of the State. No State may be subjected to economic, political or any other type of coercion to prevent the free and full exercise of this inalienable right;

(f) The right of all States, territories and peoples under foreign occupation, alien and colonial domination or *apartheid* to restitution and full compensation for the exploitation and depletion of, and damages to, the natural resources and all other resources of those States, territories and peoples;

(g) Regulation and supervision of the activities of transnational corporations by taking measures in the interest of the national economies of the countries where such transnational corporations operate on the basis of the full sovereignty of those countries;

(h) The right of the developing countries and the peoples of territories under colonial and racial domination and foreign occupation to achieve their liberation and to regain effective control over their natural resources and economic activities;

(i) The extending of assistance to developing countries, peoples and territories which are under colonial and alien domination, foreign occupation, racial discrimination or *apartheid* or are subjected to economic, political or any other type of coercive measures to obtain from them the subordination of the exercise of their sovereign rights and to secure from them advantages of any kind, and to neo-colonialism in all its forms, and which have established or are endeavouring to establish effective control over their natural resources and economic activities that have been or are still under foreign control;

(j) Just and equitable relationship between the prices of raw materials, primary commodities, manufactured and semi-manufactured goods, exported by developing countries and the prices of raw materials, primary commodities, manufactures, capital goods and equipment imported by them with the aim of bringing about sustained improvement in their unsatisfactory terms of trade and the expansion of the world economy;

(k) Extension of active assistance to developing countries by the whole international community, free of any political or military conditions;

(l) Ensuring that one of the main aims of the reformed international monetary system shall be the promotion of the development of the developing countries and the adequate flow of real resources to them;

(m) Improving the competitiveness of natural materials facing competition from synthetic substitutes;

(n) Preferential and non-reciprocal treatment for developing countries, wherever feasible, in all fields of international economic co-operation whenever possible;

(o) Securing favourable conditions for the transfer of financial resources to developing countries;

(p) Giving to the developing countries access to the achievements of modern science and technology, and promoting the transfer of technology and the creation of indigenous technology for the benefit of the developing countries in forms and in accordance with procedures which are suited to their economies;

(q) The need for all States to put an end to the waste of natural resources, including food products;

(r) The need for developing countries to concentrate all their resources for the cause of development;

(s) The strengthening, through individual and collective actions, of mutual economic, trade, financial and technical co-operation among the developing countries, mainly on a preferential basis;

(t) Facilitating the role which producers' associations may play within the framework of international co-operation and, in pursuance of their aims, *inter alia* assisting in the promotion of sustained growth of the world economy and accelerating the development of developing countries.

5. The unanimous adoption of the International Development Strategy for the Second United Nations Development Decade was an important step in the promotion of international economic co-operation on a just and equitable basis. The accelerated implementation of obligations and commitments assumed by the international community within the framework of the Strategy, particularly those concerning imperative development needs of developing countries, would contribute significantly to the fulfilment of the aims and objectives of the present Declaration.

6. The United Nations as a universal organization should be capable of dealing with problems of international economic co-operation in a comprehensive manner and ensuring equally the interests of all countries. It must have an even greater role in the establishment of a new international economic order. The Charter of Economic Rights and Duties of States, for the preparation of which the present Declaration will provide an additional source of inspiration, will constitute a significant contribution in this respect. All the States Members of the United Nations are therefore called upon to exert maximum efforts with a view to securing the implementation of the present Declaration, which is one of the principal guarantees for the creation of better conditions for all peoples to reach a life worthy of human dignity.

7. The present Declaration on the Establishment of a New International Economic Order shall be one of the most important bases of economic relations between all peoples and all nations.

2229th plenary meeting
1 May 1974

---

5. What is your reaction to this U.N. document? Are there parts with which you disagree? parts with which you agree? Why?

6. *Should* the U.S. support the creation of a New International Economic Order? Do you think it *will*?

In the following article, "Helping Others—and Ourselves," Peter G. Peterson, a former Secretary of Commerce, attempts to outline seven crucial concepts with which, he claims, Americans must be confronted "before America can play any durable and credible role in shaping a New International Economic Order."

HELPING OTHERS—AND OURSELVES

PETER G. PETERSON

Before America can play any durable and credible role in shaping a New International Economic Order, I believe we must meet head-on our popular indifference to aid to the underdeveloped world. This can be accomplished only if we move toward an approach that encompasses, among others, some of the following concepts:

1. A set of understandable and achievable long-term goals—what is it we are trying to do and by when?
Our immediate goal should focus on helping the underdeveloped countries generate sufficient internal productive capacity so that *they* can lift their poorest people to subsistence levels of food, shelter and health; still, in 1976, only slightly more than one-quarter of our bilateral aid went to the least-developed countries. But it should be clear how we help ourselves as we help others help themselves; for example, increasing the supply of resources abroad reduces inflation everywhere.

2. Aid—with conditions
We and our developed partners should make clear that we will act only if the third-world countries take specific measures, as indeed must we, to make that aid effective—for example, to expand their food production, to moderate their population growth, to distribute income and social services much more effectively to the poor, and to increase their internal savings rate.

For us, conditional aid that stimulates performance has become imperative, but to the governing elites of developing countries it may seem an intrusion. If so, let us be the ones to put a generous but tough-minded offer of aid on the table. Then, let the elites in those countries tell us—and their impoverished peoples—that meeting these minimum human needs is less central than protesting such alleged intrusions—or buying weapons.

3. Greater reliance on neutral multilateral institutions
Most Americans prefer traditional bilateral aid so as to assure more leverage, more attention to the year's political hot spots, and full, visible credit. However, neutral and rehabilitated multilateral mechanisms provide perhaps the only chance to impose essential conditions without creating constant bilateral political crises. (Up to now, human rights issues have been unilateral or bilateral, almost necessarily so. To integrate them into a fragile set of multilateral economic institutions might overload the circuit.)

4. A reciprocal system of mutual sanctions and mutual benefits
What is essential is a commitment by both sides to a new, comprehensive, reciprocal contract. We can offer more open access to our markets for their processed and manufactured goods, as well as access to our private and official technological and

© 1977 by the New York Times Company. Reprinted by permission.

monetary capital, if fairly treated. The developing countries provide us more secure access to resources, labor and markets.

The rules of unacceptable behavior must apply equally to both sides. We must be as ready as others to accept penalties if we take unilateral action in the form, for example, of export controls on soybeans.

5. A new simplicity

We could take a lesson from our own domestic welfare programs, in which too much complexity leads to corruption, waste and contradictions. For example, some of the international commodity proposals have the perverse effect of making some of the richest countries in the North richer and some of the poorest countries in the South poorer. In this vein, a New International Economic Order may inflict on us a huge international bureaucratic Parkinsonism. Thus, I am attracted to the simpler income-maintenance programs—both abroad and at home.

6. New money

Financial support by annual appropriation has either been decreasing (United States aid, at 0.25 percent of the gross national product, is at half the rate it once was and near the bottom of the list of industrialized countries) or gyrating, as have the decisions as to where the money should go. Yet, continuity and credibility are essential to the effectiveness of long-term development programs.

We should also tap new forms of "revenue sharing" that do not depend on the vagaries of the world economy or domestic politics: a tax on international resources (for example, the sale of seabed minerals), or a levy on world trade, travel, fishing, telecommunications or other activities from which nations now derive international benefits. The vast Organization of Petroleum Countries surpluses are also a vital source.

Finally, we might propose to the Soviet Union, and others, that we mutually share with the underdeveloped countries, through multilateral institutions, some of the billions that an effective disarmament agreement could yield. Such an offer might also generate some third-world pressure on lagging disarmament efforts, including their own.

7. New leadership

What we need first is conceptual leadership goals, priorities, an integrated strategy and a consolidated budget. Some still argue for "eclectic incrementalism"—an issue-by-issue or even conference by conference approach, to the current New International Economic Order negotiations. Still, what has 25 years of this produced?

We need even more: We need political leadership, with a vision of the future far beyond one's term of office; we need to mobilize our people against an enemy that is not a person or a nation. Jean Monnet put it simply: "We must attack our problems instead of each other."

American humanitarianism must be tapped, but it should not be abused. With a coherent and tough-minded approach, only the President can persuade us that a fair sharing of these burdens is in everyone's interest, that it has a good chance of working. And only the President can decide how much of his political capital he wants to spend on this immensely difficult, but equally rewarding task.

---

7. Do you agree or disagree with Peterson? Why?
8. Which of the seven concepts do you feel to be the most important? Why?

9. How does Peterson's analysis fit the NIEO as described by the original declaration? Is he consistent or inconsistent with its stated goals and objectives?

DIVERSE MODELS OF DEVELOPMENT

The demands for the NIEO and the response of the developed countries to these demands will undoubtedly affect the future of the world economy and the fate of the developing countries. Yet, in the global context of political-economic power realities and increased militance on the part of the Third World, it is important to understand the many unique forms of development approaches that are presently being constructed and implemented by the developing nations.

What is clear from these emerging development models is that the "classic" models of United States capitalism and Soviet socialism are no longer perceived as the ideal type of models to be emulated. We have only to look at countries such as Sweden, Norway, Great Britain, Yugoslavia, Mexico, Brazil, Chile, Venezuela, Cuba, Nigeria, South Africa, Tanzania, Egypt, India, Japan, and China in order to appreciate the diversity of economic system variants already operational around the globe.

The following brief articles demonstrate the diversity among nations undergoing economic transformation. First we will examine the current situations in Tanzania and Brazil. And, to conclude, we will examine in some detail the development model of the People's Republic of China.

Kaufman's article describes the general philosophy and operation of Tanzania's model "ujamaa" village of Chamwino. The "ujamaa" village concept has been the keystone to President Julius Nyerere's ten-year-old experiment in creating a non-Marxist socialism in this East African country of 16 million people.

TANZANIA HOPES MODEL VILLAGE WILL INSPIRE GROWTH OF OTHERS

MICHAEL T. KAUFMAN

CHAMWINO, Tanzania—Amid recurrent reports of shortages and unemployment in the cities, this rural cooperative village and others like it sustain the vision of a socialist, egalitarian and self-sufficient Tanzania.

It is the showpiece and model of ujamaa—the Swahili word meaning familyhood, or self-help, and the basis for the concept of establishing collective agrarian settlements. This is the basis of President Julius K. Nyerere's original program for the transformation of his nation.

Here on a hot semiarid plain, 664 families have gathered together, each with its own house and two- or three-acre garden. There is a school, a clinic, a church and

© 1977 by The New York Times Company. Reprinted by permission.

vast communal fields where cash crops are raised. There is electricity and even a telephone.

"Do not get the wrong idea," said Raymond Sangiwa, the district development director for the area at the heart of the country some 300 miles west of Dar es Salaam. "This is not typical of our 9000 villages. This is a model. Mwalimu [a term meaning teacher that is used as an honorific for President Nyerere] has come here and worked in the fields. The Government has invested a good deal in this village, but it has shown the other less-advanced villages what can be done."

FAMILIES WERE DRAWN TOGETHER

What has been done in the four years since the village was organized is impressive. Wagogo tribesmen, who traditionally lived scattered throughout the area at the mercy of an irregular rainfall, assembled here. At first they built their low flat-roofed mud and stick homes and marked off gardens.

Peter Chrysologus, the head of the village school and the secretary of the 25-man village council that governs here, pointed out that many of those huts had already given way to brick houses financed by government loans obtained by the village.

He said that in keeping with the philosophy of ujamaa, agriculture is the basis of life here. Each family is free to cultivate its two-acre or three-acre plot in any way it chooses. "They can grow what they wish and they can keep the harvest or sell their surplus," Mr. Chrysologus said.

"In addition, each family contributes three days' labor a week on the communal fields," he said. "The village council determines what shall be planted and how the yield is to be used. Some of it is obviously sold to the state buying agencies, other parts are stored for times of shortages."

PROFITS FINANCE COMMUNITY PROJECTS

Mr. Chrysologus, a gentle man who bears a strong resemblance to Mr. Nyerere, said the money raised by the cash crops is reinvested in community projects. This year there have been 11 projects, including a small poultry operation, the raising of pigs, a cooperative store and a workshop that makes doors and window frames.

Work assignments for the projects are made by the village council, and according to villagers there is no appeal from these decisions. But there is no sign that people are dissatisfied. Far from it. During the three-hour visit, residents gave every indication of being much better off than they ever had been and of knowing it.

Women, who recalled walking hours each day to fill gourds and oil cans with water, often murky water, now have taps just a few yards from their houses. Each house eventually is to be connected to a water system that draws from underground sources.

Such things are hard to quantify in the endless statistics used by government economists and international agencies trying to gauge the progress of Tanzania's experiment. The school, the clinic and the store, though rudimentary by Western standards, represent revolutionary changes here.

When he first outlined his road to a non-Marxist socialism 10 years ago, President Nyerere wrote in an essay:

"Until we have changed our way of living in the rural areas, we have changed nothing in Tanzania. We have a lot of land; our people are scattered and this is very difficult for development. It would be much easier for development, using the limited resources that we have, if people were living in compact communities.

"There is this movement to live in villages. This we would have done, socialism or no socialism. There is bound to be an inertia; many people prefer to be left alone. We are not going to leave them alone."

In fact, there have been relatively few reported instances of duress in the village program. Some huts have been burned. But as one observer put it, "Tanzania's blessing is that the lack of administrative skills and institutional discipline, which often creates difficulties, also prevents Stalinist excesses."

JOINT EFFORT IS EXPECTED TO EVOLVE

Nine million of the country's 16 million people now live in villages. In most, people live together but work alone, tilling their own plots. The premise is, however, that the people living next to each other will grow to realize the benefit of cooperative ventures.

Together, said Mr. Sangiwa, the district development director, "they can rent a tractor for a day, which they could never do on their own."

The so-called ujamaa villages have three stages of development. The village of Chamwino is said by government officials to be in the third and final stage toward full self-sufficiency and self-rule. "Soon," said Mr. Sangiwa, "the Government will give the village a certificate of occupancy, which will mean simply that they are on their own."

Another ujamaa village is a few miles down a dusty road from Chamwino. It is called Chamangali No. 2. It is in the first phase of development and, according to government officials, is much more representative of most villages. It has no electricity, no new houses, and no community center.

A BEGINNING HAS BEEN MADE

But there is a bore hole and a few centrally located water taps. As in Chamwino, most livestock is privately held, but there is a small collective herd. There are both village fields and private holdings. The village council of 25, which includes three women, has started a small scantily stocked shop. The school goes only to the third grade, but for many of the villagers it is the first schooling their children have had.

"The people here know what they have done in Chamwino," said a district official. "They would like to do the same. We may be socialists, but that is the competition we want. We want each village to have pride in itself and to feel it can be better, more productive, than any other."

---

10. Critically evaluate the philosophy and operation of the working model "ujamaa" village of Chamwino?

11. What do you find consistent and inconsistent about using "profits" to finance community projects in a socialist country like Tanzania?

12. From the brief description of the Tanzanian development plan given in this article, what would Tanzania like to see for itself come out of the creation of a New International Economic Order?

Brazil in the past ten years has been somewhat of a paradox for Western economic observers. From 1968 to 1974, Brazil was heralded over the globe as being the "Brazilian Miracle." She exhibited annual rates of growth over this time period of 10 percent per year. Yet, the growth rate was colored by the presence of a series of military dictatorships prone to the use of political repression. Nevertheless, in recent years the "Brazilian Miracle" has gone bust and the country is being suffocated under a mountain of debt now estimated at $30 billion. In order to control this situation and revive the image of prosperity, Brazil has engaged in unprecedented state intervention in the economy. Indeed, Brazil has become one of the most formidable state capitalist nations in South America. This new departure had been met with vocal criticism by members of the private business sector and foreign multinational corporations.

BRAZIL REGIME WIDENING STATE ECONOMIC CONTROL

JONATHAN KANDELL

RIO DE JANEIRO, April 10—Twelve years after the armed forces took power with a strong commitment to save and expand private enterprise, Brazil appears well on the road to creating the most successful and pervasive system of state capitalism in South America.

By some estimates, the participation of the state in the economy has equaled the levels reached in Chile under the late President Salvador Allende Gossens, in Argentina under the Peronists or in Peru under its leftist military government.

And in contrast to those floundering economic models, Brazil has evolved a skilled group of government technocrats directing ever larger and more numerous state concerns whose efficiency and profitability at times rival or surpass private enterprises.

GROWING STATE CONTROL

The phenomenon of growing state economic control under an avowedly conservative government has occurred even though virtually all Brazilian political leaders—from President Ernesto Geisel down to Cabinet ministers and technocrats—continue to reaffirm the nation's commitment to private enterprise.

But not a day goes by without an acerbic newspaper editorial, accusations by leading businessmen and strong rebuttals from government officials on the regime's intention to expand giant state concerns.

© 1977 by The New York Times Company. Reprinted by permission.

"Why not admit that we are confronting one of the gravest threats Brazilian society has ever faced?" *O Estado de São Paulo,* the leading newspaper, asked in an editorial. "During these last ten years we have verified a real escalation of statism without precedent in the history of the country and comparable only to socialist states."

Virtually every major business and industrial association has expressed similar fears during recent months.

The controversy has drawn attention from business and government circles in the United States, Western Europe and Latin America that have looked upon Brazil as a fortress of private enterprise among developing nations and as a successful alternative to populist and Marxist models of economic growth. . . .

The debate has gathered force as the economy has entered a period of the greatest uncertainty in a decade. The seven years from 1968 through 1974 produced the "Brazilian miracle" with 10 percent annual increases in national growth, but the boom has ended because rising oil prices and the recent world recession have slowed down the country's export-oriented economy.

Conservative businessmen and their political allies are concerned that state enterprises are better prepared than private companies to withstand the inflation and economic contraction now under way.

A PRIME EXAMPLE

Perhaps the prime example of the trend towards government enterprises in the heartland of Latin American capitalism is the state-owned Companhia Vale do Rio Doce.

With 21,500 employees, the company is a giant even by standards of concerns in industrialized countries. It is the world's largest exporter of iron ore. Its ten fully owned subsidiaries are also involved in shipping, reforestation, marketing, engineering consulting, geological prospecting, and mining.

Its various joint ventures with European, American, and Japanese companies include metal-pelletizing plants, bauxite and aluminum production, pulp manufacture and an iron-ore project in the northern Brazilian jungles that is being touted as the world's biggest mining development at an estimated cost of $2.7 billion.

In 1975 the company's foreign billings totaled $611 million, with net profits showing a striking 39 percent increase over 1974. The company accounted for more than 10 percent of Brazil's total exports last year.

SEEKS MONEY ABROAD

As its president, Fernando Roquette Reis, pointed out, Companhia Vale do Rio Doce is also the first Brazilian concern to venture into the international stock market, issuing debentures last year worth $25 million, which were quickly bought up in West Germany. This year, the company will issue debentures in the United States and Japan.

"We are going to need fabulous quantities of money," Mr. Roquette Reis said confidently. "We are not so foolish as to think that the internal market is capable of supplying us with these resources."

For the next five years, the company has budgeted investments of $10 billion. This represents about 10 percent of the total investment in the Brazilian economy.

There is no consensus on just how large a role the government now has in the economy. According to a study released this year by Mackenzie University in São Paulo, the government has increased its share of total investment in the economy from 15 percent at the end of World War II to 50 percent today. Other estimates by business and academic groups range from 40 to 60 percent.

CONTROL OVER CREDIT

The government's role in the economy has been mainly in basic industries and services such as electric power generation, petroleum, railroads, communications and public utilities. But there has recently been a sharp growth of government participation in manufacturing. The state also exercises enormous control over savings and credit.

The state enterprises are staffed with executives drawn from both the public and private sectors. Salaries and other perquisites—including chauffeured cars, large expense accounts and sumptuous housing, often with swimming pools—for top officers equal and often surpass those offered by private companies.

At Companhia Vale do Rio Doce, the directors reportedly receive basic salaries of $5000 to $6000 a month. The directors of Petrobras, the state oil monopoly, draw annual incomes and fringe benefits as high as $225,000 each.

"Between salaries and other benefits, the directors of public enterprises have emerged as a privileged product of the high degree of nationalization of the Brazilian economy," *Jornal do Brasil,* a leading daily, said in a recent editorial.

BEYOND PRIVATE RESOURCES

The main reason advanced to explain the extraordinary expansion of state enterprises is that they have entered areas that were beyond the financial and organizational resources of Brazilian private companies.

"We are involved in projects that require the building of hydroelectric plants, hotels, houses, churches, and even jails," Mr. Roquette Reis told a group of leading private industrialists in São Paulo last week. "Besides that, we have to attract engineers and specialized technicians to regions like the Amazon by paying them three times as much as they would make in São Paulo or Rio. What private national firm could make this sort of investment?"

"I am not a defender of a state takeover of the economy," Mr. Roquette Reis added. "But I believe that there are sectors and activities where only public enterprises can go in."

The controversy over state enterprises has uncovered a deep vein of criticism against private Brazilian capital, not only among government officials but also by businessmen themselves.

In Brazil and elsewhere in Latin America local businessmen tend to invest their money in projects with low risks and quick returns. Real estate in particular has been one of the favored outlets for Brazilian private capital throughout the recent boom years.

The luxury high-rise apartments along Rio's Ipanema and Copacabana beaches, in São Paulo, Salvador and every major city may be more lasting monuments to Brazilian private capital than factories, mining and agricultural projects.

Brazil's private companies are also criticized for their conservatism in management, organization and finance. Many companies have continued as family-owned or family-controlled enterprises, fearful of losing their grip by expanding their number of stockholders or participating in joint ventures.

Faced with increasing competition, other Brazilian concerns have chosen to sell out to foreign investors. According to a report prepared last year for the United States Senate subcommittee on multinational corporations, one-third of United States companies that entered Brazil did so by directly acquiring existing Brazilian enterprises.

Some government officials, such as the Minister of Industry and Commerce, Severo Fagundes Gomes, have justified the growing economic role of the state as a buffer against the rapid expansion of the multinationals.

Another major explanation for the rise of state enterprises is Brazil's balance-of-payments crisis. The country's foreign debt stands at more than $22 billion—the highest in Latin America—and the government is counting heavily on state enterprises to develop the fertilizers, minerals, and energy projects that will help correct the burdensome trade imbalances.

---

13. What are the advantages and disadvantages of the Brazilian government's increased state intervention into the economy?

14. How would an economic consultant from the U.S. government assess the strengths and weaknesses of the Brazilian economy? What policy suggestions would this consultant make to the Brazilian government?

15. Assuming the creation of a New International Economic Order, how would Brazil benefit from it?

China in 1949 under the leadership of Chairman Mao Tse-tung set out to transform herself from a backward feudal agrarian society into an evenly balanced socialist society. The early years of the Chinese Revolution witnessed massive land reform in the primarily peasant agricultural society. The decade of the 1950s was devoted to agricultural development and some gradual industrial development with substantial support and assistance from the Soviet Union. In 1958, the Great Leap Forward was launched in order to fully institute the complex Chinese commune system in the agricultural sector while at the same time implementing an industrialization program of "walking on two legs" which essentially gave light, medium, and heavy industry equal treatment. The Great Leap Forward was somewhat successful but resulted in general disappointment. From 1959 to 1961 the "Crisis Years" set in resulting in the Sino-Soviet split and internal ideological power struggles over the "correct" path to pursue in the future. The New Economic Policy, designed to revitalize the Chinese economy, involved the application and practice of policies termed capitalist and similar to those being implemented in the Soviet Union by the liberal reform economist Evsei Liberman. Great debate raged over these years as some argued that Mao's way was the only way to avoid the road back to capitalism that Mao and his followers argued that the Soviet Union had traveled. There was fear that uneven development with too rapid industrialization would result in a privileged minority running a vast bureaucracy thus abandoning the goals of the revolution. This running debate culminated in the Cultural Revolution, reaffirmed Mao's position, and guided the country into the early 1970s. In 1971 the first Western visitors made their way into the People's Republic of China and subsequently made their findings and impressions public. They were incredibly impressed by what they found and awed at what the Chinese people had accomplished in so little time. Today, China is again experiencing internal tensions as Mao's death has resulted in another power play for leadership. With this brief historical sketch, let us look at the article by Stanford economist John Gurley on China.

MAOIST ECONOMIC DEVELOPMENT: THE NEW MAN IN THE NEW CHINA

JOHN GURLEY

The Maoists' disagreement with the capitalist view of economic development is profound. Their emphases, values, and aspirations are quite different from those of capitalist economists. Maoist economic development occurs within the context of central planning, public ownership of industries, and agricultural coöperatives or communes. While decision making is decentralized to some extent, decisions regarding investment versus consumption, foreign trade, allocation of material inputs, and the labor supply, prices of various commodities—these and more are essentially in the hands of the state. The profit motive is officially discouraged from assuming an important role in the allocation of resources, and material incentives, while still prevalent, are downgraded.

Perhaps the most striking difference between the capitalist and Maoist views concerns goals. Maoists believe that while a principal aim of nations should be to raise the level of material welfare of the population, this should be done only within the context of the development of human beings, encouraging them to realize fully their manifold creative powers. And it should be done only on an egalitarian basis— that is, on the basis that development is not worth much unless everyone rises together; no one is to be left behind, either economically or culturally. Indeed, Maoists believe that rapid economic development is not likely to occur *unless* everyone rises together. Development as a trickle-down process is therefore rejected by Maoists, and so they reject any strong emphasis on profit motives and efficiency criteria that lead to lopsided growth.

In Maoist eyes, economic development can best the attained by giving prominence to men rather than "things...."

John Gurley, "Maoist Economic Development: The New Man in the New China," *The Center Magazine,* May, 1970. Reprinted with the permission of The Center for the Study of Democratic Institutions, Santa Barbara, Calif.

... The Maoists' emphasis, however, is quite different. First of all, while they recognize the role played by education and health in the production process, their emphasis is heavily placed on the transformation of ideas, the making of the Communist Man. Ideology, of course, may be considered as part of education in the broadest sense, but it is surely not the part that capitalist economists have in mind when they evaluate education's contribution to economic growth. Moreover, ideological training does not include the acquisition of particular skills or the training of specialists—as education and job training in capitalist countries tend to do. The Maoists believe that economic development can best be promoted by breaking down specialization, by dismantling bureaucracies, and by undermining the other centralizing and divisive tendencies that give rise to experts, technicians, authorities, and bureaucrats remote from or manipulating "the masses." Finally, Maoists seem perfectly willing to pursue the goal of transforming man even though it is temporarily at the expense of some economic growth. Indeed, it is clear that Maoists will not accept economic development, however rapid, if it is based on the capitalist principles of sharp division of labor and sharp (meaning unsavory or selfish) practices.

The proletarian worldview, which Maoists believe must replace that of the bourgeoisie, stresses that only through struggle can progress be made; that selflessness and unity of purpose will release a huge reservoir of enthusiasm, energy, and creativeness; that active participation by "the masses" in decision making will provide them with the knowledge to channel their energy most productively; and that the elimination of specialization will not only increase workers' and peasants' willingness to work hard for the various goals of society but will also increase their ability to do this by adding to their knowledge and awareness of the world around them.

... Maoists believe that each person should be devoted to "the masses" rather than to his own pots and pans, and should serve the world proletariat rather than, as the *Peking Review* has put it, reaching out with "grasping hands everywhere to seek fame, material gain, power, position, and limelight." They think that if a person is selfish, he will resist criticisms and suggestions and is likely to become bureaucratic and elitist. He will not work as hard for community or national goals as he will for narrow, selfish ones. In any case, a selfish person is not an admirable person. Thus Maoists de-emphasize material incentives, for they are the very manifestation of a selfish, bourgeois society. While selflessness is necessary to imbue man with energy and the willingness to work hard, Maoists believe this is not sufficient; man must also have the ability as well. And such ability comes from active participation—from seeing and doing. To gain knowledge, people must be awakened from their half slumber, encouraged to mobilize themselves and to take conscious action to elevate and liberate themselves. When they actively participate in decision making, when they take an interest in state affairs, when they dare to do new things, when they become good at presenting facts and reasoning things out, when they criticize and test and experiment scientifically—having discarded myths and superstitions—when they are aroused, then, says the *Peking Review,* "the socialist initiative latent in the masses [will] burst out with volcanic force and a rapid change [will take] place in production."

Finally, if men become "selfless," there will be discipline and unity of will, for these "cannot be achieved if relations among comrades stem from selfish interests and personal likes and dislikes." If men become "active," then along with extensive democracy they will gain true consciousness and ultimately freedom, in the Marxian sense of intelligent action. Together, selflessness and active participation will achieve ideal combinations of opposites: "a vigorous and lively political situation . . . is taking shape throughout our country, in which there is both centralism and democracy, both discipline and freedom, both unity of will and personal ease of mind. . . ."

. . . For Marx, specialization and bureaucratization were the very antithesis of communism. Man could not be free or truly human until these manifestations of alienation were eliminated, allowing him to become an all-round communist man. Maoists, too, have been intensely concerned with this goal, specifying it in terms of eliminating the distinction between town and countryside, mental and manual labor, and workers and peasants. The realization of the universal man is not automatically achieved by altering the forces of production, by the socialist revolution. Rather, it can be achieved only after the most intense and unrelenting ideological efforts to raise the consciousness of the masses through the creative study and creative use of Mao's thought. Old ideas, customs, and habits hang on long after the material base of the economy has been radically changed, and it takes one mighty effort after another to wipe out the bourgeois superstructure and replace it with the proletarian world outlook. This transformation of the "subjective world" will then have a tremendous impact on the "objective world. . . ."

. . . The truth is that China over the past two decades has made very remarkable economic advances (though not steadily) on almost all fronts. The basic, overriding economic fact about China is that for twenty years she has fed, clothed, and housed everyone, has kept them healthy, and has educated most. Millions have not starved; sidewalks and streets have not been covered with multitudes of sleeping, begging, hungry, and illiterate human beings; millions are not disease-ridden. To find such deplorable conditions, one does not look to China these days but, rather, to India, Pakistan, and almost anywhere else in the under-developed world. These facts are so basic, so fundamentally important, that they completely dominate China's economic picture, even if one grants all of the erratic and irrational policies alleged by her numerous critics.

The Chinese—all of them—now have what is in effect an insurance policy against pestilence, famine, and other disasters. In this respect, China has out-performed every underdeveloped country in the world; and, even with respect to the richest one, it would not be farfetched to claim that there has been less malnutrition due to maldistribution of food in China over the past twenty years than there has been in the United States. If this comes close to the truth, the reason lies not in China's grain output far surpassing her population growth—for it has not—but, rather, in the development of institutions to distribute food evenly among the population. It is also true, however, that China has just had six consecutive bumper grain crops (wheat and rice) that have enabled her to reduce wheat imports and greatly increase rice exports. On top of this, there have been large gains in the supplies of eggs, vegetables, fruits, poultry, fish, and meat. In fact, China today exports more food than she imports. The Chinese are in a much better position now than ever before to ward off natural disasters, as there has been significant progress in irrigation, flood control, and water conservation. The use of chemical fertilizers is increasing rapidly, the volume now over ten times that of the early 1950s; there have been substantial gains in the output of tractors, pumps, and other farm implements; and much progress has been made in the control of plant disease and in crop breeding.

In education, there has been a major breakthrough. All urban children and a great majority of rural children have attended primary schools, and enrolments in secondary schools and in higher education are large, in proportion to the population, compared with pre-communist days. If "school" is extended to include as well all part-time, part-study education, spare-time education, and the study groups organized by the communes, factories, street organizations, and the army, then there are schools everywhere in China.

China's gains in the medical and public-health fields are perhaps the most impressive of all. The gains are attested to by many fairly recent visitors to China. For example, G. Leslie Wilcox, a Canadian doctor, a few years ago visited medical colleges, hospitals, and research institutes, and reported in "Observations on Medical Practices" (*Bulletin of the Atomic Scientists,* June, 1966) that everywhere he found good equipment, high medical standards, excellent medical care—almost all comparable to Canadian standards. As William Y. Chen, a member of the U.S. Public Health Service, wrote in "Medicine in Public Health" (*Sciences in Communist China),* "the prevention and control of many infectious and parasitic diseases which have ravaged [China] for generations" was a "most startling accomplishment." He noted, too, that "the improvement of general environmental sanitation and the practice of personal hygiene, both in the cities and in the rural areas, were also phenomenal."

While all these gains were being made, the Chinese were devoting an unusually large amount of resources to industrial output. China's industrial production has risen on the average by at least 11 percent per year since 1950, which is an exceptionally high growth rate for an underdeveloped country. Furthermore, industrial progress is not likely to be retarded in the future by any lack of natural resources, for China is richly endowed and is right now one of the four top producers in the world of coal, iron ore, mercury, tin, tungsten, magnesite, salt, and antimony. In recent years, China has made large gains in the production of coal, iron, steel, chemical fertilizers, and oil. In fact, since the huge discoveries at the Tach'ing oilfield, China is now self-sufficient in oil and has offered to export some to Japan.

From the industrial, agricultural, and other gains, I would estimate that China's real GNP has risen on the average by at least 6 percent per year since 1949, or by at least 4 percent on a per-capita basis. This may not seem high, but it is a little better than the Soviet Union did over a comparable period (1928–1940), much better than England's record during her century of industrialization (1750–1850), when her income per capita grew at 0.5 percent per year, perhaps a bit better than Japan's performance from 1878 to 1936, certainly much superior to France's 3 percent record from 1800 to 1870, far better than India's 1.3 percent growth during 1950 to 1967; more important, it is much superior to the postwar record of almost all underdeveloped countries in the world.

This is a picture of an economy richly endowed in natural resources, but whose people are still very poor, making substantial gains in industrialization, moving ahead more slowly in agriculture, raising education and health levels dramatically, turning out increasing numbers of scientists and engineers, expanding the volume of foreign trade and the variety of products traded, and making startling progress in the development of nuclear weapons. This is a truer picture, I believe, than the bleak one drawn by some of our China experts. . . .

. . . The point is that this issue—which, I should stress, includes not only labor productivity (that is, the development of material things by human beings) but also the development of human beings themselves—this issue of generalists versus specialists, communist men versus experts, the masses versus bureaucrats, or whatever, is not to be laughed away, as it has been, in effect, by some China experts. How men, in an industrial society, should relate to machines and to each other in seeking happiness and real meaning in their lives has surely been one of the most important problems of the modern age. There is also another basic issue here: whether modern industrial society, capitalist or socialist, does in fact diminish man's essential powers, his capacity for growth in many dimensions, even though it does allocate them "efficiently" and increases his skills as a specialized input. Is man Lockean in nature—reactive to outside forces, adjusting passively to disequilibrium forces from without? Or is he essentially Leibnitzian—the source of acts, active, capable of growth, and having an inner being that is self-propelled? If the latter, how are these powers released?

The Maoists claim that the powers exist and can be released. If they are right, the implications for economic development are so important that it would take blind men on this side of the Pacific to ignore them.

---

16. Compare and contrast the view of "human nature" implicit in the capitalist and Maoist views of development.

17. What do you find impressive about China's economic development since 1949?

18. What will be the major problems facing China in the future? Will China be different now that Mao is dead?

19. What problems do you think you personally would have living in a country like China?

CONCLUSION

The future for the developing countries is thus filled with choices—how much of a commitment to make to development; what sorts of relationships to have with international institutions, MNCs and other governments; and what type of a system and development strategy to adopt. Their future is also one of uncertainty and continued problems—inflation, unemployment, overpopulation, poverty, human suffering, debt problems, the demands for the NIEO, and so on. One of the most fundamental aspects of the future political, social, and economic development of the world will be tied up in the fate of these developing nations and their struggles.

In the next Part, we extend our consideration of the future by examining some problems facing the economies of the developed world, the likely direction of the development of economics in its efforts to help us create and cope with our future, and some of the choices we face in making our own world.

KEY CONCEPTS

diffusion model
economic development
Third World
structuralist model
imperialism
dependency model

New International Economic Order
Maoist economic development
moral incentives
material incentives

REVIEW QUESTIONS

1. Define in your own words the term "economic development." What are the obstacles to development?

2. Compare and contrast the diffusion and dependency models' approaches to the problems of developing nations. Which approach do you think best examines and explains the subject? Why?

3. Assume that you are a top-level economic planner for a developing nation. Briefly, outline your development strategy and include in your economic plan the role you would like to see played by the following: the International Monetary Fund, the World Bank, multinational corporations, foreign aid, and your own government.

4. What moral and ethical questions are there in the development process? To what extent should policymakers allow these considerations to influence their decisions?

5. What do you think would be the appropriate response by the U.S. to the demands of the Third World in the proposal for an NIEO?

6. Why do you suppose it is becoming more and more difficult for any particular country's economic system to remain "pure" in the sense of being either Capitalist or Socialist?

7. Compare and contrast the positions that would be taken by economic specialists from Tanzania and Brazil with respect to their preferences in the creation of an NIEO.

8. What could the developing nations of the Third World learn from the Chinese development experience? What could the advanced industrial world learn from the Chinese development experience?

SUGGESTED READINGS

Richard Barnet and Ronald Müller, 1974. *Global Reach,* Simon and Schuster. See Part II, Chapters 6-8 for an excellent treatment of the impact of multinational corporations on developing nations.

Geoffrey Barraclough, 1976. "The Haves and the Have Nots," *New York Review of Books,* May 13. A fine in-depth treatment of the political economic realities of the developing nations in their quest for an NIEO.

Bhaskar P. Menon, 1977. *Global Dialogue: The New International Order,* Pergamon Press. A good introduction to the present U.N. dialogue on the NIEO. Also contains the original transcripts of the major resolutions passed by the U.N. pertaining to the NIEO.

Jan Tinbergen, 1976. *RIO (Reshaping the International Order),* Dutton. This is an excellent comprehensive treatment of the history and present status of the U.N. call for an NIEO.

E. L. Wheelwright and Bruce Macfarlane, 1970. *The Chinese Road to Socialism,* Monthly Review Press. A sophisticated and favorable treatment of the Chinese economic system. See Chapters 11 and 12 for a discussion of Mao's strategy and philosophy and the future of the Chinese road to socialism.

Charles K. Wilber (ed.), 1973. *The Political Economy of Development and Underdevelopment,* Random House. An excellent reader on development, presenting articles from the conservative, liberal, and radical perspectives.

THE FUTURE

PART VI

The future can rarely be predicted with precision; and the future of such a complex phenomenon as the world economy is particularly difficult to anticipate or even to visualize. When nothing is known about such a phenomenon nothing can be proven to be impossible. But as the actual state of the system and its structural properties become known and the forces and relations that govern its development and change become better understood, many of the originally envisaged futures are eliminated from the range of realistic possibilities. At the same time the distant outlines of the possible emerge more clearly and in more detail as increased knowledge and understanding are brought to bear on the subject.

However, even if the inner workings of the world economic system were fully understood and the external factors which will affect its development possibilities over the next quarter of a century were fully known, a gradual elimination of the options that first appeared to be open but upon further examination turned out to be closed cannot reduce the originally envisioned wide range of possibilities to a single inevitable path. One reason for this is that some of the factors upon which the course of future developments can be shown to depend will be controlled by purposeful national or international action guided by more or less rational choices.

Wassily Leontief *et al., The Future of the World Economy,* Oxford University Press, 1977, p. 13.

In this final part of the text, we will focus upon the future. First, we will analyze, in Chapter 24, the question "What has become of the Keynesian Revolution?" Then in Chapter 25, we will explore the issues surrounding "Economic Growth, Resources, and the Environment." And, to conclude, in Chapter 26, we will consider the visionary future contrasting the optimistic and the pessimistic viewpoints.

"The outlines of the possible." (Photograph by Steve Stamos.)

WHAT HAS BECOME OF THE KEYNESIAN REVOLUTION?

CHAPTER 24

What the bushy-bearded, heavy-handed German revolutionary did with malice aforethought and by frontal attack, the English aristocrat, a scholar of Eton and King's College, Cambridge, a director of the Bank of England, an advisor to the Chancellor of the Exchequer, a peer of the Realm, performed neatly, skillfully, and unconsciously, by flank attack.

E. E. Hale

Now, it seems that the bastard Keynesian era is coming to an end in general disillusionment; the economists have no more idea what to say than they had when the old equilibrium doctrine collapsed in the great slump. The Keynesian revolution still remains to be made both in teaching economic theory and in forming economic policy.

Joan Robinson

WHY THE QUESTION?

John Maynard Keynes published *The General Theory of Employment, Interest, and Money* in 1936. In this book, as we have already learned, he attempted to diagnose the illness of capitalism in the midst of the Great Depression and to provide a prescription to cure the ailing system. More fundamentally, Keynes provided an explanation for the massive unemployment and some guidance as to how to reduce the gross inequalities in wealth and income characteristic of capitalism in the 1930s.

Many argue that the Keynesian Revolution was Keynes's formulation of a *new* economic theory breaking with the classical and neoclassical tradition. It was new economic theory more appropriate for the time period than a dated theory incapable of explaining existing economic reality. In another sense, as the American Marxist, Paul Sweezy, has said of Keynes's importance, his "mission was to *reform* Neo-classical economics, to bring it back into contact with the real world," with which it had lost touch since the 1870s.

Keynes posited that capitalism had reached a stage of development in which high levels of unemployment and stagnation of economic growth were logical out-

John Maynard Keynes, 1883–1946

comes of the natural operation of the system as it was then constructed. More importantly, he felt that it would not deviate from this path automatically over time in a "self-correcting" manner as the dominant economic paradigm promised. In effect, Keynes proved that Say's Law was incorrect. The real secret to the capitalist economy's health, viability, and stability was the level of aggregate demand relative to productive capacity. Keynes's new approach to the concepts and functions of savings and investment put to rest the myths of the previous economic paradigm. As he suggested, the only way to ensure full employment, price stability, economic growth, a positive trade balance, and an equitable distribution of income was for the government to take a more aggressive role in the economic system by utilizing the tools of fiscal and monetary policy. It could be argued that Keynes reintroduced the science of political economy into economics. By suggesting that government spend money to ensure the proper level of aggregate demand in order to maintain full employment, he raised indirectly the question of "What should government spend the money on?" This question, as we will see, was answered over time by historical events and the exercise of political power and vested economic interest.

So there can be little doubt that there was such a thing as the "Keynesian Revolution" viewed as a new economic paradigm replacing the dying neoclassical body of thought. But many have since argued that the *real* Keynesian Revolution never occurred. Some economists maintain that what was truly revolutionary about *The General Theory* was never fully understood nor articulated by Keynes or his disciples. The late E. E. Hale, one such critic who taught economics at the University of Texas, argued that Keynes refused "to draw, or even to admit, the logical conclusions of the General Theory, but they are there nevertheless, and in plain sight for all to see." Hale further asserted that "Keynes's blindness at bottom results from his failure or refusal to recognize that he had hit upon the contradiction in the process of capital accumulation which Marx had so clearly pictured three-quarters of a century earlier." What then was this particular similarity between Keynes and Marx? Hale has summarized it as follows (as well as noting some differences).

Keynes and Marx, indeed, have much in common. *The General Theory,* like *Das Kapital,* teaches that unemployment and depression are the norms to which the capitalist economy tends. Both Keynes and Marx were aware of deficient demand and oversaving, of the declining profit rate resulting from limited investment opportunities, of the unwisdom of capital exportation. Both were highly critical of the excesses of the capitalist system. But Keynes was no socialist. For him the troubles of our society are due, not to the breakdown of a social system, but to a failure of intelligence. He is convinced that by the exercise of intelligence capitalism can be made more efficient for attaining economic ends than any alternative system yet in sight.

E. E. Hale (prepared by Ron Philips), "Some Implications of Keynes' *General Theory of Employment, Interest, and Money,*" Review of Radical Political Economics, Vol. 8, No. 4, Winter 1976.

In retrospect, economic historians have concluded that essentially what Keynes did was to rescue capitalism from its sickbed and reform it sufficiently so that it could continue to function adequately. By administering Keynesian policy tools, the business cycle could be tamed once and for all.

Leaving aside for the moment the question of the *real* Keynesian Revolution (to which we will return at the end of this chapter), let us look briefly at the historical track record of Keynesian economics as practiced in the U.S. since World War II in order to evaluate the efficacy of Keynesian economics.

A BRIEF HISTORICAL OVERVIEW: WORLD WAR II TO THE PRESENT

It took several years after some initial reluctance for the U.S. to understand, appreciate, and begin to implement the Keynesian doctrine. The U.S. found (as did Hitler's Germany years earlier) that one way to achieve full employment was to engage in deficit spending to build a vast military machine. This can be easily documented by the following data in Table 24.1:

TABLE 24.1

Year	Unemployment Rate	Government Deficit (Billions of Dollars)	Total Military Outlays (Billions of Dollars)
1933	24.9	−2.6	0.8
1939	17.2	−3.9	1.4
1940	14.6	−3.1	1.8
1941	9.9	−5.0	6.3
1942	4.7	−20.8	22.9
1943	1.9	−54.9	63.4
1944	1.2	−47.0	76.0
1945	1.9	−47.5	80.5

Source: *Economic Report of the President 1977,* pages 228 and 268; and "Statistical Appendix to Annual Report of the Treasury for the Fiscal Year Ended June 30, 1968."

Adjustment to the postwar period for the U.S. was somewhat difficult but nevertheless successful. There was a series of recessions in the time period 1949 to 1971 in which real GNP decreased and unemployment increased (see Table 24.2).

TABLE 24.2

Years	Unemployment Rate
1948–1949	5.9%
1953–1954	5.5%
1957–1958	6.8%
1960–1961	6.7%
1970–1971	6.0%

Source: *Economic Report of the President,* 1977.

We can conclude from this that indeed the cyclical behavior of American capitalism was not eliminated, but it was certainly curbed and mitigated. There were recessions, but no repeat of the depression experience of the 1930s. This is particularly impressive in light of the fact that the neoclassical–Keynesian synthesis did not really become popularly accepted theory until the publication of the First Edition of Paul Samuelson's *Principles of Economics* in 1948. This spelled out in very elementary language and analysis the integration of the "Keynesian Revolution" with the then *revived* neoclassical theory. Yet, it was not until the early 1960s that Keynesian economists were fully integrated into the policymaking institutions of the American economy. Most economists would point to the historic "tax cut" engineered by Walter Heller in 1964 as the real acceptance of Keynesian economics in the U.S.

From the early 1960s to the early years of the 1970s, economists and the economics discipline were held in great esteem. An almost euphoric sense of confidence in the practice of Keynesian economics and the strength of the American economy filled the pages of textbooks, journals, periodicals, and newspapers, as well as the corridors of businesses and government. Keynesian economics was viewed as a panacea for our economic woes of the past. The fragmented and persistent criticism by conservative Monetarists and radical Marxists alike fell on deaf ears as the U.S. economy went breezing along. With strong economic growth, almost full employment, relative price stability and U.S. international hegemony, why should anyone doubt the universal applicability of Keynesian economics and its apparent immortality?

Much to the Keynesians' surprise, though, doubt did surface and became stronger and stronger over time. In the middle of the 1960s, the U.S. found itself committed to a land war in Southeast Asia, pouring hundreds of millions of dollars ($150 billion) into this effort, while domestically the nation was literally coming apart due to urban unrest, campus rebellion, and racial strife. Indeed, the Keynesian system found itself unable to deliver the promised goals and objectives under the pressure of *internal* and *external* demands that later proved to be contradictory in terms of the maintenance of the system's stability. Recessions occurred in 1970-1971 and again in 1973-1975. By the early 1970s, the U.S. economic system was experiencing great international pressures. The defeat in Vietnam followed by persistent balance of payments problems put such pressure on the currency that the Nixon administration had little choice but to devalue the dollar twice within 18 months. This signaled to the world at large that one important institutional piece of the Keynesian synthesis in the capitalist world—the international monetary system—had collapsed.

Further exacerbating the emergent dilemma for the Keynesian system was the continued presence of a myriad of domestic problems that had surfaced in the mid-1960s. There was still poverty, racism, sexism, militarism, and environmental decay. A belligerent foreign policy still existed and caused complaint. In addition, new problems of inflation accompanied by high levels of unemployment, heightened global interdependence, the growing impoverishment of the developing world, and the growing concentration of political and economic power held by multinational corporations and the executive branch of the federal government all together brought additional pressures and problems to bear upon the ability of an economic philosophy fashioned to deal with a set of problems in the 1930s.

Indeed, many felt that University of Michigan economist Daniel Fusfeld was more than justified in 1972 in announcing the tragic disintegration of the system that had so capably prolonged the life of American capitalism. (See his article in Chapter 19). While Fusfeld and others continued to trumpet the misfortunes of Keynesian theory and policy, others fought hard to defend the system and worked diligently to repair the struggling patient, in order to restore its health and credibility.

Before considering the recent efforts on the part of the Nixon, Ford, and Carter administrations to restore stability to the economic system, let us consider the data in Table 24.3 on the U.S. economy from 1970-1977.

TABLE 24.3

Year	Balance-of-Payments Deficit (Millions of Dollars)	Unemployment Rate	Capacity Utilization in Manufacturing	Annual Rate of Inflation (CPI)	Federal Deficit (Millions of Dollars)
1970	−356	4.9	79.2	5.5	−2,845
1971	−3,957	5.9	78.0	3.4	−23,033
1972	−9,802	5.6	83.1	3.4	−23,372
1973	+22	4.9	87.5	8.8	−14,849
1974	−3,598	5.6	84.5	12.2	−4,688
1975	+11,697	8.5	73.6	7.0	−45,108
1976	−1,427	7.7	81.0	4.8	−66,461
1977	−16,000	7.0	82.4	6.8	−45,040

Source: *Economic Report of the President,* 1978.

THE NIXON-FORD YEARS AND THE COMING OF CARTER

As we have seen, by 1971, the collapse of the international monetary system was self-evident. The U.S. was forced to devalue the dollar several times in order to rectify the problems associated with continued large balance-of-payments deficits. President Nixon and his economic advisors exhibited policies that characterized the chaos of the period. Nixon, a conservative Republican, proudly professed a laissez-faire economic philosophy when he took office in 1968. But by the time that Watergate forced his resignation, he had worn all of the ideological hats of mainstream economics. Inflation was such a problem for him that the classical Monetarist solutions did not work and he was forced to institute his controversial wage and price controls. These controls were an incomes policy characteristic of very liberal Keynesians. Nixon's manipulation of the economy succeeded in getting him re-elected but did not in the long run solve the basic economic problems of inflation and unemployment. In fact, these two problems worsened simultaneously—in violation of the classic trade-off suggested by the Phillips Curve. By 1974, the year of Nixon's resignation and Gerald Ford's appointment as President, the twin evils had become one integrated phenomenon—*stagflation*.

The deep and prolonged recession of 1973-1975 greeted President Ford. With unemployment at 8.5 percent and inflation at 12.2 percent, the experienced Congressman-now-President struggled desperately to find a solution to this economic plague. After a series of Economic Summit Conferences (Fall, 1974) designed to solicit a wide range of opinion on the economy and to symbolically open the executive branch of the federal government to public interest groups, President Ford and his major advisors (Alan Greenspan, Chairman of the Council of Economic Advisors, and William Simon, Secretary of the Treasury) settled into an economic program designed to beat back the rate of inflation. This policy in effect rested ultimately upon a conservative Monetarist view of the problem. Ford was content to let Arthur Burns, Chairman of the Federal Reserve Board, implement the strategy. In conjunction with the efforts of Burns to control the money supply and interest rates, Ford would see to it that government spending would be reduced and the private sector stimulated. He never outlined a serious strategy for the unemployment problem other than suggesting that a strong private sector eventually experiencing growth and expansion would, in and of itself, create meaningful long-term employment.

Once again, as was the case in the Nixon years, the policy prescription failed to deliver. By election time in 1976, inflation and unemployment were stubbornly frozen at 7.2 and 7.7 percent, respectively, with little further relief in sight. Ford's program called for gradualism, patience, and confidence. But the American public was neither prepared to wait nor to support Ford's economic program—especially with the charismatic Georgian making promises to ensure rapid recovery, to curb inflation, and to reduce dramatically the rate of unemployment. In some sense, it could be argued that the economic problems Ford inherited were just too much for him to overcome in the time he had, even if he had employed correct policy prescriptions. For by 1976 it was readily apparent to the majority of practicing economists that something was seriously wrong with the theory and tools utilized by economists. Economic theorists and policy architects frantically beat retreats to their respective cubicles in order to reevaluate the last eight years. Only the courageous and bold came forth claiming that they understood the problems and had solutions. Indeed, the young core of economic consultants advising Jimmy Carter during his campaign and the experienced Charles L. Schultze (later to become the Chairman of the Council of Economic Advisors under Carter) proudly explained the failures of the past administrations and suggested the "new direction" to be taken by the Carter administration. What was this new direction and how did it differ from the directions taken by the previous administrations?

There was much about the Carter campaign package that could easily have been termed a "New Deal." The parallels with the early Roosevelt Administration in the 1930s are many and interesting to explore. Carter promised that his administration would behave professionally and pragmatically and would seek achievable goals. By the end of his term in 1980, he promised that unemployment would be down to 4.5 percent, inflation to 4.5 percent, the economic growth rate at 5 percent, and that the federal budget would be balanced. In addition, he promised that his administration would produce legislation calling for government reorganization, a reduction in military spending, major tax reform with some income redistribution, welfare reform, and a comprehensive energy program. For Carter the most popular of the campaign promises was to quickly reduce the rate of unemployment, especially among youth, women, and minorities. Inflation, while important, he considered secondary to the problem of unemployment. What happened after Carter took office? What economic policy does he seem to be following? How successful has be been thus far?

After the election and during the early months of getting settled, Carter and his economic advisors pursued a cautious approach in their formulations. They were quick to reassure the business community that in no circumstances would they resort to an incomes policy of wage and price controls to curb inflation. In fact, they quickly pleased and comforted the private sector by saying that inflation was now a problem that deserved *equal* attention with unemployment. Subsequently, Carter's commitment to the goal of a balanced budget by 1980 and his preoccupation with inflation had severe implications for his committment to reduce unemployment dramatically. Most economists were somewhat surprised that Carter would accept and adopt the conservative policies of Arthur Burns. The Carter administration established a business-government-labor roundtable to discuss the possibilities for voluntary cooperation to stem the tide of rising inflation. Aware that a major part of inflation is rooted in corporate market power because of high concentration of production in some sectors by a few powerful firms, Carter warned that he would utilize antitrust legislation if necessary in cases in which large firms did not behave responsibly. He further warned organized labor that it too had the responsibility to voluntarily discipline itself or face government pressure.

With respect to unemployment, especially of youth, women, and minorities, Carter proposed a dual program. He proposed a $4 billion Public Works bill to immediately alleviate the burden among the groups mentioned; and to follow this by a long-term strategy of tax cuts, government spending, and other incentives to stimulate the private sector, thereby creating meaningful long-term private employment.

Internationally, the Carter economic program was quite vague and expressed in general terms. Carter promised to maintain liberal trade and investment policies so that the U.S. could be guaranteed "a good strong domestic economy." Finally, he claimed that U.S. foreign and international policy would be guided by the highest moral and ethical principles. "Human Rights" were to be protected globally.

In the first year of Carter's administration, it was difficult to judge the ultimate success or failure of the Carter economic program. There were several disappointments in terms of campaign promises (the decision to eliminate a proposed tax rebate in 1977 and his emphasis on inflation rather than unemployment) and several successes (the cancellation of the B-1 Bomber program and the development of the Energy Plan). Observers agreed that his program was one that would take time to produce results. It was a gradual program designed to achieve results by 1980.

Some have noted that this gradual approach is not dissimilar from that of the Ford administration from 1974 to 1976. In the following article by Melville J. Ulmer, "Sorry, No Change," this parallel is developed.

SORRY, NO CHANGE

MELVILLE J. ULMER

The advice and admonitions of outgoing public officials normally have as little effect on a nation's destiny as letters to the editor of the *Tupecola* (Miss.) *Journal*. This goes as well for Gerald Ford and the larger part of the budget and economic messages he was required by law to deliver just a few days before leaving office. To the extent that a president can promptly alter the economic course of a bulky ship of state, with an immense momentum of its own, this executive responsibility is now of course entirely Jimmy Carter's. Even so, Ford's parting messages, and the plans they contain, have an importance that was no doubt unintended. They serve as a reminder that political advertising can be as deceptive as the other kind. Despite all the campaign hoopla and transition memoranda, the economic stabilization plans currently promised by President Carter turned out to be not markedly different from those of ex-President Ford, as actually pursued in the past year and proposed in his pro forma "messages."

Neither the outgoing nor the incoming president has promised full employment—not soon and not in the determinable future either. Neither one provides a substantive plan for stopping inflation, nor even to retard it. Both present a legislative package of modest stimulation, featuring tax reductions, and amounting to from $23 to $30 billion over the next two years. Even if the upper end of the range is

From *The New Republic*, Feb. 5, 1977. Reprinted by permission of *The New Republic*. © 1977, *The New Republic*.

more likely, that comes to less than one percent, annually, of our present giant-sized gross national product of $1700 billion, providing the smashing impact of a wet noodle. Both men forecast a budget deficit for fiscal 1977 (which ends this September 30, 1977) in the neighborhood of $60 billion, greater than any in history with the possible exception of 1976. Hence, regardless of the way the vote may have gone last November, the prospect would have been and still is for considerable unemployment *and* inflation, at least through the next two years. Nor is there anything, other than the usual deathless oratory of politicians, to warrant any greater hope of a stable, full employment economy in the longer run....

... In the longer run, over the next three or four years, Carter may well fulfill his pledges to reorganize the entire federal government, reform the tax system, sterilize the welfare mess, and perform similar exploits. But right now, in the broad aggregates of government spending and taxes, and in the ceaseless war against inflation and unemployment, no substantial change in tactics appears in the offing. That is the most significant element in the economic news of the last several weeks.

Why this timidity on the part of Carter, bringing him so close to the frankly conservative and cautious Ford? The answer lies in two parameters, as economists call them, that are constant for both men. The first and more fundamental is the ruling stabilization ideology. Ever since World War II conventional economists have been tied professionally to the assumed magic of Keynesian fiscal policies. Their reputations hinge upon it. Their emotions cling to it. With increasing orthodoxy and boldness, every president from Truman through Ford has used it. Now President Carter, who won office by running against "Washington," has accepted Washington's conventional wisdom, not to mention many of its proponents in key cabinet or subcabinet posts.

The conventional economic wisdom recognizes just three basic tools for stabilizing the economy. They allow public officials to give the appearance of being in command by merely pressing buttons, so to speak. The tools are tax changes (given the most stress of all), interest rate changes, and alterations in public spending which since FDR have dwindled in importance to next to nothing. When unemployment is the dominant problem, taxes and interest rates are lowered and public spending, if used at all, rises. This tactic always creates some jobs, but—with increasing embarrassment for its proponents—always stimulates inflation. When inflation draws to the forefront as the overriding problem, the opposite steps are taken. Taxes and interest rates are raised and public spending is contracted. This usually retards inflation but always creates unemployment. In this way the economy has see-sawed through cycles that have been continuous but not precisely repetitive: the swings have grown sharper, with joblessness more widespread on each downturn and inflation progressively more alarming and stubborn. This trend yields the second fixed parameter faced by both men.

The past three years have witnessed a more severe *combination* of high unemployment and briskly rising prices than ever before in modern history—roughly 8 percent of the labor force jobless and an annual inflation rate wavering between 5 and 10 percent or more. It was so for Ford when he took office in August 1974, and it is so for Carter now, despite some improvement from the worst days of 1975. Therefore, like his predecessor, the new President can't pump up the economy very much because that would excite inflation, already much too great. Nor can he dampen it down significantly, because that would spread unemployment, still at a near-depression level. Ford's answer, beginning in 1975, was to pump up the economy, but just a little. That's Carter's answer too. The strategy is to keep the economy fairly slack, even though improving modestly, tolerating considerable joblessness in the hope that inflation will gradually, somehow, subside.

That hope is virtually certain to prove groundless. There are just two possibilities. The first, though not the more likely, is that things will go according to plan at least at the start. That means that economic activity will expand only slightly, producing at best a 7-percent jobless rate even by the end of 1978. (That estimate is in line with the official projection of the Congressional Budget Office.) Will the congressmen and senators up for election in November of that year sit idly by, with unions, blacks, and others roaring? The chances are that spending bills and/or further tax cuts will become the order of the day. If enacted, as they probably will be, you can bet on a sharply accelerating price level—on top of a 6- or 7-percent inflation rate that probably will prevail a year from now. What then? The customary "cure," sooner or later, is a corrective recession.

The other possibility is that the inflationary crisis will come sooner. Business activity shows every sign at present of gathering steam on its own. Consumer spending is brisk and capital spending, heretofore lagging, has given recent evidence of revival. If that trend persists, past experience teaches, our highly excitable wage and price levels will be dancing well before the end of this year.

In short, simply pumping up the economy just a little, or three or four times as much as that, won't do. Inflation remains the ogre. There is a way out of the dilemma that would get at the structural imbalances that *cause* the difficulties. But that would involve minor surgery, or as the seers of Capitol Hill would put it, more national economic planning than the present political climate will tolerate. A compromise that would provide a partial answer, much better than none, is wage and price controls. I do not mean by this the crude and ineffective voluntary "guidelines" already mentioned *sotto voce* by some Carter advisers. When last seen in 1966 guidelines were crumbling under pressure; and were not of much use before that date. I do mean mandatory, selective controls, carefully framed to survive the long pull, and aimed at the outstanding abusers of economic power in big business and organized labor. With their help the presently impossible could be realized—an expansion to high employment without an unacceptable rate of inflation. But they won't work if delayed until *after* the wage and price elevation is much greater than it is at present. The effort would be as futile as a water pistol in a forest fire. Carter should establish controls and standards within the next 60 days. Business fears can be soothed with a new investment tax credit. Labor could be easily mollified by the repeal of right-to-work laws. Both measures are eminently supportable on independent grounds.

---

1. Why is Carter's economic program not very much different from Ford's program?

In the late 1970s, the economy was slowly recovering from the deep recession of 1973–1975. This sluggish recovery was welcomed by some because of the fear of heating up inflationary pressures. Others were frustrated by the lack of significant progress in reducing unemployment. There was also an element of *unevenness* in the recovery as the private sector was the main beneficiary while the public sector lagged and suffered greatly.

Projections for 1978–1982 by Carter's Office of Management and Budget are shown in Table 24.4.

TABLE 24.4

Long-range economic assumptions

Economic activity assumed for purposes of budget projections				
GNP (percentage change)	1979	1980	1981	1982
Current dollars	+11.3	+10.6	+9.4	+8.6
Constant dollars (1972)	+5.0	+5.2	+4.9	+4.3
Inflation (percentage change)				
GNP deflator	+6.1	+5.1	+4.3	+4.2
Consumer price index	+5.9	+5.0	+4.3	+4.3
Unemployment (yearly average)	5.7	5.2	4.8	4.5

The budget outlook 1978–1982

In billions of dollars	1978*	1979	1980	1981	1982
Projected outlays	$462.9	$498.6	$532.7	$564.8	$601.0
Projected receipts	401.4	466.8	536.6	606.9	676.5
Budget deficit or margin	−61.5	−31.8	+3.9	+42.1	+75.5

*Current estimates, including impact of Congressional action or inaction
Source: *New York Times,* July 1, 1977.

2. How would you critically evaluate Carter's economic program at this point in time?

As the Carter administration labored to develop and implement an economic program, critics lined up from all areas of the political economic spectrum to fire their critiques at him and his advisors. Thus far, it appears that conservatives, while not totally satisfied with his emergent program (particularly the Energy Plan and the decision not to deregulate natural gas), were quite satisfied with his sensitivity to the needs of the private corporate sector and the problem of inflation. Liberal Democrats in general were supportive of his program but not altogether enthusiastic. A minority faction preferred to move more slowly, while another minority faction wanted to move more aggressively, especially with regard to unemployment. In general, there was cautious optimism, buffeted by constructive criticism. The Carter administration's mid-1977 projections from the Office of Management and Budget for the time period of 1978 to 1982 are "overly optimistic" according to the major econometric forecasters. In fact, a 1977 study commissioned by the OECD countries projected that the U.S. and the major Western European nations in particular face a very difficult road ahead with sluggish growth rates into the 1980s.

In the following article, liberal Democrat Walter Heller presents his appraisal of the U.S. economy's prospects as of 1976 as well as his optimistic assessment of the economy's performance through the end of the 1970s. His carefully guarded optimism assumes certain specific preconditions. Heller hopes for, among other things, sound yet bold and imaginative economic policy bolstered by a "little bit of luck."

THE OUTLOOK

WALTER HELLER

By 1976, some of the pressures on the economy, on economists, and on economic policymakers were relenting. The peak of inflation and the trough of recession were past, and recovery was on schedule. The energy crisis had turned from a sharp pain into a dull ache. New York, if not back to health, was at least hobbling along on its crutches. And internationally the new regimen of floating rates was managing rather nicely.

Still, it was more a time of crises surmounted than of problems solved. The Keynesian prescription of aggregate demand stimulus was working rather well, spurring expansion without rekindling inflation. But prescribing successfully for an economy that has caught the pneumonia of deep recession remains far easier than curing the chronic headache of too-high unemployment coupled with too-high inflation. Once the economy's "buffer stocks" of unemployment and idled industrial capacity are absorbed by continued recovery, what is to protect us from resurging inflation?

Not that the inflation catapults of 1973–1974—food shortages, the oil uprising, the commodity scramble, decontrol, and devaluation—show any signs of being unlimbered again. Even the fears of newly skyrocketing commodity prices as the industrial economies again expand in tandem seem to be overdone. A new study by Richard Cooper and Robert Lawrence (published in *Brookings Papers*, 3: 1975) of the doubling of industrial commodity prices (other than food and oil) from mid-1972 to mid-1974—which accounted for a quarter of world inflation in that period— traces a considerable part of that roaring price runup to "a whirlpool of speculation." Primary metals prices, for example, rose 40 percent more than can be accounted for by historical relationships of prices to industrial production needs. The lesson for the future? Build up buffer stocks of strategic raw materials in slack times to throw into the speculative breach during the next commodity squeeze.

"The Outlook" is reprinted from *The Economy: Old Myths and New Realities*, by Walter W. Heller, with the permission of W. W. Norton & Company, Inc. Copyright © 1976 by W. W. Norton & Company, Inc.

Analysis of the 1973-1974 commodity price upsweep reminds us once more of how economists go about their business—in this case, isolating a specific form of the inflationary cancer, identifying its sources, and pinpointing a way of containing it. And it underscores also the vital need to disaggregate, to look at the structural micro-factors and forces that throw the macro-mechanism off balance, to look at the supply and price disturbances that disrupt aggregate demand management. The oil price explosion was only one example—albeit the most spectacular one—of sharp changes in supply prices that cause significant shifts in real income and purchasing power and require significant fiscal and monetary adjustments to compensate for the resulting effects on aggregate demand.

What inferences should the policymaker draw? First, that macro-policy will be open to disruption unless ways are found to protect its micro-flanks. Or, to put it differently, that demand management alone, relying on those buffer stocks of the jobless and excess capacity to contain inflation, is an inadequate answer in not only human but economic terms. Supply management—at this time, the building of buffer stocks of oil, food, and other strategic commodities—ought to be a basic ingredient of stabilization policy.

Second, economic policy will have to develop more delicate sensors and antennae as well as a more agile response mechanism, first, to minimize surprises and, second, to maximize the speed of response to external shocks and developing internal bottlenecks. Policymakers might still be surprised, but they would not, one hopes, be quite so dumbfounded.

The recent reform of the congressional budget process puts Congress in a new and better position to adapt its fiscal policy to changes in the economic environment. But further steps are required to lift and lengthen the sights of the political process by some more formal commitment to take the future into account. Whether this requires economic planning and programming on a national scale is an open question that the Humphrey-Javits and Humphrey-Hawkins bill and their backers in and out of Congress will keep very much alive. Out of the give-and-take on this issue, one may hope for at least a firm commitment by the White House and Congress to lengthen their perspective on economic policy—a resolve to draw on improved data, horizon-scanning, and future-focused analysis for earlier detection of emerging economic trends, threats of shortages, and danger signs in both the national and international economy.

Just as the economic future should not be left to chance, the coordination of monetary and fiscal policy must no longer be a matter of caprice. This is not to say that the Federal Reserve—probably the most independent central bank in the world—should be subordinated to the White House. But somehow, through more conscious and constructive cooperation of the White House, Congress, and Fed, must come an improved policy mix, a better fit of monetary to fiscal policy.

Under present arrangements, should the desire be, for example, to run a tougher fiscal policy and easier monetary policy—more deficits (or bigger surpluses) coupled with lower interest rates—in order to tilt expansion in the direction of greater capital investment, there is no machinery to ensure such a result. Again, the new budget procedures are an important step toward the necessary congressional cohesion for economic *entente*—and perhaps even *détente*. It puts Congress in a stronger position to strike and carry out bargains with the Federal

Reserve and the White House not just on expansionary or restrictive policy per se, but on the relative emphasis on consumption and investment and the policy mix needed to carry it out.

But no amount of improvement in structural or supply policy or in coordination of fiscal and monetary policy can surmount the abiding problem that confronts us all: how (1) to create the 12 million jobs required between now and 1980 to absorb both the stream of new entrants into the labor force and the huge pool of unemployed workers and (2) doing so without touching off a new demand inflation later in the 1970s. It cannot be done simply by pumping up the economy and assuming that the flow of demand will find its way neatly into the nooks and crannies and hollows where stubborn unemployment exists.

Policies for economic expansion via monetary-fiscal stimulus will have to be carefully coupled with structural policies to increase productivity, to remove regulatory roadblocks to competition and lower costs, to improve labor information and mobility, to train and upgrade the disadvantaged, and to tide the unemployed over with temporary jobs and retraining rather than transfer payments alone. But even with such skillful tailoring of policies, it will be difficult to keep the pressures of high aggregate demand from once again putting the price-wage and wage-wage spirals in motion before unemployment is brought down to tolerable levels.

The day when these pressures reappear may be distant—and absent the shocks of 1973-1974, there is no reason to expect inflation to be as virulent as in that benighted period. But the ominous postwar uptilt of inflation was in clear evidence before 1973 and can hardly be said to have faded away in 1976 with inflation still at levels that represented "new highs" in the 1952-1972 period. To urge bolder policies to step up expansion and cut unemployment more quickly in 1976-1977 is to claim only that such moves are consistent with moderating inflation in a slack economy, not that inflation has dropped to tolerable levels nor that it will hold still if the economy is pushed to the limits of its potential.

To claim that would be to deny that the "unstable triad"—(1) full employment, (2) price stability, and (3) full freedom of economic choice—still prevails. In the face of powerful producer groups—labor, business, farmers, and so on—no long-run policy can deliver both full employment and contain inflation without some curbing of price and wage appetites. Clearly, "disciplining" labor by high unemployment and management by shrunken markets has been progressively less effective in de-escalating wage and price advances. On both sides, there is enough clout, enough market power, to enforce income claims that add up to more than the total output pie at existing prices. And conventional price and wage policies relying on markup pricing and "fair" wages add to the downward rigidity of prices and wages.

How to moderate these claims without the harsh treatment of deep recession or prolonged stagnation remains an unanswered challenge to economic policy. Sweden has perhaps come closest to solving it in a democratic society—though not without a degree of planning and intervention that has been unacceptable in this country to date.

The challenge to ingenuity in the United States is to find a formula for lowering the norm for wage and price advances. Part of the answer ... is to impose some guidelines and restraints on the unions and businesses that wield excessive market power. And the time to install such limited restraints is precisely when the economy is operating far below its output potential. Once it gets there, it is too late—only more onerous controls will then do the job.

In the grander design, an incomes policy must seek an economic disarmament agreement in which labor and management agree to settle for slower advances in *money* income in exchange for less inflation, that is, without sacrificing *real* income. To forge such a social contract—and to provide the tax or other inducements, especially to labor, to initiate and maintain it—is at best a difficult task. But unless ways are found to de-escalate income claims, the prospect of attaining full employment without either unacceptable rates of inflation or unwanted degrees of wage-price control will remain clouded.

The U.S. economy of the mid-seventies has enough leeway for expansion to permit a long advance toward our employment and output goals without a resurgence of inflation. And a combination of good analysis and good policy could achieve some significant advances in coping with inflationary threats. But without some bold political leadership, skilled economic management, and a dose of good luck, the country will again face hard choices and uncomfortable trade-offs between jobs, prices, and controls in the late 1970s.

3. Do you agree or disagree with Heller's assessment of what needs to be done to ensure a "crisis free" future? Why?

4. To what degree do you think President Carter's economic program did or did not accomplish the specified tasks Heller feels are so vital for our future economic health and stability?

In addition to mainstream criticism, since 1968 there has been a growing body of radical literature dealing with the intensified problems of American capitalism both domestically and internationally. This literature has been written primarily by members of the Union for Radical Political Economics. Many consider themselves Marxists since they adhere in general to the methodology and philosophy of Karl Marx. These radical critics have a different point of view and one that deserves, in our opinion, a detailed treatment.

RADICAL CRITIQUE: KEYNES AND THE BUSINESS CYCLE

Keynesian economics, in spite of all that it has done for our understanding of business fluctuations, has beyond doubt left at least one major thing unexplained, and that thing is nothing less than the business cycle itself.

J. R. Hicks

Radical economists argue in general that the stagflation in our economy today is symptomatic not only of a failure of Keynesian theory and policy but also of a fundamental breakdown of American capitalism. Radical economists view American capitalism as experiencing a long-term *structural crisis*. They argue that the cyclical behavior of American capitalism since World War II (resulting in six recessions) cannot be explained by "accidental forces" or factors external to the economy. It can be explained only by a *systematic* analysis of the behavior and operation of the capitalist economy. In a sense, the rediscovery and acceptance of the business cycle by orthodox economists has yielded common ground with radical economists. They all now agree that business cycles are *inevitable* in a capitalist economic system. The difference now appears to be between the orthodox economist's belief in the capability of Keynesian theory to tame the business cycle by "fine tuning" the economy and the radical's belief that it is becoming increasingly difficult to prevent and/or ameliorate the dislocations of business cycles.

In addition, the radical critique of Keynesian theory and policy challenges the "theory of the State" implicit in the Keynesian paradigm. Keynesian economic theory posits a view of the State as the legitimate arbiter of societal conflicts resulting from interest-group political behavior and lobbying. This view of political democracy is often termed "pluralism." In a pluralist society, the State (government) acts in a neutral capacity to provide for and protect the rights and interests of the majority as well as minorities. The radical economist's theory of the State is quite different. Radicals contend that the State is little more than the institutional apparatus that serves the interests and needs of the ruling class. There is no such thing as a *neutral State*. In a capitalist economic system, the political apparatus serves the dominant economic class by mediating societal class conflicts and arbitrating conflicts between members of the dominant class itself. This is the principal function of the State. The State's overriding goal is to preserve the operation and characteristics of the American capitalist system itself with its emphasis on private ownership and free enterprise.

The radical view of the State can be best understood in the context of the "class-conflict" theory of the State as revealed in the radical theory of the "Political business cycle."

Radical economists argue that the State consciously guides the economy and cyclical instability in order to serve the needs of the dominant economic class. Cyclical instability serves a functional set of needs for the capitalist class. How do they explain this?

The business cycle describes the movement and performance of the economy as it passes through various stages of expansion and contraction. In the expansion phase, aggregate demand is high, total output of goods and services grows rapidly, and the economy approaches full employment and full utilization of productive capacity. In the contraction phase, aggregate demand is low, total output of goods and services is falling, and the economy experiences high unemployment and low levels of utilization of productive capacity.

Business cycles historically have been explained by orthodox economists in basically two different ways: (1) underconsumption or limited demand and (2) overinvestment/overproduction. What radical economists have done is to combine the two different orthodox interpretations and forge them into one single theory of the business cycle. Their explanation is the following: The primary motivation of the capitalist is the search for profits. This encourages the capitalist to invest and accumulate capital. This process stimulates economic expansion and conditions that encourage expectations of profit returns. In a way, an accelerator principle works to encourage greater and greater investment seeking higher and higher profit returns. As the expansion phase continues, distortions begin to appear. There may be overproduction of goods and services. Competition for capital results in the costs of capital increasing faster than other prices. In order to create the funds necessary for further investment capital, the capitalist must obtain or produce sufficient profits. This can be done by increasing prices for finished goods and services, thereby fueling inflationary pressures; by borrowing, thereby increasing the debt equity ratio and worsening the liquidity position of the firm; or by reducing payments to workers in the form of wages, thereby reducing their purchasing power and limiting total demand (i.e., underconsumption). This last option is difficult to do at the peak of an expansion because, as the economy approaches full employment, labor is in a stronger wage-bargaining position and more likely to demand and get high wage increases. The capitalist is faced with a "profit squeeze" from higher wage costs and higher capital costs and is thus forced, out of necessity, to alleviate these pressures by dismissing workers and reducing investment spending. This ushers in the contraction phase, or a recession. The contraction phase serves the function of curing the distortions of the previous expansion phase.

This "functional" analysis of the recession has been carefully summarized by Raford Boddy and James Crotty in the following manner:

It is the economic function of the recession to correct the imbalances of the previous expansion and thereby create the preconditions for a new one. By robbing millions of people of their jobs, and threatening the jobs of millions of others, recessions reduce worker demands and end the rise of labor costs. They eventually rebuild profit margins and stabilize prices. During recessions, inventories are cut, loans are repaid, corporate liquidity positions improve, and the deterioration in the balance of payments position is reversed. All the statements of Keynesian economists to the contrary notwithstanding, *recessions are inevitable in the unplanned economy of the United States* because they perform an essential function for which no adequate substitute has *thus far* been available.

Raford Boddy and James R. Crotty, "Who Will Plan the Planned Economy?" *The Progressive*, February, 1975.

This then is the general description of expansion and contraction and the function of recession as viewed by radical economists. It is important to note that the cause is rooted in the structure of the economy and the behavior of the capitalist class. But there are other factors that normally intensify the business cycle. These are briefly: (1) the psychological expectations of either optimism or pessimism, (2) the existence of monopoly power in the major productive sectors of the economy, (3) events or conditions related to the international economic and financial sector, and (4) speculation in money, credit, and commodity markets.

Based upon the radical analysis of the business cycle, unemployment is perceived as being *structurally* "built-in" to the normal functioning of the capitalist system. Unemployment becomes a sort of cushion or "shock-absorber" for the cyclical behavior of the system. Likewise, inflation becomes a structural characteristic of the system having less to do with the rate of growth of the money supply than with the monopolistic pricing behavior of corporations with concentrated market power in the corporate sector.

In order to explain the continued existence of the business cycle and its *politicized* nature, radicals point to major *structural* changes in American capitalism since World War II that help to shed light upon the present failures of Keynesian policy. First, they identify the growing concentration of production by corporate firms and their growing political economic power. Another feature of the concentration of production is related to the international specialization and division of labor since 1945 carried out principally by multinational corporations and other international institutions. This increased global integration of capitalism has not only increased the concentration of production but has also made U.S. domestic stabilization policy difficult as Keynesian economic policy is increasingly incapable of imposing controls and regulations on the multinational institutions. In fact, changes and events taking place in the international sector have become over time more and more troublesome for Keynesian policy to adapt to in terms of promoting growth, price stability, and full employment. For example, the OPEC price increase in 1973-1974 completely upset the macro performance of the U.S. economy.

The last factor singled out by radical economists to explain the structural transformation of American capitalism since World War II is the growng symbiotic relationship between government and business. Radicals claim that this extensive "State-Corporate" expansion prohibits the possibility of genuine democracy in America and clearly depicts an underlying class character of government functions and policies.

This then is briefly the radical view of the failure of Keynesian economic policy and the general crisis of American capitalism.

In the two articles that follow there is a more detailed explanation and analysis of the radical view of the business cycle. The first article "Who Will Plan the Planned Economy?" by Boddy and Crotty gives a good historical overview of the crisis of American capitalism since the 1950s. They emphasize the importance of international factors in the crisis and conclude that one of the few options open to the Corporate State is to engage in extensive planning of the economy that would of course, in their eyes, further propel the U.S. economy along the road to State Capitalism. The only solution to this "Crisis" and frightening trend, they conclude, is to build a mass movement dedicated to the creation of Democratic Socialism in the United States.

The second article, "What the Marxists See in the Recession," is a Business-Week summarization of the radical analysis. It also presents some criticism of the Marxist position by orthodox economists and points out some internal differences among Marxists over their analysis.

WHO WILL PLAN THE PLANNED ECONOMY?

RAFORD BODDY AND JAMES R. CROTTY

The adoption in the postwar period of Keynesian approaches to managing the economy has not changed this basic characteristic of the system, nor has the continued monopolization and concentration of market power in the hands of the major corporations lessened the potential for economic instability. Until recently these factors did moderate the fluctuations of the business cycle, but they managed to do so under what now appears to have been a set of unusually favorable conditions—conditions which are no longer in effect.

From the end of World War II until the early 1960s, the U.S. was the unchallenged leader of world capitalism and the dominant military, political, and economic power. The economic strength of China and the Soviet Union could not compare with that of the U.S. and American foreign policy was built on this fact. Western Europe and Japan, on the other hand, began the period with devastated economies; they were almost completely dependent on the U.S. for imports, particularly capital goods.

In the world of the 1950s, the U.S. could pour hundreds of billions of dollars into its military machine, waste countless billions on consumer gadgetry and planned obsolescence, and still dominate world trade, accumulate a huge corporate empire in the developed world, and maintain control of the vast natural resources of the underdeveloped world.

The world of the 1950s is gone forever. (See Sidney Lens, "Running Out of Everything," in the October 1974 issue of *The Progressive*.) American political power is now constrained by a strong Soviet Union; its economic supremacy has been challenged by Western Europe and Japan, and its assured supply of cheap raw materials has disappeared. The economic chaos we are witnessing is the re-emergence of the basic instability of our economic system—a re-emergence triggered by the desperate attempts of the U.S. to maintain its status as the unchallenged leader of world capitalism in the face of the erosion of its power monopoly.

The changing status of American imperialism has had its greatest effect on the economy through the Indochina war, though its impact would eventually have been felt even if that war had not been fought. The outpouring of military expenditures on Vietnam between 1965 and 1968 came on top of an economic expansion which had about run its course. But American imperialism demanded the pursuit of victory in Vietnam, so the Johnson administration chose to overheat the economy through 1968 by accelerating military spending while taking no effective steps to reduce private spending. The prolongation of the U.S. expansion created, in turn, an environment in which the export-oriented economies of Japan and West Germany could sustain expansions.

In other words, in order to protect the worldwide empire of the multinational corporations, the U.S. government, by extending the expansion many years beyond its "natural life," created a situation in which the distortions, pressures, and

Reprinted by permission from *The Progressive*, 408 West Gorham Street, Madison, Wisconsin 53703. Copyright © 1975, The Progressive, Inc.

imbalances in the capitalist economies were magnified to proportions which could only be eliminated by an unusually long and severe recession.

The incoming Nixon administration did engineer a recession by the end of 1969, but it only lasted five or six quarters—clearly not long enough to restore balance to the economy. The administration was forced to abandon restrictive policies in 1970 because their continuation would have resulted in an unemployment rate too high to be reduced to a politically acceptable level for the 1972 election; because corporate profits, squeezed first by five years of full-employment wage pressure and then by the initial impact of the recession, were in need of immediate relief, and because the debt and liquidity problems of many corporations and banks were too severe to respond to the usual medicine.

By 1971 the economy was clearly in crisis. Falling U.S. interest rates had triggered huge short-term capital outflows and our trade surplus had completely eroded, leading to an explosion in the U.S. payments deficit. The international monetary system was drowning in a flood of U.S. dollars. These dollars in turn were bloating the money supplies of Japan and Europe, causing both inflation and demand-induced economic expansions.

The attempt to shore up the failing U.S. empire through the war in Vietnam can thus be said to have had several important repercussions: First, by prolonging the American economic expansion for three or four years, it left the system vulnerable to its fundamental instability. Second, by laying the foundation for a decade-long expansion in the world capitalist system, it led to a world-wide commodity or raw-material inflation. Third, by accelerating the relative decline in U.S. power, it created the preconditions for the political and economic revolt of the Third World raw-material suppliers, most significantly the exporters of oil. Fourth, it led to the introduction of government economic controls through Nixon's New Economic Policy, thus signaling the end of the postwar "miracle" of the Keynesian revolution.

The increases in oil and food prices are of relatively recent origin and cannot be held responsible either for domestic inflation or for international financial crisis. But they have seriously exacerbated the existing crisis, and clearly must be taken into account.

The declining international position of the U.S. has received much comment, and now the debt and liquidity position of the U.S. economy are in the spotlight. As *Business Week* put it in a special issue on the "Debt Economy." "The U.S. is leveraged as never before. There is nearly $8 of debt per $1 of money supply, more than double the figure of twenty years ago. Corporate debt amounts to more than fifteen times after-tax profits, compared with under eight times in 1955. Household debt amounts to 93 percent of disposable income, compared with 65 percent in 1955. U.S. banks have lent billions overseas through Euro-currency markets that did not even exist in 1955."

Faced with profit levels which have probably peaked and will surely decline as the recession rolls into high gear, debt-ridden corporations will find it increasingly difficult to meet their fixed-interest obligations. A snowballing of bankruptcies could follow the failure of a few giant corporations. The inability of unemployed workers to maintain payment on their debt would only aggravate the problem.

Astounding as it may seem, even some *countries* seem in danger of bankruptcy under the tremendous pressure of mounting bills for oil imports. Italy, at the moment, is the most likely candidate. In addition to its debt to the International Monetary Fund and the central banks of other countries, Italy has borrowed $10 billion in the past few years from private international sources. Default on these massive debts would reverberate throughout the capitalist system—to what eventual effect no one is sure. Nor is it possible to forecast with any accuracy the political, economic, and financial impact of the massive accumulation of petrodollars by the oil-producing countries.

Moreover, Western Europe and Japan can no longer serve as a buffer to mitigate the impacts of a U.S. recession. They, too, are experiencing rising unemployment and falling output, bringing pressure on U.S. export markets just as our recession is pressuring *their* exports. To make matters worse, this recession-induced decline in world exports is occurring at a time when most capitalist countries have huge balance-of-payments deficits toward the oil producing countries. These deficits, coupled with declining exports, might lead to export-import controls, controls on long-term capital movements, or competitive devaluations.

With the weakening of American hegemony, it is no longer certain that the U.S. can organize and discipline its competitors in order to generate an orderly treatment of the deficit problem. The American defeat in Vietnam and the breakdown of international monetary arrangements in August 1971 have had serious consequences for the world capitalist economic order. And the political strains emerging in Greece, Great Britain, Italy, Portugal, Japan, and France—not to mention the U.S.—make it even more difficult to count on economic cooperation, as opposed to competition, in dealing with mounting economic and political dislocations. This growing economic instability is fostering political instability which threatens capitalist governments throughout the Western world.

Because American capitalists no longer have the political and economic strength to control their allies, they may turn to a strategy of exploiting the existing economic and political instability. Although the decline in American power and the coming of age of Germany and Japan were the factors that permitted the oil-producing nations to impose dramatic price increases, the most damaging effects of higher oil prices have not been felt by the U.S. Rather, the economies of Japan and Western Europe were, at least temporarily, most severely pummeled. Furthermore, since Japan and Western Europe are much more immediately dependent on their export sectors than the U.S. the prospect of severe worldwide recession poses a more direct threat to them than it does to the U.S.

Paradoxically, then, the combination of high oil prices and world recession constitutes the situation in which the strength of the U.S. relative to its allies is greatest, because of their dependence on oil imports and world markets. It has thus become possible for a U.S. recession, needed for domestic purposes, to be turned into a weapon to be used against both the oil producers and our economic rivals.

If, as recent statements by high-level American officials seem to indicate, the U.S. oil strategy is to "break" the oil producers and eventually reduce energy prices, then a huge reduction in the world demand for oil is essential. One way to guarantee such a decline in world oil demand is to have a long, deep, worldwide recession. Indeed, the mere threat of such a recession may be enough to pressure Germany, Japan, and even France into participating in a subservient way in U.S. designed and dominated international economic and political tactics in the oil conflict. Maximizing the threat of world recession may, therefore, be attractive to those concerned with the maintenance of the American empire.

But this would be a dangerous gambit because the American corporate elite clearly has fewer means at its disposal for controlling the dynamics of a worldwide recession than it has with respect to a domestic one. And the political implications of an out-of-control world depression must be sobering indeed to corporate and government leaders.

All of these strains and uncertainties make it increasingly likely that the managers of the American system will seek new tools and policies to cope with the economic and political crisis. The contradictions inherent in the attempt to "solve" the current multidimensional economic crisis through the exclusive use of orthodox monetary and fiscal tools seem overwhelming.

If the government is unwilling to risk a depression, it could choose to postpone the day of reckoning by imposing mandatory wage and price controls. Although wage-price controls are generally thought of as a mechanism used to control inflation during an economic expansion, they have attracted increased interest in the face of projections of an 8 percent unemployment rate *and* a 10 percent rise in the hourly wage rate this year [1975]. Wage controls might handle part of the job of the recession by reducing the rate of wage increase.

But these controls are themselves contradictory. The experience in Western Europe and the U.S. with temporary or on-off aggregate wage-price controls indicates that a repetition of such controls as Nixon's Phases I through IV can only promote increased instability in the system. For one thing, wage and price decisions are themselves affected by the removal of controls or the anticipation of their introduction. Under these conditions, temporary controls simply reallocate inflation over time, they do not eliminate it. Moreover, controls eventually lead to surpluses and shortages because they suppress market forces which, however socially irrational, have their own internal coherence in our system. This is perhaps best seen in the confused decision that led to the withdrawal of these forces from the market, and a subsequent mammoth increase in food prices in August 1973.

In light of these considerations, more permanent and extensive controls than we had from 1971 to 1974 appear to be required. The Democratic Party, at its miniconvention in Kansas City in December, called for "an across-the-board system of economic controls, including prices, wages, executive compensation, profits and rents." Leonard Silk reported in the *New York Times* that some leading Democrats were "moving to support a program that would put far more stress on economic planning as a means of directing industrial investment to meet critical needs...." We assume that there has been serious private discussion among the corporate elite on the same topic. And, since it is recognized that the use of planning by Japan, Germany, Sweden, and France contributed heavily to their superior economic performance in the 1960s and early 1970s, there are long-run as well as short-run forces pressuring the U.S. toward a planning imperative.

A move toward planning, it should be clear, would have profound economic and political implications. Government policy will directly determine the share of total income going to capital as opposed to labor, and perhaps the distribution of labor income among workers as well. This alone might produce considerable conflict, since organized labor could be expected to fight for its share of production. But there would be more to permanent controls than the setting of wages and prices. They could require government-directed allocation of raw materials and credit, a detailed system of tax credits and subsidies, antistrike or even anticollective-bargaining legislation, and administratively coordinated investment strategies among firms and industries.

The planning process eventually will require detailed management of the economy and of people. This can obviously lead to serious political conflict. In short, controls may not deliver us from our current crisis, but may instead create a new one, overtly political in nature.

The development of detailed economic planning within the present array of political forces in the U.S. will undoubtedly mean corporate control of the planning process, just as the introduction of federal regulatory agencies has historically meant control by and for the regulated industries. It is, therefore, more important now than ever before that the political balance of power be changed and the power of the corporate elite broken. What we need now is a democratic, socialist, national political organization to defend the interests of the majority of the American people against the fundamentally antagonistic interests of the corporations and the super-rich who own and control them.

Because the problems we face are derivatives of our capitalist institutions, neither the Republican nor the Democratic Party offers real hope to the working people of this country. These parties are committed to existing power relations, and dominated by corporate money and capitalist ideology. Democratic party reformers may wish to return to the corporate liberalism of the 1950s and 1960s, but if the arguments presented here are correct, there can be no turning back.

It seems clear that over the long run the only permanent solution to the economic instability and insecurity which derive from the monopoly, inequality, and imperialism of modern capitalism is to build a democratic, socialist society. A nationwide socialist organization will be necessary to defend ourselves in the short run and to aid us in the task of developing an egalitarian society wherein production is for use rather than profit, and decisions are collectively made by workers, not bosses.

WHAT THE MARXISTS SEE IN THE RECESSION

BUSINESSWEEK

While the majority of economists argue about when the current recession will end and how vigorous an upturn will follow, radical economists believe that the U.S. economy is in the throes of a prolonged crisis from which it will not easily or quickly emerge. Even if an upturn begins this year or next, the radicals predict that it will only lead to an even sharper collapse in a few years.

The radical movement in economics got its start in the mid-1960s, when many younger economists concluded that traditional theory was irrelevant to the major issues of the period. But radical economics stagnated when the university turmoil over Vietnam subsided. The depth of the current recession has, however, breathed a new vigor into radical economics in the U.S. Just in the past year, the radicals' organization, the Union for Radical Political Economics (URPE), has grown by 25 percent to more than 2500 members.

The recession has helped the radical movement not only by creating a renewed dissatisfaction with conventional economics, but also by sharpening the radical

Reprinted from *BusinessWeek*, June 23, 1975, with special permission. © 1975 by McGraw-Hill, Inc.

analysis of the U.S. economy. The upshot is a revival of interest in classical Marxist economics.

Not everyone in URPE claims Karl Marx as his or her major intellectual ancestor, and vigorous debates take place on the relevance of Marxism. Nonetheless, in interpreting the crisis, an analysis largely based on *Das Kapital* is rapidly gaining adherents. The emerging analysis looks like this:

The radicals view the current slide as the first genuine postwar economic crisis, not just as a somewhat deeper—but basically familiar—business cycle recession. Both Keynesian and monetarist theory treat the economy as though it were a machine that regularly cranks out a cycle of ups and downs. Some of these are deeper or longer, but they can all more or less be explained in the same way. The radicals, however, distinguish between short-term fluctuations and a true structural crisis that represents a historical turning point in the development of the capitalist system. The U.S. economy, they argue, is in the midst of such a crisis.

They point to a falling rate of profit as the basic cause of the ills plaguing the U.S. economy in the past decade—from the accelerating inflation and productivity slowdown of the late 1960s to the violent swings in business activity of the 1970s. They note that profitability has declined not only in recessions, but even in the boom of 1965–1969 (chart).

They observe that corporations went heavily into debt to finance investments in the face of the profit squeeze. They maintain that the choice for business currently is an even more dangerous level of indebtedness or cutting capital spending, production, and employment.

They claim that crises are inevitable in a capitalist system to "purge" the economy and get it back on the road to high profits. Raford Boddy of American University and James Crotty of the University of Massachusetts, in a widely used URPE analysis, argue that "it is the economic function of the recession to correct the imbalances of the previous expansion and thereby create the conditions for a new one. By robbing . . . and threatening the jobs of millions . . . recessions erode worker militancy and end the rise of labor costs. They eventually rebuild profit margins and stabilize prices."

Since the falling rate of profit is at the heart of the radical analysis, it is no surprise that the theory of profits is the subject of intense debate between radicals and their opponents. Although both sides use the same numbers, they have diametrically opposed views on what causes the profit rate to fall and what it means for the economy.

INTERNAL DYNAMICS

The radicals start from Marx's labor theory of value, and in particular from the idea that profits are just a form of surplus-value. This is defined as the time that workers spend providing capitalists with the means to expand operations, as opposed to producing goods and services for themselves. When business increases the physical capital used by each worker, the rate of profit will tend to fall. The reason: The total surplus working time, which is the source of profits, does not go up as fast as the total invested capital. Corporations, the Marxists say, try to offset this tendency by preventing real wages from rising along with the productivity gains generated by the new investment.

At this point in their analysis, the radicals supplement Marx with the theories of the late Polish-born economist Michal Kalecki, who argued that in a boom's last stages, cutting the rate of wage gain, relative to productivity growth, is exactly what business finds hard to do. This is because boom-caused tight labor markets and materials shortages both restrain productivity gains and give the workers more bargaining power to resist downward wage pressure. So, the radicals conclude, it is not external factors like the oil cartel nor policy mistakes by government officials, but rather the internal dynamics of the system itself that cause the crisis.

But in the eyes of most economists, this reliance on Marx's value theory is the basic fault in radical economics. Massachusetts Institute of Technology economist Paul A. Samuelson has been conducting a polemic for several years against the labor theory of value, which has also involved such prominent economists as Princeton's William J. Baumol and one of Japan's leading theorists, Michio Morishima. Samuelson considers Marx's theory that the source of profit is exploitation of labor as an unscientific piece of metaphysical chicanery or, at best, just a trick of definitions. To which the radicals respond that the neoclassical tradition in which Samuelson works has no satisfactory theory of the origin of profits at all.

Conventional economists see the fall in the rate of return as a result of the process of "capital deepening." This means that as more and more capital is added, the law of diminishing returns sets in, and output per unit of capital falls. These economists see no reason the rate of return should not rebound once the economy gets moving again.

CONTROLLING THE WORKERS

Nowhere are the radicals more "radical" than in how they view the government's role. While liberals generally see the government as the arbiter of the differing interests within society, the radicals argue that even when it partially incorporates pro-labor attitudes and goals, government must inevitably serve the corporations' interests. To the radicals, a Kennedy administration had a different strategy for controlling the workers than a Nixon administration. Nevertheless, both identified business's needs with the welfare of the whole population.

Many radical economists therefore argue that the government has deliberately engineered the current recession to discipline labor. They point to the persistently tight monetary and fiscal stances of the Ford administration and Federal Reserve Chairman Arthur F. Burns as evidence that the government is consciously aiming at slow growth and high unemployment over a period of several more years, until the job of lowering labor's share of total output has been accomplished.

But other radicals, while not denying that conscious decision making plays a role, argue that focusing on the conservative policy choices of the current administration risks blurring the lines between the radical analysis and that of the Keynesian liberals who call for more expansive policy and large-scale public works programs. In their view, no successful economic policy exists for a capitalist government during a genuine crisis. There is no escape from the sharpening dilemma of inflation vs. unemployment.

As they see it, loosening the fiscal and monetary strings would lead to a repetition of the 1971-1973 superboom, with rapidly accelerating inflation after the slack in capacity is taken up, and eventually to a crash of even greater magnitude than

1974–1975. Monetary ease can postpone the day of reckoning—the crisis that the system "needs" to cleanse itself—but postponement would only make the ultimate readjustment even more painful.

So, according to the radicals, rapid alternation of economic policy—what many U.S. economists have dubbed the "political business cycle" and the British know as "stop-go"—is not simply the result of malevolence or stupidity on the part of policy makers. It is, in their opinion, the expression on the policy level of the fundamental weaknesses of a capitalist economy in a period of crisis.

VIOLENT PROCESS

Contrary to a common belief, however, for Marx, there was— and is—no final economic crisis for capitalism, no "catastrophe" from which it can not escape. The crisis itself recreates the conditions for profitable production, and sets off a new long upswing in the process of capital accumulation. But the process of readjustment is violent and conflict-ridden and can involve basic changes in political and economic institutions.

To get out of crisis and resume sustained growth, the radicals claim, the system needs to force the workers to a lower standard of living relative to its productive capacity. The goal is to free a greater portion of final output for capital spending, military expenditures, and foreign investment.

The Marxists note that real earnings of the typical factory worker have grown little over the decade, and are currently falling. To maintain family income in the face of declining earnings for household heads, large numbers of married women and younger people have had to enter the labor force. Thus, say the radicals, even in years when disposable family income rises, it is only at the price of a greater total work effort.

The radicals also point out that the crisis of the private economy is matched by a "fiscal crisis" of state and local governments, which respond by laying off workers, cutting services, and raising taxes. They see this not as the consequence of mismanagement, but as part and parcel of the overall attack on the standard-of-living of working and middle class people.

THE FUTURE

But the squeeze on workers, say the radicals, will be answered increasingly by strikes, demonstrations, and possibly a leftward shift in political ideology. The government, they add, will move to control the situation in favor of business, while it attempts to moderate the crisis to prevent the development of a revolutionary situation. To do this, it will move again toward Nixon-type wage-price controls, which the radicals argue held down only wages. Moreover, they expect experiments in economic planning. But radicals do not see this as a favorable development because, on the whole, they no longer equate planning as such with socialism. As Queens College economist William Tabb puts it: "Liberal leaders neglect to point out that the question is one of who does the planning and in whose interests is the planning done." Tabb argues that planning under capitalism will simply serve to control the working class more oppressively.

The future of the radicals is to some extent tied to what happens to the economy. To be sure, an upturn in production this year would not faze them much, since they generally expect a pattern of wide swings in the economy over the next few

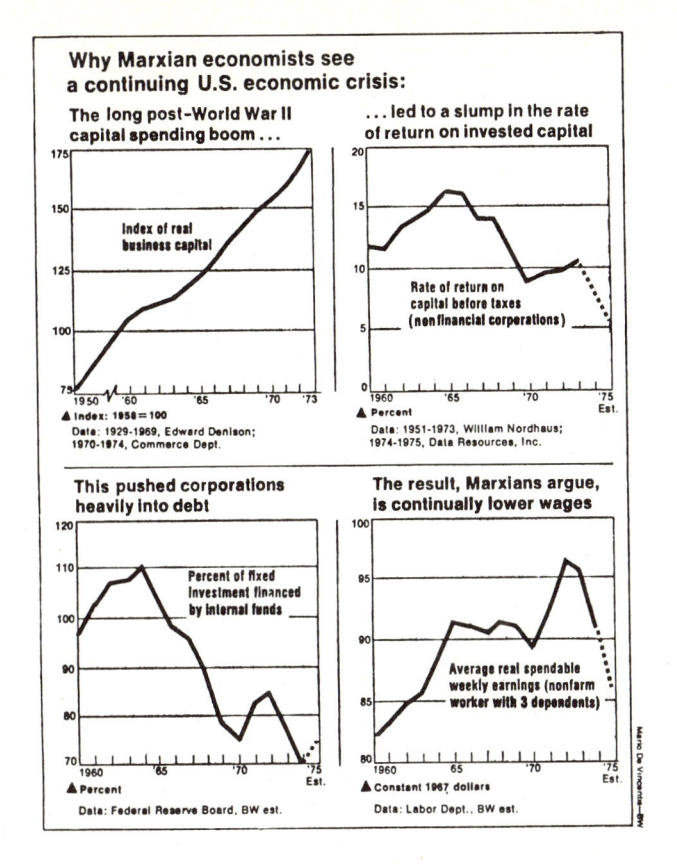

Why Marxian economists see a continuing U.S. economic crisis:

The long post–World War II capital spending boom...
Index of real business capital
Data: 1929-1969, Edward Denison; 1970-1974, Commerce Dept.
▲ Index: 1958=100

...led to a slump in the rate of return on invested capital
Rate of return on capital before taxes (nonfinancial corporations)
Data: 1951-1973, William Nordhaus; 1974-1975, Data Resources, Inc.
▲ Percent

This pushed corporations heavily into debt
Percent of fixed investment financed by internal funds
Data: Federal Reserve Board, BW est.
▲ Percent

The result, Marxians argue, is continually lower wages
Average real spendable weekly earnings (nonfarm worker with 3 dependents)
Data: Labor Dept., BW est.
▲ Constant 1967 dollars

years. But a sustained long-term growth of the system, without reemergence of crisis would reverse their growing influence among students of the "dismal science."

---

5. Why do Boddy and Crotty feel that the "declining international position of the U.S." is so important in terms of their analysis of the crisis of American capitalism?

6. Boddy and Crotty claim that the U.S. is not too far away from instituting National Economic Planning. Why do they think that this is so self-evident and why do they fear it? What would they prefer to see happen?

7. What do Marxist economists mean when they use the term, "Political Business Cycle"?

8. Critically evaluate the way in which Marxists think about recessions.

THE KEYNESIAN REVOLUTION AND THE FUTURE

Contemporary economics is in crisis because the social order is in crisis, unable to go back to the old and unwilling to strike boldly toward the new.

Daniel Fusfeld

We have now come full circle. What has become of the Keynesian Revolution? Certainly there does not seem to be at this time any conclusive evidence supporting a concrete answer to this question. Yet we can say, based upon what we have examined in this chapter and elsewhere, that there are competing theories that have created substantial controversy over this question.

In spite of the disagreements and differences in analysis, most economists would have to agree that Keynesian economics represented a disciplinary scientific revolution. Keynes did usher in a *new* body of knowledge and thought designed to analyze and solve the crisis of capitalism in the 1930s. This can safely be called the "Keynesian Revolution." Only time will tell whether or not "reformed" Keynesian economics can successfully guide capitalism through the challenges of the late 20th century. If one adopts an historical point of view, the Keynesian Revolution might be perceived as being still in its gestation period slowly maturing; or, one might choose to argue that the Keynesian Revolution is "old and tired" acting out the final stages of its life. Still others charge that the Keynesian Revolution was betrayed, Keynes was never understood, and the implications of his theory went unnoticed or ignored. What we see practiced today is not the authentic Keynes but a "bastardization" of Keynes. The real Keynes would have by now accomplished the goal of achieving full employment, tamed the business cycle, and would have eliminated the gross inequalities in income distribution. The critics who cry betrayal claim that a more radical Keynesian economics would solve most of our problems. And then there are the radical economists who posit the "slow death" of the Keynesian Revolution along with the structural crisis of modern capitalism.

Keynes in the last chapter of *The General Theory* shared some of his thoughts regarding the social philosophical implications of his masterpiece. He reflects upon: human nature and the "money-making passion" of men, the possibilities of attaining full employment through the socialization of investment, the roots of war between nations, and the future vision embodied in his work and the work of economists in general.

CONCLUDING NOTES ON THE SOCIAL PHILOSOPHY TOWARDS WHICH THE GENERAL THEORY MIGHT LEAD

JOHN MAYNARD KEYNES

The outstanding faults of the economic society in which we live are its failure to provide for full employment and its arbitrary and inequitable distribution of wealth and incomes....

... Thus our argument leads towards the conclusion that in contemporary conditions the growth of wealth, so far from being dependent on the abstinence of the rich, as is commonly supposed, is more likely to be impeded by it. One of the chief social justifications of great inequality of wealth is, therefore, removed. I am not

Excerpted from *The General Theory of Employment, Interest, and Money* by John Maynard Keynes. Reprinted by permission of Harcourt Brace Jovanovich, Inc.

saying that there are no other reasons, unaffected by our theory, capable of justifying some measure of inequality in some circumstances. But it does dispose of the most important of the reasons why hitherto we have thought it prudent to move carefully. This particularly affects our attitude towards death duties: for there are certain justifications for inequality of incomes which do not apply equally to inequality of inheritances.

For my own part, I believe that there is social and psychological justification for significant inequalities of incomes and wealth, but not for such large disparities as exist today. There are valuable human activities which require the motive of money-making and the environment of private wealth-ownership for their full fruition. Moreover, dangerous human proclivities can be canalised into comparatively harmless channels by the existence of opportunities for money-making and private wealth, which, if they cannot be satisfied in this way, may find their outlet in cruelty, the reckless pursuit of personal power and authority, and other forms of self-aggrandisement. It is better that a man should tyrannise over his bank balance than over his fellow-citizens; and whilst the former is sometimes denounced as being but a means to the latter, sometimes at least it is an alternative. But it is not necessary for the stimulation of these activities and the satisfaction of these proclivities that the game should be played for such high stakes as at present. Much lower stakes will serve the purpose equally well, as soon as the players are accustomed to them. The task of transmuting human nature must not be confused with the task of managing it. Though in the ideal commonwealth men may have been taught or inspired or bred to take no interest in the stakes, it may still be wise and prudent statesmanship to allow the game to be played, subject to rules and limitations, so long as the average man, or even a significant section of the community, is in fact strongly addicted to the money-making passion....

... In some other respects the foregoing theory is moderately conservative in its implications. For whilst it indicates the vital importance of establishing certain central controls in matters which are now left in the main to individual initiative, there are wide fields of activity which are unaffected. The State will have to exercise a guiding influence on the propensity to consume partly through its scheme of taxation, partly by fixing the rate of interest, and partly, perhaps, in other ways. Furthermore, it seems unlikely that the influence of banking policy on the rate of interest will be sufficient by itself to determine an optimum rate of investment. I conceive, therefore, that a somewhat comprehensive socialisation of investment will prove the only means of securing an approximation to full employment; though this need not exclude all manner of compromises and of devices by which public authority will cooperate with private initiative. But beyond this no obvious case is made out for a system of State Socialism which would embrace most of the economic life of the community. It is not the ownership of the instruments of production which it is important for the State to assume. If the State is able to determine the aggregate amount of resources devoted to augmenting the instruments and the basic rate of reward to those who own them, it will have accomplished all that is necessary. Moreover, the necessary measures of socialisation can be introduced gradually and without a break in the general traditions of society....

... Let us stop for a moment to remind ourselves what these advantages are. They are partly advantages of efficiency—the advantages of decentralisation and of the play of self-interest. The advantage to efficiency of the decentralisation of decisions and of the individual responsibility is even greater, perhaps, than the nineteenth century supposed; and the reaction against the appeal to self-interest may have gone too far. But, above all, individualism, if it can be purged of its defects and its abuses, is the best safeguard of personal liberty in the sense that, compared with any other system, it greatly widens the field for the exercise of personal choice. It is also the best safeguard of the variety of life, which emerges precisely from this extended field of personal choice, and the loss of which is the greatest of all the losses of the homogeneous or totalitarian state. For this variety preserves the traditions which embody the most secure and successful choices of former generations: it colours the present with the diversification of its fancy; and, being the handmaid of experiment as well as of tradition and of fancy, it is the most powerful instrument to better the future.

Whilst, therefore, the enlargement of the functions of government, involved in the task of adjusting to one another the propensity to consume and the inducement to invest, would seem to a nineteenth-century publicist or to a contemporary American financier to be a terrific encroachment on individualism, I defend it, on the contrary, both as the only practicable means of avoiding the destruction of existing economic forms in their entirety and as the condition of the successful functioning of individual initiative.

... Thus, whilst economists were accustomed to applaud the prevailing international system as furnishing the fruits of the international division of labour and harmonising at the same time the interests of different nations, there lay concealed a less benign influence; and those statesmen were moved by common sense and a correct apprehension of the true course of events, who believed that if a rich, old country were to neglect the struggle for markets, its prosperity would droop and fail. But if nations can learn to provide themselves with full employment by their domestic policy (and, we must add, if they can also attain equilibrium in the trend of their population), there need be no important economic forces calculated to set the interest of one country against that of its neighbours. There would still be room for the international division of labour and for international lending in appropriate conditions. But there would no longer be a pressing motive why one country need force its wares on another or repulse the offerings of its neighbour, not because this was necessary to enable it to pay for what it wished to purchase, but with the express object of upsetting the equilibrium of payments so as to develop a balance of trade in its own favour. International trade would cease to be what it is, namely, a desperate expedient to maintain employment at home by forcing sales on foreign markets and restricting purchases, which, if successful, will merely shift the problem of unemployment to the neighbour which is worsted in the struggle, but a willing and unimpeded exchange of goods and services in conditions of mutual advantage.

Is the fulfillment of these ideas a visionary hope? Have they insufficient roots in the motives which govern the evolution of political society? Are the interests which they will thwart stronger and more obvious than those which they will serve?

I do not attempt an answer in this place. It would need a volume of a different character from this one to indicate even in outline the practical measures in which they might be gradually clothed. But if the ideas are correct—an hypothesis on which the author himself must necessarily base what he writes—it would be a mistake, I predict, to dispute their potency over a period of time. At the present moment people are unusually expectant of a more fundamental diagnosis; more particularly ready to receive it; eager to try it out, if it should be even plausible. But apart from this contemporary mood, the ideas of economists and political philosophers, both when they are right and when they are wrong, are more powerful than is commonly understood. Indeed the world is ruled by little else. Practical men, who believe themselves to be quite exempt from any intellectual influences, are usually the slaves of some defunct economist. Madmen in authority, who hear voices in the air, are distilling their frenzy from some academic scribbler of a few years back. I am sure that the power of vested interests is vastly exaggerated compared with the gradual encroachment of ideas. Not, indeed, immediately, but after a certain interval; for in the field of economic and political philosophy there are not many who are influenced by new theories after they are twenty-five or thirty years of age, so that the ideas which civil servants and politicians and even agitators apply to current events are not likely to be the newest. But, soon or late, it is ideas, not vested interests, which are dangerous for good or evil.

9. How would you describe Keynes's view of human nature? Do you agree or disagree with him?

10. How would a Marxist economist critique this excerpt from Keynes's *The General Theory*? How would you?

11. It has been argued by some that Keynes was really a conservative. Others have on the other hand simply argued that he was a liberal. And, then, there have been those who persuasively argued that Keynes was really a radical. What do you think? Why?

Granted that the future of capitalism in general and Keynesian economics in particular are uncertain, we need to anticipate the future now with the best theory and empirical evidence we can find. As we do this, a number of difficult but obvious questions and additional variables must be firmly and soberly *integrated* into our analysis. We are just now beginning to recognize the importance of the future implications of continued economic growth; of the availability and use of natural resources, particularly those related to energy; and of the use of formalized economic planning in our economic system. We will have to consider these seriously as we attempt to analyze and predict the future. Only by doing this can we possibly hope to construct a more humane economy, as described by Daniel Fusfeld:

A humane economy requires more than prosperity and economic growth, more than efficient allocation of resources. It demands change in the framework of economic institutions to achieve greater equality and freedom. It requires dispersal of the economic power and governmental authority that support the present disposition of income, wealth, and power. It requires a social environment that brings a sense of community and fellowship into human relationships. It demands compatibility among man, his technology, and the natural environment. And all of these things must be done on a worldwide scale. These are the goals of the future, to which economists and everyone else will have to devote their energies.

Daniel Fusfeld, "Post-Post-Keynes: The Shattered Synthesis," *Saturday Review,* January 22, 1972.

KEY CONCEPTS

Keynesian revolution
Carter Economic Program
political business cycle
pluralist democracy

class conflict
profit squeeze
fiscal crisis

REVIEW QUESTIONS

1. In what way could it be said that Marx was really the first macroeconomist?

2. How would Walter Heller respond to the radical critique of American capitalism outlined in the articles by Boddy and Crotty and *BusinessWeek*?

3. If Keynes were still alive today, how, if at all, would he change the last chapter of *The General Theory*? If you could write your own concluding chapter to *The General Theory*, what would you say?

SUGGESTED READINGS

Economics Education Project of the Union for Radical Political Economics. *U.S. Capitalism in Crisis*, 1978 (URPE, 41 Union Square West, Room 901, N.Y., N.Y. 10003). A radical interpretation of the state of the economy and economics.

Michael Harrington, 1976. *The Twilight of Capitalism,* Simon and Schuster. See Part II "The Future of Karl Marx." A discussion of the contemporary relevance of Marxian economics for understanding the crisis of capitalism. See Chapter 13, "Twilight of an Epoch," for summary and conclusion.

Walter Heller, 1976. *The Economy: Old Myths and New Realities.* Norton. An easy to read and understand overview and analysis of the present condition of our economy. See Part II, "What's Right with Economics?" for a good mainstream defense of the economy.

Joan Robinson, 1962. *Economic Philosophy*, Doubleday Anchor. See Chapter 4, "The Keynesian Revolution," for an insightful analysis of Keynes.

Dwayne Ward, 1977. *Toward a Critical Political Economics*, Goodyear. See Chapter 2, "The Questioned Hegemony of Keynesian Thought," and Chapter 3, "Some Marxian Ideas on the Crises of Capitalism: Contrast with Orthodoxy."

ECONOMIC GROWTH, RESOURCES, AND THE ENVIRONMENT

CHAPTER 25

By now it should be clear that the main problems of the environment do not arise from temporary and accidental malfunctions of existing economic and social systems. On the contrary, they are the warning signs of a profound incompatibility between deeply rooted beliefs in continuous growth and the dawning recognition of the earth as a spaceship, limited in its resources and vulnerable to thoughtless mishandling. The nature of our response to these symptoms is crucial. If we refuse to recognize the cause of our trouble the result can only be increasing disillusion and growing strain upon the fragile institutions that maintain external peace and internal social cohesion. If, on the other hand, we can respond to the unprecedented challenge with informed and constructive action, the rewards will be as great as the penalties for failure.

Editors of The Ecologist

INTRODUCTION

As the last chapter emphasized, the Keynesian paradigm is now under great stress and pressure to adapt itself to the formidable challenges of the late 20th century. Our world today is experiencing rapid and unprecedented change. We have already identified some of these changes and referred to them as "structural" changes, i.e., changes that fundamentally alter the material world as well as our perceptions of it. Some of the most profound effects of these changes are on economic growth, resource availability and use, and environmental degradation. In this chapter we will examine the complex relationships among these three topics—economic growth, resources, and the environment. All have become problems in the modern era.

First, we shall place our current problems in historical perspective. Second, the "Growth versus No-Growth" controversy will be analyzed. Third, the global energy crisis will be evaluated as well as the recent response to this crisis by the Carter administration. Fourth, we will explore the unique relationship between the energy crisis and the economic crisis. And, finally, in a concluding section, we will synthesize and integrate this broad topic into a conceptual framework for assessing the future.

THE PROBLEM IN HISTORICAL PERSPECTIVE

Human beings have always been aware of and sensitive to the interrelationships between economic growth, resources, and the environment. This recognition, though, has manifested itself in different ways in different historical epochs. There have been those who feared the worst and predicted catastrophe and doom; and on the other hand, there have been the eternal optimists, confident that somehow human beings will exercise their great natural creativity and ingenuity to develop the appropriate response to a given problem at a given time.

These different points of view have been permanently etched into the cultures of peoples and societies by the works of artists, poets, musicians, architects, scientists, engineers, philosophers, and social scientists. Going back to the early 1700s in the midst of the great Scientific Revolution, we begin to see the Western world transform its view of societal development, time, space, nature, labor, and resources. Societal advancement became associated with greater specialization, division of labor, and reliance upon science and technology to greatly develop and expand the productive potential of society. This was a period of increasing secularization and materialism. Success was defined in terms of economic categories—particularly individual income, business profit, and total social output. The ideas of Adam Smith in *The Wealth of Nations* played an important role in encouraging this overriding concern with economic growth. Yet, in the midst of this period, which prepared the foundation for the Industrial Revolution, there were voices of caution and despair. One of the early classical liberal economists, the Reverend Thomas Malthus, an Englishman, predicted that geometric increases in population would eventually outstrip the available food supply that increased only arithmetically. The result could only be widespread famine unless checked by positive and preventative measures. This pessimism of the Malthusian theory, while ignored by many in his own lifetime, has resurfaced in recent years as a warning to modern society.

As the Industrial Revolution in Western Europe gained momentum, many people reflected upon the general environmental degradation associated with urbanization, industrialization, the advancement of science and technology, and economic growth. One has merely to browse through *The Condition of the Working Class in England* by Friedrich Engels or *Hard Times* by Charles Dickens to get some sense of this reaction to the slums, the pollution, and the poverty.

In this context, controversy developed over whether or not growth was controllable or even desirable in the future. The political economist, John Stuart Mill, wrote about a "stationary-state" economy and looked forward to its coming.

It is scarcely necessary to remark that a stationary condition of capital and population implies no stationary state of human improvement. There would be as much scope as ever for all kinds of mental culture, and moral and social progress; as much room for improving the Art of Living and much more likelihood of it being improved, when minds cease to be engrossed by the art of getting on.

J. S. Mill, *Principles of Political Economy*, Volume II, London: John W. Parker and son, 1857, p. 326.

1. John Stuart Mill in this excerpt is optimistic about the possibilities "of mental culture, and moral and social progress" as well as "for improving the Art of Living" in a stationary-state economy. Do you agree or disagree with him? Why?

At about the same time, Karl Marx spoke of the inherent dynamics of capitalist growth that resulted in periodic cycles of prosperity and stagnation and ultimately the collapse of the system itself. For the most part, Marx's analysis and warnings were met with hostility and ignored. By the end of the 19th century and the beginning of the 20th century, the Western world was firmly committed to a philosophy of achieving greater economic growth at whatever cost. The mastery over nature, made possible by the marvels of science and technology, was legitimized by the economic and psychological motivations of self-interest, greed, profit-seeking, and capital accumulation. These forces set in motion a veritable "growth machine" with virtually no limits, ethics, or morals.

The Modern Context

Indeed, the need for raw materials and cheap resources to fuel the growth process sent the competing nation-states of Europe all over the globe. Each hoped to acquire and control whatever resources and markets possible to ensure and maintain their own respective growth and development goals. In the process, they carved out portions of Latin America, Asia, and Africa for themselves. This period of colonialism, accompanied by two World Wars, left the global arena in a precarious state by 1945. While Europe entered a period of reconstruction, the U.S. and the Soviet Union were locked into an "ideological" struggle. This "Cold-War" mentality manifested itself in a competitive contest between the two nations. Economic growth and military power became the two major indices of ideological strength and performance. This competition legitimized the emphasis upon growth per se and military power in particular in both the U.S. and the USSR. While the two superpowers were so engaged, important events were taking place elsewhere. The early 1960s ushered in a period of de-colonization and independence for the nations of the Third World. Yet, the political independence of these nations did not mean automatic economic independence. The end result for most nations was a new stage of "neocolonialism." The interdependence of the colonial system persisted. The advanced nations maintained control over the raw materials and resources needed for their growth and prosperity.

Growing affluence in the U.S. blinded the majority of Americans (and economists) to a concern about the inherent costs and contradictions of such prosperity. Attention was first brought to the problems of a society obsessed with economic growth when John Kenneth Galbraith published *The Affluent Society*. Galbraith criticized our materialistic consumerism. He scoffed at the way the public was manipulated by the twin levers of advertising and salesmanship. In his critique,

Galbraith challenged the orthodox economist's view of consumer behavior. He argued that the consumer depicted in economic theory—the person with insatiable wants who independently and rationally decided preferences—did not exist. Galbraith suggested that consumer behavior was determined by other forces and put forth a different explanation:

> As a society becomes increasingly affluent, wants are increasingly created by the process by which they are satisfied. This may operate passively. Increases in consumption, the counterpart of increases in production, act by suggestion or emulation to create wants. Or producers may proceed actively to create wants through advertising and salesmanship. Wants thus come to depend on output. In technical terms, it can no longer be assumed that welfare is greater at an all-around higher level of production than at a lower one. It may be the same. The higher level of production has, merely, a higher level of want creation necessitating a higher level of want satisfaction.

---

2. Do you agree or disagree with John Kenneth Galbraith's analysis and critique of orthodox consumer behavior theory? Why? (Attempt to answer this question by reflecting upon your own life experience.)

Several years after Galbraith's contribution, a young Catholic priest set off across the United States to see how the American people were living in this period of prosperity. Upon his return, Michael Harrington wrote *The Other America* documenting the widespread poverty he found amidst the affluence. As his book gained notoriety, people became shocked and embarrassed that this condition existed in such a great nation. Pressure was put on policymakers to draft legislation and implement programs to eliminate this condition. While a few programs were started, the real solution for poverty and income inequality was believed to be more economic growth. This would mean more employment and income, as well as more goods and services to distribute. Such a natural and permanent solution was greatly preferred to the temporary and costly government intervention suggested by some policymakers.

In the midst of the chaos and unrest of the 1960s, the issues of ecology, environment, and growth continued to cause concern. With material prosperity, some people began to question the "quality of life" they were living. Clean air and water became just as important as having a high-paying job and a luxurious leisure-oriented life-style. As cities grew and suburbanization accelerated, the larger and more mobile population witnessed the progressive deterioration of the natural physical environment. Resource use, particularly of nonrenewable fossil energy fuels, escalated at unprecedented rates. Some Americans began to recognize the fact that with only 6 percent of the world's population, they were consuming the "lion's share" (over 30 percent) of the earth's finite resources.

Economists and other members of the scientific community began to respond to this developing crisis. In 1966, Professor Kenneth Boulding suggested in an article titled "The Economics of the Coming Spaceship Earth," that

We are now in the middle of a long process of transition in the nature of the image which man has of himself and his environment. Primitive men, and to a large extent also men of the early civilizations, imagined themselves to be living on a virtually illimitable plane. There was almost always somewhere beyond the known limits of human habitation, and over a very large part of the time that man has been on earth, there has been something like a frontier. That is, there was always some place else to go when things got too difficult, either by reason of the deterioration of the natural environment or a deterioration of the social structure in places where people happened to live. The image of the frontier is probably one of the oldest images of mankind, and it is not surprising that we find it hard to get rid of....

The closed earth of the future requires economic principles which are somewhat different from those of the open earth of the past. For the sake of picturesqueness, I am tempted to call the open economy the "cowboy economy," the cowboy being symbolic of the illimitable plains and also associated with reckless, exploitative, romantic, and violent behavior, which is characteristic of open societies. The closed economy of the future might similarly be called the "spaceman" economy, in which the earth has become a single spaceship, without unlimited reservoirs of anything, either for extraction or for pollution, and in which, therefore, man must find his place in a cyclical ecological system which is capable of continuous reproduction of material form even though it cannot escape having inputs of energy. The difference between the two types of economy becomes most apparent in the attitude towards consumption. In the cowboy economy, consumption is regarded as a good thing and production likewise; and the success of the economy is measured by the amount of the throughput from the "factors of production," a part of which, at any rate, is extracted from the reservoirs of raw materials and noneconomic objects, and another part of which is output into the reservoirs of pollution....

By contrast, in the spaceman economy ... the essential measure of the success of the economy is not production and consumption at all, but the nature, extent, quality, and complexity of the total capital stock, including in this the state of the human bodies and minds included in the system. In the spaceman economy, what we are primarily concerned with is stock maintenance, and any technological change which results in the maintenance of a given total stock with a lessened throughput (that is, less production and consumption) is clearly a gain. This idea that both production and consumption are bad things rather than good things is very strange to economists, who have been obsessed with the income-flow concepts to the exclusion, almost, of capital-stock concepts.

From "The Economics of the Coming Spaceship Earth." From Henry Jarrett (ed.), *Environmental Quality in a Growing Economy*. A Resources for the Future book published by the Johns Hopkins University Press. Copyright © 1966 by the Johns Hopkins Press.

While most mainstream economists ignored Boulding's analysis and frightening description of possible future scenarios, a talented biologist Barry Commoner was busy writing *The Closing Circle*, which, along with Rachel Carson's *Silent Spring*, had an astounding impact upon the scientific and academic community. Commoner analyzed the environmental crisis and asked that we understand the future consequences of our short-sighted urge to indulge ourselves. He challenged the capability of our market system and the "profit" motive to respond quickly and creatively to the emergent environmental crisis. "The lesson of the environmental crisis is, thus, clear. If we are to survive, ecological considerations must guide economic and political ones."

The Limits to Growth

Following close on the heels of Commoner's book was the controversial Report for the Club of Rome's Project on the Predicament of Mankind. *The Limits to Growth,* published in 1972, predicted that the human race faced an uncontrollable and disastrous collapse within 100 years unless a "global equilibrium" was established in which population and industrial growth were severely limited. A computer simulation based on five variables plotted a series of "possible" future scenarios. These variables were: (1) resource utilization and availability, (2) population growth, (3) food per capita, (4) pollution, and (5) industrial output per capita. Two of the scenarios can be seen in Figs. 25.1 and 25.2. The first illustrates the "Growth and Collapse: Doomsday Model," and the second the "Stability-Stagnation Model."

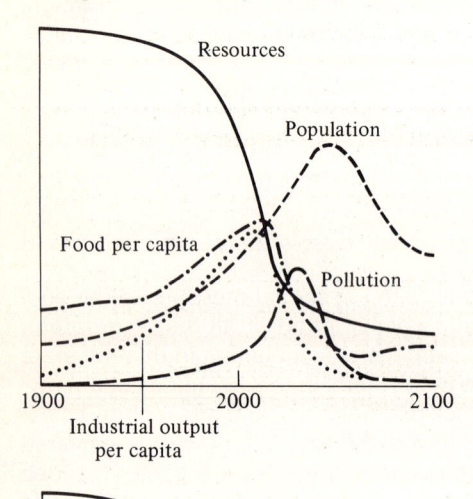

FIG. 25.1 Growth and collapse: a doomsday model.

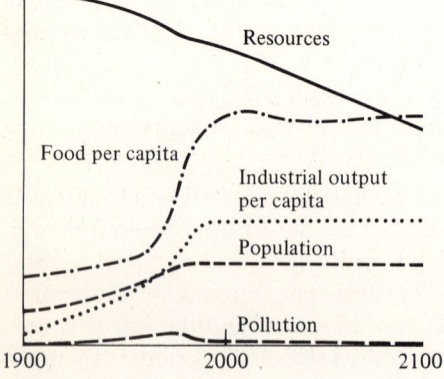

FIG. 25.2 The stability-stagnation model.

The "standard" world model run assumes no major change in the physical, economic, or social relationships that have historically governed the development of the world system. All variables plotted here follow historical values from 1900 to 1970. Food, industrial output, and population grow exponentially until the rapidly diminishing resource base forces a slowdown in industrial growth. Because of natural delays in the system, both population and pollution continue to increase for some time after the peak of industrialization. Population growth is finally halted by a rise in the death rate due to decreased food and medical services.... [Fig. 25.1]

Technological policies are added to the growth-regulating policies of the previous run to produce an equilibrium state sustainable far into the future. Technological policies include resource recycling, pollution control devices, increased lifetime of all forms of capital, and methods to restore eroded and infertile soil. Value changes include increased emphasis on food and services rather than on industrial production. [Fig. 25.2]

Dennis L. Meadows and others, *The Limits to Growth,* Washington: Potomac Associates, 1972, pp. 129, 168.

Figure 25.2 thus illustrates that a stable society can be attained with major adjustments to the primary variables.

---

3. What changes are required to achieve a stationary-state economy. What are the basic strengths and weaknesses of this strategy?

Before the global community had time to fully digest these ideas, two other events reinforced the previous prognostications of ecologists and environmentalists. In October of 1973, against the background of the Arab–Israeli conflict, the OPEC nations agreed to an oil embargo and subsequent oil price increase which quadrupled the price of oil. This show of force by the OPEC cartel spelled dire consequences for the advanced Western industrialized nations and the oil-importing nations of the Third World. It signaled a fundamental change in the power relations of the global political economy.

In the same year, E. F. Schumacher, a British economist, published *Small Is Beautiful: Economics as if People Mattered.* This popular book advanced another critique of the growth fetishism of the modern Western world. Schumacher criticized the waste and squandering of resources and the overreliance on capital and energy-intensive technology in Western production methods. He criticized as well the behavioral traits and value system that allowed this process to continue. He challeneged people to reexamine their values and life-styles. Indeed, for Schumacher the fundamental transformation necessary is a change in thinking and consciousness—a change from thinking that "more is better" to "small is beautiful." Schumacher's message made a great deal of practical sense as people recognized the immediate reality of energy shortages due to the market power of OPEC; it made even more sense in the context of the long-run future when energy supplies are going to grow ever scarcer.

The Reaction and the Recession of 1974

Yet with all of this mounting criticism and evidence, the advocates of slower growth, conservation of resources, and protection of the environment were met with fierce resistance. The Western industrialized world by 1973 had already entered into a widespread recession that was tremendously exacerbated by the OPEC embargo and eventual price increase. As the global recession intensified in 1974 and carried into 1975, some critical "rethinking" evolved on how to best accommodate environmental and resource concerns with a stagnating world economy and with critical energy resources firmly controlled by a handful of nations and multinational corporations.

It came as little surprise to onlookers that the Club of Rome at a conference in April of 1976 changed its conclusions from the first report issued three years earlier. Because of the prolonged global recession, the Club of Rome had little choice but to conclude that only further economic growth could provide the stimulus for an economic recovery thereby reducing world poverty and threats to world peace as well. In addition, at this conference, the Club of Rome previewed the conclusions of a report they had commissioned from economist Jan Tinbergen, Nobel Laureate of the Netherlands, on the creation of a new international order. The thrust of the Tinbergen report was the need for international economic planning as a substitute for the uncontrolled play of market forces. Growth should be *planned* to avoid the catastrophes hypothesized in the *Limits to Growth* argument.

While Western Europe was bogged down in the recession, the U.S. managed to initiate a "sluggish" recovery by 1976 and early 1977. Yet, in spite of the efforts by the Nixon and Ford administrations from 1968 to 1976 to make the U.S. energy-independent, the U.S. had become more and more dependent upon foreign imported oil. By 1976, the U.S. was importing almost 40 percent of its petroleum needs, as opposed to 30 percent at the height of the OPEC embargo in 1973, and only 20 percent throughout the 1960s.

In April 1977, President Carter delivered on one of his principal campaign pledges and presented to the nation his Comprehensive Energy Program. This Comprehensive Energy Program represented one synthesis of decades of work dedicated to analyzing the problems of growth, resources, and the environment. The Carter program presents itself as a "momentary" culmination of this historical process.

This Comprehensive Energy Plan contained numerous detailed proposals, certainly too many to treat here. In general, the plan called for the following: (1) conservation of energy resources and their use by utilizing the tax structure as the basis for a motivational system of rewards and penalties, (2) no immediate decontrol of domestic oil and natural gas prices, (3) an eventual end to artifical price distortions for energy without touching off dangerous inflationary pressures, (4) a massive conversion to greater reliance on coal as our primary energy resource, (5) a safe and gradual increase in our production and use of nuclear energy, (6) a commitment to fully develop alternative energy resources, particularly solar energy, (7) the development of an independent data system so that the federal government can have free and accurate access to the data necessary for monitoring the progress of the program and making decisions, (8) a firm effort to make the sacrifices and burdens "equitable" for all, (9) a commitment to prohibit "profiteering" by the energy companies, and (10) the creation of a Department of Energy to carry out and consolidate this comprehensive plan.

As one might expect, the reaction across the nation was mixed. Few disagreed with Carter's general assessment and interpretation of the problem and the need for an immediate and creative response. The disagreements and criticisms stemmed from the "specifics" and the mechanics of the implementation. Individual consumers and corporate special interest groups quickly registered their preferences in the various media.

And so, extrapolating from the best figures available, we see that the current trends, unless dramatically reversed, will inevitably lead to a situation in which the sky will fall.

Drawing by Lorenz; copyright © 1972 by The New Yorker Magazine, Inc.

The most positive outcome of this period has been the growing awareness of the inextricable interrelationships which exist among the ecosystem, the production system, and the economic system. Indeed, the energy issue has enabled us to perceive this fundamental fact of modern society and has forced us to consider a host of difficult questions. How do we now define economic growth? Is there an optimal rate of growth? Should we abandon the concept of GNP? Is there an optimal rate of population growth? How long will global resources last? What role should technology play in our future? How can we curb environmental degradation without eliminating jobs? Should we depend upon nuclear energy to save us? Is solar energy the way of the future? What institutional changes are necessary for us to meet the challenges of the future? Will the human element be adaptable to meet the uncertainties of the future? Surrounding all of these questions are three basic questions: Is sustainable (future) economic growth possible? Is it necessary? Is it desirable—does it make us any better off or happier?

Some insights into these questions can be gained by examining the "Economic Growth Controversy."

THE ECONOMIC GROWTH CONTROVERSY

The economic growth controversy is aptly summarized in the following two provocative articles. The first article by Passell and Ross, "Don't Knock the $2-Trillion Economy," makes a strong case for continued economic growth while criticizing the antigrowth advocates. The second article by E. J. Mishan, "Critique of Economic Growth," takes the position that future economic growth cannot possibly bring us any closer to the good life.

DON'T KNOCK THE $2-TRILLION ECONOMY

PETER PASSELL AND LEONARD ROSS

"Wealth," wrote John Kenneth Galbraith in *The Affluent Society*, "is not without its advantages and the case to the contrary, although it has been made, has never proved widely persuasive." But times have changed since 1958. We have become a richer nation but not, by common agreement, a happier one. The Gross National Product has gone up 64 percent; but what of the gross national pleasure?

... "You could very comfortably have stopped growing after the first World War," the British economist Ezra J. Mishan recently said ... "There was enough technology to make life quite pleasant. Cities weren't overgrown. People weren't too avaricious. You hadn't really ruined the environment as you have now, and built up entrenched industries so you can't go back."

That, in a nutshell, is the case against growth: more is less. More automobiles, cassette recorders and cook-in-a-pouch vegetables. Less satisfaction in the quality of the common life.

The case sounds simple, but it is really a sheaf of complaints misleadingly wrapped as one. Antimaterialism tells us that we have so much now that more can't really make us happier, while elitism confides that mushrooming incomes for the masses can only dilute the pleasures of those on top. Ecological conservatism says that the process of growth ruins our environment and may even risk the extinction of life. Antimaterialism warns that prosperity in the rich nations is hewn from the hides of other countries' poor.

Actually the sharp contrast in living standards between the United States and the rest of the industrialized world suggests the obvious virtues of the trillion-dollar economy. The average factory worker in Britain, earning half the wage of his Yankee counterpart, may in many respects lead an adequate existence. But he does it living with his wife and children in a three-room apartment, often without a refrigerator. The chances are good that his family shares a bathroom at the end of the hall. There is plenty of food on his dinner table, but too much of it is starch. To save money, his annual vacation is spent at a cheap seashore hotel a hundred miles from home. His kids cannot afford to go to college or, often, even to finish school.

Of course, none of this really proves that Englishmen are less happy than Americans. England may enjoy a less materialist culture than ours, and its poorly paid factory workers may be less prone to base their self-esteem on making money. To critics of growth, this cultural difference is far from accidental. Growth itself, they say, speeds up the treadmill of industrial life, creating the acquisitive values necessary to sustain it. ...

Excerpted from Peter Passell and Leonard Ross, "Don't Knock the $2-Trillion Dollar Economy," *The New York Times Magazine*, March 5, 1972. Copyright © 1972 by Peter Passell and Leonard Ross. Reprinted by permission of The Sterling Lord Agency, Inc.

Growth, then, often reflects some unappetizing values. But for the most part it does not create those values. American materialism and German regimentation could survive decades of economic stagnation. The low-growth Eisenhower years did not wean Americans from their dependence on tangible signs of success nor soften them up for an eventual change of consciousness....

Even if America could remake her culture by reducing her growth rate, it is not clear that the trade would be worth making. English values, for example, are not unambiguously preferable to our own....

Luckily, the question need not be answered. For better or worse, most Americans unambiguously cherish middle-class comforts. And the process of slowing growth is more likely to cause unnecessary ulcers than it is to alter our materialistic values. Thanks to the enormous capacity of the U.S. economy, Americans have since World War II lived better than the English live today. But the average working man is still far from achieving affluence. His take-home pay, after taxes, is about $110 a week. That suffices to keep the wolf from the door (especially if his wife also works) but buys few real luxuries. Our typical wage-earner knows quite well what to do with extra cash. He could use money for roomier housing to make the presence of his children less harassing; money for movies and restaurants and baby sitters as an alternative to Saturday night in front of the television set; money to support aging parents under a different roof.

The only way he has to get those things is through growth. The economic pie just is not big enough to go around, no matter how we choose to slice it. A reasonable growth rate, however, could easily double the average American's income in the next 25 years.

The *dolce vita* image of overabundance does not fit the facts—only 10 percent of all families make $15,000 after taxes....

... The obvious fact that a three-car garage and ski weekends in Switzerland don't guarantee happiness is a less than convincing reason for denying aspirants a chance at bourgeois living.

A less charitable interpretation of upper middle-class criticism of growth is that the elite understands it has more to lose than gain from the diffusion of the bourgeois standard throughout the United States. Wealth in America provides membership privileges in a rather exclusive club. And like most clubs, the tangible and intangible benefits of membership decline as the club expands.

Nature lovers grieve for their loss of privacy in national parks as more people can afford to make the trip. Skiers must endure endless lift lines and reckless adolescents on busy slopes where they once schussed in peace. Hit plays sell out months in advance; opera tickets are unpurchasable; *grand cru* Burgundy prices are bid up by *nouveaux* wine enthusiasts; vacationers must wait for hours to pick up mail at the London American Express.

Intangible status losses accompany these very real losses in comfort and serenity. One of the virtues of a winter vacation in the Caribbean used to be the uniqueness of sporting a tan in January. Now this sign of affluence is shared with a half-million secretaries who can afford a week at the Montego Bay Holiday Inn. What is the purpose of shopping at Tiffany's or Neiman-Marcus if everybody else does too?

Such are the rules of a democratic society that this loss of privilege is only rarely marshaled as an argument against growth. The point is transformed into generalized *Angst* about materialist values, concern for the environment, an enthusiasm for population control. Automobiles are cast as the villains of a physically and spiritually depleted society with no recognition of the mobility they symbolize for most Americans. . . .

It would be unfair to tar all the opponents of growth as elites securing their room at the top. Economic growth has real costs which must be weighed against the benefits. Few of us are immune from the irritation of pollution linked to prosperity. River water used as a coolant by thousands of factories is dumped back, warmed and reeking with chemicals. Insecticides washed off millions of farms into the national water supply threaten to make fish toxic to man. Electric power plants, garbage incinerators and automobiles defile the air with gases slicing years off the lives of city dwellers.

It is even plausible, though not very convincing, that these side effects of prosperity have completely canceled out the benefits of further material accumulation. By this reasoning, a proper accounting would show that a billion-dollar increase in output creates more than a billion dollars' worth of damage from extra pollution. Put another way, the argument implies that growth is an illusion. Each new kilowatt of electricity has less value than the house paint and human lungs destroyed by the accompanying smoke. . . .

Economists have little quarrel with the need to weigh the costs of prosperity against the benefits, but they don't believe that the solution requires a slackening of growth. Pollution, they say, doesn't come from growth but from our perverse system of incentives to industry. Today firms aren't charged for using the biosphere as a dumping ground, so they poison the air and foul the water. Any resource for which no charge is made would likewise be overused by business. If precious metals were free, every steam shovel would be made of platinum. Since nobody is charged for using the environment, its value is ignored. The answer is not to stop aiming for growth but to start charging for pollution.

If Con Ed were forced to pay for its abuse of the air, the management would learn how to clean up its own mess. . . .

A corollary to the environment arguments against growth is the notion that fuel for the economic machine is finite; the more rapidly we grow, the more we hasten the day when the earth will be stripped of all usable raw materials. This natural-limit theory of growth is at the core of the elaborate computer simulation of the world created by engineer Jay Forrester of the Massachusetts Institute of Technology, which predicts economic collapse within a few generations. As a disciple, Anthony Lewis of the *Times*, writes: "Growth is self-defeating . . . the planet cannot long sustain it. . . . To ignore that tendency, to predict that growth can go on forever, is like arguing that the earth is flat. Only the consequences are more serious."

The fallacy in this reasoning is the assumption that raw materials will always be used in the future as they are today: when the last drop of oil is burned, the last truck will sputter to a halt. But the history of technology gives us every reason to believe that long before we run out of Arabian oil we will begin extracting petroleum from the vast reserves of oil-shale rocks and tar sands. And long before we run out of those reserves, cars will be powered with other sources of energy.

Appeals to faith in technical change are more than a cheap debating technique to counter the Forrester school. The technology of substituting plentiful materials for scarce ones grows every day. Silicates made from sand replace copper and silver radio circuitry; European cattle feeds are enriched with nutrients made of natural gas converted by bacteria; mattresses are filled with polyurethane which never was closer to a Liberian rubber tree than Bayonne, N.J. Among long-range prospects is the controlled-fusion reaction. This capture of the power of the hydrogen bomb could provide all the energy we would need for several billion years. Technology, of course, is neither entirely benign nor entirely predictable. But it would be foolish to act on the assumption that science has nothing more to offer.

Critics have used similar arguments about raw materials to link growth with our drive for economic and political domination of the Third World....

This assault on growth raises two quite separate questions: Is American growth dependent on foreign raw materials? If so, does our consumption of these resources hurt the nations in which they are found?

... The American economy does use an increasing amount of the world's minerals. But that does not mean that we are becoming more dependent on them. Today, raw materials brought in from abroad constitute less than one percent of the U.S. Gross National Product, and with few exceptions these materials can be found in North America (though at somewhat higher cost).

Of course, in the process of the expansion of world trade, American companies like Anaconda, Alcoa, and Gulf have developed private stakes in the control of foreign resources. Corporate interests can more than occasionally be translated into American foreign policy; at its bleaker moments, the U.S. State Department has been the drone of Wall Street. But growth itself is not the villain and actually serves to weaken the rationale for imperialism. Gunboat diplomacy makes even less sense now for the United States than it did in 1906.

Nor is is true that American economic growth is necessarily injurious to the Third World. Underdeveloped countries need dollars to buy industrial products more than they need their own raw materials. Chile has more use for turbines and tractor parts than for mountains of copper ore. The only way it can buy these goods is through trade. A slowdown in American growth would simply mean reduced American demand for most of the products of the world's poorer nations.

So far we have spoken only of the arguments against growth—the fruits of progress, it seems to us, need not be electric can openers, sulphurous rivers, and castrated banana republics. But rapid growth as a national policy has a raison d'être more pressing than the extension of the good life beyond Scarsdale. Quite simply, growth is the only way in which America will ever reduce poverty.

The attraction of growth is that nobody gets to vote on the slice of its benefits saved for the poor. While the relative share of income that poor people get seems to be frozen, their incomes do keep pace with the economy. It's more lucrative to wash cars or wait on tables today than 20 years ago. Even allowing for inflation, the average income of the bottom 10th of the population has increased about 55 percent since 1950. Twenty more years of growth could do for the poor what the Congress won't do.

Growth is not a romantic goal, nor is it a military or strategic imperative. It offers at most a partial substitute for the measures which America should take to create a humane society. We do not argue for growth as an obsession or an object of heroic sacrifice, but simply as a sober undertaking for a nation in which scarcity is not for many a thing of the past.

CRITIQUE OF ECONOMIC GROWTH

E. J. MISHAN

THE DESIRABILITY OF SUSTAINED ECONOMIC GROWTH

Assuming that per capita growth could be maintained indefinitely at current rates, we must still ask whether such growth is desirable. Has economic growth promoted social welfare in the recent past, and is it likely to do so in the future? An odd assortment of arguments come up in this debate, a number of which are definitely "nonstarters." We can save time and heat by recognizing some of them before going any farther.

First, there is the frequent statement that technology—the main force behind current economic growth—is itself neutral. One cannot associate it with good or evil attributes and "it all depends on how man uses it." But the *potential* of science and technology is not the issue. Their *actual* effects are. Intelligent conjecture about the future presupposes some knowledge of the reach of modern science and also some idea of the probable scientific developments over the foreseeable future. From this we can speculate about some of the more likely consequences on our lives, bearing in mind the limitations of men and the driving forces of modern institutions, economic and political.

A related response, the invocation of a "challenge" to man to "face the future" or to "be worthy of his destiny," must also go off the board. Otherwise we shall find ourselves with a two-headed penny. For wherever science and technology can be seen to have created problems, the technocrats exclaim "challenge" and perceive an immediate need for more technology. We must be alert to the possibility that some of the problems inflicted upon us by the advance of technology can also be solved by using less of the existing technology.

Nor is it, for similar reasons, legitimate to argue that we should seek the "optimal," or just-right, rate of growth. One can imagine some distillation of economic growth, some essence purified of all harmful external effects, which cannot fail to result in ideal human progress. But such flights of inspiration offer no plausible picture of the future and no guide to action. Economists all know that a narrow range of adverse spillovers—such as air and water pollution, noise, congestion and tourist blight—can be reduced given some political effort. Yet in judging the quality of life over the last two decades, we obviously cannot abstract from the brute facts of expanding pollution. So, also, in debating the foreseeable future, it is not the potential ideal that is at issue, but the political likelihood of realizing significant reductions in each of the familiar forms of pollution.

The "need" to maintain the momentum of economic growth in order to enable us to do good deeds like helping the poor, promoting high culture, or expanding higher education is also not on the agenda. This argument might win ethical support even if it were agreed that economic growth actually entailed a decline in social welfare for the majority of people. But the fact is that such worthy objectives

Excerpted from E. J. Mishan, "Growth and Antigrowth: What Are the Issues?" *Challenge*, May/June 1973. Copyright © 1973 by International Arts and Sciences Press, Inc. Reprinted by permission of M. E. Sharpe, Inc.

can all be realized *without* sustained economic growth. In the United States, so much is produced which is trivial, inane, if not inimical, that we already have more than enough to transfer resources for these more meritorious purposes.

It is convenient for the professional economist to interpret people's economic behavior as reflecting their mature judgment about what is most conducive to their happiness. But I hope that he is not such a fool as really to believe it. It is also convenient for the economist to champion the right of the citizen to spend his money as he wishes. For my part, I have no objection if he prefers to sleep on a mattress stuffed with breakfast cereal. For I am not questioning his right to choose; I am questioning the consequences of his choice. We can sharpen the debate by focusing not on motivation, but only on the consequences.

Having, hopefully, cleared away some of the verbal undergrowth that tends to impede the progress of this debate, we are better able to perceive the issues that can be decisive. The issues can be divided, arbitrarily perhaps, into two categories:

1. In the first are the conventional array of adverse spillovers—air pollution, water pollution, solid waste pollution, noise, uglification of town and country—all of which have increased alarmingly since the war. The question is whether they have more than offset the "normal" expectations of welfare gains from economic growth.

2. In the second category are the remaining consequences of economic growth. How much weight is to be given to those pervasive repercussions that are less tangible and more complex than the familiar external diseconomies? Unwittingly, through the process of continually and unquestioningly adapting our style and pace of life to technological and commercial possibilities, we may be losing irrevocably traditional sources of comfort and gratification.

It is difficult to draw a balance sheet summarizing the net welfare effects of the increased output of goods and the concomitant spillovers in the last few years. Even if we had all the physical data—from the hazards of chemical pesticides to rising levels of noise, from oil-fouled beaches the world over, to forest-cropping and earth-stripping—we should, in a closely interdependent economic system, be faced with the almost impossible task of evaluation. My inclination is to describe what has been happening on the advancing pollution front in impressionistic terms, taking it for granted that the balance of the argument will be restored by the unremitting efforts of commercial advertising, establishment politicians, company chairmen, and the spate of articles in our newspapers and magazines that speak loudly of the goodies we have and of goodies yet to come.

The incidence of a single spillover alone—be it foul air, endless traffic bedlam, noise, or fear of criminal violence—can be enough to counter all of the alleged gains of economic prosperity. Let a family have five television sets, four refrigerators, three cars, two yachts, a private plane, a swimming pool, and half a million dollars' worth of securities. What enjoyment is left if it fears to stroll out of an evening, if it must take elaborate precautions against burglary, if it lives in continuous anxiety lest one or another, parent or child, be kidnapped, mutilated, or murdered? A fat bag of consumer goods, an impressive list of technical achievements, can hardly compensate for any one of such perils that have come to blight the lives of millions of Americans.

The old-fashioned notion of diminishing marginal utility of goods and the increasing marginal disutility of "bads" can also bear more emphasis. For one thing, choosing from an increasing variety of goods can be a tense and time-consuming process. For another, as Stefan Linder observes in his admirable and amusing *Harried Leisure Classes*, Americans cannot find time to make use of all the gadgets and sports gear they feel impelled to buy.

In addition, the "relative income hypothesis" (or, more facetiously, the "Jones effect") argues strongly against continued economic growth, if only because it is a predicament for which the economists can propose no remedy consistent with such growth. In an affluent society, people's satisfactions, as Thorstein Veblen observed, depend not only on the innate or perceived utility of the goods they buy but also on the status value of such goods. Thus to a person in a high consumption society, it is not only his absolute income that counts but also his *relative* income, his position in the structure of incomes. In its extreme form—and as affluence rises we draw closer to it—only relative income matters. A man would then prefer a 5 percent reduction in his own income accompanied by a 10 percent reduction in the incomes of others to a 25 percent increase in both his income and the incomes of others.

The more this attitude prevails—and the ethos of our society actively promotes it—the more futile is the objective of economic growth for society as a whole. For it is obvious that over time everybody cannot become relatively better off. The economist can, of course, continue to spin his optimal equations even in these conditions, but he has no means of measuring the loss in terms of utter futility. Since the extent of these wealth-dissipative effects are never measured, estimates over the last few years of increments of "real" income (or "measured economic welfare") must be rejected as wholly misleading.

Reflecting on the unmeasurable consequence of economic growth, Gilbert and Sullivan's dictum "Things are never what they seem" is a proper leitmotif.

Consider first the motive force behind economic growth. Bernard Shaw once remarked that "discontent is the mainspring of progress." The secret of how to keep people running is to widen the gap between their material condition and their material expectations. That gap is a fair measure of their discontent, and it was never wider than it is today. It is institutionalized by the agencies of Madison Avenue and hallowed by our system of higher education.

If continued discontent with what they have is required to keep people buying the increasing output of industry, and continued discontent with their status is necessary to keep them operating the machine, can we really believe that people are nonetheless happier as they absorb more goods? Does not the consequent struggle for status in an increasingly anonymous society become so obsessive as to cut a person off from enjoyment of the largeness of life? Does not this "virtue" of motivation act to shrivel a person's generous impulses, to make him use other people as a means to advancement, corrupting his character and his capacity for friendship?

Next, let us look at the "knowledge industry," whose products fuel the engine of economic growth. In a society that pays ritual homage to our great secular cathedrals of knowledge, the words "scientific research" are holy and scholarship is almost synonymous with saintliness. But the social consequences of the disinterested pursuit of knowledge are not all beyond dispute. The harrowing degree of specialization that results from the attempt to advance the expanding boundary of any discipline can crush the capacity of men for instinctual pleasure and can make communication between scientists, even those working in the same field, increasingly difficult.

The advance of scientific knowledge enhances the secular to the detriment of the sacred. One wonders if the loss of the great myths, the loss of belief in a benevolent deity, in reunion after death, has not contributed to a sense of desolation. One wonders also if a code of morality can be widely accepted in a society without belief in any god or in any hereafter.

As decisions are increasingly influenced by experts, democracy becomes more vulnerable. As historical knowledge grows, and hawk-eyed scholars find a vocation in debunking national heroes and popular legend, the pride of peoples in their common past is eroded and, along with it, their morale as well.

We might also want to ponder briefly some of the unexpected repercussions of a number of much-heralded inventions. Consumer innovations over the recent past and foreseeable future appear to be largely labor-saving—inventions that reduce dependence on others, or, rather, transfer dependence to a machine. Given that the machine is incomparably more efficient, can its efficiency in yielding services compensate for the inevitable loss of authentic human experience? Packaged and precooked foods save time for the busy housewife. Personal contacts necessarily decline with the spread of more efficient labor-saving devices. They have already declined with the spread of supermarkets, cafeterias, and vending machines. And they will continue to decline with the trend toward computerization in offices and factories, toward patient monitoring machines and computer-diagnoses in hospitals, toward closed-circuit television instruction, automated libraries and teaching machines.

Thus the compulsive search for efficiency, directed in the main toward innovations that save effort and time, must continue to produce for us yet more elegant instruments for our mutual estrangement. We might ask if the things commonly associated with the good life—a more settled way of natural beauty and architectual dignity, a rehabilitation of norms of propriety and taste—can ever be realized by affluent societies straining eternally to woo the consumer with ever more outlandish and expendable gadgetry and seeking eternally for faster economic growth.

If it is conceded that, once subsistence levels have been passed, the sources of man's most enduring satisfactions spring from mutual trust and affection, from sharing joy and sorrow, from giving and accepting love, from open-hearted companionship and laughter; if it is further conceded that in a civilized society the joy of living comes from the sense of wonder inspired by the unfolding of nature, from the perception of beauty inspired by great art, from the renewal of faith and hope inspired by the heroic and the good—if this much is conceded, then it is possible to believe that unremitting attempts to harness the greater part of man's energies and ingenuity to the task of amassing an ever greater assortment of material possessions can add much to people's happiness? Can it add more than it subtracts? Can it add anything?

Recognizing the darker side of economic growth, we must conclude that the game is not worth the candle. And the answer to the question of whether continued economic growth in the West brings us any closer to the good life cannot be other than a resounding No.

---

4. Passell and Ross argue that the history of technology justifies their "faith in technical change" as an answer to the nongrowth advocate's issue of finite resources. Do you agree or disagree with them? Why?

5. "Quite simply, growth is the only way in which America will ever reduce poverty." Do you agree or not? Why? What other ways might there be?

6. "We might ask if the things commonly associated with the good life—a more settled way of natural beauty and architectural dignity, a rehabilitation of norms of propriety and taste—can ever be realized by affluent societies straining eternally to woo the consumer with ever more outlandish and expendable gadgetry and seeking eternally for faster economic growth." How would you respond to this excerpt from E. J. Mishan's article?

THE ROAD AHEAD: OTHER REFLECTIONS

In the treatment of the issues of economic growth, resources, and the environment, we have thus far been terribly ethnocentric. We have considered these topics primarily from the vantage point of the U.S. and other advanced Western industrialized nations. This emphasis is important; but we cannot responsibly conclude this chapter without some consideration of these issues from an international perspective. In particular, we need to examine the impact of these issues on the developing nations of the world.

Over the past several years there has been a great deal of attention given to this problem. For example, in 1970 the United Nations produced the famous *International Development Strategy: Action Programme of the General Assembly for the Second United Nations Development Decade*. The International Development Strategy

... expressed concern with the environment and stated that national and international efforts should be intensified to arrest the deterioration of the human environment and to take measures towards its improvement, and to promote activities that will help maintain the ecological balance on which human survival depends.

In 1972, the United Nations held a conference on the Human Environment and subsequently formed the United Nations Environment Programme (UNEP). Two years later in 1974, the International Habitat and Human Settlement Foundation was established by the United Nations. And, in 1976, an international conference was held in Vancouver, B.C., on Human Settlements.

The most recent research effort from the United Nations is *The Future of the World Economy*. This study conducted by United Nations staff and coordinated by a Nobel economist, Professor Wassily Leontief of New York University, stated as its *objective* the following:

...to investigate the interrelationships between future economic growth and prospective economic issues, including questions on the availability of natural resources, the degree of pollution associated with the production of goods and services, and the economic impact of abatement policies.

In this monumental study of the global economy, the research team made use of a multiregional input-output system consisting of 2625 equations analyzing 15 different regions. Each region was characterized by 269 variables depicting the interrelations between the production and consumption of various goods and services, natural resources, export-import pools of internationally traded goods, and a region's international financial transactions. In each case, the primary focus was on the *conditions of growth* projected for 1970, 1980, 1990, and 2000 based upon specific assumptions made for different hypothetical alternatives and scenarios. The "conditions for growth" analyzed were the following: food and agriculture, adequacy of mineral resources, economic cost of pollution abatement, investment and industrialization, changes in world trade and potential payments gaps, and the creation of a new international economic order. Because the data gathered and processed in this study are unmanageable for our purposes here, we will simply focus upon some of the findings of the study as summarized below:

SUMMARY OF THE FUTURE OF THE WORLD ECONOMY
WASSILY LEONTIEF AND OTHERS

1. The principal limits to sustained economic growth and accelerated development are political, social, and institutional in character rather than physical. No insurmountable physical barriers exist within the twentieth century to the accelerated development of the developing regions;

2. The most pressing problem of feeding the rapidly increasing population of the developing regions can be solved by bringing under cultivation large areas of currently unexploited arable land and by doubling and trebling land productivity. Both tasks are technically feasible but are contingent on drastic measures of public policy favourable to such development and on social and institutional changes in the developing countries;

3. Accelerated development in developing regions is possible only under the condition that from 30 to 35 percent, and in some cases up to 40 percent, of their gross product is used for capital investment. A steady increase in the investment ratio to these levels may necessitate drastic measures of economic policy in the field of taxation and credit, increasing the role of public investment and the public sector in production and the infrastructure. Measures leading to a more equitable

income distribution are needed to increase the effectiveness of such policies. Significant social and institutional changes would have to accompany these policies. Investment resources coming from abroad would be important but are secondary as compared to the internal sources;

4. Accelerated development would lead to a continuous significant increase in the share of the developing regions in world gross product and industrial production, as compared to the relativestagnation of these shares in recent decades. Because of the high income elasticity of the demand for imports this would certainly entail a significant increase in the share of these regions in world imports to support internal development. However, the increase in their share of world exports is expected to be slower, owing to severe supply constraints in the developing regions and the relatively slower pace at which the competitive strength of their manufacturing industries would be built up. For those reasons accelerated development poses the danger of large potential trade and payments deficits in most of the developing regions;

5. There are two ways out of the balance-of-payments dilemma. One is to reduce the rates of development in accordance with the balance-of-payments constraint. Another way is to close the potential payments gap by introducing changes into the economic relations between developing and developed countries, as perceived by the Declaration on the Establishment of the New International Economic Order—namely, by stabilizing commodity markets, stimulating exports of manufacturers from the developing countries, increasing financial transfers and so on;

6. To ensure accelerated development two general conditions are necessary: first, far-reaching internal changes of a social, political, and institutional character in the developing countries, and second, significant changes in the world economic order. Accelerated development leading to a substantial reduction of the income gap between the developing and the developed countries can only be achieved through a combination of both these conditions. Clearly, each of them taken separately is insufficient, but when developed hand in hand, they will be able to produce the desired outcome.

---

7. What do you feel are the most important of these summary conclusions? Why?

With this domestic and international perspective on the problems associated with economic growth, resources, and the environment, we can now begin to integrate these considerations into a more general task—analyzing the future. As we do this several obvious questions surface: (1) What changes are really necessary? (2) How relevant are the dominant political-economic systems as we face the future? (3) How can our institutions be transformed so that we can adapt creatively for the future? (4) Will human beings be able to critically evaluate their values, beliefs, and behaviors such that the necessary changes can occur? (5) What will be the costs and benefits associated with change or the lack of change?

It is toward an examination of these questions that we now turn in our last chapter.

KEY CONCEPTS

Malthusianism
Spaceship Earth
Club of Rome

growth debate
Carter Energy Plan
International Development Strategy

REVIEW QUESTIONS

1. Analyze the emerging national energy policy of the U.S. Does it address the problems raised in this chapter? Does it raise further problems of its own?

2. In the "Economic Growth Controversy" articles, who do you feel had the best and most persuasive position—Passell and Ross or Mishan? Why?

3. Why is an international perspective so important when considering the issues of economic growth, resources and the environment?

4. What are the major implications for the advanced industrialized nations with respect to the summary conclusions of the U.N. study on *The Future of the Global Economy*?

SUGGESTED READINGS

Barry Commoner, 1976. *The Poverty of Power: Energy and the Economic Crisis*, Knopf. See Chapter 1 for an overview of the problem. See Chapter 5 for an excellent treatment of the controversy over nuclear power. Chapter 9 contains an excellent summary and the conclusions of the book.

Editors of *The Ecologist,* 1972. *Blueprint for Survival*, Signet. See Part I, Chapters 1 and 2, for a discussion of the need for change and the strategy for change. See Part III, Chapter 7, for a concluding statement—"A Legacy for Hope."

Wassily Leontief *et al.*, 1977. *The Future of the World Economy*, Oxford University Press. See Introduction and Summary, pp. 1-10. For a more technical treatment see the Technical Annexes, pp. 71-106.

Peter Passell and Leonard Ross, 1974. *The Retreat from Riches: Affluence and Its Enemies*, Viking. A good general presentation of the position taken by advocates of economic growth.

E. F. Schumacher, 1973. *Small Is Beautiful: Economics as if People Mattered,* Harper & Row. See Part I, "The Modern World," for a discussion of the problem and economists' responses to it. Chapter 4 is an interesting treatment of "Buddhist Economics." In Part II, Chapter 4 is devoted to an analysis of nuclear energy.

THE FUTURE: A PERSPECTIVE

CHAPTER 26

The future need not necessarily correspond to the vision which results from what scientists and technologists describe by extrapolating dominant tendencies in the present and by applying laws of statistical possibilities to conscious human beings. On the other hand, there is little chance that the future will coincide with those dreams, no matter how noble and humane, which assume all possibilities are open and that we are absolutely free to choose among them.

Mihailo Markovic *From Affluence to Praxis*

INTRODUCTION

This last chapter integrates and synthesizes what we have already learned. This will involve a certain willingness to be open-minded, imaginative, and creative. We will first examine the current dialogue and debate surrounding the question, "Will capitalism survive in the future?" This discussion will focus on the issue of national economic planning and the prospect for democratic socialism in the U.S. This will be followed by a more philosophical consideration of the future from a global visionary perspective. This last section will compare and contrast several competing points of view. It will conclude with an examination of the most difficult subjects of all—human nature, social change, and the future.

THE FUTURE OF AMERICAN CAPITALISM

The future of American capitalism is now in question. The recovery of the late 1970s has brought temporary relief; yet few if any economists are confident about the future. The problems of stagflation, energy, declining cities, poverty, and demands for a New International Economic Order have become permanent features of our present global order. A sober knowledge has developed in the past few years that if something significant is not done soon about these problems, there will be no escape from a chaotic and unstable future.

In this context, unemployment rates in excess of 6 percent and the fear of renewed inflation almost demand that the government take actions more expanded and more powerful than even the most liberal of Keynesian theorists would normally advocate. The debate over the future role of government has been stimulated and heightened in recent years by *two* particular events: (1) the Hawkins–Humphrey Full Employment and Balanced Economic Growth Bill and (2) a public proposal by the Initiative Committee for National Economic Planning. Both of these have received, thus far, wide discussion and mixed reactions. Conservatives cry out against further expanded powers of government intrusion into the marketplace. They argue that such measures will result in a totalitarian police state. Most liberals urge moderation and caution with a preference for avoiding such fundamental tinkering with the economy. More daring liberals demand these changes. They argue that without them there is no possibility of ever taming the vicissitudes of the business cycle. What seems to be at the center of everyone's uneasiness and skepticism is the future of American capitalism itself.

This particular theme was the subject of debate and controversy at a recent conference on the "Future of Business in America," sponsored by the University of California at Berkeley. As reported by Leonard Silk in the *New York Times,* May 5, 1977:

"We no longer have a free-enterprise system," Michael Harrington, a leading American Socialist and the author of *The Twilight of Capitalism,* told a business audience here this week. And, remarkably enough, Fletcher Byrom, chairman of the board of the Koppers Corporation and a leading business spokesman, agreed—as did many of the other businessmen present.

At this conference, Mr. Harrington went on to describe the present system in the United States as "decadent capitalism" and "welfare-dependent capitalism." He spoke of the current relevance and applicability of the work of Karl Marx. Harrington concluded his remarks by arguing for the eventual creation of "democratic socialism" in the U.S.

Although Harrington's adversary agreed that we no longer have a free-enterprise economic system, Fletcher Byrom declared that Harrington's vision of socialism was bankrupt. Byrom then articulated his vision of the future of American capitalism arguing for a "technocratic" society. Only this kind of future society can preserve what is great about capitalism, he argued. This "technocratic" society would require, among other things, longer terms in office for elected government representatives so that they could design programs and policies with longer "planning horizons."

This dialogue between Harrington and Byrom is just one isolated example of many such encounters occurring every day all over the nation. The debate thus far seems to reduce itself to the following *basic* positions viewed from the traditional conservative, liberal, and radical political economic perspectives.

Conservatives do not deny that we no longer have the classical free-enterprise economy. Many reply, "Okay, so what?" We still have the market system for exchange, individual freedom and the profit motive. So, let's just accept the changes in the system and let things go on as they are, doing the best we can. Others, in the conservative camp, blame government control and regulation for the destruction of the free-enterprise system and current problems. They adamantly call for the restoration of the original competitive economic system and the reduction of government interference in the economy. And, finally, there are those conservatives who argue persuasively for an extension of the government's role in the economy. This last group is in favor of the proposals for national economic planning. They see planning as the only way to bring predictability and stability to the economy (which they need to profitably manage their corporations).

Liberals are also worried and skeptical about the future of American capitalism. They appear to be defensive, frustrated, and embarrassed that their policies and programs do not seem to have produced satisfactory results. Most liberals are content with the present level of government involvement in the economy. Their internal disagreements stem from differences over future courses of action. The pragmatic liberals argue that we need to simply redefine our problems and accept the changes that have occurred over the past 25 years. If the problems are redefined, it makes it easier to accept as *normal* inflation and unemployment at rates of 6 to 8 percent a year permanently. Other liberals, more progressive, demand "new" solutions that require greater involvement of government in the economy. These liberals are the primary advocates for national economic planning and a commitment to full employment and balanced economic growth as the only ways to effectively solve the current problems of American capitalism.

Radicals, on the other hand, perceive American capitalism as being in a state of structural crisis and transitionary decline. Some argue that this condition is leading to inevitable collapse and that extensions of the government into the economic sector can only forestall this collapse. Many radicals feel that an emerging minority movement will grow larger and larger eventually transforming our present system into a democratic socialist system. There is a great deal of disagreement among radicals as to how this transformation can and should come about. Many feel that capitalism can be "radically reformed" over time to eventually become a democratic socialist system.

Let us examine these diverse points of view on the future of American capitalism, in the context of the debate over national economic planning.

THE PLANNING CONTROVERSY

In late 1974, the Initiative Committee for National Economic Planning was formed. The committee was composed of corporate and labor leaders, academics, and politicians. In early 1975, it issued a public statement calling for the institution of national economic planning in the United States. This would be carried out by an Office of National Economic Planning with the following responsibilities and powers:

—plenary power to accumulate, collate, and analyze detailed economic information from all sources;

—a mandate to examine major economic trends and work out realistic alternative long-term economic programs for periods of fifteen to twenty-five years, to be submitted to the President and Congress;

—a mandate to work out alternative plans of intermediate length, such as five or six years, to be submitted to the President and Congress, designed to carry us toward our long-range objectives;

—responsibility to specify the labor, resources, financing, and other economic measures needed to realize these programs and plans.

The Initiative Committee for National Economic Planning, "For a National Economic Planning System," *Challenge,* March–April 1975, pp. 51–53.

The authors of the document emphasized that this model of economic planning would be democratic and would not fundamentally alter or interfere with the cardinal institutions, principles, or operation of our capitalist economy. This ad hoc committee's statement soon became part of proposed congressional legislation. Senators Hubert H. Humphrey and Jacob Javits co-sponsored "The Balanced Growth and Economic Planning Act" in 1975. This act (and recent revisions) called for not only national economic planning but full employment as well. This act was recently still being considered by Congress.

The conservative and liberal analyses of this pending legislation can be compared and contrasted in the following dialogue between Humphrey (a sponsor of the bill) and Thomas A. Murphy, chairman of the General Motors Corporation, that appeared in the *New York Times* at the end of 1975.

NATIONAL ECONOMIC PLANNING: PRO

HUBERT H. HUMPHREY

Sensible planning has become a necessity of modern life. In a world in which populations are increasing and resources dwindling, in which shortages of food and energy threaten the well-being of millions, and in which crisis after crisis has shaken the marketplace, it is simply unthinkable for a government with budgets approaching $400 billion to act without a better system of coordination between public and private resources.

And yet, unfortunately, the United States government has become the last bastion of unplanned activity in the modern world. All other industrial nations plan and have planning systems. Businesses, universities, foundations and even individual families have realized that they have to plan in order to achieve their goals with the limited resources available. But the federal government continues to pursue an ad hoc, piecemeal approach that is not only wasteful in its inefficiency but outright harmful in its short-sightedness.

At present there are more than 50 federal offices that collect and analyze economic data. Because no single office is responsible for overseeing and integrating their activities, the data collected often lack necessary detail or appropriate standards for comparison. In many cases the data are actually incompatible or contradictory.

© 1975 by The New York Times Company. Reprinted by permission.

The confused and haphazard nature of this system makes it impossible to pursue coherent national objectives and our failure to clearly decide where we want our nation to go has wasted valuable resources.

The Balanced Growth and Economic Planning Act of 1975 is designed to fundamentally reform the government's management of its own economic policies and to enable it to better coordinate and cooperate with the private sector in the achievement of agreed-upon national goals.

The bill provides the means to formulate, systematically and comprehensively, long-term national economic goals with existing resources. It would create an economic planning board in the President's office to coordinate and analyze economic data and trends, aided by a wide range of expert advice. On the basis of those analyses, the President would be required, every two years, to submit a balanced growth plan to Congress and to the governor of each state.

Congress would be empowered to review the plan submitted, and to approve or disapprove or modify it in whole or in part. Most important, the Congressional review process is designed to involve the widest possible participation of the American people. It would solicit the views of state and local government; of labor, business and academe, and of ordinary consumers.

The plan would be designed to contribute to our most pressing national goals: full employment, price stability, balanced economic growth, a more equitable distribution of income, efficient utilization of private and public resources, balanced urban and regional development and stable international relations. It would identify the resources required to achieve these objectives and recommend legislative and administrative action.

Once agreed upon, the plan would be binding only upon the federal government. Implementation of the desired objectives in the private sector, and in states and localities, would result from voluntary cooperation. The federal role would be limited to providing assistance and guidance to the private and state-local sectors through suggesting goals, setting forth options and producing up-to-date information on economic matters about future federal actions.

America has lost much, and wasted more, because we did not begin coherent planning long ago. We have suffered again and again because we did not take the time—or have the machinery—to foresee the consequences of our actions. Examples are numerous.

Did we ever stop to reflect on how much urbanization our society really wants? Did we try to discover the optimum size of a city? Or to determine what population levels give us the most cost-effectiveness and the best living conditions? Or to avoid diseconomies of size? We did not, although these things are knowable and we had the means to understand them.

One reason for the failure to formulate national economic goals is that people get nervous about the word "planning." So deep is our commitment to free-market economics that the mere mention of planning provokes in some persons visions of "state control," "government coercion" and "creeping socialism."

But make no mistake about it: This economy is already "planned", although not in a rational or coherent way. In the private sector, where the 200 largest industrial corporations control two-thirds of industry's assets and employ fully one-half of the nation's industrial work force, decisions are made every day that profoundly affect the lives of all Americans. And they are made on the basis of planning that is expensive and confidential, and which may or may not be in the best interests of the American people.

There exist a host of free-market notions that are no longer applicable because of a general decline in competition, including the idea, as Mr. Stein puts it, that "economic planning is an inherently undemocratic process."

But it had better not be undemocratic. Increasingly, we are beginning to realize that long-term economic policy is too important to be left to the bureaucrats. We have seen the chaos and waste that result when policy is made without the involvement of Congress, states and localities and the public.

The pending legislation is not a proposal to expand the government's control over business, not a mandatory or self-operative system of restraints, but a voluntary system of coordinated economic planning based on priorities and goals in the best interests of the American people. Not a planned economy, but a planning economy.

NATIONAL ECONOMIC PLANNING: CON

THOMAS A. MURPHY

The Balanced Growth and Economic Planning Act of 1975 carries implications which are a serious threat to the welfare and freedom of our citizens and to the continued dynamic development of our national economy.

The bill seems to proceed upon the erroneous assumption that given sufficient economic information and access to public opinion, a central group can decide on appropriate priorities for the entire economy. In reality it is impossible to make such judgments on the optimal employment of society's resources.

Moreover, at any point in time the plan would accord with the broad views of only a part of the population and with the particular views of none except the few planners. Accordingly, we can anticipate that the national plan would fluctuate every few years with shifts in the party in power or in Congressional strength. . . .

. . . It is to my mind inescapable that the national planning process—however we may conceive it—would add an element of rigidity to the economy at the very time when flexibility and speed of response are more important than ever. That is, the very existence of a "plan" could impede the process of expeditiously meeting new and unforeseen challenges. This would have potentially grave consequences for all.

Some proponents of government economic planning seem to be motivated by two distinct but related notions. First, there is a school of thought that argues that because competitive markets do not function in all cases in the way simplistic, theoretical models of competition postulate, the system does not work at all. This is pure nonsense. Second, there are those who, while not denying that the market works, do not like the choices consumers make. They are quick to apply labels such as "wasteful" or "frivolous" to these choices. This is a position held by those who believe it is only their value systems or their priorities that should determine and identify the proper allocation of society's resources.

Fortunately, American consumers still exercise a remarkable freedom of choice in a market economy and our history shows clearly that this system does work. Levels of material well-being have doubled every generation. Employment has increased by a good deal more than 10 percent in every decade of the postwar period. The range of product choice available to us is truly extraordinary. Our profit-and-loss system accounts for the unending stream of new products and services seeking customer favor.

These benefits do not accrue from centralized planning but as a normal response to the market and the incentives of private enterprise. And while we should always set our sights higher, few societies have come as close as we have to eliminating poverty—one of the most enduring goals of all civilized societies.

Yet, criticism persists. In periods of economic prosperity, the marketplace is judged to be overly "materialistic"—almost as though critics consider poverty a blessing. In bad times, the free market system is condemned as an evil throwback to another century—a throwback which supposedly enriches the privileged few at the expense of the oppressed majority....

... A debate about whether planning is necessary is taking place in the energy area, one in which the motor vehicle is apparently a prime target. The fact is, the price of a gallon of gasoline increased by more than 50 percent between September 1973, and September 1975. Even allowing for the impact of the recession, it is clear that this increase has caused all car owners to use their cars more prudently. It has made fuel efficiency a major consideration in the purchase of every new car.

Both consumers and producers are responding through the marketplace to conserve energy.

This trend would no doubt continue if domestic petroleum prices were decontrolled and the sale—and therefore the production—of new cars would follow a pattern fully consistent with the nation's energy conservation requirements.

This brings me to the central danger of the proposals in the pending bill. It carries with it a faulty diagnosis of the problem, and therefore offers the wrong prescription. The faulty diagnosis is that a market economy is unstable and erratic—incapable of satisfactory economic performance without government planning. The evidence is clear that the true situation is exactly the reverse. It is primarily the erratic management of fiscal and monetary and other public policies that has kept our economic system off balance.

Whether we look at the Great Depression—when the money supply was permitted to decline by about 30 percent, the acceleration of inflation after the strictures of war-time measures were removed in 1945, or the 1974–1975 recession, the root causes are to be found in public policies—in areas where government, and only government, has authority to function.

A proposal showing promise of improving the capability of government to manage its affairs more effectively would be worthy of unqualified endorsement. If government were to manage its presently assigned responsibilities on a steadier course, many of our basic concerns about the economy—and more particularly about preserving personal freedom—would be largely resolved.

Attempts to consolidate government functions, to improve the quality of useful economic data, to remove duplication and to eliminate waste must be enthusiastically supported. The effort President Ford has encouraged to free citizens and businesses from the shackles of red tape and unnecessary, unfair, unclear, and—of particular importance—inconsistent rules and regulation is most laudable. Reducing the regulatory burden and bringing coordination and order into the governmental process would be planning of the highest order for a more smoothly functioning free society in the United States.

1. After reading the Humphrey and Murphy positions, are you for or against national economic planning? Why?
2. What impact, if any, would there be on the market system if planning as described by Humphrey were instituted in the U.S.?

While conservatives and liberals debate the issue in the above manner, radicals have adopted a different approach. William K. Tabb, a professor of economics at Queens College, has pointed out that "Liberal leaders neglect to point out that the question is one of *who does the planning and in whose interests is the planning done?*". Tabb further charges that such national economic planning would simply result in the government being used by giant corporations "to do the kind of colluding (planning) which they can't do as well by themselves." For Tabb and other radical economists, the specter of national planning in the U.S. raises fears of a possible fascist state being slowly created under the guise of democracy. Tabb more clearly outlines his personal fears in the following excerpt from an article, "Capitalist State Planning Is Not Socialism."

Once the outlines of the planned economy of monopoly capitalism are spelled out, they resemble more and more the *economic* policy of the fascist state. These policies need not be accompanied by the full political manifestations we identify with Hitler's Germany or Fascist Italy. For the policy to move toward fascism, it is necessary for the democratic forces to be discredited to the point of being, for all intents and purposes, dead.

The economic form of fascism has been described by Paul Sweezy in the following terms: "Under fascism, control over the economic system is centralized, conflicts between the different branches of capital are largely suppressed in the interest of capital as a whole, and heavy risks are pooled through the instrumentality of the state. We have here what Nazi economists have appropriately called a 'steered economy.'"

William K. Tabb, "Capitalist State Planning Is Not Socialism," in David Mermelstein (ed.), *Economics: Mainstream Readings and Radical Critiques* (3rd ed.), pp. 523–526.

3. Do you think that Tabb's fear of fascism is exaggerated or is this a real possibility given the political economic structure of the U.S. today? Why?

Radical economists in general feel that this move toward planning whether direct or indirect is a final effort by the defenders of American capitalism to prolong and preserve its future. Radicals claim that this can, at best, prolong its decline and decay. Eventually, they argue, the only real solution for the "crisis" of capitalism is a transition to democratic socialism. This point of view is well articulated in the following article by John Buell and Tom De Luca, "Let's Start Talking about Socialism."

LET'S START TALKING ABOUT SOCIALISM

JOHN BUELL AND TOM DE LUCA

Let's start talking about socialism. It has always been a dirty word in America, an "un-American" term we associate with the denial of freedom. Yet ours is the only modern industrialized nation in which socialism does not figure in the political dialogue.

The exclusion of socialism from our politics is a luxury we can no longer afford. We must start talking about socialism because the contradictions of our capitalist system become more obvious every day—and so does the inadequacy of "liberal" reform.

Despite the Keynesian revolution in economics, the unemployment rate (even as measured by government statistics) hovers at 8 percent. The progressive measures of the New Deal and the New Frontier, which promised to bring blacks and other disadvantaged minorities into the mainstream of American "affluence," have done little to diminish inequality in America. Between 1960 and 1969—the years of the New Frontier and the Great Society—the richest one-fifth of the population increased its share of national income from 43 to 45 percent. The wealthiest 5 percent of the population holds 40 percent of the national wealth, and 1 percent of the population holds 51 percent of all corporate stock. Though such disparities are often rationalized on the grounds that capitalism does provide economic growth, the real take-home pay of the average American worker is virtually the same today as it was in 1967.

Reforms of the system have brought neither economic stability nor economic justice. In fact, substantial inequality and cyclical instability are essential attributes of capitalism. Only the promise of profits and high income encourage investment, and an increase in unemployment must be encouraged from time to time to "discipline" the labor force and diminish its demands.

These inherent defects of capitalism are recognized and understood by more Americans than ever before. Several recent public opinion polls have documented profound and pervasive alienation from our corporate system. Yet the socialist alternative remains taboo; Americans associate socialism with the denial of freedom. They know that political dissidents are routinely and brutally repressed in the Soviet Union and the Eastern European nations that call themselves socialist, and they assume—and are constantly encouraged to assume—that if socialism were established in the United States, it would inevitably be accompanied by similar repression.

But socialism developed in the Soviet Union and Eastern Europe under specific and unique historic circumstances. Just as our liberal capitalism differs sub-

Reprinted by permission from *The Progressive,* 408 West Gorham Street, Madison, Wisconsin 53703. Copyright © 1977, The Progressive, Inc.

stantially from the fascist capitalism of some other nations, socialism need not embrace a Stalinist form. When we begin—as we must—to talk about a socialist transformation of America, we should talk about a form of socialism that will match our own historic experiences and expectations—a socialism that will broaden rather than restrict our freedom.

This suggestion rings strange to the American ear, for we have been taught since infancy that our market economy is the bulwark of American freedom. In this market economy, conventional wisdom maintains, we are all free to start our own business, choose our own jobs, and rise to whatever height our talents and energy will allow. Under socialism, conventional wisdom insists, the individual is rendered formless and helpless by an omnipotent state bureaucracy.

Yet freedom under capitalism is unequally distributed and severely circumscribed even for those who work successfully within the system. The "good worker" in a plant or office, for example, is caught in a bind: By functioning at optimum efficiency and maximum productivity in order to gain increased reward and recognition, the worker puts others under pressure and shows indifference to their preferences and needs. If the worker is offered promotion, he or she must somehow "weigh" the increased benefits in money and status against the likely loss of friendship and trust among co-workers. This dilemma demonstrates both the emptiness of the kind of freedom capitalism offers and the worker's intuitive understanding of this emptiness: Given capitalist freedom, how can he or she maintain dignity and trust in the eyes of co-workers and still attain the "advancement" that the system offers as incentive? The choice is between abandoning self-respect by refusing to advance or abandoning the respect of one's fellow workers.

Such dilemmas are eased, we are told, by the individual's freedom to quit his job and find a more congenial working environment. Conservative economist Milton Friedman, in a statement most liberals would accept, sees this opportunity to change jobs as an effective answer to exploitative employment: "An employe is protected from coercion by the employer because of other employers for whom he can work." This argument, like much of Friedman's reasoning, ignores the basic realities of a capitalist economy: A few people own the means of production; most people must work for someone else who extracts a profit on the employe's work; jobs must be narrow, isolating, and fragmented so that owners can maintain control over their workers. Thus, most workers are free to move only from one relatively unsatisfying job to another.

Such exploitation is justified on two major grounds: First, capitalists are entitled to the reward of profits because they assume the risks of loss. Second, capitalists perform the essential role of "efficient" management. The first argument, always morally problematic, becomes meaningless in an age when the most powerful corporations enjoy a monopoly position and successfully rely on government subsidies and bailouts to eliminate all risk.

The second argument, though more plausible, is also gravely flawed. Even if we accept the dubious proposition that efficiency is the only criterion for which jobs should be designed, the process often simply does not work. Management's notion of "efficiency" is to exert pressure on workers to labor longer and harder. The results are defective products and inefficient production. Many studies have demonstrated that broader jobs and greater worker autonomy result in increased productivity as well as enhanced worker satisfaction. But employers fear that such experiments might encourage a drive for full worker control, making the owners superfluous.

Thomas Fitzgerald, a General Motors executive writing in the *Harvard Business Review,* has candidly explained employer opposition to worker participation in decision making: "After participation has become a conscious, officially sponsored activity, participation may well go on to topics of job assignment, the allocation of rewards, or even the selection of leadership. In other words, management's present monopoly on initiating participation . . . can itself become a source of contention." Things, in other words, just might get out of hand.

Twentieth-century capitalism has, in fact, been constantly preoccupied with reorganizing the workplace in order to leave less and less control in the hands of workers and give more and more to management. The actual skills required for most jobs have been reduced to limit the worker's knowledge and diminish the worker's opportunity to market his or her talents. Today's office clerk, for example, has far more in common with a factory operative performing routinized, constricted tasks than with the clerk-bookkeeper of a century ago. Jobs and technology can be designed to promote freedom and human development, but such design does not suit the purposes of capitalism.

Unfortunately, the limitations inevitably imposed by capitalist work life also affect our "leisure" and our political freedom. Our forms of recreation are dominated by the economy's profit imperative. From vicarious sports thrills to insipid "entertainment" shows, we are bombarded with propaganda about how to behave and what to buy in order to lead the life of successful Americans. When freedom is defined in terms of the choice between an aerosol deodorant and a roll-on, we must ponder the level to which our culture has sunk. Nor is there even as much leisure as we often assume—unless we consider washing a car, driving it to work, taking it to the mechanic, or driving it to the laundromat as leisure activities.

Freedom of speech, properly the most sacred of liberal values, exists only precariously in a capitalist economy—especially as a few firms accumulate incredible concentrations of wealth and influence. Money endows capitalists with disproportionate power within the political process—power to buy elections, to hire lobbyists, to shape legislation, and to impede the effects of laws through the courts. Dissident workers can be fired and blacklisted, and when labor becomes too "militant" or local government too demanding, the large corporation can simply move its operations to "a more favorable climate."

Even the opportunity to develop coherent political perspectives and organize around essential issues is limited by mind-deadening labor, isolation from other workers, and control of the mass media by the power elite. In these circumstances, many workers come to feel that their problems—boredom, for example—are merely personal, reflecting their own inadequacy.

Freedom of thought and speech should never be dismissed by socialists as "middle-class luxuries." They are, in fact, indispensable to any humane society. But under capitalism, the opportunity to exercise fully free speech, like the opportunity to engage in fully rewarding work, is reserved to a fortunate few.

Those who defend capitalism as the bulwark of freedom ignore the problems of everyday life that confront most people in our society. This failure is a consequence not merely of class status but also of certain assumptions about man and society. Capitalists assume that people are "naturally" egoistic and competitive,

Copyright © Washington Star Syndicate, permission granted by King Features Syndicate, Inc.

and that a market economy best expresses and channels these instincts. But people's motives are shaped in important ways by the kind of society in which they live, and there have been many societies which lacked the materialism and egocentricity that characterize ours. We are, after all, instructed all our lives to "get ahead" in school and on the job, and to look to the accumulation of consumer goods as the road to personal fulfillment.

Yet the system grudgingly yields some opportunities for cooperative and creative activities. The proliferation of participant sports and do-it-yourself activities shows that there is a human potential for cooperation and creativity—a potential that is usually frustrated by the system. High rates of worker absenteeism, even during the present "recession," are an obvious indicator of profound dissatisfaction with the kind of personal growth our system allows.

Socialists do not claim that people can be angels. They will have moments of egoism and cruelty no matter how society is organized, and there will be conflict and contention. But an individual can reach his highest potential only if social institutions encourage the best instincts—those of which he or she is most proud. These benign impulses are not likely to flourish when our jobs, our schools, and our culture are designed to foster our capacity to accumulate, to compete, and to dominate. To expect a just and humane society to emerge from such "realistic" social structures is truly utopian.

Since socialists assume that human nature emerges from the kind of society in which we live, they argue that the highest freedom is not simply the ability to take one's place on the social ladder, but the opportunity to assume control over and constantly reshape the basic institutions of society. When people own the productive apparatus of society and have abolished the traditional hierarchies of the workplace, they can redesign their jobs, their leisure, their culture, and their politics in more fulfilling ways. This kind of freedom is essential to the creation of a society in which self-development and true community do not contradict but complement each other.

The development of the full human freedoms envisioned here can be found neither in the Soviet Union nor in Third World nations undergoing socialist revolutions. Yet it is premature, at least, to conclude from these experiences that democratic socialism is an impossible goal for the United States. The Soviet model is inappropriate in many important respects. The division of workers into a few who manage and the many who merely execute has not been ended there, and extreme income inequalities remain. Imperial Russia's long authoritarian tradition and the many external challenges to the Revolution during the early years help account for a repressive and hierarchical system.

Similarly, underdeveloped nations experiencing revolution today have been economically drained—often by the advanced capitalist powers. They also lack traditions of civil liberties and are witnessing attempts to crush their revolutions in the bud. But while such circumstances help explain the lack of freedom, they pose the danger that a repressive apparatus, once established, will assume a life of its own and endure much longer than historical circumstances warrant.

Though we can understand why these revolutions have failed to establish adequate civil liberties, we should not accept that failure as inevitable. Our challenge is to devise a model of democratic socialism which will encourage the full potential for human development—a model that provides the proper institutional supports for a full range of human freedoms. We cannot assume that the good will of socialist revolutionaires will suffice to preserve these freedoms.

We must admit, too, that a democratic socialist society cannot guarantee people a higher standard of living as conventionally defined. What it must do is guarantee the democratic determination of how people will live and work—and thereby ensure greater equality and a higher quality of life. In our capitalist economy, the most fundamental decisions—how much we produce, what we produce, how much we consume, what we consume—are made for us by an elite which is always guided by its quest for profits, power, and privilege. Democratic socialism would leave these decisions to the producers themselves.

That kind of society would require not only the protection of political democracy and the public ownership of key industries, but also the achievement of fundamental structural changes for which Western Europe already provides a few examples. In some industries in France, Belgium, and Italy, workers are demanding broader control of the work process. They have created factory-level committees which control training programs, demand access to company books, and redefine jobs. This is more than "job enrichment," which merely dresses up old power relations. The assumption is that all workers should participate in management and should have equally fulfilling jobs; that while specialization may be necessary, its forms can be determined by the workers themselves.

Just as nineteenth-century liberals saw property as the means by which to guarantee liberty, twentieth-century socialists should recognize that liberty is assured only when we control the work process. With more rewarding jobs and fuller control over their workplaces, workers can develop the solidarity, competence, and confidence that can make their formal political freedoms more meaningful.

Since worker control would require some decentralization of political power, ways would have to be found to integrate various economic sectors. The economy would have to be planned nationally as well as locally by associations of workers representing various sectors and regions. The federal government could make decisions about how resources would be allocated among such priorities as defense, housing, and health. Regional and local bodies could plan how these resources should best be used to meet local needs. Whenever possible, important decisions would be left to local bodies.

Healthy democratic participation at the local level is the best protection against attempts by any elite to impose its will. It is all too easy to jump from recognition of the evils of the old order to dogmatic and arbitrary new arrangements. Strong local democratic bodies must undergird the intellectual pluralism which reminds us all that our particular perceptions of the common good may be limited, or wrong. Such true federalism encourages people to develop a broad view of problems and to express their own ideas. As Tocqueville remarked, we develop a strong concern for our local communities and an ability to express ourselves only "when we treat of public affairs in public." Worker control and community involvement will, in other words, give us the potential to pursue a course of perpetual creative change.

A democratic socialist society would eliminate gross inequalities in wealth as well as work. These two concerns are inseparable. The conservative who suggests that monetary inequality is an essential incentive for work is right—in our society, where the most demeaning jobs will not be performed unless the worker daily confronts the threat of unemployment and financial ruin. When jobs are redesigned and the most tedious or dangerous work is rotated, the incentives for work need not be merely monetary. Income disparities could be reduced, and greater equality in income and work life would protect the individual from economic as well as political and psychological domination. Conflicts of interest and viewpoint would remain, but when the economic security of all is guaranteed, such divisions lose their present brutal nature. Workers, for example, would not have to support a war to protect their jobs. Thus, democratic socialism would raise the level of politics rather than eliminate it.

None of these comments should suggest, however, that socialism and the movement toward it are not fraught with dangers to freedom. Shortages, environmental crises, and nuclear blackmail are among the potential causes of war and tyranny. But in today's America, the greatest threats to peace and freedom come not from socialists but from the evolution of the capitalist system itself. However much conservatives may protest "big government," the reality is that government has been forced to expand to meet the imperatives of capitalist development.

Today, even Keynesian remedies do not suffice, and more direct form of state intervention must be found. High corporate debt, an unstable banking system, and growing economic concentration have aggravated the terms of the trade-off between unemployment and inflation. Even government economists now suggest that high rates of unemployment are needed to cool inflation. Corporate liberals have begun talking seriously about economic planning as a remedy; they realize that the constant tension of high unemployment alternating with rampant inflation is unacceptable.

Such planning may initially take the form of wage and price controls, but controls generally create shortages and economic imbalances. The government will then be impelled to allocate resources, and to become increasingly involved in various forms of corporate bailouts and economic reorganization schemes. Such measures, in turn, will require government intervention in the production process itself. Ultimately, political power will be more directly and obviously employed to control workers.

American capitalism is still immensely powerful, but it cannot control the world economy or its own cycles as easily as it did in the three decades after World War II. The enduring economic crisis is already being invoked to justify the imposition of austerity on American workers, and may soon lead to such "emergency" measures as the "temporary" suspension of basic rights, especially the right to strike. In this slide toward repression, many of the freedoms cherished by liberals will prove to be as expendable as the free market was in the face of monopoly.

We must, of course, avoid the notion that democratic socialism can solve all the problems people have. But in the face of the economic and political perils that confront us, arguments in favor of socialism and freedom are not idle chatter. The practical choice we face is whether to allow our freedoms to be curtailed by the demands of capitalism, or to resist by developing a socialist alternative.

Building a movement toward such an alternative will be a long and arduous political process. Corporate control of the mass media means that any socialist message will inevitably be distorted. The government has demonstrated its readiness to curb the freedom of those who pursue a course of dissent, and we can expect such repressive efforts to intensify as interest in the socialist alternative increases.

But the movement can draw upon and be nourished by the attempts of workers to build more responsive unions, by community pressures for better social services and equitable taxation, by organizations which resist the insane arms race and the wars that inevitably accompany it. How these disparate concerns could be focused into a participant socialist movement is a vital question, for the kind of movement built would determine, in part, whether a truly democratic socialism could become an alternative to the authoritarian socialism of Eastern Europe and the emerging corporate control of the state in the West.

An important first step is the recognition that socialism, properly construed and designed, can significantly enhance the freedom we enjoy. The time has come to begin talking about how to build such a socialism—here in the United States.

---

4. Is it possible for a truly "authentic" democratic socialism to emerge in the United States over the next few decades as Buell and De Luca suggest? Why or why not?

5. How would you "critically" evaluate the analysis and conclusions in this article?

Given this survey of recent dialogue over the future of American capitalism, we can conclude that this controversial debate will intensify over the next several years. Certainly the planning issue, in an economy plagued by stagflation, will be a major focus of attention. The discussion related to the possibility and potential shape of a movement dedicated to the creation of a socialist alternative in the U.S., while now on the periphery, will increase or decrease depending on the success or failure of our current system to adapt to the challenges of the near and distant future.

The Optimistic Vision 479

With this brief consideration of American capitalism "at the crossroads," let us now turn our attention and imaginations to the distant future and explore some of the difficult and complex questions before us.

THE VISIONARY FUTURE

What is required to contemplate the visionary future of humanity on Spaceship Earth? A willingness, an open mind, courage, a vision, a mature pessimism, a spirited optimism, a creative imagination, and certainly a host of other qualities. To a great extent, a person needs to transcend any variant of fatalistic resignation in favor of a belief that what exists today need not always be in the same shape, form, or structure. If we have learned anything from history, it is that change in society is a given. What we need to know more about is how this change takes place. How do institutions change? How do the behaviors, values, and attitudes of human beings change? How can we bring about change?

In the past, there have always been forecasters of doom as well as utopians. Neither point of view is necessarily bad or wrong per se, but we do know that the future seems to be somewhere between these two poles. Over the years various futurologists have put forth visions and scenarios. Commissions have been formed to study the future. Others have sought to share their dreams and fears through other art forms such as painting and literature. It seems that no matter what it is that people do or say about the future, the discussion inevitably gravitates toward an inquiry into the nature of human behavior and human nature itself. Indeed, this great philosophical question seems impossible to resolve satisfactorily; nevertheless it must be faced. It is to an in-depth consideration of these and other issues that this last section will address itself. This is an exercise and process that is typically excluded from economic inquiry, yet one that we feel is probably one of the most important things we can do to responsibly conclude our introduction to economics.

We will examine briefly the points of view of several people who have made major contributions toward constructing an analysis and understanding of the future of economic systems in particular but more importantly of the human race in general.

THE OPTIMISTIC VISION

Barbara Ward, famed British economist and author of *The Home of Man,* concludes in her most recent work that there is evidence to support a spirited optimism about the future of humanity. Her verdict does not leave us impaled on the horns of cynicism and despair. Nor, does she naively base her profound hope for humanity upon the faceless determination of the "technical fixers." For Ward, the real hope stems from a condition that she has recently observed across the global community. Her point is summarized in this excerpt from the Epilogue to *The Home of Man:*

In the Seventies, almost without being aware of it, the whole human family has started to discuss the humble necessary foundations of its daily life. The various international conferences may seem vast and unwieldy. There is a wariness of committees and a surfeit of rhetoric. But what is actually being discussed is the threatening growth in the world's numbers, the grain to feed them, the safe water to restore their health, work to end hopeless unemployment, the skews in income that are bitter with injustice, the energy—the safe energy—to carry on the whole human experiment. Never before has the world's housekeeping been thus discussed, and there is at least a chance that for each conference with all its preparations and explorations and with, it may be hoped, a rigorous mood to demand resulting action, the world can move from talking about its problems to beginning the forms of joint work and action which, in the long run, offer the only way of bringing into a single planetary community all the tribes and races and nations and ideologies, all the hopes and fears and energies of this fantastic human breed.

Barbara Ward, *The Home of Man*, Norton, 1976, page 289.

Much of Ward's optimism is based upon a new vision of the future made possible by recent developments in science, technology, and knowledge. She asserts that "it is just possible that this fusion of new knowledge and ancient wisdom could release a more potent explosion of moral energy than any earlier attempt to convert humanity from the false gods of greed and power." Ward, though, is cautious not to advocate or align herself with any specific ideology or economic system. She is, in fact, highly critical of all existing ideologies and systems. Ward would prefer that the peoples of the world collectively use their imaginations and creativities to create a *new* vision and response to meet the challenges ahead.

Another optimistic view of the future has been presented by L. S. Stavrianos, a retired historian and author of *The Promise of the Coming Dark Age*. Stavrianos reminds us that the history of civilization has been characterized by a sequence of continual periods of the rise and fall of empires. Each period of decay and decline has been followed by a period of transformation ushering in a new dynamic and more developed society. The present epoch, Stavrianos claims, is no exception. It is the myopia of people who have forgotten this lesson of history that explains much of the present pessimism in the world today. For Stavrianos, "this is an exhilarating moment in human history." He claims that, "today, as never before, we have the opportunity to take hold of our destiny."

As Stavrianos scans the globe, he sees many hopeful signs; or, to use the metaphor for what he calls "the participatory impulse," there is "grass growing everywhere." This refers to an emergent awareness manifesting itself in people's demands for control over their lives. Stavrianos is certain that this phenomenon will be the major catalyst for change in the future. This is already evident in *four* specific areas: (1) the trend away from Aristo-Technology to Demo-Technology, (2) the trend away from Boss Control of the work place to Worker control, (3) the trend away from representative democracy to participatory democracy, and, lastly, (4) the trend away from self-subordination to self-actualization. The common theme in *each* of these is the trend toward society that emphasizes genuine participation and democracy in every facet of human existence. The ultimate goal is to create institutions that liberate human beings and enable them to fulfill their own human potential and self-actualization goals.

> 6. What do you think of Stavrianos's argument that there is promise inherent in all our current difficulties? What manifestations of a trend toward increasing participation can you identify? Is Stavrianos correct about this? Is there also a countertrend toward increased centralization? Where is it located?

Another optimistic prognostication for the future is presented by Daniel Bell, Columbia University sociologist, futurologist, and past director of the Commission on the Year 2000. Bell has a unique view of the future compared with Ward and Stavrianos.

Bell argues that "a complex society is not changed by a flick of the wrist." For example, "considered from the viewpoint of gadgetry, the United States in the year 2000 will be more *like* the U.S. in the year 1967 than *different*." He expects changes but no significant changes capable of fundamentally altering our expectations of the future based upon the present.

What changes does Bell predict? In general, he identifies *four* sources of change: (1) technological advancement, (2) the diffusion and equalization of goods, services, and privileges in society, (3) structural developments like the further centralization of the American political system and the further emergence of the "post-industrial" service society, and (4) the relationship of the U.S. to the rest of the world. In each area, Bell expects the changes to be positive, contributing to a future society of abundance for all. He summarizes these thoughts in the following excerpt from an article, "The Future as Present Expectations."

For all these reasons, the society of the year 2000, so quickly and schematically outlined, will be more fragile, more susceptible to hostilities and to polarization along many different lines. Yet to say this is not to surrender to despair for the power to deal with these problems is also present. It resides, first, in the marvelous productive capacity of our system to generate sufficient economic resources for meeting most of the country's social and economic needs. It is latent in the flexibility of the American political system, its adaptability to change, and its ability to create new social forms to meet these challenges—public corporations, regional compacts, nonprofit organizations, responsive municipalities, and the like. The problem of the future consists in defining one's priorities and making the necessary commitments.

Daniel Bell, "The Future as Present Expectation." In Alvin Toffler (ed.), *The Futurists*, Random House, 1972, pp. 257–263.

> 7. Do you agree or disagree with Bell's optimistic analysis of the future of the U.S.? Why?

"Prometheus," by Mexican artist José Clemente Orozco. (Photograph by Steve Stamos.)

THE PESSIMISTIC VISION

In 1974, Professor Robert Heilbroner, an economist at the New School for Social Research, published *An Inquiry into the Human Prospect*. This book is one of the most powerful, provocative, and controversial scholarly essays on the subject of the future yet written. Heilbroner addressed the question, "Is there hope for man?"; and he replied, "No!"

Heilbroner pointed to three basic factors responsible for his pessimistic forecast. First, "population was expanding at unmanageable rates, especially in many parts of the underdeveloped world." Second, he noted the increased possibility of nuclear war because of the proliferation of the sales of arms globally and the increased capability of smaller nations to construct their own nuclear weapons. And third, he pointed to the environmental consequences of increased global industrial growth. He concluded that only a disciplined, monastic society would be able to adapt to long-term, convulsive change. Heilbroner's analysis was met with rage in some academic and scientific circles. Because of the controversy and alarm created by this essay, Heilbroner, one year later, decided to clarify his position and reflect upon the credibility of his analysis and conclusions. What follows is an excerpt from this article, "Second Thoughts on the Human Prospect."

SECOND THOUGHTS ON THE HUMAN PROSPECT

ROBERT L. HEILBRONER

SUSTAINED AND CONVULSIVE CHANGE

... What is important in these premises is not the particular avenues of the future that they suggest, but the fact that they indicate sustained and convulsive change as the inescapable lot of human society for a very long period to come. This overarching conclusion does indeed resist small changes in my premises. Nothing short of a total solution to the problem of population growth, nuclear danger, or economic growth would vitiate the larger anticipation of a rendezvous with forces that will subject human society to the buffets of a mighty storm.

It is in that sense that I find the overall conclusions ... however uncertain they may be in detail, stronger and more persuasive than I had originally supposed.... Whatever my mistakes of fact, however fanciful my speculations, it has become plain that my vision of a major and protracted crisis—a crisis slated to deepen and intensify rather than to lessen or disappear—is a premonition shared by many.

The common, unspoken grounds for this agreement reflect that malaise of which I spoke early in *The Human Prospect*. There seems to be a widespread sense that we are living in a period of historic exhaustion or, perhaps more accurately, in a period of historic inflection from one dominant civilizational form to another. When I explore the nature of this feeling with its pervasive mood of exhaustion, I can do no more than repeat the diagnosis of *The Human Prospect*. The malaise, I have come more and more to believe, lies in the industrial foundation on which our civilization is based. Economic growth and technical achievement, the greatest triumphs of our epoch of history, have shown themselves to be inadequate sources for collective contentment and hope. Material advance, the most profoundly distinguishing attribute of industrial capitalism and socialism alike, has proved unable to satisfy the human spirit. Not only the quest for profit but the cult of efficiency have shown themselves ultimately corrosive for human well-being. A society dominated by the machine process, dependent on factory and office routine, celebrating itself in the act of individual consumption, is finally insufficient to retain our loyalty.

I am all too aware that there is an irritating flavor of bucolic utopianism in these thoughts. But I have no intention of urging a return to the simpler ways of rural community life. That route, alas, is blocked by the very forces that produce our civilizational climacteric. Until the forces of population growth, of nuclear danger and, above all, of a runaway industrial order have been brought under control, there is very little realistic likelihood of the establishment of the small kibbutzlike communities that many would urge as the most welcome alternative to the present order. For a very long period there will be no escape from the necessity of a centralized administration for our industrial world. There is no short-run possibility

Excerpted from Robert L. Heilbroner, "Second Thoughts on the Human Prospect," *Challenge*, May–June, 1975. Copyright © 1975 by International Arts and Sciences Press, Inc. Reprinted by permission of M. E. Sharpe, Inc.

of dispersing our urban multitudes; no manner in which the immense military machines of the nation-state can be disbanded; no substitute for state authority during the period of strain in which a redivision of wealth must be achieved within nations and among them.

THE MONASTIC MODEL

Given these mighty pressures and constraints, we must think of alternatives to the present order in terms of social systems that offer a necessary degree of regimentation as well as a different set of motives and objectives. I must confess that I can picture only one such system. This is a social order that will blend a "religious" orientation and a "military" discipline. Such a monastic organization of society may be repugnant to us, but I suspect it offers the greatest promise for bringing about the profound and painful adaptations that the coming generations must make.

It is likely that China comes closest today to representing this new civilizational form. No doubt the contemporary Chinese model is as specifically "Chinese" in its monastic form as, say, Sweden or Japan are in their "capitalist" forms or the Soviet Union in its "industrial socialist" form. But I think we can discern in Chinese society certain paradigmatic elements of the future—a careful control over industrialization, an economic policy calculated to restrain rather than to whet individual consumptive appetites and, above all, an organizing religiosity expressed through the credos and observances of a socialist "church."

These speculations, I would emphasize, deal with the long-term drift of affairs. They describe the general direction in which I see the societies of the world evolving, and do not offer any timetable for this general movement. For a considerable period it is possible that, as with the disintegration of the Roman Empire, world history will be characterized by a great variety of quite dissimilar states, some retaining many features of an individualist or capitalist social order, others displaying more marked tendencies toward collectivism in both culture and economic organization. Yet, when I take the measure of the changes that must be accomplished, both within the underdeveloped world and in the industrialized nations, I cannot find a plausible alternative to the ideal-type of a monastery—a tightly disciplined, ascetic religious order—as the model which the evolving societies of the world will gradually approximate.

AUTHORITARIANISM AND DEMOCRACY

No part of my book has aroused more expressions of unhappiness than the suggestion that authoritarianism will be necessary to cope with the exigencies of the future, and I do not doubt that my present harsher description of a monastic society will evoke even sharper feelings of dismay. Here I can only offer one softening suggestion. The line between coercion and cooperation, or between necessity and freedom, is not an easy one to draw; there are armies made up of conscripts and armies made up of volunteers, churches built on dogma and churches that rest on a commonality of freely expressed beliefs. The degree of harsh authority, in other words, depends on the extent of willing self-discipline. This offers the possibility that some nation-states, endowed with unusual traditions of social unity or blessed with the good fortune of political genius, will be able to make the needed economic and social sacrifices and rearrangements with a minimum of repressive force.

This is where a faith in democracy—that is, in the public exercise of intelligence, goodwill, and self-restraint—must ultimately reside. As with many other aspects of the future, we have no "scientific" means of assessing the chances for the preservation of democracy—indeed, no means whatever other than an appeal to our intuitive judgments. Many critics have expressed a higher degree of faith than I in the resilience and adaptive capability of democratic institutions. Perhaps they are right and I am unduly pessimistic. But I do not find much evidence in history—especially in the history of nations organized under the materialistic and individualistic promptings of an industrial civilization—to encourage expectations of an easy subordination of the private interest to the public weal.

For we must remember that the required adaptations are not heroic sacrifices that, however severe, are limited in duration and promise a return to normalcy thereafter. If indeed the industrial mode of civilization is threatened from without and exhausted from within, it will have to give way to new and unaccustomed patterns that must be permanently endured. I am not, therefore, sanguine that public understanding and cooperation will make unnecessary a considerable exercise of coercive power. But at least we can see the direction in which democracy must assert itself, if this coercion is to be minimized. The great adaptational effort that must be made during the next generation or two cannot be expected to arise from the undirected impulses of individuals, each guided only by his or her private understanding of the human plight. The preservation of democratic forms can only come about as a result of intellectually farsighted and politically gifted leadership. Paradoxically, it is only through leadership that authoritarian rule can be minimized, if not wholly avoided. Unhappily, we know nothing about how such leadership evolves, much less how it can be cultivated. . . .

8. Do you agree or disagree with the main conclusions reached by Heilbroner? Why?

9. Critically evaluate Heilbroner's discussion of "Authoritarianism and Democracy." Can you think of a way to resolve this dilemma?

10. What do you like about Heilbroner's essay? What do you dislike? If you were asked to write an essay expressing your thoughts about the future of humanity, what would you have said that Heilbroner did not say in this essay?

Heilbroner's persuasive and well-argued pessimism is difficult to debate. The discussion of authoritarianism and democracy will be one of the most important issues in the coming decades. Also, his thoughts raise the seemingly timeless topic—of human nature. Indeed, much of what people say about the future presumes either explicitly or implicitly a particular view of human nature. Since this is such an important consideration, we devote the end of this last chapter to an examination of this issue.

THE FUTURE AND HUMAN NATURE

One of the most stimulating contributions to this dialogue has come from Mihailo Markovic, director of the Institute of Philosophy at the University of Belgrade in Yugoslavia.

Markovic brings a new dimension to the study of the future. His focus is not on the powers of science and technology. He is more interested in human relationships, social structures, emerging social institutions, the distribution of political power, and the adaptability of human beings. It is in these areas that he has made the greatest contribution.

In particular, he has addressed the vital issue of human nature. He analyzes human behavior and human values from the point of view of their initial development and their possible future alteration. We will examine his thinking about these issues in the following excerpt from his book, *From Affluence to Praxis*. In the last chapter, "The New Human Society and Its Organization," he addresses the question of whether human beings are basically irrational and evil.

HUMAN NATURE AND THE FUTURE

MIHAILO MARKOVIC

... The only answer which can be given by a modern dialectical thinker is: stop considering man a *thing!* He is neither a good nor a bad thing. It is not true that there is a *logos* of historical process which will inevitably make empirical man increasingly similar to an ideal harmonic, all-round entity. It is also not true that man is confronted by such a chaotic world, outside and within himself, that all his conscious striving to change, to create his world and himself anew is merely a labor of Sisyphus.

The former is not true because all known social laws hold only under definite conditions and with many deviations in individual cases. While these conditions last and while the individual is isolated he has no power to change the laws. However, associated individuals can, within the limits of their historical situation, change the conditions and create a new situation in which new laws will hold. In spite of considerable uncertainty whenever such a radical change takes place, as a matter of fact, some implications of the conscious collective engagement can be predicted. This kind of fact supports the view that both historical process and human nature have a definite structure—no matter how many—valued, and open for further change. For the same reason the second extreme conception is also not acceptable. Human freedom cannot be construed (à la early Sartre) as a total lack of any fixed content in man, lack of being something, therefore a burden and a yoke. The world is not condemned to stay eternally absurd as Camus believed. Man is not a complete stranger in his world and he differs from Sisyphus insofar as he is able to change both the world and his own nature. At least some stones remain at the brow of the hill. At least in some historical moments large masses of people act in a way which leads to considerable modifications in human nature.

Reprinted with permission from Mihailo Markovic, *From Affluence to Praxis*, The University of Michigan Press, 1974.

Change is possible because human nature is nothing but a very complex and dynamic whole, full of tension and conflict between opposite features and interests.

There is, first, a discrepancy and an interaction between interests, drives, and motives which belong to different levels of socialization: individual, group, generation, nation, class, historical epoch, and mankind as a whole. Thus, great personalities—by their character, their exceptional influence on the behavior of their class, nation, generation, and sometimes the whole epoch—contribute to the constitution of human nature as a concrete universal. Conversely, one of the fundamental effects of culture is to make individuals internalize and appropriate universal human values in a particular local, regional, national, class form.

Second, there are in man internal contradictions between positive and negative, good and evil, rational and irrational, desire for freedom and reluctance to assume responsibility, creative and destructive, social and egoistic, peaceful and aggressive. Both are human, and it is possible for these conflicting features to survive indefinitely. But it is also possible that man will act during a prolonged period of time in such a way that one would prevail over the other. We have a chance to choose, within certain limits, what kind of man we are going to be. While practically bringing to life one of several possible futures we, at the same time, consciously or involuntarily mold our own nature by fixing some of our traits, by modifying others, by creating some entirely new attitudes, needs, drives, aspirations, and values.

A historical fact which is often overlooked is that some values which have been very important in the recent past have lost their meaning and serve now to inspire revolt among the new generation. At such a moment a sudden mutation in human behavior can be observed. This is especially the case with those values which originated in powerlessness and all kinds of privation, and which have influenced human behavior for such a long time that many theoreticians took them for lasting characteristics of human nature. For example:

1. Material scarcity has brought about a hunger for goods, a lust for unlimited private property. This intemperate hunger, this typical mentality of a *homo consumens* developed especially when, for the first time in history, in industrial society, conditions were created for mass satisfaction of material needs. However, it loses a good part of its meaning in the conditions of abundance in a "postindustrial" society. In the scale of values some other things become more important. One can already observe this tendency in advanced industrial countries where people increasingly give preference to traveling and education over food and clothing.

2. A situation of powerlessness and insecurity against alienated political power gave rise to a lust for power and obvious overestimate of political authority. This kind of obsession developed on a mass scale in the most civilized countries in our century due to the introduction of various forms of semidemocracy, such as a type of society in which political power is still alienated and established in a strict hierarchical order, but at the same time open to a much larger circle of citizens. On the other hand, the rise of the will-to-power is caused by the destruction of other values: it is a substitute for a will to spiritual and creative power, it is an infallible symptom of nihilism and decay. However, it loses any meaning to the extent to which the basic political functions would be deprofessionalized and decentralized to the extent to which every individual would have real possibilities of participating in the process of management.

3. In a society in which a person is condemned to a routine technical activity which has not been freely chosen by him, and does not offer opportunity for the realization of his potential abilities, the motive of success naturally becomes the *primum movens* of all human activity, and pragmatism becomes the only relevant philosophy. Nevertheless, one can already envisage conditions under which basic changes in human motivation might take place. If an individual were to have a real possibility of choosing his place in the social division of work according to his abilities, talents, and aspirations, and if in general professional activity were reduced to a minimum and to a function of secondary importance with respect to the freely chosen activities in the leisure time, the motive of success would lose its dominant position. Success would no longer be regarded as supreme and worthy of any sacrifice, but only as a natural consequence of something much more important. This more important and indeed essential thing is the very act of creation no matter whether in science, art, politics, or personal relations. It is the act of objectification of our being according to "the laws of beauty," the satisfaction of the needs of another man, the forming of a genuine community with other men through the results of our action.

In general, the scarcity, weakness, lack of freedom, social and national insecurity, a feeling of inferiority, emptiness, and poverty to which the vast majority of people are condemned, give rise to such mechanisms of defense and compensation as national and class hatred, egoism, escape from responsibility, and aggressive and destructive behavior. Many present-day forms of evil really could be overcome in a society which would provide to each individual satisfaction of his basic vital needs, liberation from compulsory routine work, immediate participation in decision-making, a relatively free access to the sources of information, prolonged education, a possibility of appropriating genuine cultural values, and the protection of fundamental human rights.

We are not yet able to predict today, however, which new problems, tensions, and conflicts, which new forms of evil will be brought about by the so-called postindustrial society. For this reason we should be critical toward any naive technocratic optimism which expects all human problems to be solved in the conditions of material abundance.

A considerable improvement in the living conditions of individuals does not automatically entail the creation of a genuine human community, in which there is solidarity, and without which a radical emancipation of man is not possible. For it is possible to overcome poverty and still retain exploitation, to replace compulsory work with senseless and equally degrading amusement, to allow participation in insignificant processes within an essentially bureaucratic system, to let the citizens be virtually flooded by carefully selected and interpreted half-truths, to use prolonged education for a prolonged programming of human brains, to reduce morality to law, to protect certain rights without being able to create a universally human sense of duty and mutual solidarity. . . .

---

11. How would you summarize Markovic's analysis of human nature in your own words? Do you agree or disagree with his analysis and conclusions? Why?

12. How would Heilbroner respond to Markovic's discussion of human nature? Who, in your opinion, has the best developed point of view?

CONCLUSION

Congratulations! You have just completed your first course in economics. So what? Well, if we were at all successful in *our* efforts, you have not only mastered some of the most essential concepts in economics but have done so in a manner that has developed your "critical thinking" capabilities. In addition, we tried to stimulate your creativity and imagination.

It is our profound hope that with this information you will be able to become an active and responsible person taking part in the process of historical evolution. Indeed, praxis—the unification of theory and practice—should be the ultimate outcome from this exercise of learning. With a good understanding of the concepts and issues, you too can take part in the process of making history.

KEY CONCEPTS

democratic socialism
fascism
National Economic Planning

monastic model
human nature

REVIEW QUESTIONS

1. To what extent is national economic planning as discussed by Humphrey and others compatible with Buell and De Luca's description of democratic socialism?

2. Some have argued that fascism is already a reality in the United States. They argue that fascism is masked in the facade of representative democracy. What do you think?

3. How would Buell and De Luca critique Heilbroner's analysis of the future?

4. How does Markovic's analysis of human nature relate to the present emergence of a "new" critical political economics?

SUGGESTED READINGS

Michael Harrington, 1976. *The Twilight of Capitalism,* Simon and Schuster. A bit advanced, but Part II, "The Future Karl Marx," is recommended.

Robert Heilbroner, 1974. *An Inquiry into the Human Prospect,* Norton. We recommend the entire book, especially Chapter 5 "Final Reflection on the Human Prospect."

Mihailo Markovic, 1974. *From Affluence to Praxis,* University of Michigan Press. Chapter 6, "The Concept of Revolution," and Chapter 7, "The New Human Society and Its Organization," are recommended.

L. S. Stavrianos, 1976. *The Promise of the Coming Dark Age,* W. H. Freeman. Read the entire book. In particular read Chapter 7, "The Promise of the Coming Dark Age."

Barbara Ward, 1976. *The Home of Man*, Norton. Read Part VI, "The Universal City," for an excellent discussion of the possibilities before us in the future.

NAME INDEX

Arrow, Leonard, 191-194

Barnet, Richard, 208, 211
Baumol, William J., 435
Bell, Daniel, 481
Bellamy, Edward, 90-95
Blumenthal, Michael, 340
Boddy, Raford, 427, 429, 434
Boulding, Kenneth, 446-447
Breckenfeld, Gurney, 206-214
Brenner, Nathaniel, 355
Buell, John, 472
Burns, Arthur F., 298, 416, 417, 435
Byrom, Fletcher, 465

Carson, Rachel, 447
Carter, Jimmy, vi, 52, 119, 121, 122, 194, 226, 271, 352, 359
Comer, James P., 317
Commoner, Barry, vi, 447-448
Connor, John T., 199
Cooper, Richard N., 331
Crotty, James, 427, 429, 434

De Luca, Tom, 472
De Tocqueville, Alexis, 58-60
Dos Santos, Theotonio, 386
Drake, William P., 203

Engels, Friedrich, 17, 87, 99, 103, 105, 109, 110

Farnsworth, Clyde, 372
Fiske, Edward B., 129-131
Fleming, Thomas, 83-84
Ford, Gerald, vi, 52, 119, 226, 352, 359, 416
Freund, William C., 224

Friedman, Milton, 31, 36, 38, 248, 285, 296, 300
Furey, Edward B., 319
Fusfeld, Daniel, 320, 415, 437, 441

Galbraith, John Kenneth, 38, 195, 247, 262, 300, 322, 323, 445-446
Gerstenberg, Richard C., 119-202
Giscard d'Estaing, Valéry, 375
Golden, Soma, 51-55
Gordon, David, 32-37, 313
Goulet, Denis, 377, 379
Greenspan, Alan, 226, 416
Guevara, Ernesto "Che," 32
Gurley, John, 98, 110, 174, 402

Hale, E.E., 411, 412
Harrington, Michael, 446, 465
Hegel, G.W.F., 99
Heilbroner, Robert, 5, 11-12, 16-17, 23, 38, 52, 61, 97, 132, 247, 482-485
Heller, Walter, 278, 414, 422
Hereward, 43-44
Hicks, J.R., 425
Houghton, Walter E., 88-89
Humphrey, Hubert H., 467
Hunt, E.K., 6-9, 15, 23, 31, 71, 97, 110

Jevons, William Stanley, 39, 69-71

Kalecki, Michal, 434
Keen, Maurice, 44, 45, 48
Keniston, Kenneth, 221
Keynes, John Maynard, 31, 39, 80, 95-96, 225, 243, 280, 411, 438
King, Seth S., 149-154
Klein, Lawerence, 358
Kuhn, Thomas, 29, 32

Name Index

Lekachman, Robert, 229, 247, 327
Leontief, Wassily, 461

Malabre, Alfred, W. Jr., 357
Malmgren, Harold B., 351
Malthus, Thomas, 39, 81-82, 444
Mao Tse-tung, 35, 401
Markovic, Mihailo, 464, 486
Marshall, Alfred, 27, 28, 39
Marx, Karl, 3, 4, 31, 32, 39, 52, 71, 87, 98-110, 170-174, 413
Meadows, Dennis L., 449
Meany, George, 352, 356
Mill, John Stuart, 39, 67-69, 86, 237, 444
Miner, Barbara, 220
Mishan, E.J., 322, 323, 456
Moody, Bruce R., 204-205
Morishima, Michio, 435
Müller, Ronald, 208, 211
Murphy, Thomas A., 469
Myrdal, Gunnar, 322

Neff, Donald, 118-121
New York Times, vii, x, 51, 113, 125, 183, 187, 224, 354, 465, 467
Nixon, Richard M., 220, 370, 371, 416
Norman, Liane Ellison, 322
Nyerere, Julius, 395

Passell, Peter, 451-452
Phillips, A.W., 226, 302
Polanyi, Karl, 18, 23, 48
Prébisch, Raul, 385
Proudhon, P.J., 39, 85-86, 95

Ricardo, David, 39, 64-66, 237, 345, 347
Robinson, Joan, 28, 31, 71, 174, 247, 411

Rockefeller, Nelson, 41-43
Ross, Leonard, 451-452
Ruskin, John, 87-88

Samuelson, Paul, v, ix, 52, 53, 414, 435
Say, J. B., 30, 39, 80, 81-82, 95, 239
Schmeck, Harold, 113-114
Schultze, Charles, 417
Schumacher, E.F., 380, 449
Shaw, George Bernard, 88
Shultz, G., 353
Silk, Leonard, vi, x, xi-xii, 432, 465
Simon, William, 416
Smith, Adam, 16, 31, 49-61, 62-64, 73-77, 81, 83-85, 95, 96, 156, 166, 169, 183, 215, 237, 345, 444
Smith, William D., 187-191
Stavrianos, L.S., 480-481
Sweezy, Paul, 32, 174

Tabb, William K., 436, 471
Tinbergen, Jan, 450
Tobin, James, 286, 290
Trudeau, Garry, 125, 128, 132, 179

Ulmer, Melville J., 418

Veblen, Thorstein, 39, 70, 77-78
Vonnegut, Kurt, Jr., 41, 43

Ward, Barbara, 479
Webb, Beatrice, 243
Webb, Sidney, 243
Williams, Raymond, 46-48
Woolf, Leonard, 243
Woolf, Virginia, 243

SUBJECT INDEX

Absolute advantage, 345-346
Administered prices
    and inflation, 306
Advertising, 176-180
AFL-CIO
    and trade policy, 352-356
Aggregate demand, 239
Aggregate supply, 239
Agricultural surplus, *see* Economic surplus
Agriculture, 149-154
Alienation, 103
Altruism, 83. *See also* Assumptions
Antitrust, 182, 187-194
Army Corps of Engineers, 269
Appreciation
    exchange rate and, 365
Assembly line, 49-51
Assumptions, 26
    role of in theory, 26
    of self-interest, 53, 55, 57, 70, 83
    of trucking, 55, 57
    in production possibilities, 116
    in supply-and-demand analysis, 134-135
    of profit maximization and competition, 156-168
Automobile industry, 183-186
Average cost, 162-164, 164-165, 167
    and profits, 162-164
Average propensity to consume, 251-252
Average propensity to save, 252-253

Balance of payments accounts, 322-337
    current account on, 333-334
    capital account in, 334-335
    deficit in, 335-337
    gold standard and, 363
    reserve asset account in, 335
    surplus in, 335-337
    worsening of, due to dollar outflows (1960s), 367
Balance of trade, 336
Balanced-budget multiplier, 268
Banking system, 20. *See also* Commercial banks; Federal Reserve System
Big business vs. big government, 202-205, 321
Board of Governors, (Fed), 283
Bond sales
    Federal Reserve System, 293-294
    and interest rates, 271
Bottlenecks and inflation, 225-228, 306
Bourgeoisie, 15, 103, 106
Brazil, 340, 398-401
Bretton Woods System, 361
    crisis in and collapse of, 321, 322
    downfall of, 366-371
    the International Monetary Fund and, 364-365
British pound, *see* Pound sterling
Budget, deficit, *see* Deficits and surpluses
Built-in stabilizer, 365
Burke-Hartke Trade Bill, 349
Business cycles, 239-241. *See also* Economic instability
Business fluctuations, 239-240
Business Week, 433

Capital, 5, 13, 15, 66, 74
    accumulation of, 15, 33, 104, 105
    capitalist, 13, 15, 16, 33, 100, 103
    constant and variable, 170-174
    and distribution, 74
    organic composition of, 174
    and value, 66
Capital consumption allowance in GNP, 235

493

Subject Index

Capital movements in international trade, 339, 343
Capitalism, xiii, 15, 32–35, 37
  agrarian capitalism, 47
  development of American capitalism, 18–22
  and Industrial Revolution, 16–18, 83–89
  liberal and conservative defense of, 37
  Marxian analysis of, 98–109, 170–174
  monopoly capitalism, 22
  state capitalism, 22
  transition to, 9–15
Carnegie Council on Children, 220, 225–226
Carter Economic Program, 417
Carter Energy Plan, 450
Catholic church, 8, 13
Ceteris paribus, see Supply; Demand
Chicago Federal Reserve Bank on free trade, 359
Choice, 115–118,
Circular flow, 80–81, 239–240
  with leakages and injections, 244
Cities, fiscal crises of and urban policy, 274–277
Civilian goods spending, 118–124
Class, 101
Class struggle, 33–34, 58–60, 76, 99, 101–102, 104–106, 106–109, 172–173, 426
Classical economics, 29–30, 215
  classical macroeconomics, 237–241
  neoclassical economics, 69–71
Classical liberalism, 16–18
  and free trade, 349
The Club of Rome, 448
Cold War, 367
College,
  costs and benefits of, 124–131
  decision to go, 124–131
  tuition for, 135–147
Commerical bank(s), 279
  central bank and, 283
  concern over Eurodollars, 368
  deposits and, 289
  Federal Reserve Bank and, 283
  money creation and, 286–290
  reserves of, 287
  supply of money and, 285–286

See also Federal Reserve System
Commodity, 18, 62–66, 69–70
Common Market, 352
Communism, 86, 106–108
Communist Manifesto, 87, 99, 103, 105, 106–108
Comparative advantage, 345–347
Competition, 16, 76–77, 135, 156, 157, 164–168
  and consumer sovereignty and the invisible hand, 164–166
  definition of, 157
  and efficiency, 167–168
Concentration, 180–183, 196–198
Congressional Budget Office, 265
Conservative economics, 31, 35–37
Constant capital, 170–174
Consumer, 157
Consumer Price Index, 303, 308–309
Consumer sovereignty, 156, 164–166, 178–180
Consumption, 5, 24
  function and Keynesian theory, 248–252
Contradictions of capitalism, 33–34, 105–106, 106–107, 173
The corporation, 20, 22, 196–215
Cost-push theory
  inflation and, 306
  shortcoming of monetary policy and, 297
Costs, 157–159. *See also* Marginal cost; Average cost
Council of Economic Advisors (CEA), 263
Counter-countercyclical policy, 270. *See also* Fiscal policy

Debt, 270–273. *See also* National debt
Defense spending, 118–124. *See also* Militarism
Deficits and surpluses
  aggregate expenditure and, 270
  in balance of payments, 321–322
  deflationary gaps and, 305
  financing of, 270–271
  gold standard and, 363–364
  government sector and, 270, 272–273
  and post-post-Keynesianism, 321–324
  size of, 270
Deflationary gap, *see* Recessionary gap

Demand, 135–139
   change in (shift in), 146–147
   curve, 138–139
   determinants of demand (*ceteris paribus* conditions), 135–137
   quantity demanded, 138
   See also Supply
Demand deposits, 287
   expansion of, 288–290
   reserve requirements and, 287–288
   time deposits, 287
Demand for money
   income level and, 282
   See also Money demands
Demand-pull theory of inflation, 305
Democratic Socialism, 432, 472. See also Socialism
Department of Commerce, 230
Dependency model, 386–387
Depreciation, exchange rate, 365
   competitive, 372
Depression, 21, 226. See also The Great Depression
Devaluation
   exchange rates and, 337–341
   recent history of U.S. dollar and, 322
Developing countries
   floating exchange rates and, 372
   and post-post-Keynesianism, 322–323
   and trade, 342
   See also LDCs
Dialectics, 99–100
Diffusion model, 384
Dirty float, 371
Discount rate, 294
Discretionary fiscal policy, 265
   lags in, 269
Disposable income
   national income and, 233, 236
Dissaving, 250
Distribution, 5, 18, 19, 24
   of income, 72–79
   Marx's critique, 102–106
Division of labor, 54, 55–60
   in hypothetical pin factory, 55–56
   problems of, 58–60
Dollar(s),
   crisis with, 369–372
   demand-and-supply curve for, 369–370
   depreciation and, 365
   devaluation of, 337–341
   equilibrium price of, 369–370
   glut of, 367
   scarcity of, 367
   supply-and-demand curve for, 369–370
Dollar standard, de facto, see Reserve currency
Dollars & Sense, 337, 367
Dualism, 378
Dumping, 352

The Ecologist, 443
Econometric models,
   FMP (Federal Reserve–M.I.T.–Penn), 269, 295, 296
   St. Louis Federal Reserve, 270, 295, 296
Economic goals, 219
Economic development, 18–19, 380. See also Economic growth
Economic growth, 219
   controversy around, 451–460
   and inflation, 359
   and post-post-Keynesianism, 322–323
   slow growth and exchange rates, 340
   and trade, 342
   and world economy, 357
Economic instability, 21–22, 90–95
   Keynes and laissez-faire, 95–96
   Marx's theory of capitalist development, 102–106, 173
   in modern economy, 420–435
   Say vs. Malthus, 80–82
   See also Depression; Inflation; Recession; Prosperity; Business cycles
Economic interdependence, 331–343
   examples of, 331
   historical evolution and balance of payments, 322–337
   internationalization of production and, 342–343
   trade and, 341–343
Economic surplus, 5–6, 9–10, 19
Economic system, 4, 18–19. See also Capitalism; Feudalism; Socialism
Economic decision, see Choice

Subject Index

Economic theory, 25-26, 29-31, 112
   in post-post-Keynesian period, 324
   theory of supply and demand, 133-149
Economic thought, 39
   Adam Smith's contribution, 51-55
   history and development of, 39
   Jevons's contribution, 69-70
   Keynes's contribution, 95-96
   Marx's contribution, 98-109
   in post-Keynesian period, 324
Economics, viii-ix, 1-2, 23-28
   introductory, v-vii, ix-xiv. *See also*
      Radical economics; Marxian
      economics; Orthodox
      economics; Keynesian economics;
      Classical economics; Political economy
Efficiency, 111, 156, 167-168, 178-180
Employment Act (1946), 222, 263
Enclosure movement, 11-12, 46-47
Energy resources
   and decline of the dollar, 340-341
   program for, 224
Entrepreneurs, 73, 77-78
Environment
   and post-post-Keynesianism, 322-323
Equation of exchange, 237, 238
Equilibrium
   conditions for, 244, 255-256
   national income and, 253-260
   natural tendency toward, 245-246
   unemployment and, 244-246
Equilibrium exchange rate
   determination of, 337-339, 269-270
Equilibrium national income
   graphical approach to, 253-260
Eurodollars, 367-368
Exchange, 56,
   in connection with the division of labor, 56
Exchange rates
   adjustable-peg system in, 364-366
   Bretton Woods System and, 364-366
   capital movements in, 339
   depreciation and, 365
   determination of, 337-341
   devaluing of, 337-341
   dollar standard in, 366
   dirty float in, 371
   floating, 371-372
   historical experience with, 361-371
   joint float, 371
   Smithsonian Agreement on, 371
   speculative crises and, 369-371
Expenditure flow approach to the national
   income accounts, 231-232
Exploitation, 103, 104
   rate of, 172-173
Exports, 16, 20, 53
   during depression, 350
   in GNP, 232, 235,
   of jobs, 355
   tariffs and, 350
   of technology, 354
European Economic Community, 351, 352, 358
   and joint float, 371

Factors of production: land, labor, capital,
   and entrepreneurs, 5, 73, 77-78
Factory, 17, 83-89
Fascism, 471
Federal budget, receipts and outlays
   (1975-1977), 274
Federal expenditures, *see* Government
   expenditures
Federal income tax, *see* Tax(es) and
   taxation
Federal Open Market Committee (Fed), 283
Federal Reserve Banks, *see* Federal Reserve
   System
Federal Reserve policy
   1973-1974 credit squeeze, 227
Federal Reserve System, 283-284
   credit controls, 292
   discount rate and, 294
   independence of, 297-299
   interest rate regulation by, 291
   Monetarist views on, 296
   money supply and, 282-284
   open market operations of, 293
   operation of, 283-284
   reserve requirements of, 292-293
Feudalism, 5-14, 18, 47
   end of, 47
   transition from, to capitalism, 9-15, 18
Financial intermediaries (FIs), 279

The firm, 157, 196
  analysis of, 157-168
  as corporation, 196-215
Fiscal crisis, 436
Fiscal policy, 219
  balanced budget in, 268
  built-in stabilizers, 265
  countercyclical, 263
  cyclical (of state and local governments), 263, 270
  defined, 265
  discretionary, 265
  and Employment Act of 1946, 263
  gold standard and, 363
  lags in, 269-270
  Monetarist view of, 296
  national income and, 265-268
  Keynesian views of, 263
  taxation and, 266-267
  tools of, 265-268
  transfer payments and, 267-268
  new Urban Policy as example of, 274-277
  workings of, 265-270
Floating rates in foreign exchange, 371-372
Foreign trade, see International trade
The 45° line, 249
Fractional reserve system, 287
Franc, Swiss
  exchange rate for, 376
Free enterprise, see Laissez-faire; Competition
Free trade
  arguments for, 349
  defined, 349
  and MNCs, 343
  political parties and, 345
  vs. protectionism, 349-352, 353-356
  restrictions and, 359
Full-employment equilibrium, 305

GATT (General Agreement on Tariffs and Trade), 351, 360
General Agreement on Tariffs and Trade (GATT), 351, 360
General Theory of Employment, Interest and Money (Keynes), 225, 237, 246, 280, 411
General Services Administration (GSA), 259

German marks, 337, 372
Germany
  dollar crisis and, 369-370
  growth slowdown, 373
Gluts, 81-82, 90-95
Gnomes of Zurich, 361
GNP, see Gross National Product
GNP clock, 220
GNP deflator, 231
Goals, economic, 219
Gold standard, 361-364
Goods flow, 231, 232
Goods market
  in classical economics, 238-239
The government, see The State
Government bonds
  Federal Reserve System and, 293-294
  national debt and, 271
Government borrowing, 270-273
Government expenditures
  aggregate demand and, 258-260
  in fiscal policy, 265-266
  in the Great Depression, 242
  gross national product and, 235
Government financing
  alternative means of, 271
Government intervention, Monetarist and Keynesian views on, 263, 296
Government spending, see Government expenditures
Great Depression, 21, 30, 96, 226, 241-242
  balanced budget and, 242
  causes of, 241
  Smoot-Hawley tariff and, 349-350
  unemployment in, 242
Greenspan Thesis, 226-228
Gross National Product (GNP) 1973-1976, 232-233
  calculation of, 235
  changes in, 232, 233
  components of, 230-236
  corporate profits in, 233, 235
  defined, 220, 235
  deflator, 231
  government expenditures and, 232, 235
  illegal activities in, 234
  indirect taxes in, 235
  measurement of, 230-236

Subject Index

measure of economic welfare, 234
Monetarist view of, 295–296
nonmarketed economic activities and, 234
potential, 222
problems in measurement, 230–234
real vs. nominal, 231, 234
relation to net national product, national income, personal income, and disposable income, 232–233
Gross private domestic investment, 235
Group of Ten, 368, 370
Growth, economic, 219
Guilds, 8–9, 12–13, 18

Hawkins-Humphrey Full Employment Bill, 465
Historical materialism, 99–102
Human nature, 486–488
The human prospect, 482–485
Human rights, 383
Humane economy,
    requisites for, 324

Ideology, 27, 28–31
IMF, see International Monetary Fund
Immiserization, 106
Imperialism, 20, 386
Imports, 16, 53
    and inflation, 372
Income
    break-even level of, 250
    circular flow of, 231, 240, 244
    consumption as a function of, 248
    disposable, 233, 236
    equilibrium, 259
    full employment, 305
    personal, 233, 236
    See also Gross National Product; National income
Income distribution, see Distribution
Income-expenditures approach, 243–246
Income flow approach to the national income accounts, 231, 233
Incomes policy, 321
Income tax, see Tax(es) and Taxation

Independence of the Federal Reserve. See Federal Reserve System, independence of
Indirect taxes
    GNP and, 232, 235
Individual income tax, see Tax(es) and taxation
Individualism, 13–14, 18
Industrial Revolution, 16–18
    in Europe, 83–89
    in the U.S., 19
Inflation, 233, 304–313
    administered prices and, 306
    aggregate demand and, 305
    bottlenecks, 223–228
    cost-push theory of, 306
    demand-pull theory of, 305
    and economic growth, 359
    effects of, 306–312
    Eurodollars and, 368
    exchange rates and, 340–341
    exports and, 372
    fixed incomes and, 306
    income redistribution and, 306, 307–312
    market restrictions and, 228
    money and, 314
    Phillips curve and, 340
    policymakers and, 340
    post-post-Keynesianism and, 321–324
    protectionism and, 352
    profit-push and, 306
    real income and, 306
    unemployment and, 302–304
    wage push and, 306
Inflation-unemployment trade-off, 302–304
    history of, 225
    recent, 227–228
Inflationary gap, 305
Injections, 243–244
    government spending and, 258–260
    investment and, 253–256
    multiplier and, 256–258
Instability, see Economic instability
Interest, 73, 78
Interest rate
    bond sales and, 271, 294
    Federal Reserve System and, 286, 294

Subject Index 499

investment and, 291-293
  Monetarist views on, 296
  money supply and, 286
International economic issues, 329-330
International finance, 361
International Monetary Fund, 357, 358, 371
  Group of Ten and, 368-369
  purpose of, 364-366
  special drawing rights and, 375
International monetary system
  crisis in, 321-324
  See also International Monetary Fund, Bretton Woods System
International payments system, see Exchange rates
International trade, 345-360
  levels of, 357-358
Internationalization of production, 342-343
Intervention in dollar market, 373-375
Investment, 253
  changes in and the multiplier, 256-258
  defined, 253
  foreign, 339
  as injection, 254
  interest rates and, 291-293
  planned and actual, 254-255
  shortcoming of monetary policy and, 297
Investors, 73
Invisible hand, 53, 76-77, 156, 164-166, 178-180

Japan
  dollar crisis and, 369-370
  growth slowdown, 373
Joint Council on Economic Education, v, xii
Joint Economic Committee, 263
Joint float, 371

Key currency, see Reserve currency
Keynesian cross, 255
Keynesian economics, 29-30, 95-96, 411, 438
Keynesian liquidity trap, 281, 282
Keynesian model, 248-260
  overview, 243-246
  summary, 260

Keynesian theory
  consumption expenditure in, 248-252
  fundamental psychological law, 248
  money and, 279-282, 290-292
  liquidity trap, 281, 282

Labor, 5, 11-13, 17-18, 33, 73, 75
  in classical economics, 238-239
  early development of labor force, 11-13, 17-18
  labor and wages, 75
  in radical analysis of capitalism, 33
  See also Workers
Labor theory of value, 62-69,
  Marx's use of, 104-105, 170-174
Lags
  action lag in monetary policy, 294
  implementation in fiscal policy, 269
  inside lag in monetary policy, 294
  legislative in fiscal policy, 269
  outside lag in monetary policy, 294
  recognition in fiscal policy, 269
  See also Fiscal policy; Monetary policy
Laissez-faire, 16, 30, 52-55, 80-97, 168, 202-205
  and free trade, 349
Land, 5, 11-12, 18, 19, 43-44
Landowners (landlords), 73, 74, 78
Law of diminishing returns, 159-160, 163
Leakages, 243
  in the money creation process, 289-290
Lewisburg, Pennsylvania, 269
Liberal economics, 31, 35-37
Liquidity, 281
  and the gold standard, 363
Liquidity crisis
  under gold standard, 363
Liquidity preference, 281
Liquidity trap, 281-282
Lockheed, 321
Lords, 7-8, 10-12, 43

$MV = PQ$, 237-238, 295-296
M_1 and M_2 in money definitions, 285
Macroeconomic goals, 219
Macroeconomic policy, 219-228
Managed float, see Dirty float
The Manor, 7-8, 10-12, 18, 45

Manufacturing aristocracy, 58–60
Maoist economic development, 402–406
Margin requirements, 292
Marginal cost, 160–162, 164–165, 167
   and profit maximization, 160–162
Marginal propensity
   to consume, 251–252
   to save, 252–253
Marginal revenue, 160–162, 164–165, 167
   and profit maximization, 160–162
Market power, 178
Market rate of interest, *see* Interest rates
Market restrictions, and inflation, 228
Markets, 10–13, 15, 16–18, 20, 33, 133–149
   in capitalism, 33, 47
   competitive markets, 156–169
   emergence of, 10–13, 15, 16–18, 20, 47
   and exchange and division of labor, 57
   and the invisible hand, 76–77
   noncompetitive markets, 175–195
   and resource allocation, 111, 131
   theory of, 133–149
Marks, German
   exchange rate for, 337, 372
Marshall Plan, 366
Marxian economics, xi, 29–30, 87, 98–109, 170–174, 429–435
Material incentives, 402
Materialist conception of history, *see* Historical materialism
Medium of exchange, money as, 279
Mercantilism, 15–16, 17, 53–54, 84–85
Mexico, 340
Microeconomics, 111, 156
   definition of, 111
Militarism
   and post-post-Keynesianism, 322–323
The Modern *Little Red Hen,* 202–205
Monastic model, 484
Monetarism, 30, 295–296
Monetary policy, 219
   contractionary, 317
   expansionary, 291–292
   gold standard and, 364
   impact of, 296
   instruments of, 292–294
   lags in, 294–295
   Monetarist view of, 295–296

   Keynesian view of, 290–292
   objectives of, 292, 294
   policy instruments in, 292–294
   potency of, 296–297
   shortcomings, 297
Monetary rule, 296
Money, 11, 16, 19
   deposits, 287–288
   and inflation, 312
   as medium of exchange, 279
   in national income, a flexible measuring rod, 230–231
   neutrality of, 238
   precautionary demand and, 280
   quantity theory of, 237–238
   role of, 279
   as standard of deferred payment, 280
   as store of value, 280
   speculative demand and, 281
   supply of, *see* Money supply
   total demand for, 282
   transactions demand and, 280
   as unit of account, 280
   velocity of circulation, 295
   See also Money demand
Money creation process, 288–290
Money demand
   graphical display, 281–282
   precautionary motive in, 280
   speculative motive in, 281
   transactions motive in, 280
Money supply
   bond sales and purchases and, 293–294
   changes in, 285
   control over, 282–294
   decrease in, 286
   Federal Reserve and, 282–284
   increase and, 286
   interest rates and, 286, 291–293
Monopolistic competition, 179–180
Monopoly, 175–178
Moral incentives, 402
Multinational corporations, 205–214, 342–343
   and Eurodollars, 367–368
Multiplier, 245, 256–258
   balanced budget, 268
   defined, 256

derived, 257
government expenditure and, 258–260
graphic presentation of, 259
tax(es) and, 266
transfers and, 267

National debt
government spending and, 270–271
held by, 271
interest on, 224, 271
size of, 224, 270
National economic planning, 465, 466
National income, 232, 235. *See also* Gross National Product; Income
National income accounting, 220, 230–236
Neoclassical economics, *see* Classical economics
Neomercantilism, 351–352
Net exports in Keynesian model, 260
Net investment, 232
foreign, 235
Net national product, 232, 235
New Economic Policy of Nixon administration, 370
New International Economic Order (NIEO), 388–392
New York, 342, 368
Nontariff barriers to trade, 349, 358, 359
Nixon, Richard M., 220, 370, 371, 416
GNP clock, 220
New Economic Policy of, 370
Smithsonian Agreement, 371

Office of Management and Budget, 263
Oil industry, 187–194
Oligopoly, 178–179
Open Market Committee, Federal Reserve System, 283, 293
Open Market Operations, 293–294
Opportunity cost, 115, 116, 118–131, 157, 167
Organization of Petroleum Exporting Countries (OPEC), 223, 224, 372, 373, 428
Orthodox economics, xi, 29–30, 35–37. *See also* Conservative economics
Outlaws, 41, 44, 45–46

Overemployment, 324–326
Ownership, *see* Private property

Paradigm, 28–31, 32, 412
Parity value, 361
Peasants, *see* Serfs
People's Republic of China, 401
Personal consumption in Gross National Product, 235, 236
Personal income, 233, 236
Personal saving, *see* Saving
Personal taxes, *see* Tax(es) and taxation
Petrodollars, 368
Phillips curve, 224–228, 303–304
Pluralist democracy, 426
Policy
advisory groups and, 264–265
See also Fiscal policy; Monetary policy
Political business cycle, 426
Political economy, 2, 26, 28, 70, 99
Possessions, 86, 107–109
Post-Keynesian synthesis
objections to, 320
Post-post-Keynesianism, 320–324
Pound sterling
and floating exchange rates, 372
Poverty
children and families, 220
inflation and unemployment on, 317–318
level of, 223
Precautionary demand for money, 280
Priorities, 118–124
Price, 25–26, 111, 115, 131, 133–149
equilibrium price, 143–145
market determination of, 133–149
Private property, 33–34, 73, 85–86
origins of, 15, 41–48
property rights, 41–48, 103
Procyclical policy, *see* Counter-countercyclical policy
Production, 3–5, 18, 19, 24
forces of, 101–102
guidance of, in competition, 164–168
mode of, 101–102
and prices, 133
process as source of surplus value, 170–174
relations of, 101–102

Production possibilities curve, 116–117
  and gains from world trade, 347–348
Profit-push inflation, 306
Profits, 12, 13, 15, 16, 18, 34, 73, 74, 78, 156–168, 170–174
  in the corporate system, 198–202
  falling rate of, 434
  Marxian theory of, 170–174
  in noncompetitive markets, 175–180
  normal profit, 157–158, 167
  profit maximization and efficiency, 156–168
  rate of, 172–173
  squeeze, 427
  See also Capital
The Progressive, 121–123, 204, 429, 472
Proletariat, 103, 106–109
Property, see Private property
Prosperity, 21, 30
Protectionism, 349–352, 358. See also Tariff(s)
  and neomercantilism, 351–352
Protective tariff vs. free trade, 349
Protestantism, 13–14, 18
Public debt, see National debt

Quantity theory of money
  formal statement of, 237–238
Quotas defined, 349

Racial problem
  and post-post-Keynesianism, 322–324
Radical economics, xi, 31, 32–35, 425. See also Marxian economics
Rate of interest, see Interest rate
Recessionary gap, 305
Recession in business cycle
  hidden costs of, 317–320
  and protectionism, 351
  risk of, to support the dollar, 375
Regulation Q, 292
Rent, 73, 74, 78
Rental income
  as factor earnings, 73, 74, 78
  in gross national product, 232–233
Reserve asset account in balance of payments accounts, 335

Reserve requirements, 287–288, 292–293
Reserve currency, 366
Reserves for balance of payments fluctuations, 335. See also Reserve currency
Resource allocation, 111, 115, 118–124, 124–131, 133, 155, 156, 164–168, 175–195
Revaluation, see Exchange rates
Revenues, 157–159, 159–161. See also Marginal revenue
Review of Radical Political Economics, vi. See also Union for Radical Political Economics
Rule, monetary, 296

Saturday Review, 320
Saving, 249,
  link with investment, 254
  personal, 233, 236
  planned, 245
Savings function, 252–253
Say's Law, 30, 80–82, 239, 243, 412
Scarcity, 111, 113–117
Selective credit controls, 292
Self-interest, see Assumptions
Serfs, 7–8, 10–12, 17, 44, 45–47
Shortages, 144–145
  and equilibrium price, 144–145
Slavery, 5–6, 15, 20
Smithsonian Agreement, 371
Smoot-Hawley tariff, 349–350
Social Security contributions, 233, 235
Socialism, xiii, 34–35, 106–109, 472, 474
  Socialist critique of capitalism, 85–87, 90–95, 98–109
  social revolution, 106–109
Spaceship Earth, 447
Special Drawing Rights (SDRs), 335, 336
Specialization, 56, 57
Speculative demand for money, 281
Speculative crises
  exchange rates and, 339, 369–371
Standard of deferred payment
  money as, 280
Stagflation, 224, 302

Subject Index

The State, 10, 15-16, 35-36, 76, 85
    Adam Smith on need for civil government, 76
    on limits of government, 85
    and corporations, 202-205
    Marx's theory of, 106
    the rise of laissez-faire, 16, 18
    the rise of the nation-state, 10, 15-16
    the role of the state in the U.S. economy, 19-22
Stock, *see* Capital
Store of value
    money as, 280
Structural crisis, 425
Structuralist model, 385
Subsistence, 75, 104, 115
Superstructure, 101
Supply, 140-142
    change in supply (shift in supply), 147-148
    curve, 141-143
    determinants of supply (the *ceteris paribus* conditions), 140-141
    quantity supplied, 141-142
    See also Demand
Surpluses
    and equilibrium price, 144-145
Surplus value, 104, 171-174

Tanzania, 395-397
Tariffs
    arguments for, 350-356
    defined, 349
    Smoot-Hawley, 349-350
Tax(es) and taxation
    corporate income in GNP, 235
    fiscal policy and, 266-267
    personal income in GNP, 233, 236
    progressive, 265
Tax multiplier, 267
Tax reform, 223
Third World, 377
Time deposits
    reserve requirements and, 287-288
Time lags, *see* Lags
Trade
    absolute advantage in, 345-346
    comparative advantage in, 345-347
    currency values and, 338-341
    free, *see* Free trade
    gains from, 347-348
    interdependence and, 342-343
    international; *see* International trade
    nontariff barriers to, 349
    policy, Carter and, 359
    tariff and, 349
Trade-offs of unemployment and inflation, *see* Inflation-unemployment trade-off
Tradition, 5-9, 13, 18
Transactions demand for money, 280
Transfer multiplier, 268
Transfer payments
    and fiscal policy, 267-268
    in GNP, 233, 236
Treasury goals
    shortcoming of monetary policy and, 297
Truman Doctrine, 367

Underdevelopment, 384
Underemployment, 223, 316
Unemployment, 222, 225
    by age, sex, and color, 313-315
    counting and, 316
    cyclical, 313
    in Great Depression, 242
    fiscal remedies for, 302
    frictional, 313
    hidden, 313
    hidden costs of, 317-320
    inflation and, 302-327
    money supply and U.S. overemployment, 324-326
    rates, selected, 314-315
    seasonal, 313
    structural, 313
    tariffs and, 350, 352-356
Union of Radical Political Economics, 38, 425, 433, 434
Unit of account
    money as, 280
United States economic history, 20-23
    and classical economics, 239-242
Urban policy (1978), 274-277

Uses of money, 279-280
Utility, 65, 70

Value, 62-71, 72-79
  and distribution, 72-73
  in exchange, 62, 64-66
  in (use) utility, 64-66, 69-70
  See also Labor theory of value
Variable capital, 170-174
Velocity of money, 238
  and Monetarism, 295-296
  shortcomings of monetary policy and, 297
  See also Money
Versailles Peace Treaty, 243
Victorian Age, 87-89
Vietnam War
  economic growth and, 303
  fiscal and monetary policies and, 307, 310
  inflation and, 223, 307, 310, 311
  national debt and, 270, 273
  trade-offs and, 324

Wage-price controls, 311, 321, 370
Wage-price spiral, 306
Wages, 73, 75, 78
Wall Street Journal, 352
Wants, 115
Worker control, 476
Workers, 49-50, 56, 58-60, 100, 103, 106-109
World War II
  concentration of power after, 321-324
  demise of gold standard and, 364
  national debt and, 270, 272
  parity exchange rates after, 367
  world economy after, 353

Yen, Japanese
  exchange rate for, 372